AMERICAN POETRY:
THE TWENTIETH CENTURY

VOLUME TWO

AMERICAN POETRY:
THE TWENTIETH CENTURY

VOLUME TWO
E. E. Cummings to May Swenson

THE LIBRARY OF AMERICA

Some of the material in this volume is reprinted by
permission of the holders of copyright and publication rights.
Acknowledgments will be found on pages 965–73.

The paper used in this publication meets the
minimum requirements of the American National Standard for
Information Sciences—Permanence of Paper for Printed
Library Materials, ANSI Z39.48—1984.

Distributed to the trade in the United States
by Penguin Putnam Inc.
and in Canada by Penguin Books Canada Ltd.

Library of Congress Catalog Number: 99-043721
For cataloging information, see end of Index.
ISBN 1-883011-78-7

First Printing
The Library of America—116

Manufactured in the United States of America

Volume Two of
American Poetry: The Twentieth Century
was published with generous financial support
from the National Endowment for the Humanities.

Contents

E. E. CUMMINGS

(1894–1962)

All in green went my love riding
on a great horse of gold
into the silver dawn.

four lean hounds crouched low and smiling
the merry deer ran before.

Fleeter be they than dappled dreams
the swift sweet deer
the red rare deer.

Four red roebuck at a white water
the cruel bugle sang before.

Horn at hip went my love riding
riding the echo down
into the silver dawn.

four lean hounds crouched low and smiling
the level meadows ran before.

Softer be they than slippered sleep
the lean lithe deer
the fleet flown deer.

Four fleet does at a gold valley
the famished arrow sang before.

Bow at belt went my love riding
riding the mountain down
into the silver dawn.

four lean hounds crouched low and smiling
the sheer peaks ran before.

Paler be they than daunting death
the sleek slim deer
the tall tense deer.

Four tall stags at a green mountain
the lucky hunter sang before.

All in green went my love riding
on a great horse of gold
into the silver dawn.

four lean hounds crouched low and smiling
my heart fell dead before.

————————

   in Just-
   spring   when the world is mud-
   luscious the little
   lame balloonman

   whistles   far   and wee

   and eddieandbill come
   running from marbles and
   piracies and it's
   spring

   when the world is puddle-wonderful

   the queer
   old balloonman whistles
   far   and   wee
   and bettyandisbel come dancing

   from hop-scotch and jump-rope and

     it's
     spring
     and
       the

       goat-footed

     balloonMan   whistles
     far
     and
     wee

———————

Tumbling-hair
         picker of buttercups
                violets
dandelions
And the big bullying daisies
               through the field wonderful
with eyes a little sorry
Another comes
        also picking flowers

———————

Humanity i love you
because you would rather black the boots of
success than enquire whose soul dangles from his
watch-chain which would be embarrassing for both

parties and because you
unflinchingly applaud all
songs containing the words country home and
mother when sung at the old howard

Humanity i love you because
when you're hard up you pawn your
intelligence to buy a drink and when
you're flush pride keeps

you from the pawn shop and
because you are continually committing
nuisances but more
especially in your own house

Humanity i love you because you
are perpetually putting the secret of
life in your pants and forgetting
it's there and sitting down

on it
and because you are
forever making poems in the lap
of death Humanity

i hate you

———————

     O sweet spontaneous
     earth how often have
     the
     doting

         fingers of
     prurient philosophers pinched
     and
     poked

     thee
     ,has the naughty thumb
     of science prodded
     thy

       beauty   .how
     often have religions taken
     thee upon their scraggy knees
     squeezing and

buffeting thee that thou mightest conceive
gods
    (but
true

to the incomparable
couch of death thy
rhythmic
lover

    thou answerest

them only with

        spring)

    ————————

    stinging
    gold swarms
    upon the spires
    silver

      chants the litanies the
    great bells are ringing with rose
    the lewd fat bells
          and a tall

    wind
    is dragging
    the
    sea

    with

    dream

    -S

    ————————

between green
                    mountains
sings the flinger
of

fire   beyond red rivers
of fair perpetual
feet the
sinuous

            riot

the
flashing
bacchant.

partedpetaled
mouth,face
delirious.   indivisible
grace

        of dancing

        ————

Babylon slim
-ness of
evenslicing
eyes are chisels

scarlet Goes
with her
whitehot
face,gashed

by hair's blue cold

jolts of
lovecrazed abrupt

flesh split "Pretty
Baby"
to
numb rhythm before christ

———————

ta
ppin
g
toe

hip
popot
amus Back

gen
teel-ly
lugu-
bri ous

                            eyes
LOOPTHELOOP

as

fathandsbangrag

———————

Buffalo Bill 's
defunct
       who used to
       ride a watersmooth-silver
                   stallion
and break onetwothreefourfive pigeonsjustlikethat
                                  Jesus

he was a handsome man
                  and what i want to know is
how do you like your blueeyed boy
Mister Death

_____

the Cambridge ladies who live in furnished souls
are unbeautiful and have comfortable minds
(also,with the church's protestant blessings
daughters,unscented shapeless spirited)
they believe in Christ and Longfellow,both dead,
are invariably interested in so many things—
at the present writing one still finds
delighted fingers knitting for the is it Poles?
perhaps.   While permanent faces coyly bandy
scandal of Mrs. N and Professor D
. . . .the Cambridge ladies do not care,above
Cambridge if sometimes in its box of
sky lavender and cornerless,the
moon rattles like a fragment of angry candy

_____

god pity me whom(god distinctly has)
the weightless svelte drifting sexual feather
of your shall i say body?follows
truly through a dribbling moan of jazz

whose arched occasional steep youth swallows
curvingly the keenness of my hips;
or,your first twitch of crisp boy flesh dips
my height in a firm fragile stinging weather,

(breathless with sharp necessary lips)kid

female cracksman of the nifty,ruffian-rogue,
laughing body with wise breasts half-grown,
lisping flesh quick to thread the fattish drone
of I Want a Doll,
                           wispish-agile feet with slid
steps parting the tousle of saxophonic brogue.

_____

Dick Mid's large bluish face without eyebrows

sits in the kitchen nights and chews a two-bit
cigar
        waiting for the bulls to pull his joint.
Jimmie was a dude.   Dark hair and nice hands.

with a little eye that rolled and made its point

Jimmie's sister worked for Dick.   And had some rows
over percent.   The gang got shot up twice,it
operated in the hundred ands

All the chips would kid Jimmie to give them a kiss
but Jimmie lived regular. stewed three times a week.
and slept twice a week with a big toothless girl
in Yonkers.
            Dick Mid's green large three teeth leak

smoke:remembering,two pink big lips curl. . . .

how Jimmie was framed and got his

            Spring is like a perhaps hand
            (which comes carefully
            out of Nowhere)arranging
            a window,into which people look(while
            people stare
            arranging and changing placing
            carefully there a strange
            thing and a known thing here)and

            changing everything carefully

            spring is like a perhaps
            Hand in a window
            (carefully to
            and fro moving New and

Old things,while
people stare carefully
moving a perhaps
fraction of flower here placing
an inch of air there)and

without breaking anything.

––––––––––

POEM,OR BEAUTY HURTS MR. VINAL

take it from me kiddo
believe me
my country,'tis of

you,land of the Cluett
Shirt Boston Garter and Spearmint
Girl With The Wrigley Eyes(of you
land of the Arrow Ide
and Earl &
Wilson
Collars)of you i
sing:land of Abraham Lincoln and Lydia E. Pinkham,
land above all of Just Add Hot Water And Serve—
from every B.V.D.

let freedom ring

amen.   i do however protest,anent the un
-spontaneous and otherwise scented merde which
greets one(Everywhere Why)as divine poesy per
that and this radically defunct periodical.   i would

suggest that certain ideas gestures
rhymes,like Gillette Razor Blades
having been used and reused
to the mystical moment of dullness emphatically are
Not To Be Resharpened.   (Case in point

if we are to believe these gently O sweetly
melancholy trillers amid the thrillers
these crepuscular violinists among my and your
skyscrapers—Helen & Cleopatra were Just Too Lovely,
The Snail's On The Thorn enter Morn and God's
In His andsoforth

do you get me?)according
to such supposedly indigenous
throstles Art is O World O Life
a formula:example,Turn Your Shirttails Into
Drawers and If It Isn't An Eastman It Isn't A
Kodak therefore my friends let
us now sing each and all fortissimo A-
mer
i

ca,I
love,
You.   And there're a
hun-dred-mil-lion-oth-ers,like
all of you successfully if
delicately gelded(or spaded)
gentlemen(and ladies)—pretty

littleliverpill-
hearted-Nujolneeding-There's-A-Reason
americans(who tensetendoned and with
upward vacant eyes,painfully
perpetually crouched,quivering,upon the
sternly allotted sandpile
—how silently
emit a tiny violetflavoured nuisance:Odor?

ono.
comes out like a ribbon lies flat on the brush

she being Brand

-new;and you
know consequently a
little stiff i was
careful of her and(having

thoroughly oiled the universal
joint tested my gas felt of
her radiator made sure her springs were O.

K.)i went right to it flooded-the-carburetor cranked her

up,slipped the
clutch(and then somehow got into reverse she
kicked what
the hell)next
minute i was back in neutral tried and

again slo-wly;bare,ly nudg.   ing(my

lev-er Right-
oh and her gears being in
A 1 shape passed
from low through
second-in-to-high like
greasedlightning)just as we turned the corner of Divinity

avenue i touched the accelerator and give

her the juice,good

                    (it

was the first ride and believe i we was
happy to see how nice she acted right up to
the last minute coming back down by the Public
Gardens i slammed on

the
internalexpanding
&
externalcontracting
brakes Bothatonce and

brought allofher tremB
-ling
to a:dead.

stand-
;Still)

———————

on the Madam's best april the
twenty nellie

anyway and
it's flutters everything
queer;does smells he smiles is
like Out of doors he's a with
eyes and making twice the a week
you kind of,know(kind well of
A sort of the way he smile)but
and her a I mean me a
Irish,cook but well oh don't
you makes burst want to dear somehow
quickyes when(now,dark dear oh)
the iceman
how,luminously
oh how listens and,expands
my somewherealloverme heart my
the halfgloom coolish
of The what are
parks for wiggle yes has
are leap,which,anyway

give rapid lapfulls of
idiotic big hands

MEMORABILIA

stop look &

listen Venezia:incline thine
ear you glassworks
of Murano;
pause
elevator nel
mezzo del cammin' that means half-
way up the Campanile,believe

thou me cocodrillo—

mine eyes have seen
the glory of

the coming of
the Americans particularly the
brand of marriageable nymph which is
armed with large legs rancid
voices Baedekers Mothers and kodaks
—by night upon the Riva Schiavoni or in
the felicitous vicinity of the de l'Europe

Grand and Royal
Danielli their numbers

are like unto the stars of Heaven. . . .

i do signore
affirm that all gondola signore
day below me gondola signore gondola
and above me pass loudly and gondola
rapidly denizens of Omaha Altoona or what
not enthusiastic cohorts from Duluth God only,
gondola knows Cincingondolanati i gondola don't

—the substantial dollarbringing virgins

"from the Loggia where
are we angels by O yes
beautiful we now pass through the look
girls in the style of that's the
foliage what is it didn't Ruskin
says about you got the haven't Marjorie
isn't this wellcurb simply darling"

                              —O Education:O

thos cook & son

(O to be a metope
now that triglyph's here)

———————

"next to of course god america i
love you land of the pilgrims' and so forth oh
say can you see by the dawn's early my
country 'tis of centuries come and go
and are no more what of it we should worry
in every language even deafanddumb
thy sons acclaim your glorious name by gorry
by jingo by gee by gosh by gum
why talk of beauty what could be more beaut-
iful than these heroic happy dead
who rushed like lions to the roaring slaughter
they did not stop to think they died instead
then shall the voice of liberty be mute?"

He spoke.   And drank rapidly a glass of water

———————

         lis
         -ten

         you know what i mean when
         the first guy drops you know
         everybody feels sick or
         when they throw in a few gas

and the oh baby shrapnel
or my feet getting dim freezing or
up to your you know what in water or
with the bugs crawling right all up
all everywhere over you all me everyone
that's been there knows what
i mean a god damned lot of
people don't and never
never
will know,
they don't want

to
no

    ————————

my sweet old etcetera
aunt lucy during the recent

war could and what
is more did tell you just
what everybody was fighting

for,
my sister

isabel created hundreds
(and
hundreds)of socks not to
mention shirts fleaproof earwarmers

etcetera wristers etcetera,my

mother hoped that

i would die etcetera
bravely of course my father used
to become hoarse talking about how it was
a privilege and if only he
could meanwhile my

self etcetera lay quietly
in the deep mud et

cetera
(dreaming,
et
   cetera,of
Your smile
eyes knees and of your Etcetera)

_____

   Among

            these
                    red pieces of
day(against which and
quite silently hills
made of blueandgreen paper

scorchbend ingthem
-selves-U
pcurv E,into:
                anguish(clim
b)ing
s-p-i-r-a-
l
  and,disappear)
                Satanic and blasé

a black goat lookingly wanders

There is nothing left of the world but
into this noth
ing il treno per
Roma si-gnori?
jerk.
ilyr,ushes

_____

in spite of everything
which breathes and moves,since Doom
(with white longest hands
neatening each crease)
will smooth entirely our minds

—before leaving my room
i turn,and(stooping
through the morning)kiss
this pillow,dear
where our heads lived and were.

————————

since feeling is first
who pays any attention
to the syntax of things
will never wholly kiss you;

wholly to be a fool
while Spring is in the world

my blood approves,
and kisses are a better fate
than wisdom
lady i swear by all flowers. Don't cry
—the best gesture of my brain is less than
your eyelids' flutter which says

we are for each other:then
laugh,leaning back in my arms
for life's not a paragraph

And death i think is no parenthesis

————————

i sing of Olaf glad and big
whose warmest heart recoiled at war:
a conscientious object-or

his wellbelovéd colonel(trig
westpointer most succinctly bred)

took erring Olaf soon in hand;
but—though an host of overjoyed
noncoms(first knocking on the head
him)do through icy waters roll
that helplessness which others stroke
with brushes recently employed
anent this muddy toiletbowl,
while kindred intellects evoke
allegiance per blunt instruments—
Olaf(being to all intents
a corpse and wanting any rag
upon what God unto him gave)
responds,without getting annoyed
"I will not kiss your fucking flag"

straightway the silver bird looked grave
(departing hurriedly to shave)

but—though all kinds of officers
(a yearning nation's blueeyed pride)
their passive prey did kick and curse
until for wear their clarion
voices and boots were much the worse,
and egged the firstclassprivates on
his rectum wickedly to tease
by means of skilfully applied
bayonets roasted hot with heat—
Olaf(upon what were once knees)
does almost ceaselessly repeat
"there is some shit I will not eat"

our president,being of which
assertions duly notified
threw the yellowsonofabitch
into a dungeon,where he died

Christ(of His mercy infinite)
i pray to see;and Olaf,too

preponderatingly because
unless statistics lie he was
more brave than me:more blond than you.

---

twi-
        is -Light bird
ful
-ly dar
kness eats

a distance a
c(h)luck
(l)ing of just bells (touch)ing
?mind

(moon begins The
)
now,est hills er dream;new
.oh if

        when:
&
a
nd O impercept i bl

---

a clown's smirk in the skull of a baboon
(where once good lips stalked or eyes firmly stirred)
my mirror gives me,on this afternoon;
i am a shape that can but eat and turd
ere with the dirt death shall him vastly gird,
a coward waiting clumsily to cease
whom every perfect thing meanwhile doth miss;
a hand's impression in an empty glove,
a soon forgotten tune,a house for lease.
I have never loved you dear as now i love

behold this fool who,in the month of June,
having of certain stars and planets heard,
rose very slowly in a tight balloon
until the smallening world became absurd;

him did an archer spy(whose aim had erred
never)and by that little trick or this
he shot the aeronaut down,into the abyss
—and wonderfully i fell through the green groove
of twilight,striking into many a piece.
I have never loved you dear as now i love

god's terrible face,brighter than a spoon,
collects the image of one fatal word;
so that my life(which liked the sun and the moon)
resembles something that has not occurred:
i am a birdcage without any bird,
a collar looking for a dog,a kiss
without lips;a prayer lacking any knees
but something beats within my shirt to prove
he is undead who,living,noone is.
I have never loved you dear as now i love.

Hell(by most humble me which shall increase)
open thy fire!for i have had some bliss
of one small lady upon earth above;
to whom i cry,remembering her face,
i have never loved you dear as now i love

---

somewhere i have never travelled,gladly beyond
any experience,your eyes have their silence:
in your most frail gesture are things which enclose me,
or which i cannot touch because they are too near

your slightest look easily will unclose me
though i have closed myself as fingers,
you open always petal by petal myself as Spring opens
(touching skilfully,mysteriously)her first rose

or if your wish be to close me,i and
my life will shut very beautifully,suddenly,
as when the heart of this flower imagines
the snow carefully everywhere descending;

nothing which we are to perceive in this world equals
the power of your intense fragility:whose texture
compels me with the colour of its countries,
rendering death and forever with each breathing

(i do not know what it is about you that closes
and opens;only something in me understands
the voice of your eyes is deeper than all roses)
nobody,not even the rain,has such small hands

———————

                    r-p-o-p-h-e-s-s-a-g-r
              who
         a)s w(e loo)k
         upnowgath
                    PPEGORHRASS
                              eringint(o-
         aThe):l
              eA
                 !p:
    S   a
                   (r
         rIvInG   .gRrEaPsPhOs)
                                        to
         rea(be)rran(com)gi(e)ngly
         ,grasshopper;

———————

         the boys i mean are not refined
         they go with girls who buck and bite
         they do not give a fuck for luck
         they hump them thirteen times a night

         one hangs a hat upon her tit
         one carves a cross in her behind
         they do not give a shit for wit
         the boys i mean are not refined

they come with girls who bite and buck
who cannot read and cannot write
who laugh like they would fall apart
and masturbate with dynamite

the boys i mean are not refined
they cannot chat of that and this
they do not give a fart for art
they kill like you would take a piss

they speak whatever's on their mind
they do whatever's in their pants
the boys i mean are not refined
they shake the mountains when they dance

———————

as freedom is a breakfastfood
or truth can live with right and wrong
or molehills are from mountains made
—long enough and just so long
will being pay the rent of seem
and genius please the talentgang
and water most encourage flame

as hatracks into peachtrees grow
or hopes dance best on bald men's hair
and every finger is a toe
and any courage is a fear
—long enough and just so long
will the impure think all things pure
and hornets wail by children stung

or as the seeing are the blind
and robins never welcome spring
nor flatfolk prove their world is round
nor dingsters die at break of dong

and common's rare and millstones float
—long enough and just so long
tomorrow will not be too late

worms are the words but joy's the voice
down shall go which and up come who
breasts will be breasts thighs will be thighs
deeds cannot dream what dreams can do
—time is a tree(this life one leaf)
but love is the sky and i am for you
just so long and long enough

---

anyone lived in a pretty how town
(with up so floating many bells down)
spring summer autumn winter
he sang his didn't he danced his did.

Women and men(both little and small)
cared for anyone not at all
they sowed their isn't they reaped their same
sun moon stars rain

children guessed(but only a few
and down they forgot as up they grew
autumn winter spring summer)
that noone loved him more by more

when by now and tree by leaf
she laughed his joy she cried his grief
bird by snow and stir by still
anyone's any was all to her

someones married their everyones
laughed their cryings and did their dance
(sleep wake hope and then)they
said their nevers they slept their dream

stars rain sun moon
(and only the snow can begin to explain
how children are apt to forget to remember
with up so floating many bells down)

one day anyone died i guess
(and noone stooped to kiss his face)
busy folk buried them side by side
little by little and was by was

all by all and deep by deep
and more by more they dream their sleep
noone and anyone earth by april
wish by spirit and if by yes.

Women and men(both dong and ding)
summer autumn winter spring
reaped their sowing and went their came
sun moon stars rain

----

my father moved through dooms of love
through sames of am through haves of give,
singing each morning out of each night
my father moved through depths of height

this motionless forgetful where
turned at his glance to shining here;
that if(so timid air is firm)
under his eyes would stir and squirm

newly as from unburied which
floats the first who,his april touch
drove sleeping selves to swarm their fates
woke dreamers to their ghostly roots

and should some why completely weep
my father's fingers brought her sleep:
vainly no smallest voice might cry
for he could feel the mountains grow.

Lifting the valleys of the sea
my father moved through griefs of joy;
praising a forehead called the moon
singing desire into begin

joy was his song and joy so pure
a heart of star by him could steer
and pure so now and now so yes
the wrists of twilight would rejoice

keen as midsummer's keen beyond
conceiving mind of sun will stand,
so strictly(over utmost him
so hugely)stood my father's dream

his flesh was flesh his blood was blood:
no hungry man but wished him food;
no cripple wouldn't creep one mile
uphill to only see him smile.

Scorning the pomp of must and shall
my father moved through dooms of feel;
his anger was as right as rain
his pity was as green as grain

septembering arms of year extend
less humbly wealth to foe and friend
than he to foolish and to wise
offered immeasurable is

proudly and(by octobering flame
beckoned)as earth will downward climb,
so naked for immortal work
his shoulders marched against the dark

his sorrow was as true as bread:
no liar looked him in the head;
if every friend became his foe
he'd laugh and build a world with snow.

My father moved through theys of we,
singing each new leaf out of each tree
(and every child was sure that spring
danced when she heard my father sing)

then let men kill which cannot share,
let blood and flesh be mud and mire,
scheming imagine,passion willed,
freedom a drug that's bought and sold

giving to steal and cruel kind,
a heart to fear,to doubt a mind,
to differ a disease of same,
conform the pinnacle of am

though dull were all we taste as bright,
bitter all utterly things sweet,
maggoty minus and dumb death
all we inherit,all bequeath

and nothing quite so least as truth
—i say though hate were why men breathe—
because my father lived his soul
love is the whole and more than all

---

plato told

him:he couldn't
believe it(jesus

told him;he
wouldn't believe
it)lao

tsze
certainly told
him,and general
(yes

mam)
sherman;
and even
(believe it
or

not)you
told him:i told
him;we told him
(he didn't believe it,no

sir)it took
a nipponized bit of
the old sixth

avenue
el;in the top of his head:to tell

him

---

pity this busy monster,manunkind,

not. Progress is a comfortable disease:
your victim(death and life safely beyond)

plays with the bigness of his littleness
—electrons deify one razorblade
into a mountainrange;lenses extend

unwish through curving wherewhen till unwish
returns on its unself.
                    A world of made
is not a world of born—pity poor flesh

and trees,poor stars and stones, but never this
fine specimen of hypermagical

ultraomnipotence. We doctors know

a hopeless case if—listen:there's a hell
of a good universe next door;let's go

———————

a grin without a
face(a look
without an i)
be care

ful(touch noth
ing)or
it'll disapp
ear bangl

essly(into sweet
the earth)&
nobody
(including our

selves)
will reme
mber
(for 1 frac

tion of
a mo
ment)where
what how

when
who why
which
(or anything)

H. L. DAVIS
(1894–1960)

Proud Riders

We rode hard, and brought the cattle from brushy springs,
From heavy dying thickets, leaves wet as snow;
From high places, white-grassed and dry in the wind;
Draws where the quaken-asps were yellow and white,
And the leaves spun and spun like money spinning.
We poured them on to the trail, and rode for town.

Men in the fields leaned forward in the wind,
Stood in the stubble and watched the cattle passing.
The wind bowed all, the stubble shook like a shirt.
We threw the reins by the yellow and black fields, and rode,
And came, riding together, into the town
Which is by the gray bridge, where the alders are.
The white-barked alder trees dropping big leaves
Yellow and black, into the cold black water.
Children, little cold boys, watched after us—
The freezing wind flapped their clothes like windmill paddles.
Down the flat frosty road we crowded the herd:
High stepped the horses for us, proud riders in autumn.

ROLFE HUMPRHIES

(1894–1969)

Europa

The party was no good again!
Only the brilliant girls redeemed
A dull and tedious affair:
What was the matter with the men?
To her, at least, they always seemed
Embarrassed or, perhaps, afraid,
Polite, intelligent, and thin,
Never a bull-necked savage there;
So she came home and went to bed.

Exasperated, she undressed,
Shook back her hair, and tumbled in,
Pulled up the sheet again, and pressed
Its chilly edge against her breast—
She wanted so to be possessed,
And she had really never been.
Her body's manufactured ache
Kept her half-sleeping, half-awake.

She listened to the big old boats,
The ponderous deliberate hulls
Whose hoarse and raucous whistle-notes
Set up a pounding in her pulse:
They were not boats, they were not boats,
They were not boats at all, but bulls
With red and thunder-swollen throats,
They were not boats, they were not boats—

She suddenly switched on the light,
Looked at her body in the light,
Her slender body, slim and white,—
They were not boats at all, but bulls!—
She could not stand it any more,

She flung the bedclothes on the floor,
Swung herself half-around, and rose,
Hurried and firm, put on her clothes,
Slipped down the stairs and out the door.

Out in the street, she heard the blare
More nakedly across the air.
Each bull was bawling to his cow
More softly now, more softly now
Each lowing urgent bull besought her. . . .
She turned her footsteps toward the water.

And when she reached the water-front
She saw her monster, huge and blunt;
She saw the shiny river rise
Up to the level of his eyes,
He had his secrets hidden in
The water, and he did not stir,
Firm in his rut he waited her.

She dipped her fingers in the flood,
She dipped her fingers to the wrist,
Oh, what a pounding in her blood!
The water sipped and sucked and hissed
Against the fragile, paper-thin,
Red-hot sheet-metal of her skin,
Preliminary, cool, caressed
The burning nipples of her breast
As, glad because she could not swim,
She started wading out to him.

Test Paper

What do we praise?—Sunsets, and open fires,
America, and mother love, I guess;
The merry laughter of a little child,
And poems that touch the heart with tenderness.

What do we really praise?—Oh, Life and Time,
(With capitals), books that Fadiman commends,
The chromium bars, the streamlined cars and trains,
The music played for music's newest friends.

What do we praise beyond all this?—High art,
God's majesty and sacraments and grace,
The universal music of the spheres,
The mysteries of interstellar space.

Come down to earth. What is it you and I,
My love, deep in our heart of hearts, adore,
Cherish, and tend?—Each other. Not so fast.
Maybe, a little; but ourselves much more.

Last question. (On your honor.) What do all
Praise, absolutely, in this day and age?
Re-read the question; answer thoughtfully;
Write nothing on this portion of the page.

*From the Green Book of Yfan**

(Cywydd deuair fyrion)

Margaret Morse,
Mistress of horse,
Marshalled a troop
Matched, head to croup,
Marched through the dales
Mauling all males.

---

*The Green Book of Yfan, the proper name being either an archaic form of Evan or a truncated version of Myfanwy (scholars are uncertain) is a manuscript of highly dubious provenance and authenticity. Its few tattered and defaced pages contain little of poetic worth. The fragment above was presumably part of a longer alphabetical chronicle like the medieval *Battle of Fontenoy*. It seems possible that through a scribe's error two entirely different poems have been here confused, for the tone of the O, P, and possibly R, stanzas seems markedly unlike the rest.

Normandy's knights,
Noting such sights,
Never drew rein
Not till they came
North to the firth
Now called the Forth.

Ocean and oar
Opened no door.
Over the weirs
Omens and fears,
Odors of mould.
Only the old

Pity the proud.
Purple through cloud,
Peregrines knive,
Plummet and dive.
Pards on the prowl
Pybass* the owl.

Quentin the Queer,
Quaffing his beer,
Quoted a million
Quips from Quintilian.
Quince-tree and pear
Quavered in air.

Rolfe, for renown,
Wrote this all down,
Runes on a page
Rotting with age,
Ruined by Time,
Ruthless to rhyme.

*In verbs of this highly spondaic quality it is permissible license, for metrical effect, or by special dispensation from the *Penkerdd*, or Chief Poet, to transpose initial consonants, providing they are mute plosives, or plosive mutes.

EUGENE JOLAS

(1894–1952)

Mater Dolorosa

illa mala rulidala
singa rusta prilanala
buina ruli astara

ranto molo mintenolo
sira tingo frali brolo
sino rembo bustira

flinga dinas astarosa
slenga timba mulitosa
mista truna imbarun

dringa flores asirama
frils amina glinganama
doli sinta gloombarun

H. PHELPS PUTNAM

(1894–1948)

Words of an Old Woman

If you wound my hide it bleeds to enrich your crops;
After all these years I keep on giving blood
For the foreigners who called me a virgin land
And went about their business raping me.
But I think that maybe I should have been long dead,
For they gashed my body with these festering wounds,
Destroying the decent privacy of an old woman
With sperm which should have better spent itself
In the young whore they left across the sea—
I was never raped by a bull, I was never borne
To a cloudy lust on the back of a silly thought.
I was chaste and they called me virginal,
And it was unwise to make mistakes with me,
Me, a matronly woman with the Sun my paramour,
Laden and satisfied, with clear streams cooling my flesh.
I had given suck to races, wonders, and gods
And my skin was still smooth and the uplands of my body
Broad and luxuriant, and my thighs were wide to the Sun
And my body-hair luxuriant and odorous.
I was ripe and calm and my children settled down.
What had I done that my life should be used again?
I felt the bewildered Portugee breaking in,
Who spilled diseases into my ancient veins;
I felt the Spanish blade probing my side,
Pulling my guts out to the light of day
In lust for the seven cities of a feverish dream;
And I felt the French who called me heathenish,
Infesting my quietude with their earnest holy-men.
So I learned the ferocious manners of new folks
And I was sick of the day that I arose
Gleaming and fresh from the seas
And my neck alive with burning jewels of ice.
I was a tall girl with my head at one end of the world

36

And my feet at the other, beautiful,
And fit for the close embraces of the Sun.
Yes, I had cause for lament, but it was too soon;
It was little grief and small indignity—
I had not learned the extent of such disease.
The stubborn conquerors came in flotsam waves,
The low inheritors of a gimcrack world;
The unholy horde came from the northern lands,
And the acne slowly destroyed my loveliness.
I grew decrepit and my teeth fell,
My hair withered and my breast flattened,
My sweat was rancid and my baths foul;
I was foster-mother to cheap merchandise.
Listen, forced children, I will tell you this—
It is dangerous to fool with the old and the wise,
And I, who am both, am dangerous.
I have touched new flesh with my unwilling hands,
The bastards of other places and distant times;
I have molded fools in the images of men,
Making them lovelorn in all other lands,
Making them desirous with a secret homesickness,
Uneasy in my arms or in other arms.
For I have the strength of my own habitude,
I have the force of the mistress of the Sun.
I shall trouble the girlish countries over the seas;
They will wake at night and shriek in their narrow beds,
Having dreamed in sleep of my final certitude.

Hasbrouck and the Rose

Hasbrouck was there and so were Bill
And Smollet Smith the poet, and Ames was there.
After his thirteenth drink, the burning Smith,
Raising his fourteenth trembling in the air,
Said, "Drink with me, Bill, drink up to the Rose."
But Hasbrouck laughed like old men in a myth,
Inquiring, "Smollet, are you drunk? What rose?"
And Smollet said, "I drunk? It may be so;

Which comes from brooding on the flower, the flower
I mean toward which mad hour by hour
I travel brokenly; and I shall know,
With Hermes and the alchemists—but, hell,
What use is it talking that way to you?
Hard-boiled, unbroken egg, what can you care
For the enfolded passion of the Rose?"
Then Hasbrouck's voice rang like an icy bell:

"Arcane romantic flower, meaning what?
Do you know what it meant? Do I?
We do not know.
Unfolding pungent Rose, the glowing bath
Of ecstasy and clear forgetfulness;
Closing and secret bud one might achieve
By long debauchery—
Except that I have eaten it, and so
There is no call for further lunacy.
In Springfield, Massachusetts, I devoured
The mystic, the improbable, the Rose.
For two nights and a day, rose and rosette
And petal after petal and the heart,
I had my banquet by the beams
Of four electric stars which shone
Weakly into my room, for there,
Drowning their light and gleaming at my side,
Was the incarnate star
Whose body bore the stigma of the Rose.
And that is all I know about the flower;
I have eaten it—it has disappeared.
There is no Rose."

Young Smollet Smith let fall his glass; he said,
"O Jesus, Hasbrouck, am I drunk or dead?"

Bill Gets Burned

Bill Williams was in Hell without a guide
And wandering around alone and cold,
Hoping for fires, for he said, "The name
Of Hell is not enough to keep the old
Place dignified without a flame."
Bill was a hero, so he wandered on.

Then, near a city, where the apartments thinned
To suburbs, and the trolley-cars
Moved jerkily along the oily street
By clustered corners selling drugs and meat
And real-estate and tailoring and tinned
Denatured food, and by the hutches where
The rabbits bred the images of God,
Bill found a playground near a school, and there
Erect against the dusk was raised a tree,
Not blossoming, a three-armed gallows-tree.
Its fruit was only this—one empty noose,
And on the other arms two women hung
Not quite alive and yet not very dead.
"Sweet Christ, what savagery," Bill said.

And then he saw there was a troubled girl
Standing beneath the rope which dangled loose
And reaching for it with her feverish hands.
She heard Bill's step. "Come, lift me up," she cried,
Her smile was like destructive drink, "I too
Will hang, I shall be sisterly.
There is no other way, and you
Are strong and maybe good and not so wise
As I—why, you might even hang with me."

And Bill was dazed; he spoke to one of them
Who hung. "Please, tortured lady, tell
This girl that she is mad in Hell."
Which woman had no guile and answered, "No,
I cannot say it. When he kept from me
My house, my lovely garden, and my child

I suffered much; but that was long ago."
She closed her honest eyes, her hand caressed
Her noose, she said, "Oh, excellent and mild
My pain that keeps my love for me."
Bill touched her other hand and found her rings
Were hot and seared his fingers horribly.

Bill nursed his hand and would have soothed his mind,
When she, the other woman hanging there,
On whose exquisite face such great despair
Had walked as never came to Bill, said, "Boy,
They do not know, they have not been like me,
A prize producer of the race, a cow,
And served to a lusty male, to be a bed
And board and servant in his house;
For which my pay is sometimes puppy-love.
There are no flowers in Hell;
Instead of flowers each one a constant bell
Saying that time has gone and I am here,
Still young, my belly ripe with slavery.
And all this body once was like a soul,
And now my soul is only common flesh;
Thought after thought he undermined the frail
Delight, and in its place has given me
These nervous heats which are not passionate
But now most unavoidably are mine
And raise my blood to empty bawdiness."
"Enough," said Bill and closed her mouth with his,
Holding her swinging body to himself,
And murmured unheard pitying words beneath
The unlikely delicacy of his kiss.
Her hands caressed his head, her face became
Translucent with a small suffocated flame—
But suddenly was turned away from hope
And was not light; "No, go away," she said,
"For solace only tightens at my rope."

And Bill had found some fires in Hell;
His brain was scorched and all his flesh
Was cowardly with burns. And now

The female moon appeared, whose calendar
Is marked with blood, and lighted him away.
He left the unhung girl, forgetting her,
And took a taxi to the city where
He had a room engaged by telegraph,
And lay awake all night and suffered there.

CHARLES REZNIKOFF
(1894–1976)

On Brooklyn Bridge I saw a man drop dead.
It meant no more than if he were a sparrow.

Above us rose Manhattan;
below, the river spread to meet sea and sky.

———

I met in a merchant's place
Diana:
lithe body and flowerlike face.

Through the woods I had looked for her
and beside the waves.

———

The shopgirls leave their work
quietly.

Machines are still, tables and chairs
darken.

The silent rounds of mice and roaches begin.

———

How shall we mourn you who are killed and wasted,
sure that you would not die with your work unended,
as if the iron scythe in the grass stops for a flower?

———

My work done, I lean on the window-sill,
watching the dripping trees.
The rain is over, the wet pavement shines.
From the bare twigs
rows of drops like shining buds are hanging.

In the shop, she, her mother, and grandmother,
thinking at times of women at windows in still streets,
or women reading, a glow on resting hands.

The Idiot

With green stagnant eyes,
arms and legs
loose ends of string in a wind,

keep smiling at your father.

She who worked patiently,
her children grown,
lies in her grave patiently.

Epidemic

Streamers of crepe idling before doors.

Her work was to count linings—
the day's seconds in dozens.

The house-wreckers have left the door and a staircase,
now leading to the empty room of night.

Aphrodite Vrania

The ceaseless weaving of the uneven water.

April

The stiff lines of the twigs
blurred by buds.

Out of the hills the trees bulge;
the sky hangs in lumps of cloud.

How difficult for me is Hebrew:
even the Hebrew for *mother*, for *bread*, for *sun*
is foreign. How far have I been exiled, Zion.

I have learnt the Hebrew blessing before eating bread;
is there no blessing before reading Hebrew?

After I had worked all day at what I earn my living,
I was tired. Now my own work has lost another day,
I thought, but began slowly,
and slowly my strength came back to me.
Surely, the tide comes in twice a day.

The Hebrew of your poets, Zion,
is like oil upon a burn,
cool as oil;
after work,
the smell in the street at night
of the hedge in flower.
Like Solomon,
I have married and married the speech of strangers;
none are like you, Shulamite.

Though our thoughts often, we ourselves
are seldom together.
We have told each other
all that has happened; it seems to me—
for want of a better word—that we are both unlucky.
Even our meetings have been so brief
we should call them partings, and of our words
I remember most "good-by".

Among the heaps of brick and plaster lies
a girder, still itself among the rubbish.

Epitaphs

I

Drowning
I felt for a moment reaching towards me
finger tips against mine.

II

You mice,
that ate the crumbs of my freedom,
lo!

III

The clock strikes:
these are the steps of our departure.

IV

A brown oak leaf
scraping the sidewalk
frightened me.

V

Proserpine
swallowed only six seeds
of the pomegranate
and had to stay six months among the dead—
I was a glutton.

———

Millinery District

The clouds, piled in rows like merchandise,
become dark; lights are lit in the lofts;
the milliners, tacking bright flowers on straw shapes,
say, glancing out of the windows,
It is going to snow;
and soon they hear the snow scratching the panes. By night
it is high on the sills.
The snow fills up the footprints
in the streets, the ruts of wagons and of motor trucks.
Except for the whir of the car
brushing the tracks clear of snow,
the streets are hushed.
At closing time, the girls breathe deeply
the clean air of the streets
sweet after the smell of merchandise.

A dead gull in the road,
the body flattened
and the wings spread—
but not to fly out of the dust
over the waves;
and a robin dead beside a hedge,
the little claws drawn up
against the dusty bundle:
has there been a purge of Jews
among the birds?

I like this secret walking
in the fog;
unseen, unheard,
among the bushes
thick with drops;
the solid path invisible
a rod away—
and only the narrow present is alive.

Rainy Season

It has been raining for three days.
The faces of the giants
on the bill-boards
still smile,
but the gilt has been washed from the sky:
we see the iron world.

Of course, we must die.
How else will the world be rid of
the old telephone numbers
we cannot forget?

The numbers
it would be foolish—
utterly useless—
to call.

My grandfather, dead long before I was born,
died among strangers; and all the verse he wrote
was lost—
except for what
still speaks through me
as mine.

A grove of small trees, branches thick with berries,
and within it, the constant twitter of birds.
The trees of the park this cold windy day
for want of leaves
are hung with paper—strips of dirty paper.

Millinery District

Many fair hours have been buried here
to spring up again as flowers—
on hats.

Similes

Indifferent as a statue
to the slogan
scribbled on its pedestal.

The way an express train
snubs the passengers at a local station.

Like a notebook forgotten on a seat in the bus,
full of names, addresses and telephone numbers:
important, no doubt, to the owner—
but of no interest whatever
to anyone else.

Words like drops of water on a stove—
a hiss and gone.

Epitaph

Not the five feet of water to your chin
but the inch above the tip of your nose.

Free Verse

Not like flowers in the city
in neat rows or in circles
but like dandelions
scattered on a lawn.

from
Early History of a Writer

I had been bothered by a secret weariness
with meter and regular stanzas
grown a little stale. The smooth lines and rhymes
seemed to me affected, a false stress on words and syllables—
fake flowers
in the streets in which I walked.
And yet I found prose
without the burst of song and sudden dancing—
without the intensity which I wanted.
The brand-new verse some Americans were beginning to
    write—
after the French "free verse," perhaps,
or the irregular rhythms of Walt Whitman,
the English translations of the Hebrew Bible
and, earlier yet, the rough verse of the Anglo-Saxons—
seemed to me, when I first read it,
right:
not cut to patterns, however cleverly,
nor poured into ready molds,
but words and phrases flowing as the thought;
to be read just as common speech
but for stopping at the turn of each line—
and this like a rest in music or a turn in the dance.
(I found it no criticism that to read such verse as prose
was to have a kind of prose,
for that was not to read it as it was written.)
And with the even artificial beat of the old meters,
I gave up the artifice of rhyme:
not only because I had the authority of Milton
and the usage of the Elizabethans in their plays;
I liked a Doric music better.

Now, too I became friendly with one my own age,
whom I had met the summer before
thinking him just another acquaintance.
Al proved to be as helpful as my new reading.

He had come to see me at my home that summer
about to teach in the West where I had studied
five years before
that I might tell him of the place;
I had little to say and he listened
almost indifferently,
smiling half in friendship and half mockingly,
hardly looking at me with his bright blue eyes.
When he was back next summer for his vacation,
with nothing better to do, perhaps,
he came to see me again
but now we had the new verse to talk of.
I showed him what of mine had been taken for publication
in a new magazine for verse only;
but he read my verse as I had never read verse before,
scrutinizing it, phrase by phrase
and word by word, thought and image, thought and sound;
and much, if not all, that had seemed good to me
now had the dead sound of a counterfeit coin
on his marble good sense.
That was the way he had read Shakespeare at college—
without such effect, of course—
and so, except that I gave little thought
to image or sound,
was how I had read my law cases.
But, in spite of my early dislike of journalism
because of its hurried and careless writing,
I used to write verse just as carelessly—
as it flew into my head.
Now doing just what Al did,
I saw that I could use the expensive machinery
that had cost me four years of hard work at law
and which I had thought useless for my writing:
prying sentences open to look at the exact meaning;
weighing words to choose only those that had meat for my
          purpose
and throwing the rest away as empty shells.
I, too, could scrutinize every word and phrase
as if in a document or the opinion of a judge

and listen, as well, for tones and overtones,
leaving only the pithy, the necessary, the clear and plain.

Al read nothing on his knees,
and delighted in finding out for himself
what made a poem or story tick—
if it did. We began to spend much time together,
our spirits swaggering about,
blaming and praising each other's writing,
as well as that of the rest of the world—
"we poets whose lives begin in gladness."
Perhaps, if all our eager talk had been written down,
some of it would have seemed, afterwards,
as jejune as comments an arrogant self
had written in the margin of books
in those proud days when I read with a pencil.
But not all. We might, for example, talk about the story from
     the Japanese
that Lafcadio Hearn used. A man is lost in the woods.
It is going to storm. Anxious to ask his way,
he hurries up to what he takes for a peasant,
walking ahead of him in the gathering darkness.
The peasant—or whatever it is he is talking to—
turns
and the traveler sees a face without nose or eyes,
smooth as an egg, and rushes off.
Then, as he runs, stumbling, anxious now only to get away,
he sees again what he takes to be a peasant walking ahead of
     him.
He runs up, eager for any human companionship
after that earlier sight,
and blurts out what he has just seen;
and the same face turns to him again and asks:
"Was it anything like this?"
I might have said that the story was moving
because it meant that we should meet again
the horrible we thought we had escaped,
or that our secret terrors warn us
of what we shall surely face. Al said:
"Compare this with a German fairy tale.

When the Germans want to make a figure horrible,
a witch, for instance,
they enlarge the eyes, lengthen the nose, the teeth, the
          nails—
they add, they exaggerate;
but the Japanese make a more horrible figure
because less human:
they take everything away—nose, mouth, and even eyes."

I reread my verse that had been taken for publication
and found much in so few lines to change or strike out
and wrote the magazine about it,
but the editor assured me, of the longer poem,
that it was meant—
by Apollo, no doubt—
to be in quatrains, as first written,
and that the irregularities with which I proposed to remedy
          the verse
only spoiled it.
However, if changes were in order,
she suggested a number off-hand
and these I could not see at all.
In the meantime, I had sent her more verse,
of which she took another poem
to add to the two to be published,
but would not have one or two I thought the best—
better than any of mine she had taken.
The other magazines, to judge by what they were printing,
were not even worth bothering with, I thought,
with the arrogance of the young;
and for the judgment of the editor who was to print my verse
I had, by this time,
little respect.
Besides, publication in a magazine, pleasant as it would be,
seemed less important than perfection,
at least whatever degree of it I could reach.
And, as I thought about it,
it seemed to me that if I could accustom myself to working at
          my verse daily,
revising until I had a group to my own satisfaction,

and could have group after group printed,
I might in time, say, in a lifetime,
have a few poems—
the quintessence of all I had to say.
But I could not, it seemed to me,
just put my verse away in a drawer until the Messiah should
     come;
for the impulse to write—in which I had such pleasure—
and above all to revise wholeheartedly,
would be, perhaps would have to be, stimulated
by regular publication.
And again, revision year after year
of what I might have lying about
unpublished,
would become destructive merely,
rubbing out much that by constant review
would seem unnecessary
and had become tiresome.
Publication in a magazine, such as was now promised,
of a couple of poems now and then—
even as I would have them—
hardly seemed worth while.
But, since I did not hope for a publisher
to print my verse soon at his own risk
and I did not have the money to pay for a publisher's
     imprint—
nor did I relish the pretence—
why, I thought, I should print privately,
that is, pay the printer and make no pretence of having a
     publisher at all.
There was little notice to be had that way, I knew,
among the crowd of new books;
but, besides the stimulation to write and revise,
I would clear my head and heart
for new work. Yes, the work was the thing.
Large circulation is pleasant, of course,
but I did not find it necessary:
as if one has seen something exciting in the street
he must tell it—
perhaps because man is communicative—

but, after he has told his vision
once or twice,
handed on his knowledge to two or three,
he is free to go about his other business.

Besides, the urgency of war (for the country was now in the
    First World War)
made it seem advisable to arrange my affairs;
and, since my affairs were verse,
to put it, slight though in bulk and value, in order
and leave it printed behind me;
for I doubted that anyone else
would go to that trouble and any expense.
I knew two stories to strengthen me in my resolution—
one I had read and the other my mother told me;
Balzac's story of the painter who kept working at his painting
until when seen last it was only a mass of paint,
except for a beautiful hand
which showed what the painting might have been—
this for the danger of endless revision;
and my mother's story of her father
who became a kind of broker
making his little commissions on sales of cattle or wheat
and beguiled his spirit as he wandered about the countryside
writing verse in Hebrew—
until he suddenly died of influenza far from home.
And when with his bundle of clothes there was brought back
    a sheaf of papers—
his verse, the writing of thirty years—
my grandmother burnt every scrap of it, dearly as she loved
    him;
for fear that the writing which she could not read
or, if she could, did not understand,
might send her children to jail
should any of it be construed as treasonable against the Czar.
Well, I would leave no writing of mine,
if I could help it,
to the mercy of those who loved me.
I would print

and, though I knew it was an unlikely way to gain name or
    money
(not that I cared much for either),
I also knew a Chinese proverb
that one who can work ten years without recognition
will be known everywhere,
and the tradition in English verse of private publication
as the "Rubaiyat" was published and "Leaves of Grass."
Later, when I was to have much time and a little money,
I learnt how to print;
indeed, setting type by hand and running a platen-press by
    foot
is not too hard:
the great wheel turning, the rollers moving down over the
    sticky black platen,
shining arms sliding smoothly into their grooves
and the type closing on the blank paper—
to leave a printed sheet.
I would stop the wheel at each revolution,
unable to feed the press as a printer could
but, slow as I was, I would print four hundred sheets in a
    couple of hours—
more than enough.
A difficulty was room for the heavy press.
I had it in the basement of my parents' house;
when they moved, the press was dismantled,
coated with oil, stored, and finally sold—and lost.

BESSIE SMITH

(1894–1937)

Empty Bed Blues

I woke up this mornin' with an awful achin' head
I woke up this mornin' with a awful achin' head
My new man had left me just a room and a empty bed

Bought me a coffee grinder, got the best one I could find
Bought me a coffee grinder, got the best one I could find
So he could grind my coffee, 'cause he had a brand new grind

He's a deep sea diver with a stroke that can't go wrong
He's a deep sea diver with a stroke that can't go wrong
He can touch the bottom and his wind holds out so long

He knows how to thrill me and he thrills me night and day
Lord, he knows how to thrill me, he thrills me night and day
He's got a new way of lovin' almost takes my breath away

Lord, he's got that sweet somethin', and I told my gal friend
    Lou
He's got that sweet somethin', and I told my gal friend Lou
From the way she's ravin', she must have gone and tried it
    too.

When my bed get empty, make me feel awful mean and blue
When my bed get empty, make me feel awful mean and blue
My springs are gettin' rusty, sleepin' single like I do

Bought him a blanket, pillow for his head at night
Bought him a blanket, pillow for his head at night
Then I bought him a mattress so he could lay just right

He came home one evening with his spirit way up high
He came home one evening with his spirit way up high
What he had to give me made me wring my hands and cry

He give me a lesson that I never had before
He give me a lesson that I never had before
When he got through teachin' me, from my elbow down was
    sore

He boiled my first cabbage and he made it awful hot
He boiled my first cabbage and he made it awful hot
Then he put in the bacon, it overflowed the pot

When you get good lovin', never go and spread the news
Yeah, it will double cross you and leave you with them empty
    bed blues.

GENEVIEVE TAGGARD

(1894–1948)

Everyday Alchemy

Men go to women mutely for their peace;
And they, who lack it most, create it when
They make—because they must, loving their men—
A solace for sad bosom-bended heads. There
Is all the meager peace men get—no otherwhere;
No mountain space, no tree with placid leaves,
Or heavy gloom beneath a young girl's hair,
No sound of valley bell on autumn air,
Or room made home with doves along the eaves,
Ever holds peace like this, poured by poor women
Out of their heart's poverty, for worn men.

Thirst

There is a bird that hangs head-down and cries
Between the mango leaves and passion vines.
Below, a spotted serpent twines
And blunts its head against the yellowing skies.
Along the warping ground a turtle scrapes,
And tortured lie glazed fishes in marsh grass.
Across the sky that burnishes like brass
A bat veers, stupid with the yeast of grapes.

To One Loved Wholly Within Wisdom

Someone will reap you like a field,
Pile your gathered plunder,

Garner what you bring to yield,
Turn your beauty under;

In cruel usages, in such
Sickle-cutting, heaping,

Certain women toil too much,
Weary of their reaping;

Someone else may winnow you;
Someone else may plunder;

I have cut too many new
Swathes, and broken under

Soil that should have fallow lain
To be greedy either

For the shattered stalk, the stain
Where the clusters wither.

To Mr. Maunder Maunder, Professional Poet

I'll be your Gigadibs,—despise
    You, root and branch and lock and barrel;
The filmy way you use your eyes;
    The words you take for your apparel;
The way you edit with discretion;
The poetry you pick for nice
Work of a safe and sane profession.

You should be shown the edge of the sword,
    And taught to die for a stubborn phrase
Or burn on pyres for a word!
    And have swift passions, in a horde,
Run up and peer into your face
And jeer your petty, petty grace—
Have mercy on Thy Poets, Lord!

Here, learn the temper of the tool
    You wield so avid for success.

I will not touch your "beautiful"—
   Carve beauty more and rant her less . . .
The English Language is no whore—
What are you making rhyme-schemes for?

To the Powers of Desolation

O mortal boy we cannot stop
The leak in that great wall where death seeps in
With hands or bodies, frantic mouths, or sleep.
Over the wall, over the wall's top
I have seen rising waters, waters of desolation.

From my despair bibles are written, children begotten;
Women open the wrong doors; men lie in ditches retching,—
The horrible bright eyes of insanity fix on a blue fly,
Focus, enlarge. Dear mortal, escape
You cannot. I hear the drip of eternity above the quiet buzz
   of your sleep.
The waters are pouring, boiling over the wall; at the door
Where murder is under way they fall knocking on silence.
Go, that we may not hunger any more,
Or repeat again the wild ritual, the pang;
I will lie face downward
In an oblivion of waters,
Weeping in no way except in these words,
Caring then for nothing; for the blue wasp in the dabble of
   blood, perhaps, only,
While the slow waters pour.

To the Natural World: at 37

Exquisite world, powerful, joyous, splendid,
Where, almost when we learn to live, our life is ended,
Where, when we gather our trophy errors in,
And face the array and cannot again begin
To make another life less fatal, less

Like a poor travesty of some greatness,
World, you rebuke us calmly, ceaselessly,
With mute round of rising sun and mimicking sea,
With flood and ebb and taciturn refrain
In round diurnal rings, waxing to wane.
Our mortal life runs through you its swift line
Closing no circle, marking its scratch design,
Fusiform, the spindle, this is its mortal shape;—
O lovely world, midway in large landscape
I pause, look forward. Weakness with wisdom lie
Ahead with nodding age; error and energy
Behind, dim in regret and chaos where
I left my early self and got the despair
That seizes all who see how folly gone
Is their sweet youth with darkness sudden on.
World deign, for one moment, O deign to culminate
One wave in me; O in me consummate
Your surge with all beholding happy power.
So, overlapping once, here in the midway hour,
Let me watch outward splendor solemnly for
Life's brief in all this bigness, O sun's calm, O

Sea's roar.

Try Tropic

(For a Sick Generation)

Try tropic for your balm,
Try storm,
And after storm, calm.
Try snow of heaven, heavy, soft and slow,
Brilliant and warm.
Nothing will help, and nothing do much harm.

Drink iron from rare springs; follow the sun;
Go far
To get the beam of some medicinal star;
Or in your anguish run
The gauntlet of all zones to an ultimate one.

Fever and chill
Punish you still,
Earth has no zone to work against your ill.

Burn in the jewelled desert with the toad.
Catch lace
Of evening mist across your haunted face;
Or walk in upper air, the slanted road.
It will not lift that load;
Nor will large seas undo your subtle ill.

Nothing can cure and nothing kill
What ails your eyes, what cuts your pulse in two
And not kill you.

All Around the Town

It's a long way from Keats' Corner to Sandburg Ave.
Myself, I'm living now on Fearing Sq.
Eliot Park in the better part of town is for key-holders only.
It always seemed forlorn to me; perhaps some sewer leaking,
Something faintly dead under the shrubs near the band-
    stand . . .
No roller-skaters, hurdy-gurdies, cops . . . Some of my
    friends enjoy
The old-world odour. Spatted and hatted and frocked
They sit contemplating their shoe-shines, perplexed, under
    dismal yews,
Transplanted from England.
                         What a city we live in!
I hear the rents are unusually high out in the Tate section.
At the corner of Auslander and Wurdeman they say business
    is brisk.
But observe: the stucco fronts are flimsy; the paint peels.
I like Fearing Sq., myself. It is so central.

Bounding Line

Silver rubs rocks and furs the twig.
All that was little is still and big.
Attention folds and stoops
To the snail, to slants and loops—
Thread of spider arrayed on the fern.

I am frost's fleck, the grain,
The fissure, the dented vein.
Here looks the insect's eye
Against lens to magnify
The stuff of frost and chill-burn.

Large swells the hoist of shade;
Infinity far overhead.
I am frost, the rim made of shine
On the twig, mercurial line
To cut the small from the big.

Small is good, rests on the ground.
Small's to be seen, small has bound
In shape like crystal cut.
Crystal-frost lies white in the rut.
Crystal-frost rubs gaudy the twig.

Hymn to Yellow

La, la, la. To live with, to be like, to be
The serene, the level color. At ease in being. Of illusion clean.
Here is our kind. Parable of the bee's departure
On a swoon of air, lifted, guided, beguiled
To a bonfire of bloom, the yellow crest, la, la, la.
Corona horizon, utter pure, utter glow texture,
Flower goal nodding; new era's flange, la, la.

Translate us here, with the bee's literal urge,
Our lives soft bullets to this target, peace.
Large ritual—satisfaction luminous to no fraud.

Human burial, unalone, in quiet color accrued.
La, la, la into sepulcher, la, la into yellow,
Exuberance passing on, la, la, la,
Bold and bland into deathless change, the cool petal.

Bury us not in foaming snow, bury us not in brown,
Scatter us not in ash, sluice us not in green veins.
We decline to inhabit ideal blue. Divest us of love's blood,
Of red, and the splashes of rage.
                    But bury us like the bee
In calyx of yellow: to eat, to venerate the pollen, to eat
Particles, motes, specks of the dust, the yellow secret
Vibration:—living and dying in the sun's clear delicate ray.

The Weed

My sister loved milkweed, flower and plant,
Bland-toned, upsprung. The odd dim smell,
Faint fuchsia drench of color coated white
In the brown weed clusters.
                    Sister, I can't
Find you on all the long hard walks of the night . . .
(Travail of lost person always hunted for.)
Day shows the visible universe, humbles to this:
Comfort, great weed.
                    I circle down . . .
Cluster, odor, color: blast of green wind from the earth's
    great core.

Fructus

Odor of algaroba, lure of release.
The smell of red lehua and the crisp scent of maile . . .
These words and images will help you after a little
Hypnotic words emerge and bloom in the mind,
Anaesthetic names . . . Dry buzz of bees
Who make a honey eaten at early breakfast
From a comb like a broken coral . . .
Do dreams foretell the honey? Break the spell.

So I come home in the valley of Kalihi,
My bare feet on hard earth, hibiscus with stamen-tongue
Twirled in my fingers like a paper wind-mill,
A wheel of color, crimson, the petals large,
Kiss of the petal, tactile, light, intense . . .

Now I am back again. I can touch the children:
My human race, in whom was a human dwelling,
Whose names are all the races—of one skin.
For so our games ran tacit, without blur.

What brings me back with giant steps to them?
What was the feast that woke this fabulous thirst?
What was the summer fruit we found and ate
Boldly, with the children of Adam?

A game and a daily search
In the harvest of trees. We played a parable.
We possessed a valley, devoured the juicy, dense
Jewels of appetite hung in fresco sweeps
In garlands and in fountains toward the sea.

Mangoes of golden flesh, with turpentine
Peel and odor. Plums of inky stain
And the pucker of persimmons. Dates to be got
By stepping up a tree-trunk. Coconuts
With custard centres. Rose and custard apple.
Eugenia pink, lemon and little orange,

And the sacklike fig, to be ripped, to be seen, to be tasted.
How rasping sweet the suck of sugar-cane,—
Papaya and banana taken for granted.

With giant steps, in sleep and troubled pain
I return to the fabulous feast, the old communion
With bodiless hunger and thirst. Why have I come
Away from the adult world where race is war?

Here we are dipping and passing the calabash
In the ceremony of friends; I also;
But in frenzy and pain distort
The simple need, knowing how blood is shed:
                                        To sit together
Drinking the blue ocean, eating the sun
Like a fruit . . .

JEAN TOOMER

(1894–1967)

Reapers

Black reapers with the sound of steel on stones
Are sharpening scythes. I see them place the hones
In their hip-pockets as a thing that's done,
And start their silent swinging, one by one.
Black horses drive a mower through the weeds,
And there, a field rat, startled, squealing bleeds,
His belly close to ground. I see the blade,
Blood-stained, continue cutting weeds and shade.

Cotton Song

Come, brother, come. Lets lift it;
Come now, hewit! roll away!
Shackles fall upon the Judgment Day
But lets not wait for it.

God's body's got a soul,
Bodies like to roll the soul,
Cant blame God if we dont roll,
Come, brother, roll, roll!

Cotton bales are the fleecy way
Weary sinner's bare feet trod,
Softly, softly to the throne of God,
"We aint agwine t wait until th Judgment Day!

Nassur; nassur,
Hump.
Eoho, eoho, roll away!
We aint agwine t wait until th Judgment Day!"

God's body's got a soul,
Bodies like to roll the soul,
Cant blame God if we dont roll,
Come, brother, roll, roll!

Georgia Dusk

The sky, lazily disdaining to pursue
   The setting sun, too indolent to hold
   A lengthened tournament for flashing gold,
Passively darkens for night's barbecue,

A feast of moon and men and barking hounds,
   An orgy for some genius of the South
   With blood-hot eyes and cane-lipped scented mouth,
Surprised in making folk-songs from soul sounds.

The sawmill blows its whistle, buzz-saws stop,
   And silence breaks the bud of knoll and hill,
   Soft settling pollen where plowed lands fulfill
Their early promise of a bumper crop.

Smoke from the pyramidal sawdust pile
   Curls up, blue ghosts of trees, tarrying low
   Where only chips and stumps are left to show
The solid proof of former domicile.

Meanwhile, the men, with vestiges of pomp,
   Race memories of king and caravan,
   High-priests, an ostrich, and a juju-man,
Go singing through the footpaths of the swamp.

Their voices rise . . the pine trees are guitars,
   Strumming, pine-needles fall like sheets of rain . .
   Their voices rise . . the chorus of the cane
Is caroling a vesper to the stars. .

O singers, resinous and soft your songs
   Above the sacred whisper of the pines,
   Give virgin lips to cornfield concubines,
Bring dreams of Christ to dusky cane-lipped throngs.

Nullo

A spray of pine-needles,
Dipped in western horizon gold,
Fell onto a path. .
Dry moulds of cow-hoofs. .
In the forest.
Rabbits knew not of their falling,
Nor did the forest catch aflame.

Evening Song

Full moon rising on the waters of my heart,
Lakes and moon and fires,
Cloine tires,
Holding her lips apart.

Promises of slumber leaving shore to charm the moon,
Miracle made vesper-keeps,
Cloine sleeps,
And I'll be sleeping soon.

Cloine, curled like the sleepy waters where the moon-waves
    start,
Radiant, resplendently she gleams,
Cloine dreams,
Lips pressed against my heart.

Portrait in Georgia

Hair—braided chestnut,
        coiled like a lyncher's rope,
Eyes—fagots,
Lips—old scars, or the first red blisters,
Breath—the last sweet scent of cane,
And her slim body, white as the ash
        of black flesh after flame.

Seventh Street

Money burns the pocket, pocket hurts,
Bootleggers in silken shirts,
Ballooned, zooming Cadillacs,
Whizzing, whizzing down the street-car tracks.

Seventh street is a bastard of Prohibition and the War. A
crude-boned, soft-skinned wedge of nigger life breathing its
loafer air, jazz songs and love, thrusting unconscious rhythms,
black reddish blood into the white and whitewashed wood of
Washington. Stale soggy wood of Washington. Wedges rust in
soggy wood. . . . Split it! In two! Again! Shred it! . . the sun.
Wedges are brilliant in the sun; ribbons of wet wood dry and
blow away. Black reddish blood. Pouring for crude-boned
soft-skinned life, who set you flowing? Blood suckers of the
War would spin in a frenzy of dizziness if they drank your
blood. Prohibition would put a stop to it. Who set you flow-
ing? White and whitewash disappear in blood. Who set you
flowing? Flowing down the smooth asphalt of Seventh Street,

in shanties, brick office buildings, theaters, drug stores, restaurants, and cabarets? Eddying on the corners? Swirling like a blood-red smoke up where the buzzards fly in heaven? God would not dare to suck black red blood. A Nigger God! He would duck his head in shame and call for the Judgment Day. Who set you flowing?

> Money burns the pocket, pocket hurts,
> Bootleggers in silken shirts,
> Ballooned, zooming Cadillacs,
> Whizzing, whizzing down the street-car tracks.

Storm Ending

Thunder blossoms gorgeously above our heads
Great, hollow, bell-like flowers,
Rumbling in the wind,
Stretching clappers to strike our ears . .
Full-lipped flowers
Bitten by the sun
Bleeding rain
Dripping rain like golden honey—
And the sweet earth flying from the thunder.

Her Lips Are Copper Wire

whisper of yellow globes
gleaming on lamp-posts that sway
like bootleg licker drinkers in the fog

and let your breath be moist against me
like bright beads on yellow globes

telephone the power-house
that the main wires are insulate

(her words play softly up and down
dewy corridors of billboards)

then with your tongue remove the tape
and press your lips to mine
till they are incandescent

Gum

On top of two tall buildings,
   Where Seventh Street joints
The Avenue,
The city's signs:

> STAR
> J E S U S
> The Light of the World

.   .   .

> WRIGLEYS
>   eat it
>   after
>   every meal
> It Does You Good

Intermittently, their lights flash
Down upon the streets of Washington,
The sleek pat streets some asphalt spider
Spun and tired of.
Upon a fountain in the square
Where sparrows get their water,
Upon the tambourines and drum
Of the Salvation Army jawing,
Hallelujah!
The crowd
         jaws Jesus
            jawing gum.

The Gods Are Here

This is no mountain
But a house,
No rock of solitude
But a family chair,
No wilds
But life appearing
As life anywhere domesticated,
Yet I know the gods are here,
And that if I touch them
I will arise
And take majesty into the kitchen.

MARK VAN DOREN

(1894–1972)

This Amber Sunstream

This amber sunstream, with an hour to live,
Flows carelessly, and does not save itself;
Nor recognizes any entered room—
This room; nor hears the clock upon a shelf,
Declaring the lone hour; for where it goes
All space in a great silence ever flows.

No living man may know it till this hour,
When the clear sunstream, thickening to amber,
Moves like a sea, and the sunk hulls of houses
Let it come slowly through, as divers clamber,
Feeling for gold. So now into this room
Peer the large eyes, unopen to their doom.

Another hour and nothing will be here.
Even upon themselves the eyes will close.
Nor will this bulk, withdrawing, die outdoors
In night, that from another silence flows.
No living man in any western room
But sits at amber sunset round a tomb.

Axle Song

That any thing should be—
Place, time, earth, error—
And a round eye in man to see:
That was the terror.

And a true mind to try
Cube, sphere, deep, short, and long—
That was the burden of the sky's
Hoarse axle song.

Improbable the stoat—
The mouse, toad, worm, wolf, tiger;
Unthinkable the stallion's trot,
Behemoth's swagger.

Unspeakable; yet worse—
Name, look, feel, memory, and number:
Man there with his perverse
Power not to slumber.

Let things created sleep—
Rock, beast, rain, sand, and sliding river.
So growled the earth's revolving heap;
And will forever.

The Near House

Let us have deities, he said, but not as indulgence
Of a sick appetite: rare sweets in the sauce.
Temper the palate first to custom's bread,
To country wine, to fear, and a ritual faith
Repeated till it cloys not; till with knowledge
We sit again, plain brothers at the board.

Let us have gods, he said, because necessity
Clothes us; not as feathers about the brain;
No secret silk, no masking. Let them be wool
To the weather, custom's cowhide, country skin
That the sun ruddies, fearful, and tornadoes
Thicken as we kneel on sacred sand.

Let us believe, he said, in the near house,
The needful, with its rafters of raw pine
Hewn to the custom; thatched with country thunder,
And windows on the meadow side of fear.
No satin tent, no cave, no ivory windings
Burrowed away; but stoves, and an oaken door.

Midland

Under the great cold lakes, under the midmost
Parallel that Lisbon too lies under—
Vesuvius and Corinth, Ararat,
Peking and Chosen, yellow and blue seas
Enormous, then the redwoods, then high Denver—
Under the wet midnorth, under cool Canada,
Swings my own West, directionless; the temperate,
The tacit, the untold. There was I born,
There fed upon the dish of dreaming land
That feeds upon itself, forever sunk
From the far rim, from crust and outer taste,
Forever lost and pleased, as circling currents
Swim to themselves, renumbering Sargasso
Centuries a wind brings round the world.
There am I still, if no thought can escape
To edges from that soft and moving center,
That home, that floating grave of what would fly
Yet did not: my own boyhood, meditating
Unto no end, eternal where I was.

So Simple

Why are my songs so simple,
Now that I know the worst?
Nothing should delight me
In times so cursed.

And nothing does but singing,
And best that it be brief;
About the length of daydream,
Or fall of leaf.

Where I Saw the Snake

Where I saw the snake
Is where I sometimes go
In deep dreams, desiring

To see his length again
Like the sun's blackness, coiled,
Like the sun's center, pulsing,
With white fire all around.

There was no fire, though.
Only intensest black—
Blue black—not burning,
Yet what do I see now?
The body of him departing
Even as he remained:
Motionless, yet gone,

Leaving a lake of light
On the dead grass; and that
Is where I sometimes go
In deep dreams, desiring
To see him coil again,
Then straightway be elsewhere—
Not anywhere—no.

The First Poem

This is the first poem. There was none
Before it. Do not misunderstand me. This
Is the first poem ever. No hint,
No help, no host of cousin, uncle, father
Objects, no mother language, nothing to start from
Except the silence, nothing to run with save
An odd, secret excitement, a strange need
To be there with words when the heartbeat happened,
When the walls of the world, listening to each other,
Sighed, and I caught the sense of it
And fitted it to sound, as afterward
I did again when the great walls, groaning,
Grew louder; yet not deafening; the wonder
Even then was the clearness, was the joy.

ALTER BRODY

(1895–1979)

Lamentations

In a dingy kitchen
Facing a Ghetto backyard
An old woman is chanting Jeremiah's Lamentations,
Quaveringly,
Out of a Hebrew Bible.

The gaslight flares and falls. . . .

This night,
Two thousand years ago,
Jerusalem fell and the Temple was burned.
Tonight
This white-haired Jewess
Sits in her kitchen and chants—by the banks of the Hudson—
The Lament of the Prophet.

The gaslight flares and falls. . . .

Nearby,
Locked in her room,
Her daughter lies on a bed convulsively sobbing.
Her face is dug in the pillows;
Her shoulders heave with her sobs—
The bits of a photograph lie on the dresser. . . .

Winter Nocturne: The Hospital

A mass of ledged rock
Steep and brown and long
Ribbed with white streaks of snow
Rises up suddenly from among level blocks of tenements,
Lifting the red hospital buildings on its top,
Higher
Over the huddled heads of the tenements
Over the uncoiled length of the Elevated
Up to the very disc of the moon.

BABETTE DEUTSCH

(1895–1982)

"To an Amiable Child"

On upper Riverside Drive, New York, there is an enclosure containing a child's grave. It is marked by a funerary urn, the base of which bears this inscription: "Erected to the Memory of an Amiable Child, St. Claire Pollock. Died 15 July 1797, in the Fifth Year of His Age."

Was it because you'd wear
Your half-grown wisdom with a
Debonair gaiety, and laughed less than you smiled?
Or because you were tolerant
Of rainy days, of games and company you did not want?
I see you stilly radiant,
And—like delicious food, delicious play—
Loving music and motion and
Pleasure you did not understand
In voice or face or golden weather;
But sometimes for whole hours together
Hooding yourself in silence;
And when you tired of being good,
Driving them wild.
Could you go with death, making no outcry
If slow-footed, as though with nurse at bedtime?
You lie alone here.
Turfs and a quaint urn
Cover the dust of your small body.
The show
Of your inimitable ways is over.
Child, amiable centuries ago,
At your city-huddled little grave
You are remembered so:
Haunting too merrily for a ghost, you are loved
Now.

Creatures in the Zoo

Ape

His eyes are mournful, but the long lined palm
He thrusts between the bars expects the best.
His old man's face as innocent as calm,
The beggar puts compassion to the test
And fails. He grips the bars; his pained stare grows
To a brown study framed in dusty fur.
He has a cold. He sneezes, cleans his nose,
Then gravely licks a flexile forefinger.

A pause; the bald mauve hand from which men shrink,
The fingers, strong to clutch, quick to explore,
Again extended, are again refused.
The eyes, poor sorrow's jewels, seldom wink,
But to his grinning public, as before,
Show endless patience, endlessly abused.

Young Gazelle

Stiff as her Egyptian counterpart
Standing on legs of matchstick ivory,
She hides the racing of her heart,
While the black boss of her enormous eye
Flames inconsolable. Less like a deer
Than like a freckled girl, her skin's blanched gold
Drawn over little bones, her head held clear,
She listens, as if breathing were too bold.

A tremor, and she is still. Now sunny peace,
Light as the straw beneath her feet, persuades
Her pulses briefly. The terror goes—
Whipped by a childish whimsy of release,
She caracoles: a quick bound that evades
The bars. Then drops into a thrilled repose.

Lioness Asleep

Content that now the bleeding bone be swept
Out of her reach, she lay upon her side.
In a blonde void sunk deep, she slept, she slept
Bland as a child, slept, breathing like a bride.
Color of noons that shimmer as they sing
Above the dunes, her sandy flanks heaved slow.
Between her paws curled inward, billowing
Waves of desert silence seemed to flow.

The crowd was gone, the bars were gone, the cage
Thinned into air, the sawdust and the fleas
Winnowed by sleep to nothing. After food,
Absence possessed her: bliss keener than rage,
If slumber's prisoner at a bound could seize
This ghostly freedom, lapping it like blood.

Black Panther

This little panther wears a coat of soot,
Well-suited so. Stretched out along his shelf,
Still as one brooding storm, the sultry brute
Looks soft as darkness folded on itself.
His limbs, his tarry torso, are as mat
As night wanting the stars; his resting grace
Lies leashed. Alone his head's erect: pure cat
Stares, alive with danger, in that face.

From the sharp ears down to the finest hair
At his tail's tip, he might be carved of coal.
Child of the shadows, he appears as tame,
Till, from behind the grate, the gold eyes glare
With such a light as could consume the whole
To ashes and a memory of flame.

ABRAHAM LINCOLN GILLESPIE

(1895–1950)

A Purplexicon of Dissynthegrations

(Tdevelop Abut Earfluxsatisvie-Thru-Heypersieving)

punziplaze   karmasokist   DecoYen   Pompieraeian

scaruscatracery   timmedigets   outrége   Opinducts

pretensnarrant   MustEVit   spirackrete   broidevel

inducound   proleany   conclueshunning   eeriesponsybil

greak   trystsparklers   misshits   Amerdeality

Chroameo   thoualkt   dienernlarging   sklaferry

ethquikability   vichycles   eunipursonality   woarships

libigo   moodeaffex   crallrighting   sublimasturb

walloaminds   dwintrospectiv   nackuracy   infrisking

evypressoar   pronownshamentos   creallocate

selfoistenuto   bitacting   pleastic   Amerforts

negassing   stillyfrememuse   syntherile   corout

snoub   examplimations   FanelliHopper   marvellusty

broachure   sprnyde   WIldeals   equitty   sklaflout

fearl   Gallopheel   sexpect   huevents   kissimmer

willdid   puearlvoice   alcohawlic   gushot

wrympersonal   self-conscious   inshintuate   whoaman

allustration   essensual   aesthound   cosmasspection

plastrepoise   infalliable   ejaculiss   spectackle

restcue   terrifugalee   phornotgraphy   senseeminded

folksiedead   pirouethink   sklafeatus   democrapicky

keylusion   wellded   conattension   mechallous

shriekreen   pierc[i]₁lver   insite   dability   colorganise

slyting   selfpitter   IntOne   lyreams   negrowisms

meateorvalue   permcore   disjinncts   cloakull

womankneeless   vocabullery   squrdge   psychlic

factidya   spurmport   punaLludIT   philocity

precipidwell   decksquisit   initoutpourpretens

assentsualimbs   bullycose   freaxtreams   reliefaugh

ulthink   Tootons   synexdochrowth   plastraggle

bumpalludes   preocreation   missoarientations

praggressiv   ovarylease   temperanant   whoboozer

tolernjoy   repmew   chucklut   anarchetype   iotea

followswuppers   Aeolyrpegging   calculallow

hoptimystic   shrewmord   obliterary   smellspect

soneyes   decoyr   factea   readch   pleorgasm

renaissorganise   psickisms   imnexplicit   plisstening

statUresklye   purrhaps   hillycredulosity   padmirme

dykasting   raspirations   graphickle   ecstensieve

tellesclewtinates   infaccuraceize   pticklup   Expatriaints hintstructions   gadjects   tainterior   utiliterary

scourfelnthesis   harmonkey   explerimince

calligraphour   imputility   phallacious   yappetising

stintuitiv   pickuppety   tryganise   counterphit

harmonicallush   enfaithrants   prymate   graphorror

furthrallusions   sodgesire   psychrowcess   denticipate

perceptarea-ise   nousquince   abstenced   enhewge

Conductours   impklick   prepperysense   vapremote

plastcoince   reachieve   cleanxpect   arrabiffons

cerebriscretion   mischerché   looklist   himport

freequality   cerebrawl   harrigant   plastral

suberblatulence   blasexalté   bidées   goolustration

rawcoreal   writempo   sentimiews   presumaybe

siloction   aperfeeling   meticulately   vapmosphear

dontdizzymeres   nextricing   Angloaming   whirdeations

freasonable   feeligns   cernamic   flatubloso

proecursing   adjectimeagers   punditty   anonymintake

oughtobografickl   ginferences   cackontrast   artburn

snifficant   tright   Chiricous   pp<ffluktility

peopvoice   syllintrickl   happeezd   hierxoticlassic

OSCAR HAMMERSTEIN II

(1895–1960)

Ol' Man River

Dere's an ol' man called de Mississippi;
Dat's de ol' man dat I'd like to be!
What does he care if de world's got troubles?
What does he care if de land ain't free?

> Ol' Man River,
> Dat Ol' Man River,
> He mus' know sumpin'
> But don' say nuthin',
> He jes' keeps rollin',
> He keeps on rollin' along.
> He don' plant taters,
> He don' plant cotton,
> An' dem dat plants 'em
> Is soon forgotten,
> But Ol' Man River,
> He jes' keeps rollin' along.
> You an' me, we sweat an' strain,
> Body all achin' an' racked wid pain—
> Tote dat barge!
> Lif' dat bale!
> Git a little drunk,
> An' you land in jail. . . .
> Ah git weary
> An' sick of tryin';
> Ah'm tired of livin'
> An' skeered of dyin',
> But Ol' Man River,
> He jes' keeps rollin' along.

Colored folks work on de Mississippi,
Colored folks work while de white folks play,
Pullin' dem boats from de dawn to sunset,
Gittin' no rest till de Judgment Day—

Don' look up
An' don' look down—
You don' dast make
De white boss frown.
Bend your knees
An' bow your head,
An' pull dat rope
Until yo' dead.

Let me go 'way from de Mississippi,
Let me go 'way from de white man boss;
Show me dat stream called de river Jordan,
Dat's de ol' stream dat I long to cross.

Ol' Man River,
Dat Ol' Man River,
He mus' know sumpin'
But don' say nuthin',
He jes' keeps rollin',
He keeps on rollin' along.
He don' plant taters,
He don' plant cotton,
An' dem dat plants 'em
Is soon forgotten,
But Ol' Man River,
He jes' keeps rollin' along
You an' me, we sweat an' strain,
Body all achin' and racked wid pain—
Tote dat barge!
Lif' dat bale!
Git a little drunk,
An' you land in jail. . . .
Ah git weary
An' sick of tryin';
Ah'm tired of livin'
An' skeered of dyin',
But Ol' Man River,
He jes' keeps rollin' along.

LORENZ HART

(1895–1943)

Little Girl Blue

When I was very young
The world was younger than I,
As merry as a carousel.
The circus tent was strung
With ev'ry star in the sky
Above the ring I loved so well.
Now the world has grown old.
Gone are the tinsel and gold.

Sit there and count your fingers.
What can you do?
Old girl, you're through.
Sit there and count your little fingers,
Unlucky little girl blue.

Sit there and count the raindrops
Falling on you.
It's time you knew
All you can count on is the raindrops
That fall on little girl blue.

No use, old girl,
You may as well surrender.
Your hope is getting slender.
Why won't somebody send a tender
Blue Boy, to cheer a
Little girl blue?

Bewitched, Bothered and Bewildered

After one whole quart of brandy,
Like a daisy I awake.
With no Bromo Seltzer handy,
I don't even shake.
Men are not a new sensation;
I've done pretty well, I think.
But this half-pint imitation
Put me on the blink.

I'm wild again,
Beguiled again,
A simpering, whimpering child again—
Bewitched, bothered and bewildered am I.
Couldn't sleep
And wouldn't sleep
Until I could sleep where I shouldn't sleep—
Bewitched, bothered and bewildered am I.
Lost my heart, but what of it?
My mistake, I agree.
He's a laugh, but I love it
Because the laugh's on me.
A pill he is,
But still he is
All mine and I'll keep him until he is
Bewitched, bothered and bewildered
Like me.

Seen a lot—
I mean a lot—
But now I'm like sweet seventeen a lot—
Bewitched, bothered and bewildered am I.
I'll sing to him,
Each spring to him,
And worship the trousers that cling to him—
Bewitched, bothered and bewildered am I.
When he talks, he is seeking
Words to get off his chest.
Horizontally speaking,

He's at his very best.
Vexed again,
Perplexed again,
Thank God I can be oversexed again—
Bewitched, bothered and bewildered am I.

Sweet again,
Petite again,
And on my proverbial seat again—
Bewitched, bothered and bewildered am I.
What am I?
Half shot am I.
To think that he loves me
So hot am I—
Bewitched, bothered and bewildered am I.
Though at first we said, "No, sir,"
Now we're two little dears.
You might say we are closer
Than Roebuck is to Sears.
I'm dumb again
And numb again,
A rich, ready, ripe little plum again—
Bewitched, bothered and bewildered am I.

ROBERT HILLYER
(1895–1961)

Dead Man's Corner

Here is the crossroads where the slain
Were piled so deep we could not pass.
Now dreams alone renew the stain
Of blood long soaked into the grass.

If ambulance to save the maimed
Or gunwagon to maim the sound,
Both must proceed, while rightly named
The Mort Homme darkens all the ground.

As long ago wheels took the groove
In necessary roads again,
Crunching the bones that could not move
To move the limbs of living men;

With cracked and beaten lips that taste
Commands like acid but obeyed,
We still with leaden nightmare haste
Convey our shadows through the shade.

War is a most forgotten fear
But peace will not be out of mind.
We drive our ambulances here
God help us! and the road is blind.

EDMUND WILSON

(1895–1972)

Epitaphs

I
American Soldiers

All sullen and obscene, they toiled in pain.
Go, countryman of theirs: they bought you pride:
Look to it the Republic leave not vain
The deaths of those who knew not why they died.

II
American Officers and Soldiers Who Committed Suicide

What agony was yours whom here offend
These bitter graves? Turn not in scorn the face
From those who, breaking, fell before the end,
Nor yet from those whom base war rendered base.

III
A Young German

Say never that the State concerns you not,
O Artists! though you toil not for your sons.
See where I lie—I and my paints forgot—
Whom Munich bred to fall by Essen's guns.

IV
A Hospital Nurse

I, catching fevers that I could not quench,
When twenty died for two that we could save,
Was laid with dog-tagged soldiers in a trench,
    Glad of no meaner grave.

A House of the Eighties

No more in dreams as once it draws me there,
All fungus-grown and sunken in damp ground—
No more as once when waking I gazed down
On elms like water-weeds in moonlit air
Or heard the August downpour with its dull full sound—
Drenched hedges and the hillside and the night,
The largest house in sight—
And thought it sunken out of time or drowned
As hulks in Newark Bay are soaked and slowly drown.

—The ugly stained-glass window on the stair,
Dark-panelled dining-room, the guinea fowl's fierce clack,
The great gray cat that on the oven slept—
My father's study with its books and birds,
His scornful tone, his eighteenth-century words,
His green door sealed with baize
—Today I travel back
To find again that one fixed point he kept
And left me for the day
In which this other world of theirs grows dank, decays,
And founders and goes down.

The Omelet of A. MacLeish

I

And the mist: and the rain on West Rock: and
    the wind steady:
There were elms in that place: and graven
    inflexible laws:
Men of Yale: and the shudder of Tap Day: the
    need for a man to make headway

Winning a way through the door in the
    windowless walls:
And the poems that came easy and sweet with a
    blurring of Masefield
(The same that I later denied): a young man
    smooth but raw

MacLeish breaks an egg for his omelet.

Eliot alarmed me at first: but my later
    abasement:
And the clean sun of France: and the freakish
    but beautiful fashion:
Striped bathhouses bright on the sand: *Anabase*
    and *The Waste Land*:

These and the *Cantos* of Pound: O how they
    came pat!
Nimble at other men's arts how I picked up the
    trick of it:
Rode it reposed on it drifted away on it: passing

He puts plovers' eggs and truffles into his omelet.

Shores that lay dim in clear air: and the cries of
    affliction
Suave in somniferous rhythms: there was rain
    there and moons:
Leaves falling: and all of a flawless and hollow
    felicity:

In that land there were summer and autumn
    and nighttime and noon

He slips in
a few prizes
for philos-
ophers.

But all seemed alike: and the new-polished
    planets by Einstein:
And a wind out of Valéry's graveyard but it
    never blew anything loose:

And the questions and questions
                questioning
                     What am I? O
What shall I remember?
               O my people
                   a pensive dismay
What have I left unsaid?
              Till the hearer cried:

"If only MacLeish could remember if only
    could say it!" . . .

The omelet
becomes a
national
institution
and gets
into Fanny
Farmer.

And young girls came out: they were innocent
    strong in the tendons
Hungry for all that was new: and hearing their
    eyelids were hazy with

Tears and delight: and the campuses brown in
    November:
Ha but white shirt fronts pink faces: the prizes
    won:
The celluloid tower with bold intonations
    defended:

And the mean tang of Cummings turned
    saltless and sleek on the tongue:

He experi-
ments with
a new kind
of pepper-
corn.

And a Dante gone limp: and a shimmer and
    musical sound
That gleamed in the void and evoked
    approbation and wonder

That the poet need not be a madman or even a
    bounder.

II

And at last I drew close to a land dark with
    fortifications:

*He seems
likely to
lose his in-
vestment in
his omelet.*

Men shrieking outlandish reproaches till all my
    blood tingled:
It was ragged and harsh there: they hated: heart
    horribly quaked in me:

Then I thought "I have staved off the pricking
    of many a sting:
These perchance I may placate too": I put in at
    that place:
I met them with scorn and good-natured
    agreement mingled:

Their fierce cries of "Aesthete!" and "Fascist!":
    and like them I railed at the
Bankers and builders of railroads: I said "Social
    Credit":
(He's a tough lad under the verse mister all the
    same!):

And the Polacks and Dagoes and Hunkies
    undoubtedly dead:

*He is
obliged to
reopen his
omelet and
put a little
garlic in.*

And behold these savage and sybarite-baiting
    strangers
Had many among them like me well-mannered
    well-fed

Bubbling over with schoolboy heroics: their
    line had been changing:
And long in that plentiful land I dwelt honored
    in peace:
And then schoolboys from Britain came over us
    flying like angels:

Them too I courted: I labored to roughen the
    sweet
To stiffen the wilt of a style that seemed lax in
    that land:
A starch of Greek tragedy: stark Anglo-Saxon
    the beat of it:

Stock-market talk: still my numbers as
    mawkishly ran:
(Señora, I could go on like this forever:
It is a strange thing to be an American):

I was wired for sound as I started again down
    the river:
And my colons went out on the air to the clang
    of a gong:
O when shall I ring with the perilous pain and
    the fever?

A clean and clever lad
              who is doing
                     his best
                         to get on. . . .

He is doomed to go on doctoring his omelet.

JOHN DOS PASSOS

(1896–1970)

Newsreel LIII

Bye bye blackbird

ARE YOU NEW YORK'S MOST BEAUTIFUL GIRL STENOGRAPHER?

No one here can love and understand me
Oh what hard luck stories they all hand me

BRITAIN DECIDES TO GO IT ALONE

you too can quickly learn dancing at home without music and without a partner . . . produces the same results as an experienced masseur only quicker, easier and less expensive. Remember only marriageable men in the full possession of unusual physical strength will be accepted as the Graphic Apollos

Make my bed and light the light
I'll arrive late to-night

WOMAN IN HOME SHOT AS BURGLAR

Grand Duke Here to Enjoy Himself

ECLIPSE FOUR SECONDS LATE

Downtown Gazers See Corona

others are more dressy being made of rich ottoman silks, heavy satins, silk crepe or côte de cheval with ornamentation of ostrich perhaps

MAD DOG PANIC IN PENN STATION

UNHAPPY WIFE TRIES TO DIE

the richly blended beauty of the finish, both interior and exterior, can come only from the hand of an artist working towards an ideal. *Substitutes good normal solid tissue for that disfiguring fat.* He touches every point in the entire compass

99

of human need. It may look a little foolish in print but he can show you how to grow brains. If you are a victim of physical ill-being he can liberate you from pain. He can show you how to dissolve marital or conjugal problems. He is an expert in matters of sex

Blackbird bye bye

SKYSCRAPERS BLINK ON EMPTY STREETS

it was a very languid, a very pink and white Peggy Joyce in a very pink and white boudoir who held out a small white hand

THOMAS HORNSBY FERRIL

(1896–1988)

Waltz Against the Mountains

We are waltzing now into the moonlit morning
Of a city swung against the inland darkness
Of the prairie and the mountains and those lights
That stab from green to red and red to green.

The music ends. We lean against the sill
Feeling the mountains blowing over us.

What keeps on moving if your body stops?

I ask you this as if we were not new,
As if our city were an ancient city.
I ask you this in Denver, Colorado,
With a moon for the year's end over your naked shoulder.

Denver is younger than a white-haired man
Remembering yellow gold up to the grass roots.
They tell of eagles older than Denver is:
I search the crystal edges of the twilight
For birds still floating over these prairies and
These mountains that had floated over these prairies
And these mountains when there was no city here.

I walk alone down Blake Street and Wazee,
Looking for asters growing through the hub
Of a wheel that brought my city up from the prairie;
But a welder's mask with purple eyes is hanging
From a peg in a wall where a yellow ox was tied
The night the people came in a wagon to rivet
The steel of a set-back tower to a set-back tower.

I was pulling hair from the trunk of a cottonwood tree
The longhorn cattle rubbed when a sudden man
Started tossing red-hot rivets up through the leaves,

Scorching the amber varnish of the leaves.
He made the red-hot rivets stick to the sky.
I had to quiet the glowing clatter down
The frozen silence of a long long time;
I had to leave the tree and look for another.

The prairie twinkles up the Rocky Mountains.
Feel how the city sweeps against the mountains;
Some of those higher lights, I think, are stars.
Feel how the houses crowd and crack uphill.
The headlands buckle with too many houses.
They're trying to find a place where they can stand
Until the red lights turn to green again.

I'm only half as old as the city is.
I'm younger than an old box-elder tree;
I'm hardly older than the old cathedrals,
Yet I remember primroses and yucca
Out there where all those houses are tonight.
We children gathered primroses and yucca,
We gathered sand lilies and cactus blossoms.

But there's hardly a child in all the sleeping children
From here to where we think the stars begin
Who sleeps in a room where a child, his father, slumbered.

When you wake in the morning tracing a drowsy maze
In the wall paper the sunrise trembles through,
The ceiling never whispers old directions
A ceiling learns from leading old men's eyes.
Off on that prairie frozen cattle flatten
With snow you cannot tell from moonlight on
Their shoulders and with darkness-clotted skulls
And darkness sagging in their hollow flanks;
And through those mountains black above this prairie
Are other animals alive and dead,
Some warmer than the rocks and some as cold,
And we are here, moving ourselves in music.

What keeps on moving if your body stops?

Mine is a city that has never known
A woman on a high wall looking down
Forever on the firelight of her kinsmen.
You're only a woman looking out of a window;
There are no ships, no smoking sacrifices,
And what we make, we are, and it is finished.

There's hardly time to speak beyond the flesh
In a city where the young men are always finding
A better place to start a cemetery.
Yet when this darkness cools the trembling tips
Of music in your breasts and earth has found
More certain use for me than waiting for
A woman on a wall, *what keeps on moving?*

We used to know, we don't know any more.
But I have seen enough of hills and blood,
And lovers and old men and windowsills,
The bones of churches and the bones of mountains,
To know how far we may have come together,
And where we're going for a little way.

So late you came up to these mountains from
A valley by the sea you hardly know
Yet where to gather blossoms of wild plums;
But part of what you are was here before
You came, and part of what you were is gone.
Already melting snow moves through your shoulder,
Atoms of hills are warm within your shoulder,
And somewhere in your fingers that press my fingers
Are particles of corn the bison made
When their bodies clogged the river in the spring.

You are a woman younger than the city,
You are a woman older than the city,
You are the mountains changing into woman,
You are a woman changing into prairie.

See how the moon goes down behind those mountains.
The hills with every waning moon are lower.
They cannot last. They go where we are going.
They wear away to feed our lips with words.

The moon's a sand lily petal floating down
Behind the blue wall of the Rocky Mountains.
I see you as a woman on that wall,
Stepping down crumbled distances forever,
One terrace of a mountain at a time,
One terrace of a prairie at a time,
Until you join your kinsmen at the sea.

What keeps on moving while the mountains linger?

It may be something spoken at a window
About the uses of some hill we've borrowed,
Or something a welder sings to a cottonwood tree,
Or something the seasons make the lovers say
When it's summer on the plains and spring on the ranges,
And we follow weeks of lilacs up from the prairie
Into lost towns of the mountains and return
With lilacs when the hay is being cut.

Something Starting Over

You don't see buffalo skulls very much any more
On the Chugwater buttes or down the Cheyenne plains,
And when you roll at twilight over a draw,
With ages in your heart and hills in your eyes,
You can get about as much from a Model-T,
Stripped and forgotten in a sage arroyo,
As you can from asking the blue peaks over and over:
    "Will something old come back again tonight?
    Send something back to tell me what I want."

I do not know how long forever is,
But today is going to be long long ago,
There will be flint to find, and chariot wheels,

And silver saxophones the angels played,
So I ask myself if I can still remember
How a myth began this morning and how the people
Seemed hardly to know that something was starting over.

Oh, I get along all right with the old old times,
I've seen them sifting the ages in Nebraska
On Signal Butte at the head of Kiowa creek.
    (You can drink from the spring where old man Roubadeau
    Had his forge and anvil up in Cedar Valley,
    You can look back down the valley toward Scottsbluff
    And still see dust clouds on the Oregon trail.)
I entered the trench they cut through Signal Butte,
And I pulled a buffalo bone from the eight-foot layer,
And I watched the jasper shards and arrowheads
Bounce in the jigging screen through which fell dust
Of antelope and pieces of the world
Too small to have a meaning to the sifters.
One of them said, when I held the bone in my hand:
    "This may turn out to be the oldest bison
In North America," and I could have added:
    "How strange, for this is one of the youngest hands
That ever squeezed a rubber bulb to show
How helium particles shoot through water vapor."
And the dry wind out of Wyoming might have whispered:
    "Today is going to be long long ago."

I know how it smells and feels to sift the ages,
But something is starting over and I say
It's just as beautiful to see the yucca
And cactus blossoms rising out of a Ford
In a sage arroyo on the Chugwater flats,
And pretend you see the carbon dioxide slipping
Into the poverty weed, and pretend you see
The root hairs of the buffalo grass beginning
To suck the vanadium steel of an axle to pieces,
An axle that took somebody somewhere,
To moving picture theaters and banks,
Over the ranges, over the cattle-guards,

Took people to dance-halls and cemeteries—
I like to think of them that way together:
Dance-halls and cemeteries, bodies beginning
To come together in dance-halls where the people
Seem hardly to know that hymns are beginning too;
There's a hymn in the jerk of the sand-hill crawl of the
    dancers,
And all the gods are shining in their eyes;
Then bodies separating and going alone
Into the tilting uphill cemeteries,
Under the mesas, under the rimrock shadows.

I can look at an axle in a sage arroyo,
And hear them whispering, the back-seat lovers,
The old myth-makers, starting something over.

Noon

Noon is half the passion of light,
Noon is the middle prairie and the slumber,
The lull of resin weed, the yucca languor,
The wilt of sage at noon is the longest distance any nostril
    knows . . .
How far have we come to feel the shade of this tree?

IRA GERSHWIN

(1896–1983)

I Can't Get Started

I'm a glum one; it's explainable:
I met someone unattainable;
Life's a bore,
The world is my oyster no more.
All the papers, where I led the news
With my capers, now will spread the news:
"Superman
Turns Out to Be Flash in the Pan."

I've flown around the world in a plane;
I won the race from Newport to Maine;
The North Pole I have charted,
But can't get started with you.

Around a golf course I'm under par,
The Theatre Guilders want me to star;
I've got a house—a showplace—
But I get no place with you.

You're so supreme,
Lyrics I write of you;
Scheme
Just for a sight of you;
Dream
Both day and night of you,
And what good does it do?

I've been consulted by Franklin D.
And Greta Garbo's asked me to tea,
And yet I'm brokenhearted
'Cause I can't get started with you.

I do a hundred yards in ten flat;
The Duke of Kent has copied my hat;
With queens I've à la carted,
But can't get started with you.

When Democrats are all in a mess,
I hear Jim Farley's call of distress,
And I help him maneuver,
But I'm just Hoover to you.

When first we met—
How you elated me!
Pet!
You devastated me!
Yet,
Now you've deflated me
Till you're my Waterloo.

When J. P. Morgan bows, I just nod;
Green Pastures wanted me to play God.
The Siamese Twins I've parted,
But I can't get started with you.

The Himalaya Mountains I climb;
I'm written up in *Fortune* and *Time*.
New Yorker did my profile
But I've had no feel from you.

There's always "Best regards and much love"
From Mr. Lehman—you know, the Gov;
I go to ev'ry state ball,
But I'm just behind the eight ball with you.

Oh, tell me why
Am I no kick to you?
I,
Who'd always stick to you?
Fly
Through thin and thick to you?
Tell me why I'm taboo!

Oh, what a man you're keeping at bay;
I use a pound of Lifebuoy each day;
But you've got me downhearted
'Cause I can't, I can't, I can't, I can't,
I can't get started with you.

They All Laughed

The odds were a hundred to one against me,
The world thought the heights were too high to climb.
But people from Missouri never incensed me:
Oh, I wasn't a bit concerned,
For from hist'ry I had learned
How many, many times the worm had turned.

They all laughed at Christopher Columbus
When he said the world was round;
They all laughed when Edison recorded sound.

They all laughed at Wilbur and his brother
When they said that man could fly;
They told Marconi
Wireless was a phony—
It's the same old cry!

They laughed at me wanting you,
Said I was reaching for the moon;
But oh, you came through—
Now they'll have to change their tune.

They all said we never could be happy,
They laughed at us—and how!
But ho, ho, ho—
Who's got the last laugh now!

They all laughed at Rockefeller Center—
Now they're fighting to get in;
They all laughed at Whitney and his cotton gin.

They all laughed at Fulton and his steamboat,
Hershey and his choc'late bar.
Ford and his Lizzie
Kept the laughers busy—
That's how people are!

They laughed at me wanting you—
Said it would be Hello! Good-bye!
But oh, you came through—
Now they're eating humble pie.

They all said we'd never get together—
Darling, let's take a bow,
For ho, ho, ho—
Who's got the last laugh—
He, he, he—
Let's at the past laugh—
Ha, ha, ha—
Who's got the last laugh now?

RAMON GUTHRIE

(1896–1973)

Elegy for Mélusine from the Intensive Care Ward

So name her Vivian. I, scarecrow Merlin—
our Broceliande this frantic bramble of
glass and plastic tubes and stainless steel—
could count off such illusions as I have
on a quarter of my thumbs.

> (. . . *even a postcard of Viollet-le-Duc's*
> *pensive chimera signed with her initial* . . .)

I penciled out a cable: FCHRISAKE COMMA
WRITE TO ME STOP YOURE LIVING AND IM DYING.
Gray lady challenged the expletive and my assurance
that it was an Ainu epithet of endearment.
I struck out everything but WRITE—cheaper
and besides I wasn't really dying
save that I couldn't breathe too well
nor feed except on intravenous dextrose.

Still stands that I am dying, Mélusine,
and have been ever since my infancy,
but the process is more measurable now.
You can tick off the months on a calendar—
eeny, meeny, miny . . . and when you get to the end . . .

> (*Today again no word.*
> . . . *Breton Saint Anne* . . . *Black Virgin*
> *of Le Puy* . . .)

When you get to the end . . .
when you get to the end . . .
You know what *I* should like to do when I get to the end?
when I am tucked and snug and smug
with hair combed sleek for once
pants pressed   shoes shined
and tie on straight for the first time in my life?

I'd like to give one last galvanic jerk
and flip up straight and look all living beings
in the eye—all human ones, that is
(because, less lucky than are cats and cows
and bumblebees, they know that they are living)
and speak out clear: "I hate life. I who am
no longer living can speak this truth.
From my first taste of it, from the moment when
my drunken Uncle Doc dangled me by the heels
and whacked my rump, I have always hated living!"
then flop back flat into the casket with a happy
or, at least, contented or vacuous, smirk upon my face—
soundly dead for keeps this time.
That, mes amis, would be worth living long enough to see!

Every tear would dry like sizzled spit
testing a hot flatiron. The organ,
up to then simpering stately lullabies,
would burst a dozen pipes. The pallbearers
would stop dead in their tracks. (Their tracks to *where?*
Don't ask *me*: I'm only playing the lead
in this production, not directing it.)
And everybody from the preacher down
to the boy soprano would look each other in the eye
and murmur in unison:
"Why, the old bastard! Who'da thunk it of him!"
(It would be no time for grammatical niceties.)
                    Still . . .
bring on your Dead March with Muffled Drums
and Reversed Rifles and high-stepping young
Drum Majorettes with the minniest of Miniskirts.
Let Taps be played and Keeners keen.
Consume the Baked Meats with good appetite.
                    And . . .
grant me this: I *tried* to love life—
tried my damnedest but just couldn't make it.
Matter of acquired tastes you somehow can't acquire—
like some wines (Tokay, Monbazillac)
or foods (gazpacho, prune whip, lemon pie).

Fell fable of the fox that did at last
    leap high enough and the grapes
        definitely *were* sour.

                  (*. . . or an empty envelope addressed in her concise*
                                    swift runic hand.)

Red-Headed Intern, Taking Notes

Do you been or did you never? Ha!
Speakless, can you flex your omohyoid
and whinny ninety-nine? Quick now,
can you recall your grandmother's maiden name
six times rapidly? Have you a phobia of spiders?
Only fairly large and brown ones
dropping from the ceiling?
Does this happen often, would you say?
(Nurse, clamp the necrometer when I say when.
If he passes out, tickle his nose with a burning feather
and tweak his ears counterclockwise.)
No history of zombi-ism in the immediate family?
And tularemia? No recent intercourse
with a rabbit?
        (Lash him firmly to the stretcher
        and store him in the ghast house for the night.)

Scene: A Bedside in the Witches' Kitchen

DOCTOR *to his retinue of interns and residents:*
    Obvious ptoritus of the drabia.
    Although the prizzle presents no sign of rabies,
    note this pang in the upper diaphrosis.
    When kicked there hard enough, the patient utters,
    "Yoof!" and curls up like a cutworm.
    I prescribe bedcheck every hour on the hour
    with intensive catalepsis. (*Exeunt.*)

PATIENT *to Nurse:*
>My name is Marsyas, a stranger here.
>   How to explain?
>Sprächen zoo something? anything? Aard-vark? Gnu?
>you look well-meaning. If I made noises in my phlarynx
>and shaped them with my phtongue, would they have
>snignifigance to you? Or would they merely
>confuse us further? Let's go about it anagogically.
>Close your ears. Go twine your sphygnomanometer
>about some other patient or administer him his hemlock,
>while I supplicate.

>   Today is Friday.

Gamut of goddesses, Gaia, Latona, Frigg whose day it is,
cat-flanked Ishtar with the up-turned palms,
Rosmertha of the Gauls, with grief-gouged eyes
and rough-hewn cleft—
>   sister, mother, mistress of the dead,
mare-shaped Epona, you, Venus of Lespugue
in mammoth tusk, majestic at scarce a handsbreadth tall,
though not quite small enough to put into a matchbox
and walk the streets of Montparnasse with in your pocket . . .

Gamut of goddesses,
in your spare moments intercede for me . . .
>   (Breath comes scant now,
>   but by chance you may have heard,
>   my name is Marsyas) . . .
intercede for me. Let me be never born.
Let my ghost wander in brambled upland meadows.
Drizzle in evening streets, may she at times recall
our walking there, arms pressed to ribs together.

Mélusine!

E. Y. HARBURG

(1896–1981)

Brother, Can You Spare a Dime?

They used to tell me
I was building a dream
And so I followed the mob
When there was earth to plough
Or guns to bear
I was always there
Right on the job

They used to tell me
I was building a dream
With peace and glory ahead
Why should I be standing in line
Just waiting for bread?

Once I built a railroad,
Made it run
Made it race against time
Once I built a railroad
Now it's done
Brother, can you spare a dime?

Once I built a tower
To the sun
Brick and rivet and lime
Once I built a tower
Now it's done
Brother, can you spare a dime?

Once in khaki suits
Gee, we looked swell
Full of that Yankee Doodle-de-dum
Half a million boots went sloggin' thru hell
I was the kid with the drum

Say, don't you remember?
They called me "Al"
It was "Al" all the time
Say, don't you remember
I'm your pal
Buddy, can you spare a dime?

ISIDOR SCHNEIDER

(1896–1977)

Insects

Clockwork beings, winding out their lives—
souls would kill them as machines kill us.
They are not stranger to us. Their shellacked
and felted bodies built in sections, grooved
to make elastic their wire-tendoned strength,
we too have made with rougher metals
and with coarser cloth. Clanging, they fill
the booming Summer, fill the grass, the air,
an exposition of well geared machines.
They whirr and hammer; the sun's rays
dart power to them on glittering rails;
and through the pastoral night the stationed stars
now seem a swarm of midges. Trembling on
the unseen eaves of space, the milky way
swings a rumpled spider web, where, guttering,
the captured stars exert their dim,
funereal, phosphorescent light.

A History of the Cæsars

Burrowing with his teeth
Cæsar enters the curled flesh,
his nostrils launched on the perfume
rendered from the roasting out of life.

Containing the ashes of love-curdled courtesans,
and ventral ladies of senatorial class,
and gentle minions whom unbudded breasts had choked,
a high womblipped urn satiates
the pustular eye of Cæsar.

Having become buffoons with delirium,
dwarfs by doubling pain,
giants by reaches of despair,
and final statuary by sudden, moulding death,
a thousand citizens, his guests,
poisoned distinctively, made merriment for Cæsar.

The peoples have their representatives in Court,
the slaves of Cæsar,—
animals devour themselves
to bite the thornballs from their skins,—
caged kings and queens
draggle the feather of triumph from Cæsar's car
to make for him a feature advertisement.

Ruling the world like a slum landlord,
Cæsar buys plantations in Heaven.

Fleeing the monotony of surfeit,
Cæsar consumed himself.

LOUISE BOGAN

(1897–1970)

Medusa

I had come to the house, in a cave of trees,
Facing a sheer sky.
Everything moved,—a bell hung ready to strike,
Sun and reflection wheeled by.

When the bare eyes were before me
And the hissing hair,
Held up at a window, seen through a door.
The stiff bald eyes, the serpents on the forehead
Formed in the air.

This is a dead scene forever now.
Nothing will ever stir.
The end will never brighten it more than this,
Nor the rain blur.

The water will always fall, and will not fall,
And the tipped bell make no sound.
The grass will always be growing for hay
Deep on the ground.

And I shall stand here like a shadow
Under the great balanced day,
My eyes on the yellow dust, that was lifting in the wind,
And does not drift away.

Knowledge

Now that I know
How passion warms little
Of flesh in the mould,
And treasure is brittle,—

I'll lie here and learn
How, over their ground,
Trees make a long shadow
And a light sound.

Women

Women have no wilderness in them,
They are provident instead,
Content in the tight hot cell of their hearts
To eat dusty bread.

They do not see cattle cropping red winter grass,
They do not hear
Snow water going down under culverts
Shallow and clear.

They wait, when they should turn to journeys,
They stiffen, when they should bend.
They use against themselves that benevolence
To which no man is friend.

They cannot think of so many crops to a field
Or of clean wood cleft by an axe.
Their love is an eager meaninglessness
Too tense, or too lax.

They hear in every whisper that speaks to them
A shout and a cry.
As like as not, when they take life over their door-sills
They should let it go by.

The Alchemist

I burned my life, that I might find
A passion wholly of the mind,
Thought divorced from eye and bone,
Ecstasy come to breath alone.
I broke my life, to seek relief
From the flawed light of love and grief.

With mounting beat the utter fire
Charred existence and desire.
It died low, ceased its sudden thresh.
I had found unmysterious flesh—
Not the mind's avid substance—still
Passionate beyond the will.

My Voice Not Being Proud

My voice, not being proud
Like a strong woman's, that cries
Imperiously aloud
That death disarm her, lull her—
Screams for no mourning color
Laid menacingly, like fire,
Over my long desire.
It will end, and leave no print.
As you lie, I shall lie:
Separate, eased, and cured.
Whatever is wasted or wanted
In this country of glass and flint
Some garden will use, once planted.
As you lie alone, I shall lie,
O, in singleness assured,
Deafened by mire and lime.
I remember, while there is time.

Men Loved Wholly Beyond Wisdom

Men loved wholly beyond wisdom
Have the staff without the banner.
Like a fire in a dry thicket
Rising within women's eyes
Is the love men must return.
Heart, so subtle now, and trembling,
What a marvel to be wise,
To love never in this manner!
To be quiet in the fern
Like a thing gone dead and still,
Listening to the prisoned cricket
Shake its terrible, dissembling
Music in the granite hill.

Sub Contra

Notes on the tuned frame of strings
Plucked or silenced under the hand
Whimper lightly to the ear,
Delicate and involute,
Like the mockery in a shell.
Lest the brain forget the thunder
The roused heart once made it hear,—
Rising as that clamor fell,—
Let there sound from music's root
One note rage can understand,
A fine noise of riven things.
Build there some thick chord of wonder;
Then, for every passion's sake,
Beat upon it till it break.

Cassandra

To me, one silly task is like another.
I bare the shambling tricks of lust and pride.
This flesh will never give a child its mother,—
Song, like a wing, tears through my breast, my side,
And madness chooses out my voice again,
Again. I am the chosen no hand saves:
The shrieking heaven lifted over men,
Not the dumb earth, wherein they set their graves.

Winter Swan

It is a hollow garden, under the cloud;
Beneath the heel a hollow earth is turned;
Within the mind the live blood shouts aloud;
Under the breast the willing blood is burned,
Shut with the fire passed and the fire returned.
But speak, you proud!
Where lies the leaf-caught world once thought abiding,
Now but a dry disarray and artifice?
Here, to the ripple cut by the cold, drifts this
Bird, the long throat bent back, and the eyes in hiding.

Dark Summer

Under the thunder-dark, the cicadas resound.
The storm in the sky mounts, but is not yet heard.
The shaft and the flash wait, but are not yet found.

The apples that hang and swell for the late comer,
The simple spell, the rite not for our word,
The kisses not for our mouths,—light the dark summer.

Late

The cormorant still screams
Over cave and promontory.
Stony wings and bleak glory
Battle in your dreams.
Now sullen and deranged,
Not simply, as a child,
You look upon the earth
And find it harrowed and wild.
Now, only to mock
At the sterile cliff laid bare,
At the cold pure sky unchanged,
You look upon the rock,
You look upon the air.

Song

It is not now I learn
To turn the heart away
From the rain of a wet May
Good for the grass and leaves.
Years back I paid my tithe
And earned my salt in kind,
And watched the long slow scythe
Move where the grain is lined,
And saw the stubble burn
Under the darker sheaves.
Whatever now must go
It is not the heart that grieves.
It is not the heart—the stock,
The stone,—the deaf, the blind—
That sees the birds in flock
Steer narrowed to the wind.

Short Summary

Listen but once to the words written out by my hand
In the long line fit only for giving ease
To the tiresome heart. I say: Not again shall we stand
Under green trees.

How we stood, in the early season, but at the end of day,
In the yes of new light, but at the twice-lit hour,
Seeing at one time the shade deepened all one way
And the breaking flower;

Hearing at one time the sound of the night-fall's reach
And that checked breath bound to the mouth and caught
Back to the mouth, closing its mocking speech:
Remind me not.

Soon to dark's mid-most pitch the divided light
Ran. The balance fell, and we were not there.
It was early season; it was the verge of night;
It was our land;
It was evening air.

Roman Fountain

Up from the bronze, I saw
Water without a flaw
Rush to its rest in air,
Reach to its rest, and fall.

Bronze of the blackest shade,
An element man-made,
Shaping upright the bare
Clear gouts of water in air.

O, as with arm and hammer,
Still it is good to strive
To beat out the image whole,
To echo the shout and stammer
When full-gushed waters, alive,
Strike on the fountain's bowl
After the air of summer.

Evening-Star

Light from the planet Venus, soon to set,
Be with us.

Light, pure and round, without heat or shadow,
Held in the cirrous sky, at evening:
Accompany what we do.

Be with us;
Know our partial strength.
Serve us in your own way,
Brief planet, shining without burning.

Light, lacking words that might praise you;
Wanting and breeding sighs only.

Baroque Comment

From loud sound and still chance;
From mindless earth, wet with a dead million leaves;
From the forest, the empty desert, the tearing beasts,
The kelp-disordered beaches;
Coincident with the lie, anger, lust, oppression and death in
　　many forms:

Ornamental structures, continents apart, separated by seas;
Fitted marble, swung bells; fruit in garlands as well as on the
　　branch;
The flower at last in bronze, stretched backward, or curled
　　within;
Stone in various shapes: beyond the pyramid, the contrived
　　arch and the buttress;
The named constellations;
Crown and vesture; palm and laurel chosen as noble and
　　enduring;
Speech proud in sound; death considered sacrifice;
Mask, weapon, urn; the ordered strings;
Fountains; foreheads under weather-bleached hair;
The wreath, the oar, the tool,
The prow;
The turned eyes and the opened mouth of love.

Kept

Time for the wood, the clay,
The trumpery dolls, the toys
Now to be put away:
We are not girls and boys.

What are these rags we twist
Our hearts upon, or clutch
Hard in the sweating fist?
They are not worth so much.

But we must keep such things
Till we at length begin
To feel our nerves their strings,
Their dust, our blood within.

The dreadful painted bisque
Becomes our very cheek.
A doll's heart, faint at risk,
Within our breast grows weak.

Our hand the doll's, our tongue.

Time for the pretty clay,
Time for the straw, the wood.
The playthings of the young
Get broken in the play,
Get broken, as they should.

Heard by a Girl

Something said: You have nothing to fear
From those long fine bones, and that beautiful ear.

From the mouth, and the eyes set well apart
There's nothing can come which will break your heart.

From the simple voice, the indulgent mind,
No venom breeds to defeat your kind.

And even, it said, those hands are thin
And large, well designed to clasp within

Their fingers (and O what more do you ask?)
The secret and the delicate mask.

Several Voices Out of a Cloud

Come, drunks and drug-takers; come, perverts unnerved!
Receive the laurel, given, though late, on merit; to whom and
    wherever deserved.

Parochial punks, trimmers, nice people, joiners true-blue,
Get the hell out of the way of the laurel. It is deathless. And it
    isn't for you.

Musician

Where have these hands been,
By what delayed,
That so long stayed
Apart from the thin

Strings which they now grace
With their lonely skill?
Music and their cool will
At last interlace.

Now with great ease, and slow,
The thumb, the finger, the strong
Delicate hand plucks the long
String it was born to know.

And, under the palm, the string
Sings as it wished to sing.

Zone

We have struck the regions wherein we are keel or reef.
The wind breaks over us,
And against high sharp angles almost splits into words,
And these are of fear or grief.

Like a ship, we have struck expected latitudes
Of the universe, in March.
Through one short segment's arch
Of the zodiac's round
We pass,
Thinking: Now we hear
What we heard last year,
And bear the wind's rude touch
And its ugly sound
Equally with so much
We have learned how to bear.

Night

The cold remote islands
And the blue estuaries
Where what breathes, breathes
The restless wind of the inlets,
And what drinks, drinks
The incoming tide;

Where shell and weed
Wait upon the salt wash of the sea,
And the clear nights of stars
Swing their lights westward
To set behind the land;

Where the pulse clinging to the rocks
Renews itself forever;
Where, again on cloudless nights,
The water reflects
The firmament's partial setting;

—O remember
In your narrowing dark hours
That more things move
Than blood in the heart.

Morning

I.

The robins' green-blue eggs
Being the complementary color
To the robins' rosy breast—
Is it a vision in the eye, a resolution in the blood
That calls back these birds, to cherish and to guard?

2.

The clever and as though instructed
Tendril of convolvulus
Having chosen the rosebranch for the support of its
        ascending spiral
Succeeds in avoiding
All but the smaller thorns.

The Dragonfly

You are made of almost nothing
But of enough
To be great eyes
And diaphanous double vans;
To be ceaseless movement,
Unending hunger
Grappling love.

Link between water and air,
Earth repels you.
Light touches you only to shift into iridescence
Upon your body and wings.

Twice-born, predator,
You split into the heat.
Swift beyond calculation or capture
You dart into the shadow
Which consumes you.

You rocket into the day.
But at last, when the wind flattens the grasses,
For you, the design and purpose stop.

And you fall
With the other husks of summer.

EMANUEL CARNEVALI

(1897–1942?)

Sermon

Chao-Mong-Mu freely laid his hands over the sky:
You do not know how to lay your hands over the breasts of
    your beloved.

Chao-Mong-Mu made the tree dance at his will:
You do not know how to hug a rough tree and say "darling"
    to it.

Chao-Mong-Mu magnificently ran a shaft of sunlight to
    smash against the treetops:
You walk carefully, carefully, and fend off the sunlight with
    your grey clothes, although you're very poor.

Chao-Mong-Mu painted a sky that was a pink-fleshed vase;
    then he became a very small thing and hid in the vase:
You build yourselves immense houses to live in, and you are
    afraid even there.

Serenade

Come on, don't be afraid you'll spoil me
if you light the gas in your room
and show me
that you have heard my cries.

Are you so poor in kisses
that you're so stingy with them;
and is your heart so ravaged!
that you won't let me pick there
one or two flowers
to stick in my jacket's
button-hole?

I play my serenade
beating with my clenched fist
on a gong and a drum.
What I want is to give you
the sound of what a man is.

I love my eyes and lips
better than yours;
besides, the dampness of the night
pierces my shoes.

I can be as capricious
as you can be, don't worry!

Come on, open that window
or I'll go home.

Kiss

You think you can leave the matter to your lips
and they don't work right
and then
it's two deadmen shaking hands
saying "Howdydo Sir?"

Almost a God

I am dying under this heat
but there may be worse.

I love my wife
but I should love her more.

I love my sweetheart but her love should be more universal.
One word describes her but I do not know which word.

All shorter than something else:
All is more God-like than something else.

There is competition in the chaos,
which is very foolish.

I am in doubt as a bent willow branch
nodding to the water.

I admire the devil for he leaves things unfinished.
I admire God for he finishes everything.

BLIND LEMON JEFFERSON

(1897–1929)

Long Distance Moan

I'm flying to South Carolina
                              I gotta go there this time
I'm flying to South Carolina
                              I gotta go there this time
Woman in Dallas Texas
                      is 'bout to make me lose my mind

Long distance, long distance
                           will you please give me a credit call
Long distance, long distance
                          will you give me a please cr-credit call
Want to talk to my gal in South Carolina
                          who looks like a Indian squaw

Just want to ask my baby
                       what in the world is she been doing
I want to ask my baby
                    what in the world is she been doing
Give your loving to another joker
                        and it's sure gonna be my ruin

Hey long distance
                  I can't help but moan
Mmmmmmmmmmmmmmmm
                      I can't help but moan
My baby's voice sound so sweet
                      oh I'm gonna break this telephone

You don't know you love
                  your rider till she is so far from you
You don't know you love your rider
                      until she's so far from you

135

You can get long distance moan
                  and you don't care what you do

I say no use standing and buzzing
                  to get my brownie off my mind
No use standing and bawling
                  get my baby off my mind
This long distance moan
                  about to worry me to death this time

WALTER LOWENFELS

(1897–1976)

from
Elegy in the Manner of a Requiem in Memory of D. H. Lawrence

Among the Luminals

So I fled into the thing for him
north with a lash

past your frozen Jesus
your Orpheus in abattoir

remember me apostles!

north beyond the fathers
dropping among the cycles
the sweat of pearls among the ices.
Caught trapped
without a word among the luminals?
O Master what rituals of what seasons?

Frozen as the winds blow
above the sky below the roots
among the needles and the cones
an elegy of untranslation
excellent among the trees
high among the sea fauna
and the weeds that wave
among the corals and the shoals.

So I bled into a melt
above the blades above the wrecks
a plankton along the reefs
a stir among the muscles

above the Morris-dancing of the Islanders
among the movers and the ridden
    and the heaven-borne.

Forgive us sea-petals
and remember us not
    as you will not
lipped by the wave
sea-moulded among the waxes.
The straw is in the wind
running like an idiot with moss in the ears.

    What nightmare of the time?
island universes
    dark with exotic blooms
over quicksilver streams
vanishing at the touch?
or this hysteria of others?
moving like the desert locusts in the spring
to the first lake
into death by water
    from drought.

            O parched O thirsting
take lime
    bathe among the heather
be brilliant among the juices.
Build thee less stately mansions
in the groves among the oranges
and forget the visions
for long life among the turtles.

So I made the poem
and otherwise lay chained with others
doomed to ever-lasting dungeons
among the tattered and the torn
writhing below the spires
in the cells below the fastness
staked to the dankness of the soil
devising plans for killing rats

for evading stenches
    and seeping poisons
and stabbing for the heart
to sustain a brother
    in the flesh
blood-drinking
    swimming with Athena
west of Andromeda
    O spires O temples

So your human yolk
flowers like a crab with anemone
only inwardly like the crystal of a cancer
and cracks in the shell
for not being born.

But it acts like a loving thing
like a living thing
              like an angel
full of good habits.
           And this
I was too much my cousin
    lay by myself
bred only white mice
    all my dreams
one length of Asia less familiar
and there across the continents
the sperm of the mind
struck from its roots
fertilized monstrosities
    among the vacuums.

And this is the service!
Fouled in the penis
a penitentiary of too closeness
cursed and soaring
          among the centuries
    among the vectors
among the walkers and the riders and the heaven-borne.

DAVID McCORD

(1897–1997)

Waiter

By and by
God caught his eye.

History of Education

The decent docent doesn't doze:
He teaches standing on his toes.
His student dassn't doze—and does,
And that's what teaching is and was.

JOHN WHEELWRIGHT

(1897–1940)

Slow Curtain

Two lovers face one another
    actor and actress
    author and conjoint authoress
    manager, promptress
    property man and make-up woman.
It is an amateur performance
    but the piece is well written
    but the lines imply the business
    but the piece means little
    but the last two words read:
    They kiss.
The actors are their own audience.
    As actors, they are artists
    As audience, they are critics.
    They have read the play beforehand
    in order to do it justice,
    and they know the final stage directions
    are impossible.
The piece comes to an end.
    The lovers face one another.
    Neither moves a muscle.
There is no applause.

Why Must You Know?

—"What was that sound we heard
fall on the snow?"
—"It was a frozen bird.
Why must you know?
All the dull earth knows the good
that the air, with claws and wings
tears to the scattered questionings

which burn in fires of our blood."
—"Let the air's beak and claws
   carry my deeds
far, where no springtime thaws
   the frost for their seeds."
—"One could fathom every sound
that the circling blood can tell
who heard the diurnal syllable,
while lying close against the ground."
—"My flesh, bone and sinew
   now would discern
hidden waters in you
   Earth, waters that burn."
—"One who turns to earth again
finds solace in its weight; and deep
hears the blood forever keep
the silence between drops of rain."

Would You Think?

Does the sound or the silence make
music? When no ripples pass
over watery trees; like painted glass
lying beneath a quiet lake;
   would you think the real forest lay
   only in the reflected
   trees, which are protected
   by non-existence from the air of day?
Our blood gives voice to earth and shell,
they speak but in refracted sounds.
The silence of the dead resounds,
but what they say we cannot tell.
   Only echoes of what they taught
   are heard by living ears.
   The tongue tells what it hears
   and drowns the silence which the dead besought.
The questioning, circumambient light
the answering, luminiferous doubt

listen, and whisper it about
until the mocking stars turn bright.
  Tardy flowers have bloomed long
  but they have long been dead.
  Now on the ice, like lead
  hailstones drop loud, with a rattlesnake's song.

Fish Food

An Obituary to Hart Crane

As you drank deep as Thor, did you think of milk or wine?
Did you drink blood, while you drank the salt deep?
Or see through the film of light, that sharpened your rage
      with its stare,
a shark, dolphin, turtle? Did you not see the Cat
who, when Thor lifted her, unbased the cubic ground?
You would drain fathomless flagons to be slaked with
      vacuum—
The sea's teats have suckled you, and you are sunk far
in bubble-dreams, under swaying translucent vines
of thundering interior wonder. Eagles can never now
carry parts of your body, over cupped mountains
as emblems of their anger, embers to fire self-hate
to other wonders, unfolding white, flaming vistas.

Fishes now look upon you, with eyes which do not gossip.
Fishes are never shocked. Fishes will kiss you, each
fish tweak you; every kiss take bits of you away,
till your bones alone will roll, with the Gulf Stream's swell.
So has it been already, so have the carpers and puffers
nibbled your carcass of fame, each to his liking. Now
in tides of noon, the bones of your thought-suspended
      structures
gleam as you intended. Noon pulled your eyes with small
magnetic headaches; the will seeped from your blood. Seeds
of meaning popped from the pods of thought. And you fall.
  And the unseen

churn of Time changes the pearl-hued ocean;
like a pearl-shaped drop, in a huge water-clock
falling; from *came* to *go*, from *come* to *went*. And you fell.

Waters received you. Waters of our Birth in Death dissolve
   you.
Now you have willed it, may the Great Wash take you.
As the Mother-Lover takes your woe away, and cleansing
grief and you away, you sleep, you do not snore.
Lie still. Your rage is gone on a bright flood
away; as, when a bad friend held out his hand
you said, "Do not talk any more. I know you meant no
   harm."
What was the soil whence your anger sprang, who are deaf
as the stones to the whispering flight of the Mississippi's
   rivers?
What did you see as you fell? What did you hear as you sank?
Did it make you drunken with hearing?
I will not ask any more. You saw or heard no evil.

Come Over and Help Us

A Rhapsody

I

Our masks are gauze / and screen our faces for those unlike
   us only,
Who are easily deceived. / Pierce through these masks to our
   unhidden tongues
And watch us scold, / scold with intellectual lust; / scold
Ourselves, our foes, our friends; / Europe, America, Boston;
   and all that is not
Boston; / till we reach a purity, fierce as the love of God;— /
   Hate.
Hate, still fed by the shadowed source; / but fallen, stagnant
   fallen;
Sunk low between thin channels; rises, rises; / swells to burst

Its walls; and rolls out deep and wide. / Hate rules our
    drowning Race.
Any freed from our Tyrant; / abandon their farms, forsake
    their Country, *become American.*

We, the least subtle of Peoples, / lead each only one life at a
    time,—
Being never, never anything but sincere; / yet we trust our
    honesty
So little that we dare not depart from it,— / knowing it to
    need habitual stimulation.
And living amid a world of Spooks, / we summon another
    to us
Who is (in some sort) our Clown,— / as he affords us
    amusement.
O! sweet tormentor, Doubt! longed-for and human, / leave
    us some plausible
Evil motive, however incredible. / The Hate in the World
    outside our World
(Envious, malicious, vindictive) / makes our Hate gleam in
    the splendor
Of a Castrate / who with tongue plucked out; / arms, legs
    sawed off;
Eyes and ears, pierced through; / still thinks / thinks
By means of all his nutriment, / with intense, exacting
    Energy, terrible, consuming.
Madness, we so politely placate / as an every-day
    inconvenience
We shun in secret. / Madness is sumptuous; Hate, ascetic.
Those only who remain sane, / taste the flavor of Hate.
Strong Joy, we forbid ourselves / and deny large pleasurable
    objects,
But, too shrewd to forego amusement, / we enjoy all joys
    which, dying, leave us teased.
So spare us, sweet Doubt, our tormentor, / the Arts, our
    concerts, and novels;
The theater, sports, the exotic Past; / to use to stave off
    Madness,
To use as breathing spells, / that our drug's tang may not
    die.

We are not tireless; *ı* distract us from thin ecstasy, that we
    may hate
If with less conviction, *ı* with some result, some end,—
So pure ourselves; so clear our passion; *ı* *pure, clear, alone.*

II

The New Englander leaves New England *ı* to flaunt his drab
    person
Before Latin decors *ı* and Asiatic back-drops.
Wearies. *ı* Returns to life,—life tried for a little while.
A poor sort of thing *ı* (filling the stomach; emptying the
    bowels;
Bothering to speak to friends on the street; *ı* filling the
    stomach again;
Dancing, drinking, whoring) *ı* forms the tissue of this
    fabric.—
(Marriage; society; business; charity;— *ı* *Life, and life*
    refused.)

The New Englander appraises sins, *ı* finds them beyond his
    means, *ı* and hoards.
Likewise, he seldom spends his goodness *ı* on someone
    ignoble as he,
But, to make an occasion, he proves himself *ı* that he is
    equally ignoble.
Then he breaks his fast! *ı* Then he ends his thirsting!
He censors the Judge. *ı* He passes judgment on the
    Censor. *ı* No language is left.
His lone faculty, Condemnation,—condemned. *ı* Nothing is
    left to say.
Proclaim an Armistice *ı* Through Existence, livid, void, *ı*
    let silence flood.

Ask the Silent One your question. *ı* (He is stupid in misery
No more than the talkative man, who talks through his
    hat.) *ı* Ask the question.
If he replied at all, *ı* it would be to remark that he never
    could despise
Anyone so much as himself *ı* should he once give way to
    Self-pity.

A different act of faith is his,— */* the white gesture of
    Humility.
He knows his weakness. */* He is well-schooled */* and he
    never forgets the shortest
Title of his Knowledge. */* The jailer of his Soul sees Pride. */*
    He sees
Tears, never. */* The Silent One is so eaten away
He cannot make that little effort */* which surrender to
    external Fact
Requires, */* but looks out always only with one wish,— */* *to*
    realize he exists.

Lo! a Desire! */* A Faint motive! */* A motive (however faint)
    beyond disinterestedness.
Faint. */* It is faint. */* But the boundary is clear. */* Desire, oh
    desire further!
Past that boundary lies Annihilation */* where the Soul
Breaks the monotonous-familiar */* and man wakes to the
    shocking
Unastounded company of other men. */* But the Silent One
    would not pass
Where the Redmen have gone. */* He would live without
    end. That,— */* *the ultimate nature of Hell.*

Anathema. Maranatha!

Oh for that rose of Bolshevism which holds
memory of its own budding,—and not this;—
this drooping prophecy of wormed potpourri,
Moscow's abomination of desolation;—
zig-zag marshlight of illth,
too "practical" five year planner of,—defeat;—
up-start Pope fanned by peacock lies:
"Were we ever wrong? No. We were never wrong.
We offer no resistance to Fascism.
We were correct before, during, and after.
What we could not do, Nazism has done.
We have committed no mistakes."

Infallible dunce, ineffably vincible,
we'll burn your cancer to a root in us.
As our waxing forces upon nature wax
force in ourselves, our forces over others wane,
and though your lamp'll never out, it fades . . .
fades before searchlight material humane.

Flivvers herd fireflies down the sumac slope;
the trees stir; the tides turn; the cloud
theater-curtain closes across the Moon;
and a landward sea wind lifts over the lawn,
with dancing leaves, the tilth that Spring thaws lent the brine;
while (to a Westland gale and heat lightnings
a-rumble over Coffin's Beach, laden
with hay scent of storm) the flotsam rubbish pile
bursts once more into flame. Flame doubled now
where late were the acid Moon and one star mirrored.
The tempest's cribbed abundance bursts its bin;
plum trees drop worm-soft fruit and ratted bark.
Thunder begins the night. In three days, it may clear.
The stars will bud.

In the Bathtub, to Mnemosyne

Away in this chambered secret, I'll draw sound
out of its cistern, pavement sealed, and drink
life water from rivuletted water life
of here excluded wind and sun. Intrude
your person, knock, or voice without a message
of great joy or doom,—I'll answer your sweet rattle
with unfond silence, or present at your fond touch
a hollow turtle shell, or vacant snake skin.

Esprit d'Escalier

That drop of sweat which is sliding down my mouth
tastes like a tear. Is my lip cut? was her cheek?
It was a tear, fool. Fool, you did not see
once through empty freight train conversation
her Jack and Jill tears fall down to defer
breaking that telegram her pulse was ticking
to her ears. They were, then, sweat and blood? Her tears
taste, in my mouth, of death and birth and salt.

I, when she ask me a question, or make reply
think only what I think; while she is thinking
our future, past, our present one dimension.
O! everything I'd say cuts with primal woe;
nor shall I ever tell the taste of my own sweat
from the tang of tears or blood, or taste of that spit.

Cross Questions

How do I know why you ask me, "How *are* you?
How *are* you? How are you? *How are*
you?" You do not care how I am. You
do not care who I am. You do not
really care what I think,—taking care not to, really.
"Do you, really?" you say, "Do you, really? Do
you think that you think that? Do
you doo? Doo you?"

How would I know if (in fear of fear) somehow
someone should ask you to bother to keep something
secret, you would not bother even to deny?
I am too busy finding who is not I.
Again? Do not start this all over again.
Please, I am still busy finding out them I please.

STEPHEN VINCENT BENÉT

(1898–1943)

from
John Brown's Body

American muse, whose strong and diverse heart
So many men have tried to understand
But only made it smaller with their art,
Because you are as various as your land,

As mountainous-deep, as flowered with blue rivers,
Thirsty with deserts, buried under snows,
As native as the shape of Navajo quivers,
And native, too, as the sea-voyaged rose.

Swift runner, never captured or subdued,
Seven-branched elk beside the mountain stream,
That half a hundred hunters have pursued
But never matched their bullets with the dream,

Where the great huntsmen failed, I set my sorry
And mortal snare for your immortal quarry.

You are the buffalo-ghost, the broncho-ghost
With dollar-silver in your saddle-horn,
The cowboys riding in from Painted Post,
The Indian arrow in the Indian corn,

And you are the clipped velvet of the lawns
Where Shropshire grows from Massachusetts sods,
The grey Maine rocks—and the war-painted dawns
That break above the Garden of the Gods.

The prairie-schooners crawling toward the ore
And the cheap car, parked by the station-door.

Where the skyscrapers lift their foggy plumes
Of stranded smoke out of a stony mouth
You are that high stone and its arrogant fumes,
And you are ruined gardens in the South

And bleak New England farms, so winter-white
Even their roofs look lonely, and the deep
The middle grainland where the wind of night
Is like all blind earth sighing in her sleep.

A friend, an enemy, a sacred hag
With two tied oceans in her medicine-bag.

They tried to fit you with an English song
And clip your speech into the English tale.
But, even from the first, the words went wrong,
The catbird pecked away the nightingale.

The homesick men begot high-cheekboned things
Whose wit was whittled with a different sound
And Thames and all the rivers of the kings
Ran into Mississippi and were drowned.

They planted England with a stubborn trust.
But the cleft dust was never English dust.

Stepchild of every exile from content
And all the disavouched, hard-bitten pack
Shipped overseas to steal a continent
With neither shirts nor honor to their back.

Pimping grandee and rump-faced regicide,
Apple-cheeked younkers from a windmill-square,
Puritans stubborn as the nails of Pride,
Rakes from Versailles and thieves from County Clare,

The black-robed priests who broke their hearts in vain
To make you God and France or God and Spain.

These were your lovers in your buckskin-youth.
And each one married with a dream so proud
He never knew it could not be the truth
And that he coupled with a girl of cloud.

And now to see you is more difficult yet
Except as an immensity of wheel
Made up of wheels, oiled with inhuman sweat
And glittering with the heat of ladled steel.

All these you are, and each is partly you,
And none is false, and none is wholly true.

from the Invocation

John Brown's body lies a-mouldering in the grave.
He will not come again with foolish pikes
And a pack of desperate boys to shadow the sun.
He has gone back North. The slaves have forgotten his eyes.
John Brown's body lies a-mouldering in the grave.
John Brown's body lies a-mouldering in the grave.
Already the corpse is changed, under the stone,
The strong flesh rotten, the bones dropping away.
Cotton will grow next year, in spite of the skull.
Slaves will be slaves next year, in spite of the bones.
Nothing is changed, John Brown, nothing is changed.

*"There is a song in my bones. There is a song
In my white bones."*

I hear no song. I hear
Only the blunt seeds growing secretly
In the dark entrails of the preparate earth,
The rustle of the cricket under the leaf,
The creaking of the cold wheel of the stars.

*"Bind my white bones together—hollow them
To skeleton pipes of music. When the wind
Blows from the budded Spring, the song will blow."*

I hear no song. I only hear the roar
Of the Spring freshets, and the gushing voice
Of mountain-brooks that overflow their banks,
Swollen with melting ice and crumbled earth.

*"That is my song.
It is made of water and wind. It marches on."*

No, John Brown's body lies a-mouldering,
A-mouldering.

*"My bones have been washed clean
And God blows through them with a hollow sound,
And God has shut his wildfire in my dead heart."*

I hear it now,
Faint, faint as the first droning flies of March,
Faint as the multitudinous, tiny sigh
Of grasses underneath a windy scythe.

"It will grow stronger."

It has grown stronger. It is marching on.
It is a throbbing pulse, a pouring surf,
It is the rainy gong of the Spring sky
Echoing,
John Brown's body,
John Brown's body.
But still it is not fierce. I find it still
More sorrowful than fierce.

*"You have not heard it yet. You have not heard
The ghosts that walk in it, the shaking sound."*

Strong medicine,
Bitter medicine of the dead,
I drink you now. I hear the unloosed thing,
The anger of the ripe wheat—the ripened earth
Sullenly quaking like a beaten drum

From Kansas to Vermont. I hear the stamp
Of the ghost-feet. I hear the ascending sea.

> "Glory, Glory Hallelujah,
> Glory, Glory, Hallelujah,
> Glory, Glory, Hallelujah!"

What is this agony of the marching dust?
What are these years ground into hatchet blades?

"Ask the tide why it rises with the moon,
My bones and I have risen like that tide
And an immortal anguish plucks us up
And will not hide us till our song is done."

The phantom drum diminishes—the year
Rolls back. It is only winter still, not spring,
The snow still flings its white on the new grave,
Nothing is changed, John Brown, nothing is changed
John . . . Brown . . .

from *Book One*

American Names

I have fallen in love with American names,
The sharp names that never get fat,
The snakeskin-titles of mining-claims,
The plumed war-bonnet of Medicine Hat,
Tucson and Deadwood and Lost Mule Flat.

Seine and Piave are silver spoons,
But the spoonbowl-metal is thin and worn,
There are English counties like hunting-tunes
Played on the keys of a postboy's horn,
But I will remember where I was born.

I will remember Carquinez Straits,
Little French Lick and Lundy's Lane,

The Yankee ships and the Yankee dates
And the bullet-towns of Calamity Jane.
I will remember Skunktown Plain.

I will fall in love with a Salem tree
And a rawhide quirt from Santa Cruz,
I will get me a bottle of Boston sea
And a blue-gum nigger to sing me blues.
I am tired of loving a foreign muse.

Rue des Martyrs and Bleeding-Heart-Yard,
Senlis, Pisa, and Blindman's Oast,
It is a magic ghost you guard
But I am sick for a newer ghost,
Harrisburg, Spartanburg, Painted Post.

Henry and John were never so
And Henry and John were always right?
Granted, but when it was time to go
And the tea and the laurels had stood all night,
Did they never watch for Nantucket Light?

I shall not rest quiet in Montparnasse.
I shall not lie easy at Winchelsea.
You may bury my body in Sussex grass,
You may bury my tongue at Champmédy.
I shall not be there. I shall rise and pass.
Bury my heart at Wounded Knee.

Cotton Mather

1663–1728

Grim Cotton Mather
Was always seeing witches,
Daylight, moonlight,
They buzzed about his head,
Pinching him and plaguing him
With aches and pains and stitches,
Witches in his pulpit,
Witches by his bed.

Nowadays, nowadays,
We'd say that he was crazy,
But everyone believed him
In old Salem town
And nineteen people
Were hanged for Salem witches
Because of Cotton Mather
And his long, black gown.

Old Cotton Mather
Didn't die happy.
He could preach and thunder,
He could fast and pray,
But men began to wonder
If there *had* been witches—
When he walked in the streets
Men looked the other way.

Daniel Boone

1735–1820

When Daniel Boone goes by, at night,
The phantom deer arise
And all lost, wild America
Is burning in their eyes.

Metropolitan Nightmare

It rained quite a lot, that spring. You woke in the morning
And saw the sky still clouded, the streets still wet,
But nobody noticed so much, except the taxis
And the people who parade. You don't, in a city.
The parks got very green. All the trees were green
Far into July and August, heavy with leaf,
Heavy with leaf and the long roots boring and spreading,
But nobody noticed that but the city gardeners
And they don't talk.
                        Oh, on Sundays, perhaps, you'd notice:
Walking through certain blocks, by the shut, proud houses
With the windows boarded, the people gone away,
You'd suddenly see the queerest small shoots of green
Poking through cracks and crevices in the stone
And a bird-sown flower, red on a balcony,
But then you made jokes about grass growing in the streets
And politics and grass-roots—and there were songs
And gags and a musical show called "Hot and Wet."
It all made a good box for the papers. When the flamingo
Flew into a meeting of the Board of Estimate,
The new Mayor acted at once and called the photographers.
When the first green creeper crawled upon Brooklyn Bridge,
They thought it was ornamental. They let it stay.

That was the year the termites came to New York
And they don't do well in cold climates—but listen, Joe,
They're only ants and ants are nothing but insects.
It was funny and yet rather wistful, in a way
(As Heywood Broun pointed out in the *World-Telegram*)
To think of them looking for wood in a steel city.
It made you feel about life. It was too divine.
There were funny pictures by all the smart, funny artists
And Macy's ran a terribly clever ad:
"The Widow's Termite" or something.
                                      There was no
Disturbance. Even the Communists didn't protest
And say they were Morgan hirelings. It was too hot,
Too hot to protest, too hot to get excited,

An even, African heat, lush, fertile and steamy,
That soaked into bone and mind and never once broke.
The warm rain fell in fierce showers and ceased and fell.
Pretty soon you got used to its always being that way.

You got used to the changed rhythm, the altered beat,
To people walking slower, to the whole bright
Fierce pulse of the city slowing, to men in shorts,
To the new sun-helmets from Best's and the cops' white
        uniforms,
And the long noon-rest in the offices, everywhere.
It wasn't a plan or anything. It just happened.
The fingers tapped the keys slower, the office-boys
Dozed on their benches, the bookkeeper yawned at his desk.
The A. T. & T. was the first to change the shifts
And establish an official siesta-room,
But they were always efficient. Mostly it just
Happened like sleep itself, like a tropic sleep,
Till even the Thirties were deserted at noon
Except for a few tourists and one damp cop.
They ran boats to see the big lilies on the North River
But it was only the tourists who really noticed
The flocks of rose-and-green parrots and parrakeets
Nesting in the stone crannies of the Cathedral.
The rest of us had forgotten when they first came.

There wasn't any real change, it was just a heat spell,
A rain spell, a funny summer, a weather-man's joke,
In spite of the geraniums three feet high
In the tin-can gardens of Hester and Desbrosses.
New York was New York. It couldn't turn inside out.
When they got the news from Woods Hole about the Gulf
        Stream,
The *Times* ran an adequate story.
But nobody reads those stories but science-cranks.

Until, one day, a somnolent city-editor
Gave a new cub the termite yarn to break his teeth on.
The cub was just down from Vermont, so he took the time.
He was serious about it. He went around.

He read all about termites in the Public Library
And it made him sore when they fired him.
                                        So, one evening,
Talking with an old watchman, beside the first
Raw girders of the new Planetopolis Building
(Ten thousand brine-cooled offices, each with shower)
He saw a dark line creeping across the rubble
And turned a flashlight on it.
                              "Say, buddy," he said,
"You better look out for those ants. They eat wood, you
    know,
They'll have your shack down in no time."
                                        The watchman spat.
"Oh, they've quit eating wood," he said, in a casual voice,
"I thought everybody knew that."
                                —and, reaching down,
He pried from the insect jaws the bright crumb of steel.

MALCOLM COWLEY

(1898–1989)

Winter Tenement

When everything but love was spent
we climbed five flights above the street
and wintered in a tenement.
It had no bathroom and no heat
except a coal fire in the grate
that we kept burning night and day
until the fire went out in May.

There in a morning ritual,
clasping our chilblained hands, we joked
about the cobwebs on the wall,
the toilet in the public hall,
    the fire that always smoked.
We shivered as we breakfasted,
then to get warm went back to bed.

In the black snows of February
that rickety bed an arm's-length wide
became our daylong sanctuary,
our Garden of Eden, till we spied
one spring morning at our bedside,
    resting on his dull sword,
the rancorous angel of the bored.

"We raised this cockroach shrine to love,"
I said; "here let his coffin lie.
Get up, put coffee on the stove
to drink in memory of love,
then take the uptown train, while I
sit here alone to speculate
and poke the ashes in the grate."

Ernest

Safe is the man with blunderbuss
who stalks the hippopotamus
on Niger's bank, or scours the veldt
to rape the lion of his pelt;

but deep in peril he who sits
at home to rack his lonely wits
and there do battle, grim and blind
against the jackals of the mind.

HARRY CROSBY
(1898–1929)

Vision

I exchange eyes with the Mad Queen

the mirror crashes against my face and
bursts into a thousand suns
    all over the city flags crackle and bang
fog horns scream in the harbor
    the wind hurricanes through the window
    and I begin to dance the dance of the
Kurd Shepherds

    I stamp upon the floor
    I whirl like dervishes

colors revolve dressing and undressing
I lash them with my fury
stark white with iron black
harsh red with blue
marble green with bright orange
and only gold remains naked

columns of steel rise and plunge
emerge and disappear
pistoning in the river of my soul
    thrusting upwards
    thrusting downwards
    thrusting inwards
    thrusting outwards
      penetrating

    I roar with pain

black-footed ferrets disappear into holes

the sun tattooed on my back
begins to spin
   faster and faster
   whirring whirling
throwing out a glory of sparks
sparks shoot off into space
sparks into shooting stars
shooting stars collide with comets

     Explosions
   Naked Colors Explode
     into
   Red Disaster

I crash out through the
window naked, widespread
upon a
   Heliosaurus
I uproot an obelisk and plunge
it into the ink-pot of the
Black Sea
I write the word
     SUN
across the dreary palimpsest
of the world
I pour the contents of the
Red Sea down my throat
I erect catapults and
lay siege to the cities of the world
I scatter violent disorder
throughout the kingdoms of the world
I stone the people of the world
I stride over mountains
I pick up oceans like thin cards
and spin them into oblivion
I kick down walled cities
I hurl giant firebrands against governments

I thrust torches through the eyes of the law
   I annihilate museums
   I demolish libraries
   I oblivionize skyscrapers
I become hard as adamant
indurated in solid fire
rigid with hatred

I bring back the wizards and the sorcerers
the necromancers
the magicians
I practise witchcraft
I set up idols
with a sharp-edged sword
I cut through the crowded streets
comets follow in my wake
stars make obeisance to me
the moon uncovers her
nakedness to me

I am the harbinger of a
New Sun World
I bring the Seed of a
   New Copulation
I proclaim the Mad Queen

I stamp out vast empires
I crush palaces in my rigid
   hands
I harden my heart against
   churches

I blot out cemeteries
I feed the people with
stinging nettles
I resurrect madness
I thrust my naked sword
between the ribs of the world
I murder the world!

Photoheliograph

(for Lady A.)

black black black black black
black black black black black
black black black black black
black black black black black
black black SUN black black
black black black black black
black black black black black
black black black black black
black black black black black
black black black black black

HORACE GREGORY

(1898–1982)

from
Chorus for Survival

8

The Meek Shall Disinherit the Earth.

Darkness in rain:
traffic in asphalt mirrors on the Square
gathers before it mounts Fifth Avenue
north through the white-arc'd Victory in stone
toward Five O'clock.
                    A voice in air:
"Come talk to me at 61, my attic
an antique stairway-landing in the sky:
'Loaf and invite the soul,' the deer that strays
into our hands, the silver beast
with wary, child-like eyes, yet innocent—
we'll talk until another day's begun."

And through the rain I saw his house loom up,
an old ship harbored into alien time,
dry-docked in broken timber, the bricks fallen,
steel hawsers giving way, the cornice sprung:
and as one stepped inside, one heard the wind.
I saw him leaning from the top-flight floor:
"I have been ill, been poor, yet when night enters
this room that holds the hours I lie awake,
something like youth returns: there is a tumult
of warmth within my veins . . . and then the tide,
music inspired by a golden bird—
that winged bough whose day is always spring
whose fiery chariot is the song unheard
leaping the ashes of Time's Illium
from dark to dark, that lives in fire,

166

climbs fire that flames upon an iron tree,
takes flight within a dream,
and is the hurricane in deepening calm.

I sometimes feel that I have lived forever in this room:
the rent unpaid, yet I am fed and watered
like a geranium on that window sill—
by landlady, charwoman, or foolish girl
who disappears at noon
leaving her alms behind.
But if I leave the room, wherever I go
I hear a whisper: 'Don't come again;
your face is too well known:
you are Herman Melville of the Customs House,
bright in oblivion and yet unseen.'

In a far reach of the room I sometimes hear
Shakespeare and Dante risen from the shades:
perpetual oak and olive sheltering
the delicate laurel of middle-aged spring,
May in October and an early frost:
the grasses changed to glittering white hair.
No, I'm not bitter: I am always friendly.
I always threaten meekness everywhere,
my face the preternaturally calm
forgiving smile . . .
                    Last night I saw a flame
pour out of darkness over eastern heavens:
the earth had perished on the farther shore,
an ocean wilderness on either hand . . .
The sound of that sea shall be my requiem."

12

Among the shades I heard my father's father:
"I am a tall man, handsome for my years:
Astute, four score and ten, my six foot three
Mounting to steer the horses beggars ride,
Ex-Dubliner, astronomer, engineer

From thick green growing turf where I was born
Where blackbird armies wheeled down from the clouds
Breaking the sky through fractured sunlit rain
Until the violet long archaic twilight
Empties its shadows over hill and plain.
I built my bridges to oblivion
Even here across young lakes, across the sea . . .
Get out of my grave: there is nothing here—
Take your hands away—I want none of you: sons,
Grandsons, cousins and fools.
                      Put the spade aside,
No treasures here: the inhabitant's gone,
Nor nakedness, nor sins, nor flesh, nor worms,
Nor rings, nor jewels, nor gold.
The grave has a clever way of keeping secrets,
Everything lost in dust and a few odd bones:
And the last pawn-tickets dust,
And long lost ancestors in deeper dust
Under the green-mossed ruins of family pride.
Be careful with that spade. It is made of iron:
It awakes destruction.
If ever there is another resurrection,
I have the great cold strength to stand alone."

The Cage of Voices

Hear them, hear them—all
Of them are back again:
The schoolmaster and the boys
And girls, the white-haired
Middle-aged red face, the faces
Of the young, laughing, laughing,
Laughing behind closed doors,
Or on stairs, or in the hall.
Hear them, they know, they tell
All you have done, where
You have been and why;
All are talking, talking,
Chattering in the next room.

This is more than a dream:
It is something that is awake
Within a dream; it wakes
And follows you out of bed,
Out of the room, out of the house
And down the street. Hear
Them through an open window,
An open door. Stand in the street
And the shop windows look
At your eyes and hands and what
You wear. They know the secret.

That little girl with the pale
Sharp face and small green eye
Could, if you ask her, tell
Everything: her lips are moving,
She talks in whispers, but an hour
Later, she is a sibyl
Speaking through the walls—
She is merely one of them.
Hear them: they have disguised
Their voices to make you think
They are talking of someone else,
Not you, nor yours, but of
Some other death, some other life;
Yet, if you listen closely,
Closely as when the ear discerns
The stirring of the wind
Within a yellow leaf, or is
Almost certain of a crying
Whisper in the rain—

                        you shall hear
Them speak as voices call
In sleep; they have returned
And you must hear.

MELVIN B. TOLSON

(1898–1966)

from
Libretto for the Republic of Liberia

Ti

O Calendar of the Century,
red-letter the Republic's birth!
O Hallelujah,
oh, let no *Miserere*
venom the spinal cord of Afric earth!
Selah!
"Ecce homo!"
the blind men cowled in azure rant
before the Capitol,
between the Whale and Elephant,
where no longer stands Diogenes' hearse
readied for the ebony mendicant,
nor weeping widow Europe with her hands
making the multitudinous seas incarnadine
or earth's *massebôth* worse:
O Great White World, thou boy of tears, omega hounds
lap up the alpha laugh and *du-haut-en-bas* curse.
Selah!

O Africa, Mother of Science
. . . *lachen mit yastchekes* . . .
What dread hand,
to make tripartite one august event,
sundered Gondwanaland?
What dread grasp crushed your biceps and
back upon the rack
chaos of chance and change
fouled in Malebolgean isolation?
What dread *elboga* shoved your soul
into the *tribulum* of retardation?

170

melamin or melanin dies to the world and dies:
Rome casketed herself in Homeric hymns.
Man's culture in barb and Arab lies:
The Jordan flows into the Tiber,
the Yangtze into the Thames,
the Ganges into the Mississippi, the Niger
into the Seine.
Judge of the Nations, spare us: yet,
fool latins, alumni of one school,
on Clochan-na-n'all, say *Phew*
. . . *Lest we forget! Lest we forget!* . . .
to dusky peers of Roman, Greek, and Jew.
Selah!

Elders of Agâ's House, keening
at the Eagles' feast, cringing
before the Red Slayer, shrinking
from the blood on Hubris' pall—
carked by cracks of myriad curbs,
hitherto, against the Wailing Wall
of Ch'in, the blind men cried:
All cultures crawl
walk hard
fall,
flout
under classes under
Lout,
enmesh in ethos, in *masôreth*, the poet's flesh,
intone the Mass of the class as the requiem of the mass,
serve *adola mentis* till the crack of will,
castle divorcee Art in a blue-blood moat,
read the flesh of grass
into bulls and bears,
let Brahmin pens kill
Everyman the Goat,
write Culture's epitaph in *Notes* upstairs.
O Cordon Sanitaire,
thy brain's tapeworm, extract, thy eyeball's mote!
Selah!

Between pavilions
small and great
sentineled from capital to stylobate
by crossbow, harquebus, cannon, or Pegasus' bomb
. . . *and none went in and none went out* . . .
hitherto the State,
in spite of Sicilian Vespers, stout
from slave, feudal, bourgeois, or soviet grout,
has hung its curtain—scrim, foulard, pongee,
silk, lace, or iron—helled in by Sancho's fears
of the bitter hug of the Great Fear, Not-To-Be—
oscuro Luzbel,
with no bowels of mercy,
in the starlight
de las canteras sin auroras.
Behind the curtain, aeon after aeon,
he who doubts the white book's colophon
is Truth's, if not Laodicean, wears
the black flower T of doomed Laocoön.
Before hammer and sickle or swastika, two
worlds existed: the Many, the Few.
They sat at Delos', at Vienna's, at Yalta's, ado:
Macbeth, without three rings, as host
to Banquo's ghost.
Selah!

Like some gray ghoul from Alcatraz,
old Profit, the bald rake *paseq*, wipes the bar,
polishes the goblet vanity,
leers at the tigress Avarice
as
she harlots roués from afar:
swallowtails unsaved by loincloths,
famed enterprises prophesying war,
hearts of rags (*Hanorish tharah sharinas*) souls of chalk,
laureates with sugary grace in zinc buckets of verse,
myths rattled by the blueprint's talk,
ists potted and pitted by a feast,
Red Ruin's skeleton horsemen, four abreast
. . . galloping . . .

Marx, the exalter, would not know his East
. . . galloping . . .
nor Christ, the Leveler, His West.
Selah!

O Age of Tartuffe
. . . *a lighthouse with no light atop* . . .
O Age, *pesiq*, O Age,
kinks internal and global stinks
fog the bitter black estates of Buzzard and Og.
A Dog, I'd rather be, o sage, a Monkey or a Hog.
O Peoples of the Brinks,
come with the hawk's resolve,
the skeptic's optic nerve, the prophet's *tele* verve
and Oedipus' guess, to solve
the riddle of
the Red Enigma and the White Sphinx.
Selah!

O East . . . *el grito de Dolores* . . . O West,
pacts, disemboweled, crawl off to die;
white books, *fiers instants promis à la faux*,
in sick bay choke on mulligan truth and lie;
the knife of Rousseau hacks the anatomy
of the fowl necessity;
dead eyes accuse red Desfourneau,
whose sit-down strike gives High-Heels vertigo;
the wind blows through the keyhole
and the fettered pull down the shades;
while *il santo* and *pero* hone phillipics,
Realpolitik explodes the hand grenades
faits accomplis
in the peace of parades;
caught in the blizzard *divide et impera*,
the little gray cattle cower
before the Siamese wolves,
pomp and power;
Esperanto trips the heels of Greek;
in brain-sick lands, the pearls too rich for swine
the claws of the anonymous seek;

the case Caesarean, Lethean brew
nor instruments obstetrical at hand,
the midwife of the old disenwombs the new.
Selah!

The *Höhere* of Gaea's children
is beyond the *dérèglement de tous les sens*, is beyond
gold fished from cesspools, the *galerie des rois*,
the seeking of cows, *apartheid*, Sisyphus' despond,
the Ilande intire of itselfe with *die Schweine* in mud,
the potter's wheel that stocks the potter's field,
Kchesinskaja's balcony with epitaphs in blood,
deeds hostile all, O Caton, to hostile eyes,
the breaking of foreheads against the walls,
gazing at navels, thinking with thighs

.   .   .

The *Höhere* of God's stepchildren
is beyond the sabotaged world, is beyond
das Diktat der Menschenverachtung,
la muerte sobre el esqueleto de la nada,
the pelican's breast rent red to feed the young,
summer's third-class ticket, the *Revue des morts*,
the skulls trepanned to hold ideas plucked from dung,
Dives' crumbs in the church of the unchurched,
absurd life shaking its ass's ears among
the colors of vowels and Harrar blacks
with Nessus shirts from Europe on their backs

.   .   .

The *Höhere* of X's children
is beyond Heralds' College, the *filets d'Arachné*, is beyond
maggot democracy, the *Mal éternel*, the Bells of Ys,
the doddering old brigades with aorist medicines of poetry,
the *Orizaba* with its Bridge of Sighs,
the *oasis d'horreur dans un déserte d'ennui*,
the girasol rocks of Secunderabad,
Yofan's studio and *Shkola Nenavisti*,
the *ototoi*—in Crimson Tapestries—of the *hoi polloi*,
Euboean defeats

in the Sausage Makers' bout
the fool himself himself finds out
and in the cosmos of his chaos
repeats.
Selah!

The *Höhere* of one's pores *En Masse*
. . . Christians, Jews, *ta ethne* . . .
makes as apishly
brazen as the brag and brabble of brass
the flea's fiddling
on the popinjay,
the pollack's pout
in the net's hurray,
the jerboa's feat
in the fawn and the flout
of
Quai d'Orsay,
White House,
Kremlin,
Downing Street.
Again black Aethiop reaches at the sun, O Greek.
Things-as-they-are-for-us, *nullius in verba*,
speak!
O East, O West,
on tenotomy bent,
Chang's tissue is
Eng's ligament!
Selah!

Between Yesterday's wars
now hot now cold
the grief-in-grain of Man
dripping dripping dripping
from the Cross of Iron
dripping
drew jet vampires
of the Skull;
Between Yesterday's wills of Tanaka, between
golden goblet and truckling trull

and the ires
of rivers red with the reflexes of fires,
the ferris wheel
of race, of caste, of class
dumped and alped cadavers till the ground
fogged the Pleiades with Gila rot: Today the mass,
the Beast with a Maginot Line in its Brain,
the staircase Avengers of base alloy,
the *vile canaille—Gorii!*—the *Bastard-rasse*,
the *uomo qualyque*, the *hoi barbaroi*,
the *raya* in the *Oeil de Boeuf*,
the *vsechelovek*, the *descamisados*, the *hoi polloi*,
the Raw from the Coliseum of the Cooked,
Il Duce's Whore, Vardaman's Hound—
unparadised nobodies with maps of Nowhere
ride the merry-go-round!
Selah!

from
Harlem Gallery

Alpha

The Harlem Gallery, an Afric pepper bird,
awakes me at a people's dusk of dawn.
The age altars its image, a dog's hind leg,
and hazards the moment of truth in pawn.
The Lord of the House of Flies,
jaundice-eyed, synapses purled,
wries before the tumultuous canvas,
The Second of May—
by Goya:
the dagger of Madrid
vs.
the scimitar of Murat.
In Africa, in Asia, on the Day
of Barricades, alarm birds bedevil the Great White World,
a Buridan's ass—not Balaam's—between no oats and hay.

Sometimes a Roscius as tragedian,
sometimes a Kean as clown,
without Sir Henry's flap to shield my neck,
I travel, from oasis to oasis, man's Saharic up-and-down.

As a Hambletonian gathers his legs for a leap,
dead wool and fleece wool
I have mustered up from hands
now warm or cold: a full
rich Indies' cargo;
but often I hear a dry husk-of-locust blues
descend the tone ladder of a laughing goose,
syncopating between
the faggot and the noose:
"Black Boy, O Black Boy,
is the port worth the cruise?"

Like the lice and maggots of the apples of Cain
on a strawberry tree,
the myth of the Afroamerican past
exacts the parasite's fee.

Sometimes the spirit wears away
in the dust bowl of abuse,
like the candied flesh of the barrel cactus which
the unpitying pitch
of a Panhandle wind
leaves with unpalatable juice.

Although the gaffing *"Tò tí?"* of the Gadfly girds
the I-ness of my humanness and Negroness,
the clockbird's
jackass laughter
in sun, in rain,
at dusk of dawn,
mixes with the pepper bird's reveille in my brain,
where the plain is twilled and the twilled is plain.

Mu

Hideho Heights
and I, like the brims of old hats,
slouched at a sepulchered table in the Zulu Club.
Frog Legs Lux and his Indigo Combo
spoke with tongues that sent their devotees
out of this world!

Black and brown and yellow fingers flashed,
like mirrored sunrays of a heliograph,
on clarinet and piano keys, on cornet valves.

Effervescing like acid on limestone,
Hideho said:
"O White Folks, O Black Folks,
the dinosaur imagined its extinction meant
the death of the piss ants."

Cigarette smoke
—opaque veins in Carrara marble—
magicked the habitués into
humoresques and grotesques.
Lurid lights
spraying African figures on the walls
ecstasied maids and waiters,
pickups and stevedores—
with delusions
of Park Avenue grandeur.

Once, twice,
Hideho sneaked a swig.
"On the house," he said, proffering the bottle
as he lorded it under the table.
Glimpsing the harpy eagle at the bar,
I grimaced,
"I'm not the house snake of the Zulu Club."

A willow of a woman,
bronze as knife money,

executed, near our table, the Lenox Avenue Quake.
Hideho winked at me and poked
that which
her tight Park Avenue skirt vociferously advertized.
Peacocking herself, she turned like a ballerina,
her eyes blazing drops of rum on a crêpe suzette.
"Why, you—"
A sanitary decree, I thought. "Don't *you* me!" he fumed.
The lips of a vixen exhibited a picadill flare.
"*What* you smell isn't cooking," she said.
Hideho sniffed.
"Chanel No. 5," he scoffed,
"from Sugar Hill."
I laughed and clapped him on the shoulder.
"A bad metaphor, *poet.*"
His jaws closed
like an alligator squeezer.
"She's a willow," I emphasized,
"a willow by a cesspool."
Hideho mused aloud,
"Do I hear The Curator rattle Eliotic bones?"

Out of the Indigo Combo
flowed rich and complex polyrhythms.
Like surfacing bass,
exotic swells and softenings
of the veld vibrato
emerged.
.   .   .
Was that Snakehips Briskie
gliding out of the aurora australis of the Zulu Club
into the kaleidoscopic circle?
.   .   .
Etnean gasps!
Vesuvian acclamations!
.   .   .
Snakehips poised himself—
Giovanni Gabrieli's
single violin against his massed horns.
.   .   .

The silence of the revelers was the arrested
hemorrhage of an artery
grasped by bull forceps.
I felt Hideho's breath against my ear.
"The penis act in the Garden of Eden," he confided.

. . .

Convulsively, unexampledly,
Snakehips' body and soul
began to twist and untwist like a gyrating rawhide—
began to coil, to writhe
like a prismatic-hued python
in the throes of copulation.

Eyes bright as the light
at Eddystone Rock,
an ebony Penthesilea
grabbed her tiger's-eye yellow-brown
beanpole Sir Testiculus of the evening
and gave him an Amazonian hug.
He wilted in her arms
like a limp morning-glory.
"The Zulu Club is in the groove," chanted Hideho,
"and the cats, the black cats, are *gone!*"

In the *ostinato*
of stamping feet and clapping hands,
the Promethean bard of Lenox Avenue became a
lost loose-leaf
as memory vignetted
Rabelaisian I's of the Boogie-Woogie dynasty
in barrel houses, at rent parties,
on riverboats, at wakes:
The Toothpick, Funky Five, and Tippling Tom!
Ma Rainey, Countess Willie V., and Aunt Harriet!
Speckled Red, Skinny Head Pete, and Stormy Weather!
Listen, Black Boy.
Did the High Priestess at 27 rue de Fleurus
assert, "The Negro suffers from nothingness"?
Hideho confided like a neophyte on The Walk,
"Jazz is the marijuana of the Blacks."

In the *tribulum* of dialectics, I juggled the idea;
then I observed,
"Jazz is the philosophers' egg of the Whites."

Hideho laughed from below the Daniel Boone rawhide belt
he'd redeemed, in a Dallas pawn shop,
with part of the black-market
loot set loose
in a crap game
by a Yangtze ex-coolie who,
in a Latin Quarter dive below Telegraph Hill,
out-Harvarded his Alma Mater.

. . .

Frog Legs Lux and his Indigo Combo
let go
with a wailing pedal point
that slid into
Basin Street Blues
like Ty Cobb stealing second base:
Zulu,
King of the Africans,
arrives on Mardi Gras morning;
the veld drum of Baby Dodds'
great-grandfather
in Congo Square
pancakes the first blue note
in a callithump of the USA.
And now comes the eve of Ash Wednesday.
Comus on parade!
All God's children revel
like a post-Valley Forge
charivari in Boston celebrating the nuptials of
a gay-old-dog minuteman with a lusty maid.

. . .

Just as
the bourgeois adopted
the lyric-winged piano of Liszt in the court at Weimar
for the solitude of his
aeried apartment,
Harlem chose

for its cold-water flat
the hot-blues cornet of King Oliver
in his cart
under the
El pillars of the Loop.
. . .

The yanking fishing rod
of Hideho's voice
jerked me out of my bird's-foot violet romanticism.
He mixed Shakespeare's image with his own
and caricatured me:
"Yonder Curator has a lean and hungry look;
he thinks too much.
Such blackamoors are dangerous to
the Great White World!"
. . .

With a dissonance
from the Weird Sisters,
the jazz diablerie
boiled down and away
in the vacuum pan
of the Indigo Combo.

LÉONIE ADAMS

(1899–1988)

April Mortality

Rebellion shook an ancient dust,
And bones, bleached dry of rottenness,
Said: Heart, be bitter still, nor trust
The earth, the sky, in their bright dress.

Heart, heart, dost thou not break to know
This anguish thou wilt bear alone?
We sang of it an age ago,
And traced it dimly upon stone.

With all the drifting race of men
Thou also art begot to mourn
That she is crucified again,
The lonely Beauty yet unborn.

And if thou dreamest to have won
Some touch of her in permanence,
'Tis the old cheating of the sun,
The intricate lovely play of sense.

Be bitter still, remember how
Four petals, when a little breath
Of wind made stir the pear-tree bough,
Blew delicately down to death.

Ghostly Tree

O breech, unbind your yellow leaf, for deep
The honeyed time lies sleeping, and lead shade
Seals up the eyelids of its golden sleep.
Long are your flutes, chimes, little bells, at rest,
And here is only the cold scream of the fox,

Only the hunter following on the hound;
While your quaint-plumaged,
The bird that your green summer boughs lapped round,
Bends south its soft bright breast.

Before the winter and the terror break,
Scatter the leaf that broadened with the rose
Not for a tempest, but a sigh, to take.
Four nights to exorcise the thing that stood
Bound by these frail which dangle at your branch,
They ran a frosty dagger to its heart;
And it, wan substance,
No more remembered it might cry or start
Or stain a point with blood.

The Rounds and Garlands Done

Now the golden looks are spent
And light no more will brim from the large air,
But green and changeling drips from the little round
Of the close branch;
And the shadow, born of nothing,
Glides over the green ground.

Day that cast the lovely looks is sped;
And from the turf, circled with white dew,
The lovers and the children are gone,
Leaving the wreath, the bouquet fresh, looped up with
        grasses;
All the golden looks are spent,
And the time of the rounds and the garlands done.

High from a drowning heart the waters' cry
Rises subdued to silver and is lost
On the pure bell of silence, and the petal
Whose sweetness drooped the spray,
Drained now of lustre, rides
Upon a soundless wind
More light than any ghost.

The Moon and Spectator

In the dead of the night
I got from my bed;
The air stretched hollow,
A theatre of the dead.

The night was half sunk and the wind gone,
The passion of the wind had gone down;
But the boughs shaken a little, blanched a little,
Spectrally, by the moon.

The moon performed her march fantastic,
The harrier of clouds, a flame half seen,
Or full in the high sky, the royal sables being spread,
A withered queen.

The moon, that chill frame, I saw enact
Her rite commemorative of a bound ghost,
And thought of a night wildly born, outliving storm,
And its tears lost.

Almost without pulse, a spectator to the moon,
A dream of some fashion set the body awake,
But called to the heart in the deeps of sleep how rising
From sleep again it would break.

Fragmentary Stars

So wide the wells of darkness sink,
These having their own light, that are lost with the light,
Appear immersed in mournfulness over the night,
Like things that in sleep will come to the mind's brink:
The bright Aldebaran, and seven that hover,
Seven wild and pale, clouding their brightness over,
And the flame that fell with summer, and the rose of stars
    returning,
Like tears piercing the sky;

Glittering without cause, for the piece of a legend,
Wept, I know not why.
O lovely and forgotten,
Gathered only of sleep,
All night upon the lids set burning,
Shaken from the lids at morning.

The Horn

While coming to the feast I found
A venerable silver-throated horn,
Which were I brave enough to sound,
Then all, as from that moment born,
Would breathe the honey of this clime,
And three times merry in their time
Would praise the virtue of the horn.

The mist is risen like thin breath;
The young leaves of the ground smell chill,
So faintly are they strewn on death,
The road I came down a west hill;
But none can name as I can name
A little golden-bright thing, flame,
Since bones have caught their marrow chill.

And in a thicket passed me by,
In the black brush, a running hare,
Having a spectre in his eye,
That sped in darkness to the snare;
And who but I can know in pride
The heart, set beating in the side,
Has but the wisdom of a hare?

The Figurehead

This that is washed with weed and pebblestone
Curved once a dolphin's length before the prow,
And I who read the land to which we bore
In its grave eyes, question my idol now,
What cold and marvelous fancy it may keep,
Since the salt terror swept us from our course,
Or if a wisdom later than the storm,
For old green ocean's tinctured it so deep;
And with some reason to me on this strand
The waves, the ceremonial waves have come
And stooped their barbaric heads, and all spread out
Their lovely arms before them, and are gone,
Leaving their murderous tribute on the sand.

Grapes Making

Noon sun beats down the leaf; the noon
Of summer burns along the vine
And thins the leaf with burning air,
Till from the underleaf is fanned,
And down the woven vine, the light.
Still the pleached leaves drop layer on layer
To wind the sun on either hand,
And echoes of the light are bound,
And hushed the blazing cheek of light,
The hurry of the breathless noon,
And from the thicket of the vine
The grape has pressed into its round.

The grape has pressed into its round,
And swings, aloof chill green, clean won
Of light, between the sky and ground;
Those hid, soft-flashing lamps yet blind,
Which yield an apprehended sun.
Fresh triumph in a courteous kind,
Having more ways to be, and years,

And easy, countless treasuries,
You whose all-told is still no sum,
Like a rich heart, well-said in sighs,
The careless autumn mornings come,
The grapes drop glimmering to the shears.

Now shady sod at heel piles deep,
An overarching shade, the vine
Across the fall of noon is flung;
And here beneath the leaves is cast
A light to colour noonday sleep,
While cool, bemused the grape is swung
Beneath the eyelids of the vine;
And deepening like a tender thought
Green moves along the leaf, and bright
The leaf above, and leaf has caught,
And emerald pierces day, and last
The faint leaf vanishes to light.

HART CRANE

(1899–1932)

Chaplinesque

We make our meek adjustments,
Contented with such random consolations
As the wind deposits
In slithered and too ample pockets.

For we can still love the world, who find
A famished kitten on the step, and know
Recesses for it from the fury of the street,
Or warm torn elbow coverts.

We will sidestep, and to the final smirk
Dally the doom of that inevitable thumb
That slowly chafes its puckered index toward us,
Facing the dull squint with what innocence
And what surprise!

And yet these fine collapses are not lies
More than the pirouettes of any pliant cane;
Our obsequies are, in a way, no enterprise.
We can evade you, and all else but the heart:
What blame to us if the heart live on.

The game enforces smirks; but we have seen
The moon in lonely alleys make
A grail of laughter of an empty ash can,
And through all sound of gaiety and quest
Have heard a kitten in the wilderness.

For the Marriage of Faustus and Helen

> *"And so we may arrive by Talmud skill*
> *And profane Greek to raise the building up*
> *Of Helen's house against the Ismaelite,*
> *King of Thogarma, and his habergeons*
> *Brimstony, blue and fiery; and the force*
> *Of King Abaddon, and the beast of Cittim;*
> *Which Rabbi David Kimchi, Onkelos,*
> *And Aben Ezra do interpret Rome."*
> —THE ALCHEMIST.

I

The mind has shown itself at times
Too much the baked and labeled dough
Divided by accepted multitudes.
Across the stacked partitions of the day—
Across the memoranda, baseball scores,
The stenographic smiles and stock quotations
Smutty wings flash out equivocations.

The mind is brushed by sparrow wings;
Numbers, rebuffed by asphalt, crowd
The margins of the day, accent the curbs,
Convoying divers dawns on every corner
To druggist, barber and tobacconist,
Until the graduate opacities of evening
Take them away as suddenly to somewhere
Virginal perhaps, less fragmentary, cool.

> *There is the world dimensional for*
> *those untwisted by the love of things*
> *irreconcilable . . .*

And yet, suppose some evening I forgot
The fare and transfer, yet got by that way
Without recall,—lost yet poised in traffic.
Then I might find your eyes across an aisle,
Still flickering with those prefigurations—
Prodigal, yet uncontested now,
Half-riant before the jerky window frame.

There is some way, I think, to touch
Those hands of yours that count the nights
Stippled with pink and green advertisements.
And now, before its arteries turn dark
I would have you meet this bartered blood.
Imminent in his dream, none better knows
The white wafer cheek of love, or offers words
Lightly as moonlight on the eaves meets snow.

Reflective conversion of all things
At your deep blush, when ecstasies thread
The limbs and belly, when rainbows spread
Impinging on the throat and sides . . .
Inevitable, the body of the world
Weeps in inventive dust for the hiatus
That winks above it, bluet in your breasts.

The earth may glide diaphanous to death;
But if I lift my arms it is to bend
To you who turned away once, Helen, knowing
The press of troubled hands, too alternate
With steel and soil to hold you endlessly.
I meet you, therefore, in that eventual flame
You found in final chains, no captive then—
Beyond their million brittle, bloodshot eyes;
White, through white cities passed on to assume
That world which comes to each of us alone.

Accept a lone eye riveted to your plane,
Bent axle of devotion along companion ways
That beat, continuous, to hourless days—
One inconspicuous, glowing orb of praise.

II

Brazen hypnotics glitter here;
Glee shifts from foot to foot,
Magnetic to their tremulo.
This crashing opera bouffe,
Blest excursion! this ricochet

From roof to roof—
Know, Olympians, we are breathless
While nigger cupids scour the stars!

A thousand light shrugs balance us
Through snarling hails of melody.
White shadows slip across the floor
Splayed like cards from a loose hand;
Rhythmic ellipses lead into canters
Until somewhere a rooster banters.

Greet naïvely—yet intrepidly
New soothings, new amazements
That cornets introduce at every turn—
And you may fall downstairs with me
With perfect grace and equanimity.
Or, plaintively scud past shores
Where, by strange harmonic laws
All relatives, serene and cool,
Sit rocked in patent armchairs.

O, I have known metallic paradises
Where cuckoos clucked to finches
Above the deft catastrophes of drums.
While titters hailed the groans of death
Beneath gyrating awnings I have seen
The incunabula of the divine grotesque.
This music has a reassuring way.

The siren of the springs of guilty song—
Let us take her on the incandescent wax
Striated with nuances, nervosities
That we are heir to: she is still so young,
We cannot frown upon her as she smiles,
Dipping here in this cultivated storm
Among slim skaters of the gardened skies.

III

Capped arbiter of beauty in this street
That narrows darkly into motor dawn,—
You, here beside me, delicate ambassador
Of intricate slain numbers that arise
In whispers, naked of steel;
                    religious gunman!
Who faithfully, yourself, will fall too soon,
And in other ways than as the wind settles
On the sixteen thrifty bridges of the city:
Let us unbind our throats of fear and pity.

                    We even,
Who drove speediest destruction
In corymbulous formations of mechanics,—
Who hurried the hill breezes, spouting malice
Plangent over meadows, and looked down
On rifts of torn and empty houses
Like old women with teeth unjubilant
That waited faintly, briefly and in vain:

We know, eternal gunman, our flesh remembers
The tensile boughs, the nimble blue plateaus,
The mounted, yielding cities of the air!

That saddled sky that shook down vertical
Repeated play of fire—no hypogeum
Of wave or rock was good against one hour.
We did not ask for that, but have survived,
And will persist to speak again before
All stubble streets that have not curved
To memory, or known the ominous lifted arm
That lowers down the arc of Helen's brow
To saturate with blessing and dismay.

A goose, tobacco and cologne—
Three winged and gold-shod prophecies of heaven,
The lavish heart shall always have to leaven
And spread with bells and voices, and atone
The abating shadows of our conscript dust.

Anchises' navel, dripping of the sea,—
The hands Erasmus dipped in gleaming tides,
Gathered the voltage of blown blood and vine;
Delve upward for the new and scattered wine,
O brother-thief of time, that we recall.
Laugh out the meager penance of their days
Who dare not share with us the breath released,
The substance drilled and spent beyond repair
For golden, or the shadow of gold hair.

Distinctly praise the years, whose volatile
Blamed bleeding hands extend and thresh the height
The imagination spans beyond despair,
Outpacing bargain, vocable and prayer.

Voyages

I

Above the fresh ruffles of the surf
Bright striped urchins flay each other with sand.
They have contrived a conquest for shell shucks,
And their fingers crumble fragments of baked weed
Gaily digging and scattering.

And in answer to their treble interjections
The sun beats lightning on the waves,
The waves fold thunder on the sand;
And could they hear me I would tell them:

O brilliant kids, frisk with your dog,
Fondle your shells and sticks, bleached
By time and the elements; but there is a line
You must not cross nor ever trust beyond it
Spry cordage of your bodies to caresses
Too lichen-faithful from too wide a breast.
The bottom of the sea is cruel.

II

—And yet this great wink of eternity,
Of rimless floods, unfettered leewardings,
Samite sheeted and processioned where
Her undinal vast belly moonward bends,
Laughing the wrapt inflections of our love;

Take this Sea, whose diapason knells
On scrolls of silver snowy sentences,
The sceptred terror of whose sessions rends
As her demeanors motion well or ill,
All but the pieties of lovers' hands.

And onward, as bells off San Salvador
Salute the crocus lustres of the stars,
In these poinsettia meadows of her tides,—
Adagios of islands, O my Prodigal,
Complete the dark confessions her veins spell.

Mark how her turning shoulders wind the hours,
And hasten while her penniless rich palms
Pass superscription of bent foam and wave,—
Hasten, while they are true,—sleep, death, desire,
Close round one instant in one floating flower.

Bind us in time, O Seasons clear, and awe.
O minstrel galleons of Carib fire,
Bequeath us to no earthly shore until
Is answered in the vortex of our grave
The seal's wide spindrift gaze toward paradise.

III

Infinite consanguinity it bears—
This tendered theme of you that light
Retrieves from sea plains where the sky
Resigns a breast that every wave enthrones;
While ribboned water lanes I wind
Are laved and scattered with no stroke
Wide from your side, whereto this hour
The sea lifts, also, reliquary hands.

And so, admitted through black swollen gates
That must arrest all distance otherwise,—
Past whirling pillars and lithe pediments,
Light wrestling there incessantly with light,
Star kissing star through wave on wave unto
Your body rocking!
                and where death, if shed,
Presumes no carnage, but this single change,—
Upon the steep floor flung from dawn to dawn
The silken skilled transmemberment of song;

Permit me voyage, love, into your hands . . .

IV

Whose counted smile of hours and days, suppose
I know as spectrum of the sea and pledge
Vastly now parting gulf on gulf of wings
Whose circles bridge, I know, (from palms to the severe
Chilled albatross's white immutability)
No stream of greater love advancing now
Than, singing, this mortality alone
Through clay aflow immortally to you.

All fragrance irrefragibly, and claim
Madly meeting logically in this hour
And region that is ours to wreathe again,
Portending eyes and lips and making told
The chancel port and portion of our June—

Shall they not stem and close in our own steps
Bright staves of flowers and quills to-day as I
Must first be lost in fatal tides to tell?

In signature of the incarnate word
The harbor shoulders to resign in mingling
Mutual blood, transpiring as foreknown
And widening noon within your breast for gathering

All bright insinuations that my years have caught
For islands where must lead inviolably
Blue latitudes and levels of your eyes,—

In this expectant, still exclaim receive
The secret oar and petals of all love.

V

Meticulous, past midnight in clear rime,
Infrangible and lonely, smooth as though cast
Together in one merciless white blade—
The bay estuaries fleck the hard sky limits.

—As if too brittle or too clear to touch!
The cables of our sleep so swiftly filed,
Already hang, shred ends from remembered stars.
One frozen trackless smile. . . What words
Can strangle this deaf moonlight? For we

Are overtaken. Now no cry, no sword
Can fasten or deflect this tidal wedge,
Slow tyranny of moonlight, moonlight loved
And changed . . . "There's

Nothing like this in the world," you say,
Knowing I cannot touch your hand and look
Too, into that godless cleft of sky
Where nothing turns but dead sands flashing.

"—And never to quite understand!" No,
In all the argosy of your bright hair I dreamed
Nothing so flagless as this piracy.

But now
Draw in your head, alone and too tall here.
Your eyes already in the slant of drifting foam;
Your breath sealed by the ghosts I do not know:
Draw in your head and sleep the long way home.

VI

Where icy and bright dungeons lift
Of swimmers their lost morning eyes,
And ocean rivers, churning, shift
Green borders under stranger skies,

Steadily as a shell secretes
Its beating leagues of monotone,
Or as many waters trough the sun's
Red kelson past the cape's wet stone;

O rivers mingling toward the sky
And harbor of the phœnix' breast—
My eyes pressed black against the prow,
—Thy derelict and blinded guest

Waiting, afire, what name, unspoke,
I cannot claim: let thy waves rear
More savage than the death of kings,
Some splintered garland for the seer.

Beyond siroccos harvesting
The solstice thunders, crept away,
Like a cliff swinging or a sail
Flung into April's inmost day—

Creation's blithe and petalled word
To the lounged goddess when she rose
Conceding dialogue with eyes
That smile unsearchable repose—

Still fervid covenant, Belle Isle,
—Unfolded floating dais before
Which rainbows twine continual hair—
Belle Isle, white echo of the oar!

The imaged Word, it is, that holds
Hushed willows anchored in its glow.
It is the unbetrayable reply
Whose accent no farewell can know.

Repose of Rivers

The willows carried a slow sound,
A sarabande the wind mowed on the mead.
I could never remember
That seething, steady leveling of the marshes
Till age had brought me to the sea.

Flags, weeds. And remembrance of steep alcoves
Where cypresses shared the noon's
Tyranny; they drew me into hades almost.
And mammoth turtles climbing sulphur dreams
Yielded, while sun-silt rippled them
Asunder . . .

How much I would have bartered! the black gorge
And all the singular nestings in the hills
Where beavers learn stitch and tooth.
The pond I entered once and quickly fled—
I remember now its singing willow rim.

And finally, in that memory all things nurse;
After the city that I finally passed
With scalding unguents spread and smoking darts
The monsoon cut across the delta
At gulf gates . . . There, beyond the dykes

I heard wind flaking sapphire, like this summer,
And willows could not hold more steady sound.

The Wine Menagerie

Invariably when wine redeems the sight,
Narrowing the mustard scansions of the eyes,
A leopard ranging always in the brow
Asserts a vision in the slumbering gaze.

Then glozening decanters that reflect the street
Wear me in crescents on their bellies. Slow
Applause flows into liquid cynosures:
—I am conscripted to their shadows' glow.

Against the imitation onyx wainscoting
(Painted emulsion of snow, eggs, yarn, coal, manure)
Regard the forceps of the smile that takes her.
Percussive sweat is spreading to his hair. Mallets,
Her eyes, unmake an instant of the world . . .

What is it in this heap the serpent pries—
Whose skin, facsimile of time, unskeins
Octagon, sapphire transepts round the eyes;
—From whom some whispered carillon assures
Speed to the arrow into feathered skies?

Sharp to the windowpane guile drags a face,
And as the alcove of her jealousy recedes
An urchin who has left the snow
Nudges a cannister across the bar
While August meadows somewhere clasp his brow.

Each chamber, transept, coins some squint,
Remorseless line, minting their separate wills—
Poor streaked bodies wreathing up and out,
Unwitting the stigma that each turn repeals:
Between black tusks the roses shine!

New thresholds, new anatomies! Wine talons
Build freedom up about me and distill
This competence—to travel in a tear
Sparkling alone, within another's will.

Until my blood dreams a receptive smile
Wherein new purities are snared; where chimes
Before some flame of gaunt repose a shell
Tolled once, perhaps, by every tongue in hell.
—Anguished, the wit that cries out of me:

"Alas,—these frozen billows of your skill!
Invent new dominoes of love and bile . . .
Ruddy, the tooth implicit of the world
Has followed you. Though in the end you know
And count some dim inheritance of sand,
How much yet meets the treason of the snow.

"Rise from the dates and crumbs. And walk away,
Stepping over Holofernes' shins—
Beyond the wall, whose severed head floats by
With Baptist John's. Their whispering begins.

"—And fold your exile on your back again;
Petrushka's valentine pivots on its pin."

At Melville's Tomb

Often beneath the wave, wide from this ledge
The dice of drowned men's bones he saw bequeath
An embassy. Their numbers as he watched,
Beat on the dusty shore and were obscured.

And wrecks passed without sound of bells,
The calyx of death's bounty giving back
A scattered chapter, livid hieroglyph,
The portent wound in corridors of shells.

Then in the circuit calm of one vast coil,
Its lashings charmed and malice reconciled,
Frosted eyes there were that lifted altars;
And silent answers crept across the stars.

Compass, quadrant and sextant contrive
No farther tides . . . High in the azure steeps
Monody shall not wake the mariner.
This fabulous shadow only the sea keeps.

THE BRIDGE

From going to and fro in the earth,
and from walking up and down in it.
THE BOOK OF JOB

To
Brooklyn Bridge

How many dawns, chill from his rippling rest
The seagull's wings shall dip and pivot him,
Shedding white rings of tumult, building high
Over the chained bay waters Liberty—

Then, with inviolate curve, forsake our eyes
As apparitional as sails that cross
Some page of figures to be filed away;
—Till elevators drop us from our day . . .

I think of cinemas, panoramic sleights
With multitudes bent toward some flashing scene
Never disclosed, but hastened to again,
Foretold to other eyes on the same screen;

And Thee, across the harbor, silver-paced
As though the sun took step of thee, yet left
Some motion ever unspent in thy stride,—
Implicitly thy freedom staying thee!

Out of some subway scuttle, cell or loft
A bedlamite speeds to thy parapets,
Tilting there momently, shrill shirt ballooning,
A jest falls from the speechless caravan.

Down Wall, from girder into street noon leaks,
A rip-tooth of the sky's acetylene;
All afternoon the cloud-flown derricks turn . . .
Thy cables breathe the North Atlantic still.

And obscure as that heaven of the Jews,
Thy guerdon . . . Accolade thou dost bestow
Of anonymity time cannot raise:
Vibrant reprieve and pardon thou dost show.

O harp and altar, of the fury fused,
(How could mere toil align thy choiring strings!)
Terrific threshold of the prophet's pledge,
Prayer of pariah, and the lover's cry,—

Again the traffic lights that skim thy swift
Unfractioned idiom, immaculate sigh of stars,
Beading thy path—condense eternity:
And we have seen night lifted in thine arms.

Under thy shadow by the piers I waited;
Only in darkness is thy shadow clear.
The City's fiery parcels all undone,
Already snow submerges an iron year . . .

O Sleepless as the river under thee,
Vaulting the sea, the prairies' dreaming sod,
Unto us lowliest sometime sweep, descend
And of the curveship lend a myth to God.

I
Ave Maria

Venient annis, saecula seris,
Quibus Oceanus vincula rerum
Laxet et ingens pateat tellus
Tethysque novos detegat orbes
Nec sit terris ultima Thule.

—SENECA

Be with me, Luis de San Angel, now—
Witness before the tides can wrest away
The word I bring, O you who reined my suit
Into the Queen's great heart that doubtful day;
For I have seen now what no perjured breath
Of clown nor sage can riddle or gainsay;—
To you, too, Juan Perez, whose counsel fear
And greed adjourned,—I bring you back Cathay!

Columbus,
alone, gazing
toward Spain,
invokes the
presence of
two faithful
partisans of
his quest . . .

Here waves climb into dusk on gleaming mail;
Invisible valves of the sea,—locks, tendons
Crested and creeping, troughing corridors
That fall back yawning to another plunge.
Slowly the sun's red caravel drops light
Once more behind us. . . . It is morning there—
O where our Indian emperies lie revealed,
Yet lost, all, let this keel one instant yield!

I thought of Genoa; and this truth, now proved,
That made me exile in her streets, stood me
More absolute than ever—biding the moon
Till dawn should clear that dim frontier, first seen
—The Chan's great continent. . . . Then faith, not fear
Nigh surged me witless. . . . Hearing the surf near—
I, wonder-breathing, kept the watch,—saw
The first palm chevron the first lighted hill.

And lowered. And they came out to us crying,
"The Great White Birds!" (O Madre Maria, still
One ship of these thou grantest safe returning;

Assure us through thy mantle's ageless blue!)
And record of more, floating in a casque,
Was tumbled from us under bare poles scudding;
And later hurricanes may claim more pawn. . . .
For here between two worlds, another, harsh,

This third, of water, tests the word; lo, here
Bewilderment and mutiny heap whelming
Laughter, and shadow cuts sleep from the heart
Almost as though the Moor's flung scimitar
Found more than flesh to fathom in its fall.
Yet under tempest-lash and surfeitings
Some inmost sob, half-heard, dissuades the abyss,
Merges the wind in measure to the waves,

Series on series, infinite,—till eyes
Starved wide on blackened tides, accrete—enclose
This turning rondure whole, this crescent ring
Sun-cusped and zoned with modulated fire
Like pearls that whisper through the Doge's hands
—Yet no delirium of jewels! O Fernando,
Take of that eastern shore, this western sea,
Yet yield thy God's, thy Virgin's charity!

—Rush down the plenitude, and you shall see
Isaiah counting famine on this lee!

.   .   .

An herb, a stray branch among salty teeth,
The jellied weeds that drag the shore,—perhaps
Tomorrow's moon will grant us Saltes Bar—
Palos again,—a land cleared of long war.
Some Angelus environs the cordage tree;
Dark waters onward shake the dark prow free.

.   .   .

O Thou who sleepest on Thyself, apart
Like ocean athwart lanes of death and birth,
And all the eddying breath between dost search
Cruelly with love thy parable of man,—
Inquisitor! incognizable Word
Of Eden and the enchained Sepulchre,

Into thy steep savannahs, burning blue,
Utter to loneliness the sail is true.

Who grindest oar, and arguing the mast
Subscribest holocaust of ships, O Thou
Within whose primal scan consummately
The glistening seignories of Ganges swim;—
Who sendest greeting by the corposant,
And Teneriffe's garnet—flamed it in a cloud,
Urging through night our passage to the Chan;—
Te Deum laudamus, for thy teeming span!

Of all that amplitude that time explores,
A needle in the sight, suspended north,—
Yielding by inference and discard, faith
And true appointment from the hidden shoal:
This disposition that thy night relates
From Moon to Saturn in one sapphire wheel:
The orbic wake of thy once whirling feet,
Elohim, still I hear thy sounding heel!

White toil of heaven's cordons, mustering
In holy rings all sails charged to the far
Hushed gleaming fields and pendant seething wheat
Of knowledge,—round thy brows unhooded now
—The kindled Crown! acceded of the poles
And biassed by full sails, meridians reel
Thy purpose—still one shore beyond desire!
The sea's green crying towers a-sway, Beyond

And kingdoms
            naked in the
                        trembling heart—
      Te Deum laudamus
                        O Thou Hand of Fire

II
Powhatan's Daughter

*"—Pocahuntus, a well-featured but wanton yong girle . . .
of the age of eleven or twelve years, get the boyes forth with her
into the market place, and make them wheele, falling on their
hands, turning their heels upwards, whom she would followe,
and wheele so herself, naked as she was, all the fort over."*

The Harbor Dawn

Insistently through sleep—a tide of voices—
They meet you listening midway in your dream,
The long, tired sounds, fog-insulated noises:
Gongs in white surplices, beshrouded wails,
Far strum of fog horns . . . signals dispersed in
    veils.

400 years and more . . . or is it from the soundless shore of sleep that time

And then a truck will lumber past the wharves
As winch engines begin throbbing on some deck;
Or a drunken stevedore's howl and thud below
Comes echoing alley-upward through dim snow.

And if they take your sleep away sometimes
They give it back again. Soft sleeves of sound
Attend the darkling harbor, the pillowed bay;
Somewhere out there in blankness steam

Spills into steam, and wanders, washed away
—Flurried by keen fifings, eddied
Among distant chiming buoys—adrift. The sky,

Cool feathery fold, suspends, distills
This wavering slumber. . . . Slowly—
Immemorially the window, the half-covered chair
Ask nothing but this sheath of pallid air.

And you beside me, blessèd now while sirens
Sing to us, stealthily weave us into day—
Serenely now, before day claims our eyes
Your cool arms murmurously about me lay.

recalls you to your love, there in a waking dream to merge your seed

While myriad snowy hands are clustering at the panes—

> *your hands within my hands are deeds;*
> *my tongue upon your throat—singing*
> *arms close; eyes wide, undoubtful*
> > *dark*
> > > *drink the dawn—*
> *a forest shudders in your hair!*

—with whom?

The window goes blond slowly. Frostily clears.
From Cyclopean towers across Manhattan waters
—Two—three bright window-eyes aglitter, disk
The sun, released—aloft with cold gulls hither.

Who is the woman with us in the dawn? . . . whose is the flesh our feet have moved upon?

The fog leans one last moment on the sill.
Under the mistletoe of dreams, a star—
As though to join us at some distant hill—
Turns in the waking west and goes to sleep.

Van Winkle

Macadam, gun-grey as the tunny's belt,
Leaps from Far Rockaway to Golden Gate:
Listen! the miles a hurdy-gurdy grinds—
Down gold arpeggios mile on mile unwinds.

Streets spread past store and factory—sped by sunlight and her smile . . .

Times earlier, when you hurried off to school,
—It is the same hour though a later day—
You walked with Pizarro in a copybook,
And Cortes rode up, reining tautly in—
Firmly as coffee grips the taste,—and away!

There was Priscilla's cheek close in the wind,
And Captain Smith, all beard and certainty,
And Rip Van Winkle bowing by the way,—
"Is this Sleepy Hollow, friend—?" And he—

Like Memory, she is time's truant, shall take you by the hand . . .

And Rip forgot the office hours,
> *and he forgot the pay;*

Van Winkle sweeps a tenement
way down on Avenue A,—

The grind-organ says . . . Remember, remember
The cinder pile at the end of the backyard
Where we stoned the family of young
Garter snakes under . . . And the monoplanes
We launched—with paper wings and twisted
Rubber bands . . . Recall—recall

the rapid tongues
That flittered from under the ash heap day
After day whenever your stick discovered
Some sunning inch of unsuspecting fibre—
It flashed back at your thrust, as clean as fire.

And Rip was slowly made aware
that he, Van Winkle, was not here
nor there. He woke and swore he'd seen Broadway
a Catskill daisy chain in May—

So memory, that strikes a rhyme out of a box,
Or splits a random smell of flowers through glass—
Is it the whip stripped from the lilac tree
One day in spring my father took to me,
Or is it the Sabbatical, unconscious smile
My mother almost brought me once from church
And once only, as I recall—?

It flickered through the snow screen, blindly
It forsook her at the doorway, it was gone
Before I had left the window. It
Did not return with the kiss in the hall.

Macadam, gun-grey as the tunny's belt,
Leaps from Far Rockaway to Golden Gate. . . .
Keep hold of that nickel for car-change, Rip,—
Have you got your "*Times*"—?
And hurry along, Van Winkle—it's getting late!

The River

Stick your patent name on a signboard
brother—all over—going west—young man
Tintex—Japalac—Certain-teed Overalls ads   *. . . and past*
and lands sakes! under the new playbill ripped   *the din and*
in the guaranteed corner—see Bert Williams   *slogans of*
   what?   *the year—*
Minstrels when you steal a chicken just
save me the wing for if it isn't
Erie it ain't for miles around a
Mazda—and the telegraphic night coming on Thomas

a Ediford—and whistling down the tracks
a headlight rushing with the sound—can you
imagine—while an EXPRESS makes time like
SCIENCE — COMMERCE and the HOLYGHOST
RADIO ROARS IN EVERY HOME WE HAVE THE NORTHPOLE
WALLSTREET AND VIRGINBIRTH WITHOUT STONES OR
WIRES OR EVEN RUNning brooks connecting ears
and no more sermons windows flashing roar
breathtaking—as you like it . . . eh?

        So the 20th Century—so
whizzed the Limited—roared by and left
three men, still hungry on the tracks, ploddingly
watching the tail lights wizen and converge, slip-
ping gimleted and neatly out of sight.

  .   .   .   .

The last bear, shot drinking in the Dakotas
Loped under wires that span the mountain stream.
Keen instruments, strung to a vast precision
Bind town to town and dream to ticking dream.   *to those*
But some men take their liquor slow—and count   *whose*
—Though they'll confess no rosary nor clue—   *addresses*
The river's minute by the far brook's year.   *are never near*
Under a world of whistles, wires and steam
Caboose-like they go ruminating through
Ohio, Indiana—blind baggage—
To Cheyenne tagging . . . Maybe Kalamazoo.

Time's rendings, time's blendings they construe
As final reckonings of fire and snow;
Strange bird-wit, like the elemental gist
Of unwalled winds they offer, singing low
My Old Kentucky Home and *Casey Jones,*
Some Sunny Day. I heard a road-gang chanting so.
And afterwards, who had a colt's eyes—one said,
"Jesus! Oh I remember watermelon days!" And sped
High in a cloud of merriment, recalled
"—And when my Aunt Sally Simpson smiled," he drawled—
"It was almost Louisiana, long ago."
"There's no place like Booneville though, Buddy,"
One said, excising a last burr from his vest,
"—For early trouting." Then peering in the can,
"—But I kept on the tracks." Possessed, resigned,
He trod the fire down pensively and grinned,
Spreading dry shingles of a beard. . . .

                                        Behind
My father's cannery works I used to see
Rail-squatters ranged in nomad raillery,
The ancient men—wifeless or runaway
Hobo-trekkers that forever search
An empire wilderness of freight and rails.
Each seemed a child, like me, on a loose perch,
Holding to childhood like some termless play.
John, Jake or Charley, hopping the slow freight
—Memphis to Tallahassee—riding the rods,
Blind fists of nothing, humpty-dumpty clods.

Yet they touch something like a key perhaps.
From pole to pole across the hills, the states
—They know a body under the wide rain;   *but who have*
Youngsters with eyes like fjords, old reprobates   *touched her,*
With racetrack jargon,—dotting immensity   *knowing her*
They lurk across her, knowing her yonder breast   *without name*
Snow-silvered, sumac-stained or smoky blue—
Is past the valley-sleepers, south or west.
—As I have trod the rumorous midnights, too,

And past the circuit of the lamp's thin flame
(O Nights that brought me to her body bare!)
Have dreamed beyond the print that bound her name.
Trains sounding the long blizzards out—I heard
Wail into distances I knew were hers.
Papooses crying on the wind's long mane
Screamed redskin dynasties that fled the brain,
—Dead echoes! But I knew her body there,
Time like a serpent down her shoulder, dark,
And space, an eaglet's wing, laid on her hair.

Under the Ozarks, domed by Iron Mountain,
The old gods of the rain lie wrapped in pools
Where eyeless fish curvet a sunken fountain   *nor the*
And re-descend with corn from querulous crows.   *myths of her*
Such pilferings make up their timeless eatage,   *fathers . . .*
Propitiate them for their timber torn
By iron, iron—always the iron dealt cleavage!
They doze now, below axe and powder horn.

And Pullman breakfasters glide glistening steel
From tunnel into field—iron strides the dew—
Straddles the hill, a dance of wheel on wheel.
You have a half-hour's wait at Siskiyou,
Or stay the night and take the next train through.
Southward, near Cairo passing, you can see
The Ohio merging,—borne down Tennessee;
And if it's summer and the sun's in dusk
Maybe the breeze will lift the River's musk
—As though the waters breathed that you might know
Memphis Johnny, Steamboat Bill, Missouri Joe.
Oh, lean from the window, if the train slows down,
As though you touched hands with some ancient clown,
—A little while gaze absently below
And hum *Deep River* with them while they go.

Yes, turn again and sniff once more—look see,
O Sheriff, Brakeman and Authority—
Hitch up your pants and crunch another quid,
For you, too, feed the River timelessly.

And few evade full measure of their fate;
Always they smile out eerily what they seem.
I could believe he joked at heaven's gate—
Dan Midland—jolted from the cold brake-beam.

Down, down—born pioneers in time's despite,
Grimed tributaries to an ancient flow—
They win no frontier by their wayward plight,
But drift in stillness, as from Jordan's brow.

You will not hear it as the sea; even stone
Is not more hushed by gravity . . . But slow,
As loth to take more tribute—sliding prone
Like one whose eyes were buried long ago

The River, spreading, flows—and spends your dream.
What are you, lost within this tideless spell?
You are your father's father, and the stream—
A liquid theme that floating niggers swell.

Damp tonnage and alluvial march of days—
Nights turbid, vascular with silted shale
And roots surrendered down of moraine clays:
The Mississippi drinks the farthest dale.

O quarrying passion, undertowed sunlight!
The basalt surface drags a jungle grace
Ochreous and lynx-barred in lengthening might;
Patience! and you shall reach the biding place!

Over De Soto's bones the freighted floors
Throb past the City storied of three thrones.
Down two more turns the Mississippi pours
(Anon tall ironsides up from salt lagoons)

And flows within itself, heaps itself free.
All fades but one thin skyline 'round . . . Ahead
No embrace opens but the stinging sea;
The River lifts itself from its long bed,

Poised wholly on its dream, a mustard glow
Tortured with history, its one will—flow!
—The Passion spreads in wide tongues, choked and slow,
Meeting the Gulf, hosannas silently below.

The Dance

The swift red flesh, a winter king—
Who squired the glacier woman down the sky?
She ran the neighing canyons all the spring;
She spouted arms; she rose with maize—to die.

And in the autumn drouth, whose burnished
　　hands
With mineral wariness found out the stone
Where prayers, forgotten, streamed the mesa
　　sands?
He holds the twilight's dim, perpetual throne.

Mythical brows we saw retiring—loth,
Disturbed and destined, into denser green.
Greeting they sped us, on the arrow's oath:
Now lie incorrigibly what years between . . .

There was a bed of leaves, and broken play;
There was a veil upon you, Pocahontas, bride—
O Princess whose brown lap was virgin May;
And bridal flanks and eyes hid tawny pride.

I left the village for dogwood. By the canoe
Tugging below the mill-race, I could see
Your hair's keen crescent running, and the blue
First moth of evening take wing stealthily.

What laughing chains the water wove and threw!
I learned to catch the trout's moon whisper; I
Drifted how many hours I never knew,
But, watching, saw that fleet young crescent die,—

Then you shall see her truly —your blood remembering its first invasion of her secrecy, its first encounters with her kin, her chieftain lover . . . his shade that haunts the lakes and hills

And one star, swinging, take its place, alone,
Cupped in the larches of the mountain pass—
Until, immortally, it bled into the dawn.
I left my sleek boat nibbling margin grass . . .

I took the portage climb, then chose
A further valley-shed; I could not stop.
Feet nozzled wat'ry webs of upper flows;
One white veil gusted from the very top.

O Appalachian Spring! I gained the ledge;
Steep, inaccessible smile that eastward bends
And northward reaches in that violet wedge
Of Adirondacks!—wisped of azure wands,

Over how many bluffs, tarns, streams I sped!
—And knew myself within some boding shade:—
Grey tepees tufting the blue knolls ahead,
Smoke swirling through the yellow chestnut glade . . .

A distant cloud, a thunder-bud—it grew,
That blanket of the skies: the padded foot
Within,—I heard it; 'til its rhythm drew,
—Siphoned the black pool from the heart's hot root!

A cyclone threshes in the turbine crest,
Swooping in eagle feathers down your back;
Know, Maquokeeta, greeting; know death's best;
—Fall, Sachem, strictly as the tamarack!

A birch kneels. All her whistling fingers fly.
The oak grove circles in a crash of leaves;
The long moan of a dance is in the sky.
Dance, Maquokeeta: Pocahontas grieves . . .

And every tendon scurries toward the twangs
Of lightning deltaed down your saber hair.
Now snaps the flint in every tooth; red fangs
And splay tongues thinly busy the blue air . . .

Dance, Maquokeeta! snake that lives before,
That casts his pelt, and lives beyond! Sprout, horn!
Spark, tooth! Medicine-man, relent, restore—
Lie to us,—dance us back the tribal morn!

Spears and assemblies: black drums thrusting on—
O yelling battlements,—I, too, was liege
To rainbows currying each pulsant bone:
Surpassed the circumstance, danced out the siege!

And buzzard-circleted, screamed from the stake;
I could not pick the arrows from my side.
Wrapped in that fire, I saw more escorts wake—
Flickering, sprint up the hill groins like a tide.

I heard the hush of lava wrestling your arms,
And stag teeth foam about the raven throat;
Flame cataracts of heaven in seething swarms
Fed down your anklets to the sunset's moat.

O, like the lizard in the furious noon,
That drops his legs and colors in the sun,
—And laughs, pure serpent, Time itself, and moon
Of his own fate, I saw thy change begun!

And saw thee dive to kiss that destiny
Like one white meteor, sacrosanct and blent
At last with all that's consummate and free
There, where the first and last gods keep thy tent.

    .   .   .   .

Thewed of the levin, thunder-shod and lean,
Lo, through what infinite seasons dost thou gaze—
Across what bivouacs of thine angered slain,
And see'st thy bride immortal in the maize!

Totem and fire-gall, slumbering pyramid—
Though other calendars now stack the sky,
Thy freedom is her largesse, Prince, and hid
On paths thou knewest best to claim her by.

High unto Labrador the sun strikes free
Her speechless dream of snow, and stirred again,
She is the torrent and the singing tree;
And she is virgin to the last of men . . .

West, west and south! winds over Cumberland
And winds across the llano grass resume
Her hair's warm sibilance. Her breasts are fanned
O stream by slope and vineyard—into bloom!

And when the caribou slant down for salt
Do arrows thirst and leap? Do antlers shine
Alert, star-triggered in the listening vault
Of dusk?—And are her perfect brows to thine?

We danced, O Brave, we danced beyond their farms,
In cobalt desert closures made our vows . . .
Now is the strong prayer folded in thine arms,
The serpent with the eagle in the boughs.

Indiana

The morning glory, climbing the morning long   *. . . and read*
   Over the lintel on its wiry vine,   *her in a*
Closes before the dusk, furls in its song   *mother's*
            As I close mine . . .   *farewell gaze.*

And bison thunder rends my dreams no more
   As once my womb was torn, my boy, when you
Yielded your first cry at the prairie's door . . .
            Your father knew

Then, though we'd buried him behind us, far
   Back on the gold trail—then his lost bones stirred . . .
But you who drop the scythe to grasp the oar
            Knew not, nor heard

How we, too, Prodigal, once rode off, too—
   Waved Seminary Hill a gay good-bye . . .
We found God lavish there in Colorado
       But passing sly.

The pebbles sang, the firecat slunk away
   And glistening through the sluggard freshets came
In golden syllables loosed from the clay
       His gleaming name.

A dream called Eldorado was his town,
   It rose up shambling in the nuggets' wake,
It had no charter but a promised crown
       Of claims to stake.

But we,—too late, too early, howsoever—
   Won nothing out of fifty-nine—those years—
But gilded promise, yielded to us never,
       And barren tears . . .

The long trail back! I huddled in the shade
   Of wagon-tenting looked out once and saw
Bent westward, passing on a stumbling jade
       A homeless squaw—

Perhaps a halfbreed. On her slender back
   She cradled a babe's body, riding without rein.
Her eyes, strange for an Indian's, were not black
       But sharp with pain

And like twin stars. They seemed to shun the gaze
   Of all our silent men—the long team line—
Until she saw me—when their violet haze
       Lit with love shine . . .

I held you up—I suddenly the bolder,
   Knew that mere words could not have brought us nearer.
She nodded—and that smile across her shoulder
       Will still endear her

As long as Jim, your father's memory, is warm.
    Yes, Larry, now you're going to sea, remember
You were the first—before Ned and this farm,—
            First-born, remember—

And since then—all that's left to me of Jim
    Whose folks, like mine, came out of Arrowhead.
And you're the only one with eyes like him—
            Kentucky bred!

I'm standing still, I'm old, I'm half of stone!
    Oh, hold me in those eyes' engaging blue;
There's where the stubborn years gleam and atone,—
            Where gold is true!

Down the dim turnpike to the river's edge—
    Perhaps I'll hear the mare's hoofs to the ford . . .
Write me from Rio . . . and you'll keep your pledge;
            I know your word!

Come back to Indiana—not too late!
    (Or will you be a ranger to the end?)
Good-bye . . . Good-bye . . . oh, I shall always wait
    You, Larry, traveller—
                    stranger,
                        son,
                            —my friend—

III
Cutty Sark

O, the navies old and oaken,
O, the Temeraire no more!
                    —MELVILLE

I met a man in South Street, tall—
a nervous shark tooth swung on his chain.
His eyes pressed through green glass
—green glasses, or bar lights made them
so—
        shine—
            GREEN—
                        eyes—
stepped out—forgot to look at you
or left you several blocks away—

in the nickel-in-the-slot piano jogged
"Stamboul Nights"—weaving somebody's nickel—sang—

        O Stamboul Rose—dreams weave the rose!

            Murmurs of Leviathan he spoke,
            and rum was Plato in our heads . . .

"It's *S.S. Ala*—Antwerp—now remember kid
to put me out at three she sails on time.
I'm not much good at time any more keep
weakeyed watches sometimes snooze—" his bony hands
got to beating time . . . "A whaler once—
I ought to keep time and get over it—I'm a
Democrat—I know what time it is—No
I don't want to know what time it is—that
damned white Arctic killed my time . . ."

        O Stamboul Rose—drums weave—

"I ran a donkey engine down there on the Canal
in Panama—got tired of that—
then Yucatan selling kitchenware—beads—
have you seen Popocatepetl—birdless mouth
with ashes sifting down—?
                              and then the coast again . . ."

> *Rose of Stamboul O coral Queen—*
> *teased remnants of the skeletons of cities—*
> *and galleries, galleries of watergutted lava*
> *snarling stone—green—drums—drown—*

Sing!
"—that spiracle!" he shot a finger out the door . . .
"O life's a geyser—beautiful—my lungs—
No—I can't live on land—!"

I saw the frontiers gleaming of his mind;
or are there frontiers—running sands sometimes
running sands—somewhere—sands running . . .
Or they may start some white machine that sings.
Then you may laugh and dance the axletree—
steel—silver—kick the traces—and know—

> *ATLANTIS ROSE drums wreathe the rose,*
> *the star floats burning in a gulf of tears*
> *and sleep another thousand—*

                              interminably
long since somebody's nickel—stopped—
playing—

A wind worried those wicker-neat lapels, the
swinging summer entrances to cooler hells . . .
Outside a wharf truck nearly ran him down
—he lunged up Bowery way while the dawn
was putting the Statue of Liberty out—that
torch of hers you know—

I started walking home across the Bridge . . .

   ·   ·   ·   ·   ·

Blithe Yankee vanities, turreted sprites, winged
           British repartees, skil-
ful savage sea-girls
that bloomed in the spring—Heave, weave
those bright designs the trade winds drive . . .

   Sweet opium and tea, Yo-ho!
   Pennies for porpoises that bank the keel!
   Fins whip the breeze around Japan!

Bright skysails ticketing the Line, wink round the Horn
to Frisco, Melbourne . . .
       Pennants, parabolas—
clipper dreams indelible and ranging,
baronial white on lucky blue!

   Perennial-*Cutty*-trophied-*Sark*!

Thermopylae, Black Prince, Flying Cloud through Sunda
—scarfed of foam, their bellies veered green esplanades,
locked in wind-humors, ran their eastings down;

   at Java Head freshened the nip
   (sweet opium and tea!)
   and turned and left us on the lee . . .

Buntlines tusseling (91 days, 20 hours and anchored!)
         Rainbow, Leander
(last trip a tragedy)—where can you be
Nimbus? and you rivals two—

    a long tack keeping—

         Taeping?
         Ariel?

IV
Cape Hatteras

The seas all crossed,
weathered the capes, the voyage done . . .
— WALT WHITMAN

Imponderable the dinosaur
             sinks slow,
                the mammoth saurian
                    ghoul, the eastern
                        Cape . . .
While rises in the west the coastwise range,
                slowly the hushed land—
Combustion at the astral core—the dorsal change
Of energy—convulsive shift of sand . . .
But we, who round the capes, the promontories
Where strange tongues vary messages of surf
Below grey citadels, repeating to the stars
The ancient names—return home to our own
Hearths, there to eat an apple and recall
The songs that gypsies dealt us at Marseille
Or how the priests walked—slowly through Bombay—
Or to read you, Walt,—knowing us in thrall

To that deep wonderment, our native clay
Whose depth of red, eternal flesh of Pocahontas—
Those continental folded aeons, surcharged
With sweetness below derricks, chimneys, tunnels—
Is veined by all that time has really pledged us . . .
And from above, thin squeaks of radio static,
The captured fume of space foams in our ears—
What whisperings of far watches on the main
Relapsing into silence, while time clears
Our lenses, lifts a focus, resurrects
A periscope to glimpse what joys or pain
Our eyes can share or answer—then deflects
Us, shunting to a labyrinth submersed
Where each sees only his dim past reversed . . .

But that star-glistered salver of infinity,
The circle, blind crucible of endless space,
Is sluiced by motion,—subjugated never.
Adam and Adam's answer in the forest
Left Hesperus mirrored in the lucid pool.
Now the eagle dominates our days, is jurist
Of the ambiguous cloud. We know the strident rule
Of wings imperious . . . Space, instantaneous,
Flickers a moment, consumes us in its smile:
A flash over the horizon—shifting gears—
And we have laughter, or more sudden tears.
Dream cancels dream in this new realm of fact
From which we wake into the dream of act;
Seeing himself an atom in a shroud—
Man hears himself an engine in a cloud!

"—Recorders ages hence"—ah, syllables of faith!
Walt, tell me, Walt Whitman, if infinity
Be still the same as when you walked the beach
Near Paumanok—your lone patrol—and heard the wraith
Through surf, its bird note there a long time falling . . .
For you, the panoramas and this breed of towers,
Of you—the theme that's statured in the cliff,
O Saunterer on free ways still ahead!
Not this our empire yet, but labyrinth
Wherein your eyes, like the Great Navigator's without ship,
Gleam from the great stones of each prison crypt
Of canyoned traffic . . . Confronting the Exchange,
Surviving in a world of stocks,—they also range
Across the hills where second timber strays
Back over Connecticut farms, abandoned pastures,—
Sea eyes and tidal, undenying, bright with myth!

The nasal whine of power whips a new universe . . .
Where spouting pillars spoor the evening sky,
Under the looming stacks of the gigantic power house
Stars prick the eyes with sharp ammoniac proverbs,
New verities, new inklings in the velvet hummed
Of dynamos, where hearing's leash is strummed . . .
Power's script,—wound, bobbin-bound, refined—

Is stropped to the slap of belts on booming spools, spurred
Into the bulging bouillon, harnessed jelly of the stars.
Towards what? The forked crash of split thunder parts
Our hearing momentwise; but fast in whirling armatures,
As bright as frogs' eyes, giggling in the girth
Of steely gizzards—axle-bound, confined
In coiled precision, bunched in mutual glee
The bearings glint,—O murmurless and shined
In oilrinsed circles of blind ecstasy!

Stars scribble on our eyes the frosty sagas,
The gleaming cantos of unvanquished space . . .
O sinewy silver biplane, nudging the wind's withers!
There, from Kill Devils Hill at Kitty Hawk
Two brothers in their twinship left the dune;
Warping the gale, the Wright windwrestlers veered
Capeward, then blading the wind's flank, banked and spun
What ciphers risen from prophetic script,
What marathons new-set between the stars!
The soul, by naphtha fledged into new reaches
Already knows the closer clasp of Mars,—
New latitudes, unknotting, soon give place
To what fierce schedules, rife of doom apace!

Behold the dragon's covey—amphibian, ubiquitous
To hedge the seaboard, wrap the headland, ride
The blue's cloud-templed districts unto ether . . .
While Iliads glimmer through eyes raised in pride
Hell's belt springs wider into heaven's plumed side.
O bright circumferences, heights employed to fly
War's fiery kennel masked in downy offings,—
This tournament of space, the threshed and chiselled height,
Is baited by marauding circles, bludgeon flail
Of rancorous grenades whose screaming petals carve us
Wounds that we wrap with theorems sharp as hail!

Wheeled swiftly, wings emerge from larval-silver hangars.
Taut motors surge, space-gnawing, into flight;
Through sparkling visibility, outspread, unsleeping,
Wings clip the last peripheries of light . . .

Tellurian wind-sleuths on dawn patrol,
Each plane a hurtling javelin of winged ordnance,
Bristle the heights above a screeching gale to hover;
Surely no eye that Sunward Escadrille can cover!
There, meaningful, fledged as the Pleiades
With razor sheen they zoom each rapid helix!
Up-chartered choristers of their own speeding
They, cavalcade on escapade, shear Cumulus—
Lay siege and hurdle Cirrus down the skies!
While Cetus-like, O thou Dirigible, enormous Lounger
Of pendulous auroral beaches,—satellited wide
By convoy planes, moonferrets that rejoin thee
On fleeing balconies as thou dost glide,
—Hast splintered space!

                              Low, shadowed of the Cape,
Regard the moving turrets! From grey decks
See scouting griffons rise through gaseous crepe
Hung low . . . until a conch of thunder answers
Cloud-belfries, banging, while searchlights, like fencers,
Slit the sky's pancreas of foaming anthracite
Toward thee, O Corsair of the typhoon,—pilot, hear!
Thine eyes bicarbonated white by speed, O Skygak, see
How from thy path above the levin's lance
Thou sowest doom thou hast nor time nor chance
To reckon—as thy stilly eyes partake
What alcohol of space . . ! Remember, Falcon-Ace,
Thou hast there in thy wrist a Sanskrit charge
To conjugate infinity's dim marge—
Anew . . !

          But first, here at this height receive
The benediction of the shell's deep, sure reprieve!
Lead-perforated fuselage, escutcheoned wings
Lift agonized quittance, tilting from the invisible brink
Now eagle-bright, now
                    quarry-hid, twist-
                              -ing, sink with
Enormous repercussive list-
                    -ings down

Giddily spiralled
                    gauntlets, upturned, unlooping
In guerrilla sleights, trapped in combustion gyr-
Ing, dance the curdled depth
                              down whizzing
Zodiacs, dashed
                    (now nearing fast the Cape!)
                                   down gravitation's
                                        vortex into crashed
. . . . dispersion . . . into mashed and shapeless debris. . . .
By Hatteras bunched the beached heap of high bravery!
          .   .   .   .   .   .

The stars have grooved our eyes with old persuasions
Of love and hatred, birth,—surcease of nations . . .
But who has held the heights more sure than thou,
O Walt!—Ascensions of thee hover in me now
As thou at junctions elegiac, there, of speed
With vast eternity, dost wield the rebound seed!
The competent loam, the probable grass,—travail
Of tides awash the pedestal of Everest, fail
Not less than thou in pure impulse inbred
To answer deepest soundings! O, upward from the dead
Thou bringest tally, and a pact, new bound
Of living brotherhood!

                    Thou, there beyond—
Glacial sierras and the flight of ravens,
Hermetically past condor zones, through zenith havens
Past where the albatross has offered up
His last wing-pulse, and downcast as a cup
That's drained, is shivered back to earth—thy wand
Has beat a song, O Walt,—there and beyond!
And this, thine other hand, upon my heart
Is plummet ushered of those tears that start
What memories of vigils, bloody, by that Cape,—
Ghoul-mound of man's perversity at balk
And fraternal massacre! Thou, pallid there as chalk
Hast kept of wounds, O Mourner, all that sum
That then from Appomattox stretched to Somme!

Cowslip and shad-blow, flaked like tethered foam
Around bared teeth of stallions, bloomed that spring
When first I read thy lines, rife as the loam
Of prairies, yet like breakers cliffward leaping!
O, early following thee, I searched the hill
Blue-writ and odor-firm with violets, 'til
With June the mountain laurel broke through green
And filled the forest with what clustrous sheen!
Potomac lilies,—then the Pontiac rose,
And Klondike edelweiss of occult snows!
White banks of moonlight came descending valleys—
How speechful on oak-vizored palisades,
As vibrantly I following down Sequoia alleys
Heard thunder's eloquence through green arcades
Set trumpets breathing in each clump and grass tuft—'til
Gold autumn, captured, crowned the trembling hill!

Panis Angelicus! Eyes tranquil with the blaze
Of love's own diametric gaze, of love's amaze!
Not greatest, thou,—not first, nor last,—but near
And onward yielding past my utmost year.
Familiar, thou, as mendicants in public places;
Evasive—too—as dayspring's spreading arc to trace is:—
Our Meistersinger, thou set breath in steel;
And it was thou who on the boldest heel
Stood up and flung the span on even wing
Of that great Bridge, our Myth, whereof I sing!

Years of the Modern! Propulsions toward what capes?
But thou, *Panis Angelicus,* hast thou not seen
And passed that Barrier that none escapes—
But knows it leastwise as death-strife?—O, something green,
Beyond all sesames of science was thy choice
Wherewith to bind us throbbing with one voice,
New integers of Roman, Viking, Celt—
Thou, Vedic Caesar, to the greensward knelt!

And now, as launched in abysmal cupolas of space,
Toward endless terminals, Easters of speeding light—
Vast engines outward veering with seraphic grace

On clarion cylinders pass out of sight
To course that span of consciousness thou'st named
The Open Road—thy vision is reclaimed!
What heritage thou'st signalled to our hands!

And see! the rainbow's arch—how shimmeringly stands
Above the Cape's ghoul-mound, O joyous seer!
Recorders ages hence, yes, they shall hear
In their own veins uncancelled thy sure tread
And read thee by the aureole 'round thy head
Of pasture-shine, *Panis Angelicus!*

                                        yes, Walt,
Afoot again, and onward without halt,—
Not soon, nor suddenly,—no, never to let go
      My hand
                  in yours,
                        Walt Whitman—
                                    so—

V
Three Songs

The one Sestos, the other Abydos hight.
                        —MARLOWE

Southern Cross

I wanted you, nameless Woman of the South,
No wraith, but utterly—as still more alone
The Southern Cross takes night
And lifts her girdles from her, one by one—
High, cool,
            wide from the slowly smoldering fire
Of lower heavens,—
                        vaporous scars!

Eve! Magdalene!
            or Mary, you?

Whatever call—falls vainly on the wave.
O simian Venus, homeless Eve,
Unwedded, stumbling gardenless to grieve
Windswept guitars on lonely decks forever;
Finally to answer all within one grave!

And this long wake of phosphor,
                              iridescent
Furrow of all our travel—trailed derision!
Eyes crumble at its kiss. Its long-drawn spell
Incites a yell. Slid on that backward vision
The mind is churned to spittle, whispering hell.

I wanted you . . . The embers of the Cross
Climbed by aslant and huddling aromatically.
It is blood to remember; it is fire
To stammer back . . . It is
God—your namelessness. And the wash—

All night the water combed you with black
Insolence. You crept out simmering, accomplished.
Water rattled that stinging coil, your
Rehearsed hair—docile, alas, from many arms.
Yes, Eve—wraith of my unloved seed!

The Cross, a phantom, buckled—dropped below the dawn.
Light drowned the lithic trillions of your spawn.

National Winter Garden

Outspoken buttocks in pink beads
Invite the necessary cloudy clinch
Of bandy eyes. . . . No extra mufflings here:
The world's one flagrant, sweating cinch.

And while legs waken salads in the brain
You pick your blonde out neatly through the smoke.
Always you wait for someone else though, always—
(Then rush the nearest exit through the smoke).

Always and last, before the final ring
When all the fireworks blare, begins
A tom-tom scrimmage with a somewhere violin,
Some cheapest echo of them all—begins.

And shall we call her whiter than the snow?
Sprayed first with ruby, then with emerald sheen—
Least tearful and least glad (who knows her smile?)
A caught slide shows her sandstone grey between.

Her eyes exist in swivellings of her teats,
Pearls whip her hips, a drench of whirling strands.
Her silly snake rings begin to mount, surmount
Each other—turquoise fakes on tinselled hands.

We wait that writhing pool, her pearls collapsed,
—All but her belly buried in the floor;
And the lewd trounce of a final muted beat!
We flee her spasm through a fleshless door. . . .

Yet, to the empty trapeze of your flesh,
O Magdalene, each comes back to die alone.
Then you, the burlesque of our lust—and faith,
Lug us back lifeward—bone by infant bone.

Virginia

O rain at seven,
Pay-check at eleven—
Keep smiling the boss away,
Mary (what are you going to do?)
Gone seven—gone eleven,
And I'm still waiting you—

O blue-eyed Mary with the claret scarf,
Saturday Mary, mine!

It's high carillon
From the popcorn bells!
Pigeons by the million—

And Spring in Prince Street
Where green figs gleam
By oyster shells!

O Mary, leaning from the high wheat tower,
    Let down your golden hair!

    High in the noon of May
    On cornices of daffodils
    The slender violets stray.
    Crap-shooting gangs in Bleecker reign,
    Peonies with pony manes—
    Forget-me-nots at windowpanes:

Out of the way-up nickel-dime tower shine,
                Cathedral Mary,
                        shine!—

VI
Quaker Hill

*I see only the ideal. But no ideals
have ever been fully successful on
this earth.*

—ISADORA DUNCAN

*The gentian weaves her fringes,
The maple's loom is red.*
                —EMILY DICKINSON

Perspective never withers from their eyes;
They keep that docile edict of the Spring
That blends March with August Antarctic skies:
These are but cows that see no other thing
Than grass and snow, and their own inner being
Through the rich halo that they do not trouble
Even to cast upon the seasons fleeting
Though they should thin and die on last year's stubble.

And they are awkward, ponderous and uncoy . . .
While we who press the cider mill, regarding them—
We, who with pledges taste the bright annoy
Of friendship's acid wine, retarding phlegm,
Shifting reprisals ('til who shall tell us when
The jest is too sharp to be kindly?) boast
Much of our store of faith in other men
Who would, ourselves, stalk down the merriest ghost.

Above them old Mizzentop, palatial white
Hostelry—floor by floor to cinquefoil dormer
Portholes the ceilings stack their stoic height.
Long tiers of windows staring out toward former
Faces—loose panes crown the hill and gleam
At sunset with a silent, cobwebbed patience . . .
See them, like eyes that still uphold some dream
Through mapled vistas, cancelled reservations!

High from the central cupola, they say
One's glance could cross the borders of three states;
But I have seen death's stare in slow survey
From four horizons that no one relates . . .
Weekenders avid of their turf-won scores,
Here three hours from the semaphores, the Czars
Of golf, by twos and threes in plaid plusfours
Alight with sticks abristle and cigars.

This was the Promised Land, and still it is
To the persuasive suburban land agent
In bootleg roadhouses where the gin fizz
Bubbles in time to Hollywood's new love-nest pageant.
Fresh from the radio in the old Meeting House
(Now the New Avalon Hotel) volcanoes roar
A welcome to highsteppers that no mouse
Who saw the Friends there ever heard before.

What cunning neighbors history has in fine!
The woodlouse mortgages the ancient deal
Table that Powitzky buys for only nine-
Ty-five at Adams' auction,—eats the seal,

The spinster polish of antiquity . . .
Who holds the lease on time and on disgrace?
What eats the pattern with ubiquity?
Where are my kinsmen and the patriarch race?

The resigned factions of the dead preside.
Dead rangers bled their comfort on the snow;
But I must ask slain Iroquois to guide
Me farther than scalped Yankees knew to go:
Shoulder the curse of sundered parentage,
Wait for the postman driving from Birch Hill
With birthright by blackmail, the arrant page
That unfolds a new destiny to fill. . . .

So, must we from the hawk's far stemming view,
Must we descend as worm's eye to construe
Our love of all we touch, and take it to the Gate
As humbly as a guest who knows himself too late,
His news already told? Yes, while the heart is wrung,
Arise—yes, take this sheaf of dust upon your tongue!
In one last angelus lift throbbing throat—
Listen, transmuting silence with that stilly note

Of pain that Emily, that Isadora knew!
While high from dim elm-chancels hung with dew,
That triple-noted clause of moonlight—
Yes, whip-poor-will, unhusks the heart of fright,
Breaks us and saves, yes, breaks the heart, yet yields
That patience that is armour and that shields
Love from despair—when love foresees the end—
Leaf after autumnal leaf
                    break off,
                              descend—
                                        descend—

VII
The Tunnel

To Find the Western path
Right thro' the Gates of Wrath.
                                    —BLAKE

Performances, assortments, résumés—
Up Times Square to Columbus Circle lights
Channel the congresses, nightly sessions,
Refractions of the thousand theatres, faces—
Mysterious kitchens. . . . You shall search them all.
Someday by heart you'll learn each famous sight
And watch the curtain lift in hell's despite;
You'll find the garden in the third act dead,
Finger your knees—and wish yourself in bed
With tabloid crime-sheets perched in easy sight.

       Then let you reach your hat
       and go.
       As usual, let you—also
       walking down—exclaim
       to twelve upward leaving
       a subscription praise
       for what time slays.

Or can't you quite make up your mind to ride;
A walk is better underneath the L a brisk
Ten blocks or so before? But you find yourself
Preparing penguin flexions of the arms,—
As usual you will meet the scuttle yawn:
The subway yawns the quickest promise home.

Be minimum, then, to swim the hiving swarms
Out of the Square, the Circle burning bright—
Avoid the glass doors gyring at your right,
Where boxed alone a second, eyes take fright
—Quite unprepared rush naked back to light:
And down beside the turnstile press the coin
Into the slot. The gongs already rattle.

And so
of cities you bespeak
subways, rivered under streets
and rivers. . . . In the car
the overtone of motion
underground, the monotone
of motion is the sound
of other faces, also underground—

"Let's have a pencil Jimmy—living now
at Floral Park
Flatbush—on the fourth of July—
like a pigeon's muddy dream—potatoes
to dig in the field—travlin the town—too—
night after night—the Culver line—the
girls all shaping up—it used to be—"

Our tongues recant like beaten weather vanes.
This answer lives like verdigris, like hair
Beyond extinction, surcease of the bone;
And repetition freezes—"What

"what do you want? getting weak on the links?
fandaddle daddy don't ask for change—IS THIS
FOURTEENTH? it's half past six she said—if
you don't like my gate why did you
swing on it, why *didja*
swing on it
anyhow—"

And somehow anyhow swing—

The phonographs of hades in the brain
Are tunnels that re-wind themselves, and love
A burnt match skating in a urinal—
Somewhere above Fourteenth TAKE THE EXPRESS
To brush some new presentiment of pain—

"But I want service in this office SERVICE
I said—after
the show she cried a little afterwards but—"

Whose head is swinging from the swollen strap?
Whose body smokes along the bitten rails,
Bursts from a smoldering bundle far behind
In back forks of the chasms of the brain,—
Puffs from a riven stump far out behind
In interborough fissures of the mind . . . ?

And why do I often meet your visage here,
Your eyes like agate lanterns—on and on
Below the toothpaste and the dandruff ads?
—And did their riding eyes right through your side,
And did their eyes like unwashed platters ride?
And Death, aloft,—gigantically down
Probing through you—toward me, O evermore!
And when they dragged your retching flesh,
Your trembling hands that night through Baltimore—
That last night on the ballot rounds, did you,
Shaking, did you deny the ticket, Poe?

For Gravesend Manor change at Chambers Street.
The platform hurries along to a dead stop.

The intent escalator lifts a serenade
Stilly
Of shoes, umbrellas, each eye attending its shoe, then
Bolting outright somewhere above where streets
Burst suddenly in rain. . . . The gongs recur:
Elbows and levers, guard and hissing door.
Thunder is galvothermic here below. . . . The car
Wheels off. The train rounds, bending to a scream,
Taking the final level for the dive
Under the river—
And somewhat emptier than before,
Demented, for a hitching second, humps; then
Lets go. . . . Toward corners of the floor
Newspapers wing, revolve and wing.
Blank windows gargle signals through the roar.

And does the Daemon take you home, also,
Wop washerwoman, with the bandaged hair?
After the corridors are swept, the cuspidors—

The gaunt sky-barracks cleanly now, and bare,
O Genoese, do you bring mother eyes and hands
Back home to children and to golden hair?

Daemon, demurring and eventful yawn!
Whose hideous laughter is a bellows mirth
—Or the muffled slaughter of a day in birth—
O cruelly to inoculate the brinking dawn
With antennae toward worlds that glow and sink;—
To spoon us out more liquid than the dim
Locution of the eldest star, and pack
The conscience navelled in the plunging wind,
Umbilical to call—and straightway die!

O caught like pennies beneath soot and steam,
Kiss of our agony thou gatherest;
Condensed, thou takest all—shrill ganglia
Impassioned with some song we fail to keep.
And yet, like Lazarus, to feel the slope,
The sod and billow breaking,—lifting ground,
—A sound of waters bending astride the sky
Unceasing with some Word that will not die . . . !

    .   .   .   .   .

A tugboat, wheezing wreaths of steam,
Lunged past, with one galvanic blare stove up the River.
I counted the echoes assembling, one after one,
Searching, thumbing the midnight on the piers.
Lights, coasting, left the oily tympanum of waters;
The blackness somewhere gouged glass on a sky.
And this thy harbor, O my City, I have driven under,
Tossed from the coil of ticking towers. . . . Tomorrow,
And to be. . . . Here by the River that is East—
Here at the waters' edge the hands drop memory;
Shadowless in that abyss they unaccounting lie.
How far away the star has pooled the sea—
Or shall the hands be drawn away, to die?

Kiss of our agony Thou gatherest,
                  O Hand of Fire
                        gatherest—

VIII
Atlantis

Music is then the knowledge of that which
relates to love in harmony and system.
                                        —PLATO

Through the bound cable strands, the arching path
Upward, veering with light, the flight of strings,—
Taut miles of shuttling moonlight syncopate
The whispered rush, telepathy of wires.
Up the index of night, granite and steel—
Transparent meshes—fleckless the gleaming staves—
Sibylline voices flicker, waveringly stream
As though a god were issue of the strings. . . .

And through that cordage, threading with its call
One arc synoptic of all tides below—
Their labyrinthine mouths of history
Pouring reply as though all ships at sea
Complighted in one vibrant breath made cry,—
"Make thy love sure—to weave whose song we ply!"
—From black embankments, moveless soundings hailed,
So seven oceans answer from their dream.

And on, obliquely up bright carrier bars
New octaves trestle the twin monoliths
Beyond whose frosted capes the moon bequeaths
Two worlds of sleep (O arching strands of song!)—
Onward and up the crystal-flooded aisle
White tempest nets file upward, upward ring
With silver terraces the humming spars,
The loft of vision, palladium helm of stars.

Sheerly the eyes, like seagulls stung with rime—
Slit and propelled by glistening fins of light—
Pick biting way up towering looms that press
Sidelong with flight of blade on tendon blade
—Tomorrows into yesteryear—and link
What cipher-script of time no traveller reads

But who, through smoking pyres of love and death,
Searches the timeless laugh of mythic spears.

Like hails, farewells—up planet-sequined heights
Some trillion whispering hammers glimmer Tyre:
Serenely, sharply up the long anvil cry
Of inchling aeons silence rivets Troy.
And you, aloft there—Jason! hesting Shout!
Still wrapping harness to the swarming air!
Silvery the rushing wake, surpassing call,
Beams yelling Aeolus! splintered in the straits!

From gulfs unfolding, terrible of drums,
Tall Vision-of-the-Voyage, tensely spare—
Bridge, lifting night to cycloramic crest
Of deepest day—O Choir, translating time
Into what multitudinous Verb the suns
And synergy of waters ever fuse, recast
In myriad syllables,—Psalm of Cathay!
O Love, thy white, pervasive Paradigm . . . !

We left the haven hanging in the night—
Sheened harbor lanterns backward fled the keel.
Pacific here at time's end, bearing corn,—
Eyes stammer through the pangs of dust and steel.
And still the circular, indubitable frieze
Of heaven's meditation, yoking wave
To kneeling wave, one song devoutly binds—
The vernal strophe chimes from deathless strings!

O Thou steeled Cognizance whose leap commits
The agile precincts of the lark's return;
Within whose lariat sweep encinctured sing
In single chrysalis the many twain,—
Of stars Thou art the stitch and stallion glow
And like an organ, Thou, with sound of doom—
Sight, sound and flesh Thou leadest from time's realm
As love strikes clear direction for the helm.

Swift peal of secular light, intrinsic Myth
Whose fell unshadow is death's utter wound,—
O River-throated—iridescently unborne
Through the bright drench and fabric of our veins;
With white escarpments swinging into light,
Sustained in tears the cities are endowed
And justified conclamant with ripe fields
Revolving through their harvests in sweet torment.

Forever Deity's glittering Pledge, O Thou
Whose canticle fresh chemistry assigns
To wrapt inception and beatitude,—
Always through blinding cables, to our joy,
Of thy white seizure springs the prophecy:
Always through spiring cordage, pyramids
Of silver sequel, Deity's young name
Kinetic of white choiring wings . . . ascends.

Migrations that must needs void memory,
Inventions that cobblestone the heart,—
Unspeakable Thou Bridge to Thee, O Love.
Thy pardon for this history, whitest Flower,
O Answerer of all,—Anemone,—
Now while thy petals spend the suns about us, hold—
(O Thou whose radiance doth inherit me)
Atlantis,—hold thy floating singer late!

So to thine Everpresence, beyond time,
Like spears ensanguined of one tolling star
That bleeds infinity—the orphic strings,
Sidereal phalanxes, leap and converge:
—One Song, one Bridge of Fire! Is it Cathay,
Now pity steeps the grass and rainbows ring
The serpent with the eagle in the leaves . . . ?
Whispers antiphonal in azure swing.

———————

O Carib Isle!

The tarantula rattling at the lily's foot
Across the feet of the dead, laid in white sand
Near the coral beach—nor zigzag fiddle crabs
Side-stilting from the path (that shift, subvert
And anagrammatize your name)—No, nothing here
Below the palsy that one eucalyptus lifts
In wrinkled shadows—mourns.

                                    And yet suppose
I count these nacreous frames of tropic death,
Brutal necklaces of shells around each grave
Squared off so carefully. Then

To the white sand I may speak a name, fertile
Albeit in a stranger tongue. Tree names, flower names
Deliberate, gainsay death's brittle crypt. Meanwhile
The wind that knots itself in one great death—
Coils and withdraws. So syllables want breath.

But where is the Captain of this doubloon isle
Without a turnstile? Who but catchword crabs
Patrols the dry groins of the underbrush?
What man, or What
Is Commissioner of mildew throughout the ambushed
      senses?
His Carib mathematics web the eyes' baked lenses!

Under the poinciana, of a noon or afternoon
Let fiery blossoms clot the light, render my ghost
Sieved upward, white and black along the air
Until it meets the blue's comedian host.

Let not the pilgrim see himself again
For slow evisceration bound like those huge terrapin
Each daybreak on the wharf, their brine caked eyes;
—Spiked, overturned; such thunder in their strain!
And clenched beaks coughing for the surge again!

Slagged of the hurricane—I, cast within its flow,
Congeal by afternoons here, satin and vacant.
You have given me the shell, Satan,—carbonic amulet
Sere of the sun exploded in the sea.

The Broken Tower

The bell-rope that gathers God at dawn
Dispatches me as though I dropped down the knell
Of a spent day—to wander the cathedral lawn
From pit to crucifix, feet chill on steps from hell.

Have you not heard, have you not seen that corps
Of shadows in the tower, whose shoulders sway
Antiphonal carillons launched before
The stars are caught and hived in the sun's ray?

The bells, I say, the bells break down their tower;
And swing I know not where. Their tongues engrave
Membrane through marrow, my long-scattered score
Of broken intervals . . . And I, their sexton slave!

Oval encyclicals in canyons heaping
The impasse high with choir. Banked voices slain!
Pagodas, campaniles with reveilles outleaping—
O terraced echoes prostrate on the plain! . . .

And so it was I entered the broken world
To trace the visionary company of love, its voice
An instant in the wind (I know not whither hurled)
But not for long to hold each desperate choice.

My word I poured. But was it cognate, scored
Of that tribunal monarch of the air
Whose thigh embronzes earth, strikes crystal Word
In wounds pledged once to hope,—cleft to despair?

The steep encroachments of my blood left me
No answer (could blood hold such a lofty tower
As flings the question true?)—or is it she
Whose sweet mortality stirs latent power?—

And through whose pulse I hear, counting the strokes
My veins recall and add, revived and sure
The angelus of wars my chest evokes:
What I hold healed, original now, and pure . . .

And builds, within, a tower that is not stone
(Not stone can jacket heaven)—but slip
Of pebbles,—visible wings of silence sown
In azure circles, widening as they dip

The matrix of the heart, lift down the eye
That shrines the quiet lake and swells a tower . . .
The commodious, tall decorum of that sky
Unseals her earth, and lifts love in its shower.

THOMAS A. DORSEY

(1899–1993)

Take My Hand, Precious Lord

Precious Lord, take my hand,
Lead me on, let me stand,
I am tired, I am weak, I am worn.
Through the storm, through the night
Lead me on to the light,
Take my hand, precious Lord,
Lead me home.

When my way grows drear,
Precious Lord, linger near.
When my life is almost gone,
Hear my cry, hear my call,
Hold my hand lest I fall.
Take my hand, precious Lord,
Lead me home.

When the darkness appears
And the night draws near,
And the day is past and gone,
At the river I stand,
Guide my feet, hold my hand.
Take my hand, precious Lord,
Lead me home.

HILDEGARDE FLANNER

(1899–1987)

Dumb

Silence braided her fingers in my hair
And put her ankles close to mine in bed.
She hushed a silver sparrow in his song
And laid against my throat her fragile head.

"I conquered today," she said, "as yesterday,
And now we two shall rest as one tonight.
A girl with silence in her arms,
(Lie quietly!) is a lovely sight."

And so I rest with silence in my arms,
Her hair across my breath when I would weep.
I cannot even force my tongue to pray
That she will leave me in my sleep.

Moment

I saw a young deer standing
Among the languid ferns.
Suddenly he ran—
And his going was absolute,
Like the shattering of icicles
In the wind.

Fern Song

Had I the use of thought equivalent
To moist hallucination of a flute
I could be saying how
A certain music in my woods has driven
A certain female fern to tear
In panic from her good black root.

But no transparency of clear intent
Assisting me,
I only guessed at what the singer meant
That hour I heard his intervals prolong
Beyond security of common song
Into a raving sweetness coming closer
While the lyric animal himself
Was still remote,
Since thrush may have a mile of music
In one inch of throat.

Frog Song

You would not guess it is the voice
That croons warm water from the ice
And melts the season to reverse
Stiff white its fatal trip into excess.

You would not guess it is the voice
Roused by planets in their course
Who sweep their burning manes across
Spring's muddy flowers and soiling of the snows.

You would not guess it is the voice
That can be heard through prison wall,
It can though, can with sorrow drill
And spread a marshy hum in a dark place.

You would not guess it is the voice
That stirs a woman past her prime
To kneel on the scanty path to come
And thank the cold frog in his slime
Who does not know his stupid rank
But throbs as vivid as a lark—
That's it, she quietly thinks,
Full utterance and little time,

That is the voice.

True Western Summer

Corporeal summer, no marvel is lost
In your obsession to be real.
To love you has been my boast
In the bald days of cactus and hawk
Where never a brook in liquid shade rolls green,
Nor softly to my heart rambles the rain,
And to love you humbly under the feet of the quail,
By fallen acacia seed and brown bud,
And in the poor kingdom of the crowned toad,
Whose wealth is drought,
There to love you well,
Even where shadow that gives no shade
Lies dark as obsidian strewn
There to love you still,
And now to love in alarm and delight
Seeing the little stone in the field
Tremble and soar to your meaning alive
Alive in the top of the sky,
And to love you more as a ravish of light
Feasts on the literal and the revealed
Leaving only of truth the passionate skull
Small and perfect where it fell.

JANET LEWIS

(1899–1998)

from
The Indians in the Woods

The Indians in the Woods

Ah, the woods, the woods
Where small things
Are distinct and visible,

The berry plant,
The berry leaf, remembered
Line for line.

There are three figures
Walking in the woods
Whose feet press down
Needle and leaf and vine.

The Grandmother Remembers

Ah, the cold, cold days
When we lived
On wintergreen berries and nuts,
On caraway seeds.

The deer went over the grass
With wet hooves
To the river to drink.

Their shadows passed
Our tent.

Nightfall Among Poplars

As light grew horizontal,
I, among bracken,
Felt the cold ripples
Among bracken stems.

The quick dry spider
Ran across my hand.

Manibush and the Grandmother

With keen ankles
Dividing weed and weed
He shakes the dry seed
From the grass.

Fox feet, and five
Bare leather paws
And small sharp claws
Accompany him.

From the blue spruce
Tree where the wind blows
I watch the flashing
In the grass.

He Goes Away Again

In thorny juniper
The wind is cold,

In thorny juniper.

Shadows
Of stones grow white with evening.

The deer, the deer
Among the withered asters.

The spider,
Making tight her web.

One Sits in the Woods

Gradual, continual approach
Of some one through the woods,
But no one comes.

The thin flame
Shoots up
Among grasses.

Violets, color of stone,
Minute and scarce
Where the great ants climb.

Exodus at Evening

Light came sideways
Into the hole;
The badger's children
Creeping sideways out.

Down they went
To bushes in the valley,
Treading silky yarrow.

Girl Help

Mild and slow and young,
She moves about the room,
And stirs the summer dust
With her wide broom.

In the warm, lofted air,
Soft lips together pressed,
Soft wispy hair,
She stops to rest.

And stops to breathe,
Amid the summer hum,
The great white lilac bloom
Scented with days to come.

The Reader

Sun creeps under the eaves,
And shines on the bare floor
While he forgets the earth.

Cool ashes on the hearth,
And all so still save for
The soft turning of leaves.

A creature fresh from birth
Clings to the screen door,
Heaving damp heavy wings.

Winter Garden

Child, dream of a pomegranate tree
Weighted with ruby, showered with gold,
Dream of a fig tree under the cold
And cloudy sky
Lifting its curved and silver boughs
Like a roofless house
For birds that be
Tardily in November here;
Dream of a spare
And twisted vine—
The grape—and ivy for the hair,
And honeysuckle, stubborn twine;
And of the firm and hidden shape
Of the green orange deep in the tree;
And dreaming, in my garden be.

I have bestowed calendulas
That brighten beside reddening haws,
And rooted out the hoarhound grey,
And pulled the nettle from our way,
And torn my hand on bramble berry.
Then, if a drop, red as a cherry,
Of blood upon my finger show,
It is a seal set to a vow
To ward and to cherish even as now,
Now that you sleep your joy to replenish,
Each branch, each varied lifting bough,
That not a leaf in your garden perish.

Helen Grown Old

We have forgotten Paris, and his fate.
We have not much inquired
If Menelaus from the Trojan gate
Returning found the long desired
Immortal beauty by his hearth. Then late,

Late, long past the morning hour,
Could even she recapture from the dawn
The young delightful love? When the dread power
That forced her will was gone,
When fell the last charred tower,

When the last flame had faded from the cloud,
And by the darkening sea
The plain lay empty of the arméd crowd,
Then was she free
Who had been ruled by passion blind and proud?

Then did she find with him whom first she chose
Before the desperate flight,
At last, repose
In love still radiant at the edge of night,
As fair as in the morning? No one knows.

No one has cared to say. The story clings
To the tempestuous years, by passion bound,
Like Helen. No one brings
A tale of quiet love. The fading sound
Is blent of falling embers, weeping kings.

For the Father of Sandro Gulotta

When I called the children from play
Where the westering sun
Fell level between the leaves
       of olive and bay,
There, where the day lilies stand,
I paused
       to touch with a curious hand
The single blossom, furled,
That with morning had opened wide,
The long bud tinged
       with gold of an evening sky.

All day, and only one day,
It drank the sunlit air.
In one long day
All that it needed to do in this world
It did, and at evening precisely curled
The tender petals to shield
From wind, from dew,
The pollen-laden heart.
Sweet treasure gathered apart
From our grief, from our longing view,
Who shall say if the day was too brief,
For the flower, if time lacked?
Had it not, like the children, all Time
In their long, immortal day?

The Ancient Ones: Betátakin

Time stays, they said. We go.
They moved through Time as through a room
Under the great arch of Betátakin.

We cannot hear their voices.
What words they spoke
To echo here, to rise along the walls
Of this steep canyon,
Are gone; and yet the jay,
The warbler speak their notes
And the wind blows, whirling the aspen leaves,
Brushing the thick short needles of these pines,
And by the path
The small flowers still are bright—
Vetch, bluer than turquoise,
Clustering white stars;
And all the leaves are new, early in May,
Small, perfectly shaped, each to its odd design,
And gleaming; and the porcupine
Climbs from his tree with easy slumberous grace.
His quills shine in the early light,
A halo, as he goes
Into the mist of green.

Time stays, the canyon stays;
Their houses stay, split rock
Mortared with clay, and small.
And the shards, grey, plain or painted,
In the pale roseate dust reveal, conceal
The patterns of their days,
Speak of the pure form of the shattered pot.

We do not recreate, we rediscover
The immortal form, that, once created,
Stands unchanged
In Time's unchanging room.

Garden Note I, Los Altos

A spring storm shakes the old peach tree,
Making the branches glisten,
Scattering the dark petals,
While the cherry,
Young as any bride,
Holds fast her white clusters.

Garden Note II, March

Nothing more hesitant
Than the way the poplar seedlings take.
Nothing more certain than the intention
Behind their wanderings. They float
Over the grass, over the roof, and beyond
My garden, beyond this day,
As I saw them years ago,
On this same ground,
Under this same tree.

JOSEPH MONCURE MARCH

(1899–1977)

from
The Wild Party

The gang was there when midnight came.
The studio was lit by candle-flame;
Dim: mysterious: shrouded.
Unbidden shadow-guests swarmed
About the room. They huddled crowded
In every corner; raised deformed
Ungainly shoulders, hideous, tall
Necks and heads against the wall.
Enormous blurred hands kept stealing
Spider-like, across the ceiling;
Crossing with sharp, prismatic masses
Of light from swaying spectre glasses.
The flames flickered:
The shadows leapt:
They rushed forward boldly;
Swept
Triumphant
Across white faces:
Wavered, retreated;
Turned, defeated,
And shrank back to darker places.

The party was getting under way
Stiffly, slowly.
The way they drank was unholy.
They hovered around the glass-filled tray
Ravenously,
Like birds of prey.
White, intense;
With mask-like faces
Frozen in rigid, gay grimaces.
They chattered and laughed

Stony-eyed:
Impatient:
Hasty:
Preoccupied.

They drank swiftly, as though they might
Drop dead before they were properly tight.

Christ,
What a crew!
Take a look at Madelaine True;
Her eyes slanted. Her eyes were green;
Heavy-lidded; pouched: obscene.
Eyes like a snake's:
Like a stagnant pool
Filled with slime.
Her mouth was cruel:
A scar
In red,
That had recently opened and bled.
Her body was marvellous:
A miracle had fused it:
The whole world had seen it—
And a good part had used it.
People bought their seats in advance
For fifteen dollars,
Glad of the chance
To see her dance.
Women adored her.
Less often, a man:
And the more fool he—
She was Lesbian.

Then Jackie:
Perfectly formed of face,
Slim, elegant,
Full of grace:
Leaving a subtle trail of scent
Floating behind him as he went.
A soft-shoe dancer

With a special act.
New York, or Paris—
His house was packed.
He had two cars.
He had been behind bars
For theft, public nuisance, rape:
Once extra for trying escape.
Too bad?
Nonsense!
He was fun.
A good sport:
The only son
Of some unheard-of preacher father
Who had kicked him out as too much bother.
Of course—
(The Black Horse)
His hips were jaunty,
And his gestures too dextrous.
A versatile lad!
He was ambisextrous.

By contrast—Eddie:
A short, squat brute,
Gorilla-like: hirsute:
With eyes deep set,
A nose battered
Flat on one side,
And teeth scattered.
The bones about his cheeks and eyes
Protruded grimly, oversize.
A boxer, you'd guess—
And right.
The man could certainly fight.
Aggressive; fast;
Punishment-proof:
Each hand held a kick like a mule's hoof.
He might have been champion—
He had the cunning:
But drink had put him out of the running.
Away from the ring, he was easy-going;

Good-natured—if sober—
And given to blowing.
But after he'd had his tenth Scotch,
A man to be careful of
And watch:
And when he was mixing gin and rum—
A man to keep well away from.

His woman at present was Mae.
She was blonde, and slender, and gay:
A passionate flirt,
So dumb that it hurt,
And better for night than for day.

Behold the Brothers d'Armano:
Otherwise, Oscar and Phil.
They sang:
They played the piano:
They functioned together with skill.
They lisped.
Their voices were shrill.
They were powdered,
Rouged,
Sleek of hair:
They must have worn
Pink silk underwear.
They clung together with arms laced
Each about the other's waist:
Stood around in anguished poses.
They rated
A shower of paper roses;
Lavender lights,
And the stink of joss.
Suffering Moses,
What a loss!

Watch Dolores:
Dark, tall,
Slim,
Wrapped in a Spanish shawl;

With a Spanish comb making a flare
Of crimson against her smooth, black hair.
A singer
Without a voice:
But she rode in a Rolls-Royce.
She made herself up, and out, to be
Of Spanish aristocracy.
(As a matter of fact,
If one only knew,
She was somewhat Negro
And a great deal Jew.)
In each eye lurked
What she thought was a dagger;
And she walked with a slink
Mixed with a swagger.
She was swell to sleep with.
Her toe-nails were scarlet.
She looked like—and had been—
A Mexican harlot.

There were others, of course:
A dozen or so.
Sally,
With Butter and Eggs in tow—
He had seen her first two nights ago
In the chorus of a summer musical show.

And the usual two
Loud Jew
Theatrical managers stood engrossed
Bewailing high production cost.
Each of them had suffered most.
In twenty minutes both had lost
The sum of sixty million dollars—
With gestures:
After which they sighed,
And drank
Panting:
Tragic-eyed:
Mopping at sadly wilted collars.

Nadine:
Mae's kid sister.
Fourteen:
No man had kissed her.
Excitement made her wide-eyed:
She was so thrilled to be there
She could have died!
She was quite pretty
And she looked older.
She knew only
What had been told her.

And of course, Burrs:
Natty in grey,
With a breath you could smell a yard away:
Putting his better foot foremost
And trying to be the perfect host.

The rest were simply repetitions
Of the more notorious. Slim editions:
Less practised; less hardened:
Less vicious; less strong:
Just a nice crowd trying to get along.

But to-night, Queenie surpassed them all.
Exquisite in black;
Radiant;
Tall;
With a face of ivory,
And blurred gold for hair:
She was something to kneel before, in prayer.

"My god, Queenie; you're looking swell!"

Quoth Queenie:
"I'm feeling slick as hell!"

VLADIMIR NABOKOV

(1899–1977)

from
Lolita

Wanted, wanted: Dolores Haze.
Hair: brown. Lips: scarlet.
Age: five thousand three hundred days.
Profession: none, or "starlet."

Where are you hiding, Dolores Haze?
Why are you hiding, darling?
(I talk in a daze, I walk in a maze,
I cannot get out, said the starling).

Where are you riding, Dolores Haze?
What make is the magic carpet?
Is a Cream Cougar the present craze?
And where are you parked, my car pet?

Who is your hero, Dolores Haze?
Still one of those blue-caped star-men?
Oh the balmy days and the palmy bays,
And the cars, and the bars, my Carmen!

Oh Dolores, that juke-box hurts!
Are you still dancin', darlin'?
(Both in worn levis, both in torn T-shirts,
And I, in my corner, snarlin').

Happy, happy is gnarled McFate
Touring the States with a child wife,
Plowing his Molly in every State
Among the protected wild life.

My Dolly, my folly! Her eyes were *vair*,
And never closed when I kissed her.
Know an old perfume called *Soleil Vert*?
Are you from Paris, mister?

L'autre soir un air froid d'opéra m'alita:
Son fêlé—bien fol est qui s'y fie!
Il neige, le décor s'écroule, Lolita!
Lolita, qu'ai-je fait de ta vie?

Dying, dying, Lolita Haze,
Of hate and remorse, I'm dying.
And again my hairy fist I raise,
And again I hear you crying.

Officer, officer, there they go—
In the rain, where that lighted store is!
And her socks are white, and I love her so,
And her name is Haze, Dolores.

Officer, officer, there they are—
Dolores Haze and her lover!
Whip out your gun and follow that car.
Now tumble out, and take cover.

Wanted, wanted: Dolores Haze.
Her dream-gray gaze never flinches.
Ninety pounds is all she weighs
With a height of sixty inches.

My car is limping, Dolores Haze,
And the last long lap is the hardest,
And I shall be dumped where the weed decays,
And the rest is rust and stardust.

On Translating "Eugene Onegin"

1

What is translation? On a platter
A poet's pale and glaring head,
A parrot's screech, a monkey's chatter,
And profanation of the dead.
The parasites you were so hard on
Are pardoned if I have your pardon,
O, Pushkin, for my stratagem:
I travelled down your secret stem,
And reached the root, and fed upon it;
Then, in a language newly learned,
I grew another stalk and turned
Your stanza patterned on a sonnet,
Into my honest roadside prose—
All thorn, but cousin to your rose.

2

Reflected words can only shiver
Like elongated lights that twist
In the black mirror of a river
Between the city and the mist.
Elusive Pushkin! Persevering,
I still pick up Tatiana's earring,
Still travel with your sullen rake.
I find another man's mistake,
I analyze alliterations
That grace your feasts and haunt the great
Fourth stanza of your Canto Eight.
This is my task—a poet's patience
And scholiastic passion blent:
The shadow of your monument.

LYNN RIGGS

(1899–1954)

Santo Domingo Corn Dance

The Chorus

"Bring rain,
As we bring now
Our gift of dance and song
To You—who dance not, nor sing—
Bring rain!"

The Dancers

Bodies
Reddened, and gourds,
Rain girdles, ornaments,
The skins of foxes—what should please
You more?

Portent

But look!
Where the line whips
Like rain in corn, like clouds
Wind beaten, or like the frown
Upon His brow!

Song of the Bodies

"I am
Naked before
You, High One—look! Hear me!
As I stamp this ground worn smooth
By feet.

"Not as
  A supplicant
  I shake the doors of earth—
  Let the green corn spring to meet
  My tread!"

The Clouds

Just now
Across the line
Of these red men there swept—
Like wings of thunder at the sun—
Shadows!

The Koshari

As if
Their feet were struck
With scorn, their hands with pride—
Koshari glide, halt, grimace, grin,
And turn.

The Child Dancer

"But that
  I am a child,
  I should not notice the branch
  Of spruce tied on his arm
  In my eyes."

The Orchard

Beyond
The baking roofs,
A barren mountain points
Still higher, though its feet are white
With bloom.

Rain

One drum—
Note more, one voice,
One slant of bodies,
And my tears will fall like rain
Upon this ground.

ALLEN TATE

(1899–1979)

Mr. Pope

When Alexander Pope strolled in the city
Strict was the glint of pearl and gold sedans.
Ladies leaned out more out of fear than pity
For Pope's tight back was rather a goat's than man's.

Often one thinks the urn should have more bones
Than skeletons provide for speedy dust,
The urn gets hollow, cobwebs brittle as stones
Weave to the funeral shell a frivolous rust.

And he who dribbled couplets like a snake
Coiled to a lithe precision in the sun
Is missing. The jar is empty; you may break
It only to find that Mr. Pope is gone.

What requisitions of a verity
Prompted the wit and rage between his teeth
One cannot say. Around a crooked tree
A moral climbs whose name should be a wreath.

Ode to the Confederate Dead

Row after row with strict impunity
The headstones yield their names to the element,
The wind whirrs without recollection;
In the riven troughs the splayed leaves
Pile up, of nature the casual sacrament
To the seasonal eternity of death;
Then driven by the fierce scrutiny
Of heaven to their election in the vast breath,
They sough the rumour of mortality.

Autumn is desolation in the plot
Of a thousand acres where these memories grow
From the inexhaustible bodies that are not
Dead, but feed the grass row after rich row.
Think of the autumns that have come and gone!—
Ambitious November with the humors of the year,
With a particular zeal for every slab,
Staining the uncomfortable angels that rot
On the slabs, a wing chipped here, an arm there:
The brute curiosity of an angel's stare
Turns you, like them, to stone,
Transforms the heaving air
Till plunged to a heavier world below
You shift your sea-space blindly
Heaving, turning like the blind crab.

    Dazed by the wind, only the wind
    The leaves flying, plunge

You know who have waited by the wall
The twilight certainty of an animal,
Those midnight restitutions of the blood
You know—the immitigable pines, the smoky frieze
Of the sky, the sudden call: you know the rage,
The cold pool left by the mounting flood,
Of muted Zeno and Parmenides.
You who have waited for the angry resolution
Of those desires that should be yours tomorrow,
You know the unimportant shrift of death
And praise the vision
And praise the arrogant circumstance
Of those who fall
Rank upon rank, hurried beyond decision—
Here by the sagging gate, stopped by the wall.

    Seeing, seeing only the leaves
    Flying, plunge and expire

Turn your eyes to the immoderate past,
Turn to the inscrutable infantry rising

Demons out of the earth—they will not last.
Stonewall, Stonewall, and the sunken fields of hemp,
Shiloh, Antietam, Malvern Hill, Bull Run.
Lost in that orient of the thick and fast
You will curse the setting sun.

   Cursing only the leaves crying
   Like an old man in a storm

You hear the shout, the crazy hemlocks point
With troubled fingers to the silence which
Smothers you, a mummy, in time.

                         The hound bitch
Toothless and dying, in a musty cellar
Hears the wind only.

                      Now that the salt of their blood
Stiffens the saltier oblivion of the sea,
Seals the malignant purity of the flood,
What shall we who count our days and bow
Our heads with a commemorial woe
In the ribboned coats of grim felicity,
What shall we say of the bones, unclean,
Whose verdurous anonymity will grow?
The ragged arms, the ragged heads and eyes
Lost in these acres of the insane green?
The gray lean spiders come, they come and go;
In a tangle of willows without light
The singular screech-owl's tight
Invisible lyric seeds the mind
With the furious murmur of their chivalry.

   We shall say only the leaves
   Flying, plunge and expire

We shall say only the leaves whispering
In the improbable mist of nightfall
That flies on multiple wing:
Night is the beginning and the end

And in between the ends of distraction
Waits mute speculation, the patient curse
That stones the eyes, or like the jaguar leaps
For his own image in a jungle pool, his victim.

What shall we say who have knowledge
Carried to the heart? Shall we take the act
To the grave? Shall we, more hopeful, set up the grave
In the house? The ravenous grave?

                    Leave now
The shut gate and the decomposing wall:
The gentle serpent, green in the mulberry bush,
Riots with his tongue through the hush—
Sentinel of the grave who counts us all!

The Twelve

There by some wrinkled stones round a leafless tree
With beards askew, their eyes dull and wild
Twelve ragged men, the council of charity
Wandering the face of the earth a fatherless child,
Kneel, at their infidelity aghast,
For where was it, somewhere in Syria
Or Palestine when the streams went red,
The victor of Rome, his arms outspread,
His eyes cold with that inhuman ecstasy,
Cried the last word, the accursèd last
Of the forsaken that seared the western heart
With the fire of the wind, the thick and the fast
Whirl of the damned in the heavenly storm:
Now the wind's empty and the twelve living dead
Look round them for that promontory Form
Whose mercy flashed from the sheet-lightning's head,
But the twelve lie in the sand by the dry rock
Seeing nothing—the sand, the tree, rocks
Without number—and turn away the face
To the mind's briefer and more desert place.

Last Days of Alice

Alice grown lazy, mammoth but not fat,
Declines upon her lost and twilight age;
Above in the dozing leaves the grinning cat
Quivers forever with his abstract rage:

Whatever light swayed on the perilous gate
Forever sways, nor will the arching grass,
Caught when the world clattered, undulate
In the deep suspension of the looking-glass.

Bright Alice! always pondering to gloze
The spoiled cruelty she had meant to say
Gazes learnedly down her airy nose
At nothing, nothing thinking all the day.

Turned absent-minded by infinity
She cannot move unless her double move—
The All-Alice of the world's entity
Smashed in the anger of her hopeless love,

Love for herself who, as an earthly twain,
Pouted to join her two in a sweet one:
No more the second lips to kiss in vain
The first she broke, plunged through the glass alone—

Alone to the weight of impassivity,
Incest of spirit, theorem of desire,
Without will as chalky cliffs by the sea,
Empty as the bodiless flesh of fire:

All space, that heaven is a dayless night,
A nightless day driven by perfect lust
For vacancy, in which her bored eyesight
Stares at the drowsy cubes of human dust.

—We too back to the world shall never pass
Through the shattered door, a dumb shade-harried crowd
Being all infinite, function, depth and mass
Without figure, a mathematical shroud

Hurled at the air—blessèd without sin!
O God of our flesh, return us to Your wrath,
Let us be evil could we enter in
Your grace, and falter on the stony path!

The Wolves

There are wolves in the next room waiting
With heads bent low, thrust out, breathing
At nothing in the dark: between them and me
A white door patched with light from the hall
Where it seems never (so still is the house)
A man has walked from the front door to the stair.
It has all been forever. A beast claws the floor.
I have brooded on angels and archfiends
But no man has ever sat where the next room's
Crowded with wolves, and for the honor of man
I affirm that never have I before. Now while
I have looked for the evening star at a cold window
And whistled when Arcturus spilt his light,
I've heard the wolves scuffle, and said: So this
Is man; so—what better conclusion is there—
The day will not follow night, and the heart
Of man has a little dignity, but less patience
Than a wolf's, and a duller sense that cannot
Smell its own mortality. (This and other
Meditations will be suited to other times
After dog silence howls my epitaph)
Now remember courage, go to the door,
Open it and see whether coiled on the bed
Or cringing by the wall a savage beast
Maybe with golden hair, with deep eyes
Like a bearded spider on a sunlit floor
Will snarl—and man can never be alone.

Aeneas at Washington

I myself saw furious with blood
Neoptolemus, at his side the black Atridae,
Hecuba and the hundred daughters, Priam
Cut down, his filth drenching the holy fires.
In that extremity I bore me well,
A true gentleman, valorous in arms,
Disinterested and honourable. Then fled:
That was a time when civilization
Run by the few fell to the many, and
Crashed to the shout of men, the clang of arms:
Cold victualing I seized, I hoisted up
The old man my father upon my back,
In the smoke made by sea for a new world
Saving little—a mind imperishable
If time is, a love of past things tenuous
As the hesitation of receding love.

(To the reduction of uncitied littorals
We brought chiefly the vigor of prophecy
Our hunger breeding calculation
And fixed triumphs)

                        The thirsty dove I saw
In the glowing fields of Troy, hemp ripening
And tawny corn, the thickening Blue Grass
All lying rich forever in the green sun.
I see all things apart, the towers that men
Contrive I too contrived long, long ago.
Now I demand little. The singular passion
Abides its object and consumes desire
In the circling shadow of its appetite.
There was a time when the young eyes were slow,
Their flame steady beyond the firstling fire,
I stood in the rain, far from home at nightfall
By the Potomac, the great Dome lit the water,
The city my blood had built I knew no more

While the screech-owl whistled his new delight
Consecutively dark.

                    Stuck in the wet mire
Four thousand leagues from the ninth buried city
I thought of Troy, what we had built her for.

The Ivory Tower

Let us begin to understand the argument.
There is a solution to everything: Science.
Separate those evils strictly social
From other evils that are eventually social.
It ends in all evils being social: Deduction.
Is not marriage a social institution,
(*Un contrat social*) Is not prostitution
An institution? Abolish (1) marriage, (2) poverty.
We understand everything: Dialectic.
We who get plenty to eat and get it
Advertising the starvation of others
Understand everything not including
Ourselves: we have enough to eat. Oedipus
Was necessarily an example—everything
Is an example—of capitalism pooped
By decay; King Lear, of neurotic senility
Bred of tyrannous escape from reality;
Cleopatra, of the unadjusted girl.
Everybody but us is an example of capitalism.
We are understanding the argument
That we have got to make men slaves
Of their bellies in order to get them fed.
The sole problem is the problem of hunger
(Or the distribution of commodities)
And a beast came out of the sea
And a fire came out of the night
To them that were not hungry
The commodities being well distributed
And the prostate thrives a little, then delays,

The hour of light is brief, then decays;
But light must be a social institution
Even if we are not sure what the other
Is (*pro*, forth; *stare*, to stand).
We know everything to know on sea or land.
And on the mountains by the sea
There was enacted tragedy
(Or maybe in a hollow by a tree),
Both man and woman were well-fed
When he had brought her hot to bed
But he was largely make-believe
And she no better than a sieve;
Soon the uneconomic woe
That love engenders crushed them, so
That every time they drank or ate
They cursed the board where food was set.
Axel's Castle, the text they took,
Was a most remarkable book
But yet in spite of Mr. Wilson
Beef and cheese washed down by Pilsen
Did not adjust the sexual act
To truths of economic fact,
So was produced this tragedy
In a far tower of ivory
Where, O young men, late in the night
All you who drink light and stroke the air
Come back, seeking the night, and cry
To strict Rapunzel to let down her hair.

The Mediterranean

Quem das finem, rex magne, dolorum?

Where we went in the boat was a long bay
A slingshot wide, walled in by towering stone—
Peaked margin of antiquity's delay,
And we went there out of time's monotone:

Where we went in the black hull no light moved
But a gull white-winged along the feckless wave,
The breeze, unseen but fierce as a body loved,
That boat drove onward like a willing slave:

Where we went in the small ship the seaweed
Parted and gave to us the murmuring shore,
And we made feast and in our secret need
Devoured the very plates Aeneas bore:

Where derelict you see through the low twilight
The green coast that you, thunder-tossed, would win,
Drop sail, and hastening to drink all night
Eat dish and bowl—to take that sweet land in!

Where we feasted and caroused on the sandless
Pebbles, affecting our day of piracy,
What prophecy of eaten plates could landless
Wanderers fulfil by the ancient sea?

We for that time might taste the famous age
Eternal here yet hidden from our eyes
When lust of power undid its stuffless rage;
They, in a wineskin, bore earth's paradise.

Let us lie down once more by the breathing side
Of Ocean, where our live forefathers sleep
As if the Known Sea still were a month wide—
Atlantis howls but is no longer steep!

What country shall we conquer, what fair land
Unman our conquest and locate our blood?
We've cracked the hemispheres with careless hand!
Now, from the Gates of Hercules we flood

Westward, westward till the barbarous brine
Whelms us to the tired land where tasseling corn,
Fat beans, grapes sweeter than muscadine
Rot on the vine: in that land were we born.

Sonnets at Christmas

I

This is the day His hour of life draws near,
Let me get ready from head to foot for it
Most handily with eyes to pick the year
For small feed to reward a feathered wit.
Some men would see it an epiphany
At ease, at food and drink, others at chase
Yet I, stung lassitude, with ecstasy
Unspent argue the season's difficult case
So: Man, dull critter of enormous head,
What would he look at in the coiling sky?
But I must kneel again unto the Dead
While Christmas bells of paper white and red,
Figured with boys and girls spilt from a sled,
Ring out the silence I am nourished by.

II

Ah, Christ, I love you rings to the wild sky
And I must think a little of the past:
When I was ten I told a stinking lie
That got a black boy whipped; but now at last
The going years, with an accurate glow,
Reverse like balls englished upon green baize—
Let them return, let the round trumpets blow
The ancient crackle of the Christ's deep gaze.
Deafened and blind, with senses yet unfound,
Am I, untutored to the after-wit
Of knowledge, knowing a nightmare has no sound;
Therefore with idle hands and head I sit
In late December before the fire's daze
Punished by crimes of which I would be quit.

The Swimmers

SCENE: *Montgomery County,*
Kentucky, July 1911

Kentucky water, clear springs: a boy fleeing
 To water under the dry Kentucky sun,
 His four little friends in tandem with him, seeing

Long shadows of grapevine wriggle and run
 Over the green swirl; mullein under the ear
 Soft as Nausicaä's palm; sullen fun

Savage as childhood's thin harmonious tear:
 O fountain, bosom source undying-dead
 Replenish me the spring of love and fear

And give me back the eye that looked and fled
 When a thrush idling in the tulip tree
 Unwound the cold dream of the copperhead.

—Along the creek the road was winding; we
 Felt the quicksilver sky. I see again
 The shrill companions of that odyssey:

Bill Eaton, Charlie Watson, "Nigger" Layne
 The doctor's son, Harry Duèsler who played
 The flute; and Tate, with water on the brain.

Dog-days: the dusty leaves where rain delayed
 Hung low on poison-oak and scuppernong,
 And we were following the active shade

Of water, that bells and bickers all night long.
 "No more'n a mile," Layne said. All five stood still.
 Listening, I heard what seemed at first a song;

Peering, I heard the hooves come down the hill.
 The posse passed, twelve horse; the leader's face
 Was worn as limestone on an ancient still.

Then, as sleepwalkers shift from a hard place
   In bed, and rising to keep a formal pledge
   Descend a ladder into empty space,

We scuttled down the bank below a ledge
   And marched stiff-legged in our common fright
   Along a hog-track by the riffle's edge:

Into a world where sound shaded the sight
   Dropped the dull hooves again; the horsemen came
   Again, all but the leader. It was night

Momently and I feared: eleven same
   Jesus-Christers unmembered and unmade,
   Whose Corpse had died again in dirty shame.

The bank then levelling in a speckled glade,
   We stopped to breathe above the swimming-hole;
   I gazed at its reticulated shade

Recoiling in blue fear, and felt it roll
   Over my ears and eyes and lift my hair
   Like seaweed tossing on a sunk atoll.

I rose again. Borne on the copper air
   A distant voice green as a funeral wreath
   Against a grave: "That dead nigger there."

The melancholy sheriff slouched beneath
   A giant sycamore; shaking his head
   He plucked a sassafras twig and picked his teeth:

"We come too late." He spoke to the tired dead
   Whose ragged shirt soaked up the viscous flow
   Of blood in which It lay discomfited.

A butting horse-fly gave one ear a blow
   And glanced off, as the sheriff kicked the rope
   Loose from the neck and hooked it with his toe

Away from the blood.—I looked back down the slope:
    The friends were gone that I had hoped to greet.—
    A single horseman came at a slow lope

And pulled up at the hanged man's horny feet;
    The sheriff noosed the feet, the other end
    The stranger tied to his pommel in a neat

Slip-knot. I saw the Negro's body bend
    And straighten, as a fish-line cast transverse
    Yields to the current that it must subtend.

The sheriff's Goddamn was a murmured curse
    Not for the dead but for the blinding dust
    That boxed the cortège in a cloudy hearse

And dragged it towards our town. I knew I must
    Not stay till twilight in that silent road;
    Sliding my bare feet into the warm crust,

I hopped the stonecrop like a panting toad
    Mouth open, following the heaving cloud
    That floated to the court-house square its load

Of limber corpse that took the sun for shroud.
    There were three figures in the dying sun
    Whose light were company where three was crowd.

My breath crackled the dead air like a shotgun
    As, sheriff and the stranger disappearing,
    The faceless head lay still. I could not run

Or walk, but stood. Alone in the public clearing
    This private thing was owned by all the town,
    Though never claimed by us within my hearing.

EDWARD DAHLBERG

(1900–1977)

February Ground

I

Ocean begat ground,
And the rocks of the new continent slept
As if they were still bellied in the jagged deep.
The Americas were the last to have risen
From the two great seas,
Yet the people are ancient,
The detritus of Asia, Tyre, Carthage, the Pyrenees.
The forest became their deity and larder.
The woods gave off a remembrance of saline origins,
Providing them with untutored grape-vines
As edible as the clusters of Jericho;
There were walnuts, chestnuts, berries, brachen,
Brushwood for savage gruel and medicine.
The woods are pernicious gods,
And the mountains are a dead hymn,
But the hills could father us if we knew them.

The rivers, bays, ponds, the isthmus,
The animal mouths of the lakes
Were still raw from ocean and disuse.
The Niagara River has the leap of the mountain cat;
The St. Lawrence rises in great sheets of water,
The Superior and the Illinois empty into the Huron,
But where is our source?
The Erie pours into Lake Frontenac,
And as it dwindles it is known as the Niagara River,
But what is our name?
The Outaoutantoi is a large branch of the Fatal River.
Know that the journey is to be made alone.
What right have we to the old funeral mounds,
The mastodons of Ohio,

283

And the bones of tigers in the Carolina savannas?
Are we the woolly cattle of the Platte,
Scythian beast, with mad, hirsute head,
And a war-hump between its shoulders,
Stupid, battle animals of the mesa?

North America is the February hemisphere
With rivers and skies of great water claws,
And bluffs that are steep rapids.
The woods lie close to the soul,
And only the moon to light its lakes
And oppose its shaggy head-winds.
There is no roadstead,
No passage out
Save beyond the furied bar outside Caudebac.

II

La Salle adopted the same sea-vein
As Colón, De Soto, Cortés.
The voyage was mild,
All sorrows were in the latitude of Finisterre.
But where is the gentlest zone for human anguish?
The Island of Pines abounds in turtle-doves, parrots,
And among the trees run wild swine,
Ithaca for homecoming Odysseus.
But the soldiers of La Salle disembarked,
And boiling an alligator ate of it.

February is the month of private dying;
The corn-seed of the Illinois tribe
Was interred in the ground;
It is the time for hiding the mother
In the funeral blankets;
The prairie sleeps,
And the huts of sewn flat reeds
Are warmed by fires of bison-dung.
In March the barrow greens,
And the rocks awaken,
And the mud chants;

Ruined snows produce worms.
Men cure their hopes by patience,
Which is the springing up of sod and sprouting;
Destiny has the February stone,
And man is naked until his Nemesis,
And the journey to his great waters.

The Illinois chief, Chassagoac,
Warned La Salle to shun the great river,
Cumber'd with bars, rapids, and serpents.
Each neighbor counsels man to flee his soul
And be content with a journal of gullet and discharge.
Save for the rains and ice
The Mississippi has a mild mother's bosom,
And loins, two leagues in breadth,
Of love and forgiveness.

Walt Whitman

Sing the Alpha forest gods,
Sorrel, purslane, and the uncured sassafras;
We forsook the soft, doved waters of Venus and Daphne,
And the oaks of Ilium
To quarry our Ghost in the marsh.
Concord was unsown violets and bog-cress;
At Nona the waters smelled of the fox.
Sorrow was our father and hope;
Penury sang in our pockets.
We sowed affliction in rank marl,
And called this Adam's ground.
Then came the cities of Cush and Ham,
And the granaries of shrewd Pul.

The midwest was a Mesopotamian corral for Laban;
Omaha, a stable for the cattle of Job;
Roanoke and St. Joseph were as Erech and Calneh;
The Missouri was laden with the boats of Tarshish.
Togmarah sold mules and horses to Kansas City,

The mart for the melons and the leeks
That shone as emeralds in Paradise.
Venus came from the bins of Joplin,
Fragrant with rye, oats and papaw.

There was a man named Walt Whitman,
Prophetic goat and Buddha of the states,
An evangelist of the rank gullet,
And the pagan works of Phallus.
An Old Testament Balaam was he,
And as lickerous as the Angels
Who parted the thighs of the daughters of men.
He strode the cities of Shinar
As though they were the oaks at Mamre.
At Sodom he sat at the gates as Lot,
Strewing his affections as palms and boughs.
Gaza and Akkad comforted his navel.

Every aged man was father Adam;
He went soft upon the ground
Lest he trample Abel's blood.
Among the thorns he grieved anew for Manasseh.
Did the Pharisee he kissed moult the canting hands?
Nimrod has giant laughing shoulders
Which hide the sinews of Cain.

We cannot bear each other,
For we are immense territory,
And our malignant folly was to mew us up in cities,
And take away our ocean past.
For the sign of Cain is solitude,
And he that goes in the earth apart
Grieves as the worm.

We are still mostly landless,
And a water people,
For we are not yet earth-born children,
And our Abraham, Isaac and Jacob
Are New Mexico, Arizona and Texas,
Residual sand and flood clay,

And the red that came out of it,
Iroquois and Algonquin,
Which means the blood, we slew.
Now the long wastes of flats,
And the terrible inland oceans
Are like our fierce black and gray burial cities.
The country is still more than half whale,
For we go to water quicker than to fire or to blood,
And we are a kinless people
Still suffering for the flood sins.
Whitman, our Adam, has died in our loins.

YVOR WINTERS

(1900–1968)

Two Songs of Advent

I

On the desert, between pale mountains, our cries—
Far whispers creeping through an ancient shell.

II

Coyote, on delicate mocking feet,
Hovers down the canyon, among the mountains,
His voice running wild in the wind's valleys.

Listen! listen! for I enter now your thought.

The Magpie's Shadow

O saisons, ô châteaux!

I. IN WINTER

Myself
Pale mornings, and
I rise.

Still Morning
Snow air—my fingers curl.

Awakening
New snow, O pine of dawn!

Winter Echo
Thin air! My mind is gone.

The Hunter
Run! in the magpie's shadow.

No Being
I, bent. Thin nights receding.

II. IN SPRING

Spring
I walk out the world's door.

May
Oh, evening in my hair!

Spring Rain
My doorframe smells of leaves.

Song
Why should I stop
for spring?

III. IN SUMMER AND AUTUMN

Sunrise
Pale bees! Oh, whither now?

Fields
I did not pick
a flower.

At Evening
Like leaves my feet passed by.

Cool Nights
At night bare feet on flowers!

Sleep
Like winds my eyelids close.

The Aspen's Song
The summer holds me here.

The Walker
In dream my feet are still.

Blue Mountain
A deer walks that mountain.

God of Roads
I, peregrine of noon.

September
Faint gold! O think not here!

A Lady
She's sun on autumn leaves.

Alone
I saw day's shadow strike.

A Deer
The trees rose in the dawn.

Man in Desert
His feet run as eyes blink.

Desert
The tented autumn, gone!

The End
Dawn rose, and desert shrunk.

High Valleys
In sleep I filled these lands.

Awaiting Snow
The well of autumn—dry.

The Solitude of Glass

No ferns, but
Fringed rock
Spreads on hills
To cover us.

On stone of pollen
At the bend of sight
Stiff rocks
Cast violet eyes

Like rays of shadow,
Roam
Impenetrable
In a cold of glass—

The sun, a lichen
Spreading on the sky
For days
Behind the cold;

The burros,
Like iron-filings
Gathered to
The adamant.

October

The houses
Are more bare
And nothing
Dims the hills.

October
Comes and goes
And in the moonlight
I wait for winter.

The silence
Is like moonlight
In one thing:
That it hides nothing.

Vacant Lot

Tough hair like dead
grass over new and
hooves quick and
impatient the he-goat
looks round him
over frozen mud

                    but
          finds no mate

                    hardeyed
          and savage he
          turns back and nips
          the bitter grass

The Cold

Frigidity the hesitant
uncurls its tentacles
into a furry sun.
The ice expands
into an insecurity
that should appal
yet I remain, a son
of stone and of a
commentary, I, an epitaph,
astray in this
oblivion, this
inert labyrinth
of sentences that
dare not end. It
is high noon and
all is the more quiet
where I trace
the courses of the Crab
and Scorpion, the Bull,
the Hunter, and the Bear—
with front of steel
they cut an aperture
so clear across the
cold that it cannot
be seen: there is no
smoky breath, no
breath at all.

Nocturne

Moonlight on stubbleshining
hills
whirls down upon me finer than geometry
and at my very
eyes it blurs and softens like a dream

In leafblack houses
linen smooth with sleep
and folded by cold life itself for limbs so definite

their passion is
persistent like a pane of glass

about their feet the clustered
birds are sleeping
heavy with incessant life

The dogs swim close to earth

A kildee rises
dazed and rolled amid the sudden blur of sleep
above the dayglare of the fields
goes screaming
off toward darker hills.

The Barnyard

The wind appears
and disappears
like breath on a mirror
and between the hills
is only cold
that lies
beneath the stones
and in the grass.

The sleeping dog
becomes a
knot of twinging turf.
It was the
spring that left
this rubbish
and these scavengers
for ice to kill—
this old man
wrinkled in
the fear of Hell, the
child that staggers
straight into
the clotting cold
with short fierce cries.

Wild Sunflower

Sunflower! gross of leaf and porous,
gummy, raw,
with unclean edges,

                    fury
of the broken but unbeaten
earth, it leers
beside our door!

                Grip
hard to the dry
airy logs, scoured
clean with sun. Hold fast
to what you are, in spite of
the wormseething loam,
the boiling land. And give
me love, slow love
that draws the turgid
loam up into the sun!

                              But
  fiercely this thing
  grows, is hairy, is
  unfinished at the edges,
  gulps the sun and earth, will
  not be beaten
  down nor turn away.

The Realization

Death. Nothing is simpler. One is dead.
The set face now will fade out; the bare fact,
Related movement, regular, intact,
Is reabsorbed, the clay is on the bed.
The soul is mortal, nothing: the dim head
On the dim pillow, less. But thought clings flat
To this, since it can never follow that
Where no precision of the mind is bred.

Nothing to think of between you and All!
Screaming processionals of infinite
Logic are grinding down receding cold!
O fool! Madness again! Turn not, for it
Lurks in each paintless cranny, and you sprawl
Blurring a definition. Quick! you are old.

Apollo and Daphne

Deep in the leafy fierceness of the wood,
Sunlight, the cellular and creeping pyre,
Increased more slowly than aetherial fire:
But it increased and touched her where she stood.
The god had seized her, but the powers of good
Struck deep into her veins; with rending flesh
She fled all ways into the grasses' mesh
And burned more quickly than the sunlight could.

And all her heart broke stiff in leafy flame
That neither rose nor fell, but stood aghast;
And she, rooted in Time's slow agony,
Stirred dully, hard-edged laurel, in the past;
And, like a cloud of silence or a name,
The god withdrew into Eternity.

The Fable

Beyond the steady rock the steady sea,
In movement more immovable than station,
Gathers and washes and is gone. It comes,
A slow obscure metonymy of motion,
Crumbling the inner barriers of the brain.
But the crossed rock braces the hills and makes
A steady quiet of the steady music,
Massive with peace.

And listen, now:
The foam receding down the sand silvers
Between the grains, thin, pure as virgin words,
Lending a sheen to Nothing, whispering.

The Fall of Leaves

The green has suddenly
Divided to pure flame,
Leaf-tongued from tree to tree.
Yea, where we stood it came.

This change may have no name,
Yet it was like a word
Spoken, and none to blame,
Alive where shadow stirred.

So was the instant blurred.
But as we waited there
The slow cry of a bird
Built up a scheme of air.

The vision of despair
Starts at the moment's bound,
Seethes from the vibrant air
With slow autumnal sound

Into the burning ground.

The Slow Pacific Swell

Far out of sight, forever stands the sea,
Bounding the land with pale tranquillity.
When a small child, I watched it from a hill
At thirty miles or more. The vision still
Lies in the eye, soft blue and far away:
The rain has washed the dust from April day;
Paint-brush and lupine lie against the ground;
The wind above the hill-top has the sound
Of distant water in unbroken sky;
Dark and precise, the little steamers ply—
Firm in direction, they seem not to stir.
That is illusion. The artificer
Of quiet, Distance, holds me in a vise
And holds the ocean steady to my eyes.

Once when I rounded Flattery, the sea
Hove its loose weight, like sand, to tangle me
Upon the washing deck, to crush the hull;
Subsiding, dragged flesh at the bone. The skull
Felt the retreating wash of dreaming hair.
Half drenched in dissolution, I lay bare.
I scarcely pulled myself erect; I came
Back slowly, slowly knew myself the same.
That was the ocean. From the ship we saw

Grey whales for miles. The long sweep of the jaw,
The blunt head plunging clean above the wave.
And one rose in a tent of sea and gave
A darkening shudder; water fell away;
The whale stood shining, and then sunk in spray.

A landsman, I. The sea is but a sound.
I would be near it on a sandy mound,
And hear the steady rushing of the deep
While I lay stinging in the sand with sleep.
I have lived inland long. The land is numb.
It stands beneath the feet, and one may come
Walking securely, till the sea extends
Its limber margin, and precision ends.
By night a chaos of commingling power,
The whole Pacific hovers hour by hour.
The slow Pacific swell stirs on the sand,
Sleeping to sink away, withdrawing land,
Heaving and wrinkled in the moon, and blind,
Or gathers seaward, ebbing out of mind.

To a Young Writer

Achilles Holt: Stanford, 1930

Here for a few short years
Strengthen affections; meet,
Later, the dull arrears
Of age, and be discreet.

The angry blood burns low.
Some friend of lesser mind
Discerns you not; but so
Your solitude's defined.

Write little; do it well.
Your knowledge will be such,
At last, as to dispel
What moves you overmuch.

By the Road to the Sunnyvale Air-Base

The calloused grass lies hard
Against the cracking plain:
Life is a grayish stain;
The salt-marsh hems my yard.

Dry dikes rise hill on hill:
In sloughs of tidal slime
Shell-fish deposit lime,
Wild sea-fowl creep at will.

The highway, like a beach,
Turns whiter, shadowy, dry:
Loud, pale against the sky,
The bombing planes hold speech.

Yet fruit grows on the trees;
Here scholars pause to speak;
Through gardens bare and Greek,
I hear my neighbor's bees.

Elegy on a Young Airedale Bitch
Lost Two Years Since in the Salt-Marsh

Low to the water's edge
You plunged: the tangled herb
Locked feet and mouth, a curb
Tough with the salty sedge.

Half dog and half a child,
Sprung from that roaming bitch,
You flung through dike and ditch,
Betrayed by what was wild.

The old dogs now are dead,
Tired with the hunt and cold,
Sunk in the earth and old.
But your bewildered head,

Led by what heron cry,
Lies by what tidal stream?—
Drenched with ancestral dream,
And cast ashore to dry.

On Teaching the Young

The young are quick of speech.
Grown middle-aged, I teach
Corrosion and distrust,
Exacting what I must.

A poem is what stands
When imperceptive hands,
Feeling, have gone astray.
It is what one should say.

Few minds will come to this.
The poet's only bliss
Is in cold certitude—
Laurel, archaic, rude.

Time and the Garden

The spring has darkened with activity.
The future gathers in vine, bush, and tree:
Persimmon, walnut, loquat, fig, and grape,
Degrees and kinds of color, taste, and shape.
These will advance in their due series, space
The season like a tranquil dwelling-place.
And yet excitement swells me, vein by vein:
I long to crowd the little garden, gain
Its sweetness in my hand and crush it small
And taste it in a moment, time and all!
These trees, whose slow growth measures off my years,
I would expand to greatness. No one hears,

And I am still retarded in duress!
And this is like that other restlessness
To seize the greatness not yet fairly earned,
One which the tougher poets have discerned—
Gascoigne, Ben Jonson, Greville, Raleigh, Donne,
Poets who wrote great poems, one by one,
And spaced by many years, each line an act
Through which few labor, which no men retract.
This passion is the scholar's heritage,
The imposition of a busy age,
The passion to condense from book to book
Unbroken wisdom in a single look,
Though we know well that when this fix the head,
The mind's immortal, but the man is dead.

In Praise of California Wines

Amid these clear and windy hills
Heat gathers quickly and is gone;
Dust rises, moves, and briefly stills;
Our thought can scarcely pause thereon.

With pale bright leaf and shadowy stem,
Pellucid amid nervous dust,
By pre-Socratic stratagem,
Yet sagging with its weight of must,

The vineyard spreads beside the road
In repetition, point and line.
I sing, in this dry bright abode,
The praises of the native wine.

It yields the pleasure of the eye,
It charms the skin, it warms the heart;
When nights are cold and thoughts crowd high,
Then 'tis the solvent for our art.

When worn for sleep the head is dull,
When art has failed us, far behind,
Its sweet corruption fills the skull
Till we are happy to be blind.

So may I yet, as poets use,
My time being spent, and more to pay,
In this quick warmth the will diffuse,
In sunlight vanish quite away.

To the Moon

Goddess of poetry,
Maiden of icy stone
With no anatomy,
Between us two alone
Your light falls thin and sure
On all that I propound.

Your service I have found
To be no sinecure;
For I must still inure
My words to what I find,
Though it should leave me blind
Ere I discover how.

What brings me here? Old age.
Here is the written page.
What is your pleasure now?

STERLING A. BROWN

(1901–1989)

Long Gone

I laks yo' kin' of lovin',
   Ain't never caught you wrong,
But it jes' ain' nachal
   Fo' to stay here long;

It jes' ain' nachal
   Fo' a railroad man,
With a itch fo' travelin'
   He cain't understan'. . . .

I looks at de rails,
   An' I looks at de ties,
An' I hears an ole freight
   Puffin' up de rise,

An' at nights on my pallet,
   When all is still,
I listens fo' de empties
   Bumpin' up de hill;

When I oughta be quiet,
   I is got a itch
Fo' to hear de whistle blow
   Fo' de crossin' or de switch,

An' I knows de time's a-nearin'
   When I got to ride,
Though it's homelike and happy
   At yo' side.

You is done all you could do
   To make me stay;
'Tain't no fault of yours I'se leavin'—
   I'se jes dataway.

I don't know which way I'm travelin'—
   Far or near,

All I knows fo' certain is
   I cain't stay here.

Ain't no call at all, sweet woman,
   Fo' to carry on—
Jes' my name and jes' my habit
   To be Long Gone. . . .

Scotty Has His Say

Whuh folks, whuh folks; don' wuk muh brown too hahd!

   'Cause Ise crazy 'bout muh woman,
   An' ef yuh treats huh mean,
   I gonna sprinkle goofy dus'
   In yo' soup tureen.

Whuh folks, whuh folks; don' wuk muh brown too hahd!
Muh brown what's tendin' chillen in yo' big backyahd.

   Oh, dat gal is young an' tender.
   So jes' don' mistreat huh please,
   Or I'll put a sprig of pisen ivy
   In yo' B.V.D.'s.

   I got me a Blackcat's wishbone,
   Got some Blackcat's ankle dus',
   An' yuh crackers better watch out
   Ef I sees yo' carcass fus'—

Whuh folks, whuh folks; don' wuk muh brown too hahd!
Muh brown what's wringin' chicken necks in yo' backyahd.

   'Cause muh brown an' me, we'se champeens
   At de St. Luke's Hall;
   An' yo' cookin' an' yo' washin'
   Jes' ain't in it, not at all,

   Wid de way we does de Chahlston,
   De Black Bottom an' cake walkin',
   Steppin' on de puppies' tail;
   Whuh folks, ain' no need in talkin',—

You is got muh purty brownskin
In yo' kitchen an' yo' yahd,
Lemme tell yuh rebs one sho thing
Doncha wuk muh brown too hahd—

Whuh folks, whuh folks; don' wuk muh brown too hahd!
Who's practisin' de Chahlston in yo' big backyahd.

Sister Lou

Honey
When de man
Calls out de las' train
You're gonna ride,
Tell him howdy.

Gather up yo' basket
An' yo' knittin' an' yo' things,
An' go on up an' visit
Wid frien' Jesus fo' a spell.

Show Marfa
How to make yo' greengrape jellies,
An' give po' Lazarus
A passel of them Golden Biscuits.

Scald some meal
Fo' some rightdown good spoonbread
Fo' li'l box-plunkin' David.

An' sit aroun'
An' tell them Hebrew Chillen
All yo' stories. . . .

Honey
Don't be feared of them pearly gates,
Don't go 'round to de back,
No mo' dataway
Not evah no mo'.

Let Michael tote yo' burden
An' yo' pocketbook an' evahthing
'Cept yo' Bible,
While Gabriel blows somp'n
Solemn but loudsome
On dat horn of his'n.

Honey
Go straight on to de Big House,
An' speak to yo' God
Widout no fear an' tremblin'.

Then sit down
An' pass de time of day awhile.

Give a good talkin' to
To yo' favorite 'postle Peter,
An' rub the po' head
Of mixed-up Judas,
An' joke awhile wid Jonah.

Then, when you gits de chance,
Always rememberin' yo' raisin',
Let 'em know youse tired
Jest a mite tired.

Jesus will find yo' bed fo' you
Won't no servant evah bother wid yo' room.
Jesus will lead you
To a room wid windows
Openin' on cherry trees an' plum trees
Bloomin' everlastin'.

An' dat will be yours
Fo' keeps.

Den take yo' time. . . .
Honey, take yo' bressed time.

Southern Road

Swing dat hammer—hunh—
Steady, bo';
Swing dat hammer—hunh—
Steady, bo';
Ain't no rush, bebby,
Long ways to go.

Burner tore his—hunh—
Black heart away;
Burner tore his—hunh—
Black heart away;
Got me life, bebby,
An' a day.

Gal's on Fifth Street—hunh—
Son done gone;
Gal's on Fifth Street—hunh—
Son done gone;
Wife's in de ward, bebby,
Babe's not bo'n.

My ole man died—hunh—
Cussin' me;
My ole man died—hunh—
Cussin' me;
Ole lady rocks, bebby,
Huh misery.

Doubleshackled—hunh—
Guard behin';
Doubleshackled—hunh—
Guard behin';
Ball an' chain, bebby,
On my min'.

White man tells me—hunh—
Damn yo' soul;
White man tells me—hunh—

Damn yo' soul;
Got no need, bebby,
To be tole.

Chain gang nevah—hunh—
Let me go;
Chain gang nevah—hunh—
Let me go;
Po' los' boy, bebby,
Evahmo'. . . .

Memphis Blues

I

Nineveh, Tyre,
Babylon,
Not much lef'
Of either one.
All dese cities
Ashes and rust,
De win' sing sperrichals
Through deir dus'. . .
Was another Memphis
Mongst de olden days,
Done been destroyed
In many ways. . . .
Dis here Memphis
It may go;
Floods may drown it;
Tornado blow;
Mississippi wash it
Down to sea—
Like de other Memphis in
History.

2

Watcha gonna do when Memphis on fire,
   Memphis on fire, Mistah Preachin' Man?
Gonna pray to Jesus and nebber tire,
   Gonna pray to Jesus, loud as I can,
      Gonna pray to my Jesus, oh, my Lawd!

Watcha gonna do when de tall flames roar,
   Tall flames roar, Mistah Lovin' Man?
Gonna love my brownskin better'n before—
   Gonna love my baby lak a do right man,
      Gonna love my brown baby, oh, my Lawd!

Watcha gonna do when Memphis falls down,
   Memphis falls down, Mistah Music Man?
Gonna plunk on dat box as long as it soun',
   Gonna plunk dat box fo' to beat de ban',
      Gonna tickle dem ivories, oh, my Lawd!

Watcha gonna do in de hurricane,
   In de hurricane, Mistah Workin' Man?
Gonna put dem buildings up again,
   Gonna put em up dis time to stan',
      Gonna push a wicked wheelbarrow, oh, my Lawd!

Watcha gonna do when Memphis near gone,
   Memphis near gone, Mistah Drinkin' Man?
Gonna grab a pint bottle of Mountain Corn,
   Gonna keep de stopper in my han',
      Gonna get a mean jag on, oh, my Lawd!

Watcha gonna do when de flood roll fas',
   Flood roll fas', Mistah Gamblin' Man?
Gonna pick up my dice fo' one las' pass—
   Gonna fade my way to de lucky lan',
      Gonna throw my las' seven—oh, my Lawd!

3

Memphis go
By Flood or Flame;
Nigger won't worry
All de same—
Memphis go
Memphis come back,
Ain' no skin
Off de nigger's back.
All dese cities
Ashes, rust. . . .
De win' sing sperrichals
Through deir dus'.

Ma Rainey

1

When Ma Rainey
Comes to town,
Folks from anyplace
Miles aroun',
From Cape Girardeau,
Poplar Bluff,
Flocks in to hear
Ma do her stuff;
Comes flivverin' in,
Or ridin' mules,
Or packed in trains,
Picknickin' fools. . . .
That's what it's like,
Fo' miles on down,
To New Orleans delta
An' Mobile town,
When Ma hits
Anywheres aroun'.

2

Dey comes to hear Ma Rainey from de little river settlements,
From blackbottom cornrows and from lumber camps;
Dey stumble in de hall, jes' a-laughin' an' a-cacklin',
Cheerin' lak roarin' water, lak wind in river swamps.

An' some jokers keeps deir laughs a-goin' in de crowded
        aisles,
An' some folks sits dere waitin' wid deir aches an' miseries,
Till Ma comes out before dem, a-smilin' gold-toofed smiles
An' Long Boy ripples minors on de black an' yellow keys.

3

O Ma Rainey,
Sing yo' song;
Now you's back
Whah you belong,
Git way inside us,
Keep us strong. . . .
O Ma Rainey,
Li'l an' low;
Sing us 'bout de hard luck
Roun' our do';
Sing us 'bout de lonesome road
We mus' go. . . .

4

I talked to a fellow, an' the fellow say,
"She jes' catch hold of us, somekindaway.
She sang Backwater Blues one day:
        'It rained fo' days an' de skies was dark as night,
        Trouble taken place in de lowlands at night.

        'Thundered an' lightened an' the storm begin to roll
        Thousan's of people ain't got no place to go.

        'Den I went an' stood upon some high ol' lonesome hill,
        An' looked down on the place where I used to live.'

An' den de folks, dey natchally bowed dey heads an' cried,
Bowed dey heavy heads, shet dey moufs up tight an' cried,
An' Ma lef' de stage, an' followed some de folks outside."

Dere wasn't much more de fellow say:
She jes' gits hold of us dataway.

Slim in Atlanta

Down in Atlanta,
  De whitefolks got laws
For to keep all de niggers
  From laughin' outdoors.

      Hope to Gawd I may die
        If I ain't speakin' truth
      Make de niggers do deir laughin'
        In a telefoam booth.

Slim Greer hit de town
  An' de rebs got him told,—
"Dontcha laugh on de street,
  If you want to die old."

      Den dey showed him de booth,
        An' a hundred shines
      In front of it, waitin'
        In double lines.

Slim thought his sides
  Would bust in two,
Yelled, "Lookout, everybody,
  I'm coming through!"

      Pulled de other man out,
        An' bust in de box,
      An' laughed four hours
        By de Georgia clocks.

Den he peeked through de door,
    An' what did he see?
Three hundred niggers there
    In misery.—

            Some holdin' deir sides,
                Some holdin' deir jaws,
            To keep from breakin'
                De Georgia laws.

An' Slim gave a holler,
    An' started again;
An' from three hundred throats
    Come a moan of pain.

            An' everytime Slim
                Saw what was outside,
            Got to whoopin' again
                Till he nearly died.

An' while de poor critters
    Was waitin' deir chance,
Slim laughed till dey sent
    Fo' de ambulance.

            De state paid de railroad
                To take him away;
            Den, things was as usural
                In Atlanta, Gee A.

Children's Children

When they hear
These songs, born of the travail of their sires,
Diamonds of song, deep buried beneath the weight
Of dark and heavy years;
They laugh.

When they hear
Saccharine melodies of loving and its fevers,
Soft-flowing lies of love everlasting;
Conjuring divinity out of gross flesh itch;
They sigh
And look goggle-eyed
At one another.

They have forgotten, they have never known,
Long days beneath the torrid Dixie sun
In miasma'd riceswamps;
The chopping of dried grass, on the third go round
In strangling cotton;
Wintry nights in mud-daubed makeshift huts,
With these songs, sole comfort.

They have forgotten
What had to be endured—

That they, babbling young ones,
With their paled faces, coppered lips,
And sleek hair cajoled to Caucasian straightness,
Might drown the quiet voice of beauty
With sensuous stridency;

And might, on hearing these memoirs of their sires,
Giggle,
And nudge each other's satin clad
Sleek sides. . . .

Chillen Get Shoes

Hush little Lily,
    Don't you cry;
You'll get your silver slippers
    Bye and bye.

Moll wears silver slippers
    With red heels,
And men come to see her
    In automobiles.

Lily walks wretched,
    Dragging her doll,
Worshipping stealthily
    Good-time Moll;

Envying bitterly
    Moll's fine clothes,
And her plump legs clad
    In openwork hose.

Don't worry, Lily,
    Don't you cry;
You'll be like Moll, too,
    Bye and bye.

Sporting Beasley

Good glory, give a look at Sporting Beasley
Strutting, oh my Lord.

Tophat cocked one side his bulldog head,
Striped four-in-hand, and in his buttonhole
A red carnation; Prince Albert coat
Form-fitting, corset like; vest snugly filled,
Gray morning trousers, spotless and full-flowing,
White spats and a cane.

Step it, Mr. Beasley, oh step it till the sun goes down.

Forget the snippy clerks you wait upon,
Tread clouds of glory above the heads of pointing
    children,
Oh, Mr. Peacock, before the drab barnfowl of the world.

Forget the laughter when at the concert
You paced down the aisle, your majesty,
Down to Row A, where you pulled out your opera
     glasses.

Majesty. . . .

It's your turn now, Sporting Beasley,
Step it off.

The world is a ragbag; the world
Is full of heathens who haven't seen the light;
Do it, Mr. Missionary.

Great glory, give a look.

Oh Jesus, when this brother's bill falls due,
When he steps off the chariot
And flicks the dust from his patent leathers with his silk
     handkerchief,
When he stands in front of the jasper gates, patting his
     tie,

And then paces in
Cane and knees working like well-oiled slow-timed
     pistons;

Lord help us, give a *look* at him.

Don't make him dress up in no night gown, Lord.
Don't put no fuss and feathers on his shoulders, Lord.

Let him know it's heaven.

Let him keep his hat, his vest, his elkstooth, and
     everything.

Let him have his spats and cane
Let him have his spats and cane.

Cabaret

(*1927, Black & Tan Chicago*)

Rich, flashy, puffy-faced,
Hebrew and Anglo-Saxon,
The overlords sprawl here with their glittering darlings.
The smoke curls thick, in the dimmed light
Surreptitiously, deaf-mute waiters
Flatter the grandees,
Going easily over the rich carpets,
Wary lest they kick over the bottles
Under the tables.

The jazzband unleashes its frenzy.

> *Now, now,*
> *To it, Roger; that's a nice doggie,*
> *Show your tricks to the gentlemen.*

The trombone belches, and the saxophone
Wails curdlingly, the cymbals clash,
The drummer twitches in an epileptic fit

> Muddy water
> Round my feet
> Muddy water

The chorus sways in.
The 'Creole Beauties from New Orleans'
(By way of Atlanta, Louisville, Washington, Yonkers,
With stop-overs they've used nearly all their lives)
Their creamy skin flushing rose warm,
O, le bal des belles quarteronnes!
Their shapely bodies naked save
For tattered pink silk bodices, short velvet tights,
And shining silver-buckled boots;
Red bandannas on their sleek and close-clipped hair;

To bring to mind (aided by the bottles under the tables)
Life upon the river—

          Muddy water, river sweet

(Lafitte the pirate, instead,
And his doughty diggers of gold)

            There's peace and happiness there
            I declare

(In Arkansas,
Poor half-naked fools, tagged with identification numbers,
Worn out upon the levees,
Are carted back to the serfdom
They had never left before
And may never leave again)

        Bee—dap—ee—DOOP, dee—ba—dee—BOOP

The girls wiggle and twist

      Oh you too,
      Proud high-stepping beauties,
      Show your paces to the gentlemen.
      A prime filly, seh.
      What am I offered, gentlemen, gentlemen. . . .

            I've been away a year today
            To wander and roam
            I don't care if it's muddy there

(Now that the floods recede,
What is there left the miserable folk?
Oh time in abundance to count their losses,
There is so little else to count.)

            Still it's my home, sweet home

From the lovely throats
Moans and deep cries for home:
Nashville, Toledo, Spout Springs, Boston,
Creoles from Germantown;—
The bodies twist and rock;
The glasses are filled up again. . . .

(In Mississippi
The black folk huddle, mute, uncomprehending,
Wondering 'how come the good Lord
Could treat them this a way')

> shelter
> Down in the Delta

(Along the Yazoo
The buzzards fly over, over, low,
Glutted, but with their scrawny necks stretching,
Peering still.)

> I've got my toes turned Dixie ways
> Round that Delta let me laze

The band goes mad, the drummer throws his sticks
At the moon, a *papier-mâché* moon,
The chorus leaps into wierd posturings,
The firm-fleshed arms plucking at grapes to stain
Their coralled mouths; seductive bodies weaving
Bending, writhing, turning

> My heart cries out for
> MUDDY WATER

(Down in the valleys
The stench of the drying mud
Is a bitter reminder of death.)

> Dee da dee DAAAAH

Old Lem

I talked to old Lem
and old Lem said:
    "They weigh the cotton
    They store the corn
        We only good enough
        To work the rows;
    They run the commissary
    They keep the books
        We gotta be grateful
        For being cheated;
    Whippersnapper clerks
    Call us out of our name
        We got to say mister
        To spindling boys
    They make our figgers
    Turn somersets
    We buck in the middle
        Say, "Thankyuh, sah."
        They don't come by ones
        They don't come by twos
        But they come by tens.

    "They got the judges
    They got the lawyers
    They got the jury-rolls
    They got the law
        They don't come by ones
    They got the sheriffs
    They got the deputies
        They don't come by twos
    They got the shotguns
    They got the rope
        We git the justice
        In the end
        And they come by tens.

"Their fists stay closed
Their eyes look straight
   Our hands stay open
   Our eyes must fall
      They don't come by ones
They got the manhood
They got the courage
      They don't come by twos
   We got to slink around
   Hangtailed hounds.
They burn us when we dogs
They burn us when we men
      They come by tens . . .

"I had a buddy
Six foot of man
Muscled up perfect
Game to the heart
      They don't come by ones
Outworked and outfought
Any man or two men
      They don't come by twos
He spoke out of turn
At the commissary
They gave him a day
To git out the county
He didn't take it.
He said 'Come and get me.'
They came and got him
      And they came by tens.
He stayed in the county—
He lays there dead.

      They don't come by ones
      They don't come by twos
      But they come by tens."

ROBERT FRANCIS

(1901–1987)

A Broken View

Newcomers on the hill have cut the trees
That broke their view. Now they have all the west
From north in an unbroken sweep to south.
Outdoors or out of windows looking westward
Anywhere there is the west, the view.
An afternoon ago we stood with them
And saw their view. Hills beyond hills shading
From green to blue and clouds from white to blue.
Open places of pasture on the hills
And sky among the clouds. It was enough
For anyone to love for all a lifetime.

Yet we were thinking (though we didn't say so
And wouldn't of course have said so ever to them
Or even wished to) how we loved a broken
View better, a view broken by trees,
Under and over and through the branches of trees.
A view that didn't give you everything
At once or anything too easily.
One that changed as you went from window to window
And changed again as you went from month to month,
Closing in in spring and opening
In fall.

What we felt was not regret.
We had no sighs for trees that were not there.
Trees grow again in time or others grow
To take their places, more slowly than a house
Is built, but still they grow. Young trees were growing
Among the stumps there even while we looked
Over their heads.
Perhaps we had a view
Through time, like a view trembling through leaves, of a time

323

When not these newcomers but a child of theirs
Or a child of that child living on the hill,
Growing up with trees upon the hill
Might see as we had seen, loving both trees
And view, loving them more each for the other.

Onion Fields

Far inland from the sea the onion fields
Flow as the sea flows level to the sky.
Something blue of the sea is in their green.
Something bright of the sun on little waves
Of water is in the ripple of their leaves.
Stand with me here awhile until the white
Kerchiefs of the weeding women are whitecaps
And the long red barns boats—until there are
Only boats and whitecaps and white clouds
And a blue-green sea off to the blue of sky.
Wind from the onion fields is welcomer
Than any sweetness. We stand and breathe as we stand
On a shore and breathe the saltness of the sea.

Earthworm

My spading fork turning the earth turns
This fellow out—without touching him this time.
Robbed of all resistance to his progress
He squirms awhile in the too-easy air
Before an ancient and implicit purpose
Starts him traveling in one direction
Reaching out, contracting, reaching out,
Contracting—a clean and glistening earth-pink.
He has turned more earth than I have with my fork.
He has lifted more earth than all men have or will.
Breaking the earth in spring men break his body.
And it is broken in the beaks of birds.

He has become and will again become
The flying and singing of birds. Yet another spring
I shall find him working noiselessly in the earth.
When I am earth again he will be there.

Slow

I have been watching slow things the long afternoon,
The thickening pad of snow out on the windowsill
That grows so slowly we can never see it grow
Although we say we can. All that we know is that
It *has* grown and most probably *will* grow so long
As the snow falls. And that is quite enough to know.
Then it will go and that will be a slow thing too
Whether it goes in sun or rain, whether a wind
Is or is not blowing. It always has been so.
And what is slower than this short, gray afternoon?
Slower than the way the sun, almost snowed in,
Begins by being low and ends by being low
And never sets or so it seems? Such a slow sun.
Nor is there much to show for *my* long afternoon
Except perhaps that I've been growing I suppose.
Only the unremarkable growth that must be, though,
Which isn't much, Heaven knows, for anyone to show.

By Night

After midnight I heard a scream.
I was awake. It was no dream.
But whether it was bird of prey
Or prey of bird I could not say.
I never heard that sound by day.

The Curse

Hell is a red barn on a hill
With another hill behind the barn
Of dung. The road is stones and dust
And in the road are harpy-hens,
A hound, bones of cattle, flies.

Suddenly on Sunday morning
Out of the dew and stillness, a voice
Out of the barn God-damning cows
At milking. Whoever passes shivers
In the sun and hurries on.

While I Slept

While I slept, while I slept and the night grew colder
She would come to my room, stepping softly
And draw a blanket about my shoulder
While I slept.

While I slept, while I slept in the dark, still heat
She would come to my bedside, stepping coolly
And smooth the twisted, troubled sheet
While I slept.

Now she sleeps, sleeps under quiet rain
While nights grow warm or nights grow colder.
And I wake, and sleep, and wake again
While she sleeps.

The Sound I Listened For

What I remember is the ebb and flow of sound
That summer morning as the mower came and went
And came again, crescendo and diminuendo,
And always when the sound was loudest how it ceased

A moment while he backed the horses for the turn,
The rapid clatter giving place to the slow click
And the mower's voice. That was the sound I listened for.
The voice did what the horses did. It shared the action
As sympathetic magic does or incantation.
The voice hauled and the horses hauled. The strength of one
Was in the other and in the strength was no impatience.
Over and over as the mower made his rounds
I heard his voice and only once or twice he backed
And turned and went ahead and spoke no word at all.

As Easily As Trees

As easily as trees have dropped
Their leaves, so easily a man,
So unreluctantly, might drop
All rags, ambitions, and regrets
Today and lie with leaves in sun.
So he might sleep while they began,
Falling or blown, to cover him.

Waxwings

Four Tao philosophers as cedar waxwings
chat on a February berrybush
in sun, and I am one.

Such merriment and such sobriety—
the small wild fruit on the tall stalk—
was this not always my true style?

Above an elegance of snow, beneath
a silk-blue sky a brotherhood of four
birds. Can you mistake us?

To sun, to feast, and to converse
and all together—for this I have abandoned
all my other lives.

Pitcher

His art is eccentricity, his aim
How not to hit the mark he seems to aim at,

His passion how to avoid the obvious,
His technique how to vary the avoidance.

The others throw to be comprehended. He
Throws to be a moment misunderstood.

Yet not too much. Not errant, arrant, wild,
But every seeming aberration willed.

Not to, yet still, still to communicate
Making the batter understand too late.

Cypresses

At noon they talk of evening and at evening
Of night, but what they say at night
Is a dark secret.

Somebody long ago called them the Trees
Of Death and they have never forgotten.
The name enchants them.

Always an attitude of solitude
To point the paradox of standing
Alone together.

How many years they have been teaching birds
In little schools, by little skills,
How to be shadows.

Swimmer

I

Observe how he negotiates his way
With trust and the least violence, making
The stranger friend, the enemy ally.
The depth that could destroy gently supports him.
With water he defends himself from water.
Danger he leans on, rests in. The drowning sea
Is all he has between himself and drowning.

II

What lover ever lay more mutually
With his beloved, his always-reaching arms
Stroking in smooth and powerful caresses?
Some drown in love as in dark water, and some
By love are strongly held as the green sea
Now holds the swimmer. Indolently he turns
To float.—The swimmer floats, the lover sleeps.

Farm Boy After Summer

A seated statue of himself he seems.
A bronze slowness becomes him. Patently
The page he contemplates he doesn't see.

The lesson, the long lesson, has been summer.
His mind holds summer as his skin holds sun.
For once the homework, all of it, was done.

What were the crops, where were the fiery fields
Where for so many days so many hours
The sun assaulted him with glittering showers?

Expect a certain absence in his presence.
Expect all winter long a summer scholar,
For scarcely all its snows can cool that color.

Museum Vase

For W. A.

It contains nothing.
We ask it
To contain nothing.

Having transcended use
It is endlessly
Content to be.

Still it broods
On old burdens—
Wheat, oil, wine.

LINDLEY WILLIAMS HUBBELL

(1901–1994)

Ordovician Fossil Algae

This is the oldest book
That I can read with pleasure.
The Cambrian trilobite
Is an unpleasant sight,
As for Pre-Cambrian algae I look and look
And cannot see them, though I'm told they're there.

But these
Exquisite fern-like forms
Printed upon the rock,
These fragile plants that have survived the storms
Of some odd billion years
Move me almost to tears.

So I come here often
To see these delicate stems
Breathed on the rock like frost crystals on a window,
But permanently,
But forever.
This rock is my favorite book, my favorite picture,
My dependable scripture,
My sense of wholeness, a billion years at my elbow.

Sounds

To me the sound of falling rain
Is very beautiful,
But Japanese prefer the sound of snow
Which I can't hear at all.

A student who sat facing me on the Osaka express

Under his persistent look I closed my eyes,
pretending to doze.

When I opened them he was still staring
so I resumed the pose.

Sitting there with closed eyes, I thought:
Look your fill.

I have no defences left
and no concealment. I am what you see,

an old man, twisted and ugly,
and as unconcerned as a tree.

Beer Bottles

Irving Katzenstein told me a poem once
that had been written by a friend of his:

> There are more paintings in the world
> Than empty beer bottles.

I have forgotten the name of the man who wrote it
and now that Irving is gone I'll never know,
but I think of it so often, changing it to:

> There are more poems in the world
> Than empty beer bottles.

So many millions of poems have been written!
What happens to them all? Who reads them?
I remember so many I have loved at one time or another
and then lost somewhere along the way.

I remember a poem by Edgar Fawcett that gave me
some of my most satisfactory sex fantasies
when I was a boy (I found it in the virginal bookcase
of my maiden aunts) and a little later
an exquisite small book in green covers, called
A Cabinet of Jade, by David O'Neil
(he was George O'Neil's uncle and now they are both
        forgotten)
then there were the wonderful poems of Walter Conrad
        Arensberg,
now forgotten, though he himself is not,
being the most illustrious collector of Duchamp
(he also had some very peculiar theories about Dante and
        Shakespeare)
and there was Mina Loy, whom Ezra Pound
considered as good a poet as Marianne Moore,
now quite forgotten (she might make a come-back, though)
and there were the six-syllable poems of Yvor Winters,
the dada poems of Louis Aragon
and of Elsa, Baroness von Freytag-Loringhoven,
and that great-souled woman, Charlotte Perkins Stetson,
who wrote the poem about the recalcitrant butterfly:

> I do not want to be a fly!
> I want to be a worm!

and the New England woman, whoever she was, who wrote:

> I don't know whether I'm High Church
> And I don't know whether I'm Low.

and I remember a lovely poem by Helen Frazee-Bower
who disappointed me when I rediscovered her forty years
        later
by having become a tub-thumping, come-to-Jesus evangelist,
and a noble poem by George Brandon Saul who afterwards
did something about Yeats, the last I heard of him
he was working in an advertising agency in Hartford.

And there are the long poems:

> "between 1650 and 1670
> French poets produced as many as
> forty epic poems"

and the English are not far behind. Who reads them?
Who reads, for example, Sir Richard Blackmore?
As for me, for *The Light of Asia* and *Towards Democracy*
I would gladly sacrifice:

> *Paradise Lost*
> *Paradise Regained*
> *The Prelude*
> and *The Excursion*

and Sir Christopher Hatton wrote *The Silver Swan*.
There is no greater lyric poem in English.
He must have written lots of other poems.
What happened to them all? Where are they now?

Beer bottles . . .   beer bottles . . .

Waka

> I am not a person.
> I am a succession of persons
> Held together by memory.
>
> When the string breaks,
> The beads are scattered.

LAURA RIDING

(1901–1991)

An Ancient Revisits

They told me, when I lived, because my art
To them seemed wide and spacious as the air,
That time would be pervaded everywhere
With it, until no work would have a part
That had not once awakened in my heart,
That everything would crooked be or fair
As it inherited its proper share
From me and could that share again impart.
But this strange present world is not of me.
If I could find somewhere a secret sign,
That one might say: In this an Ancient sings,
I should acknowledge then my legacy
And love to call this modern fabric mine.
Perhaps, once, in my sleep, I dreamed such things?

As Well As Any Other

As well as any other, Erato,
I can dwell separately on what we know
In common secrecy,
And celebrate the old, adoréd rose,
Retell—oh why—how similarly grows
The last leaf of the tree.

But for familiar sense what need can be
Of my most singular device or me,
If homage may be done
(Unless it is agreed we shall not break
The patent silence for mere singing's sake)
As well by anyone?

Mistrust me not, then, if I have begun
Unwontedly and if I seem to shun
Unstrange and much-told ground:
For in peculiar earth alone can I
Construe the word and let the meaning lie
That rarely may be found.

Prisms

What is beheld through glass seems glass.

The quality of what I am
Encases what I am not,
Smoothes the strange world.
I perceive it slowly,
In my time,
In my material,
As my pride,
As my possession:
The vision is love.

When life crashes like a cracked pane,
Still shall I love
Even the strange dead as the living once.
Death also sees, though distantly,
And I must trust then as now
A prism—of another kind,
Through which one may not put one's hands to touch.

Lucrece and Nara

Astonished stood Lucrece and Nara,
Face flat to face, one sense and smoothness.
'Love, is this face or flesh,
Love, is this you?'
One breath drew the dear lips close

And whispered,
'Nara, is there a miracle can last?'
'Lucrece, is there a simple thing can stay?'

Unnoticed as a single raindrop
Broke each dawn until
Blindness as the same day fell.
'How is the opalescence of my white hand, Nara?
Is it still pearly-cool?'
'How is the faintness of my neck, Lucrece?
Is it blood shy with warmth, as always?'

Ghostly they clung and questioned
A thousand years, not yet eternal,
True to their fading,
Through their long watch defying
Time to make them whole, to part them.

A gentle clasp and fragrance played and hung
A thousand years and more
Around earth closely.
'Earth will be long enough,
Love has no elsewhere.'

And when earth ended, was devoured
One shivering midsummer
At the dissolving border,
A sound of light was felt.
'Nara, is it you, the dark?'
'Lucrece, is it you, the quiet?'

O Vocables of Love

O vocables of love,
O zones of dreamt responses
Where wing on wing folds in
The negro centuries of sleep
And the thick lips compress
Compendiums of silence—

Throats claw the mirror of blind triumph,
Eyes pursue sight into the heart of terror.
Call within call
Succumbs to the indistinguishable
Wall within wall
Embracing the last crushed vocable,
The spoken unity of efforts.

O vocables of love,
The end of an end is an echo,
A last cry follows a last cry.
Finality of finality
Is perfection's touch of folly.
Ruin unfolds from ruin.
A remnant breeds a universe of fragment.
Horizons spread intelligibility
And once more it is yesterday.

Faith Upon the Waters

A ghost rose when the waves rose,
When the waves sank stood columnwise
And broken: archaic is
The spirituality of sea,
Water haunted by an imagination
Like fire previously.

More ghost when no ghost,
When the waves explain
Eye to the eye

And dolphins tease,
And the ventriloquist gulls
Their angular three-element cries.

Fancy ages.
A death-bed restlessness inflames the mind
And a warm mist attacks the face
With mortal premonition.

Sea, False Philosophy

Foremost of false philosophies,
The sea harangues the daft,
The possessed logicians of romance.
Their swaying gaze, that swaying mass
Embrace in everlasting loss—
Sea is the spurned dust
Sifted with fine renunciation
Into a metaphor,
A slow dilution.

The drifting rhythms mesmerize
The speechless book of dreams.
The lines intone but are not audible.
The course is overtrue and knows
Neither a wreckage nor a sequel.

Optimisms in despair
Embark upon this apathetic frenzy.
Brains baffled in their eyes
Rest on this picture of monotony
And swoon with thanks.
Ah, hearts whole so peculiarly,
Heaven keep you by such argument
Persuaded and unbroken,
Heaven keep you if it can
As visions widen to a watery zero
And prophecy expands into extinction.

The Map of Places

The map of places passes.
The reality of paper tears.
Land and water where they are
Are only where they were
When words read *here* and *here*
Before ships happened there.

Now on naked names feet stand,
No geographies in the hand,
And paper reads anciently,
And ships at sea
Turn round and round.
All is known, all is found.
Death meets itself everywhere.
Holes in maps look through to nowhere.

Chloe or . . .

Chloe or her modern sister, Lil,
Stepping one day over the fatal sill,
Will say quietly: 'Behold the waiting equipage!'
Or whistle Hello and end an age.

For both these girls have that cold ease
Of women overwooed, half-won, hard to please.
Death is one more honour they accept
Quizzically, ladies adept

In hiding what they feel, if they feel at all.
It can scarcely have the importance of a ball,
Is less impressive than the least man
Chloe, smiling, turns pale, or Lil tweaks with her fan.

Yet, they have been used so tenderly.
But the embarrassment of the suit will be
Death's not theirs. They will avoid aggression
As usual, be saved by self-possession.

Both of them, or most likely, Lil,
No less immortal, will
Refuse to see anything distressing,
Keep Death, like all the others, guessing.

Take Hands

Take hands.
There is no love now.
But there are hands.
There is no joining now,
But a joining has been
Of the fastening of fingers
And their opening.
More than the clasp even, the kiss
Speaks loneliness,
How we dwell apart,
And how love triumphs in this.

The World and I

This is not exactly what I mean
Any more than the sun is the sun.
But how to mean more closely
If the sun shines but approximately?
What a world of awkwardness!
What hostile implements of sense!
Perhaps this is as close a meaning
As perhaps becomes such knowing.
Else I think the world and I
Must live together as strangers and die—
A sour love, each doubtful whether
Was ever a thing to love the other.
No, better for both to be nearly sure
Each of each—exactly where
Exactly I and exactly the world
Fail to meet by a moment, and a word.

The Wind, the Clock, the We

The wind has at last got into the clock—
Every minute for itself.
There's no more sixty,
There's no more twelve,
It's as late as it's early.

The rain has washed out the numbers.
The trees don't care what happens.
Time has become a landscape
Of suicidal leaves and stoic branches—
Unpainted as fast as painted.
Or perhaps that's too much to say,
With the clock devouring itself
And the minutes given leave to die.

The sea's no picture at all.
To sea, then: that's time now,
And every mortal heart's a sailor
Sworn to vengeance on the wind,
To hurl life back into the thin teeth
Out of which first it whistled,
An idiotic defiance of it knew not what
Screeching round the studying clock.

Now there's neither ticking nor blowing.
The ship has gone down with its men,
The sea with the ship, the wind with the sea.
The wind at last got into the clock,
The clock at last got into the wind,
The world at last got out of itself.

At last we can make sense, you and I,
You lone survivors on paper,
The wind's boldness and the clock's care
Become a voiceless language,
And I the story hushed in it—
Is more to say of me?
Do I say more than self-choked falsity
Can repeat word for word after me,
The script not altered by a breath
Or perhaps meaning otherwise?

Nothing So Far

Nothing so far but moonlight
Where the mind is;
Nothing in that place, this hold,
To hold;
Only their faceless shadows to announce
Perhaps they come—
Nor even do they know
Whereto they cast them.

Yet here, all that remains
When each has been the universe:
No universe, but each, or nothing.
Here is the future swell curved round
To all that was.

What were we, then,
Before the being of ourselves began?
Nothing so far but strangeness
Where the moments of the mind return.
Nearly, the place was lost
In that we went to stranger places.

Nothing so far but nearly
The long familiar pang
Of never having gone;
And words below a whisper which
If tended as the graves of live men should be
May bring their names and faces home.

It makes a loving promise to itself,
Womanly, that there
More presences are promised
Than by the difficult light appear.
Nothing appears but moonlight's morning—
By which to count were as to strew
The look of day with last night's rid of moths.

Divestment of Beauty

She, she and she and she—
Which of these is not lovely?
In her long robe of glamour now
And her beauty like a ribbon tied
The wisdom of her head round?

To call these 'women'
Is homage of the eye:
Such sights to greet as natural,
Such beings to proclaim
Companion to expectance.

But were they now who take
This gaudy franchise from
The accolade of stilted vision
Their lady-swaddlings to unwrap
And shed the timorous scales of nakedness—

It were a loathsome spectacle, you think?
Eventual entrails of deity
Worshipful eye offending?
It were the sign, man,
To pluck the loathsome eye,

Forswear the imbecile
Theology of loveliness,
Be no more doctor in antiquities—
Chimeras of the future
In archaic daze embalmed—

And grow to later youth,
Felling the patriarchal leer
That it lie reft of all obscenities
While she and she, she, she, disclose
The recondite familiar to your candour.

Because of Clothes

Without dressmakers to connect
The good-will of the body
With the purpose of the head,
We should be two worlds
Instead of a world and its shadow
The flesh.

The head is one world
And the body is another—
The same, but somewhat slower
And more dazed and earlier,
The divergence being corrected
In dress.

There is an odour of Christ
In the cloth: below the chin
No harm is meant. Even, immune
From capital test, wisdom flowers
Out of the shaded breast, and the thighs
Are meek.

The union of matter with mind
By the method of raiment
Destroys not our nakedness
Nor muffles the bell of thought.
Merely the moment to its dumb hour
Is joined.

Inner is the glow of knowledge
And outer is the gloom of appearance.
But putting on the cloak and cap
With only the hands and the face showing,
We turn the gloom in and the glow forth
Softly.

Wherefore, by the neutral grace
Of the needle, we possess our triumphs
Together with our defeats
In a single balanced couplement:
We pause between sense and foolishness,
And live.

With the Face

With the face goes a mirror
As with the mind a world.
Likeness tells the doubting eye
That strangeness is not strange.
At an early hour and knowledge
Identity not yet familiar
Looks back upon itself from later,
And seems itself.

To-day seems now.
With reality-to-be goes time.
With the mind goes a world.
With the heart goes a weather.
With the face goes a mirror
As with the body a fear.
Young self goes staring to the wall
Where dumb futurity speaks calm,
And between then and then
Forebeing grows of age.

The mirror mixes with the eye.
Soon will it be the very eye.
Soon will the eye that was
The very mirror be.
Death, the final image, will shine
Transparently not otherwise
Than as the dark sun described
With such faint brightnesses.

ARNA BONTEMPS

(1902–1973)

Reconnaissance

After the cloud embankments,
the lamentation of wind
and the starry descent into time,
we came to the flashing waters and shaded our eyes
from the glare.

Alone with the shore and the harbor,
the stems of the cocoanut trees,
the fronds of silence and hushed music,
we cried for the new revelation
and waited for miracles to rise.

Where elements touch and merge,
where shadows swoon like outcasts on the sand
and the tried moment waits, its courage gone—
there were we

In latitudes where storms are born.

Southern Mansion

Poplars are standing there still as death
and ghosts of dead men
meet their ladies walking
two by two beneath the shade
and standing on the marble steps.

There is a sound of music echoing
through the open door
and in the field there is
another sound tinkling in the cotton:
chains of bondmen dragging on the ground.

The years go back with an iron clank,
a hand is on the gate,
a dry leaf trembles on the wall.
Ghosts are walking.
They have broken roses down
and poplars stand there still as death.

Dark Girl

Easy on your drums,
easy wind and rain,
and softer on your horns—
she will not dance again.

Come easy little leaves
without a ghost of sound
from the China trees
to the fallow ground.

Easy, easy drums
and sweet leaves overhead,
easy wind and rain—
your dancing girl is dead.

A Black Man Talks of Reaping

I have sown beside all waters in my day.
I planted deep, within my heart the fear
that wind or fowl would take the grain away.
I planted safe against this stark, lean year.

I scattered seed enough to plant the land
in rows from Canada to Mexico
but for my reaping only what the hand
can hold at once is all that I can show.

Yet what I sowed and what the orchard yields
my brother's sons are gathering stalk and root;
small wonder then my children glean in fields
they have not sown, and feed on bitter fruit.

KENNETH FEARING

(1902–1961)

Green Light

Bought at the drug store, very cheap; and later pawned.
    After a while, heard on the street; seen in the park.
    Familiar but not quite recognized.
    Followed and taken home and slept with.
    Traded or sold. Or lost.
Bought again at the corner drug store,
    At the green light, at the patient's demand, at nine o'clock.
    Re-read and memorized and re-wound.
    Found unsuitable.
    Smashed, put together, and pawned.
Heard on the street, seen in a dream, heard in the park, seen
      by the light of day,
    Carefully observed one night by a secret agent of the Greek
      Hydraulic Mining Commission, in plain clothes, off
      duty.
    The agent, in broken English, took copious notes. Which
      he lost.
    Strange and yet ordinary.
    Sad, but true.
True; or exaggerated; or true;
    As the people laugh and the sparrows fly;
    As the people change and the sea stays;
    As the people go;
    As the lights go on and it is night, and it is serious, and it is
      just the same;
    As some one dies and it is serious and just the same;
    As a girl knows and it is small; and true;
    As a butcher knows and it is true; and pointless;
    As an old man knows and it is comical; and true;
    As the people laugh, as the people think, as the people
      change,
    It is serious and the same; exaggerated; or true.

Bought at the drug store on the corner
  Where the wind blows and the motors go by and it is night
      or day.
  Bought for the hero's pride.
  Bought to instruct the animals in the zoo.
  Bought to impress the statuary in the park.
  Bought for the spirit of the nation's splendid cultural
      heritage.
  Bought to use as a last resort.
  Bought at a cut rate, at a cheap demand, at the green light,
      at nine o'clock.
  Borrowed or bought, to look well. To ennoble. To prevent
      disease. To have.
  Broken or sold. Or given away.

Evening Song

(For. H. R.)

Go to sleep McKade.
  Fold up the day. It was a bright scarf.
  Put it away.
  Take yourself apart like a house of cards.
It is time to be a grey mouse under a tall building.
  Go there. Go there now.
  Look at the huge nails. Run behind the pipes.
  Scamper in the walls.
  Crawl toward the beckoning girl, her breasts are warm.
  But here is a dead man. A lunatic?
  Kill him with your pistol. Creep past him to the girl.
Sleep, McKade.
  Throw one arm across the bed. Wind your watch.
  You are a gentleman and important.
  Yawn. Go to sleep.
The continent, turning from the sun, is dark and quiet.
  Your ticker waits for tomorrow morning
  And you are alive now.
  It will be a long time before they put McKade under the
      sod.

Sometime, but not now.
Sometime, though. Sometime for certain.
Take apart your brain,
    Close the mouths in it that have been hungry, they are fed
        for a while.
    Go to sleep, you are a gentleman McKade, alive and sane,
    A gentleman of position.
Tip your hat to the lady.
    Speak to the mayor.
    You are a personal friend of the mayor's, are you not?
    True, a friend of the mayor's.
    And you met the Queen of Roumania? True.
Then go to sleep.
    Be a dog sleeping in the old sun.
    Be a dog dreaming in the old sun by the Appian Way.
    Be a dog lying in the meadow watching soldiers pass on the
        road.
    Follow the girl who beckons to you.
    Run from the man with the dagger. It will split your bones.
    Be terrified.
    Curl up and dream on the pavement of Fifth Avenue in the
        old sun.
    Sleep, McKade.
    Yawn. Go to sleep.

1933

You heard the gentleman, with automatic precision, speak the
        truth.
    Cheers. Triumph.
    And then mechanically it followed the gentleman lied.
    Deafening applause. Flashlights, cameras, microphones.
        Floral tribute. Cheers.

Down Mrs. Hogan's alley, your hand with others reaching
        among the ashes, cinders, scrapiron, garbage, you
        found the rib of sirloin wrapped in papal documents.
        Snatched it. Yours by right, the title clear.

Looked up. Saw lips twitch in the smiling head thrust from
the museum window. "A new deal."

And ran. Escaped. You returned the million dollars. You
restored the lady's virginity.
You were decorated 46 times in rapid succession by the
King of Italy. Took a Nobel prize. Evicted again, you
went downtown, slept at the movies, stood in the
breadline, voted yourself a limousine.
Rage seized the Jewish Veterans of Foreign Wars. In
footnotes, capitals, Latin, italics, the poet of the
Sunday supplements voiced steamheated grief. The
RFC expressed surprise.
And the news, at the Fuller Brush hour, leaked out.
Shouts. Cheers. Stamping of feet. Blizzard of confetti.
Thunderous applause.

But the stocks were stolen. The pearls of the actress, stolen
again. The bonds embezzled.
Inexorably, the thief pursued. Captured inexorably. Tried.
Inexorably acquitted.
And again you heard the gentleman, with automatic
precision, speak the truth.
Saw, once more, the lady's virginity restored.

In the sewers of Berlin, the directors prepared, the room dark
for the seance, she a simple Baroness, you a lowly
millionaire, came face to face with John D. Christ.
Shook hands, his knife at your back, your knife at his. Sat
down.
Saw issue from his throat the ectoplasm of Pius VIII, and
heard "A test of the people's faith." You said amen,
voted to endorse but warned against default, you
observed the astral form of Nicholas II, and heard
"Sacred union of all." Saw little "Safe for democracy"
Nell. Listened to Adolph "Safety of France and
society" Thiers.
And beheld the faith, the union of rags, blackened hands,
stacked carrion, breached barricades in flame,

no default, credit restored, Union Carbide 94 3/8, call
    money 10%, disarm, steel five points up, rails rise,
    Dupont up, disarm, disarm, and heard again,
ghost out of ghost out of ghost out of ghost,
the voice of the senator reverberate through all the
    morgues of all the world, echo again for liberty in the
    catacombs of Rome, again sound through the
    sweatshops, ghettoes, factories, mines, hunger again
    repealed, circle the London cenotaph once more
    annulling death, saw ten million dead returned to life,
    shot down again, again restored,

Heard once more the gentleman speak, with automatic
    precision, the final truth,
once more beheld the lady's virginity, the lady's decency,
    the lady's purity, the lady's innocence,
paid for, certified, and restored.

Crawled amorously into bed. Felt among the maggots for the
    mouldering lips. The crumbled arms. Found them.
Tumult of cheers. Music and prayer by the YMCA. Horns,
    rockets. Spotlight.
The child was nursed on government bonds. Cut its teeth
    on a hand grenade. Grew fat on shrapnel. Bullets.
    Barbed wire. Chlorine gas. Laughed at the bayonet
    through its heart.

These are the things you saw and heard, these are the things
    you did, this is your record,
you.

Escape

Acid for the whorls of the fingertips; for the face, a surgeon's
    knife; oblivion to the name;
eyes, hands, color of hair, condition of teeth, habits,
    haunts, the subject's health;
wanted or not, guilty or not guilty, dead or alive, did you
    see this man

Walk in a certain distinctive way through the public streets or
        the best hotels,
    turn and go,
    escape from marshals, sheriffs, collectors, thugs; from the
        landlord's voice or a shake of the head; leave an
        afternoon beer; go from an evening cigar in a
        wellknown scene,
    walk, run, slip from the earth into less than air?

Gone from the teletype, five-feet ten; lost from the headlines,
        middle-aged, grey, posed as a gentleman;
    a drawling voice in a blue serge suit, fled from the radio,
        forehead scarred,

Tear up the letters and bury the clothes, throw away the keys,
        file the number from the gun, burn the record of
        birth, smash the name from the tomb, bathe the
        fingers in acid, wrap the bones in lime,
    forget the street, the house, the name, the day,

But something must be saved from the rise and fall of the
        copper's club; something must be kept from the
        auctioneer's hammer; something must be guarded
        from the rats and the fire on the city dump;
    something, for warmth through the long night of death;
        something to be saved from the last parade through
        granite halls and go, go free, arise with the voice that
        pleads not guilty,
    go with the verdict that ascends forever beyond steel-
        barred windows into blue, deep space,

Guilty of vagrancy, larceny, sedition, assault,
    tried, convicted, sentenced, paroled, imprisoned, released,
        hunted, seized,
    under what name and last seen where? And in what
        disguise did the soiled, fingerprinted, bruised,
        secondhand, worndown, scarred, familiar disguise
        escape?

No name, any name, nowhere, nothing, no one, none.

Dirge

1-2-3 was the number he played but today the number came
    3-2-1;
  bought his Carbide at 30 and it went to 29; had the favorite
    at Bowie but the track was slow—

O, executive type, would you like to drive a floating power,
    knee-action, silk-upholstered six? Wed a Hollywood
    star? Shoot the course in 58? Draw to the ace, king,
    jack?
  O, fellow with a will who won't take no, watch out for
    three cigarettes on the same, single match; O,
    democratic voter born in August under Mars, beware
    of liquidated rails—

Denouement to denouement, he took a personal pride in the
    certain, certain way he lived his own, private life,
  but nevertheless, they shut off his gas; nevertheless, the
    bank foreclosed; nevertheless, the landlord called;
    nevertheless, the radio broke,

And twelve o'clock arrived just once too often,
  just the same he wore one grey tweed suit, bought one
    straw hat, drank one straight Scotch, walked one short
    step, took one long look, drew one deep breath,
  just one too many,

And wow he died as wow he lived,
  going whop to the office and blooie home to sleep and biff
    got married and bam had children and oof got fired,
  zowie did he live and zowie did he die,

With who the hell are you at the corner of his casket, and
    where the hell we going on the right-hand silver knob,
    and who the hell cares walking second from the end
    with an American Beauty wreath from why the hell
    not,

Very much missed by the circulation staff of the New York
      Evening Post; deeply, deeply mourned by the B.M.T.,

Wham, Mr. Roosevelt; pow, Sears Roebuck; awk, big dipper;
      bop, summer rain;
  bong, Mr., bong, Mr., bong, Mr., bong.

Portrait

The clear brown eyes, kindly and alert, with 20-20 vision, give
      confident regard to the passing world through R. K.
      Lampert & Company lenses framed in gold
  his soul, however, is all his own
    Arndt Brothers necktie and hat (with feather) supply a
      touch of youth

With his soul his own, he drives, drives, chats and drives the
      second and third bicuspids, lower right, replaced by
      bridgework, while two incisors have porcelain
      crowns

(Render unto federal, state, and city Caesar, but not unto
      time
  render nothing unto time until Amalgamated Death serves
      final notice, in proper form

The vault is ready
  the will has been drawn by Clagget, Clagget, Clagget &
      Brown
    the policies are adequate, Confidential's best,
      reimbursing for disability, partial or complete, with
      double indemnity should the end be a pure and
      simple accident)

Nothing unto time
  nothing unto change
    nothing unto fate
      nothing unto you, and nothing unto me, or to any
      other known or unknown party or parties, living or
      deceased

But Mercury shoes, with special arch supports, take much of
    the wear and tear
  on the course, a custombuilt driver corrects a tendency to
    slice
    love's ravages have been repaired (it was a textbook case)
      by Drs. Schultz, Lightner, Mannheim, and Goode
    while all of it is enclosed in excellent tweed, with Mr.
      Baumer's personal attention to the shoulders and
      the waist

And all of it now roving, chatting amiably through space in a
    Plymouth 6
  with his soul (his own) at peace, soothed by Walter
    Lippmann, and sustained by Haig & Haig.

American Rhapsody (4)

First you bite your fingernails. And then you comb your hair
  again. And then you wait. And wait.
(They say, you know, that first you lie. And then you steal,
  they say. And then, they say, you kill.)

Then the doorbell rings. Then Peg drops in. And Bill. And
  Jane. And Doc.
And first you talk, and smoke, and hear the news and have a
  drink. Then you walk down the stairs.
And you dine, then, and go to a show after that, perhaps, and
  after that a night spot, and after that come home again,
  and climb the stairs again, and again go to bed.

But first Peg argues, and Doc replies. First you dance the
  same dance and you drink the same drink you always
  drank before.
And the piano builds a roof of notes above the world.
And the trumpet weaves a dome of music through space. And
  the drum makes a ceiling over space and time and night.
And then the table-wit. And then the check. Then home
  again to bed.
But first, the stairs.

And do you now, baby, as you climb the stairs, do you still
    feel as you felt back there?
Do you feel again as you felt this morning? And the night
    before? And then the night before that?

(They say, you know, that first you hear voices. And then you
    have visions, they say. Then, they say, you kick and
    scream and rave.)
Or do you feel: What is one more night in a lifetime of
    nights?
What is one more death, or friendship, or divorce out of two,
    or three? Or four? Or five?
One more face among so many, many faces, one more life
    among so many million lives?

But first, baby, as you climb and count the stairs (and they
    total the same) did you, sometime or somewhere, have a
    different idea?
Is this, baby, what you were born to feel, and do, and be?

Literary

I sing of simple people and the hardier virtues, by Associated
    Stuffed Shirts & Company, Incorporated, 358 West 42d
    Street, New York, brochure enclosed
  of Christ on the Cross, by a visitor to Calvary, first class
art deals with eternal, not current verities, revised from last
    week's Sunday supplement
  guess what we mean, in *The Literary System*, and a
    thousand noble answers to a thousand empty
    questions, by a patriot who needs the dough.

And so it goes.
  Books are the key to magic portals. Knowledge is power.
    Give the people light.
  Writing must be such a nice profession.
  Fill in the coupon. How do you know? Maybe you can be a
    writer, too.

How Do I Feel?

Get this straight, Joe, and don't get me wrong.
Sure, Steve, O.K., all I got to say is, when do I get the
    dough?

Will you listen for a minute? And just shut up? Let a guy
    explain?
Go ahead, go ahead, I won't say a word.

Will you just shut up?
O.K., I tell you, whatever you say, it's O.K. with me.

What's O.K. about it, if that's the way you feel?
What do you mean, how I feel? What do you know, how I
    feel?

Listen, Joe, a child could understand, if you'll listen for a
    minute without butting in, and don't get so sore.
You got to collect it first before you lay it out, sure, I know,
    you can't be left on a limb yourself.

Me? On a limb? For a lousy fifty bucks?
Take it easy, Steve, I'm just saying

I'm just telling you
Wait, listen

Now listen, wait, will you listen for a minute? That's all I ask.
    Yes or no?
O.K., Steve, O.K.

O.K.?
O.K., O.K.

O.K., then, and you won't get sore?
O.K., Steve. All I got to say is, when do I get the dough?

Art Review

Recently displayed at the Times Square station, a new
    Vandyke on the face-cream girl.
(Artist unknown. Has promise, but lacks the brilliance shown
    by the great masters of the Elevated age)
The latest wood carving in a Whelan telephone booth, titled
    "O Mortal Fools WA 9-5090," shows two winged hearts
    above an ace of spades.
(His meaning is not entirely clear, but this man will go far)
A charcoal nude in the rear of Flatbush Ahearn's Bar & Grill,
    "Forward to the Brotherhood of Man," has been boldly
    conceived in the great tradition.
(We need more, much more of this)
Then there is the chalk portrait, on the walls of a waterfront
    warehouse, of a gentleman wearing a derby hat:
    "Bleecker Street Mike is a doublecrossing rat."
(Morbid, but powerful. Don't miss)

Know then by these presents, know all men by these signs
    and omens, by these simple thumbprints on the throat of
    time,
Know that Pete, the people's artist, is ever watchful,
That Tuxedo Jim has passed among us, and was much
    displeased, as always,
That George the Ghost (no man has ever seen him) and Billy
    the Bicep boy will neither bend nor break,
That Mr. Harkness of Sunnyside still hopes for the best, and
    has not lost his human touch,
That Phantom Phil, the master of them all, has come and
    gone, but will return, and all is well.

Reception Good

Now, at a particular spot on the radio dial, "—in this corner,
    wearing purple trunks,"
Mingles, somehow, with the news that "—powerful enemy
    units have been surrounded in the drive—"

And both of these with the information that "—there is a way
    to avoid having chapped and roughened hands."

Such are the new and complex harmonies, it seems, of a
    strange and still more complex age;
It is not that the reception is confused or poor, but rather it is
    altogether too clear and good,

And no worse, in any case, than that other receiving set, the
    mind,
Forever faithfully transmitting the great and little impulses
    that arrive, however wavering or loud, from near and far:
"It is an ill wind—" it is apt to report, underscoring this with
    "—the bigger they are the harder they fall," and
    simultaneously reminding, darkly, that "Things are
    seldom as they seem,"

Reconciling, with ease, the irreconcilable,
Piecing together fragments of a flashing past with clouded
    snapshots of the present and the future,
("Something old, something new," its irrelevant announcer
    states. "Something borrowed, something blue.")

Fashioning a raw, wild symphony of a wedding march, a
    drinking song, and a dirge,
Multiplying enormous figures with precision, then raising the
    question: But after all, what is a man?
Somehow creating hope and fresh courage out of ancient
    doubt.

"Both boys are on their feet, they're going to it," the radio
    reports,
"—the sinking was attended by a heavy loss of life—"
"—this amazing cream for quick, miraculous results."

How many pieces are there, in a simple jigsaw puzzle?
How many phases of a man's life can crowd their way into a
    single moment?
How many angels, actually, can dance on the point of a pin?

Beware

Someone, somewhere, is always starting trouble,
Either a relative, or a drunken friend, or a foreign state.
Trouble it is, trouble it was, trouble it will always be.
Nobody ever leaves well enough alone.

It begins, as a rule, with an innocent face and a trivial remark:
"There are two sides to every question," or "Sign right here,
    on the dotted line,"
But it always ends with a crash of glass and a terrible shout—
No one, no one lets sleeping dragons sleep.

And it never happens, when the doorbell rings, that you find
    a troupe of houris standing on your stoop.
Just the reverse.
So beware of doorbells. (And beware, beware of houris, too)
And you never receive a letter that says: "We enclose,
    herewith, our check for a million."
You know what the letter always says, instead.
So beware of letters. (And anyway, they say, beware of great
    wealth)

Be careful of doorbells, be cautious of telephones, watch out
    for genial strangers, and for ancient friends;
Beware of dotted lines, and mellow cocktails; don't touch
    letters sent specifically to you;
Beware, especially, of innocent remarks;
Beware of everything,
Damn near anything leads to trouble,
Someone is always, always stepping out of line.

4 A.M.

It is early evening, still, in Honolulu, and in London, now, it
    must be well past dawn,
But here in the Riviera Café, on a street that has been lost
    and forgotten long ago, as the clock moves steadily
    toward closing time,
The spark of life is very low, if it burns at all—

And here we are, four lost and forgotten customers in this
    place that surely will never again be found,
Sitting, at ten-foot intervals, along this lost and forgotten bar
(Wishing the space were further still, for we are still too close
    for comfort),
Knowing that the bartender, and the elk's head, and the
    picture of some forgotten champion
(All gazing at something of interest beyond us and behind us,
    but very far away),
Must somehow be aware of us, too, as we stare at the cold
    interior of our lives reflected in the mirror beneath and
    in back of them—

Hear how lonely the radio is, as its voice talks on and on,
    unanswered,
How its music proves again that one's life is either too
    humdrum or too exciting, too empty or too full, too
    this, too that;
Only the cat that has been sleeping in the window, now
    yawning and stretching and trotting to the kitchen to
    sleep again,
Only this living toy knows what we feel, knows what we are,
    really knows what we merely think we know—

And soon, too soon, it will be closing time, the door will be
    locked,
Leaving each of us alone, then, with something too ravaging
    for a name
(Our golden, glorious futures, perhaps)—

Lock the door now and put out the lights, before some
    terrible stranger enters and puts, to each of us, a
    question that must be answered with the truth—

They say the Matterhorn at dawn, and the Northern Lights
    of the Arctic, are things that should be seen;
They say, they say—in time, you will hear them say anything,
    and everything;

What would the elk's head, or the remote bartender say, if
    they could speak?
The booth where last night's love affair began, the spot
    where last year's homicide occurred, are empty now, and
    still.

Bryce & Tomlins

Every need analyzed, each personal problem weighed,
    carefully, and solved according to the circumstance of
    each
(No investment too great. No question too small)
In confidence, at no cost, embarrassment, or obligation to
    you—

Offering maximum safety
(At 5%)
Full protection against change and chance, rust, moths, and
    the erratic flesh
(Trusts in perpetuity. Impartial executors of long-range wills)
Year after year, security in spite of the treacherous currents of
    impulse, yours and others',
Despite the swiftest tide of affairs—

Rails, chemicals, utilities, steel,
Listed or unlisted, let these stand guard through the shadowy
    times to be,
The heavy parchment with its exact phrases proof you shall
    walk this day's path, identically, tomorrow,
That as long as you wish you may see these streets and parks
    with the same eyes,
The same mood as today—

As though your features, yours, were stamped on the wind,
    yet more lasting than bronze,
The voice, free as always, yet recorded forever,
Your being, yours, still with its problems stronger than even
    the chemicals or the steel—

Decades of experience behind each portfolio can protect that
    future,
Filled with its unfinished business, incomplete desire, and still
    with the stubborn will to protect that future—

All of this, plus 5% of this, until the end of time.

LANGSTON HUGHES

(1902–1967)

The Negro Speaks of Rivers

(To W. E. B. DuBois)

I've known rivers:
I've known rivers ancient as the world and older than the flow
    of human blood in human veins.

My soul has grown deep like the rivers.

I bathed in the Euphrates when dawns were young.
I built my hut near the Congo and it lulled me to sleep.
I looked upon the Nile and raised the pyramids above it.
I heard the singing of the Mississippi when Abe Lincoln went
    down to New Orleans, and I've seen its muddy bosom
    turn all golden in the sunset.

I've known rivers:
Ancient, dusky rivers.

My soul has grown deep like the rivers.

Aunt Sue's Stories

Aunt Sue has a head full of stories.
Aunt Sue has a whole heart full of stories.
Summer nights on the front porch
Aunt Sue cuddles a brown-faced child to her bosom
And tells him stories.

Black slaves
Working in the hot sun,
And black slaves
Walking in the dewy night,

And black slaves
Singing sorrow songs on the banks of a mighty river
Mingle themselves softly
In the flow of old Aunt Sue's voice,
Mingle themselves softly
In the dark shadows that cross and recross
Aunt Sue's stories.

And the dark-faced child, listening,
Knows that Aunt Sue's stories are real stories.
He knows that Aunt Sue
Never got her stories out of any book at all,
But that they came
Right out of her own life.

And the dark-faced child is quiet
Of a summer night
Listening to Aunt Sue's stories.

When Sue Wears Red

When Susanna Jones wears red
Her face is like an ancient cameo
Turned brown by the ages.

Come with a blast of trumpets,
    Jesus!

When Susanna Jones wears red
A queen from some time-dead Egyptian night
Walks once again.

Blow trumpets, Jesus!

And the beauty of Susanna Jones in red
Burns in my heart a love-fire sharp like pain.

Sweet silver trumpets,
    Jesus!

Young Prostitute

Her dark brown face
Is like a withered flower
On a broken stem.
Those kind come cheap in Harlem
So they say.

My People

The night is beautiful,
So the faces of my people.

The stars are beautiful,
So the eyes of my people.

Beautiful, also, is the sun.
Beautiful, also, are the souls of my people.

Dream Variations

To fling my arms wide
In some place of the sun,
To whirl and to dance
Till the white day is done.
Then rest at cool evening
Beneath a tall tree
While night comes on gently,
    Dark like me—
That is my dream!

To fling my arms wide
In the face of the sun,
Dance! Whirl! Whirl!
Till the quick day is done.
Rest at pale evening . . .
A tall, slim tree . . .
Night coming tenderly
    Black like me.

Subway Face

That I have been looking
For you all my life
Does not matter to you.
You do not know.

You never knew.
Nor did I.
Now you take the Harlem train uptown;
I take a local down.

I, Too

I, too, sing America.

I am the darker brother.
They send me to eat in the kitchen
When company comes,
But I laugh,
And eat well,
And grow strong.

Tomorrow,
I'll sit at the table
When company comes.
Nobody'll dare
Say to me,
"Eat in the kitchen,"
Then.

Besides,
They'll see how beautiful I am
And be ashamed—

I, too, am America.

Suicide's Note

The calm,
Cool face of the river
Asked me for a kiss.

Summer Night

The sounds
Of the Harlem night
Drop one by one into stillness.
The last player-piano is closed.
The last victrola ceases with the
"Jazz Boy Blues."
The last crying baby sleeps
And the night becomes
Still as a whispering heartbeat.
I toss
Without rest in the darkness,
Weary as the tired night,
My soul
Empty as the silence,
Empty with a vague,
Aching emptiness,
Desiring,
Needing someone,
Something.

I toss without rest
In the darkness
Until the new dawn,
Wan and pale,
Descends like a white mist
Into the court-yard.

Strange Hurt

In times of stormy weather
She felt queer pain
That said,
"You'll find rain better
Than shelter from the rain."

Days filled with fiery sunshine
Strange hurt she knew
That made
Her seek the burning sunlight
Rather than the shade.

In months of snowy winter
When cozy houses hold,

She'd break down doors
To wander naked
In the cold.

A House in Taos

Rain

Thunder of the Rain God:
    And we three
    Smitten by beauty.

Thunder of the Rain God:
    And we three
    Weary, weary.

Thunder of the Rain God:
    And you, she, and I
    Waiting for nothingness.

Do you understand the stillness
    Of this house
    In Taos
Under the thunder of the Rain God?

Sun

That there should be a barren garden
About this house in Taos
Is not so strange,
But that there should be three barren hearts
In this one house in Taos—
Who carries ugly things to show the sun?

Moon

Did you ask for the beaten brass of the moon?
We can buy lovely things with money,
You, she, and I,
Yet you seek,
As though you could keep,
This unbought loveliness of moon.

Wind

Touch our bodies, wind.
Our bodies are separate, individual things.
Touch our bodies, wind,
But blow quickly
Through the red, white, yellow skins
Of our bodies
To the terrible snarl,
Not mine,
Not yours,
Not hers,
But all one snarl of souls.
Blow quickly, wind,
Before we run back

Into the windlessness—
With our bodies—
Into the windlessness
Of our house in Taos.

Railroad Avenue

Dusk dark
On Railroad Avenue.
Lights in the fish joints,
Lights in the pool rooms.
A box-car some train
Has forgotten
In the middle of the
Block.
A player piano,
A victrola.
   942
   Was the number.
A boy
Lounging on a corner.
A passing girl
With purple powdered skin.
   Laughter
   Suddenly
   Like a taut drum.
   Laughter
   Suddenly
   Neither truth nor lie.
   Laughter
Hardening the dusk dark evening.
   Laughter
Shaking the lights in the fish joints,
Rolling white balls in the pool rooms,
And leaving untouched the box-car
Some train has forgotten.

Sea Calm

How still,
How strangely still
The water is today.
It is not good
For water
To be so still that way.

Drum

Bear in mind
That death is a drum
Beating for ever
Till the last worms come
To answer its call,
Till the last stars fall,
Until the last atom
Is no atom at all,
Until time is lost
And there is no air
And space itself
Is nothing nowhere,
Death is a drum,
A signal drum,
Calling all life
To come! Come!
Come!

Cubes

In the days of the broken cubes of Picasso
And in the days of the broken songs of the young men
A little too drunk to sing
And the young women
A little too unsure of love to love—
I met on the boulevards of Paris
An African from Senegal.

God
Knows why the French
Amuse themselves bringing to Paris
Negroes from Senegal.

It's the old game of the boss and the bossed,
                boss and the bossed,
                        amused
                        and
                        amusing,
                worked and working,
Behind the cubes of black and white,
                                black and white,
                        black and white

But since it is the old game,
For fun
They give him the three old prostitutes of France—
Liberty, Equality, Fraternity—
And all three of 'em sick
In spite of the tax to the government
And the legal houses
And the doctors
And the *Marseillaise*.

Of course, the young African from Senegal
Carries back from Paris
A little more disease
To spread among the black girls in the palm huts.
He brings them as a gift
                disease—
From light to darkness
                        disease—
From the boss to the bossed
                        disease—
From the game of black and white
                disease

From the city of the broken cubes of Picasso
                    d
                     i
                      s
                     e
                      a
                       s
                      e

Little Lyric (Of Great Importance)

I wish the rent
Was heaven sent.

Evil

Looks like what drives me crazy
Don't have no effect on you—
But I'm gonna keep on at it
Till it drives you crazy, too.

Songs

I sat there singing her
Songs in the dark.

She said,
I do not understand
The words.

I said,
There are
No words.

Luck

Sometimes a crumb falls
From the tables of joy,
Sometimes a bone
Is flung.

To some people
Love is given,
To others
Only heaven.

Curious

I can see your house, babe,
But I can't see you.
I can see your house,
But I can't see you.
When you're in your house, baby
Tell me, what do you do?

American Heartbreak

I am the American heartbreak—
Rock on which Freedom
Stumps its toe—
The great mistake
That Jamestown
Made long ago.

from
Montage of a Dream Deferred

STREET SONG

Jack, if you got to be a rounder
Be a rounder right—
Just don't let mama catch you
Makin' rounds at night.

125TH STREET

Face like a chocolate bar
full of nuts and sweet.

Face like a jack-o'-lantern,
candle inside.

Face like slice of melon,
grin that wide.

DIVE

Lenox Avenue
by daylight
runs to dive in the Park
but faster . . .
faster . . .
after dark.

WARNING: AUGMENTED

Don't let your dog curb you!
    Curb your doggie
    Like you ought to do,
But don't let that dog curb you!
    You may play folks cheap,
    Act rough and tough,
    But a dog can tell

When you're full of stuff.
Them little old mutts
Look all scraggly and bad,
But they got more sense
Than some people ever had.
Cur dog, fice dog, kerry blue—
Just don't let your dog curb you!

UP-BEAT

In the gutter
boys who try
might meet girls
on the fly
as out of the gutter
girls who will
may meet boys
copping a thrill
while from the gutter
both can rise:
But it requires
plenty eyes.

JAM SESSION

Letting midnight
out on bail
pop-a-da
having been
detained in jail
oop-pop-a-da
for sprinkling salt
on a dreamer's tail
pop-a-da

BE-BOP BOYS

Imploring Mecca
to achieve
six discs
with Decca.

TAG

Little cullud boys
      with fears,
      frantic,
nudge their draftee years.

Pop-a-da!

THEME FOR ENGLISH B

The instructor said,

> *Go home and write*
> *a page tonight.*
> *And let that page come out of you—*
> *Then, it will be true.*

I wonder if it's that simple?
I am twenty-two, colored, born in Winston-Salem.
I went to school there, then Durham, then here
to this college on the hill above Harlem.
I am the only colored student in my class.
The steps from the hill lead down into Harlem,
through a park, then I cross St. Nicholas,
Eighth Avenue, Seventh, and I come to the Y,
the Harlem Branch Y, where I take the elevator
up to my room, sit down, and write this page:

It's not easy to know what is true for you or me
at twenty-two, my age. But I guess I'm what
I feel and see and hear, Harlem, I hear you:

hear you, hear me—we two—you, me, talk on this page.
(I hear New York, too.) Me—who?
Well, I like to eat, sleep, drink, and be in love.
I like to work, read, learn, and understand life.
I like a pipe for a Christmas present,
or records—Bessie, bop, or Bach.
I guess being colored doesn't make me *not* like
the same things other folks like who are other races.
So will my page be colored that I write?
Being me, it will not be white.
But it will be
a part of you, instructor.
You are white—
yet a part of me, as I am a part of you.
That's American.
Sometimes perhaps you don't want to be a part of me.
Nor do I often want to be a part of you.
But we are, that's true!
As I learn from you,
I guess you learn from me—
although you're older—and white—
and somewhat more free.

This is my page for English B.

COLLEGE FORMAL: RENAISSANCE CASINO

Golden girl
in a golden gown
in a melody night
in Harlem town
lad tall and brown
tall and wise
college boy smart
eyes in eyes
the music wraps
them both around
in mellow magic
of dancing sound

till they're the heart
of the whole big town
gold and brown

LOW TO HIGH

How can you forget me?
But you do!
You said you was gonna take me
Up with you—
Now you've got your Cadillac,
you done forgot that you are black.
How can you forget me
When I'm you?

But you do.

How can you forget me,
fellow, say?
How can you low-rate me
this way?
You treat me like you damn well please,
Ignore me—though I pay your fees.
How can you forget me?

But you do.

BOOGIE: I A.M.

Good evening, daddy!
I know you've heard
The boogie-woogie rumble
Of a dream deferred
Trilling the treble
And twining the bass
Into midnight ruffles
Of cat-gut lace.

HIGH TO LOW

God knows
We have our troubles, too—
One trouble is you:
you talk too loud,
cuss too loud,
look too black,
don't get anywhere,
and sometimes it seems
you don't even care.
The way you send your kids to school
stockings down,
(not Ethical Culture)
the way you shout out loud in church,
(not St. Phillip's)
and the way you lounge on doorsteps
just as if you were down South,
(not at 409)
the way you clown—
the way, in other words,
you let me down—
me, trying to uphold the race
and you—
well, you can see,
we have our problems,
too, with you.

LADY'S BOOGIE

See that lady
Dressed so fine?
She ain't got boogie-woogie
On her mind—

But if she was to listen
I bet she'd hear,
Way up in the treble
The tingle of a tear.

Be-Bach!

SO LONG

So long
is in the song
and it's in the way you're gone
but it's like a foreign language
in my mind
and maybe was I blind
I could not see
and would not know
you're gone so long
so long.

DEFERRED

This year, maybe, do you think I can graduate?
I'm already two years late.
Dropped out six months when I was seven,
a year when I was eleven,
then got put back when we come North.
To get through high at twenty's kind of late—
But maybe this year I can graduate.

Maybe now I can have that white enamel stove
I dreamed about when we first fell in love
eighteen years ago.
But you know,
rooming and everything
then kids,
cold-water flat and all that.
But now my daughter's married
And my boy's most grown—
quit school to work—
and where we're moving
there ain't no stove—
Maybe I can buy that white enamel stove!

Me, I always did want to study French.
It don't make sense—
I'll never go to France,

but night schools teach French.
Now at last I've got a job
where I get off at five,
in time to wash and dress,
so, s'il vous plaît, I'll study French!

Someday,
I'm gonna buy two new suits
at once!

All I want is
one more bottle of gin.

All I want is to see
my furniture paid for.

All I want is a wife who will
work with me and not against me. Say,
baby, could you see your way clear?

Heaven, heaven, is my home!
This world I'll leave behind
When I set my feet in glory
I'll have a throne for mine!

I want to pass the civil service.

I want a television set.

You know, as old as I am,
I ain't never
owned a decent radio yet?

I'd like to take up Bach.

> *Montage*
> *of a dream*
> *deferred.*

Buddy, have you heard?

REQUEST

Gimme $25.00
and the change.
I'm going
where the morning
and the evening
won't bother me.

SHAME ON YOU

If you're great enough
and clever enough
the government might honor you.
But the people will forget—
Except on holidays.

A movie house in Harlem named after Lincoln,
Nothing at all named after John Brown.
Black people don't remember
any better than white.

If you're not alive and kicking,
shame on you!

WORLD WAR II

What a grand time was the war!
        Oh, my, my!
What a grand time was the war!
        My, my, my!
In wartime we had fun,
Sorry that old war is done!
What a grand time was the war,
        My, my!

Echo:
        Did
        Somebody
        Die?

MYSTERY

When a chile gets to be thirteen
and ain't seen Christ yet,
she needs to set on de moaner's bench
night and day.

Jesus, lover of my soul!

Hail, Mary, mother of God!

Let me to thy bosom fly!

Amen! Hallelujah!

Swing low, sweet chariot,
Coming for to carry me home.

Sunday morning where the rhythm flows,
how old nobody knows—
yet old as mystery,
older than creed,
basic and wondering
and lost as my need.

    Eli, eli!

    Te deum!

    Mahomet!

    Christ!

Father Bishop, Effendi, Mother Horne,
Father Divine, a Rabbi black
as black was born,
a jack-leg preacher, a Ph.D.

    The mystery
    and the darkness
    and the song
    and me.

SLIVER OF SERMON

When pimps out of loneliness cry:
    Great God!
Whores in final weariness say:
    Great God!
    Oh, God!
    My God!

    Great
    God!

TESTIMONIAL

If I just had a piano,
if I just had a organ,
if I just had a drum,
how I could praise my Lord!

But I don't need no piano,
    neither organ
    nor drum
for to praise my Lord!

PASSING

On sunny summer Sunday afternoons in Harlem
when the air is one interminable ball game
and grandma cannot get her gospel hymns
from the Saints of God in Christ
on account of the Dodgers on the radio,
on sunny Sunday afternoons
when the kids look all new
and far too clean to stay that way,
and Harlem has its
washed-and-ironed-and-cleaned-best out,
the ones who've crossed the line
to live downtown
miss you,
Harlem of the bitter dream,
since their dream has
come true.

NIGHTMARE BOOGIE

I had a dream
and I could see
a million faces
black as me!
A nightmare dream:
Quicker than light
All them faces
Turned dead white!
Boogie-woogie,
Rolling bass,
Whirling treble
of cat-gut lace.

SUNDAY BY THE COMBINATION

I feel like dancin', baby,
till the sun goes down.

But I wonder where
the sunrise
Monday morning's gonna be?

I feel like dancin'!
Baby, dance with me!

CASUALTY

He was a soldier in the army,
But he doesn't walk like one.
He walks like his soldiering
Days are done.

Son! . . . Son!

NIGHT FUNERAL IN HARLEM

Night funeral
In Harlem:

*Where did they get
Them two fine cars?*

Insurance man, he did not pay—
His insurance lapsed the other day—
Yet they got a satin box
For his head to lay.

Night funeral
In Harlem:

*Who was it sent
That wreath of flowers?*

Them flowers came
from that poor boy's friends—
They'll want flowers, too,
When they meet their ends.

Night funeral
In Harlem:

*Who preached that
Black boy to his grave?*

Old preacher man
Preached that boy away—
Charged Five Dollars
His girl friend had to pay.

Night funeral
In Harlem:

When it was all over
And the lid shut on his head

and the organ had done played
and the last prayers been said
and six pallbearers
Carried him out for dead
And off down Lenox Avenue
That long black hearse done sped,
    The street light
    At his corner
    Shined just like a tear—
That boy that they was mournin'
Was so dear, so dear
To them folks that brought the flowers,
To that girl who paid the preacher man—
It was all their tears that made
    That poor boy's
    Funeral grand.

    Night funeral
    In Harlem.

———

HARLEM [2]

What happens to a dream deferred?

    Does it dry up
    like a raisin in the sun?
    Or fester like a sore—
    And then run?
    Does it stink like rotten meat?
    Or crust and sugar over—
    like a syrupy sweet?

    Maybe it just sags
    like a heavy load.

    Or does it explode?

GOOD MORNING

Good morning, daddy!
I was born here, he said,
watched Harlem grow
until colored folks spread
from river to river
across the middle of Manhattan
out of Penn Station
dark tenth of a nation,
planes from Puerto Rico,
and holds of boats, chico,
up from Cuba Haiti Jamaica,
in buses marked New York
from Georgia Florida Louisiana
to Harlem Brooklyn the Bronx
but most of all to Harlem
dusky sash across Manhattan
I've seen them come dark
     wondering
     wide-eyed
     dreaming
out of Penn Station—
but the trains are late.
The gates open—
     Yet there're bars
     at each gate.

     What happens
     to a dream deferred?

Daddy, ain't you heard?

SAME IN BLUES

I said to my baby,
Baby, take it slow.
I can't, she said, I can't!
I got to go!

> *There's a certain*
> *amount of traveling*
> *in a dream deferred.*

Lulu said to Leonard,
I want a diamond ring.
Leonard said to Lulu,
You won't get a goddamn thing!

> *A certain*
> *amount of nothing*
> *in a dream deferred.*

Daddy, daddy, daddy,
All I want is you.
You can have me, baby—
but my lovin' days is through.

> *A certain*
> *amount of impotence*
> *in a dream deferred.*

Three parties
On my party line—
But that third party,
Lord, ain't mine!

> *There's liable*
> *to be confusion*
> *in a dream deferred.*

From river to river,
Uptown and down,
There's liable to be confusion
when a dream gets kicked around.

COMMENT ON CURB

You talk like
they don't kick
dreams around
downtown.

> *I expect they do—*
> *But I'm talking about*
> *Harlem to you!*

LETTER

Dear Mama,
> *Time I pay rent and get my food*
and laundry I don't have much left
but here is five dollars for you
to show you I still appreciates you.
My girl-friend send her love and say
she hopes to lay eyes on you sometime in life.
Mama, it has been raining cats and dogs up
here. Well, that is all so I will close.
> *Your son baby*
>> *Respectably as ever,*
>> *Joe*

ISLAND [2]

Between two rivers,
North of the park,
Like darker rivers
The streets are dark.

Black and white,
Gold and brown—
Chocolate-custard
Pie of a town.

Dream within a dream,
Our dream deferred.

Good morning, daddy!

Ain't you heard?

OGDEN NASH

(1902–1971)

Spring Comes to Murray Hill

I sit in an office at 244 Madison Avenue,
And say to myself you have a responsible job, havenue?
Why then do you fritter away your time on this doggerel?
If you have a sore throat you can cure it by using a good
    goggeral,
If you have a sore foot you can get it fixed by a chiropodist
And you can get your original sin removed by St. John the
    Bopodist,
Why then should this flocculent lassitude be incurable?
Kansas City, Kansas, proves that even Kansas City needn't
    always be Missourible.
Up up my soul! This inaction is abdominable.
The pilgrims settled Massachusetts in 1620 when they landed
    on a stone hummock.
Maybe if they were here now they would settle my stomach.
Oh, if I only had the wings of a bird
Instead of being confined on Madison Avenue I could soar in
    a jiffy to Second or Third.

Reflection on Ice-Breaking

Candy
Is dandy
But liquor
Is quicker.

The Terrible People

People who have what they want are very fond of telling
    people who haven't what they want that they really don't
    want it,
And I wish I could afford to gather all such people into a
    gloomy castle on the Danube and hire half a dozen
    capable Draculas to haunt it.
I don't mind their having a lot of money, and I don't care
    how they employ it,
But I do think that they damn well ought to admit they enjoy it.
But no, they insist on being stealthy
About the pleasures of being wealthy,
And the possession of a handsome annuity
Makes them think that to say how hard it is to make both
    ends meet is their bounden duity.
You cannot conceive of an occasion
Which will find them without some suitable evasion.
Yes indeed, with arguments they are very fecund;
Their first point is that money isn't everything, and that they
    have no money anyhow is their second.
Some people's money is merited,
And other people's is inherited,
But wherever it comes from,
They talk about it as if it were something you got pink gums
    from.
This may well be,
But if so, why do they not relieve themselves of the burden
    by transferring it to the deserving poor or to me?
Perhaps indeed the possession of wealth is constantly
    distressing,
But I should be quite willing to assume every curse of wealth
    if I could at the same time assume every blessing.
The only incurable troubles of the rich are the troubles that
    money can't cure,
Which is a kind of trouble that is even more troublesome if
    you are poor.
Certainly there are lots of things in life that money won't buy,
    but it's very funny—
Have you ever tried to buy them without money?

Song of the Open Road

I think that I shall never see
A billboard lovely as a tree.
Perhaps, unless the billboards fall,
I'll never see a tree at all.

Very Like a Whale

One thing that literature would be greatly the better for
Would be a more restricted employment by authors of simile
    and metaphor.
Authors of all races, be they Greeks, Romans, Teutons or
    Celts,
Can't seem just to say that anything is the thing it is but have
    to go out of their way to say that it is like something else.
What does it mean when we are told
That the Assyrian came down like a wolf on the fold?
In the first place, George Gordon Byron had had enough
    experience
To know that it probably wasn't just one Assyrian, it was a lot
    of Assyrians.
However, as too many arguments are apt to induce apoplexy
    and thus hinder longevity,
We'll let it pass as one Assyrian for the sake of brevity.
Now then, this particular Assyrian, the one whose cohorts
    were gleaming in purple and gold,
Just what does the poet mean when he says he came down
    like a wolf on the fold?
In heaven and earth more than is dreamed of in our
    philosophy there are a great many things,
But I don't imagine that among them there is a wolf with
    purple and gold cohorts or purple and gold anythings.
No, no, Lord Byron, before I'll believe that this Assyrian was
    actually like a wolf I must have some kind of proof;
Did he run on all fours and did he have a hairy tail and a big
    red mouth and big white teeth and did he say Woof woof
    woof?

Frankly I think it very unlikely, and all you were entitled to
    say, at the very most,
Was that the Assyrian cohorts came down like a lot of
    Assyrian cohorts about to destroy the Hebrew host.
But that wasn't fancy enough for Lord Byron, oh dear me no,
    he had to invent a lot of figures of speech and then
    interpolate them,
With the result that whenever you mention Old Testament
    soldiers to people they say Oh yes, they're the ones that a
    lot of wolves dressed up in gold and purple ate them.
That's the kind of thing that's being done all the time by
    poets, from Homer to Tennyson;
They're always comparing ladies to lilies and veal to venison.
How about the man who wrote,
Her little feet stole in and out like mice beneath her petticoat?
Wouldn't anybody but a poet think twice
Before stating that his girl's feet were mice?
Then they always say things like that after a winter storm
The snow is a white blanket. Oh it is, is it, all right then, you
    sleep under a six-inch blanket of snow and I'll sleep
    under a half-inch blanket of unpoetical blanket material
    and we'll see which one keeps warm,
And after that maybe you'll begin to comprehend dimly
What I mean by too much metaphor and simile.

A Necessary Dirge

Sometimes it's difficult, isn't it, not to grow grim and
    rancorous
Because man's fate is so counter-clockwise and cantankerous.
Look at all the noble projects that die a-borning,
Look how hard it is to get to sleep at night and then how
    hard it is to wake up in the morning!
How easy to be unselfish in the big things that never come up
    and how hard in the little things that come up daily and
    hourly, oh yes,

Such as what heroic pleasure to give up the last seat in a
    lifeboat to a mother and babe, and what an irritation to
    give some housewife your seat on the Lexington Avenue
    Express!
How easy for those who do not bulge
To not overindulge!
O universe perverse, why and whence your perverseness?
Why do you not teem with betterness instead of worseness?
Do you get your only enjoyment
Out of humanity's annoyment?
Because a point I would like to discuss
Is, why wouldn't it be just as easy for you to make things easy
    for us?
But no, you will not listen, expostulation is useless,
Home is the fisherman empty-handed, home is the hunter
    caribouless and mooseless.
Humanity must continue to follow the sun around
And accept the eternal run-around.
Well, and if that be the case, why come on humanity!
So long as it is our fate to be irked all our life let us just keep
    our heads up and take our irking with insouciant
    urbanity.

Portrait of the Artist as a Prematurely Old Man

It is common knowledge to every schoolboy and even every
    Bachelor of Arts,
That all sin is divided into two parts.
One kind of sin is called a sin of commission, and that is very
    important,
And it is what you are doing when you are doing something
    you ortant,
And the other kind of sin is just the opposite and is called a
    sin of omission and is equally bad in the eyes of all right-
    thinking people, from Billy Sunday to Buddha,
And it consists of not having done something you shuddha.
Well, there are more ways than one to kill a cat,
And offhand you'd think there were more kinds of sin than
    that,

But I suppose that once upon a time there was somebody
    somewhere who just wouldn't be pacified
Until they got sin classified,
So now even if you are a combination of Casanova and
    Bluebeard and Jesse James and Benedict Arnold and an
    oriental magician
Still, the only kind of sin you can pull out of the hat is a sin
    either of om- or com-mission.
I might as well give you my opinion of these two kinds of sin
    as long as, in a way, against each other we are pitting
    them,
And that is, don't bother your head about sins of commission
    because however sinful, they must at least be fun or else
    you wouldn't be committing them.
It is the sin of omission, the second kind of sin,
That lays eggs under your skin.
The way you get really painfully bitten
Is by the insurance you haven't taken out and the checks you
    haven't added up the stubs of and the appointments you
    haven't kept and the bills you haven't paid and the letters
    you haven't written,
And they start piling up and up and up on top of you,
Till you are so bowed down that unless you get up on a
    ladder the bald spot of a midget standing on its head in a
    cellar is about the only thing of which you can get a
    proper view.
Also, about sins of omission there is one particularly painful
    lack of beauty,
Namely, it isn't as though it had been a riotous red letter day
    or night every time you neglected to do your duty;
You didn't get a wicked forbidden thrill
Every time you let a policy lapse or forgot to pay a bill;
You didn't slap the lads in the tavern on the back and loudly
    cry Whee,
Let's all fail to write just one more letter before we go home,
    and this round of unwritten letters is on me.
No, you never get any fun
Out of the things you haven't done,
But they are the things that I do not like to be amid,

Because the suitable things you didn't do give you a lot more
    trouble than the unsuitable things you did.
The moral is that it is probably better not to sin at all, but if
    some kind of sin you must be pursuing,
Well, remember to do it by doing rather than by not doing.

The Germ

A mighty creature is the germ,
Though smaller than the pachyderm.
His customary dwelling place
Is deep within the human race.
I cannot help but wonder at
The oddness of his habitat.
His childish pride he often pleases
By giving people strange diseases.
Do you, my poppet, feel infirm?
You probably contain a germ.

Glossina Morsitans, or, the Tsetse

A *Glossina morsitans* bit rich Aunt Betsy.
Tsk tsk, tsetse.

Samson Agonistes

I test my bath before I sit,
And I'm always moved to wonderment
That what chills the finger not a bit
Is so frigid upon the fundament.

Inter-Office Memorandum

The only people who should really sin
Are the people who can sin with a grin,
Because if sinning upsets you,
Why, nothing at all is what it gets you.
Everybody certainly ought to eschew all offences however
venial
As long as they are conscience's menial.
Some people suffer weeks of remorse after having committed
the slightest peccadillo,
And other people feel perfectly all right after feeding their
husbands arsenic or smothering their grandmother with
a pillow.
Some people are perfectly self-possessed about spending their
lives on the verge of delirium tremens,
And other people feel like hanging themselves on a coathook
just because they took that extra cocktail and amused
their fellow guests with recitations from the poems of
Mrs. Hemans.
Some people calmly live a barnyard life because they find
monogamy dull and arid,
And other people have sinking spells if they dance twice in an
evening with a lady to whom they aren't married.
Some people feel forever lost if they are riding on a bus and
the conductor doesn't collect their fare,
And other people ruin a lot of widows and orphans and all
they think is, Why there's something in this business of
ruining widows and orphans, and they go out and ruin
some more and get to be a millionaire.
Now it is not the purpose of this memorandum, or song,
To attempt to define the difference between right and wrong;
All I am trying to say is that if you are one of the
unfortunates who recognize that such a difference exists,
Well, you had better oppose even the teensiest temptation
with clenched fists,
Because if you desire peace of mind it is all right to do wrong
if it never occurs to you that it is wrong to do it,
Because you can sleep perfectly well and look the world in the
eye after doing anything at all so long as you don't rue it,

While on the other hand nothing at all is any fun
So long as you yourself know it is something you shouldn't
have done.
There is only one way to achieve happiness on this terrestrial
ball,
And that is to have either a clear conscience, or none at all.

Which the Chicken, Which the Egg?

He drinks because she scolds, he thinks;
She thinks she scolds because he drinks;
And neither will admit what's true,
That he's a sot and she's a shrew.

EVE TRIEM

(1902–1992)

For Paul

I make no moan or outcry, just don't sleep.
The rain staining, etching the windowpane,
takes care of tears. Awake without hope
he will drink the morning with me, intone
a comment to my rhyme. What a lot of breath
went into the loving and now it's dying
we have to think of. The ghost on his path—
I refuse to believe what it is saying,

recalling the heron-river, books read aloud,
the nights we talked, sending the moon away.
The weedy places we rolled in and hid,
each to the other changing dark to glow.
You cannot lose me, said his ringing Yes
between the death-sweat and my forlorn kiss.

COUNTEE CULLEN

(1903–1946)

Yet Do I Marvel

I doubt not God is good, well-meaning, kind,
And did He stoop to quibble could tell why
The little buried mole continues blind,
Why flesh that mirrors Him must some day die,
Make plain the reason tortured Tantalus
Is baited by the fickle fruit, declare
If merely brute caprice dooms Sisyphus
To struggle up a never-ending stair.
Inscrutable His ways are, and immune
To catechism by a mind too strewn
With petty cares to slightly understand
What awful brain compels His awful hand.
Yet do I marvel at this curious thing:
To make a poet black, and bid him sing!

Atlantic City Waiter

With subtle poise he grips his tray
    Of delicate things to eat;
Choice viands to their mouths half way,
    The ladies watch his feet

Go carving dexterous avenues
    Through sly intricacies;
Ten thousand years on jungle clues
    Alone shaped feet like these.

For him to be humble who is proud
    Needs colder artifice;
Though half his pride is disavowed,
    In vain the sacrifice.

Sheer through his acquiescent mask
  Of bland gentility,
The jungle flames like a copper cask
  Set where the sun strikes free.

Incident

(For Eric Walrond)

Once riding in old Baltimore,
  Heart-filled, head-filled with glee,
I saw a Baltimorean
  Keep looking straight at me.

Now I was eight and very small,
  And he was no whit bigger,
And so I smiled, but he poked out
  His tongue, and called me, "Nigger."

I saw the whole of Baltimore
  From May until December;
Of all the things that happened there
  That's all that I remember.

Heritage

(For Harold Jackman)

What is Africa to me:
Copper sun or scarlet sea,
Jungle star or jungle track,
Strong bronzed men, or regal black
Women from whose loins I sprang
When the birds of Eden sang?
One three centuries removed
From the scenes his fathers loved,
Spicy grove, cinnamon tree,
What is Africa to me?

So I lie, who all day long
Want no sound except the song
Sung by wild barbaric birds,
Goading massive jungle herds,
Juggernauts of flesh that pass
Trampling tall defiant grass
Where young forest lovers lie,
Plighting troth beneath the sky.
So I lie, who always hear,
Though I cram against my ear
Both my thumbs, and keep them there,
Great drums throbbing through the air.
So I lie, whose fount of pride,
Dear distress, and joy allied,
Is my somber flesh and skin,
With the dark blood dammed within
Like great pulsing tides of wine
That, I fear, must burst the fine
Channels of the chafing net
Where they surge and foam and fret.

Africa? A book one thumbs
Listlessly, till slumber comes.
Unremembered are her bats
Circling through the night, her cats
Crouching in the river reeds,
Stalking gentle flesh that feeds
By the river brink; no more
Does the bugle-throated roar
Cry that monarch claws have leapt
From the scabbards where they slept.
Silver snakes that once a year
Doff the lovely coats you wear,
Seek no covert in your fear
Lest a mortal eye should see;
What's your nakedness to me?
Here no leprous flowers rear
Fierce corollas in the air;
Here no bodies sleek and wet,
Dripping mingled rain and sweat,
Tread the savage measures of

Jungle boys and girls in love.
What is last year's snow to me,
Last year's anything? The tree
Budding yearly must forget
How its past arose or set—
Bough and blossom, flower, fruit,
Even what shy bird with mute
Wonder at her travail there,
Meekly labored in its hair.
One three centuries removed
From the scenes his fathers loved,
Spicy grove, cinnamon tree,
What is Africa to me?

So I lie, who find no peace
Night or day, no slight release
From the unremittant beat
Made by cruel padded feet
Walking through my body's street.
Up and down they go, and back,
Treading out a jungle track.
So I lie, who never quite
Safely sleep from rain at night—
I can never rest at all
When the rain begins to fall;
Like a soul gone mad with pain
I must match its weird refrain;
Ever must I twist and squirm,
Writhing like a baited worm,
While its primal measures drip
Through my body, crying, "Strip!
Doff this new exuberance.
Come and dance the Lover's Dance!"
In an old remembered way
Rain works on me night and day.

Quaint, outlandish heathen gods
Black men fashion out of rods,
Clay, and brittle bits of stone,
In a likeness like their own,
My conversion came high-priced;

I belong to Jesus Christ,
Preacher of humility;
Heathen gods are naught to me.

Father, Son, and Holy Ghost,
So I make an idle boast;
Jesus of the twice-turned cheek,
Lamb of God, although I speak
With my mouth thus, in my heart
Do I play a double part.
Ever at Thy glowing altar
Must my heart grow sick and falter,
Wishing He I served were black,
Thinking then it would not lack
Precedent of pain to guide it,
Let who would or might deride it;
Surely then this flesh would know
Yours had borne a kindred woe.
Lord, I fashion dark gods, too,
Daring even to give You
Dark despairing features where,
Crowned with dark rebellious hair,
Patience wavers just so much as
Mortal grief compels, while touches
Quick and hot, of anger, rise
To smitten cheek and weary eyes.
Lord, forgive me if my need
Sometimes shapes a human creed.

All day long and all night through,
One thing only must I do:
Quench my pride and cool my blood,
Lest I perish in the flood.
Lest a hidden ember set
Timber that I thought was wet
Burning like the dryest flax,
Melting like the merest wax,
Lest the grave restore its dead.
Not yet has my heart or head
In the least way realized
They and I are civilized.

For My Grandmother

This lovely flower fell to seed;
Work gently, sun and rain;
She held it as her dying creed
That she would grow again.

For a Lady I Know

She even thinks that up in heaven
Her class lies late and snores,
While poor black cherubs rise at seven
To do celestial chores.

For One Who Gayly Sowed His Oats

My days were a thing for me to live,
For others to deplore;
I took of life all it could give:
Rind, inner fruit, and core.

For Hazel Hall, American Poet

Soul-troubled at the febrile ways of breath,
Her timid breast shot through with faint alarm,
"Yes, I'm a stranger here," she said to Death,
"It's kind of you to let me take your arm."

From the Dark Tower

(To Charles S. Johnson)

We shall not always plant while others reap
The golden increment of bursting fruit,
Not always countenance, abject and mute,
That lesser men should hold their brothers cheap;
Not everlastingly while others sleep
Shall we beguile their limbs with mellow flute,
Not always bend to some more subtle brute;
We were not made eternally to weep.

The night whose sable breast relieves the stark,
White stars is no less lovely being dark,
And there are buds that cannot bloom at all
In light, but crumple, piteous, and fall;
So in the dark we hide the heart that bleeds,
And wait, and tend our agonizing seeds.

EDWIN DENBY

(1903–1983)

The Subway

The subway flatters like the dope habit,
For a nickel extending peculiar space:
You dive from the street, holing like a rabbit,
Roar up a sewer with a millionaire's face.

Squatting in the full glare of the locked express
Imprisoned, rocked, like a man by a friend's death,
O how the immense investment soothes distress,
Credit laps you like a huge religious myth.

It's a sound effect. The trouble is seeing
(So anaesthetized) a square of bare throat
Or the fold at the crotch of a clothed human being:
You'll want to nuzzle it, crop at it like a goat.

That's not in the buy. The company between stops
Offers you security, and free rides to cops.

A New York Face

The great New York bridges reflect its faces
Personality scoots across one like tiny
Traffic intent from Brooklyn—it stays spacious
Aggrandized, in gales splendidly whining.

And adrift as figures on roof and pier-end
Stare at the gigantic delicacy, a face
So hangs its enormous ghost above the spent
Lover, too vacant for safety too still for sex.

In echoing darkness their dimensions become sleep—
River and dark neighborhood and skyscraper shape,
A hall-bedroom; faces all night inert in the leap
Of their fate so enlarge into grace without hope.

New York faces have a structure wide as this
Undisturbed by subway or by secret kiss.

———————

I had heard it's a fight. At the first clammy touch
You yell, you wrestle with it, it kicks you
In the stomach, squeezes your eyes, in agony you clutch
At a straw, you rattle, and that will fix you.

I don't know. The afternoon it touched me
It sneaked up like it was a sweet thrill
Inside my arms and back so I let it come just a wee
Mite closer, though I knew what it was, hell.

Was it sweet! Then like a cute schoolkid
Who does it the first time, I decided it was bad
Cut out the liquor, went to the gym, and did
What a man naturally does, as I mostly had.

The crazy thing, so crazy it gives me a kick:
I can't get over that minute of dying so quick.

Smelling or feeling of the several holes
Above the jawbone and below the belly
Suggests to searching lovers that the soul's
A slippery gumdrop filled with a sweet jelly.

A mouth tastes spicy like geraniums
Eyes like sweet trout, ears like snails to eat
And when it's lower down the lover comes
He's washed all through by something awfully sweet.

And though in the full course of his research
Each lover must deceive himself at will
Must falsify, forget, betray, besmirch
Debase and doublecross and nearly kill,

Yet licking their lips all lovers are agreed
The soul's a something very sweet indeed.

DUDLEY FITTS

(1903–1968)

"Ya se van los pastores"

Lady, the shepherds have all gone
To Extremadura, taking their sheep with them,

Their musical instruments also, their singing:
We shall not see them again.

Therefore bring lute, flute, or other melodious machine,
And we shall sit under this plane-tree and perform upon it.

There is no help for it: use your eyes:

ι e shepherds, Lady, have gone into Extremadura,
Eastward, into sunrise.

BREWSTER GHISELIN

(b. 1903)

Shore Bird

What bird unknown,
Turnstone or plover, feeds
On the wet sea-waste
Near the gray waves rising,
Gleans in the midst of the foam
The heaped red weed,
And quick from the shining hail
And snow of the wave
Speeds in the zebra flashing of its flight?

Bath of Aphrodite

She rises among boulders. Naked, alone,
In freshets of the seacliff wind she stands;
She comes rose-golden over the color of stones,
Down to the wide plane of the seaward sand.

And what are these . . . visitants that pass her?
Shorebirds with wings like thin
Fins against the morning.

She wades in shallows warmer than the air
And sees the long push of the promised foam,
She feels the chill that draws her breath like fear,
And wading slowly feels for the deeper cold. . . .

What voices twitter and fade along that shore?
The godwit and the killdeer and the curlew,
The turnstone and the willet.

And now the water is silvering to her knees.
Over the sunmarks flurried about her feet
She sees a hundred harmless fishes flit
In the autumn of the glass-sharp morning sea.

What birds are those that ride the rising seas?
Slow shorelong pelicans
Fanned by the shoreward green.

Her thighs curved like the Venus's-shell submerge.
She wades into deep waves, her body drowns
Up to the lifted breasts and lifting arms;
Foam floats the tendrils of her tightening curls.

What birds are these that fall with never a swerve?
Far waves where morning burns,
Terns shatter into glass.

Now the rich moment, as she leans and swims
Folded into a hissing slope of foam:
The sea receives the shape that once it gave:
Her gold and roses to its dazzle of waves,
The shadow of all her secrets to its shade.

The Food of Birds

I

The cuckoo snatches at the hairy worm
In Audubon's paradise. The hawk bites blood.
The heron probes the wounded marsh. The swan
Feeds like a dredge.
But Time is eaten by the mockingbird.

II

From leaning weeds a goldfinch takes its seed.
Sanderling needles selvage in the sand.
With folded dive, a pelican bags the sea
And gargles fins.
Time's taste is gargled by the mockingbird.

III

Flycatcher snips ephemerid from the light.
On sweet and heavy bees the kingbird feeds.
The soft owl fattens on the feel of fur
Softer than he.
Men share the wafer of the mockingbird.

The Net Breaker

I laid down my long net in the big tide.
The brown web streamed like a dropped sail in the water
Yet seemed small as lace. It lifted and rode,
Widened and lagged. Then it began to flash,
Shivering, gleamed, and sank with a long shudder.
I never knew what hurried and held it hard.
The weight of a million? Or one vaster shape?
The slack of it rose, floating the Niles of calm,
Idling over the rolling of the deepened ocean.

Learning the Language

The diphthongs are honey, the dentals are resin
Between the teeth: and, testing, I can see:
This country comes into my standing car
Like the scent of orange blossoms,
Like dust blown from the plow,
Like the woman who asks—and enters, as the barrier rises
From the crossing and naked rails while one
Slate-dark train flows from the station
Away toward emptier plains, more pallid
Distance piled with mountains of haze.
Under the lintel of cloth over her brow the eyes,
That were keeping their counsel, black as a cave whose own
    darkness is its door, change:
In the blank of their shadow, a brazier is breathed on.

LORINE NIEDECKER

(1903–1970)

Remember my little granite pail?
The handle of it was blue.
Think what's got away in my life—
Was enough to carry me thru.

———————

The clothesline post is set
yet no totem-carvings distinguish the Niedecker tribe
from the rest; every seventh day they wash:
worship sun; fear rain, their neighbors' eyes;
raise their hands from ground to sky,
and hang or fall by the whiteness of their all.

———————

There's a better shine
on the pendulum
than is on my hair
and many times

· ·   · ·

I've seen it there.

———————

What horror to awake at night
and in the dimness see the light.
            Time is white
            mosquitoes bite
I've spent my life on nothing.

The thought that stings. How are you, Nothing,
sitting around with Something's wife.

        Buzz and burn
        is all I learn
I've spent my life on nothing.

I'm pillowed and padded, pale and puffing
lifting household stuffing—
        carpets, dishes
        benches, fishes
I've spent my life in nothing.

        Paul
          when the leaves
            fall

      from their stems
        that lie thick
          on the walk

      in the light
        of the full note
          the moon

      playing
        to leaves
          when they leave

      the little
        thin things
          Paul

The death of my poor father
leaves debts
and two small houses.

To settle this estate
a thousand fees arise—
I enrich the law.

Before my own death is certified,
recorded, final judgement
judged

taxes taxed
I shall own a book
of old Chinese poems

and binoculars
to probe the river
trees.

———————

Woman in middle life
raises hot fears—

a few cool years after these
then who'll remember

flash to black
I gleamed?

———————

He lived—childhood summers
        thru bare feet
then years of money's lack
        and heat

beside the river—out of flood
        came his wood, dog
woman, lost her, daughter—
        prologue

to planting trees. He buried carp
        beneath the rose
where grass-still
        the marsh rail goes.

To bankers on high land
    he opened his wine tank.
He wished his only daughter
    to work in the bank

but he'd given her a source
    to sustain her—
a weedy speech,
    a marshy retainer.

———————

I rose from marsh mud,
algae, equisetum, willows,
sweet green, noisy
birds and frogs

to see her wed in the rich
rich silence of the church,
the little white slave-girl
in her diamond fronds.

In aisle and arch
the satin secret collects.
United for life to serve
silver. Possessed.

The Graves

You were my mother, thorn apple bush,
armed against life's raw push.
But you my father catalpa tree
stood serene as now—he refused to see
that the other woman, the hummer he shaded
    hotly cared
for his purse petals falling—
    his mind in the air.

———————

My friend tree
I sawed you down
but I must attend
an older friend
the sun

———————

The men leave the car
to bring us green-white lilies
      by woods
These men are our woods
yet I grieve

I'm swamp
as against a large pine-spread—
his clear No marriage
      no marriage
friend

———————

My life is hung up
in the flood
   a wave-blurred
          portrait

Don't fall in love
with this face—
   it no longer exists
        in water
           we cannot fish

———————

Get a load
   of April's
        fabulous

frog rattle—
   lowland freight cars
      in the night

Poet's Work

Grandfather
  advised me:
    Learn a trade

I learned
  to sit at desk
    and condense

No layoff
  from this
    condensery

———————

I married

in the world's black night
for warmth
    if not repose.
    At the close—
someone.

I hid with him
from the long range guns.
    We lay leg
    in the cupboard, head
in closet.

A slit of light
at no bird dawn—
    Untaught
    I thought
he drank

too much.
I say
    I married
    and lived unburied.
I thought—

My Life By Water

My life
   by water—
      Hear

spring's
   first frog
      or board

out on the cold
   ground
      giving

Muskrats
   gnawing
      doors

to wild green
   arts and letters
      Rabbits

raided
   my lettuce
      One boat

two—
   pointed toward
      my shore

thru birdstart
   wingdrip
      weed-drift

of the soft
   and serious—
      Water

————————

Far reach
  of sand
          A man

bends to inspect
  a shell
          Himself

part coral
  and mud
          clam

————————

Stone
and that hard
contact—
the human

On the mossed
massed quartz
on which spruce
grew dense

I met him
We were thick
We said good-bye
on The Passing Years
River

Sewing a Dress

The need
these closed-in days

to move before you
smooth-draped
and color-elated

in a favorable wind

Paean to Place

*And the place
was water*

Fish
    fowl
        flood
    Water lily mud
My life

in the leaves and on water
My mother and I
             born
in swale and swamp and sworn
to water

My father
thru marsh fog
    sculled down
        from high ground
saw her face

at the organ
bore the weight of lake water
    and the cold—
he seined for carp to be sold
that their daughter

might go high
on land
    to learn
Saw his wife turn
deaf

and away
She
    who knew boats
      and ropes
no longer played

She helped him string out nets
for tarring
    And she could shoot
      He was cool
to the man

who stole his minnows
by night and next day offered
    to sell them back
      He brought in a sack
of dandelion greens

if no flood
No oranges—none at hand
    No marsh marigolds
      where the water rose
He kept us afloat

I mourn her not hearing canvasbacks
their blast-off rise
    from the water
        Not hearing sora
rails's sweet

spoon-tapped waterglass-
descending scale-
    tear-drop-tittle
        Did she giggle
as a girl?

His skiff skimmed
the coiled celery now gone
    from these streams
        due to carp
He knew duckweed

fall-migrates
toward Mud Lake bottom
    Knew what lay
        under leaf decay
and on pickerel weeds

before summer hum
To be counted on:
    new leaves
        new dead
leaves

He could not
—like water bugs—
    stride surface tension
        He netted
loneliness

As to his bright new car
my mother—her house
   next his—averred:
        A hummingbird
can't haul

Anchored here
in the rise and sink
   of life—
        middle years' nights
he sat

beside his shoes
rocking his chair
   Roped not 'looped
       in the loop
of her hair'

I grew in green
slide and slant
   of shore and shade
       Child-time—wade
thru weeds

Maples to swing from
Pewee-glissando
   sublime
       slime-
song

Grew riding the river
Books
   at home-pier
       Shelley could steer
as he read

I was the solitary plover
a pencil
    for a wing-bone
From the secret notes
I must tilt

upon the pressure
execute and adjust
    In us sea-air rhythm
'We live by the urgent wave
of the verse'

Seven year molt
for the solitary bird
    and so young
Seven years the one
dress

for town once a week
One for home
    faded blue-striped
as she piped
her cry

Dancing grounds
my people had none
    woodcocks had—
    backland-
air around

Solemnities
such as what flower
    to take
    to grandfather's grave
unless

water lilies—
he who'd bowed his head
    to grass as he mowed
    Iris now grows
on fill

for the two
and for him
    where they lie
    How much less am I
in the dark then they?

Effort lay in us
before religions
    at pond bottom
        All things move toward
the light

except those
that freely work down
    to oceans' black depths
        In us an impulse tests
the unknown

River rising—flood
Now melt and leave home
    Return—broom wet
        naturally wet
Under

soak-heavy rug
water bugs hatched—
    no snake in the house
        Where were they?—
she

who knew how to clean up
after floods
    he who bailed boats, houses
        Water endows us
with buckled floors

You with sea water running
in your veins sit down in water
    Expect the long-stemmed blue
        speedwell to renew
itself

O my floating life
Do not save love
    for things
        Throw *things*
to the flood

ruined
by the flood
    Leave the new unbought—
        all one in the end—
water

I possessed
the high word:
    The boy my friend
        played his violin
in the great hall

On this stream
my moonnight memory
    washed of hardships
        maneuvers barges
thru the mouth

of the river
They fished in beauty
    It was not always so
        In Fishes
red Mars

rising
rides the sloughs and sluices
    of my mind
        with the persons
on the edge

———

Not all harsh sounds displease—
Yellowhead blackbirds cough
    through reeds and fronds
as through pronged bronze

Darwin

I

His holy
    slowly
        mulled over
  matter

not all 'delirium
    of delight'
        as were the forests
  of Brazil

'Species are not
    (it is like confessing
        a murder)
  immutable'

He was often becalmed
    in this Port Desire by illness
        or rested from species
  at billiard table

As to Man
    'I believe Man . . .
        in the same predicament
  with other animals'

II

Cordilleras to climb—Andean
    peaks 'tossed about
        like the crust
  of a broken pie'

Icy wind
    Higher, harder
        Chileans advised eat onions
  for shortness of breath

Heavy on him:
    Andes miners carried up
        great loads—not allowed
  to stop for breath

Fossil bones near Santa Fe
    Spider-bite-scauld
        Fever
  Tended by an old woman

'Dear Susan . . .
    I am ravenous
        for the sound
  of the pianoforte'

III

FitzRoy blinked—
    sea-shells on mountain tops!
        The laws of change
  rode the seas

without the good captain
    who could not concede
        land could rise from the sea
  until—before his eyes

earthquake—
    Talcahuana Bay drained out—
        all-water wall
  up from the ocean

—six seconds—
    demolished the town
        The will of God?
  Let us pray

And now the Galapagos Islands—
    hideous black lava
        The shore so hot
  it burned their feet

through their boots
    Reptile life
        Melville here later
  said the chief sound was a hiss

A thousand turtle monsters
    drive together to the water
        Blood-bright crabs hunt ticks
  on lizards' backs

Flightless cormorants
    Cold-sea creatures—
        penguins, seals
  here in tropical waters

Hell for FitzRoy
    but for Darwin Paradise Puzzle
        with the jig-saw gists
  beginning to fit

IV

Years . . . balancing
    probabilities
        I am ill, he said
  and books are slow work

Studied pigeons
    barnacles, earthworms
        Extracted seeds
  from bird dung

Brought home Drosera—
    saw insects trapped
        by its tentacles—the fact
  that a plant should secrete

an acid acutely akin
    to the digestive fluid
        of an animal! Years
  till he published

He wrote Lyell: Don't forget
    to send me the carcass
        of your half-bred African cat
  should it die

V

I remember, he said
    those tropical nights at sea—
        we sat and talked
  on the booms

Tierra del Fuego's
    shining glaciers translucent
        blue clear down
  (almost) to the indigo sea

(By the way Carlyle
    thought it most ridiculous
        that anyone should care
  whether a glacier

moved a little quicker
    or a little slower
        or moved at all)
  Darwin

sailed out
    of Good Success Bay
        to carcass-
conclusions—

the universe
    not built by brute force
        but designed by laws
  The details left

to the working of chance
    'Let each man hope
        and believe
  what he can'

CARL RAKOSI

(b. 1903)

The January of a Gnat

Snow panels, ice pipes, house the afternoon
whose poised arms lift prayer with the elm's antennae.
She has her wind of swift burrs, whose spiel is gruff,
scanning the white mind of the winter moon
with her blank miles. Her voice is lower
than the clovers or the bassviol of seastuff.

So void moons make a chaste anabasis
across the stalks of star and edelweiss
while Volga nixies and a Munich six
o'clock hear in the diaphane the rise
of one bassoon.
                            So the immense frosts fix
their vacant death, bugs spray the roots like lice.
High blizzards broom the cold for answer
to their ssh of vapors and their vowel ooo.

Amulet

You are ideal,
o figurette,
and cool as camphor.
Your eyes are set
in small blue jadework
and your head stings
like a drop of witchhazel.

Bless the white throat
of this lady
drinking clabber milk
at a buffet lunch.

Figures in an Ancient Ink

In the dense scopes
Jupiter progenitor,
perfumed a Christian,
fishes in the reefs
with ancient weights
or sometimes wanders
an apocryphal white goat.

And Hrothgar the wandering scop,
heartrover among your fathers,
sails the North Sea
with a load of deerhides
      and bird feathers
and two thousand tods
      of whalebone for the Danes.

And Saracen physicians
under a pecan tree
discuss the heart.

These unconnected images no doubt
once represented agents
and fellows bearing yokes,
but that is not the way
they speak to me.

I made them
but took away their speech
and gave them instead a precious
patina of ancient associations.
That is how they got their mystery
and speak to me.

What, am I in love then
with my own images, an Onan
wrapped in their protective strangeness?
shrinking from what failure?

Strange that such a patina should be
more durable than the actual Hrothgar!

The Lobster

Eastern Sea, 100 fathoms,
green sand, pebbles,
broken shells.

Off Suno Saki 60 fathoms,
gray sand, pebbles,
bubbles rising.

Plasma-bearer
and slow-
motion benthos!

The fishery vessel *Ion*
drops anchor here
                collecting
plankton smears and fauna.

Plasma-bearer, visible
sea purge,
          sponge and kelpleaf.
Halicystus the Sea Bottle

resembles emeralds
and is the largest
cell in the world.

Young sea horse
Hippocampus twenty
minutes old—

nobody has ever
seen this marine
freak blink.

It radiates on
terminal vertebra
a comb of twenty

upright spines
and curls
its rocky tail.

Saltflush lobster
bull encrusted swims

backwards from the rock.

Lying in Bed on a Summer Morning

How pleasant are the green
and brown tiles
of my neighbor's roof.
The branches of his elm tree
stretch across
and make a delightful
composition,
                    the angle
of the roof
                the exact plane
which the branch needs
to be interesting.
Le mot juste? la branche juste!

And you, my dark spruce,
dominate the left side
of this composition.
You are clannish but authentic
and stand, uncompromising,
for the family of trees.

And all at once the early birds
all break out chirping
as when the bidding opens
on the stock exchange.
                        Then one,
the long sweet warble
of a finch.

Oh stay!
And then a chant from down the street,
two boys triumphant,
very small in thick thick glasses:
"We got a bird nest! We got a bird nest!"
But a younger brother,
left behind and clobbered
when the mother was not looking
saw his chance to singsong back
(ah, sweet revenge):
                    "But
a woodpecker didn't make that nest!"

And now I come to you, sky.
What is there between us?

For one, I love El Greco,
who was your painter.

Your blue is clear
as on the first day.

In your presence I am man
and feel as if I
                    could live forever.

Young Girl

on her way to the beach,
walking daintily in bare feet
to avoid the stones.

Titania's gauze
forms a cute skirt,
                    so short
it takes the breath away
and opens in front

to admit man
to her shapely legs
                    walking brightly
in inexorable scissor movement
through his child taboos.

At thirteen she
already swings her hips,
ostensibly to keep her balance,
and re-enacts the secret
of man's bed.
She smiles and shoots
implacable seduction
straight into the eyes.

A nimbus envelops her girdle.

Oh stay!

Disclose your meaning.

"I like the way you look at me.
The lubricities of your mind."

Hold it, grandpa.
From where I stood, it sounded more like
"How delightful
that you noticed my new swimming suit!
It makes me feel like a woman."

Touché!

But was it so far out to imagine
that in the safety of that dark,
rather old-fashioned, sensitive
homuncio look in the poet's eyes,
having only a moment,
she let the panther out
of her pubic lair
to show that she was nubile,
and became ionized herself?

It was a great day
for Patrick Henry
                    Junior High.

Such bitter-sweet discombobulations
in a moment turn men into Pierrots.

Americana 3

On Washington's Birthday Yancey the haberdasher
ran a full-page ad under a banner headline
in deference to the boy who could not tell a lie:
IT'S TIME WE QUIT FOOLING YOU
                              Yancey's had a false front.
It was ten feet shorter inside than out.
To correct this, he was knocking walls down, moving fixtures,
putting in new lights and introducing a new heating system
in order to give his customers the opportunity
to be seduced by accessories of the finest quality.

Atta boy, merchant! Down the hatch!

One time in Boot Hollow Little Ab Yancey challenged Foggy
      Dell
and his companions Homer Bullteeter and Slappy Henstep.
Crowing like cocks they accepted the challenge
and flapped their wings.
                          Then Ab rose up and neighed like a
                          horse:
"I'm the yellow flower of the forest
all brimstone but the head and that's aquafortis"
and rode them down like lightning through a crab-apple
      orchard.

"We're satisfied," they conceded. "You're a beauty!"

To an Anti-Semite

So you fought for the Jews
in the last war
and have become a patriot again!

Why you thick-skulled liar,
as impossible to offend
as to trust with an order,

you were never within
three thousand miles
of the front.

You fought the war
in Camp McKinley,
cleaning stables

and stealing out
into the moonlight
with the kitchen maids.

Discoveries, Trade Names,
Genitals, and Ancient Instruments

If there is no connection between the wild
                                        hemp of Kashmir
and the plectrum on a Persian lute,
                            the mind
will make one before the mallet comes down
                                    on the cymbalo.
As the young people have discovered,
it can also make a Pax Americana
out of genitals and meditation.
So while it notes that Ghulan Quadir Zardar,
                                    the Hasheesh King,
has been arrested in a taxi on his way to Srinagar,
let's steal a gay name from a love potion
and call ourselves HI-JOHN THE CONQUEROR ROOT.

Two Variations on a Theme

I

What's his offense?

He's young
and lies with women

in his imagination.
The apprehension of death
grips him by the neck.
He'll go as close to an old man
as to a blubber washed up

on the beach.

II

What's his offense?

He will not look.
The face is too old.
He will not look.

Instructions to the Player

Cellist,
easy on that bow.
Not too much weeping.

Remember that the soul
is easily agitated
and has a terror of shapelessness.
It will venture out
but only to a doe's eye.

Let the sound out
inner *misterioso*
but from a distance
like the forest at night.

And do not forget
                 the pause between.
That is the sweetest
and has the nature of infinity.

The Avocado Pit

a complete earth
                 hard as stone
the size of a plum
                 Pompeian red,
darkened and faded
                 like an old Roman mural
from the bath house
                 of Menander,
golden brown
                 with delicate veins
as if the earth
                 had cracked with age
or we were looking
                 at the rivers
from a satellite.

R. P. BLACKMUR

(1904–1965)

Redwing

What is that island, say you, stark and black—
A Cythera in northern exile? sung
Only by sailors on the darkward tack
Or till the channel buoy give safety tongue?
    Here is no Eldorado on the wane:
    New Sirens draw us in, in silent seine.

Men do not come to live here, but to spend
Memory, time, and the long sense of flight,
And find by spendthrift each one image friend
That might outlast him and himself benight:
    In spending tides, spent winds, and unspent seas
    Find out the flowering desert dark, soul's ease.

Redwing was driven so and so drawn in,
A bearded fisher in his own annoy
Hearing without all hallowèd within,
The hermit prison-crying in the boy,
    The broken promise cutting the inward grain,
    The heart throstling the sweet-tormented brain.

Redwing was jilted forty years ago;
What wilted waits for water still, what winced
Still tenders when his fingers free and fro
The mooring-buoy, and he, each fair tide since,
    Full-bearded, full awry, takes second sight
    Of exile in the black isle, Jordan's Delight.

(Once I was with him, he within me yet,
When while the ash of dawn was colding through
And the ashen tiller stick was creaking wet
He sang of Oh, the foggy, foggy dew!—
    Then felt, and lost, the long, low-running swell
    That buoyed his words up, voice that made them spell.)

All broken ground and ledges to the east
Awash and breaking, this island has a loom
Never to be forgotten from the west
And never to be left without sea-room.
 O Redwing, by your ruddled beard I swear
 Jordan shall wreck you yet, and wrecking spare.

This stony garden crossed by souring cries—
Gull bleat, hawk shriek, mouse and eagle screams—
Retrieves, O Redwing, silence in your eyes:
It is excruciation that redeems;
 Redeems, O Redwing, by your blood I swear,
 The still brain from anhungered sirens there.

———

   One grey and foaming day
   I looked from my lee shore
   landwards and across the bay:
   my eyes grew small and sore.

   Low in the low sea-waves
   the coastline sank from sight;
   the viewless, full sea-graves
   stood open like the night:

   (sea waters are most bare
   when darkness spreads her trawl,
   the sea-night winds her snare
   either for ship or soul).

   Once along this coast
   my fathers made their sail
   and were with all hands lost,
   outweathered in a gale.

   Now from long looking I
   have come on second sight,
   there where the lost shores lie
   the sea is breeding night.

Mirage

The wind was in another country, and
the day had gathered to its heart of noon
the sum of silence, heat, and stricken time.
Not a ripple spread. The sea mirrored
perfectly all the nothing in the sky.
We had to walk about to keep our eyes
from seeing nothing, and our hearts from stopping
at nothing. Then most suddenly we saw
horizon on horizon lifting up
out of the sea's edge a shining mountain
sun-yellow and sea-green; against it surf
flung spray and spume into the miles of sky.
Somebody said mirage, and it was gone,
but there I have been living ever since.

Seas Incarnadine

Wind was not, flat was, but was imminent.
The long grey swells reddened with the dawn,
I saw the black spar-buoy on Leighton's shoal
lifted on red water and dip from sight.
The breaking of the seas below was dull.
I on my cliff stood up in all my blood
confessing the sudden murder in my heart
to the dark tangle of rock and spray beneath.
Had I friend there I would have cast him down.

Red vanished and the shrunken sun sky-lost.
Like mountain night wind was, sheer-fallen, black.
I could not see nor hear nor breathe, but held,
sea-crucified, back-nailed against granite,
wind-fast, tight-drenched, flat-flailed, a sacrifice
vainly surrendered to unpropitiable seas.

Seas would not take me. All I saw of glory,
where twenty fathoms broke gigantic black

backs to shrieking smother, fathoms in air,
made me run out of blood entirely. I was
the only prisoner in a world set free.

Since There's No Help . . .

What of the beauty that these hands have held,
is there no help that they preserve it still,
and can be seized, as when great silence welled,
more than a memory, almost at will?
Is there no help, if I see in these eyes
the drunken weather of the headlong heart,
the radiance of wordless intimacies,
brim to the flood? It is no help to part.

You, Michael, were but righting wrong with wrong.
Why should I pocket my imploring hands,
why seal my inner ear to inmost song
or quench the radiance in which she stands?
    Such would be parting: an insensate night
    that perjures, with its pain, the soul's delight.

The Communiqués from Yalta

Not heart, not soul, and not their joined intent,
not these alone, but the whole process, breaking;
these are not salvo sounds, but fire raking
all hope, all memory, all undertaking.

—Who mocks the mockers when mockery is spent?
When will this dry tree I clutch be done shaking?

[Luke xxiii, 31]

The Groundhog

In June, amid the golden fields,
I saw a groundhog lying dead.
Dead lay he; my senses shook,
And mind outshot our naked frailty.
There lowly in the vigorous summer
His form began its senseless change,
And made my senses waver dim
Seeing nature ferocious in him.
Inspecting close his maggots' might
And seething cauldron of his being,
Half with loathing, half with a strange love,
I poked him with an angry stick.
The fever arose, became a flame
And Vigour circumscribed the skies,
Immense energy in the sun,
And through my frame a sunless trembling.
My stick had done nor good nor harm.
Then stood I silent in the day
Watching the object, as before;
And kept my reverence for knowledge
Trying for control, to be still,
To quell the passion of the blood;
Until I had bent down on my knees
Praying for joy in the sight of decay.
And so I left; and I returned
In Autumn strict of eye, to see
The sap gone out of the groundhog,
But the bony sodden hulk remained.
But the year had lost its meaning,
And in intellectual chains
I lost both love and loathing,
Mured up in the wall of wisdom.
Another summer took the fields again
Massive and burning, full of life,
But when I chanced upon the spot
There was only a little hair left,
And bones bleaching in the sunlight
Beautiful as architecture;

I watched them like a geometer,
And cut a walking stick from a birch.
It has been three years, now.
There is no sign of the groundhog.
I stood there in the whirling summer,
My hand capped a withered heart,
And thought of China and of Greece,
Of Alexander in his tent;
Of Montaigne in his tower,
Of Saint Theresa in her wild lament.

'I Walked Over the Grave of Henry James'

I walked over the grave of Henry James
But recently, and one eye kept the dry stone.
The other leaned on boys at games away,
My soul was balanced in my body cold.

I am one of those prodigals of hell
Whom ten years have seen cram with battle;
Returns to what he canted from, grants it good,
As asthma makes itself a new resolution.

I crushed a knob of earth between my fingers,
This is a very ordinary experience.
A name may be glorious but death is death,
I thought, and took a street-car back to Harvard Square.

The Fury of Aerial Bombardment

You would think the fury of aerial bombardment
Would rouse God to relent; the infinite spaces
Are still silent. He looks on shock-pried faces.
History, even, does not know what is meant.

You would feel that after so many centuries
God would give man to repent; yet he can kill
As Cain could, but with multitudinous will,
No farther advanced than in his ancient furies.

Was man made stupid to see his own stupidity?
Is God by definition indifferent, beyond us all?
Is the eternal truth man's fighting soul
Wherein the Beast ravens in its own avidity?

Of Van Wettering I speak, and Averill,
Names on a list, whose faces I do not recall
But they are gone to early death, who late in school
Distinguished the belt feed lever from the belt holding pawl.

On a Squirrel Crossing the Road
in Autumn, in New England

It is what he does not know,
Crossing the road under the elm trees,
About the mechanism of my car,
About the Commonwealth of Massachusetts,
About Mozart, India, Arcturus,

That wins my praise. I engage
At once in whirling squirrel-praise.

He obeys the orders of nature
Without knowing them.
It is what he does not know
That makes him beautiful.
Such a knot of little purposeful nature!

I who can see him as he cannot see himself
Repose in the ignorance that is his blessing.

It is what man does not know of God
Composes the visible poem of the world.

                    . . . Just missed him!

La Crosse at Ninety Miles an Hour

Better to be the rock above the river,
The bluff, brown and age-old sandstone,
Than the broad river winding to the Gulf.

The river looks like world reality
And has the serenity of wide and open things.
It is a river of even ice today.

Winter men in square cold huts have cut
Round holes to fish through: I saw it as a boy.
They have a will to tamper with the river.

Up on the high bluffs nothing but spirit!
It is there I would be, where an Indian scout was
Long ago, now purely imaginary.

It is a useless and heaven-depended place,
Commodious rock to lock the spirit in,
Where it gazes on the river and the land.

Better to be rock-like than river-like;
Water is a symbol will wear us all away.
Rock comes to the same end, more slowly so.

Rock is the wish of the spirit, heavy symbol,
Something to hold to beyond worldly use.
I feel it in my bones, kinship with vision,

And on the brown bluffs above the Mississippi
In the land of my deepest, earliest memories,
Rushing along at ninety miles an hour,

I feel the old elation of the imagination.
Strong talk of the river and the rock.
Small division between the world and spirit.

Gnat on My Paper

He has two antennae,
They search back and forth,
Left and right, up and down.

He has four feet,
He is exploring what I write now.

This is a living being,
Is this a living poem?

His life is a quarter of an inch.
I could crack him any moment now.

Now I see he has two more feet,
Almost too delicate to examine.

He is still sitting on this paper,
An inch away from An.

Does he know who I am,
Does he know the importance of man?

He does not know or sense me,
His antennae are still sensing.

I wonder if he knows it is June,
The world in its sensual height?

How absurd to think
That he never thought of Plato.

He is satisfied to sit on this paper,
For some reason he has not flown away.

Small creature, gnat on my paper,
Too slight to be given a thought,

I salute you as the evanescent,
I play with you in my depth.

What, still here? Still evanescent?
You are my truth, that vanishes.

Now I put down this paper,
He has flown into the infinite.
He could not say it.

JOHN HOLMES

(1904–1962)

The Old Professor

It isn't the young men sprawling in chairs I mind.
(Though when I was a student we sat straight.)
It isn't that I mind much the coughing, or cutting
My classes, or ignorant ignorance of the past.
(When I was a student, we said Sir, stood to recite.)
It isn't that I mind ideas. I had some, too,
And was told it wasn't right, and it wouldn't do,
And it couldn't be, and I had them just the same.
It isn't the clothes. It isn't the swing music.
But sometimes I walk the college streets at night,
Hands rammed into topcoat pockets, collar up,
Kicking the leaves before me, cursing the College,
Cursing the dull dear young indifferent damned,
The boys and girls who never wanted to know,
And never will, but can be passed in the course.

Four and a Half

The griefs of a little boy are forever.
His rages are a death-blow given.
In his throat and eyes the loneliness
Of a small boy is a weather-driven
Ache. Joy in a little boy
Is a handbell whirled and ringing.
His delight makes more delight.
Growing, greeting, gathering,
A little boy invents amazing words
For the world. The name of never
Is not one. And watch his eyes.
He knows a humming world-forever
Word but cannot say it yet.

The labors of a little boy are all
In carrying something somewhere else,
And back, and reaching to be tall.
His afternoons and evenings are
Thrust forward against sleep as far
As ingenious eagerness can go.
His mornings never end.
Under skies that never bend
He asks to see, and help, and know.
He dabbles noise and water. Tries
The world's worth by running on
Its grass hard. Trusts. And has not
Time to ask why yesterday is gone.

LOUIS ZUKOFSKY

(1904–1978)

I Sent Thee Late

Vast, tremulous;
Grave on grave of water-grave:

Past.

Futurity no more than duration
Of a wave's rise, fall, rebound
Against the shingles, in ever repeated mutation
Of emptied returning sound.

Poem beginning "The"

Because I have had occasion to remember, quote, paraphrase, I
dedicate this poem to Anyone and Anything I have unjustifiably
forgotten. Also to J. S. Bach—309, Bede's *Ecclesiastical History*—
248, 291, Max Beerbohm—245, Beethoven's *Ninth Symphony*—
310–312, Broadway—134, Geoffrey Chaucer—1st Movement, Title,
College Cheer—45, E. E. Cummings' *Is Five*—38, Dante—66,
Norman Douglas' *South Wind*—14, Elijah, the Prophet—24, T. S.
Eliot's *The Waste Land* and *The Sacred Wood*—25–27, John Erskine—
184, 185, Heinrich Heine—266, 267, 269, 316, Robert Herrick—187,
188, Horace—141, Horses—224–237, Aldous Huxley's *Those Barren
Leaves*—12, 18, Henry James—2nd Movement, Title, Jewish Folk
Song—191, 270–280, James Joyce—13, 20, 28, 29, D. H. Lawrence—
8, 19, 133, Christopher Marlowe's *Edward II*—46, 47, Modern
Advertising—163, George Moore—24, Marianne Moore—22, Mus-
solini—74, 75, Myself—130, 142, 167, 309, Obvious—Where the
Reference is Obvious, Walter Pater's *Renaissance*—165, *Peer Gynt*—
281–285, Poe's *Helen*—168–182, Popular Non-Sacred Song—4, 5, 36,
37, 288, 289, Ezra Pound—15, 18, Power of the Past, Present, and

Figures and References following dashes are to lines in *Poem beginning
"The"*.

Future—Where the reference is to the word Sun, E. A. Robinson's *Children of the Night*—132, Sophocles—6, Oswald Spengler—132, Max Stirner—199–202, Symbol of our Relatively Most Permanent Self, Origin and Destiny—Wherever the reference is to the word Mother, *The Bible*—1–3, 9, 313, 314, The Bolsheviki—203, 323, The French Language—31, 33, 51, 292, The King's English—166, *The Merchant of Venice*—250–265, The Yellow Menace—241–242, University Extension—70, Villon—21, Franz Werfel—68, Virginia Woolf's *Mrs. Dalloway*—52, Yehoash—110–129, 205–223, 318–330.

First Movement: "And out of olde bokes, in good feith"

1   The
2   Voice of Jesus I. Rush singing
3   in the wilderness
4   A boy's best friend is his mother,
5   It's your mother all the time.
6   Residue of Oedipus-faced wrecks
7   Creating out of the dead,—
8   From the candle flames of the souls of dead mothers
9   Vide the legend of thin Christ sending her out of the
               temple,—
10   Books from the stony heart, flames rapping the stone,
11   Residue of self-exiled men
12   By the Tyrrhenian.
13   Paris.
14   But everywhere only the South Wind, the sirocco, the
               broken Earth-face.
15   The broken Earth-face, the age demands an image of its
               life and contacts,
16   Lord, lord, not that we pray, are sure of the question,
17   But why are our finest always dead?
18   And why, Lord, this time, is it Mauberly's Luini in
               porcelain, why is it Chelifer,

19   Why is it Lovat who killed Kangaroo,
20   Why Stephen Daedalus with the cane of ash,
21   But why les neiges?
22   And why, if all of Mary's Observations have been made
23   Have not the lambs become more sapient drinking of
          the spring;
24   Kerith is long dry, and the ravens that brought the
          prophet bread
25   Are dust in the waste land of a raven-winged evening.
26   And why if the waste-land has been explored, travelled
          over, circumscribed,
27   Are there only wrathless skeletons exhumed new planted
          in its sacred wood,
28   Why—heir, long dead—Odysseus, wandering of ten
          years
29   Out-journeyed only by our Stephen, bibbing of a day,
30   O why is that to Hecuba as Hecuba to he!

31   You are cra-a-zee on the subject of babies, says she,
32   That is because somehow our authors have been given a
          woman's intuition.
33   Il y a un peu trop de femme in this South Wind.
34   And on the cobblestones, bang, bang, bang, myself like
          the wheels—
35   The tram passes singing
36   O do you take this life as your lawful wife,
37   I do!
38   O the Time is 5
39   I do!
40   O the Time is 5
41   I do!
42   O do you take these friends as your loves to wive,
43   O the Time is 5
44   I do!

45   For it's the hoo-doos, the somethin' voo-doos
46   And not Kings onelie, but the wisest men
47   Graue Socrates, what says Marlowe?

48 For it was myself seemed held
49 Beating—beating—
50 Body trembling as over an hors d'oeuvres—
51
52 And the dream ending—Dalloway! Dalloway—
53 The blind portals opening, and I awoke!

54 Let me be
55 Not by art have we lived,
56 Not by graven images forbidden to us
57 Not by letters I fancy,
58 Do we dare say
59 With Spinoza grinding lenses, Rabbaisi,
60 After living on Cathedral Parkway?

Second Movement: International Episode

61 This is the aftermath
62 When Peter Out and I discuss the theatre.
63 Evenings, our constitutional.
64 We both strike matches, both in unison,
65   to light one pipe, my own.
66 'Tis, 'tis love, that makes the world go round and love is
            what I dream.
67 Peter is polite and I to me am almost as polite as Peter.
68 Somehow, in Germany, the Jew goat-song is
          unconvincing—
69   How the brain forms its visions thinking incessantly
            of the things,
70 Not the old Greeks anymore,—
71   the things themselves a shadow world scarce shifting
            the incessant thought—
72 Time, time the goat were an offering,
73 Eh, what show do we see tonight, Peter?
74 "Il Duce: I feel God deeply."
75   Black shirts—black shirts—some power is so
            funereal.

76   Lion-heart, frate mio, and so on in two languages
77   the thing itself a shadow world.
78   Goldenrod
79   Of which he is a part,
80   Sod
81   He hurried over
82   Underfoot,
83   Make now
84   His testament of sun and sky
85   With clod
86   To root what shoot
87   It sends to run the sun,
88   The sun-sky blood.
89   My loves there is his mystery beyond your loves.
90   Uncanny are the stars,
91   His slimness was as evasive
92   And his grimness was not yours,

93   Do you walk slowly the halls of the heavens,
94   Or saying that you do, lion-hearted not ours,
95   Hours, days, months, past from us and gone,
96   Lion-heart not looked upon, walk with the stars.
97   Or have these like old men acknowledged
98   No kin but that grips of death,
99   Of being dying only to live on with them
100 Entirely theirs,
101 And so quickly grown old that we on earth like stems
         raised dark
102 Feel only the lull, heave, phosphor change, death, the
103 One follow, the other, the end?

104 Our candles have been buried beneath these waters,
105 Their lights are his,
106 Ship-houses on the waters he might have lived near.
107 Steady the red light and it makes no noise whatever.
108 Damn it! they have made capital of his flesh and bone.
109 What, in revenge, can dead flesh and bone make
         capital?

110 And his heart is dry
111 Like the teeth of a dead camel
112 But his eyes no longer blink
113 Not even as a blind dog's.

114 With the blue night shadows on the sand
115 May his kingdom return to him,
116 The Bedouin leap again on his *asilah*,
117 The expanse of heaven hang upon his shoulder
118 As an embroidered texture,
119 Behind him on his saddle sit the night
120 Sing into his ear:

121 Swifter than a tiger to his prey,
122 Lighter than the storm wind, dust or spray,
123 The Bedouin bears the Desert-Night,
124 Big his heart and young with life,
125 Younger yet his gay, wild wife
126   The Desert-Night.

127 Some new trappings for his steed,
128 All the stars in dowry his meed
129   From the Desert-Night.

130 I've changed my mind, Zukofsky,
131 How about some other show—
132 "The Queen of Roumania", "Tilbury", "The West-
             Decline",
133 "Hall's Mills", "The Happy Quetzalcoatl",
134 "Near Ibsen", "Dancing with H. R. H.", "Polly Wants
             a New Fur Coat",
135 "The Post Office"—
136 Speaking of the post office, the following will handicap
             you for the position,
137   my dear Peter,
138 Your weight less than one hundred twenty-five pounds,
139 One half of a disabled veteran, and probably
140   the whole of an unknown soldier,
141 That's indomitaeque morti for you.

142   Is it true what you say, Zukofsky,
143   Sorry to say, My Peter Out.

144   "Tear the Codpiece Off, A Musical Comedy",
145   Likewise, "Panting for Pants",
146   "The Dream That Knows No Waking".

Third Movement: In Cat Minor

147   Hard, hard the cat-world.
148   On the stream Vicissitude
149   Our milk flows lewd.

150   We'll cry, we'll cry,
151   We'll cry the more
152   And wet the floor,

153   Megrow, megrow,
154   Around around
155   The only sound

156   The prowl, our prowl,
157   Of gentlemen cats
158   With paws like spats

159   Who weep the nights
160   Till the nights are gone—
161   —And r-r-run—the Sun!

Fourth Movement: More "Renaissance"

162   Is it the sun you're looking for,
163   Drop in at Askforaclassic, Inc.,
164   Get yourself another century,
165   A little frost before sundown,
166   It's the times don'chewknow,
167   And if you're a Jewish boy, then be your Plato's Philo.

168   Engprof, thy lectures were to me
169   Like those roast flitches of red boar
170   That, smelling, one is like to see
171   Through windows where the steam's galore
172   Like our own "Cellar Door".

173   On weary bott'm long wont to sit,
174   Thy graying hair, thy beaming eyes,
175   Thy heavy jowl would make me fit
176   For the Pater that was Greece,
177   The siesta that was Rome.

178   Lo! from my present—say not—itch
179   How statue-like I see thee stand
180   Phi Beta Key within thy hand!
181   Professor—from the backseats which
182   Are no man's land!

183   Poe,
184   Gentlemen, don'chewknow,
185   But never wrote an epic.

Fifth Movement: Autobiography

186   Speaking about epics, mother,
187   How long ago is it since you gathered mushrooms,
188   Gathered mushrooms while you mayed.
189   Is it your mate, my father, boating.
190   A stove burns like a full moon in a desert night.
191   Un in hoyze is kalt. You think of a new grave.
192   In the fields, flowers.
193   Night on the bladed grass, bayonets dewed.
194   Is it your mate, my father, boating.
195   Speaking about epics, mother,—
196   Down here among the gastanks, ruts, cemetery-
      tenements—
197   It is your Russia that is free.

198 And I here, can I say only—
199   "So then an egoist can never embrace a party
200   Or take up with a party?
201   Oh, yes, only he cannot let himself
202   Be embraced or taken up by the party."
203 It is your Russia that is free, mother.
204 Tell me, mother.

205 Winged wild geese, where lies the passage,
206 In far away lands lies the passage.
207 Winged wild geese, who knows the pathway?
208 Of the winds, asking, we shall say:
209 Wind of the South and wind of the North
210 Where has our sun gone forth?
211 Naked, twisted, scraggly branches,
212 And dark, gray patches through the branches,
213 Ducks with puffed-up, fluttering feathers
214 On a cobalt stream.
215 And faded grass that's slowly swaying.
216 A barefoot shepherd boy
217 Striding in the mire:
218 Swishing indifferently a peeled branch
219 On jaded sheep.
220 An old horse strewn with yellow leaves
221 By the edge of the meadow
222 Draws weakly with humid nostrils
223 The moisture of the clouds.
224 Horses that pass through inappreciable woodland,
225 Leaves in their manes tangled, mist, autumn green,
226 Lord, why not give these bright brutes—your good
                  land—
227 Turf for their feet always, years for their mien.
228 See how each peer lifts his head, others follow,
229 Mate paired with mate, flanks coming full they crowd,
230 Reared in your sun, Lord, escaping each hollow
231 Where life-struck we stand, utter their praise aloud.
232 Very much Chance, Lord, as when you first made us,
233 You might forget them, Lord, preferring what
234 Being less lovely where sadly we fuss?

235 Weed out these horses as tho they were not?
236 Never alive in brute delicate trembling
237 Song to your sun, against autumn assembling.

238 If horses could but sing Bach, mother,—
239 Remember how I wished it once—
240 Now I kiss you who could never sing Bach, never read
      Shakespeare.

241 In Manhattan here the Chinamen are yellow in the
      face, mother,
242 Up and down, up and down our streets they go yellow
      in the face,
243 And why is it the representatives of your, my, race are
      always hankering for food, mother?
244 We, on the other hand, eat so little.
245 Dawn't you think Trawtsky rawthaw a darrling,
246 I ask our immigrant cousin querulously.
247 Naw! I think hay is awlmawst a Tchekoff.
248 But she has more color in her cheeks than the Angles—
      Angels—mother,—
249 They have enough, though. We should get some more
      color, mother.
250 If I am like them in the rest, I should resemble them in
      that, mother,
251 Assimilation is not hard,
252 And once the Faith's askew
253 I might as well look Shagetz just as much as Jew.
254 I'll read their Donne as mine,
255 And leopard in their spots
256 I'll do what says their Coleridge,
257 Twist red hot pokers into knots.
258 The villainy they teach me I will execute
259 And it shall go hard with them,
260 For I'll better the instruction,
261 Having learned, so to speak, in their colleges.
262   It is engendered in the eyes
263   With gazing fed, and fancy dies
264   In the cradle where it lies
265   In the cradle where it lies

266 I, Senora, am the Son of the Respected Rabbi,
267 Israel of Saragossa,
268 Not that the Rabbis give a damn,
269 Keine Kadish wird man sagen.

Half-Dozenth Movement: Finale, and After

270 Under the cradle the white goat stands, mother,
271 What will the goat be saddled with, mother?
272   Almonds, raisins
273 What will my heart be bartering, mother,
274   Wisdom, learning.
275 Lullaby, lullaby, lullaby, lullaby.
276 These are the words of the prophet, mother,
277 Likely to save me from Tophet, mother—
278 What will my heart be burning to, mother,
279   Wisdom, learning.
280 By the cat and the well, I swear, my Shulamite!
281 In my faith, in my hope, and in my love.
282 I will cradle thee, I will watch thee,
283 Sleep and dream thou, dear my boy!
284   (Presses his cheek against her mouth.)
285 I must try to fare forth from here.
286 I do not forget you,
287 I am just gone out for to-night,
288 The Royal Stag is abroad,
289 I am gone out hunting,
290 The leaves have lit by the moon.
291 Even in their dirt, the Angles like Angels are fair,
292 Brooks Nash, for instance, faisant un petit bruit, mais
          tres net,
293 Saying, He who is afraid to do that should be denied
          the privilege,
294 And where the automobile roads with the gasoline
          shine,
295 Appropriately the katydid—
296 Ka-ty did .   .   .   .   Ka-ty didn't. . . .

297 Helen Gentile,
298 And did one want me; no.
299 But wanted me to take one? yes.
300 And should I have kissed one? no.
301 That is, embraced one first
302 And holding closely one, then kissed one? yes.
303 Angry against things' iron I ring
304 Recalcitrant prod and kick.
305 Oh, Baedekera Schönberg, you here
306   dreaming of the relentlessness of motion
307 As usual,
308 One or two dead in the process what does it matter.

309 Our God immortal such Life as is our God,
310 Bei dein Zauber, by thy magic I embrace thee,
311 Open Sesame, Ali Baba, I, thy firefly, little errant star,
        call here,
312 By thy magic I embrace thee.

313 O my son Sun, my son, my son Sun! would God
314 I had died for thee, O Sun, my son, my son!

315 I have not forgotten you, mother,—
316 It is a lie—Aus meinen grossen leiden mach ich die
        kleinen lieder,
317 Rather they are joy, against nothingness joy—
318 By the wrack we shall sing our Sun-song
319 Under our feet will crawl
320 The shadows of dead worlds,
321 We shall open our arms wide,
322 Call out of pure might—
323 Sun, you great Sun, our Comrade,
324 From eternity to eternity we remain true to you,
325 A myriad years we have been,
326 Myriad upon myriad shall be.

327 How wide our arms are,
328 How strong,
329 A myriad years we have been,
330 Myriad upon myriad shall be.

Not much more than being,
Thoughts of isolate, beautiful
Being at evening, to expect
        at a river-front:

A shaft dims
With a turning wheel;

Men work on a jetty
By a broken wagon;

Leopard, glowing-spotted,
    The summer river—
Under: The Dragon:

Cocktails
and signs of
"ads"

flashing,
light's waterfalls,

Bacchae
among electric lights

will swarm the crowds
streamers of the lighted

skyscrapers

nor tripping
over underbrush

but upon pavement

and not with thyrsus
shall they prick

the body of their loves
but waist to waist

laugh out in gyre—
announced then upon stairs,

not upon hills,
will be their flight

when passed turnstiles,
having dropped

coins
they've sprinted up

where on the air (elevated)
waves flash—and out—

leap
signaling—lights below

Ferry

Gleams a green lamp
In the fog:
Murmur in almost
A dialogue

Siren and signal
Siren to signal.

Parts the shore from the fog,
Rise there, tower on tower,
Signs of stray light
And of power.

Siren to signal
Siren to signal.

Hour-gongs and the green
Of the lamp.

Plash. Night. Plash. Sky.

Tibor Serly

Red varnish
Warm flitch

Of cello,
They play

Scroll before
Them—Sound

Breaks the
Sunset!—Kiss

With wide
Eyes—With

Their music
The (no?)

Pit, weather
Of tears

Which plagues
Us—Bodies

Of waves
Whose crests

Spear air,
Here rolls

The sea—
Go chase

It—a
Salt pact

Ranged over
Bars—white

Ribs pervade
In constant

Measures the
Rounds—Its

Wet frosting,
A kiss

Opens nothing,
Bend head

No! lips
Not this

An assumed
Poise among

Crowds! Blue—
Withdraws sunset—

Tones sound—
Pluck—dissonant—

Stops sing
The welter

———————

in that this happening
    is not unkind
it put to
    shame every kindness

mind, mouths, their words
    people, put sorrow
        on
    its body

before sorrow it came
    and before every kindness,
happening for every sorrow
    before every kindness;

———————

To my wash-stand
in which I wash
    my left hand
and my right hand

To my wash-stand
whose base is Greek
    whose shaft
is marble and is fluted

To my wash-stand
whose wash-bowl
    is an oval
in a square

To my wash-stand
whose square is marble
    and inscribes two
smaller ovals to left and right for soap

Comes a song of
water from the right faucet and the left
    my left and my
right hand mixing hot and cold

Comes a flow which
if I have called a song
    is a song
entirely in my head

a song out of imagining
modillions descried above
    my head   a frieze
of stone completing what no longer

is my wash-stand
since its marble has completed
    my getting up each morning
my washing before going to bed

my look into a mirror
to glimpse half an oval
    as if its half
were half-oval in my head   and the

climates of many
inscriptions human heads shapes'
    horses' elephants' (tusks) others'
scratched in marble tile

so my wash-stand
in one particular breaking of the
    tile at which I have
looked and looked

has opposed to my head
the inscription of a head
    whose coinage is the
coinage of the poor

observant in waiting
in their getting up mornings
and in their waiting
going to bed

carefully attentive
to what they have
and to what they do not
have

when a flow of water
doubled in narrow folds
occasions invertible counterpoints
over a head   and

an age in a wash-stand
and in their own heads

———————

When the crickets
sound like fifty water-taps
forsaken at once

the inclemency
of the inhuman noises
is the earth's

with its roadways
over cabins in the forests

the sheets smell
of sweet milk

all the waters
of the world

we are going
to sleep to sleep

———————

It's hard to see but think of a sea
Condensed into a speck.
And there are waves—
Frequencies of light,
Others that may be heard.
The one is one sea, the other a second.
There are electric stresses across condensers
That wear them down till they can stand no strain,
Are of no force and as unreclaimed
            as the bottom of the sea
Unless the space the stresses cross be air,
            that can be patched.
Large and small condensers,
Passing in the one instance frequencies
            that can be turned to sound,
In the other, alternations that escape,
So many waves of a speck of sea or what,
Or a graph the curve of a wave beyond all sound,
An open circuit where no action—
Like that of the retina made human by light—
Is recorded otherwise
Than having taken a desired path a little way
And tho infinitely a mote to be uncontained for ever.
This science is then like gathering flowers of the weed
One who works with me calls birdseed
That are tiny and many on one stem
They shed to the touch tho on a par
            with the large flower
That picked will find a vase.
I see many things at one time
            the harder the concepts get,
Or nothing
Which is a forever become me over forty years.
I am like another, and another, who has finished learning
And has just begun to learn.
If I turn pages back
A child may as well be staring with me
Wondering at the meaning
I turn to last
Perhaps.

The lines of this new song are nothing
But a tune making the nothing full
Stonelike become more hard than silent
The tune's image holding in the line.

Can a mote of sunlight defeat its purpose
When thought shows it to be deep or dark?

See sun, and think shadow.

(Ryokan's scroll)

dripping
words

off

a
long
while

the
first
snow

out
off
where
blue

eyes

the
cherry
tree's
petals

Xenophanes

Water, cold, and sweet, and pure
And yellow loaves are near at hand,
Wine that makes a rosy hand
Fire in winter, the little pulse.

Eating a little pulse, who are you?
How old? The hands of all are clean.
Why first pour wine into the cup?
Water first and the wine above.

Better than the strength of horses,
I come back to my other words:
The hound, "Stop beating him, I said,
I knew him when I heard his voice."

For now the floor and cups are clean,
The aired earth at the feet is seen,
The rainbow, violet, red, pale green,
Men making merry should first hymn—

"As To How Much"

Of the right way
That branches may be
Described—
Laden with snow—
What proscribed
A limit long ago?

We do not know
Of any we see—
Inscribed
Here bark is next snow.
Love is so. Thrived.
And we do not know. No.

As to how much
Such love may be
Ascribed
To bark or snow
You proscribed
Some music long ago.

Shang Cup

From a libation cup
of bronze
which stands

on a thought
its three feet are man—

so any pair of two
make wonder, sign

a writing of that stance
seen from all planes

as the base
cradling the cup

with half-circle
of an ancient ear
the handle—

a turtle dove
sings in jade
nests part of the lid

closed on the lip

but its beak and wings
raised to heaven

           this way
           the eye of it
           looks up

           singing
           come sip
           I drink.

"A" 11

for Celia and Paul

River that must turn full after I stop dying
Song, my song, raise grief to music
Light as my loves' thought, the few sick
So sick of wrangling: thus weeping,
Sounds of light, stay in her keeping
And my son's face—this much for honor.

Freed by their praises who make honor dearer
Whose losses show them rich and you no poorer
Take care, song, that what stars' imprint you mirror
Grazes their tears; draw speech from their nature or
Love in you—faced to your outer stars—purer
Gold than tongues make without feeling
Art new, hurt old: revealing
The slackened bow as the stinging
Animal dies, thread gold stringing
The fingerboard pressed in my honor.

Honor, song, sang the blest is delight knowing
We overcome ills by love. Hurt, song, nourish
Eyes, think most of whom you hurt. For the flowing
River 's poison where what rod blossoms. Flourish
By love's sweet lights and sing *in them I flourish.*

No, song, not any one power
May recall or forget, our
Love to see your love flows into
Us. If Venus lights, your words spin, to
Live our desires lead us to honor.

Graced, your heart in nothing less than in death, go—
I, dust—raise the great hem of the extended
World that nothing can leave; having had breath go
Face my son, say: 'If your father offended
You with mute wisdom, my words have not ended
His second paradise where
His love was in her eyes where
They turn, quick for you two—sick
Or gone cannot make music
You set less than all. Honor

His voice in me, the river's turn that finds the
Grace in you, four notes first too full for talk, leaf
Lighting stem, stems bound to the branch that binds the
Tree, and then as from the same root we talk, leaf
After leaf of your mind's music, page, walk leaf
Over leaf of his thought, sounding
His happiness: song sounding
The grace that comes from knowing
Things, her love our own showing
Her love in all her honor.'

from
"A" 12

In peace
200-year spruce at least
For a fiddle for Paul:
Save
The heart of the wood so to speak
And who belongs to it.

Paul to Paul,
Recall surely,
Carved, not the chips of the process,
Whence are the stems?
He sang sometimes, my son,
When we let him talk,
A chance lilt,
After prayers—
A shred, a repeated word, his whole world—
As, like Bottom,
You might blunder on *tumblesalt*
For *somersault*, Paul.
"They sang this way in deep Russia"
He'd say and carry the notes
Recalling the years
Fly. Where stemmed
The Jew among strangers?
As the hummingbird
Can fly backwards
Also forwards—
How else could it keep going?
Speech moved to sing
To echo the stranger
A tear in an eye
The quick hand wiped off—
Casually:
"I loved to hear them."

As I love:
My poetics.
"Little fish," he grieved
For his wife.
He prayed to the full moon
Over the prow
Alone on that trip
Not seasick.
He returned
For a last look
At Most

After the fire.
His boy wept
And would not let him go.
But he kissed and kissed him and crossed
The Atlantic again alone
This time to
Bring the family over.
What did he not do?
He had kept dogs
Before he rolled logs
On the Niemen.
He swam
Dogpaddle
(Dexter, Paracelsus!)
What a blessing:
He saw Rabbi
Yizchok Elchonon
Walking
On the wharf
In Kovno.
The miracle of his first job
On the lower East Side:
Six years night watchman
In a men's shop
Where by day he pressed pants
Every crease a blade
The irons weighed
At least twenty pounds
But moved both of them
Six days a week
From six in the morning
To nine, sometimes eleven at night,
Or midnight;
Except Fridays
When he left, enough time before sunset
Margolis begrudged.
His own business
My father told Margolis
Is to keep Sabbath.

"Sleep," he prayed
For his dead.
Sabbath.

Moses released the horse
For one day from his harness
So that a man might keep pace.

A shop bench his bed,
He rose rested at four.
Half the free night
Befriended the mice:
Singing Psalms
As they listened.
A day's meal
A slice of bread
And an apple,
The evenings
What matter?
His boots shone.
Gone and out of fashion
His beard you stroked, Paul,
With the Sabbath Prince Albert.
I never saw more beautiful fingers
Used to lift bootstraps.
A beard that won over
A jeering Italian
Who wanted to pluck it—
With the love
His dark brown eyes
Always found in others.
Everybody loves Reb Pinchos
Because he loves everybody,
How many strangers—
He knew so many—
Said that to me
Every Sabbath
He took me—
I was a small boy—
To the birdstore-window to see

The blue-and-yellow Polly
The cardinal, the
Orchard oriole.

Everybody loved Reb Pinchos
Because he loved everybody.
Simple.
You must, myself,
As father of Nicomachus
Say very little
Except: such were his actions.

My life for yours.
Goodness dies—
The humming bird flies forward.
Buried beneath blue sky, bright sunlight.
You'll remember:
The eleventh of April
    1950.
The twelfth—
Snow flurries—
Tasting all unseasonable weather early
Alongside his "little fish"
There 23 years before him.
John Donne in his death-shroud
A saintly face in praying shawl—
He died happy
If you want to know
What he looked like,
Scop,
What are you asking?
He retired on old age pension—
$26 a month—
At 81—not too late,
He did not covet charity—
Or what has become of it—
And supported his children
Not sure now whether to
Put 91 or 95
On his tombstone.

He had forgotten birthright and birthday,
Who can remember
When every new day
May be turned into account.
What do you await?
If occasion warranted
He could tender his hand to a Polish countess
Playing the glass harmonica
And she wouldn't take offense.
His clasp pocketbook is in a lower drawer
Of his old chiffonier no one wanted.
$3 and some pennies
Saved for the synagogue—
He had hoped for more
But gave away
What he could not spare
To his bungling children—
Praising and showing their photos
They gave him.
The street never wide enough for him,
Taking a diagonal to cross it,
To open and close the synagogue
For over six times ten years
Until three days before he died—
A longer journey than Odysseus'.
Now his namesake says:
"If it's not my kind of words
    I don't want to hear them."
He died certain—
With such the angel of death does not wrestle—
And alone,
Not to let me see death:
"Isn't visiting over?
Go home,
Celia must be anxious,
Kiss Paul."

Measure, tacit is.
Listen to the birds—
And what do the birds sing.

He never saw a movie.
A rich sitter, a broad wake.
Not a sign that he is not here,
Yet a sign, to what side of the window
He sat by, creaks outside.
A speech tapped off music.
Draw off—
Still in the eye of—
              an acacia.
Division: wits so undivided.
A source knows a tree
              still not in the earth
In no hurry to shadow the living
He opens the gates of the synagogue
As time never heard
Lifting up the voice.
Actions things; themselves; doing.

HOWARD BAKER

(1905–1990)

Advice to a Man Who Lost a Dog

Don't hunt too anxiously a wilful hound;
Don't hope to hear the hot expectant sound
Or see him in the brush turn leaping round
    To give a token of reply
    Promptly to your cry:

Things called must take their time about complying;
Things summoned come, but as they come they're trying
Each dangling scent though it be false and dying:
    Since blood has ancient ghosts to lay
    Let's grant the blood its way.

The ranging dog is like the red leaves driven
Over a wall, vine-covered and frost-riven,
To the devouring cedar thicket given;
    The woodbine's scarlet leaf compels
    His wild autumnal spells.

Stop by the brook and take your thoughts to school,
Scan your reflection in a quiet pool—
Does the dog's quest mark him the greater fool?
    What of the men who thus have gazed?
    The wisdom they have praised?

Think, when you hunt him on the windy brow
Where the lean settler led his shaggy cow
And questing yielded to the tranquil plow,
    That that fine poise bequeathed alone
    A cellar overgrown.

If you don't find him, for the spirit's sake
Go get the blanket from the car and make

His bed where he last was. When you awake
 Tonight, you'll seem to see him there,
 Curled tight in flowing air.

Tomorrow try more habitable land.
By a back-door perhaps he'll take his stand,
Pleasant but cautious to the stranger's hand;
 As he had been unquenched and wild,
 Exhausted now and mild.

Sappho's Leap

There is a white cliff, sea-worn, temple-scarred,
Off Greece, where a pale victim annually
Went to his death, tossed outward on a hard
Meticulous arc between the shrine and sea,
His frantic forearms threaded to a cloud
Of sparrows, or a hide of airy sweep.
Later, these orgies spent and disavowed,
The cliff assumed the name of Sappho's Leap.

No one believes that Sappho leapt toward death
From this white rock . . . yet he who loves must own
To dreams of birdwings and the sea's harsh breath
In which he's sometimes thrower, sometimes thrown . . .
Whoever loves can't ever put behind
The harrowing sweet history of his kind.

FRANK MARSHALL DAVIS

(1905–1987)

Christ Is a Dixie Nigger

You tell me Christ was born nearly twenty centuries ago in a
    little one horse town called Bethlehem . . . your artists
    paint a man as fair as another New White Hope
Well, you got it all wrong . . . facts twisted as hell . . . see?

Let me tell you wise guys something
I've got my own ideas . . . I've got a better Christ and a big-
    ger Christ . . . one you can put your hands on today or to-
    morrow.

My Christ is a Dixie nigger black as midnight, black as the
    roof of a cave's mouth
My Christ is a black bastard . . . maybe Joe did tell the
    neighbors God bigged Mary . . . but he fooled nobody
    . . . they all knew Christ's father was Mr. Jim who owns
    the big plantation . . . and when Christ started bawling
    out back in the cabins Mr. Jim made all three git
You see, I know
Christ studied medicine up North in Chicago then came back
    to Mississippi a good physician with ideas for gettin' the
    races together . . . he lectured in the little rundown
    schoolhouses awaiting Rosenwald money . . . he talked of
    the brotherhood and equality of man and of a Constitution
    giving everybody a right to vote and some of the nigger lis-
    teners told their white folks . . . then they found how
    Christ healed a white woman other doctors gave up for lost
    . . . the two things together got him in the calaboose
They called him a Communist and a menace to the Existing
    Relationship Between Black and White in the South
Sheriff and judge debated whether to open the hoosegow and
    tell reporters the mob stormed the jail or let the state lynch
    him on the gallows
Anyhow they got him

Maybe the rope was weak or Christ was too strong to die
    . . . I don't know
They cut him down and they patched him up . . . he hid
    in the swamps until he got well enough to get around
    again . . . then he lectured a little more . . . and faded out
Whether he went to heaven or Harlem or the white folks
    broke his neck and hid the corpse somewhere is a question
    they still ask—
See what I mean?

I don't want any of your stories about somebody running
    around too long ago to be anything but a highly publicised
    memory
Your pink priests who whine about Pilate and Judas and
    Gethsemane I'd like to hogtie and dump into the stinking
    cells to write a New Testament around the Scottsboro Boys
Subdivide your million dollar temples into liquor taverns and
    high class whore-houses . . . my nigger Christ can't get
    past the door anyway

Remember this, you wise guys
Your tales about Jesus of Nazareth are no-go with me
    I've got a dozen Christs in Dixie all bloody and black . . .

Sam Jackson

The moon was a thick slab of yellow cheese between thin
    slices of toasted clouds

The night air spilled steak and coffee smells from a sack of
    odors hauled from the Elite Cafe

Beneath penniless Sam Jackson's window two dogs argued
    like nations over a morsel found in a garbage can

Strong Hunger slashed Sam's belly with eagle talons until he
    staggered wounded and sore to the street

Daily papers itemed: "An unidentified Negro was shot and in-
    stantly killed late last night by Officer Patrick Riley while
    trying to break into the rear of the Dew Drop Inn . . ."

DOROTHY FIELDS

(1905–1974)

I Can't Give You Anything But Love

Gee, but it's tough to be broke, kid,
It's not a joke, kid, it's a curse;
My luck is changing, it's gotten
From simply rotten, to something worse.

Who knows some day I will win too,
I'll begin to reach my prime;
Now though I see what our end is
All I can spend is just my time.

I can't give you anything but love, baby,
That's the only thing I've plenty of, baby,
Dream awhile, scheme awhile,
We're sure to find
Happiness and I guess
All those things you've always pined for.

Gee, I'd like to see you looking swell, baby,
Diamond bracelets Woolworth doesn't sell, baby,
Till that lucky day, you know darned well, baby,
I can't give you anything but love.

STANLEY KUNITZ

(b. 1905)

The Science of the Night

I touch you in the night, whose gift was you,
My careless sprawler,
And I touch you cold, unstirring, star-bemused,
That are become the land of your self-strangeness.
What long seduction of the bone has led you
Down the imploring roads I cannot take
Into the arms of ghosts I never knew,
Leaving my manhood on a rumpled field
To guard you where you lie so deep
In absent-mindedness,
Caught in the calcium snows of sleep?

And even should I track you to your birth
Through all the cities of your mortal trial,
As in my jealous thought I try to do,
You would escape me—from the brink of earth
Take off to where the lawless auroras run,
You with your wild and metaphysic heart.
My touch is on you, who are light-years gone.
We are not souls but systems, and we move
In clouds of our unknowing
                              like great nebulae.
Our very motives swirl and have their start
With father lion and with mother crab.

Dreamer, my own lost rib,
Whose planetary dust is blowing
Past archipelagoes of myth and light,
What far Magellans are you mistress of
To whom you speed the pleasure of your art?
As through a glass that magnifies my loss
I see the lines of your spectrum shifting red,

The universe expanding, thinning out,
Our worlds flying, oh flying, fast apart.

From hooded powers and from abstract flight
I summon you, your person and your pride.
Fall to me now from outer space,
Still fastened desperately to my side;
Through gulfs of streaming air
Bring me the mornings of the milky ways
Down to my threshold in your drowsy eyes;
And by the virtue of your honeyed word
Restore the liquid language of the moon,
That in gold mines of secrecy you delve.
Awake!
       My whirling hands stay at the noon,
Each cell within my body holds a heart
And all my hearts in unison strike twelve.

The Dragonfly

Fallen, so freshly fallen
From his estates of air,
He made on the gritty path
A five-inch funeral car,
New Hampshire's lesser dragon
In the grip of his kidnapers.
A triumph of *chinoiserie*
He seemed, in green and gold
Enameling, pin-brained,
With swizzle-stick for tail,
The breastplate gemmed between.
What a gallantry of pomp
In that royal spread of wings!—
Four leaves of thinnest mica,
Or, better, of the skin
Of water, if water had a skin.
Semaphores, at rest,
Of the frozen invisible,

They caught a glinting light
In the hairlines of their scripture
When a vagrom current stirred
And made them feign to flutter.
It was a slow progress,
A thing of fits and starts,
With bands of black attendants
Tugging at the wings
And under the crested feelers
At the loose-hinged head
(So many eyes he had, which were
The eyes?), still others pushing
From behind, where a pair
Of ornamental silks
That steered him in his flights
Gave tenuous pincer-hold.
Admire, I said to myself,
How he lords it over them,
Grounded though he may be
After his blue-sky transports;
But see how they honor him,
His servants at the feast,
In a passion of obsequies,
With chomping mandibles
And wildly waving forelegs
Telegraphing news abroad
Of their booty's worth; oh praise this
Consummate purity
Of the bestriding will!
In a scaled-down mythology
These myrmidons could stand
For the separate atoms of St. George
(Why not?). And fancy drove
Me on, my science kneeling
Before such witless tools,
To pay my tithe of awe
And read the resurrection-sign
In the motion of the death.
But then I saw,
When an imperceptible gust

Abruptly hoisted sails
And flipped my hero over . . .
In the reversal of the scene
I saw the sixfold spasm
Of his tucked-in claws,
The cry of writhing nerve-ends,
And down his membrane-length
A tide of gray pulsation.
I wheeled. The scorpion sun,
Stoking its belly-fires,
Exploded overhead, and the rain
Came down: scales, tortuous wires,
Flakings of green and gold.

The Testing-Tree

I

On my way home from school
        up tribal Providence Hill
                past the Academy ballpark
where I could never hope to play
        I scuffed in the drainage ditch
                among the sodden seethe of leaves
hunting for perfect stones
        rolled out of glacial time
                into my pitcher's hand;
then sprinted lickety-
        split on my magic Keds
                from a crouching start,
scarcely touching the ground
        with my flying skin
                as I poured it on
for the prize of the mastery
        over that stretch of road,
                with no one no where to deny
when I flung myself down
        that on the given course
                I was the world's fastest human.

2

Around the bend
        that tried to loop me home
                dawdling came natural
across a nettled field
        riddled with rabbit-life
                where the bees sank sugar-wells
in the trunks of the maples
        and a stringy old lilac
                more than two stories tall
blazing with mildew
        remembered a door in the
                long teeth of the woods.
All of it happened slow:
        brushing the stickseed off,
                wading through jewelweed
strangled by angel's hair,
        spotting the print of the deer
                and the red fox's scats.

Once I owned the key
        to an umbrageous trail
                thickened with mosses
where flickering presences
        gave me right of passage
                as I followed in the steps
of straight-backed Massassoit
        soundlessly heel-and-toe
                practicing my Indian walk.

3

Past the abandoned quarry
        where the pale sun bobbed
                in the sump of the granite,
past copperhead ledge,
        where the ferns gave foothold,
                I walked, deliberate,

on to the clearing,
 with the stones in my pocket
  changing to oracles
and my coiled ear tuned
 to the slightest leaf-stir.
  I had kept my appointment.
There I stood in the shadow,
 at fifty measured paces,
  of the inexhaustible oak,
tyrant and target,
 Jehovah of acorns,
  watchtower of the thunders,
that locked King Philip's War
 in its annulated core
  under the cut of my name.
Father wherever you are
 I have only three throws
  bless my good right arm.
In the haze of afternoon,
 while the air flowed saffron,
  I played my game for keeps—
for love, for poetry,
 and for eternal life—
  after the trials of summer.

4

In the recurring dream
 my mother stands
  in her bridal gown
under the burning lilac,
 with Bernard Shaw and Bertie
  Russell kissing her hands;
the house behind her is in ruins;
 she is wearing an owl's face
  and makes barking noises.
Her minatory finger points.
 I pass through the cardboard doorway
  askew in the field

and peer down a well
    where an albino walrus huffs.
        He has the gentlest eyes.
If the dirt keeps sifting in,
    staining the water yellow,
        why should I be blamed?
Never try to explain.
    That single Model A
        sputtering up the grade
unfurled a highway behind
    where the tanks maneuver,
        revolving their turrets.
In a murderous time
    the heart breaks and breaks
        and lives by breaking.
It is necessary to go
    through dark and deeper dark
        and not to turn.
I am looking for the trail.
    Where is my testing-tree?
        Give me back my stones!

The Catch

    It darted across the pond
    toward our sunset perch,
    weaving in, up, and around
    a spindle of air,
    this delicate engine
    fired by impulse and glitter,
    swift darning-needle,
    gossamer dragon,
    less image than thought,
    and the thought come alive.
    Swoosh went the net
    with a practiced hand.
    "Da-da, may I look too?"
    You may look, child,

all you want.
This prize belongs to no one.
But you will pay all
your life for the privilege,
all your life.

The Quarrel

The word I spoke in anger
weighs less than a parsley seed,
but a road runs through it
that leads to my grave,
that bought-and-paid-for lot
on a salt-sprayed hill in Truro
where the scrub pines
overlook the bay.
Half-way I'm dead enough,
strayed from my own nature
and my fierce hold on life.
If I could cry, I'd cry,
but I'm too old to be
anybody's child.
Liebchen,
with whom should I quarrel
except in the hiss of love,
that harsh, irregular flame?

Route Six

The city squats on my back.
I am heart-sore, stiff-necked,
exasperated. That's why
I slammed the door,
that's why I tell you now,
in every house of marriage
there's room for an interpreter.

Let's jump into the car, honey,
and head straight for the Cape,
where the cock on our housetop crows
that the weather's fair,
and my garden waits for me
to coax it into bloom.
As for those passions left
that flare past understanding,
like bundles of dead letters
out of our previous lives
that amaze us with their fevers,
we can stow them in the rear
along with ziggurats of luggage
and Celia, our transcendental cat,
past-mistress of all languages,
including Hottentot and silence.
We'll drive non-stop till dawn,
and if I grow sleepy at the wheel,
you'll keep me awake by singing
in your bravura Chicago style
Ruth Etting's smoky song,
"Love Me or Leave Me,"
belting out the choices.

Light glazes the eastern sky
over Buzzards Bay.
Celia gyrates upward
like a performing seal,
her glistening nostrils aquiver
to sniff the brine-spiked air.
The last stretch toward home!
Twenty summers roll by.

Touch Me

Summer is late, my heart.
Words plucked out of the air
some forty years ago
when I was wild with love
and torn almost in two
scatter like leaves this night
of whistling wind and rain.
It is my heart that's late,
it is my song that's flown.
Outdoors all afternoon
under a gunmetal sky
staking my garden down,
I kneeled to the crickets trilling
underfoot as if about
to burst from their crusty shells;
and like a child again
marveled to hear so clear
and brave a music pour
from such a small machine.
What makes the engine go?
Desire, desire, desire.
The longing for the dance
stirs in the buried life.
One season only,
                    and it's done.
So let the battered old willow
thrash against the windowpanes
and the house timbers creak.
Darling, do you remember
the man you married? Touch me,
remind me who I am.

PHYLLIS McGINLEY

(1905–1978)

Twelfth Night

Down from the window take the withered holly.
Feed the torn tissue to the literal blaze.
Now, now at last are come the melancholy
Anticlimactic days.

Here in the light of morning, hard, unvarnished,
Let us with haste dismantle the tired tree
Of ornaments a trifle chipped and tarnished.
Pretend we do not see

How all the room seems shabbier and meaner
And all the house a little less than snug.
Fold up the tinsel. Run the vacuum cleaner
Over the littered rug.

Nothing is left. The postman passes by, now,
Bearing no gifts, no kind or seasonal word.
The icebox yields no wing, no nibbled thigh, now,
From any festive bird.

Sharp in the streets the north wind plagues its betters,
While Christmas snow to gutters is consigned.
Nothing remains except the thank-you letters,
Most tedious to the mind,

And the bright gadget which must wait no longer
To be exchanged (by stealth) at Lewis & Conger.

Spring Comes to the Suburbs

Now green the larch; the hedges green,
   And early jonquils go a-begging.
The thoughtful man repairs his screen,
   The child emerges from his legging.

By daylight now, commuters come
   Homeward. The grackle, unimpeded,
Forsakes his charitable crumb
   To loot the lawn that's newly seeded.

Tulips are mocked for their display
   By periwinkles' self-effacement,
And benedicts on ladders sway,
   Fetching the storm sash to the basement.

Still slumbers the lethargic bee,
   The rosebush keeps its winter tag on,
But hatless to the A & P
   The shopper rides in station wagon.

Once more Good Humor's wheedling bell
   Brings out the spendthrift in the miser,
And everywhere's the lovely smell
   Of showers and soil and fertilizer.

The 5:32

She said, If tomorrow my world were torn in two,
Blacked out, dissolved, I think I would remember
(As if transfixed in unsurrendering amber)
This hour best of all the hours I knew:

When cars came backing into the shabby station,
Children scuffing the seats, and the women driving
With ribbons around their hair, and the trains arriving,
And the men getting off with tired but practiced motion.

Yes, I would remember my life like this, she said:
Autumn, the platform red with Virginia creeper,
And a man coming toward me, smiling, the evening paper
Under his arm, and his hat pushed back on his head;

And wood smoke lying like haze on the quiet town,
And dinner waiting, and the sun not yet gone down.

Portrait of Girl with Comic Book

Thirteen's no age at all. Thirteen is nothing.
It is not wit, or powder on the face,
Or Wednesday matinées, or misses' clothing,
Or intellect, or grace.
Twelve has its tribal customs. But thirteen
Is neither boys in battered cars nor dolls,
Not *Sara Crewe*, or movie magazine,
Or pennants on the walls.

Thirteen keeps diaries and tropical fish
(A month, at most); scorns jumpropes in the spring;
Could not, would fortune grant it, name its wish;
Wants nothing, everything;
Has secrets from itself, friends it despises;
Admits none to the terrors that it feels;
Owns half a hundred masks but no disguises;
And walks upon its heels.

Thirteen's anomalous—not that, not this:
Not folded bud, or wave that laps a shore,
Or moth proverbial from the chrysalis.
Is the one age defeats the metaphor.
Is not a town, like childhood, strongly walled
But easily surrounded; is no city.
Nor, quitted once, can it be quite recalled—
Not even with pity.

KENNETH REXROTH

(1905–1982)

Spring, Coast Range

The glow of my campfire is dark red and flameless,
The circle of white ash widens around it.
I get up and walk off in the moonlight and each time
I look back the red is deeper and the light smaller.
Scorpio rises late with Mars caught in his claw;
The moon has come before them, the light
Like a choir of children in the young laurel trees.
It is April; the shad, the hot headed fish,
Climbs the rivers; there is trillium in the damp canyons;
The foetid adder's tongue lolls by the waterfall.
There was a farm at this campsite once, it is almost gone now.
There were sheep here after the farm, and fire
Long ago burned the redwoods out of the gulch,
The Douglas fir off the ridge; today the soil
Is stony and incoherent, the small stones lie flat
And plate the surface like scales.
Twenty years ago the spreading gulley
Toppled the big oak over onto the house.
Now there is nothing left but the foundations
Hidden in poison oak, and above on the ridge,
Six lonely, ominous fenceposts;
The redwood beams of the barn make a footbridge
Over the deep waterless creek bed;
The hills are covered with wild oats
Dry and white by midsummer.
I walk in the random survivals of the orchard.
In a patch of moonlight a mole
Shakes his tunnel like an angry vein;
Orion walks waist deep in the fog coming in from the ocean;
Leo crouches on the hills.
There are tiny hard fruits already on the plum trees.
The purity of the apple blossoms is incredible.
As the wind dies down their fragrance

Clusters around them like thick smoke.
All the day they roared with bees, in the moonlight
They are silent and immaculate.

Andrée Rexroth

Died October, 1940

Now once more grey mottled buckeye branches
Explode their emerald stars,
And alders smoulder in a rosy smoke
Of innumerable buds.
I know that spring again is splendid
As ever, the hidden thrush
As sweetly tongued, the sun as vital—
But these are the forest trails we walked together,
These paths, ten years together.
We thought the years would last forever,
They are all gone now, the days
We thought would not come for us are here.
Bright trout poised in the current—
The racoon's track at the water's edge—
A bittern booming in the distance—
Your ashes scattered on this mountain—
Moving seaward on this stream.

The Signature of All Things

I

My head and shoulders, and my book
In the cool shade, and my body
Stretched bathing in the sun, I lie
Reading beside the waterfall—
Boehme's 'Signature of all Things.'
Through the deep July day the leaves
Of the laurel, all the colors

Of gold, spin down through the moving
Deep laurel shade all day. They float
On the mirrored sky and forest
For a while, and then, still slowly
Spinning, sink through the crystal deep
Of the pool to its leaf gold floor.
The saint saw the world as streaming
In the electrolysis of love.
I put him by and gaze through shade
Folded into shade of slender
Laurel trunks and leaves filled with sun.
The wren broods in her moss domed nest.
A newt struggles with a white moth
Drowning in the pool. The hawks scream,
Playing together on the ceiling
Of heaven. The long hours go by.
I think of those who have loved me,
Of all the mountains I have climbed,
Of all the seas I have swum in.
The evil of the world sinks.
My own sin and trouble fall away
Like Christian's bundle, and I watch
My forty summers fall like falling
Leaves and falling water held
Eternally in summer air.

2

Deer are stamping in the glades,
Under the full July moon.
There is a smell of dry grass
In the air, and more faintly,
The scent of a far off skunk.
As I stand at the wood's edge,
Watching the darkness, listening
To the stillness, a small owl
Comes to the branch above me,
On wings more still than my breath.
When I turn my light on him,
His eyes glow like drops of iron,

And he perks his head at me,
Like a curious kitten.
The meadow is bright as snow.
My dog prowls the grass, a dark
Blur in the blur of brightness.
I walk to the oak grove where
The Indian village was once.
There, in blotched and cobwebbed light
And dark, dim in the blue haze,
Are twenty Holstein heifers,
Black and white, all lying down,
Quietly together, under
The huge trees rooted in the graves.

3

When I dragged the rotten log
From the bottom of the pool,
It seemed heavy as stone.
I let it lie in the sun
For a month; and then chopped it
Into sections, and split them
For kindling, and spread them out
To dry some more. Late that night;
After reading for hours,
While moths rattled at the lamp,
The saints and the philosophers
On the destiny of man;
I went out on my cabin porch,
And looked up through the black forest
At the swaying islands of stars.
Suddenly I saw at my feet,
Spread on the floor of night, ingots
Of quivering phosphorescence,
And all about were scattered chips
Of pale cold light that was alive.

Lyell's Hypothesis Again

'An attempt to Explain the Former
Changes of the Earth's Surface by
Causes Now in Operation'
subtitle of Lyell—PRINCIPLES OF GEOLOGY

I

The mountain road ends here,
Broken away in the chasm where
The bridge washed out years ago.
The first scarlet larkspur glitters
In the first patch of April
Morning sunlight. The engorged creek
Roars and rustles like a military
Ball. Here by the waterfall,
Insuperable life, flushed
With the equinox, sentient
And sentimental, falls away
To the sea and death. The tissue
Of sympathy and agony
That binds the flesh in its Nessus' shirt;
The clotted cobweb of unself
And self; sheds itself and flecks
The sun's bed with darts of blossom
Like flagellant blood above
The water bursting in the vibrant
Air. This ego, bound by personal
Tragedy and the vast
Impersonal vindictiveness
Of the ruined and ruining world,
Pauses in this immortality,
As passionate, as apathetic,
As the lava flow that burned here once;
And stopped here; and said, 'This far
And no further.' And spoke thereafter
In the simple diction of stone.

2

Naked in the warm April air,
We lie under the redwoods,
In the sunny lee of a cliff.
As you kneel above me I see
Tiny red marks on your flanks
Like bites, where the redwood cones
Have pressed into your flesh.
You can find just the same marks
In the lignite in the cliff
Over our heads. *Sequoia*
Langsdorfii before the ice,
And *sempervirens* afterwards
There is little difference,
Except for all those years.
Here in the sweet, moribund
Fetor of spring flowers, washed,
Flotsam and jetsam together,
Cool and naked together,
Under this tree for a moment,
We have escaped the bitterness
Of love, and love lost, and love
Betrayed. And what might have been,
And what might be, fall equally
Away with what is, and leave
Only these ideograms
Printed on the immortal
Hydrocarbons of flesh and stone.

It Is a German Honeymoon

They are stalking humming birds
The jewels of the new world
The rufous hummingbird dives
Along his parabola
Of pure ether. We forgot—
An imponderable and

Invisible elastic
Crystal is the womb of space.
They wait with poised cameras
Focused telescopic lens
Beyond the crimson trumpet vine.
He returns squealing against
The sky deeper than six billion
Light years, and plunges through sun
Blaze to the blood red flower womb.
A whirling note in the lens of space.
"Birds are devas," says Morris
Graves, "They live in a world
Without Karma." No grasping,
No consequence, only the
Grace of the vectors that form
The lattices of the unending
Imponderable crystal.
The blond and handsome young man
And woman are happy, they
Love each other, when they have
Gone around the world they will
Sit in the Grunewald and
Look at a picture of a
California hummingbird.
Nobody can swim across
The Great River. Turn your back
And study the spotted wall.
Turn around on the farther shore.
Nine dice roll out, one by one.
The mouse eats them. They never were.
The hundred flowers put their
Heads together, yellow stamens and
Swelling pistils. Between them
In midspace they generate
A single seed. You cannot
Find it in a telescope.
Found, you could not see it in
An electron microscope.

On Flower Wreath Hill

I

An aging pilgrim on a
Darkening path walks through the
Fallen and falling leaves, through
A forest grown over the
Hilltop tumulus of a
Long dead princess, as the
Moonlight grows and the daylight
Fades and the Western Hills turn
Dim in the distance and the
Lights come on, pale green
In the streets of the hazy city.

II

Who was this princess under
This mound overgrown with trees
Now almost bare of leaves?
Only the pine and cypress
Are still green. Scattered through the
Dusk are orange wild kaki on
Bare branches. Darkness, an owl
Answers the temple bell. The
Sun has passed the crossroads of
Heaven.
      There are more leaves on
The ground than grew on the trees.
I can no longer see the
Path; I find my way without
Stumbling; my heavy heart has
Gone this way before. Until
Life goes out memory will
Not vanish, but grow stronger
Night by night.
      Aching nostalgia—
In the darkness every moment

Grows longer and longer, and
I feel as timeless as the
Two thousand year old cypress.

III

The full moon rises over
Blue Mount Hiei as the orange
Twilight gives way to dusk.
Kamo River is full with
The first rains of Autumn, the
Water crowded with colored
Leaves, red maple, yellow gingko,
On dark water, like Chinese
Old brocade. The Autumn haze
Deepens until only the
Lights of the city remain.

IV

No leaf stirs. I am alone
In the midst of a hundred
Empty mountains. Cicadas,
Locusts, katydids, crickets,
Have fallen still, one after
Another. Even the wind
Bells hang motionless. In the
Blue dusk, widely spaced snowflakes
Fall in perfect verticals.
Yet, under my cabin porch,
The thin, clear Autumn water
Rustles softly like fine silk.

V

This world of ours, before we
Can know its fleeting sorrows,
We enter it through tears.
Do the reverberations
Of the evening bell of
The mountain temple ever

Totally die away?
Memory echoes and reechoes
Always reinforcing itself.
No wave motion ever dies.
The white waves of the wake of
The boat that rows away into
The dawn, spread and lap on the
Sands of the shores of all the world.

VI

Clustered in the forest around
The royal tumulus are
Tumbled and shattered gravestones
Of people no one left in
The world remembers. For the
New Year the newer ones have all been cleaned
And straightened and each has
Flowers or at least a spray
Of bamboo and pine.
It is a great pleasure to
Walk through fallen leaves, but
Remember, you are alive,
As they were two months ago.

VII

Night shuts down the misty mountains
With fine rain. The seventh day
Of my seventieth year,
Seven-Seven-Ten, my own
Tanabata, and my own
Great Purification. Who
Crosses in midwinter from
Altair to Vega, from the
Eagle to the Swan, under the earth,
Against the sun? Orion,
My guardian king, stands on
Kegonkyoyama.
So many of these ancient
Tombs are the graves of heroes

Who died young. The combinations
Of the world are unstable
By nature. Take it easy.
Nirvana.
Change rules the world forever.
And man but a little while.

VIII

Oborozuki,
Drowned Moon,
The half moon is drowned in mist
Its hazy light gleams on leaves
Drenched with warm mist. The world
Is alive tonight. I am
Immersed in living protoplasm,
That stretches away over
Continents and seas. I float
Like a child in the womb. Each
Cell of my body is
Penetrated by a
Strange electric life. I glow
In the dark with the moon drenched
Leaves, myself a globe
Of St. Elmo's fire.

I move silently on the
Wet forest path that circles
The shattered tumulus.
The path is invisible.
I am only a dim glow
Like the tumbled and broken
Gravestones of forgotten men
And women that mark the way.
I sit for a while on one
Tumbled sotoba and listen
To the conversations of
Owls and nightjars and tree frogs.
As my eyes adjust to the
Denser darkness I can see

That my seat is a cube and
All around me are scattered
Earth, water, air, fire, ether.
Of these five elements
The moon, the mist, the world, man
Are only fleeting compounds
Varying in power, and
Power is only insight
Into the void—the single
Thought that illuminates the heart.
The heart's mirror hangs in the void.

Do there still rest in the broken
Tumulus ashes and charred
Bones thrown in a corner by
Grave robbers, now just as dead?
She was once a shining flower
With eyebrows like the first night's moon,
Her white face, her brocaded
Robes perfumed with cypress and
Sandalwood; she sang in the Court
Before the Emperor, songs
Of China and Turkestan.
She served him wine in a cup
Of silver and pearls, that gleamed
Like the moonlight on her sleeves.
A young girl with black hair
Longer than her white body—
Who never grew old. Now owls
And nightjars sing in a mist
Of silver and pearls.

The wheel
Swings and turns counterclockwise.
The old graspings live again
In the new consequences.
Yet, still, I walk this same path
Above my cabin in warm
Moonlit mist, in rain, in
Autumn wind and rain of maple

Leaves, in spring rain of cherry
Blossoms, in new snow deeper
Than my clogs. And tonight in
Midsummer, a night enclosed
In an infinite pearl.
Ninety-nine nights over
Yamashina Pass, and the
Hundredth night and the first night
Are the same night. The night
Known prior to consciousness,
Night of ecstasy, night of
Illumination so complete
It cannot be called perceptible.

Winter, the flowers sleep on
The branches. Spring, they awake
And open to probing bees.
Summer, unborn flowers sleep
In the young seeds ripening
In the fruit. The mountain pool
Is invisible in the
Glowing mist. But the mist-drowned
Moon overhead is visible
Drowned in the invisible water.

Mist-drenched, moonlit, the sculpture
Of an orb spider glitters
Across the path. I walk around
Through the bamboo grass. The mist
Dissolves everything else, the
Living and the dead, except
This occult mathematics of light.
Nothing moves. The wind that blows
Down the mountain slope from
The pass and scatters the spring
Blossoms and the autumn leaves
Is still tonight. Even the
Spider's net of jewels has ceased
To tremble. I look back at
An architecture of pearls

And silver wire. Each minute
Droplet reflects a moon, as
Once did the waterpails of
Matsukaze and Murasame.

And I realize that this
Transcendent architecture
Lost in the forest where no one passes
Is itself the Net of Indra,
The compound infinities of infinities,
The Flower Wreath,
Each universe reflecting
Every other, reflecting
Itself from every other,
And the moon the single thought
That populates the Void.
The night grows still more still. No
Sound at all, only a flute
Playing soundlessly in the
Circle of dancing gopis.

from
The Love Poems of Marichiko

I

I sit at my desk.
What can I write to you?
Sick with love,
I long to see you in the flesh.
I can write only,
"I love you. I love you. I love you."
Love cuts through my heart
And tears my vitals.
Spasms of longing suffocate me
And will not stop.

III

Oh the anguish of these secret meetings
In the depth of night,
I wait with the shoji open.
You come late, and I see your shadow
Move through the foliage
At the bottom of the garden.
We embrace—hidden from my family.
I weep into my hands.
My sleeves are already damp.
We make love, and suddenly
The fire watch loom up
With clappers and lantern.
How cruel they are
To appear at such a moment.
Upset by their apparition,
I babble nonsense
And can't stop talking
Words with no connection.

IV

You ask me what I thought about
Before we were lovers.
The answer is easy.
Before I met you
I didn't have anything to think about.

XI

Uguisu sing in the blossoming trees.
Frogs sing in the green rushes.
Everywhere the same call
Of being to being.
Somber clouds waver in the void.
Fishing boats waver in the tide.
Their sails carry them out.
But ropes, as of old, woven

With the hair of their women,
Pull them back
Over their reflections on the green depths,
To the ports of love.

XXIII

I wish I could be
Kannon of eleven heads
To kiss you, Kannon
Of the thousand arms,
To embrace you forever.

XXIV

I scream as you bite
My nipples, and orgasm
Drains my body, as if I
Had been cut in two.

XXV

Your tongue thrums and moves
Into me, and I become
Hollow and blaze with
Whirling light, like the inside
Of a vast expanding pearl.

XXXI

Some day in six inches of
Ashes will be all
That's left of our passionate minds,
Of all the world created
By our love, its origin
And passing away.

XXXII

I hold your head tight between
My thighs, and press against your
Mouth, and float away
Forever, in an orchid
Boat on the River of Heaven.

XXXIII

I cannot forget
The perfumed dusk inside the
Tent of my black hair,
As we awoke to make love
After a long night of love.

XXXIV

Every morning, I
Wake alone, dreaming my
Arm is your sweet flesh
Pressing my lips.

XLII

How many lives ago
I first entered the torrent of love,
At last to discover
There is no further shore.
Yet I know I will enter again and again.

LI

Did you take me because you loved me?
Did you take me without love?
Or did you just take me
To experiment on my heart?

LIII

Without me you can only
Live at random like
A falling pachinko ball.
I am your wisdom.

LV

The night is too long to the sleepless.
The road is too long to the footsore.
Life is too long to a woman
Made foolish by passion.
Why did I find a crooked guide
On the twisted paths of love?

LVI

This flesh you have loved
Is fragile, unstable by nature
As a boat adrift.
The fires of the cormorant fishers
Flare in the night.
My heart flares with this agony.
Do you understand?
My life is going out.
Do you understand?
My life.
Vanishing like the stakes
That hold the nets against the current
In Uji River, the current and the mist
Are taking me.

LVII

Night without end. Loneliness.
The wind has driven a maple leaf
Against the shoji. I wait, as in the old days,
In our secret place, under the full moon.
The last bell crickets sing.
I found your old love letters,
Full of poems you never published.
Did it matter? They were only for me.

LVIII

Half in a dream
I become aware
That the voices of the crickets
Grow faint with the growing Autumn.
I mourn for this lonely
Year that is passing
And my own being
Grows fainter and fades away.

LIX

I hate this shadow of a ghost
Under the full moon.
I run my fingers through my greying hair,
And wonder, have I grown so thin?

LX

Chilled through, I wake up
With the first light. Outside my window
A red maple leaf floats silently down.
What am I to believe?
Indifference?
Malice?
I hate the sight of coming day
Since that morning when
Your insensitive gaze turned me to ice
Like the pale moon in the dawn.

BYRON VAZAKAS

(1905–1987)

The Pavilion on the Pier

A sunstruck spray sifts back breakwater waves,
while out the bay a cackling naphtha launch
slits water whitely up the back. I squint
behind sun glasses with their green ground glass,
and stomp the steel-strut pier whose fish hooks hook
the fish, our kindred; and stuffed seagulls dive
to rise like mermaids at the Hippodrome.
Horse-hair horizons pencil-line my eyes
till backward, on the boardwalk, grandma rides
her wicker rolling chair, and bats the breeze.
And backward, on a fatal figure-eight,
I'm somersaulted to a child again.
Head over heels . . . still, clammy hands hold tight
that waltz with mother, like a record grooved
three-quarter time in pity. But the salt
air heals the salt rubbed in by coming back,
till recognition rounds a sheepish grin
at mother as a whalebone collared *Madame
X*, the unknown woman; and the looking back
sands down disaster to a souvenir
of polk-a-dotted parasols above the beach
where mother sits forever for her photograph.

Epitaph for the Old Howard

Off Scollay Square, back from the subway, stands
the last stand of the last Burlesque. Its doors
are boarded; and its boards are bare. And like
a charge, the license for its license hangs
suspended over Howard Street. Where trefoil
and the quatrefoil of Gothic windows

framed a church, new worshippers of sex
observed its ancient rituals. From pit
and balcony, their eyes, like ghostly lovers,
love untouched. Their ghosts return. Desire
returns like echoed ragtime tapping through
a haunted house. Now furtive footsteps shuffle
through more red-light exits till their sex is
on the town. Turned inside out, desire's dim
audiences disperse to crumpled tabloids
in the street, and tabloids on newsstands.
The street recovers what the Burlesque lost.
Tired trouper, darkened derelict, the
Howard Athenaeum's sign creaks windily,
Ya got a light? Ya got a dime?

ROBERT PENN WARREN

(1905–1989)

The Return: An Elegy

The east wind finds the gap bringing rain:
Rain in the pine wind shaking the stiff pine.
Beneath the wind the hollow gorges whine
The pines decline
Slow film of rain creeps down the loam again
Where the blind and nameless bones recline.

> they are conceded to the earth's absolute chemistry
> they burn like faggots in—of damp and dark—the
> monstrous bulging flame.
> calcium phosphate lust speculation faith treachery
> it walked upright with habitation and a name
> *tell me its name*

The pines, black, like combers plunge with spray
Lick the wind's unceasing keel
It is not long till day
The boughs like hairy swine in slaughter squeal
And lurch beneath the thunder's livid heel.
The pines, black, snore *what does the wind say?*

> *tell me its name*

I have a name: I am not blind.
Eyes, not blind, press to the Pullman pane
Survey the driving dark and silver taunt of rain.
What will I find
What will I find beyond the snoring pine?
O eyes locked blind in death's immaculate design
Shall fix their last distrust in mine

give me the nickels off your eyes
from your hands the violets
let me bless your obsequies
if you possessed conveniently enough three eyes
then I could buy a pack of cigarettes

In gorges where the dead fox lies the fern
Will rankest loop the battened frond and fall
Above the bare and tushèd jaws that turn
Their insolence unto the gracious catafalque and pall.
It will be the season when milkweed blossoms burn.

the old bitch is dead
what have I said!
I have only said what the wind said
wind shakes a bell the hollow head

By dawn, the wind, the blown rain
Will cease their antique concitation.
It is the hour when old ladies cough and wake,
The chair, the table, take their form again
Earth begins the matinal exhalation

does my mother wake

Pines drip without motion
The hairy boughs no longer shake
Shaggy mist, crookbacked, ascends
Round hairy boughs the mist with shaggy fingers bends.
No wind: no rain:
Why do the steady pines complain?
Complain

the old fox is dead
what have I said

Locked in the roaring cubicle
Over the mountains through darkness hurled
I race the daylight's westward cycle
Across the groaning rooftree of the world.
The mist is furled.

a hundred years they took this road
the lank hunters then men hard-eyed with hope:
ox breath whitened the chill air: the goad
fell: here on the western slope
the hungry people the lost ones took their abode
here they took their stand:
alders bloomed on the road to the new land
here is the house the broken door the shed
the old fox is dead

The wheels hum hum
The wheels: I come I come
Whirl out of space through time O wheels
Pursue down backward time the ghostly parallels
Pursue past culvert cut embankment semaphore
Pursue down gleaming hours that are no more.
The pines, black, snore

    turn backward turn backward o time in your flight
    and make me a child again just for tonight
    good lord he's wet the bed come bring a light

What grief hath the mind distilled?
The heart is unfulfilled
The hoarse pine stilled
I cannot pluck
Out of this land of pine and rock
Of the fallen pine cone
Of red bud their season not yet gone
If I could pluck
(In drouth the lizard will blink on the hot limestone)

    the old fox is dead
    what is said is said
    heaven rest the hoary head
    what have I said!
     . . . I have only said what the wind said
    honor thy father and mother in the days of thy youth
    for time uncoils like the cottonmouth

If I could pluck
Out of the dark that whirled
Over the hoarse pine over the rock
Out of the mist that furled
Could I stretch forth like God the hand and gather
For you my mother
If I could pluck
Against the dry essential of tomorrow
To lay upon the breast that gave me suck
Out of the dark the dark and swollen orchid of this sorrow.

Bearded Oaks

The oaks, how subtle and marine,
Bearded, and all the layered light
Above them swims; and thus the scene,
Recessed, awaits the positive night.

So, waiting, we in the grass now lie
Beneath the languorous tread of light:
The grasses, kelp-like, satisfy
The nameless motions of the air.

Upon the floor of light, and time,
Unmurmuring, of polyp made,
We rest; we are, as light withdraws,
Twin atolls on a shelf of shade.

Ages to our construction went,
Dim architecture, hour by hour:
And violence, forgot now, lent
The present stillness all its power.

The storm of noon above us rolled,
Of light the fury, furious gold,
The long drag troubling us, the depth:
Dark is unrocking, unrippling, still.

Passion and slaughter, ruth, decay
Descend, minutely whispering down,
Silted down swaying streams, to lay
Foundation for our voicelessness.

All our debate is voiceless here,
As all our rage, the rage of stone;
If hope is hopeless, then fearless fear,
And history is thus undone.

Our feet once wrought the hollow street
With echo when the lamps were dead
At windows, once our headlight glare
Disturbed the doe that, leaping, fled.

I do not love you less that now
The caged heart makes iron stroke,
Or less that all that light once gave
The graduate dark should now revoke.

We live in time so little time
And we learn all so painfully,
That we may spare this hour's term
To practice for eternity.

Where the Slow Fig's Purple Sloth

Where the slow fig's purple sloth
Swells, I sit and meditate the
Nature of the soul, the fig exposes,
To the blaze of afternoon, one haunch
As purple-black as Africa, a single
Leaf the rest screens, but through it, light
Burns, and for the fig's bliss
The sun dies, the sun
Has died forever—far, oh far—
For the fig's bliss, thus.

                    The air
Is motionless, and the fig,
Motionless in that imperial and blunt
Languor of glut, swells, and inward
The fibers relax like a sigh in that
Hot darkness, go soft, the air
Is gold.

             When you
Split the fig, you will see
Lifting from the coarse and purple seed, its
Flesh like flame, purer
Than blood.

             It fills
The darkening room with light.

Audubon: A Vision

To Allen and Helen Tate

*Thou tellest my wanderings: put thou my tears into thy bottle:
are they not in thy book?*

                                        PSALM 56:8

            *I caught at his strict shadow
            and the shadow released itself
            with neither haste nor anger.
            But he remained silent.*
                        Carlos Drummond de Andrade:
                        "Travelling in the Family"
                        Translated by Elizabeth Bishop

*Jean Jacques Audubon, whose name was anglicized when, in his youth,
he was sent to America, was early instructed in the official version of his
identity: that he was the son of the sea captain Jean Audubon and a first
wife, who died shortly after his birth in Santo Domingo, and that the
woman who brought him up in France was a second wife. Actually, he
was the son of Jean Audubon and his mistress during the period when*

Jean Audubon was a merchant and slave-dealer in Santo Domingo, and the woman who raised him was the wife his father had left behind him in France while he was off making his fortune. By the age of ten Audubon knew the true story, but prompted, it would seem, by a variety of impulses, including some sound practical ones, he encouraged the other version, along with a number of flattering embellishments. He was, indeed, a fantasist of talent, but even without his help legends accreted about him. The most famous one—that he was the lost Dauphin of France, the son of the feckless Louis XVI and Marie Antoinette—did not, in fact, enter the picture until after his death, in 1851.

I. Was Not the Lost Dauphin

[A]

Was not the lost dauphin, though handsome was only
Base-born and not even able
To make a decent living, was only
Himself, Jean Jacques, and his passion—what
Is man but his passion?

      Saw,
Eastward and over the cypress swamp, the dawn,
Redder than meat, break;
And the large bird,
Long neck outthrust, wings crooked to scull air, moved
In a slow calligraphy, crank, flat, and black against
The color of God's blood spilt, as though
Pulled by a string.

      Saw
It proceed across the inflamed distance.

Moccasins set in hoar frost, eyes fixed on the bird,
Thought: "On that sky it is black."
Thought: "In my mind it is white."
Thinking: "*Ardea occidentalis*, heron, the great one."

Dawn: his heart shook in the tension of the world.

Dawn: and what is your passion?

[B]

October: and the bear,
Daft in the honey-light, yawns.

The bear's tongue, pink as a baby's, out-crisps to the curled
    tip,
It bleeds the black blood of the blueberry.

The teeth are more importantly white
Than has ever been imagined.

The bear feels his own fat
Sweeten, like a drowse, deep to the bone.

Bemused, above the fume of ruined blueberries,
The last bee hums.

The wings, like mica, glint
In the sunlight.

He leans on his gun. Thinks
How thin is the membrane between himself and the world.

II. The Dream He Never Knew the End Of

[A]

Shank-end of day, spit of snow, the call,
A crow, sweet in distance, then sudden
The clearing: among stumps, ruined cornstalks yet standing,
    the spot
Like a wound rubbed raw in the vast pelt of the forest. There
Is the cabin, a huddle of logs with no calculation or craft:
The human filth, the human hope.

                        Smoke,
From the mud-and-stick chimney, in that air, greasily
Brims, cannot lift, bellies the ridgepole, ravels
White, thin, down the shakes, like sputum.

He stands,
Leans on his gun, stares at the smoke, thinks: "Punk-wood."
Thinks: "Dead-fall half-rotten." Too sloven,
That is, to even set axe to clean wood.

His foot,
On the trod mire by the door, crackles
The night-ice already there forming. His hand
Lifts, hangs. In imagination, his nostrils already
Know the stench of that lair beyond
The door-puncheons. The dog
Presses its head against his knee. The hand
Strikes wood. No answer. He halloos. Then the voice.

[B]

What should he recognize? The nameless face
In the dream of some pre-dawn cock-crow—about to say
    what,
Do what? The dregs
Of all nightmare are the same, and we call it
Life. He knows that much, being a man,
And knows that the dregs of all life are nightmare.

Unless.

Unless what?

[C]

The face, in the air, hangs. Large,
Raw-hewn, strong-beaked, the haired mole
Near the nose, to the left, and the left side by firelight
Glazed red, the right in shadow, and under the tumble and
    tangle
Of dark hair on that head, and under the coarse eyebrows,
The eyes, dark, glint as from the unspecifiable
Darkness of a cave. It is a woman.

She is tall, taller than he.
Against the gray skirt, her hands hang.

"Ye wants to spend the night? Kin ye pay?
Well, mought as well stay then, done got one a-ready,
And leastwise, ye don't stink like no Injun."

[D]

The Indian,
Hunched by the hearth, lifts his head, looks up, but
From one eye only, the other
An aperture below which blood and mucus hang, thickening
    slow.

"Yeah, a arrow jounced back off his bowstring.
Durn fool—and him a Injun." She laughs.

                          The Indian's head sinks.
So he turns, drops his pack in a corner on bearskin, props
The gun there. Comes back to the fire. Takes his watch out.
Draws it bright, on the thong-loop, from under his hunter's-
    frock.
It is gold, it lives in his hand in the firelight, and the woman's
Hand reaches out. She wants it. She hangs it about her neck.

And near it the great hands hover delicately
As though it might fall, they quiver like moth-wings, her eyes
Are fixed downward, as though in shyness, on that gleam,
    and her face
Is sweet in an outrage of sweetness, so that
His gut twists cold. He cannot bear what he sees.

Her body sways like a willow in spring wind. Like a girl.

The time comes to take back the watch. He takes it.
And as she, sullen and sunken, fixes the food, he becomes
    aware
That the live eye of the Indian is secretly on him, and
    soundlessly
The lips move, and when her back is turned, the Indian
Draws a finger, in delicious retardation, across his own throat.

After food, and scraps for his dog, he lies down:
In the corner, on bearskins, which are not well cured,
And stink, the gun by his side, primed and cocked.

Under his hand he feels the breathing of the dog.

The woman hulks by the fire. He hears the jug slosh.

[E]

The sons come in from the night, two, and are
The sons she would have. Through slit lids
He watches. Thinks: "Now."

The sons
Hunker down by the fire, block the firelight, cram food
Into their large mouths, where teeth
Grind in the hot darkness, their breathing
Is heavy like sleep, he wants to sleep, but
The head of the woman leans at them. The heads
Are together in firelight.

He hears the jug slosh.

Then hears,
Like the whisper and *whish* of silk, that other
Sound, like a sound of sleep, but he does not
Know what it is. Then knows, for,
Against firelight, he sees the face of the woman
Lean over, and the lips purse sweet as to bestow a kiss, but
This is not true, and the great glob of spit
Hangs there, glittering, before she lets it fall.

The spit is what softens like silk the passage of steel
On the fine-grained stone. It whispers.

When she rises, she will hold it in her hand.

[F]

With no sound, she rises. She holds it in her hand.
Behind her the sons rise like shadow. The Indian
Snores.

He thinks: "Now."

And knows
He has entered the tale, knows
He has entered the dark hovel
In the forest where trees have eyes, knows it is the tale
They told him when he was a child, knows it
Is the dream he had in childhood but never
Knew the end of, only
The scream.

[G]

But no scream now, and under his hand
The dog lies taut, waiting. And he, too, knows
What he must do, do soon, and therefore
Does not understand why now a lassitude
Sweetens his limbs, or why, even in this moment
Of fear—or is it fear?—the saliva
In his mouth tastes sweet.

"Now, now!" the voice in his head cries out, but
Everything seems far away, and small.

He cannot think what guilt unmans him, or
Why he should find the punishment so precious.

It is too late. Oh, oh, the world!

Tell me the name of the world.

[H]

The door bursts open, and the travelers enter:
Three men, alert, strong, armed. And the Indian
Is on his feet, pointing.

He thinks
That now he will never know the dream's ending.

[I]

Trussed up with thongs, all night they lie on the floor there.
The woman is gagged, for she had reviled them.
All night he hears the woman's difficult breath.

Dawn comes. It is gray. When he eats,
The cold corn pone grinds in his throat, like sand. It sticks
      there.

Even whiskey fails to remove it. It sticks there.

The leg-thongs are cut off the tied-ones. They are made to
      stand up.
The woman refuses the whiskey. Says: "What fer?"
The first son drinks. The other
Takes it into his mouth, but it will not go down.

The liquid drains, slow, from the slack side of the mouth.

[J]

They stand there under the long, low bough of the great oak.
Eastward, low over the forest, the sun is nothing
But a circular blur of no irradiation, somewhat paler
Than the general grayness. Their legs
Are again bound with thongs.

They are asked if they want to pray now. But the woman:
"If'n it's God made folks, then who's to pray to?"
And then: "Or fer?" And bursts into laughing.

For a time it seems that she can never stop laughing.

But as for the sons, one prays, or tries to. And one
Merely blubbers. If the woman
Gives either a look, it is not
Pity, nor even contempt, only distance. She waits,

And is what she is,

And in the gray light of morning, he sees her face. Under
The tumbled darkness of hair, the face
Is white. Out of that whiteness
The dark eyes stare at nothing, or at
The nothingness that the gray sky, like Time, is, for
There is no Time, and the face
Is, he suddenly sees, beautiful as stone, and

So becomes aware that he is in the manly state.

[K]

The affair was not tidy: bough low, no drop, with the clients
Simply hung up, feet not much clear of the ground, but not
Quite close enough to permit any dancing.
The affair was not quick: both sons long jerking and farting,
     but she,
From the first, without motion, frozen
In a rage of will, an ecstasy of iron, as though
This was the dream that, lifelong, she had dreamed toward.

                                                        The face,
Eyes a-glare, jaws clenched, now glowing black with
     congestion
Like a plum, had achieved,
It seemed to him, a new dimension of beauty.

[L]

There are tears in his eyes.
He tries to remember his childhood.
He tries to remember his wife.
He can remember nothing.

His throat is parched. His right hand,
Under the deerskin frock, has been clutching the gold watch.

The magic of that object had been,
In the secret order of the world, denied her who now hangs
     there.

He thinks: "What has been denied me?"
Thinks: "There is never an answer."

Thinks: "The question is the only answer."

He yearns to be able to frame a definition of joy.

[M]

And so stood alone, for the travelers
Had disappeared into the forest and into
Whatever selves they were, and the Indian,
Now bearing the gift of a gun that had belonged to the
     hanged-ones,
Was long since gone, like smoke fading into the forest,
And below the blank and unforgiving eye-hole
The blood and mucus had long since dried.

He thought: "I must go."

                    But could not, staring
At the face, and stood for a time even after
The first snowflakes, in idiotic benignity,
Had fallen. Far off, in the forest and falling snow,
A crow was calling.

So stirs, knowing now
He will not be here when snow
Drifts into the open door of the cabin, or,
Descending the chimney, mantles thinly
Dead ashes on the hearth, nor when snow thatches
These heads with white, like wisdom, nor ever will he
Hear the infinitesimal stridor of the frozen rope
As wind shifts its burden, or when

The weight of the crow first comes to rest on a rigid shoulder.

III. We Are Only Ourselves

We never know what we have lost, or what we have found.
We are only ourselves, and that promise.
Continue to walk in the world. Yes, love it!

He continued to walk in the world.

IV. The Sign Whereby He Knew

[A]

His life, at the end, seemed—even the anguish—simple.
Simple, at least, in that it had to be,
Simply, what it was, as he was,
In the end, himself and not what
He had known he ought to be. The blessedness!—

To wake in some dawn and see,
As though down a rifle barrel, lined up
Like sights, the self that was, the self that is, and there,
Far off but in range, completing that alignment, your fate.

Hold your breath, let the trigger-squeeze be slow and steady.

The quarry lifts, in the halo of gold leaves, its noble head.

This is not a dimension of Time.

[B]

In this season the waters shrink.

The spring is circular and surrounded by gold leaves
Which are fallen from the beech tree.

Not even a skitter-bug disturbs the gloss
Of the surface tension. The sky

Is reflected below in absolute clarity.
If you stare into the water you may know

That nothing disturbs the infinite blue of the sky.

[C]

Keep store, dandle babies, and at night nuzzle
The hazelnut-shaped sweet tits of Lucy, and
With the piratical mark-up of the frontier, get rich.

But you did not, being of weak character.

You saw, from the forest pond, already dark, the great
        trumpeter swan
Rise, in clangor, and fight up the steep air where,
In the height of last light, it glimmered, like white flame.

The definition of love being, as we know, complex,
We may say that he, after all, loved his wife.

The letter, from campfire, keelboat, or slum room in New
        Orleans,
Always ended, "God bless you, dear Lucy." After sunset,

Alone, he played his flute in the forest.

[D]

Listen! Stand very still and,
Far off, where shadow
Is undappled, you may hear

The tushed boar grumble in his ivy-slick.

Afterward, there is silence until
The jay, sudden as conscience, calls.

The call, in the infinite sunlight, is like
The thrill of the taste of—on the tongue—brass.

[E]

The world declares itself. That voice
Is vaulted in—oh, arch on arch—redundancy of joy, its end
Is its beginning, necessity
Blooms like a rose. Why,

Therefore, is truth the only thing that cannot
Be spoken?

It can only be enacted, and that in dream,
Or in the dream become, as though unconsciously, action,
      and he stood,

At dusk, in the street of the raw settlement, and saw
The first lamp lit behind a window, and did not know
What he was. Thought: "I do not know my own name."

He walked in the world. He was sometimes seen to stand
In perfect stillness, when no leaf stirred.

Tell us, dear God—tell us the sign
Whereby we may know the time has come.

V. The Sound of That Wind

[A]

He walked in the world. Knew the lust of the eye.

Wrote: "Ever since a Boy I have had an astonishing
                      desire
                 to see Much of the World and particularly
                 to acquire a true knowledge of the Birds of
                      North America."

He dreamed of hunting with Boone, from imagination
     painted his portrait.
He proved that the buzzard does not scent its repast, but
     sights it.
He looked in the eye of the wounded white-headed eagle.

Wrote: ". . . the Noble Fellow looked at his Ennemies
                 with a Contemptible Eye."

At dusk he stood on a bluff, and the bellowing of buffalo
Was like distant ocean. He saw
Bones whiten the plain in the hot daylight.

He saw the Indian, and felt the splendor of God.

Wrote: ". . . for there I see the Man Naked from his
                 hand and yet free from acquired Sorrow."

Below the salt, in rich houses, he sat, and knew insult.
In the lobbies and couloirs of greatness he dangled,
And was not unacquainted with contumely.

Wrote: "My Lovely Miss Pirrie of Oackley Passed by
                      Me
                 this Morning, but did not remember how
                      beautifull
                 I had rendered her face once by Painting it
                 at her Request with Pastelles."

Wrote: ". . . but thanks to My humble talents I can
run
the gantlet throu this World without her help."

And ran it, and ran undistracted by promise of ease,
Nor even the kind condescension of Daniel Webster.

Wrote: ". . . would give me a fat place was I willing to
have one; but I love indepenn and piece more
than humbug and money."

And proved same, but in the end, entered
On honor. Far, over the ocean, in the silken salons,
With hair worn long like a hunter's, eyes shining,
He whistled the bird-calls of his distant forest.

Wrote: ". . . in my sleep I continually dream of birds."

And in the end, entered into his earned house,
And slept in a bed, and with Lucy.

                        But the fiddle
Soon lay on the shelf untouched, the mouthpiece
Of the flute was dry, and his brushes.

                        His mind
Was darkened, and his last joy
Was in the lullaby they sang him, in Spanish, at sunset.

He died, and was mourned, who had loved the world.

Who had written: ". . . a world which though wicked
enough
in all conscience is *perhaps* as good
as worlds unknown."

[B]

So died in his bed, and
Night leaned, and now leans,
Off the Atlantic, and is on schedule.

Grass does not bend beneath that enormous weight
That with no sound sweeps westward. In the Mississippi,
On a mud bank, the wreck of a great tree, left
By flood, lies, the root-system and now-stubbed boughs
Lifting in darkness. It
Is white as bone. That whiteness
Is reflected in dark water, and a star
Thereby.

      Later,
In the shack of a sheep-herder, high above the Bitterroot,
The light goes out. No other
Light is visible.

The Northwest Orient plane, New York to Seattle, has
     passed, winking westward.

[c]

For everything there is a season.

But there is the dream
Of a season past all seasons.

In such a dream the wild-grape cluster,
High-hung, exposed in the gold light,
Unripening, ripens.

Stained, the lip with wetness gleams.

I see your lip, undrying, gleam in the bright wind.

I cannot hear the sound of that wind.

VI. Love and Knowledge

Their footless dance
Is of the beautiful liability of their nature.
Their eyes are round, boldly convex, bright as a jewel,
And merciless. They do not know

Compassion, and if they did,
We should not be worthy of it. They fly
In air that glitters like fluent crystal
And is hard as perfectly transparent iron, they cleave it
With no effort. They cry
In a tongue multitudinous, often like music.

He slew them, at surprising distances, with his gun.
Over a body held in his hand, his head was bowed low,
But not in grief.

He put them where they are, and there we see them:
In our imagination.

What is love?

One name for it is knowledge.

VII. *Tell Me a Story*

[A]

Long ago, in Kentucky, I, a boy, stood
By a dirt road, in first dark, and heard
The great geese hoot northward.

I could not see them, there being no moon
And the stars sparse. I heard them.

I did not know what was happening in my heart.

It was the season before the elderberry blooms,
Therefore they were going north.

The sound was passing northward.

[B]

Tell me a story.

In this century, and moment, of mania,
Tell me a story.

Make it a story of great distances, and starlight.

The name of the story will be Time,
But you must not pronounce its name.

Tell me a story of deep delight.

Birth of Love

Season late, day late, sun just down, and the sky
Cold gunmetal but with a wash of live rose, and she,
From water the color of sky except where
Her motion has fractured it to shivering splinters of silver,
Rises. Stands on the raw grass. Against
The new-curdling night of spruces, nakedness
Glimmers and, at bosom and flank, drips
With fluent silver. The man,

Some ten strokes out, but now hanging
Motionless in the gunmetal water, feet
Cold with the coldness of depth, all
History dissolving from him, is
Nothing but an eye. Is an eye only. Sees

The body that is marked by his use, and Time's,
Rise, and in the abrupt and unsustaining element of air,
Sway, lean, grapple the pond-bank. Sees
How, with that posture of female awkwardness that is,
And is the stab of, suddenly perceived grace, breasts bulge
     down in
The pure curve of their weight and buttocks
Moon up and, in that swelling unity,
Are silver, and glimmer. Then

The body is erect, she is herself, whatever
Self she may be, and with an end of the towel grasped in each
    hand,
Slowly draws it back and forth across back and buttocks, but
With face lifted toward the high sky, where
The over-wash of rose color now fails. Fails, though no star
Yet throbs there. The towel, forgotten,
Does not move now. The gaze
Remains fixed on the sky. The body,

Profiled against the darkness of spruces, seems
To draw to itself, and condense in its whiteness, what light
In the sky yet lingers or, from
The metallic and abstract severity of water, lifts. The body,
With the towel now trailing loose from one hand, is
A white stalk from which the face flowers gravely toward the
    high sky.
This moment is non-sequential and absolute, and admits
Of no definition, for it
Subsumes all other, and sequential, moments, by which
Definition might be possible. The woman,

Face yet raised, wraps,
With a motion as though standing in sleep,
The towel about her body, under the breasts, and,
Holding it there, hieratic as lost Egypt and erect,
Moves up the path that, stair-steep, winds
Into the clamber and tangle of growth. Beyond
The lattice of dusk-dripping leaves, whiteness
Dimly glimmers, goes. Glimmers and is gone, and the man,

Suspended in his darkling medium, stares
Upward where, though not visible, he knows
She moves, and in his heart he cries out that, if only
He had such strength, he would put his hand forth
And maintain it over her to guard, in all
Her out-goings and in-comings, from whatever
Inclemency of sky or slur of the world's weather
Might ever be. In his heart
He cries out. Above

Height of the spruce-night and heave of the far mountain, he
    sees
The first star pulse into being. It gleams there.

I do not know what promise it makes to him.

Evening Hawk

From plane of light to plane, wings dipping through
Geometries and orchids that the sunset builds,
Out of the peak's black angularity of shadow, riding
The last tumultuous avalanche of
Light above pines and the guttural gorge,
The hawk comes.

        His wing
Scythes down another day, his motion
Is that of the honed steel-edge, we hear
The crashless fall of stalks of Time.

The head of each stalk is heavy with the gold of our error.

Look! look! he is climbing the last light
Who knows neither Time nor error, and under
Whose eye, unforgiving, the world, unforgiven, swings
Into shadow.

        Long now,
The last thrush is still, the last bat
Now cruises in his sharp hieroglyphics. His wisdom
Is ancient, too, and immense. The star
Is steady, like Plato, over the mountain.

If there were no wind we might, we think, hear
The earth grind on its axis, or history
Drip in darkness like a leaking pipe in the cellar.

Heart of Autumn

Wind finds the northwest gap, fall comes.
Today, under gray cloud-scud and over gray
Wind-flicker of forest, in perfect formation, wild geese
Head for a land of warm water, the *boom*, the lead pellet.

Some crumple in air, fall. Some stagger, recover control,
Then take the last glide for a far glint of water. None
Knows what has happened. Now, today, watching
How tirelessly *V* upon *V* arrows the season's logic,

Do I know my own story? At least, they know
When the hour comes for the great wing-beat. Sky-strider,
Star-strider—they rise, and the imperial utterance,
Which cries out for distance, quivers in the wheeling sky.

That much they know, and in their nature know
The path of pathlessness, with all the joy
Of destiny fulfilling its own name.
I have known time and distance, but not why I am here.

Path of logic, path of folly, all
The same—and I stand, my face lifted now skyward,
Hearing the high beat, my arms outstretched in the tingling
Process of transformation, and soon tough legs,

With folded feet, trail in the sounding vacuum of passage,
And my heart is impacted with a fierce impulse
To unwordable utterance—
Toward sunset, at a great height.

Vision

The vision will come—the Truth be revealed—but
Not even its vaguest nature you know—ah, truth

About what? But deep in the sibilant dark
That conviction irregularly

Gleams like fox-fire in sump-woods where,
In distance, lynx-scream or direful owl-stammer

Freezes the blood in a metaphysical shudder—which
Might be the first, feather-fine brush of Grace. Such

An event may come with night rain on roof, season changing
And bed too wide; or, say, when the past is de-fogged

And old foot tracks of folly show fleetingly clear before
Rationalization again descends, as from seaward.

Or when the shadow of pastness teasingly
Lifts and you recollect having caught—when, when?—

A glint of the nature of virtue like
The electrically exposed white of a flicker's

Rump feathers at the moment it flashes for the black thicket.
Or when, even, in a section of the city

Where no acquaintance would ever pass,
You watch snowflakes slash automobile lights

As you move toward the first
Illicit meeting, naturally at a crummy

Café. Your pace slows. You see her
Slip from the cab, dash for the door, dark fur coat

Collar up, head down. Inside,
As you order two highballs,

All eyes seem to focus on you. Drinks come, but
There is nothing to say. Hands

Do, damply, clasp—though no bed yet. Each stares
Into the other's eyes, desire like despair, and doom

Grows slow, and fat, and dark, like a burgundy begonia.
Soon you will watch the pale silken flash

Of well-turned ankles beneath dark fur,
As she hurries away on her stolen time, cab-hunting, and the
    future

Scarcely breathes. Your chest is a great clot. Perhaps then.
Oh, no. It may not happen, in fact, until

A black orderly, white-coated, on rubber soles, enters
    at 5 A.M.
The hospital room, suds and razor in hand, to shave,

With no word of greeting, the area the surgeon
Will penetrate. The robot departs. No one

Comes yet. Do not give up hope.
There is still time. Watch dawn blur the window.

Can it be that the vision has, long back, already come—
And you just didn't recognize it?

Muted Music

As sultry as the cruising hum
Of a single fly lost in the barn's huge, black
Interior, on a Sunday afternoon, with all the sky
Ablaze outside—so sultry and humming
Is memory when in barn-shade, eyes shut,
You lie in hay, and wonder if that empty, lonely,
And muted music was all the past was, after all.
Does the past now cruise your empty skull like
That blundering buzz at barn-height—which is dark
Except for the window at one gable, where
Daylight is netted gray with cobwebs, and the web
Dotted and sagged with blunderers that once could cruise
    and hum?

What do you really know
Of that world of decision and
Action you once strove in? What
Of that world where now
Light roars, while you, here, lulled, lie
In a cunningly wrought and mathematical

Box of shade, and try, of all the past, to remember
Which was *what*, *what*, *which*. Perhaps
That sultry hum from the lone bumbler, cruising high
In shadow, is the only sound that truth can make,
And into that muted music you soon sink
To hear at last, at last, what you have strained for
All the long years, and sometimes at dream-verge thought

You heard—the song the moth sings, the babble
Of falling snowflakes (in a language
No school has taught you), the scream
Of the reddening bud of the oak tree

As the bud bursts into the world's brightness.

STANLEY BURNSHAW

(b. 1906)

End of the Flower-World

Fear no longer for the lone gray birds
That fall beneath the world's last autumn sky,
Mourn no more the death of grass and tree.

These will be as they have ever been:
Substance of springtime; and when flower-world ends,
They will go back to earth, and wait, and be still,

Safe with the dust of birds long dead, with boughs
Turned ashes long ago, that still are straining
To leave their tombs and find the hills again,

Flourish again, mindless of the people—
The strange ones now on a leafless earth
Who seem to have no care for things in blossom.

Fear no more for trees, but mourn instead
The children of these strange, sad men: their hearts
Will hear no music but the song of death.

Bread

This that I give you now,
This bread that your mouth receives,
Never knows that its essence
Slept in the hanging leaves

Of a waving wheatfield thriving
With the sun's light, soil, and the rain,
A season ago, before knives
And wheels took life from the grain

That leaf might be flour—and the flour
Bread for the breathers' need . . .
Nor cared that some night one breather
Might watch how each remnant seed

Invades the blood, to become
Your tissue of flesh, and molests
Your body's secrets, swift-changing
To arms and the mounds of your breasts,

To thigh, hand, hair, to voices,
Your heart and your woman's mind . . .
For whatever the bread, do not grieve now
That soon a flash of the wind

May hurry away what remains
Of this quiet valiance of grass:
It entered your body, it fed you
So that you too can pass

From valiance to quiet, from thriving
To silenced flesh, and to ground:
Such is our meager cycle
That turns but a single round

For the deathless flesh of the earth,
For the signless husks of men dead,
For the folded oceans and mountains,
For birds, and fields, and for bread.

WARING CUNEY

(1906–1976)

No Images

She does not know
her beauty,
she thinks her brown body
has no glory.

If she could dance
naked
under palm trees
and see her image in the river,
she would know.

But there are no palm trees
on the street,
and dish water gives back
no images.

The Death Bed

All the time they were praying
He watched the shadow of a tree
Flicker on the wall.

There is no need of prayer
He said,
No need at all.

The kin-folk thought it strange
That he should ask them from a dying bed.
But they left all in a row
And it seemed to ease him
To see them go.

There were some who kept on praying
In a room across the hall,
And some who listened to the breeze
That made the shadows waver
On the wall.

He tried his nerve
On a song he knew
And made an empty note
That might have come,
From a bird's harsh throat.

And all the time it worried him
That they were in there praying,
And all the time he wondered
What it was they could be saying.

Conception

Jesus' mother never had no man.
God came to her one day an' said,
"Mary, chile, kiss ma han'."

JOSEPH KALAR

(1906–1972)

Papermill

Not to be believed, this blunt savage wind
Blowing in chill empty rooms, this tornado
Surging and bellying across the oily floor
Pushing men out in streams before it;
Not to be believed, this dry fall
Of unseen fog drying the oil
And emptying the jiggling greasecups;
Not to be believed, this unseen hand
Weaving a filmy rust of spiderwebs
Over these turbines and grinding gears,
These snarling chippers and pounding jordans;
These fingers placed to lips saying shshsh;
Keep silent, keep silent, keep silent;
Not to be believed hardly, this clammy silence
Where once feet stamped over the oily floor,
Dinnerpails clattered, voices rose and fell
In laughter, curses, and songs. Now the guts
Of this mill have ceased their rumbling, now
The fires are banked and red changes to black,
Steam is cold water, silence is rust, and quiet
Spells hunger. Look at these men, now,
Standing before the iron gates, mumbling,
"Who could believe it? Who could believe it?"

RICHMOND LATTIMORE

(1906–1984)

North Philadelphia Trenton and New York

Thin steel, in paired lines forever mated, cuts,
forks and crosses, catches blue light, threads a station and a
    yard,
finds a bridge across the winter Schuylkill lithograph,
slips by the winter boardings, the chimney pots, the dirty
windowpanes and chimneys cut aslant for factories
either way aside.

                Now square your panes, look
large to wheel the brittle gray, the deep
horizon up. The prison steps into your square, and runs
    beside,
and drops away. The nunnery, the monastery after it,
fleetly shine, dip, recover, and are gone,
as houses in precise astonished rows come out,
sit up and solidify, stare, and are politely wheeled away.
Under bridge and under wheel the Delaware floats down
ice cakes, watched by the gilt glitter of the Capitol.

North now, sky change on earth angle altering,
color of iron blooms on spinneys, Breughel snow and brown
    tree
authenticate the high parallel.

                  In North Jersey, flat, endlessly
arranged in silver gas cylinders, shine of plane wing, deep
dirty and deliberate rivers grope between meadows
where the catkins keep good order and the posters march
    beside you,
and the turnpike loping near on legs of pylons stays to race you,
and the hill with houses slides to meet you.

                    The tunnel: you are gone,
and the bright winter sky as from a tube of indigo is squeezed
    away.

Vergil Georgics I. 489–514

Therefore Philippi saw once more the Roman battalions
clash upon each other with weapons matched; and the high
    gods
deigned twice over that with our blood the wide fields of
    Haemus
and Emathia be made fat and flourish. Surely the time shall
come when in those reaches the farmer following the
    plowshare
cramped to earth shall come on javelins thin with rust-rot
or with the weight of the mattock turn up hollow helmets.
Gods of our fathers grown to our soil, O Romulus, Vesta
mother and savior of Tuscany, Tiber, Rome's Palatine ridges,
deny not that this young man at least shall be healer
to our collapsed world. We have paid enough long since in
    our own
blood for the sins and the treachery of Troy and Laomedon.
Now long since the kingdom of the sky has envied you,
    Caesar,
us and you, is sick of bringing to pass the triumphs of
    mortals,
right sometimes and sometimes wicked; the world at warfare
so many times; so many faces of cruelty; never the farmer's
right he merits; the tillers swept away and the fields gone
foul, the curved reaping-hooks beaten stark into sword-
    blades.
From the east Euphrates, from the north Germany stirs to
    battle.
Close cities have broken their links of peace and go armed
    now
for civil strife; the savagery of bloody Mars fills the whole
    globe.
As when chariots for racing have burst from their caverned
stalls, go wild abroad, and with vain hands clutching the
    guide-reins
helpless the charioteer is carried at the will of his horses.

HELENE JOHNSON

(1907–1995)

Bottled

Upstairs on the third floor
Of the 135th Street library
In Harlem, I saw a little
Bottle of sand, brown sand
Just like the kids make pies
Out of down at the beach.
But the label said: "This
Sand was taken from the Sahara desert."
Imagine that! The Sahara desert!
Some bozo's been all the way to Africa to get some sand.

And yesterday on Seventh Avenue
I saw a darky dressed fit to kill
In yellow gloves and swallow tail coat
And swirling a cane. And everyone
Was laughing at him. Me, too,
At first, till I saw his face
When he stopped to hear a
Organ grinder grind out some jazz.
Boy! You should a seen that darky's face!
It just shone. Gee, he was happy!
And he began to dance. No
Charleston or Black Bottom for him.
No sir. He danced just as dignified
And slow. No, not slow either.
Dignified and proud! You couldn't
Call it slow, not with all the
Cuttin' up he did. You would a died to see him.

The crowd kept yellin' but he didn't hear,
Just kept on dancin' and twirlin' that cane
And yellin' out loud every once in a while.
I know the crowd thought he was coo-coo.

But say, I was where I could see his face,
And somehow, I could see him dancin' in a jungle,
A real honest-to-cripe jungle, and he wouldn't have on them
Trick clothes—those yaller shoes and yaller gloves
And swallow-tail coat. He wouldn't have no nothing.
And he wouldn't be carrying no cane.
He'd be carrying a spear with a sharp fine point
Like the bayonets we had "over there."
And the end of it would be dipped in some kind of
Hoodoo poison. And he'd be dancin' black and naked and
　　gleaming.
And he'd have rings in his ears and on his nose
And bracelets and necklaces of elephants' teeth.
Gee, I bet he'd be beautiful then all right.
No one would laugh at him then, I bet.
Say! That man that took that sand from the Sahara desert
And put it in a little bottle on a shelf in the library,
That's what they done to this shine, ain't it? Bottled him—
Trick shoes, trick coat, trick cane, trick everything—all glass—
But inside—
Gee, that poor shine!

Sonnet to a Negro in Harlem

You are disdainful and magnificent—
Your perfect body and your pompous gait,
Your dark eyes flashing solemnly with hate,
Small wonder that you are incompetent
To imitate those whom you so despise—
Your shoulders towering high above the throng,
Your head thrown back in rich, barbaric song,
Palm trees and mangoes stretched before your eyes.
Let others toil and sweat for labor's sake
And wring from grasping hands their meed of gold.
Why urge ahead your supercilious feet?
Scorn will efface each footprint that you make.
I love your laughter arrogant and bold.
You are too splendid for this city street!

Magalu

Summer comes.
The ziczac hovers
'Round the greedy-mouthed crocodile.
A vulture bears away a foolish jackal.
The flamingo is a dash of pink
Against dark green mangroves,
Her slender legs rivalling her slim neck.
The laughing lake gurgles delicious music in its throat
And lulls to sleep the lazy lizard,
A nebulous being on a sun-scorched rock.
In such a place,
In this pulsing, riotous gasp of color,
I met Magalu, dark as a tree at night,
Eager-lipped, listening to a man with a white collar
And a small black book with a cross on it.
Oh Magalu, come! Take my hand and I will read you poetry,
Chromatic words,
Seraphic symphonies,
Fill up your throat with laughter and your heart with song.
Do not let him lure you from your laughing waters,
Lulling lakes, lissome winds.
Would you sell the colors of your sunset and the fragrance
Of your flowers, and the passionate wonder of your forest
For a creed that will not let you dance?

LINCOLN KIRSTEIN

(1907–1996)

Gloria

If you doan mind, would you please Mind moving over,
    please.
Thank YOU. There's Plenty of room for All us girls. Jeez,
   hon, I'm Sorry; really. So how should *I* know. I thought
   we was All girls here, though now I see you are Not
but can take the Joke. What a Relief! For about One
second I was scared you'd Sock me; but honest, hon,
    you Do remind me of Someone I knew years ago:
    just your type although you yourself might'n think so—

I mean super-fishulee—crew cut, all your
Classs. It's that clean-cut Navy Look; it always sure
   beats Me, though I was Army, but it wasn't the Real me.
   I adore Navy. The Most. The U.S. Navy—
but what admiral would want me? I'm asking you, man:
does this Interest you? Oh, you, Stop! So . . . I can
    pro-ceed? Sometimes it's quite Hard to know who is
      honestly
    inerstid. Fred was the First I knew when he

Joins the Navy and such a Good Kid, naughty but nice,
wild And cute; wicked, he's just the kind you look Twice
   at, but he never got into no trouble Untillll
   he was in Service. Then, mann, did he get his Fillll!
This all Begins *Years* before, but let's Skip all that;
I was living in a little cold-water flat;
    I was being Alone, then. Fred, sometimes, spent the night;
    he was working Out of Town and doing All Right—

Sold National Advertising for some Large Concern,
not High Pay but he was just beginning to Learn.
    One day, we weren't even At War yet, he wanders in;

"Gloria," he grins, "I dood it." He done it, En-
listed. I was Dumb-Founded. I gave him a big kiss;
We got Screamin. Imagine! In *Uniform* This
 One would look like sheer Mad heaven; simply cannot beat
 your Navy blue-and-gold or that old Navy neat-

Nessss. You All look ssoo Damn *clean.* Why does Army *never*
in spite of all them soapy showers look Ever
 clean? Fred done his first bootcamp bit way out at Great
  Lakes.
 Tough, but made it—WAIT! Your're Leaving! Now, for
  Land sakes,
You need One More Beer. Now *please.* This one's on Meee.
 Now then . . .
I lost my apartment. Bitchy landlady, when
 I spend Weeks ripping plaster, Complete two-coat painting,
 and Entire interior Ree-Decorating—

The Back Room apple-green, trim in Black; the front, a brick
 wall
hung with a *Huge* baroque mirror. Sooo, after all
 this, she raise the Rent. She said I wasn't a good Bet.
 I paid on the Dot. I should be living there Yet.
But let's not talk about Meee. Fred's at Norfolk, now onnn.
I didn't hear One word for Weeks. I thought; he's GONE
 and Shipped Out, but then, smack: in the middle of the
  Night
 a *telegram* phones. It's from Fred all right, all right.

"Come Norfolk At Once. *Difficulties.*" My Poor dear Fred.
I couldn't sleep a Wink, just lay Thinking, in bed
 And scared Green, and I mean for Himmm, not at all for
  Meee. . . .
 By mistake he'd written a Letter, you seee. . . .
To my Old addresss, since he hadn't my New addressss—
Wrote on the envelope his *Own* addresss. I guesss
 That landlady Did it, but we'd never rightfully Know;
 it was opened by Errorr. I never saw it, though

Fred said it was Something Like as how he'd Met this Marrr-
velous mahogany-haired marine, some Gay Barrr,
    and went up In Smoke. It *worked*. And this young kid
    Liked Fred;
    sensational. Fred went out of his fucking Headdd,
drew his profile for me: crew cut, big jaw, cute lad;
Fred was a good draftsman; the Firm he worked for had
    thought him Talented for layouts. He sketched Very Good;
    he could have been a Great Illustrator, he could.

His letter must have been One Wow of a camperooo
with this marine's Portrait and Full Description tooo
    describing Everything. What's this letter do Then?
    Gets itself turned over to CID—you know: Those Men
who confront Fred with it, without Warning, just like That:
"*You* Wrote This?" His own commanding officer asked:
    "What
    is the Meaning of *this*?" Fred said: "Well, sir, it don't
    Meannn
    Nothing. It's just a Joke—in Bad Taste." Get that quean.

Who'd believe Fred? There wasn't One small Shadow of
    doubt
what his Whole silly sincere letter was About.
    They didn't exactly Arrest him; held him Confined
    in the best hotel. He started to Lose his Mind,
wired Meee. Then, it wasn't easy to catch a plane quick:
Norfolk, wartime, two-motor plane. I was Quite sick:
    I get sick when it's at all bumpy, sometimes when Not.
    I thought: Gloria, if Ize in some Christless spot

Who'd I turn to? Fred, natch. So the Least poor I could do—
try and help Himmm. Hotel room in Norfolk with *Whooo*
    but a marine guard. Get the Picture? I had to get
    permission from his commandant before they'd let
me Innn. They left the door Open so they could listen and
needn't Buggg it. Now I begin to Understand
    it's a Court-Martial offenssse; but—they better Be Sure
    and Prove it. Just get us a good lawyer, but your

Sainted Mother now found that Some people are just Viiile.
They had No idea of letting Fred stand trialll;
   without no Prrooof, just this letter and sketch, like Fred
     said:
   a joke; in rather poor Taste. Fred was real well bred;
slips me a note: tells me: "Go this certain gay bar Where"
his marine would sure probably Beee—but when?—there-
   sooo, if Anyone asked Questions not to say One Thing,
   quel horreur, though Fred said Jack would Nnneverrr sing.

I'll do anything for Friends, but I didn't know:
What Could I do? CID watched wherever I'd go;
   Was this *smart*? I'm a sensible girl; curious, too,
   how this one would Look, for Fred's a Real Expert and you
Are curious when somebody's Gorgeous. You wanta Seee.
I'm only Human: would this, his, Jack—be for Meee?
   Hon . . . Bar was filled with mad numbers. Remember
   the warrr?
   Like a friggin floor show. But no Jack. I drank farrr

Into the night. Next morning I saw Fred, my poor friend,
in a Horrible state. He looked just like the *End*.
   Those lousy CID's. What had they now Gone and Done?
   You wouldn't Believe it. My grey hair *curled*. That SON
of a bitch the marine guard who brung in poor Fred's food
wasn't allowed to talk to him; this same guy who'd
   been sent in last night, late, with an old hospital tray:
   milk and fruit; then this marine slips Away.

At the time Fred didn't notice. He was too Down to eat—
finds on his plate a thoughtful extra-added Treattt:
   a loaded service revolver. Man, I never knew
   what the old United States Navy could *do* to you.
Soooo . . . your Sainted Mother had Quite a time keeping
    Fred
From putting a bullet through his pretty head.
   I pleaded with him, begged really: the best I could;
   they'd nothing on him At All; so What is the good

In *Suicide*? He wrote a letter. Assuming it's true
(which it was)—it's not the First time. It's nothing New.
    But Fred Collapsed. He broke down. He cried, he cried
      and cried.
    But no hari-kari. I saw his captain, Lied
like a real character witness, though I couldn't quite telll
what Cap thought. Told him about Fred's broads. Oh
      welll. . . .
    I got down on my Kneeess. I prayed for Common Sense.
    This captain, splendid man, loved Fred; was just Immense;

Said Fred was a good man for a good job—in his Way;
told me, very kind: Go back. You tell him: O.K.
    they'd fix something up, but for High Heaven's Sweet Sake
    don't write no more *Letters*. This time he'd get a break.
This puts hope into Freddy-boy. He cheers up a bit,
saw the light; then on in we laughed a lot at it.
    I smuggled beer; gave some to that marine guard and he
    winked. From then on in, it went rather Easily.

But Fred had an Idea proving he's not so Bright;
in some ways he's stupid. Now he thought it all right
    since he's in the Clear and since I had to get Back
    (I was just a working girl, didn't want the sack),
I should cruise that bar again, try to make One last try,
see if I could actually contact this guy;
    couldn't Bear to think he'd never see Junior anywhere.
    How'd I tell which jack Jack was with all them jacks there?

But he needn't ask mother *twice*. I went. Found myself one
Sensational number. No kin to Jack, though *fun*.
    We had beers. You can't help try to make some Try.
    I didn't tell Fred. Him so Depressed. Why should I?
That's about *It*. Today, he'll still say I saved his life;
us camping, I cast myself as his divorced wife,
    we kid about Him paying Me my own alimony. . . .
    End of Story? Not quite. (One more beer?) . . . I agree:

Hasn't much *Point*. That's The point of this here story:
they let him resign for the good of Old Glory.
  Soooo . . . then what does this Foooll do? Joins the
    Marines, he does:
  Ferocious combat training. It was
Murder. Shave you. Beat you. Feed you live ammunition.
Fred did great. He had military ambition.
  So then some Bastard dug up his old Papers and found
  his Navy Records and, natch, they could make it sound

Bad. Marines chuck him out. You think That's it? You ain't
    seen
Nothing yet. Sooo, now he joins the merchant marine:
  him a mere merchant seaman after all he's been Through.
  Then They got his records Too. They chuck him out
    Toooo.
My poor Freddy was now a three-time loser for Keeps.
He gave up. I got drafted but you needn't weep
  for your Sainted Mother. Europe? A Ball, for three years.
  Fred? Took it like a Man. Shed no more tears,

Just sat the rest of This war out. Grim fairy tale?
Fred a failure? No, sir, though I watched him fail
  three times, perfectly cast as that Navy juvenile,
  adoring the Service, a good officer, while
when I spoke to his sweet commandant I *did* get Notions
that old salt Liked Fred. Honest, hon, the fucking ocean's
  Fulll of Strange fish. After the war, Fred makes more than
    me,
  a first-rate illustrator and No tragedy.

I see him less when I get back from Over Seas. . . .
Now—you Leaving? Please, hon; please. Sir, one more. Sir.
    Please.

P.O.E.

THIS IS IT and so: so long.
 We're soldiers now, all set to sail.
We may not sing one sad old song
 Herded within a dark dock-rail.

Self-pity pools its furtive tear;
 Expect the Worst, discount the Best.
Insurance as a form of fear
 Tickles the terror in each chest.

So: THIS IS IT—yet not the sheer
 Crude crisis we've been trained to take,
For many a female volunteer
 Doles out thin cocoa with thick cake.

They've parked their limousines the while;
 Their natty uniform is spick
And span, their hairdo and their smile
 Pronounces patriotic chic;

And THIS IS IT for these dames too.
 We strive to fake a grateful note
But goddam duffel bag and pack,
 Gas mask, rifle, helmet, coat

Too heavy are, so each sad sack
 Must flop and gripe: This is *some* shit.
Up On Your Feet, our orders crack.
 It's All Aboard for THIS IS IT.

CONSTANCE CARRIER

(1908–1991)

A Point of View

One world at a time, remarked Thoreau,
speaking more in rebuke than in sorrow.
The pious who heard him had reckoned
he was close to the brink of a second,
but for all of their coaxing and coaching
he wouldn't guess what was approaching.
He had studied this life: he had tried
to get at its roots, and he died
prepared to give equal attention
to life in another dimension
if the gods should endow him with such.
But two at a time was too much.

The pious were pained at the weight
he put on the earthly estate—
on the daily and deadly prosaic:
the lives that men lead in Passaic,
Paducah, Peru, and Penn Yan;
and the men who survive as they can,
too busy, too bored, or too blind
to get the word *living* defined.
But Thoreau was that kind of mystic
whose marvels are all realistic:
he never laid claim to have found
the dove, the bay horse or the hound,
and he ventured no views on tomorrow.

One world at a time, remarked Thoreau.

Clause for a Covenant

Title conveyed, seal set,
still it is wise to let
the thicket grow,
nor mow all grass to stubble:
permit the reeds to blow,
the branch to bend above its watery double,

lest the benevolent hand,
clearing this close-grown land,
letting the white
hot light into this tangle,
too sharp, too burning bright,
leave the earth dead under the cold blade's angle.

To their own daimon yield
these coverts long-concealed—
his native, strange,
unchanging sanctuary:
let him in freehold range,
safe, and invisible, and solitary.

Elegy

Here where the elm trees were
is only empty air.

Where once they stood
how blunt the buildings are!

Where the trees were,
sky itself has fled
far overhead.

We have lost the leafy shield
between us and that space,
that lonely tract, revealed,
that light too straitly shed—

and lost as well the lace,
the filigree, that gave
the works of man a grace
not theirs by right.

The world is smaller and larger
with the tall trees gone.
Through sunlight yellow as pollen
we walk where the elms have fallen.

We walk in too much light.

Laudare

Death, let me praise you now
while I have breath to praise
the dark on which I measure
the brightness of my days.

O lapidary death
who cut and faceted
this diamond I hold
that else were glass instead—

O contrapuntal death
resolving every chord;
the soundless antiphon;
the dominant restored—

O necromancer death
who charms my love from me—
what lover's faith compares
with your fidelity?

Let me then praise you now;
let me all homage give
to this my master death
by whose dark grace I live.

Helianthus

The great whorl-centered sun
rides here in miniature—
sextant upon a stalk,
all the corona flames
tangible, lapped and rayed.
As water to the moon
obedient, it moves
to trace upon the air
the single truth it knows.

A bee, no less intent,
riding that tethered wheel,
reaping that yellow heart,
hovers between two suns.

ALTON DELMORE

(1908–1964)

The Girl by the River

I met a fair maiden so sweet and so fair
Where the white flowers bloomed on the shore
And one of these flowers was fixed in her hair
I can still see that flower she wore

> The girl by the river she meets me no more
> No more do the white flowers grow
> Perhaps she will meet me on some distant shore
> She's gone where the white flowers go

We made a nice couple, we talked and we sang
So sweet was her laughter to hear
But the beautiful flowers so white without name
Grew closer and to her more dear

> The girl by the river she meets me no more
> No more do the white flowers grow
> Perhaps she will meet me on some distant shore
> She's gone where the white flowers go

Through spring and through summer we capered around
Through the beautiful white flowers there
In autumn they faded and could not be found
And my darling she showed a strange fear

> The girl by the river she meets me no more
> No more do the white flowers grow
> Perhaps she will meet me on some distant shore
> She's gone where the white flowers go

We'd made our plans for a wedding to be
She told me that she would be mine

One day she vanished and now I can't find
My darling, my sweetheart divine

The girl by the river she meets me no more
No more do the white flowers grow
Perhaps she will meet me on some distant shore
She's gone where the white flowers go

JOSEPHINE JACOBSEN

(b. 1908)

Poems for My Cousin

I. I Took My Cousin to Prettyboy Dam

I took my cousin to Prettyboy Dam.
A boxer was swimming for sticks, the ripples
Blew from the left, and beer cans glittered
Under the poison-ivy.

We talked of pelota; and of how the tendrils of vines
Curl opposite ways in the opposite hemispheres.
My cousin was dying. By this I mean
The rate of his disengagement was rapid.

There was a haze of heat, and August boys
Chunked rocks at a bottle that bobbed on the water.
The slow hours enclosed the flight of instants,
Melted the picnic-ice.

Everything he saw differently, and more clearly than I.
The joined dragon-flies, the solid foam of the fall;
The thin haste of the ant at my foot,
And me, as I looked at him.

We were close beside each other, speaking of
Pelota, chaining cigarettes when the matches were gone.
But we saw different things, since one could not say
    "Wait . . ."
Nor the other "Come . . ."

II. The Four Faces of My Cousin

My cousin had four faces.

One was the face which grimaced
In laughter or anger—mobile to danger,
Fun or sudden love;

Made up of flaws, joys, private
Recall; of a benediction
Or so, and sudden love;

With the harassed grain, and strains
Of wretched encounters, the thought
Of difficult heaven, and sudden love.

The second, was the blast of agony:
Contorted, it glared without sight
When the sheet was turned from the face

By familiar fingers. It glared
Without rest under the harsh gesture
Of death, and the mouth was frantic for its breath.

The third, silent, and silently watched
By the crucified man, had tiny pulses
Of light on its false tranquility—

The candle's mark. It was a good mask,
Composed to duty and not unbeautiful
Below the poised and frilly inner lid.

But the gray-white was wrong, and the faint rouge
On a dead man's lips—(and the fingers
Curled stiffly, shared the face's error.)

The fourth face of my cousin I have never
Seen. This is the secret accurate intended
Face I must wait for.

III. Arrival of My Cousin

My cousin is arrived in
the green city of the dead.
It slopes, shapes itself
in hilly contours, and the summer light
lights all the white stones, crosses and angels of granite.

Thousands or tens of thousands
in the cool grass, under the flight
of birds, of shadows of birds; the shadow
of flight in the sunny marble,
the bird-notes, bird-calls, dew-clear;
The blue and white sky is bent over my cousin,
in the green city of the dead.

Traffic sweats and stalls on Oliver Street,
and Hargrove, Dolphin, Bethel Streets; the dirty bars
sweat, and the usual accidents in the accident-rooms
are glazed by July, as are the gutters and the junk-man's
horse, jerked up the tar-soft mountain of July.
My cousin, however, is in
the green city of the dead.

Not being of a primitive tribe
I speak in metaphor when I find my cousin,
cloud-free, granite-still, in
the green bird-rich city, bounded
by the sweating streets, and the houses, and rooms,
and the people in streets, houses, rooms,
and their eyes.
By the body of Christ we ate, his absence
is evident:
But I speak of the token, the image
I was given for identity;
that word of flesh, like a name, a sound,
is what I speak of.

Infinitely not of the alley, the gutter, the traffic,
the sweating problem that walks
the pavement, sits in the room—
is the token, the word, the vanishing image of my cousin
under blue sky, white cloud, grass, bird-call, stone angel
in the green city of the dead.

Yellow

Yellow became alive.
Materialization took place.
First logically with lemons,
then fresh butter.
Also a chair-leg.
After that it appeared
to carve the curve of clouds
and, as sun, shatter them.
The stars grew yellower
yellow whirls on wheels on whirls
leaves flew yellow
the corn sprang
yellow and the crows
winged with a yellow nimbus.
Finally his face
had brilliant yellow
in its grain.
Outside the madhouse hung the yellow sun.

GEORGE OPPEN

(1908–1984)

Discrete Series

The knowledge not of sorrow, you were
    saying, but of boredom
Is—aside from reading speaking
    smoking——
Of what, Maude Blessingbourne it was,
    wished to know when, having risen,
"approached the window as if to see
    what really was going on";
And saw rain falling, in the distance
    more slowly,
The road clear from her past the window-
    glass——
Of the world, weather-swept, with which
    one shares the century.

————

I

White. From the
Under arm of T

The red globe.

Up
Down. Round
Shiny fixed
Alternatives

From the quiet

Stone floor . . .

2

Thus
Hides the

Parts—the prudery
Of Frigidaire, of
Soda-jerking——

Thus

Above the

Plane of lunch, of wives
Removes itself
(As soda-jerking from
the private act

Of
Cracking eggs);

big-Business

————

The evening, water in a glass
Thru which our car runs on a higher road.

Over what has the air frozen?

Nothing can equal in polish and obscured
        origin that dark instrument
A car
        (Which.
Ease; the hand on the sword-hilt

————

Her ankles are watches
(Her arm-pits are causeways for water)

When she steps
She walks on a sphere

Walks on the carpet, dressing.
Brushing her hair

Her movement accustomed, abstracted,
Declares this morning a woman's
"My hair, scalp——"

———

1

The three wide
Funnels raked aft, and the masts slanted

      the
Deck-hand slung in a bosun's chair
Works on this 20th century chic and
        efficiency
Not evident at "The Sailor's Rest."

2

The lights, paving——
This important device
Of a race

Remains till morning.

      Burns
Against the wall.
He has chosen a place
With the usual considerations,
Without stating them.
Buildings.

———

The mast
Inaudibly soars; bole-like, tapering:
Sail flattens from it beneath the wind.
The limp water holds the boat's round
                                    sides. Sun
Slants dry light on the deck.
                          Beneath us glide
Rocks, sands, and unrimmed holes.

————

Closed car—closed in glass——
At the curb,
Unapplied and empty:
A thing among others
Over which clouds pass and the
                          alteration of lighting,
An overstatement
Hardly an exterior.
Moving in traffic
This thing is less strange——
Tho the face, still within it,
Between glasses—place, over which
                          time passes—a false light.

————

Who comes is occupied
Toward the chest (in the crowd moving
            opposite
Grasp of me)
                    In firm overalls
The middle-aged man sliding
Levers in the steam-shovel cab,——
Lift (running cable) and swung, back
Remotely respond to the gesture before last
Of his arms fingers continually——
Turned with the cab. But if I (how goes
                it?)——
                    The asphalt edge

Loose on the plateau,
Horse's classic height cartless
See electric flash of streetcar,
The fall is falling from electric burst.

———

Party on Shipboard

Wave in the round of the port-hole
Springs, passing,—arm waved,
Shrieks, unbalanced by the motion——
Like the sea incapable of contact
Save in incidents (the sea is not
    water)
Homogeneously automatic—a green capped
    white is momentarily a half mile
    out——
The shallow surface of the sea, this,
Numerously—the first drinks——
The sea is a constant weight
In its bed. They pass, however, the sea
Freely tumultuous.

———

This land:
The hills, round under straw;
A house

With rigid trees

And flaunts
A family laundry,
And the glass of windows

———

Semaphoring chorus,
The width of the stage. The usher from it:
Seats' curving rows two sides by distant
          phosphor. And those 'filled';
Man and wife, removing gloves
Or overcoat. Still faces already lunar.

————

The edge of the ocean,
The shore: here
Somebody's lawn,
By the water.

————

Tug against the river——
Motor turning, lights
In the fast water off the bow-wave:
Passes slowly.

————

She lies, hip high,
On a flat bed
While the after-
Sun passes.

Plant, I breathe——
                    O Clearly,
Eyes legs arms hands fingers,
Simple legs in silk.

————

Civil war photo:
Grass near the lens;
Man in the field
In silk hat. Daylight.
The cannon of that day
In our parks.

———

As I saw
There
Year ago——
If there's a bird
On the cobbles;
One I've not seen

———

Bolt
In the frame
Of the building——
A ship
Grounds
Her immense keel
Chips
A stone
Under fifteen feet
Of harbor
Water——
The fiber of this tree
Is live wood
Running into the
Branches and leaves
In the air.

———

From this distance thinking toward you,
Time is recession

Movement of no import
Not encountering you

Save the pulse cumulates a past
And your pulse separate doubly.

———

Town, a town,
But location
Over which the sun as it comes to it;
Which cools, houses and lamp-posts,
          during the night, with the roads——
Inhabited partly by those
Who have been born here,
Houses built——. From a train one sees
          him in the morning, his morning;
Him in the afternoon, straightening——
People everywhere, time and the work
          pauseless:
One moves between reading and re-reading,
The shape is a moment.
From a crowd a white powdered face,
Eyes and mouth making three——
Awaited—locally—a date.

———

Near your eyes——
Love at the pelvis
Reaches the generic, gratuitous
                    (Your eyes like snail-tracks)

Parallel emotions,
We slide in separate hard grooves
Bowstrings to bent loins,
                    Self moving
Moon, mid-air.

———

Fragonard,
Your spiral women
By a fountain

'1732'

Your picture lasts thru us

                    its air
Thick with succession of civilizations;
And the women.

————

No interval of manner
Your body in the sun.
You? A solid, this that the dress
                    insisted,
Your face unaccented, your mouth a mouth?
                    Practical knees:
It is you who truly
Excel the vegetable,
The fitting of grasses—more bare than
                    that.
Pointedly bent, your elbow on a car-edge
Incognito as summer
Among mechanics.

————

'O city ladies'
Your coats wrapped,
Your hips a possession

Your shoes arched
Your walk is sharp

Your breasts
        Pertain to lingerie

The fields are road-sides,
Rooms outlast you.

————

Bad times:
The cars pass
By the elevated posts
And the movie sign.
A man sells post-cards.

————

It brightens up into the branches
And against the same buildings

A morning:
His job is as regular.

————

On the water, solid——
The singleness of a toy——

A tug with two barges.

O what O what will
Bring us back to
Shore,
     the shore

Coiling a rope on the steel deck

————

Drawing

Not by growth
     But the
Paper, turned, contains
This entire volume

————

Deaths everywhere——
The world too short for trend is land——
   In the mouths,
         Rims

In this place, two geraniums
In your window-box
Are his life's eyes.

———

Written structure,
Shape of art,
More formal
Than a field would be
(existing in it)——
Her pleasure's
Looser;
'O—'

    'Tomorrow?'—

Successive
Happenings
(the telephone)

Eclogue

The men talking
Near the room's center. They have said
More than they had intended.

Pinpointing in the uproar
Of the living room

An assault
On the quiet continent.

Beyond the window
Flesh and rock and hunger

Loose in the night sky
Hardened into soil

Tilting of itself to the sun once more, small
Vegetative leaves
And stems taking place

Outside—O small ones,
To be born!

Image of the Engine

1

Likely as not a ruined head gasket
Spitting at every power stroke, if not a crank shaft
Bearing knocking at the roots of the thing like a pile-driver:
A machine involved with itself, a concentrated
Hot lump of a machine
Geared in the loose mechanics of the world with the valves
        jumping
And the heavy frenzy of the pistons. When the thing stops,
Is stopped, with the last slow cough
In the manifold, the flywheel blundering
Against compression, stopping, finally
Stopped, compression leaking
From the idle cylinders will one imagine
Then because he can imagine
That squeezed from the cooling steel
There hovers in that moment, wraith-like and like a plume of
        steam, an aftermath,
A still and quiet angel of knowledge and of comprehension.

2

Endlessly, endlessly,
The definition of mortality

The image of the engine

That stops.
We cannot live on that.
I know that no one would live out
Thirty years, fifty years if the world were ending
With his life.
The machine stares out,
Stares out
With all its eyes

Thru the glass
With the ripple in it, past the sill
Which is dusty—If there is someone
In the garden!
Outside, and so beautiful.

3

What ends
Is that.
        Even companionship
Ending.

'I want to ask if you remember
When we were happy!' As tho all travels

Ended untold, all embarkations
Foundered.

4

On that water
Grey with morning
The gull will fold its wings
And sit. And with its two eyes
There as much as anything
Can watch a ship and all its hallways
And all companions sink.

5

Also he has set the world
In their hearts. From lumps, chunks,

We are locked out: like children, seeking love
At last among each other. With their first full strength
The young go search for it,

Native in the native air.
But even in the beautiful bony children
Who arise in the morning have left behind
Them worn and squalid toys in the trash

Which is a grimy death of love. The lost
Glitter of the stores!
The streets of stores!
Crossed by the streets of stores
And every crevice of the city leaking
Rubble: concrete, conduit, pipe, a crumbling
Rubble of our roots

                    But they will find
In flood, storm, ultimate mishap:
Earth, water, the tremendous
Surface, the heart thundering
Absolute desire.

From Disaster

Ultimately the air
Is bare sunlight where must be found
The lyric valuables. From disaster

Shipwreck, whole families crawled
To the tenements, and there

Survived by what morality
Of hope

Which for the sons
Ends its metaphysic
In small lawns of home.

Psalm

Veritas sequitur . . .

In the small beauty of the forest
The wild deer bedding down—
That they are there!

        Their eyes
Effortless, the soft lips
Nuzzle and the alien small teeth
Tear at the grass

        The roots of it
Dangle from their mouths
Scattering earth in the strange woods.
They who are there.

        Their paths
Nibbled thru the fields, the leaves that shade them
Hang in the distances
Of sun

        The small nouns
Crying faith
In this in which the wild deer
Startle, and stare out.

The Occurrences

The simplest
Words say the grass blade
Hides the blaze
Of a sun
To throw a shadow
In which the bugs crawl
At the roots of the grass;

Father, father
Of fatherhood
Who haunts me, shivering
Man most naked
Of us all, O father

          watch
At the roots
Of the grass the creating
Now   that tremendous
plunge

Route

'the void eternally generative'
the *Wen Fu* of Lu Chi

I

Tell the beads of the chromosomes like a rosary,
Love in the genes, if it fails

We will produce no sane man again

I have seen too many young people become adults, young
       friends become old people, all that is not ours,

The sources
And the crude bone

—we say

Took place

Like the mass of the hills.

'The sun is a molten mass'. Therefore

Fall into oneself—?

Reality, blind eye
Which has taught us to stare—

Your elbow on a car-edge
Incognito as summer,

I wrote. Not you but a girl
At least

Clarity, clarity, surely clarity is the most beautiful
          thing in the world,
A limited, limiting clarity

I have not and never did have any motive of poetry
But to achieve clarity

2

Troubled that you are not, as they say,
Working—
I think we try rather to understand,
We try also to remain together

There is a force of clarity, it is
Of what is not autonomous in us,
We suffer a certain fear

Things alter, surrounded by a depth
And width

The unreality of our house in moonlight
Is that if the moonlight strikes it
It is truly there tho it is ours

    3

Not to reduce the thing to nothing—

I might at the top of my ability stand at a window
and say, look out; out there is the world.

Not the desire for approval nor even for love—O,
that trap! From which escaped, barely—if it fails

We will produce no sane man again

    4

Words cannot be wholly transparent. And that is the
       'heartlessness' of words.

Neither friends nor lovers are coeval . . .

as for a long time we have abandoned those in
       extremity and we find it unbearable that we should
       do so . . .

The sea anemone dreamed of something, filtering the sea
       water thru its body,

Nothing more real than boredom—dreamlessness, the
       experience of time, never felt by the new arrival,
       never at the doors, the thresholds, it is the native

Native in native time . . .

The purity of the materials, not theology, but to present
       the circumstances

5

In Alsace, during the war, we found ourselves on the edge of the Battle of the Bulge. The front was inactive, but we were spread so thin that the situation was eerily precarious. We hardly knew where the next squad was, and it was not in sight—a quiet and deserted hill in front of us. We dug in near a farmhouse. Pierre Adam, tho he was a journeyman mason, lived with his wife and his children in that farmhouse.

During the occupation the Germans had declared Alsace a part of Greater Germany. Therefore they had drafted Alsatian men into the German army. Many men, learning in their own way that they were to be called, dug a hole. The word became a part of the language: *faire un trou*. Some men were in those holes as long as two and three years. It was necessary that someone should know where those holes were; in winter it was impossible for a man to come out of his hole without leaving footprints in the snow. While snow was actually falling, however, a friend could come to the hole with food and other help. Pierre, whom many people trusted, knew where some two dozen of those holes were.

The Germans became aware that men were going into hiding, and they began to make reprisals. If the man was young and unmarried, they killed his parents. If the man was married, they took his wife into Germany to the army brothels, it was said. They took the children into Germany, and it was not certain whether those children would remember where they came from. Pierre told me this story:

Men would come to Pierre and they would say: I am thinking of making a hole. Pierre would say: yes. They would say then: but if I do they will kill my parents; or: they will take my wife and my children. Then Pierre would say, he told me: *if you dig a hole, I will help you.*

He knew, of course, what he was telling me. You must try to put yourself into those times. If one thought he knew anything, it was that a man should not join the Nazi army. Pierre

himself learned, shortly before the Americans arrived, that he
was about to be drafted. He and his wife discussed the chil-
dren. They thought of tattooing the children's names and ad-
dresses on their chests so that perhaps they could be found
after the war. But they thought that perhaps the tattooing
would be cut out of the children . . . They did not, finally,
have to make that decision, as it turned out. But what a con-
versation between a man and his wife—

There was an escape from that dilemma, as, in a way, there
always is. Pierre told me of a man who, receiving the notifica-
tion that he was to report to the German army, called a cele-
bration and farewell at his home. Nothing was said at that
party that was not jovial. They drank and sang. At the proper
time, the host got his bicycle and waved goodbye. The house
stood at the top of a hill and, still waving and calling
farewells, he rode with great energy and as fast as he could
down the hill, and, at the bottom, drove into a tree.

It must be hard to do. Probably easier in an automobile.
There is, in an automobile, a considerable time during which
you cannot change your mind. Riding a bicycle, since in those
woods it is impossible that the tree should be a redwood, it
must be necessary to continue aiming at the tree right up to
the moment of impact. Undoubtedly difficult to do. And, of
course, the children had no father. Thereafter.

6

Wars that are just? A simpler question: In the event,
will you or will you not want to kill a German. Because,
in the event, if you do not want to, you won't.

. . . and my wife reading letters she knew were two weeks
late and did not prove I was not dead while she read. Why
did I play all that, what was I doing there?

We are brothers, we are brothers?—these things are
composed of a moral substance only if they are untrue. If
these things are true they are perfectly simple, perfectly

impenetrable, those primary elements which can only be
named.

A man will give his life for his friend provided he wants
to.

In all probability a man will give his life for his child
provided his child is an infant.

. . . One man could not understand me because I was saying
simple things; it seemed to him that nothing was being
said. I was saying: there is a mountain, there is a lake

A picture seen from within. The picture is unstable, a
moving picture, unlimited drift. Still, the picture
exists.

The circumstances:

        7

And if at 80

He says what has been commonly said
It is for the sake of old times, a cozy game

He wishes to join again, an unreasonable speech
Out of context

        8

Cars on the highway filled with speech,
People talk, they talk to each other;

Imagine a man in the ditch,
The wheels of the overturned wreck
Still spinning—

I don't mean he despairs, I mean if he does not
He sees in the manner of poetry

9

The cars run in a void of utensils
—the powerful tires—beyond
Happiness

Tough rubbery gear of invaders, of the descendents
Of invaders, I begin to be aware of a countryside
And the exposed weeds of a ditch

The context is history
Moving toward the light of the conscious

And beyond, culvert, blind curb, there are also names
For these things, language in the appalling fields

I remember my father as a younger man than I am now,
My mother was a tragic girl
Long ago, the autonomous figures are gone,
The context is the thousands of days

10

Not the symbol but the scene this pavement leads
To roadsides—the finite

Losing its purposes
Is estranged

All this is reportage.

If having come so far we shall have
Song

Let it be small enough.

Virgin
what was there to be thought

comes by the road

11

Tell the life of the mind, the mind creates the finite.

All punishes him. I stumble over these stories—
Progeny, the possibility of progeny, continuity

Or love that tempted him

He is punished by place, by scene, by all that holds
all he has found, this pavement, the silent symbols

Of it, the word it, never more powerful than in this
moment. Well, hardly an epiphany, but there the thing
is all the same

All this is reportage

12

To insist that what is true is good, no matter, no matter,
        a definition—?

That tree
        whose fruit . . .

The weight of air
Measured by the barometer in the parlor,
Time remains what it was

Oddly, oddly insistent

haunting the people in the automobiles,

shining on the sheetmetal,

open and present, unmarred by indifference,

wheeled traffic, indifference,
the hard edge of concrete continually crumbling

into gravel in the gravel of the shoulders,
Ditches of our own country

Whom shall I speak to

13

Department of Plants and Structures—obsolete, the old name
In this city, of the public works

Tho we meant to entangle ourselves in the roots of the world

An unexpected and forgotten spoor, all but indestructible
        shards

To owe nothing to fortune, to chance, nor by the power of
        his heart
Or her heart to have made these things sing
But the benevolence of the real

Tho there is no longer shelter in the earth, round helpless
        belly
Or hope among the pipes and broken works

'Substance itself which is the subject of all our planning'

And by this we are carried into the incalculable

14

There was no other guarantee

Ours aren't the only madmen tho they have burned
        thousands
of men and women alive, perhaps no madder than most

Strange to be here, strange for them also, insane and criminal,
who hasn't noticed that, strange to be man, we have come
rather far

We are at the beginning of a radical depopulation of the earth

Cataclysm . . . cataclysm of the plains, jungles, the cities

Something in the soil exposed between two oceans

As Cabeza de Vaca found a continent of spiritual despair
in campsites

His miracles among the Indians heralding cataclysm

Even Cortés greeted as revelation . . . No I'd not emigrate,
I'd not live in a ship's bar wherever we may be headed

These things at the limits of reason, nothing at the limits
of dream, the dream merely ends, by this we know it is the
real

That we confront

But So As By Fire

The darkness of trees
Guards this life
Of the thin ground
That covers the rock ledge

Among the lanes and magic
Of the Eastern woods

The beauty of silence
And broken boughs

And the homes of small animals

The green leaves
Of young plants
Above the dark green moss
In the sweet smell of rot

The pools and the trickle of freshwater

First life,   rotting life
Hidden starry life it is not yet

A mirror
Like our lives

We have gone
As far as is possible

Whose lives reflect light
Like mirrors

One had not thought
To be afraid

Not of shadow but of light

Summon one's powers

In Memoriam
Charles Reznikoff

who wrote
in the great world

small for this is a way

to enter
the light on the kitchen

tables wide-

spread as the mountains'
light this is

heroic this is
the poem

to write

in the great
world small

THEODORE ROETHKE

(1908–1963)

The Heron

The heron stands in water where the swamp
Has deepened to the blackness of a pool,
Or balances with one leg on a hump
Of marsh grass heaped above a muskrat hole.

He walks the shallow with an antic grace.
The great feet break the ridges of the sand,
The long eye notes the minnow's hiding place.
His beak is quicker than a human hand.

He jerks a frog across his bony lip,
Then points his heavy bill above the wood.
The wide wings flap but once to lift him up.
A single ripple starts from where he stood.

The Bat

By day the bat is cousin to the mouse.
He likes the attic of an aging house.

His fingers make a hat about his head.
His pulse beat is so slow we think him dead.

He loops in crazy figures half the night
Among the trees that face the corner light.

But when he brushes up against a screen,
We are afraid of what our eyes have seen:

For something is amiss or out of place
When mice with wings can wear a human face.

Cuttings

Sticks-in-a-drowse droop over sugary loam,
Their intricate stem-fur dries;
But still the delicate slips keep coaxing up water;
The small cells bulge;

One nub of growth
Nudges a sand-crumb loose,
Pokes through a musty sheath
Its pale tendrilous horn.

Cuttings
(later)

This urge, wrestle, resurrection of dry sticks,
Cut stems struggling to put down feet,
What saint strained so much,
Rose on such lopped limbs to a new life?

I can hear, underground, that sucking and sobbing,
In my veins, in my bones I feel it,—
The small waters seeping upward,
The tight grains parting at last.
When sprouts break out,
Slippery as fish,
I quail, lean to beginnings, sheath-wet.

Root Cellar

Nothing would sleep in that cellar, dank as a ditch,
Bulbs broke out of boxes hunting for chinks in the dark,
Shoots dangled and drooped,
Lolling obscenely from mildewed crates,
Hung down long yellow evil necks, like tropical snakes.
And what a congress of stinks!—

Roots ripe as old bait,
Pulpy stems, rank, silo-rich,
Leaf-mould, manure, lime, piled against slippery planks.
Nothing would give up life:
Even the dirt kept breathing a small breath.

Old Florist

That hump of a man bunching chrysanthemums
Or pinching-back asters, or planting azaleas,
Tamping and stamping dirt into pots,—
How he could flick and pick
Rotten leaves or yellowy petals,
Or scoop out a weed close to flourishing roots,
Or make the dust buzz with a light spray,
Or drown a bug in one spit of tobacco juice,
Or fan life into wilted sweet-peas with his hat,
Or stand all night watering roses, his feet blue in rubber
    boots.

Frau Bauman, Frau Schmidt, and Frau Schwartze

Gone the three ancient ladies
Who creaked on the greenhouse ladders,
Reaching up white strings
To wind, to wind
The sweet-pea tendrils, the smilax,
Nasturtiums, the climbing
Roses, to straighten
Carnations, red
Chrysanthemums; the stiff
Stems, jointed like corn,
They tied and tucked,—
These nurses of nobody else.
Quicker than birds, they dipped
Up and sifted the dirt;

They sprinkled and shook;
They stood astride pipes,
Their skirts billowing out wide into tents,
Their hands twinkling with wet;
Like witches they flew along rows
Keeping creation at ease;
With a tendril for needle
They sewed up the air with a stem;
They teased out the seed that the cold kept asleep,—
All the coils, loops, and whorls.
They trellised the sun; they plotted for more than themselves.

I remember how they picked me up, a spindly kid,
Pinching and poking my thin ribs
Till I lay in their laps, laughing,
Weak as a whiffet;
Now, when I'm alone and cold in my bed,
They still hover over me,
These ancient leathery crones,
With their bandannas stiffened with sweat,
And their thorn-bitten wrists,
And their snuff-laden breath blowing lightly over me in my
    first sleep.

My Papa's Waltz

The whiskey on your breath
Could make a small boy dizzy;
But I hung on like death:
Such waltzing was not easy.

We romped until the pans
Slid from the kitchen shelf;
My mother's countenance
Could not unfrown itself.

The hand that held my wrist
Was battered on one knuckle;

At every step you missed
My right ear scraped a buckle.

You beat time on my head
With a palm caked hard by dirt,
Then waltzed me off to bed
Still clinging to your shirt.

The Lost Son

1. The Flight

At Woodlawn I heard the dead cry:
I was lulled by the slamming of iron,
A slow drip over stones,
Toads brooding wells.
All the leaves stuck out their tongues;
I shook the softening chalk of my bones,
Saying,
Snail, snail, glister me forward,
Bird, soft-sigh me home,
Worm, be with me.
This is my hard time.

Fished in an old wound,
The soft pond of repose;
Nothing nibbled my line,
Not even the minnows came.

Sat in an empty house
Watching shadows crawl,
Scratching.
There was one fly.

Voice, come out of the silence.
Say something.
Appear in the form of a spider
Or a moth beating the curtain.

Tell me:
Which is the way I take;
Out of what door do I go,
Where and to whom?

      Dark hollows said, lee to the wind,
      The moon said, back of an eel,
      The salt said, look by the sea,
      Your tears are not enough praise,
      You will find no comfort here,
      In the kingdom of bang and blab.

Running lightly over spongy ground,
Past the pasture of flat stones,
The three elms,
The sheep strewn on a field,
Over a rickety bridge
Toward the quick-water, wrinkling and rippling.

Hunting along the river,
Down among the rubbish, the bug-riddled foliage,
By the muddy pond-edge, by the bog-holes,
By the shrunken lake, hunting, in the heat of summer.

The shape of a rat?
      It's bigger than that.
      It's less than a leg
      And more than a nose,
      Just under the water
      It usually goes.

Is it soft like a mouse?
Can it wrinkle its nose?
Could it come in the house
On the tips of its toes?

      Take the skin of a cat
      And the back of an eel,
      Then roll them in grease,—
      That's the way it would feel.

It's sleek as an otter
With wide webby toes
Just under the water
It usually goes.

2. The Pit

Where do the roots go?
      Look down under the leaves.
Who put the moss there?
      These stones have been here too long.
Who stunned the dirt into noise?
      Ask the mole, he knows.
I feel the slime of a wet nest.
      Beware Mother Mildew.
Nibble again, fish nerves.

3. The Gibber

At the wood's mouth,
By the cave's door,
I listened to something
I had heard before.

Dogs of the groin
Barked and howled,
The sun was against me,
The moon would not have me.

The weeds whined,
The snakes cried,
The cows and briars
Said to me: Die.

What a small song. What slow clouds. What dark water.
Hath the raine a father? All the caves are ice. Only the snow's
    here.
I'm cold. I'm cold all over. Rub me in father and mother.
Fear was my father, Father Fear.
His look drained the stones.

What gliding shape
Beckoning through halls,
Stood poised on the stair,
Fell dreamily down?

From the mouths of jugs
Perched on many shelves,
I saw substance flowing
That cold morning.

Like a slither of eels
That watery cheek
As my own tongue kissed
My lips awake.

Is this the storm's heart? The ground is unstilling itself.
My veins are running nowhere. Do the bones cast out their
    fire?
Is the seed leaving the old bed? These buds are live as birds.
Where, where are the tears of the world?
Let the kisses resound, flat like a butcher's palm;
Let the gestures freeze; our doom is already decided.
All the windows are burning! What's left of my life?
I want the old rage, the lash of primordial milk!
Goodbye, goodbye, old stones, the time-order is going,
I have married my hands to perpetual agitation,
I run, I run to the whistle of money.

Money money money
Water water water

How cool the grass is.
Has the bird left?
The stalk still sways.
Has the worm a shadow?
What do the clouds say?

These sweeps of light undo me.
Look, look, the ditch is running white!
I've more veins than a tree!
Kiss me, ashes, I'm falling through a dark swirl.

4. The Return

The way to the boiler was dark,
Dark all the way,
Over slippery cinders
Through the long greenhouse.

The roses kept breathing in the dark.
They had many mouths to breathe with.
My knees made little winds underneath
Where the weeds slept.

There was always a single light
Swinging by the fire-pit,
Where the fireman pulled out roses,
The big roses, the big bloody clinkers.

Once I stayed all night.
The light in the morning came slowly over the white
Snow.
There were many kinds of cool
Air.
Then came steam.

Pipe-knock.

Scurry of warm over small plants.
Ordnung! ordnung!
Papa is coming!

A fine haze moved off the leaves;
Frost melted on far panes;
The rose, the chrysanthemum turned toward the light.
Even the hushed forms, the bent yellowy weeds
Moved in a slow up-sway.

5

It was beginning winter,
An in-between time,
The landscape still partly brown:
The bones of weeds kept swinging in the wind,
Above the blue snow.

It was beginning winter,
The light moved slowly over the frozen field,
Over the dry seed-crowns,
The beautiful surviving bones
Swinging in the wind.

Light traveled over the wide field;
Stayed.
The weeds stopped swinging.
The mind moved, not alone,
Through the clear air, in the silence.

> Was it light?
> Was it light within?
> Was it light within light?
> Stillness becoming alive,
> Yet still?

A lively understandable spirit
Once entertained you.
It will come again.
Be still.
Wait.

Four for Sir John Davies

I
The Dance

Is that dance slowing in the mind of man
That made him think the universe could hum?

The great wheel turns its axle when it can;
I need a place to sing, and dancing-room,
And I have made a promise to my ears
I'll sing and whistle romping with the bears.

For they are all my friends: I saw one slide
Down a steep hillside on a cake of ice,—
Or was that in a book? I think with pride:
A caged bear rarely does the same thing twice
In the same way: O watch his body sway!—
This animal remembering to be gay.

I tried to fling my shadow at the moon,
The while my blood leaped with a wordless song.
Though dancing needs a master, I had none
To teach my toes to listen to my tongue.
But what I learned there, dancing all alone,
Was not the joyless motion of a stone.

I take this cadence from a man named Yeats;
I take it, and I give it back again:
For other tunes and other wanton beats
Have tossed my heart and fiddled through my brain.
Yes, I was dancing-mad, and how
That came to be the bears and Yeats would know.

II
The Partner

Between such animal and human heat
I find myself perplexed. What is desire?—
The impulse to make someone else complete?
That woman would set sodden straw on fire.
Was I the servant of a sovereign wish,
Or ladle rattling in an empty dish?

We played a measure with commingled feet:
The lively dead had taught us to be fond.
Who can embrace the body of his fate?

Light altered light along the living ground.
She kissed me close, and then did something else.
My marrow beat as wildly as my pulse.

I'd say it to my horse: we live beyond
Our outer skin. Who's whistling up my sleeve?
I see a heron prancing in his pond;
I know a dance the elephants believe.
The living all assemble! What's the cue?—
Do what the clumsy partner wants to do!

Things loll and loiter. Who condones the lost?
This joy outleaps the dog. Who cares? Who cares?
I gave her kisses back, and woke a ghost.
O what lewd music crept into our ears!
The body and the soul know how to play
In that dark world where gods have lost their way.

III
The Wraith

Incomprehensible gaiety and dread
Attended what we did. Behind, before,
Lay all the lonely pastures of the dead;
The spirit and the flesh cried out for more.
We two, together, on a darkening day
Took arms against our own obscurity.

Did each become the other in that play?
She laughed me out, and then she laughed me in;
In the deep middle of ourselves we lay;
When glory failed, we danced upon a pin.
The valley rocked beneath the granite hill;
Our souls looked forth, and the great day stood still.

There was a body, and it cast a spell,—
God pity those but wanton to the knees,—
The flesh can make the spirit visible;
We woke to find the moonlight on our toes.

In the rich weather of a dappled wood
We played with dark and light as children should.

What shape leaped forward at the sensual cry?—
Sea-beast or bird flung toward the ravaged shore?
Did space shake off an angel with a sigh?
We rose to meet the moon, and saw no more.
It was and was not she, a shape alone,
Impaled on light, and whirling slowly down.

IV
The Vigil

Dante attained the purgatorial hill,
Trembled at hidden virtue without flaw,
Shook with a mighty power beyond his will,—
Did Beatrice deny what Dante saw?
All lovers live by longing, and endure:
Summon a vision and declare it pure.

Though everything's astonishment at last,
Who leaps to heaven at a single bound?
The links were soft between us; still, we kissed;
We undid chaos to a curious sound:
The waves broke easy, cried to me in white;
Her look was morning in the dying light.

The visible obscures. But who knows when?
Things have their thought: they are the shards of me;
I thought that once, and thought comes round again;
Rapt, we leaned forth with what we could not see.
We danced to shining; mocked before the black
And shapeless night that made no answer back.

The world is for the living. Who are they?
We dared the dark to reach the white and warm.
She was the wind when wind was in my way;
Alive at noon, I perished in her form.
Who rise from flesh to spirit know the fall:
The word outleaps the world, and light is all.

Elegy for Jane

(My Student, Thrown by a Horse)

I remember the neckcurls, limp and damp as tendrils;
And her quick look, a sidelong pickerel smile;
And how, once startled into talk, the light syllables leaped for
    her,
And she balanced in the delight of her thought,
A wren, happy, tail into the wind,
Her song trembling the twigs and small branches.
The shade sang with her;
The leaves, their whispers turned to kissing;
And the mould sang in the bleached valleys under the rose.

Oh, when she was sad, she cast herself down into such a pure
    depth,
Even a father could not find her:
Scraping her cheek against straw;
Stirring the clearest water.

My sparrow, you are not here,
Waiting like a fern, making a spiney shadow.
The sides of wet stones cannot console me,
Nor the moss, wound with the last light.

If only I could nudge you from this sleep,
My maimed darling, my skittery pigeon.
Over this damp grave I speak the words of my love:
I, with no rights in this matter,
Neither father nor lover.

The Waking

I wake to sleep, and take my waking slow.
I feel my fate in what I cannot fear.
I learn by going where I have to go.

We think by feeling. What is there to know?
I hear my being dance from ear to ear.
I wake to sleep, and take my waking slow.

Of those so close beside me, which are you?
God bless the Ground! I shall walk softly there,
And learn by going where I have to go.

Light takes the Tree; but who can tell us how?
The lowly worm climbs up a winding stair;
I wake to sleep, and take my waking slow.

Great Nature has another thing to do
To you and me; so take the lively air,
And, lovely, learn by going where to go.

This shaking keeps me steady. I should know.
What falls away is always. And is near.
I wake to sleep, and take my waking slow.
I learn by going where I have to go.

I Knew a Woman

I knew a woman, lovely in her bones,
When small birds sighed, she would sigh back at them;
Ah, when she moved, she moved more ways than one:
The shapes a bright container can contain!
Of her choice virtues only gods should speak,
Or English poets who grew up on Greek
(I'd have them sing in chorus, cheek to cheek).

How well her wishes went! She stroked my chin,
She taught me Turn, and Counter-turn, and Stand;
She taught me Touch, that undulant white skin;
I nibbled meekly from her proffered hand;
She was the sickle; I, poor I, the rake,
Coming behind her for her pretty sake
(But what prodigious mowing we did make).

Love likes a gander, and adores a goose:
Her full lips pursed, the errant note to seize;
She played it quick, she played it light and loose;
My eyes, they dazzled at her flowing knees;
Her several parts could keep a pure repose,
Or one hip quiver with a mobile nose
(She moved in circles, and those circles moved).

Let seed be grass, and grass turn into hay:
I'm martyr to a motion not my own;
What's freedom for? To know eternity.
I swear she cast a shadow white as stone.
But who would count eternity in days?
These old bones live to learn her wanton ways:
(I measure time by how a body sways).

A Walk in Late Summer

I

A gull rides on the ripples of a dream,
White upon white, slow-settling on a stone;
Across my lawn the soft-backed creatures come;
In the weak light they wander, each alone.
Bring me the meek, for I would know their ways;
I am a connoisseur of midnight eyes.
The small! The small! I hear them singing clear
On the long banks, in the soft summer air.

2

What is there for the soul to understand?
The slack face of the dismal pure inane?
The wind dies down; my will dies with the wind,
God's in that stone, or I am not a man!
Body and soul transcend appearances
Before the caving-in of all that is;
I'm dying piecemeal, fervent in decay;
My moments linger—that's eternity.

3

A late rose ravages the casual eye,
A blaze of being on a central stem.
It lies upon us to undo the lie
Of living merely in the realm of time.
Existence moves toward a certain end—
A thing all earthly lovers understand.
That dove's elaborate way of coming near
Reminds me I am dying with the year.

4

A tree arises on a central plain—
It is no trick of change or chance of light.
A tree all out of shape from wind and rain,
A tree thinned by the wind obscures my sight.
The long day dies; I walk the woods alone;
Beyond the ridge two wood thrush sing as one.
Being delights in being, and in time.
The evening wraps me, steady as a flame.

The Rose

1

There are those to whom place is unimportant,
But this place, where sea and fresh water meet,
Is important—
Where the hawks sway out into the wind,
Without a single wingbeat,
And the eagles sail low over the fir trees,
And the gulls cry against the crows
In the curved harbors,
And the tide rises up against the grass
Nibbled by sheep and rabbits.

A time for watching the tide,
For the heron's hieratic fishing,
For the sleepy cries of the towhee,

The morning birds gone, the twittering finches,
But still the flash of the kingfisher, the wingbeat of the scoter,
The sun a ball of fire coming down over the water,
The last geese crossing against the reflected afterlight,
The moon retreating into a vague cloud-shape
To the cries of the owl, the eerie whooper.
The old log subsides with the lessening waves,
And there is silence.

I sway outside myself
Into the darkening currents,
Into the small spillage of driftwood,
The waters swirling past the tiny headlands.
Was it here I wore a crown of birds for a moment
While on a far point of the rocks
The light heightened,
And below, in a mist out of nowhere,
The first rain gathered?

II

As when a ship sails with a light wind—
The waves less than the ripples made by rising fish,
The lacelike wrinkles of the wake widening, thinning out,
Sliding away from the traveler's eye,
The prow pitching easily up and down,
The whole ship rolling slightly sideways,
The stern high, dipping like a child's boat in a pond—
Our motion continues.

But this rose, this rose in the sea-wind,
Stays,
Stays in its true place,
Flowering out of the dark,
Widening at high noon, face upward,
A single wild rose, struggling out of the white embrace of the
    morning-glory,
Out of the briary hedge, the tangle of matted underbrush,
Beyond the clover, the ragged hay,
Beyond the sea pine, the oak, the wind-tipped madrona,

Moving with the waves, the undulating driftwood,
Where the slow creek winds down to the black sand of the
    shore
With its thick grassy scum and crabs scuttling back into their
    glistening craters.

And I think of roses, roses,
White and red, in the wide six-hundred-foot greenhouses,
And my father standing astride the cement benches,
Lifting me high over the four-foot stems, the Mrs. Russells,
    and his own elaborate hybrids,
And how those flowerheads seemed to flow toward me, to
    beckon me, only a child, out of myself.

What need for heaven, then,
With that man, and those roses?

III

What do they tell us, sound and silence?
I think of American sounds in this silence:
On the banks of the Tombstone, the wind-harps having their
    say,
The thrush singing alone, that easy bird,
The killdeer whistling away from me,
The mimetic chortling of the catbird
Down in the corner of the garden, among the raggedy lilacs,
The bobolink skirring from a broken fencepost,
The bluebird, lover of holes in old wood, lilting its light song,
And that thin cry, like a needle piercing the ear, the insistent
    cicada,
And the ticking of snow around oil drums in the Dakotas,
The thin whine of telephone wires in the wind of a Michigan
    winter,
The shriek of nails as old shingles are ripped from the top of a
    roof,
The bulldozer backing away, the hiss of the sandblaster,
And the deep chorus of horns coming up from the streets in
    early morning.

I return to the twittering of swallows above water,
And that sound, that single sound,
When the mind remembers all,
And gently the light enters the sleeping soul,
A sound so thin it could not woo a bird,

Beautiful my desire, and the place of my desire.

I think of the rock singing, and light making its own silence,
At the edge of a ripening meadow, in early summer,
The moon lolling in the close elm, a shimmer of silver,
Or that lonely time before the breaking of morning
When the slow freight winds along the edge of the ravaged
   hillside,
And the wind tries the shape of a tree,
While the moon lingers,
And a drop of rain water hangs at the tip of a leaf
Shifting in the wakening sunlight
Like the eye of a new-caught fish.

IV

I live with the rocks, their weeds,
Their filmy fringes of green, their harsh
Edges, their holes
Cut by the sea-slime, far from the crash
Of the long swell,
The oily, tar-laden walls
Of the toppling waves,
Where the salmon ease their way into the kelp beds,
And the sea rearranges itself among the small islands.

Near this rose, in this grove of sun-parched, wind-warped
   madronas,
Among the half-dead trees, I came upon the true ease of
   myself,
As if another man appeared out of the depths of my being,
And I stood outside myself,
Beyond becoming and perishing,
A something wholly other,

As if I swayed out on the wildest wave alive,
And yet was still.
And I rejoiced in being what I was:
In the lilac change, the white reptilian calm,
In the bird beyond the bough, the single one
With all the air to greet him as he flies,
The dolphin rising from the darkening waves;

And in this rose, this rose in the sea-wind,
Rooted in stone, keeping the whole of light,
Gathering to itself sound and silence—
Mine and the sea-wind's.

The Thing

Suddenly they came flying, like a long scarf of smoke,
Trailing a thing—what was it?—small as a lark
Above the blue air, in the slight haze beyond,
A thing in and out of sight,
Flashing between gold levels of the late sun,
Then throwing itself up and away from the implacable swift
    pursuers,

Confusing them once flying straight into the sun
So they circled aimlessly for almost a minute,
Only to find, with their long terrible eyes
The small thing diving down toward a hill,
Where they dropped again
In one streak of pursuit.

Then the first bird
Struck;
Then another, another,
Until there was nothing left,
Not even feathers from so far away.

And we turned to our picnic
Of veal soaked in marsala and little larks arranged on a long
    platter,

And we drank the dry harsh wine
While I poked with a stick at a stone near a four-pronged
    flower,
And a black bull nudged at a wall in the valley below,
And the blue air darkened.

In a Dark Time

In a dark time, the eye begins to see,
I meet my shadow in the deepening shade;
I hear my echo in the echoing wood—
A lord of nature weeping to a tree.
I live between the heron and the wren,
Beasts of the hill and serpents of the den.

What's madness but nobility of soul
At odds with circumstance? The day's on fire!
I know the purity of pure despair,
My shadow pinned against a sweating wall.
That place among the rocks—is it a cave,
Or winding path? The edge is what I have.

A steady storm of correspondences!
A night flowing with birds, a ragged moon,
And in broad day the midnight come again!
A man goes far to find out what he is—
Death of the self in a long, tearless night,
All natural shapes blazing unnatural light.

Dark, dark my light, and darker my desire.
My soul, like some heat-maddened summer fly,
Keeps buzzing at the sill. Which I is *I*?
A fallen man, I climb out of my fear.
The mind enters itself, and God the mind,
And one is One, free in the tearing wind.

RICHARD WRIGHT

(1908–1960)

I Have Seen Black Hands

I am black and I have seen black hands, millions and millions
    of them—
Out of millions of bundles of wool and flannel tiny black
    fingers have reached restlessly and hungrily for life.
Reached out for the black nipples at the black breasts of black
    mothers,
And they've held red, green, blue, yellow, orange, white, and
    purple toys in the childish grips of possession,
And chocolate drops, peppermint sticks, lollypops, wineballs,
    ice cream cones, and sugared cookies in fingers sticky
    and gummy,
And they've held balls and bats and gloves and marbles and
    jack-knives and sling-shots and spinning tops in the thrill
    of sport and play,
And pennies and nickels and dimes and quarters and
    sometimes on New Year's, Easter, Lincoln's Birthday,
    May Day, a brand new green dollar bill.
They've held pens and rulers and maps and tablets and books
    in palms spotted and smeared with ink,
And they've held dice and cards and half-pint flasks and cue
    sticks and cigars and cigarettes in the pride of new
    maturity . . .

II

I am black and I have seen black hands, millions and millions
    of them—
They were tired and awkward and calloused and grimy and
    covered with hangnails,
And they were caught in the fast-moving belts of machines
    and snagged and smashed and crushed,
And they jerked up and down at the throbbing machines
    massing taller and taller the heaps of gold in the banks of
    bosses,

And they piled higher and higher the steel, iron, the lumber,
    wheat, rye, the oats, corn, the cotton, the wool, the oil,
    the coal, the meat, the fruit, the glass, and the stone until
    there was too much to be used,
And they grabbed guns and slung them on their shoulders
    and marched and groped in trenches and fought and
    killed and conquered nations who were customers for
    the goods black hands had made,
And again black hands stacked goods higher and higher until
    there was too much to be used,
And then the black hands held trembling at the factory gates
    the dreaded lay-off slip,
And the black hands hung idle and swung empty and grew
    soft and got weak and bony from unemployment and
    starvation,
And they grow nervous and sweaty, and opened and shut in
    anguish and doubt and hesitation and irresolution . . .

III

I am black and I have seen black hands, millions and millions
    of them—
Reaching hesitantly out of days of slow death for the goods
    they had made, but the bosses warned that the goods
    were private and did not belong to them,
And the black hands struck desperately out in defence of life
    and there was blood, but the enraged bosses decreed
    that this too was wrong,
And the black hands felt the cold steel bars of the prison they
    had made, in despair tested their strength and found that
    they could neither bend nor break them,
And the black hands fought and scratched and held back but
    a thousand white hands took them and tied them,
And the black hands lifted palms in mute and futile
    supplication to the sodden faces of mobs wild in the
    revelries of sadism,
And the black hands strained and clawed and struggled in
    vain at the noose that tightened about the black throat,
And the black hands waved and beat fearfully at the tall
    flames that cooked and charred the black flesh . . .

IV

I am black and I have seen black hands
Raised in fists of revolt, side by side with the white fists of
     white workers,
And some day—and it is only this which sustains me—
Some day there shall be millions and millions of them,
On some red day in a burst of fists on a new horizon.

The FB Eye Blues

That old FB eye
Tied a bell to my bed stall
Said old FB eye
Tied a bell to my bed stall
Each time I love my baby, gover'ment knows it all.

Woke up this morning
FB eye under my bed
Said I woke up this morning
FB eye under my bed
Told me all I dreamed last night, every word I said.

Everywhere I look, Lord
I see FB eyes
Said everywhere I look, Lord
I find FB eyes
I'm getting sick and tired of gover'ment spies.

My mama told me
A rotten egg'll never fry
Said my mama told me
A rotten egg'll never fry
And everybody knows a cheating dog'll never thrive.

Got them blues, blues, blues
Them mean old FB eye blues
Said I got them blues, blues, blues
Them dirty FB eye blues
Somebody tell me something, some good news.

If he'd been a snake, Lord
He'd a jumped up and bit me
Said if he'd been a snake, Lord
He'd a jumped up and bit me
But old FB eye just hauled off and hit me.

Now kittens like milk
and rats love cheese
Said kittens like milk
And rats sure love their cheese
Wonder what FB eye loves crawling on his knees?

Grasshopper likes to spit
In a bloodhound's eye
Said grasshopper likes to spit
In a bloodhound's eye.
Lord, let that grasshopper meet the FB eye.

Breaks my heart in two, Lord
And I just can't forget
Said it breaks my heart, Lord
And I just can't forget
Old jealous FB eye ain't ended yet.

Selected Haiku

I am nobody:
A red sinking autumn sun
Took my name away.

————

For you, O gulls,
I order slaty waters
And this leaden sky!

———

O finicky cat,
Forgive me for this spring rain
That disgusts you so!

———

On winter mornings
The candle shows faint markings
Of the teeth of rats.

———

From a red tile roof
A cat is licking beads of dew
In a humid dawn.

———

A bloody knife blade
Is being licked by a cat
At hog-killing time.

———

The sound of the rain,
Blotted out now and then
By a sticky cough.

———

The spring lingers on
In the scent of a damp log
Rotting in the sun.

———

A bursting ripe plum
Forms a pool upon a leaf
From which sparrows drink.

———

Just enough of rain
To bring the smell of silk
From umbrellas.

———

A twisting tendril
Tilting off into sunshine,
Winding on itself.

———

The consumptive man,
Who lives in the room next door,
Did not cough today.

———

Bulging yellow clouds:
Between peals of spring thunder,
Deep white silences.

———

The chill autumn dusk
Grows colder as yellow lights
Come on in skyscrapers.

———

Rustling dry paper
Sounding in an empty room
Is a cold mountain.

———

The stars are dredging
The bottom of the spring river
For bits of blue steel.

———

A wild winter wind
Is tearing itself to shreds
On barbed-wire fences.

———

From the woods at night
Comes the sound of something walking
Over fallen leaves.

———

From under the house
My cat comes with dusty fur
And cobwebbed whiskers.

HELEN ADAM

(1909–1993)

Mune Rune

Sing, women o' the Earth,
Sing doun the mune.
When a' seas are motionless,
Then will she droon.

Yon jealous virgin,
Auld in heaven serene;
Spying on Earth's lovers
Wi' avid een.

Forge me a black dirk
Tae fling at the sky.
Weave me a spider's web
That will float sae high.

Sing, women o' the Earth,
Sing doun the mune.
Sisters, she's bound tae fa'
Sudden and sune.

His lane let the lordly sun
In the heavens move
Till not a hert on Earth
Remembers love.

Frae every breaking wave
Her wierd we'll dree.
Droon, droon the goddess
In her ain siller sea,

Never tae lure agin
The unborn tae the breast.
Then shall a' women laugh
And the seas rest.

646

And there shall be
No more moonlight.
And there shall be
No more moonlight.

And there shall be
No more opposites
Over a' the Earth.

The Huntsman

Dame Lud dwelt deep in the haunted shade
O' lanely woods whaur the red deer strayed;

A widow noble, and rich, and great,
Wi' one fair daughter tae share her state.

Luke Ramsey rode as a huntsman bold
About the woodlands gloomy and old.

Dame Lud was touched by the blind God's dart.
She loved Luke Ramsey wi' a' her heart.

"Oh! were ye loath, or were ye afraid
Tae hunt wi' me while the dawn delayed?

I called ye, Luke, when the red deer ran.
What garred ye tarry, my braw young man?"

"Ye ken, Dame Lud, I never was slow
Tae hunt the stag wi' arrow and bow,

Tae hunt and ride wi' my lady proud.
But sairly I feared the thunder cloud."

"Ye lie, Luke Ramsey! Boldly ye lie!
Ye did na' fear the glower o' the sky.

Ye did na' fear the rain frae the west.
Ye lay, at dawn, on my daughter's breast."

"Your daughter has hair o' cracklin' gold.
A' night it glaiked in my dreaming hold.

Your daughter's face is bonnie as noon.
And bliss it is in her arms tae droon.

The bonds that held me I needs must break,
Yet kiss me once for our auld love's sake.

Your gentle daughter I mean tae wed.
And now, between us, the truth is said."

Dame Lud laid hold o' her daughter's hand
And led her up tae the lochan strand.

"My daughter, your hair that burns by night
Mun douse its fires in the water's flight.

Your face is fair, Aye, bonnie as noon.
'Tis dule sic beauty sae deep mun droon."

"Alas! sweet mither, pity my youth!"
"On me, false daughter, did ye ha' ruth?

Ye micht ha' pitied my mortal drouth,
Or ever ye kissed Luke Ramsey's mouth."

The lochan mists ha' hidden the twa.
A curlew scritches frae far awa.

The water quivers in widening rings.
Tae the hands o' murder the live hair clings.

"Hallo! my huntsman, wake wi' the sun,
And ride wi' me whaur the red deer run."

"The air, Dame Lud, is rilling wi' dew,
Yet I am ready to ride wi' you.

We won't gae doun through the woodlands wide
But we'll gae up tae the lochan side.

The hidden loch in the misty wild,
Whaur a cruel mither micht droon her child.

Hark! a' the green waves flicker like flame
And a' the white waves whisper your name.

'Dame Lud, Dame Lud,' they whisper and flee,
'Afore the morrow Dame Lud mun dee.' "

"Oh! kill me, Luke, in the woodlands wide,
But kill me not by the lochan side

For though the loch be never sae deep
Beside my daughter I will na' sleep."

He's drooned Dame Lud in the water clear.
He's spurred his horse and ridden in fear.

"Now may the Dog Star glitter by day
If ever again I hunt sic prey!"

Shallow-Water Warning

My love was walking in the sun
Beyond a golden meadow.
She led me where the ripples run,
I thought the water shallow
Reflecting only summer sky.
So light the chains that bound me,
So like a god on Earth was I
Before my darling drowned me.

Upon a flowery bed we lay,
Familiar joys exploring,
Till in her arms at earliest day,
I heard the surf rise roaring.
I saw, too late, triumphant snow
Whose splendours still astound me;
Wild glories I was doomed to know
For there my darling drowned me.

The white surf at the world's end,
I heard its heavenly thunder,
Forgetting every earthly friend
But her who pushed me under.
She left my body on the beach
Where fallen angels found me,
They screamed, and scrambled for my bones
After my darling drowned me.

JAMES AGEE

(1909–1955)

Not met and marred with the year's whole turn of grief,
But easily on the mercy of the morning
Fell this still folded leaf:

Small that never Summer spread
Demented on the dusty heat;
And sweet that never Fall
Wrung sere and tarnished red;
Safe now that never knew
Stunning Winter's bitter blue
It fell fair in the fair season:

Therefore with reason
Dress all in cheer and lightly put away
   With music and glad will
This little child that cheated the long day
   Of the long day's ill:
Who knows this breathing joy, heavy on us all,
   Never, never, never.

———————

So it begins. Adam is in his earth
Tempted, and fallen, and his doom made sure
O, in the very instant of his birth:
Whose deathly nature must all things endure.
The hungers of his flesh, and mind, and heart,
That governed him when he was in the womb,
These ravenings multiply in every part:
And shall release him only to the tomb.
Meantime he works the earth, and builds up nations,
And trades, and wars, and learns, and worships chance,
And looks to God, and weaves the generations
Which shall his many hungerings advance
When he is sunken dead among his sins.
Adam is in this earth. So it begins.

Now stands our love on that still verge of day
Where darkness loiters leaf to leaf releasing
Lone tree to silvering tree: then slopes away
Before the morning's deep-drawn strength increasing
Till the sweet land lies burnished in the dawn:
But sleeping still: nor stirs a thread of grass:
Large on the low hill and the spangled lawn
The pureleaved air dwells passionless as glass:
So stands our love new found and unaroused,
Appareled in all peace and innocence,
In all lost shadows of love past still drowsed
Against foreknowledge of such immanence
As now, with earth outshone and earth's wide air,
Shows each to other as this morning fair.

This little time the breath and bulk of being
Are met in me: who from the eldest shade
Of all undreamt am raised forth into seeing
As I may see, the state of all things made:
In sense and dream and death to make my heart
Wise in the loveliness and natural health
Of all, and God, upon the void a part:
Likewise to celebrate this commonwealth:
Believing nothing, and believing all,
In love, in detestation, but most
In naught to sing of all: to recall
What wisdom was before I was this ghost:
Such songs I shall not make nor truths shall know:
And once more mindless into truth shall go.

To Walker Evans

Against time and the damages of the brain
Sharpen and calibrate. Not yet in full,
Yet in some arbitrated part
Order the façade of the listless summer.

Spies, moving delicately among the enemy,
The younger sons, the fools,
Set somewhat aside the dialects and the stained skins of
      feigned madness,
Ambiguously signal, baffle, the eluded sentinel.

Edgar, weeping for pity, to the shelf of that sick bluff,
Bring your blind father, and describe a little;
Behold him, part wakened, fallen among field flowers shallow
But undisclosed, withdraw.

Not yet that naked hour when armed,
Disguise flung flat, squarely we challenge the fiend.
Still, comrade, the running of beasts and the ruining heaven
Still captive the old wild king.

Wake up Threeish,
   Clean up the sink
Air out the bedroom
   Pour out a drink
Drink to the daylight
   Sit down and think
I'm Open All Night.

Go to the movies,
   Stroll in the park
Watch the kids playing
   Wait for the dark,
Then I remember
   A fellow named Clark
I'm Open All Night.

Buy me a mirror
   Make up the bed
Order the White Rock
   Get my self fed
Prink up and sit down
   And wish I was dead
I'm Open All Night.

MARY BARNARD

(b. 1909)

Shoreline

The sea has made a wall for its defence
of falling water. Those whose impertinence
leads them to its moving ledges
it rejects. Those who surrender
it will with the next wave drag under.

Sand is the beginning and the end
of our dominion.

The way to the dunes is easy.
The shelving sand is stiffened in the rain
and loosened again in the sun's fingers.
Children, lustful of the glistening hours,
drink and are insatiate. Wind under the eyelids,
confusion walling the ears, their bodies glow
in the cold wash of the beach.
                    And after,
they walk with rigid feet the planked street of the town.
They miss the slipping texture of the sand
and a sand pillow under the hollow instep.
They are unmoved by fears
that breed in darkening kitchens at sundown
following storm, and they rebel
against cold waiting in the wind and rain
for the late sail.

             Did you, as I,
condemn the coastal fog and long for islands
seen from a sail's shadow?
                  The dunes lie
more passive to the wind than water is.
This, then, the country of our choice.
It is infertile, narrow, prone
under a dome of choral sound:
water breaking upon water.

655

Litter of bare logs in the drift—
the sea has had its sharp word with them.
Wild roses, wild strawberries cover the dune shoulder.
It is a naked restless garden that descends
from the crouched pine
to shellfish caught in flat reflecting sands.

We lose the childish avarice of horizons. The sea ends
against another shore. The cracked ribs of a wreck
project from the washed beach.
Under the shell-encrusted timbers
dripping brine
plucks at the silence of slant chambers
opening seaward. What moving keel remembers
such things as here are buried under sand?

The transitory ponds and smooth bar slide
easily under the advancing tide,
emerging with the moon's
turning.
          Clear lagoons
behind the shattered hulk, thin
movements of sea grass on the dune rim
bending against cloud, these things are ours.
Submissive to the sea and wind,
resistful of all else, sand
is the beginning and the end
of our dominion.

Logging Trestle

Neither cloud nor rain casts
a chill into the valley
like that of a trestle fallen into disuse.

The rails move out from the hillside
across the piling lengthening its stroke
where ground slopes riverward.

Abruptly, the rails terminate.
Sky opens between the cross-ties lifted
each upon five upright timbers. The gray wood

leads the eye to nothing further.
The broken column stands against cloud
as though an abandoned wharf extended into wind.

The Field

Sweep the mind
                    clean
like a field of dry stubble
when the constellations
of daisies have been mown.

Let it be lit by stars
rooted outside the seasons . . .

To the flesh of the field
alive with worm and seed
tomorrow is in the night wind;
while drought or rain
spirals towards earth
mortal stirrings demand
horoscopes of the stars.

Weather is all.

Static

I wanted to hear
Sappho's laughter
and the speech of
her stringed shell.

What I heard was
whiskered mumble-
ment of grammarians:

Greek pterodactyls
and Victorian dodos.

The Solitary

The lone drake, upended,
nibbles the pond bottom,
red legs paddling the air.

He sleeps on the rock wall
by the spillway, balanced
on one foot, head hidden.

In the shadowed shallows
under sycamore boughs
the encircling ripples

have one center: himself.
Intruders, including
mallards of his own race,

beautiful strangers, drive
him to frenzied attack,
quacking, snapping, churning

the pond. When they have gone
bright wavelets unbroken
to the rim spread round him.

Probably Nobody

Twenty crows
(charred paper)
litter the
frosted ground.

Small yellow
apples gleam
nakedly through
bare twigs.

Who'll buy red
rose haws white
snowberries

or a crane
mirrored in
slough water?

The Pleiades

They are heard as a choir of seven
shining voices; they descend
like a flock of wild swans to the water.

The white wing plumage folds;
they float on the lake—seven
stars reflected among the reeds.

Tonight, the Seven Little Sisters,
daughters of the Moon, will come down
to bathe or wash their summer dresses.

They wear costumes of the seven
rainbow colors, they wear feather
mantles they can lift in sea winds

raised by their singing, and so rise
flying, soaring, until they fade
as the moon dawns; their voices dwindle

and die out in the North Woods, over
Australian bush, from Spartan
dancing grounds and African beaches.

They have returned to the sky
for the last time, and even
Electra's weeping over Troy is stilled.

What girl or star sings now
like a swan on the Yellow River?

Lethe

Above the brink
of that lamentable river I shall lean,
hesitant, unwilling to drink,
as I remember there for the last time.

Will a few drops on the tongue,
like a whirling flood submerge cities,
like a sea, grind pillars to sand?
Will it wash the color from the lips and the eyes
beloved? It were a thousand pities
thus to dissolve
the delicate sculpture of a lifted hand,
to fade the dye
of the world's color, to quench forever
the fires of earth in this river.

The living will forget
more quickly than I,
dead, lingering with lips unwet
above Lethe.

JOHNNY MERCER

(1909–1976)

Blues in the Night

My mama done tol' me
When I was in knee pants
My mama done tol' me—son
A woman'll sweet talk,
And give ya the big eye,
But when the sweet talkin's done
A woman's a two-face
A worrisome thing who'll leave ya t'sing
The blues in the night.

Now the rain's a-fallin',
Hear the train a-callin',
Whooee,
(My mama done tol' me)
Hear that lonesome whistle
Blowin' 'cross the trestle,
Whooee,
(My mama done tol' me)
A whooee-duh-whooee,
Ol' clickety clack's
A-echoin' back
The blues in the night,
The evenin' breeze'll start
The trees to cryin'
And the moon'll hide its light,
When you get the blues in the night.

Take my word, the mocking bird'll
Sing the saddest kind of song,
He knows things are wrong
And he's right.

From Natchez to Mobile,
From Memphis to St. Jo,
Where ever the four winds blow;
I been in some big towns
An' heard me some big talk,
But there is one thing I know,
A woman's a two-face,
A worrisome thing
Who'll leave ya t'sing
The blues in the night.
My mama was right,
There's blues in the night.

Midnight Sun

Your lips were like a red and ruby chalice,
Warmer than the summer night,
The clouds were like an alabaster palace
Rising to a snowy height.
Each star its own aurora borealis,
Suddenly you held me tight,
I could see the midnight sun.

I can't explain the silver rain that found me,
Or was that a moonlight veil?
The music of the universe around me,
Or was that a nightingale?
And then your arms miraculously found me,
Suddenly the sky turned pale,
I could see the midnight sun.

Was there such a night,
It's a thrill I still don't quite believe,
But after you were gone,
There was still some stardust on my sleeve.

The flame of it may dwindle to an ember,
And the stars forget to shine,

And we may see the meadow in December,
Icy white and crystalline.
But, oh, my darling, always I'll remember,
When your lips were close to mine,
And I saw the midnight sun.

ELDER OLSON

(1909–1992)

The Four Black Bogmen

O she took the babe still slick from the waterbag,
Bathed it and swathed it and cradled it then
In a willow basket and carried it
Through the pit-black woods to a fog-roofed fen.
There amid plashy ferns she laid it
And watched the slug-black ooze slip in.

An old man rose from the smoking rushes:
"O why do you walk on the tip-over tussocks
And heaving hummocks of slippery quags?
Think twice when you do what you came to do
Or the four black bogmen who set such snags
Will track you down and switch shapes with you.

"Every one of the four is a sharp shape-trader
Who can look like a toad or a bubble in the bog,
A snipe on a stick or a snail on a stalk,
A worm in a web or a bead in the fog."
"O how do you know, you old swamp-squatter?"
"I am the first." And he grabbed, and he had her.

O she watched as he swanked in her shape through the
    swamp,
Then shaky and old, she hobbled away
Till she tripped on the roots of a big-toed stump,
And there as she stuck, the slick roots quickened,
Slipped round like blacksnakes, that trap of a tree
Hissed in her ear, "I am the second."

O a bad shape sat in her sticks like a bird,
Yet what could trouble a root-rotten tree?
Through the misty forest stumbled a rickety

664

Cripple of a leper, bagging wood,
Who clutched at a branch as if to break it; the
Lipless mouth said, "I am the third."

O now on a leper's pegs she pottered
To stop her trick in the nick, if she could;
In the snake-black mire, in the coiling mud,
There was the child, choking in muck.
O how she snatched, how she cuddled! It shuddered,
Clung with its bog-black claws, and spoke.

EDWIN ROLFE

(1909–1954)

Casualty

It seemed
the sky was a harbor, into which rode
black iron cruisers, silently, their guns
poised like tiger-heads on turret-haunches.

It seemed the sky was an olive grove, ghostly
in moonlight, and Very-light, with deadly crossfire
splitting it, proving a new theorem with rifles,
unknown in any recalled geometry.

And then he woke, choking. Saw sky as sky
in purest moonlight; and the searchlight beams paled
against it, and he heard Tibidábo's guns
burst against space. Then one bomb, shrieking,

found the thin axis of his whirling fears,
the exact center.

Paris—Christmas 1938

You will remember, when the bombs
invade your softest midnight dream,
when terror flowing through your limbs
brings madness to your vulnerable room;

you will remember, when you stare at walls
familiar, patterned in a memorized
design, and watch the plaster as it falls,
abrupt, concussive—and you shrink back dazed

and all your body, that a moment past
was quiet, relaxed upon the comforting bed,
will stiffen, flex in fear; a host
of insane images will bring the dead

of many cities back to life again:
the dead you pleasantly ignored, and hid
from self and others; you will clutch the lone
solace of men who soon too will be dead

and count your sins, and know that they were crimes,
and curse your quiet, and respect, at last, these dead;
yes, you will remember—when the initial bombs
insanely fall into *your* life—Madrid.

First Love

Again I am summoned to the eternal field
green with the blood still fresh at the roots of flowers,
green through the dust-rimmed memory of faces
that moved among the trees there for the last time
before the final shock, the glazed eye, the hasty mound.

But why are my thoughts in another country?
Why do I always return to the sunken road through corroded
    hills,
with the Moorish castle's shadow casting ruins over my
    shoulder
and the black-smocked girl approaching, her hands laden
    with grapes?

I am eager to enter it, eager to end it.
Perhaps this one will be the last one.
And men afterward will study our arms in museums
and nod their heads, and frown, and name the inadequate
    dates
and stumble with infant tongues over the strange place-
    names.

But my heart is forever captive of that other war
that taught me first the meaning of peace and of comradeship

and always I think of my friend who amid the apparition of
        bombs
saw on the lyric lake the single perfect swan.

BUKKA WHITE

(1909–1977)

Fixin' to Die

I'm lookin' far in mind, b'lieve I'm fixin' to die, b'lieve I'm
fixin' to die,
I'm lookin' far in mind, b'lieve I'm fixin' to die,
I know I was born to die, but I hate to leave my children
cryin'.

Jes' as sho' as we livin' today, sho' we's born to die, sho' we's
born to die,
Jes' as sho' we live, sho' we's born to die,
I know I was born to die, but I hate to leave my children
cryin'.

Your mother treated me, children, like I was her baby child,
was her baby child,
Your mother treated me like I was her baby child,
That's why I tried so hard to come back home to die.

So many nights at the fireside, how my children's mama
would cry, how my children's mama would cry,
So many nights at the fireside, how my children's mama
would cry,
'Cause I told the mother I had to say goodbye.

Look over yonder on the buryin' ground, on the buryin'
ground,
Look over yonder on the buryin' ground,
Yonder stand ten thousand, standin' to see them let me
down.

Mother, take my children back befo' they let me down, befo'
they let me down,
Mother, take my children back fo' they let me down,
Ain't no use them screamin' and cryin' on the graveyard
ground.

ROBERT FITZGERALD

(1910–1985)

Manuscript with Illumination

Several of us are quiet in a ring
Kneeling with taws tight to our dirty thumbs
Or sunlight splitting the serge-shine
Of knickerbockers. Several will be
Braggarts in the shouting yard, or telling
Tremulous others they may see a woman.
Afternoon and dust behind the furnace
Drive the smallest ones to madness. They whack
Lathes in laughter, are afraid. One trussed
Feels his face grow purple, left alone
Cries like a martyr and plots murder.

Among us there will come stately men
Demanding the years of the popes, the seven
Capital sins, or morning in the sacristy.
About their straight cassocks and their pride
Nuns flutter, black and white, the floating doves.
A month's dear guilt is harvest to these men,
Who take our terror, flowers of our terror,
Into God's peace, drowsy with murmured Latin.
There will be several pure before the shutter.

Grace of a happy death.

Several of us are quiet, there is one
Lives with a bitch in Ephesus, another
Dealer in jewels and watches toward the sunrise.
That one, a milksop whiner, is grown ruddy
With iron shots and sunning in the south;
The elevated trembles for his friend
Who counts in a cold room items of love.
Glory in his sweet fold of ancestors
Makes one weep, as anchor chains in mist

Rush from winches for a final landfall.
Others have copious mail, deep marriages.

How earth pulls us and pulls the moon
Our bones know casually. We are diminished
Who grow with treasure of certainty toward
Delicate gestures, smiling in the rooms;
Likewise our desperate shifts for
Appeasement of the beast, the spirit,
Walking in darkness and the check from home,
Waste us wanderers. Several will be
Sheeted in wards, others give autographs,
And one perhaps will live in a cool place,
Devoted to Greek participial loveliness.

Grant them peace.

Sunlight through lightning, and the violins
Falling before the flute. This is the evening
Prophesied by our hearts, and now our love
Builds over summer drouth its structural silence.
There is nothing now but applause of leaves
For the moth's splendor, for the singing
Lute, for crimes ignoble on the stair,
And for our prayers, dubious and tender.

Horae

I

It pales. As if a look,
Invisible, came in the east.
In some far vale a rooster
Expels his cry of life.

Now dark but not formless
On the grey meads the trees
Lean and are looming soft.

In those towers of night
Ruffling things awake
Their declaration and chuckle.

Starpoint fades from the dew.

To every mile that sleeps
The cock's barbaric cry
And the wind comes cool.

Shiver of day break.

II

Now air, gentle pillager
In the citadels of summer,
Lifts a leaf here and there.
Sun holds the cornfield still
In his dream of the real.

From a wavering of bees
One droning steers away,
Elated in his golden car.
A cow stumbles and streams,
Reaching the meadow.

Tiny brutality in the grass
Manipulates the foe
Sawing and champing. Oh, soundless.

What burning contemplation
Rests in these distances?
What is seen by the leaves
Mirrored as in fair water
Millionfold?—as the eye of man
Finds itself in myriads.

III

The limber shadow is longer.
Air moves now breathing
In the plumes of corn.

Gnats on their elastics
Are busy with evening.
Heavy with night, the owl
Floats through the forest.

Shadow takes all the grass.

Beyond indigo mountains
Golden sheaves are fastened
Lightly on the infinite
West. What joy or feast
Has these for ornament?
What reclining host?

They sink away in peace.

Et Quidquid Aspiciebam Mors Erat

In this and whatever days to come
The transparent world and its motions
Compose a sheer void. How could
That be removed upon which every
Animate joy was founded? What
Thrives now but the vile face of nature
Made up by the sun to idiot glory?
Let it sway and blow its intrinsic
Monotony of vapors, seasons,
Tumblebugs and blind men; let me
Weep and curse those begetting fools,
And honorably weep my life long.

You would not cover me over
With the dropping indecent clods,
You sanctimonious bastards: take
Such of my hatred as is left
When I have cursed the aspergent
Water shaker with his stole, his
Sotto voce Latin sing song;
You craving, self-important ghouls,
Let me alone, or I will show you
The savage green sprouting
Through the obscene holes of your eyes.

Gone out of the air, not gone
Out of my nightly vision, yet
With desperate years to be corrupted
There too, wasted, thinned
To the damned ghost of your convention—
You win in the end—he who was
So distinguished for patience.
For suffering, for valor,
Of such sensible pale fingers,
A humorous, wise man.

Hereby I curse this hard city
And its whoring, golfing, political
Poker-playing men, all those
Who were schoolfellows or friends
In the old time, and never,
Though good churchgoers, visited him.
And I engrave here my small blessing
On that large silent decent one
Who thought it friendliness to do so;
Him and few others I would spare,
But let the rest go rot in a worse
Hell than even their own world is.
Yet their unawareness is his grace,
If grace be in this charnel progress:
His ten-year sickroom I say
Shames with life their death forever,
And all is death elsewhere.

Farewell

Furius and Aurelius, aides to Catullus,
Whether he penetrate the ultimate Indies
Where the rolling surf on the shores of morning
    Beats and again beats:

Or in the land of bedouin, the soft Arabs,
Or Parthians, the ungentlemanly archers,
Or where the Nile with seven similar streamlets
    Colors the clear sea;

Or if he cross the loftier Alpine passes
And view the monuments of almighty Caesar,
The Rhine, and France, and even those remotest
    Shuddersome British—

Friends, prepared for all of these, whatever
Province the celestial ones may wish me—
Take a little bulletin to my mistress,
    Unpleasantly worded:

Let her live and thrive with her fornicators
Of whom she hugs three hundred in an evening,
With no true love for any, leaving them broken-
    Winded the same way.

She need not, as in the old days, look for my love.
By her own fault it died, like a fallen flower
At the field's edge, after the passing harrow
    Touched it and left it.

Mutations

I

The absolute dark: and if you say, A cloud—
I say: I've spun abroad, often, with them.
What though I cherish her, tanned thigh,
Stovelight of pleasure: I who saw the sea
With more than wind making it seethe, the waves
Fawning towards her beauty? I who smiled
At festal summer, jested, remarked the morning,
Smile now for nothing, like a jaded Punch:
Nerve-net, bone-dangle, visceral-slick piping
My too-late company, my table friends.

II

Child cries at nightfall, man when beyond himself
Cast by his love, which is his loneliness.
Nightly he watches the fan-silken beams
Mix their bright haze and waver over hills,
And lies with her against his darkness then.

History

It is Leviathan, mountain and world,
Yet in its grandeur we perceive
This flutter of the impalpable arriving
Like moths and heartbeats, flakes of snow
Falling on wool, or clouds of thought
Trailing rain in the mind: some old one's dream
Of hauling canvas, or the joy of swording
Hard rascals with a smack—for lordly blood
Circulates tenderly and will seep away;
And the winds blowing across the day
From quarters numberless, going where words go
And songs go, even the holy songs, or where
Leaves, showering, go with the spindling grasses.

Into this mountain shade everything passes.
The slave lays down his bones here and the hero,
Thrown, goes reeling with blinded face;
The long desired opens her scorched armpits.
A mountain; so a gloom and air of ghosts,
But charged with utter light if this is light,
A feathery mass, where this beholding
Shines among lustrous fiddles and codices,
Or dusky angels painted against gold
With lutes across their knees. Magical grain
Bound up in splay sheaves on an evening field,
And a bawling calf butchered—these feed
The curious coil of man. A man, this man,
Bred among lakes and railway cars and smoke,
The salt of childhood on his wintry lips,
His full heart ebbing toward the new tide
Arriving, arriving, in laughter and cries,
Down the chaotic dawn and eastern drift,
Would hail the unforeseen, and celebrate
On the great mountainside those sprites,
Tongues of delight, that may remember him—
The yet unborn, trembling in the same rooms,
Breakfasting before the same grey windows,
Lying, grieving again; yet all beyond him,
Who knew he lived in rough Jehovah's breath,
And burned, a quiet wick in a wild night,
Loving what he beheld and will behold.

Souls Lake

The evergreen shadow and the pale magnolia
Stripping slowly to the air of May
Stood still in the night of the honey trees.
At rest above a star pool with my friends,
Beside that grove most fit for elegies,
I made my phrase to out-enchant the night.

The epithalamion, the hush were due,
For I had fasted and gone blind to see
What night might be beyond our passages;
Those stars so chevalier in fearful heaven
Could not but lay their steel aside and come
With a grave glitter into my low room.

Vague though the population of the earth
Lay stretched and dry below the cypresses,
It was not round-about but in my night,
Bone of my bone, as an old man would say;
And all its stone weighed my mortality;
The pool would be my body and my eyes,

The air my garment and material
Whereof that wateriness and mirror lived—
The colorable, meek and limpid world.
Though I had sworn my element alien
To the pure mind of night, the cold princes,
Behold them there, and both worlds were the same.

The heart's planet seemed not so lonely then,
Seeing what kin it found in that reclining.
And ah, though sweet the catch of your chorales,
I heard no singing there among my friends;
But still were the great waves, the lions shining,
And infinite still the discourse of the night.

South Side

The sun in the south ranges a winter heaven
Of crooked sticks and smoke, a silver glare
Low and blinding in the hard cold.
Go down any street: it has long darkened,
Abiding your bleary eye with patience,
Your pity with a crazed forgotten cupola,
Stained by the truths of rain and switch-engines:
A home for the aged. Cut through any yard,

The grey mud when it melts will run gold
Into a morning gutter but soon go black—
The drain of a smelly thaw. Now the frost
Holds, and the winter, and the winter sun,
As a single stranger, ducking against the sting
That blows across lots, comes, and at a corner
Heaves his old overcoat apart, scrabbling
Up from his hip a sticky ball of handkerchief:
Out for an airing on Sunday afternoon.

Spring Shade

The April winds rise, and the willow whips
Lash one another's green in rinsing light.
The dream eludes the waking finger tips.

Buffets the breakfast pane and flashes white
As a mercury arc the sun in the silver ware.
A screen door slams. Today the May flies bite.

Odor of lilac on the billowing air
Enters the child's room. Robin Red Breast grieves
The man of memory in his iron chair.

A girl in watered blue, as he conceives,
And shy from study on the garden grass,
Turned a great page of sunprint and new leaves,

Closing the volume. You may leave the class,
The Teacher seemed to say. And he was Dunce.
Now all the colored crayons break, alas,

And all the daffodils blow black at once.

FRANK LOESSER

(1910–1969)

Luck, Be a Lady

They call you Lady Luck
But there is room for doubt
At times you have a very unladylike way of running out
You're on this date with me
The pickings have been lush
And yet before this evening is over
You might give me the brush
You might forget your manners
You might refuse to stay and so
The best that I can do is pray

Luck, be a lady tonight
Luck, be a lady tonight
Luck, if you've ever been a lady to begin with
Luck, be a lady tonight

Luck, let a gentleman see
How nice a dame you can be
I know the way you've treated other guys you've been with
Luck, be a lady with me

A lady doesn't leave her escort
It isn't fair, it isn't nice
A lady doesn't wander all over the room
And blow on some other guy's dice

So let's keep the party polite
Never get out of my sight
Stick with me, baby, I'm the fellow you came in with
Luck, be a lady
Luck, be a lady
Luck, be a lady tonight

A lady wouldn't flirt with strangers
She'd have a heart, she'd have a soul
A lady wouldn't make little snake eyes at me
When I've bet my life on this roll

So let's keep the party polite
Never get out of my sight
Stick with me, baby, I'm the fellow you came in with
Luck, be a lady
Luck, be a lady
Luck, be a lady tonight

ROSALIE MOORE

(b. 1910)

The Mind's Disguise

The mind's disguise is permanence.
Whether on rock, or on wrecked surfaces,
Wrests the uncluttered wind for the needed enemy,
Watches with many turns at once,
Confronts a century.

Learn early, unletter
Your alphabet decision,
Coming down to
Accident's corner of fence:
Enigma, protector of mighty.

And the winged, divisible sorrow,
Granted, almost—like love,
Is shunt from the high forbidder,
Forehead of No.

Memory of Quiet

Still as a moth face on the water,
This flower in air is.

White as the marsh behind the moon
In Ares.

In the room, the petals fall, but do not alter:
Lie like ladles.
Some ball of glass created out of this
Blows through our objects:
Holds, as a bowl its lilies,
Us from the troubled season.

We recall that,
    and the boat slid—
The unheard drop of leaves furnishing the world;
And saw, by the lantern's thorn,
The serpent water
Lit, and the rice-small face.

Oh quakeless seemed
The rim of that flower by moon throw.

Like an under-ocean moon, tall from sea ground,
This memory from a watery height
Sinks silver down.

Height

The heron moonlight feathers the full air.

Across this light lying like unturned feathers
I see the precipice night.
The waters clear. What was not clear before
Is clear with a clearness of cliffs.

Flying is strict and casual.
The snowstorm in its glass breaks harder
Than moons their swan snow.

    Considering
How all the slow birds go from us
In our own slipped-axe minute of flying.

CHARLES OLSON

(1910–1970)

La Préface

The dead in via
              in vita nuova
                    in the way
You shall lament who know they are as tender as the horse is.
You, do not you speak who know not.

        "I will die about April 1st . . ." going off
        "I weigh, I think, 80 lbs . . ." scratch
        "My name is NO RACE" address
         Buchenwald   new Altamira cave
         With a nail they drew the object of the hunt.

Put war away with time, come into space.
It was May, precise date, 1940. I had air my lungs could
    breathe.
He talked, via stones   a stick   sea rock   a hand of earth.
It is now, precise, repeat. I talk of Bigmans organs
he, look, the lines! are polytopes.
And among the DPs—deathhead
                       at the apex
                            of the pyramid.

Birth in the house is the One of Sticks, cunnus in the crotch.
Draw it thus: (   ) 1910 (
It is not obscure. We are the new born, and there are no
    flowers.
Document means there are no flowers
                        and no parenthesis.

It is the radical, the root, he and I, two bodies
We put our hands to these dead.

The closed parenthesis reads: the dead bury the dead,
                and it is not very interesting.

Open, the figure stands at the door, horror his
and gone, possessed, o new Osiris, Odysseus ship.
He put the body there as well as they did whom he killed.

Mark that arm. It is no longer gun.
We are born not of the buried but these unburied dead
crossed stick, wire-led, Blake Underground

The Babe
      the Howling Babe

These Days

    whatever you have to say, leave
    the roots on, let them
    dangle

    And the dirt

        Just to make clear
        where they come from

In Cold Hell, in Thicket

In cold hell, in thicket, how
abstract (as high mind, as not lust, as love is) how
strong (as strut or wing, as polytope, as things are
constellated) how
strung, how cold
can a man stay (can men) confronted
thus?

All things are made bitter, words even
are made to taste like paper, wars get tossed up
like lead soldiers used to be
(in a child's attic) lined up
to be knocked down, as I am,

by firings from a spit-hardened fort, fronted
as we are, here, from where we must go

God, that man, as his acts must, as there is always
a thing he can do, he can raise himself, he raises
on a reed he raises his

Or, if it is me, what
he has to say

    1

What has he to say?
In hell it is not easy
to know the traceries, the markings
(the canals, the pits, the mountings by which space
declares herself, arched, as she is, the sister,
awkward stars drawn for teats to pleasure him, the brother
who lies in stasis under her, at ease as any monarch or
a happy man

How shall he who is not happy, who has been so made
    unclear,
who is no longer privileged to be at ease, who, in this brush,
    stands
reluctant, imageless, unpleasured, caught in a sort of hell,
    how
shall he convert this underbrush, how turn this unbidden
    place
how trace and arch again
the necessary goddess?

    2

The branches made against the sky are not of use, are
already done, like snow-flakes, do not, cannot service
him who has to raise   (Who puts this on, this damning of his
    flesh?)
he can, but how far, how sufficiently far can he raise the
    thickets of
this wilderness?

How can he change, his question is
these black and silvered knivings, these
awkwardnesses?

How can he make these blood-points into panels,
        into sides
for a king's, for his own
for a wagon, for a sleigh, for the beak of, the
        running sides of
a vessel fit for
moving?

How can he make out, he asks,
of this low eye-view,
size?

And archings traced and picked enough to hold
to stay, as she does, as he, the brother, when,
here where the mud is, he is frozen, not daring
where the grass grows, to move his feet from fear
he'll trespass on his own dissolving bones, here
where there is altogether too much remembrance?

3

The question, the fear he raises up himself against
(against the same each act is proffered, under the eyes
each fix, the town of the earth over, is managed) is: Who
am I?

Who am I but by a fix, and another,
a particle, and the congery of particles carefully picked one by
        another,

                as in this thicket, each
                smallest branch, plant, fern, root
                —roots lie, on the surface, as nerves are laid open—
                must now (the bitterness of the taste of her) be
                isolated, observed, picked over, measured, raised
                as though a word, an accuracy were a pincer!
                                                this

is the abstract, this
is the cold doing, this
is the almost impossible

So shall you blame those
who give it up, those who say
it isn't worth the struggle?

(Prayer
Or a death as going over to—shot by yr own
        forces—to
a greener place?

                    Neither
any longer
usable)

        By fixes only (not even any more by shamans)
        can the traceries
        be brought out

                    II
ya, selva oscura, but hell now
is not exterior, is not to be got out of, is
the coat of your own self, the beasts
emblazoned on you   And who
can turn this total thing, invert
and let the ragged sleeves be seen
by any bitch or common character?   Who
can endure it where it is, where the beasts are met,
where yourself is, your beloved is, where she
who is separate from you, is not separate, is not
goddess, is, as your core is,
the making of one hell

                where she moves off, where she is
                no longer arch

        (this is why he of whom we speak does not move, why
        he stands so awkward where he is, why

his feet are held, like some ragged crane's
off the nearest next ground, even from
the beauty of the rotting fern his eye
knows, as he looks down, as,
in utmost pain if cold can be so called,
he looks around this battlefield, this
rotted place where men did die, where boys
and immigrants have fallen, where nature
(the years that she's took over)
does not matter, where

             that men killed, do kill, that woman kills
             is part, too, of his question

2

That it is simple, what the difference is—
that a man, men, are now their own wood
and thus their own hell and paradise
that they are, in hell or in happiness, merely
something to be wrought, to be shaped, to be carved, for use,
    for
others

does not in the least lessen his, this unhappy man's
obscurities, his
confrontations

He shall step, he
will shape, he
is already also
moving off

        into the soil, on to his own bones

he will cross

        (there is always a field,
        for the strong there is always
        an alternative)

                        But a field
          is not a choice, is
          as dangerous as a prayer, as a death, as any
          misleading, lady

He will cross

          And is bound to enter (as she is)
          a later wilderness.
                            Yet
          what he does here, what he raises up
          (he must, the stakes are such
                                        this at least
          is a certainty, this
          is a law, is not one of the questions, this
          is what was talked of as
          —what was it called, demand?)

He will do what he now does, as she will, do
carefully, do
without wavering,
without
          as even the branches,
          even in this dark place, the twigs
                                        how
          even the brow
of what was once to him a beautiful face

as even the snow-flakes waver in the light's eye

          as even forever wavers (gutters
          in the wind of loss)

          even as he will forever waver

          precise as hell is, precise
          as any words, or wagon,
          can be made

The Moon Is the Number 18

is a monstrance,
the blue dogs bay,
and the son sits,
grieving

is a grinning god, is
the mouth of, is
the dripping moon

while in the tower the cat
preens
and all motion
is a crab

and there is nothing he can do but what they do, watch
the face of waters, and fire

> The blue dogs paw,
> lick the droppings, dew
>
> or blood, whatever
> results are. And night,
> the crab, rays round
> attentive as the cat to catch
> human sound
>
> The blue dogs rue,
> as he does, as he would howl, confronting
> the wind which rocks what was her, while prayers
> striate the snow, words blow
> as questions cross fast, fast

as flames, as flames form, melt
along any darkness

Birth is an instance as is a host, namely, death

The moon has no air

In the red tower
in that tower where she also sat
in that particular tower where watching & moving
    are,
there,
there where what triumph there is, is: there
is all substance, all creature
all there is against the dirty moon, against
number, image, sortilege—

alone with cat & crab,
and sound is, is, his
conjecture

Merce of Egypt

I

I sing the tree is a heron
I praise long grass.
I wear the lion skin
over the long skirt
to the ankle. The ankle
is a heron

I look straightly backward. Or I bend to the side straightly
to raise the sheaf
up the stick of the leg
as the bittern's leg, raised
as slow as
his neck grows

as the wheat. The presentation,
the representation,
is flat

I am followed by women and a small boy in white carrying
    a duck,
all have flat feet and, foot before foot, the women with
    black wigs
And I intent
upon idlers,
and flowers

2

      the sedge
as tall as I am, the rushes
as I am

     as far as I am animal, antelope
with such's attendant carnivores

              and rows of beaters
drive the game to the hunter, or into nets,
where it is thick-wooded or there are open spaces
with low shrubs

3

I speak downfall, the ball of my foot
on the neck of the earth, the hardsong
of the rise of all trees, the jay
who uses the air. I am the recovered sickle
with the grass-stains still on the flint of its teeth.
I am the six-rowed barley
they cut down.

I am tree. The boy of the back of my legs
is roots. I am water fowl
when motion is the season of my river, and the wild boar
casts me. But my time
is hawkweed,

4

I hold what the wind blows, and silt.
I hide in the swamps of the valley to escape civil war,
and marauding soldiers. In the new procession
I am first, and carry wine
made of dandelions. The new rites
are my bones

I built my first settlement
in groves

5

       as they would flail crops
when the spring comes, and flood, the tassels
rise, as my head

As the Dead Prey Upon Us

As the dead prey upon us,
they are the dead in ourselves,
awake, my sleeping ones, I cry out to you,
disentangle the nets of being!

I pushed my car, it had been sitting so long unused.
I thought the tires looked as though they only needed air.
But suddenly the huge underbody was above me, and the rear
    tires
were masses of rubber and thread variously clinging together

as were the dead souls in the living room, gathered
about my mother, some of them taking care to pass
beneath the beam of the movie projector, some record
playing on the victrola, and all of them
desperate with the tawdriness of their life in hell

I turned to the young man on my right and asked, "How is
        it,
there?" And he begged me protestingly don't ask, we are
        poor
poor. And the whole room was suddenly posters and
        presentations
of brake linings and other automotive accessories, cardboard
displays, the dead roaming from one to another
as bored back in life as they are in hell, poor and doomed
to mere equipments

                        my mother, as alive as ever she was, asleep
when I entered the house as I often found her in a rocker
under the lamp, and awaking, as I came up to her, as she ever
        had

I found out she returns to the house once a week, and with
        her
the throng of the unknown young who center on her as
        much in death
as other like suited and dressed people did in life

O the dead!

                and the Indian woman and I
                enabled the blue deer
                to walk

                and the blue deer talked,
                in the next room,
                a Negro talk

                it was like walking a jackass,
                and its talk
                was the pressing gabber of gammers
                of old women

and we helped walk it around the room
because it was seeking socks
or shoes for its hooves
now that it was acquiring

human possibilities

In the five hindrances men and angels
stay caught in the net, in the immense nets
which spread out across each plane of being, the multiple nets
which hamper at each step of the ladders as the angels
and the demons
and men
go up and down

        Walk the jackass
        Hear the victrola
        Let the automobile
        be tucked into a corner of the white fence
        when it is a white chair. Purity

is only an instant of being, the trammels

recur

In the five hindrances, perfection
is hidden
        I shall get
        to the place
        10 minutes late.

        It will be 20 minutes
        of 9. And I don't know,

        without the car,

        how I shall get there

O peace, my mother, I do not know
how differently I could have done
what I did or did not do.

> That you are back each week
> that you fall asleep
> with your face to the right
>
> that you are as present there
> when I come in as you were
> when you were alive
>
> that you are as solid, and your flesh
> is as I knew it, that you have the company
> I am used to your having
>
> but o, that you all find it
> such a cheapness!

o peace, mother, for the mammothness
of the comings and goings
of the ladders of life

The nets we are entangled in. Awake,
my soul, let the power into the last wrinkle
of being, let none of the threads and rubber of the tires
be left upon the earth. Let even your mother
go. Let there be only paradise

The desperateness is, that the instant
which is also paradise (paradise
is happiness) dissolves
into the next instant, and power
flows to meet the next occurrence

> Is it any wonder
> my mother comes back?
> Do not that throng
> rightly seek the room
> where they might expect

happiness? They did not complain
of life, they obviously wanted
the movie, each other, merely to pass
among each other there,
where the real is, even to the display cards,
to be out of hell

The poverty
of hell

O souls, in life and in death,
awake, even as you sleep, even in sleep
know what wind
even under the crankcase of the ugly automobile
lifts it away, clears the sodden weights of goods,
equipment, entertainment, the foods the Indian woman,
the filthy blue deer, the 4 by 3 foot 'Viewbook,'
the heaviness of the old house, the stuffed inner room
lifts the sodden nets

and they disappear as ghosts do,
as spider webs, nothing
before the hand of man

The vent! You must have the vent,
or you shall die. Which means
never to die, the ghastliness

of going, and forever
coming back, returning
to the instants which were not lived

O mother, this I could not have done,
I could not have lived what you didn't,
I am myself netted in my own being

I want to die. I want to make that instant, too,
perfect

O my soul, slip
the cog

II

The death in life (death itself)
is endless, eternity
is the false cause

The knot is other wise, each topological corner
presents itself, and no sword
cuts it, each knot is itself its fire

each knot of which the net is made
is for the hands to untake
the knot's making. And touch alone

can turn the knot into its own flame

        (o mother, if you had once touched me

        o mother, if I had once touched you)

The car did not burn. Its underside
was not presented to me
a grotesque corpse. The old man

merely removed it as I looked up at it,
and put it in a corner of the picket fence
like was it my mother's white dog?

or a child's chair

        The woman,
        playing on the grass,
        with her son (the woman next door)

        was angry with me whatever it was
        slipped across the playpen or whatever
        she had out there on the grass

And I was quite flip in reply
that anyone who used plastic
had to expect things to skid

and break, that I couldn't worry
that her son might have been hurt
by whatever it was I sent skidding

down on them.

It was just then I went into my house
and to my utter astonishment
found my mother sitting there

as she always had sat, as must she always
forever sit there her head lolling
into sleep? Awake, awake my mother

what wind will lift you too
forever from the tawdriness,
make you rich as all those souls

crave crave crave

to be rich?

They are right. We must have
what we want. We cannot afford
not to. We have only one course:

the nets which entangle us are flames

O souls, burn
alive, burn now

that you may forever
have peace, have

what you crave

O souls,
go into everything,
let not one knot pass
through your fingers

let not any they tell you
you must sleep as the net
comes through your authentic hands

What passes
is what is, what shall be, what has
been, what hell and heaven is
is earth to be rent, to shoot you
through the screen of flame which each
        knot
hides as all knots are a wall ready
to be shot open by you

                        the nets of being
are only eternal if you sleep as your hands
ought to be busy. Method, method

I too call on you to come
to the aid of all men, to women most
who know most, to woman to tell
men to awake. Awake, men,
awake

I ask my mother
to sleep. I ask her
to stay in the chair.
My chair
is in the corner of the fence.
She sits by the fireplace made of paving stones. The blue deer
need not trouble either of us.

And if she sits in happiness the souls
who trouble her and me
will also rest. The automobile

has been hauled away.

Variations Done for Gerald Van De Wiele

1. Le Bonheur

dogwood flakes
what is green

the petals
from the apple
blow on the road

mourning doves
mark the sway
of the afternoon, bees
dig the plum blossoms

the morning
stands up straight, the night
is blue from the full of the April moon

iris and lilac, birds
birds, yellow flowers
white flowers, the Diesel
does not let up dragging
the plow

      as the whippoorwill,
the night's tractor, grinds
his song

      and no other birds but us
are as busy (O saisons, o chateaux!

Délires!

      What soul
is without fault?

Nobody studies
happiness

Every time the cock crows
I salute him

I have no longer any excuse
for envy. My life

has been given its orders: the seasons
seize

the soul and the body, and make mock
of any dispersed effort. The hour of death

is the only trespass

11. The Charge

dogwood flakes
the green

the petals from the apple-trees
fall for the feet to walk on

the birds are so many they are
loud, in the afternoon

they distract, as so many bees do
suddenly all over the place

With spring one knows today to see
that in the morning each thing

is separate but by noon
they have melted into each other

and by night only crazy things
like the full moon and the whippoorwill

and us, are busy. We are busy
if we can get by that whiskered bird,

that nightjar, and get across, the moon
is our conversation, she will say

what soul
isn't in default?

can you afford not to make
the magical study

which happiness is? do you hear
the cock when he crows? do you know the charge,

that you shall have no envy, that your life
has its orders, that the seasons

seize you too, that no body and soul are one
if they are not wrought

in this retort? that otherwise efforts
are efforts? And that the hour of your flight

will be the hour of your death?

III. Spring

The dogwood
lights up the day.

The April moon
flakes the night.

Birds, suddenly,
are a multitude

The flowers are ravined
by bees, the fruit blossoms

are thrown to the ground, the wind
the rain forces everything. Noise—

even the night is drummed
by whippoorwills, and we get

as busy, we plow, we move,
we break out, we love. The secret

which got lost neither hides
nor reveals itself, it shows forth

tokens. And we rush
to catch up. The body

whips the soul. In its great desire
it demands the elixir

In the roar of spring,
transmutations. Envy

drags herself off. The fault of the body and the soul
—that they are not one—

the matutinal cock clangs
and singleness: we salute you

season of no bungling

from
The Maximus Poems

Letter 3

Tansy buttons, tansy
for my city
Tansy for their noses

Tansy for them,
tansy for Gloucester to take the smell
of all owners,
the smell

Tansy
for all of us

       Let those who use words cheap, who use us cheap
       take themselves out of the way
       Let them not talk of what is good for the city

       Let them free the way for me, for the men of the Fort
       who are not hired, who buy the white houses

       Let them cease putting out words in the public print
       so that any of us have to leave, so that my Portuguese
          leave,
       leave the Lady they gave us, sell their schooners
       with the greyhounds aft, the long Diesels
       they put their money in, leave Gloucester
       in the present shame of,
       the wondership stolen by,
       ownership

Tansy from Cressy's
I rolled in as a boy
and didn't know it was
tansy

1

Did you know, she sd, growing up there,
how rare it was? And it turned out later she meant exactly the
     long field
drops down from Ravenswood where the land abrupts,
this side of Fresh Water Cove, and throws out
that wonder of my childhood, the descending green does run
so,
by the beach

                    where they held the muster Labor Day, and the
                         engine teams
                    threw such arcs of water

                                        runs with summer with
     tansy

     2

I was not born there, came, as so many of the people came,
from elsewhere. That is, my father did. And not from the
     Provinces,
not from Newfoundland. But we came early enough. When
     he came,
there were three hundred sail could fill the harbor,
if they were all in, as for the Races, say
Or as now the Italians are in, for San Pietro,
and the way it is from Town Landing, all band-concert,
and fireworks

So I answered her: Yes,
I knew (I had that to compare to it,
was Worcester)

As the people of the earth are now, Gloucester
is heterogeneous, and so can know polis
not as localism, not that mu-sick (the trick
of corporations, newspapers, slick magazines, movie houses,
the ships, even the wharves, absentee-owned

they whine to my people, these entertainers, sellers

they play upon their bigotries (upon their fears

these   they have the nerve
to speak of that lovely hour
the Waiting Station, 5 o'clock, the Magnolia bus, Al Levy
on duty (the difference
from 1 o'clock, all the women getting off
the Annisquam-Lanesville,
and the letter carriers

5:40, and only the lollers
in front of the shoe-shine parlor

these, right in the people's faces (and not at all as the gulls do
      it,
who do it straight, do it all over the "Times" blowing
the day after, or the "Summer Sun" catching on pilings,
      floating
off the Landing, the slime
the low tide reveals, the smell
then

          3

The word does intimidate. The pay-check does.
But to use either, as cheap men

o tansy city, root city
let them not make you
as the nation is

I speak to any of you, not to you all, to no group, not to you
      as citizens
as my Tyrian might have. Polis now
is a few, is a coherence not even yet new (the island of this
      city
is a mainland now of who? who can say who are
citizens?

Only a man or a girl who hear a word
and that word meant to mean not a single thing the least
          more than
what it does mean (not at all to sell any one anything, to keep
          them anywhere,
not even
in this rare place

          Root person in root place, hear one tansy-covered boy
                    tell you
what any knowing man of your city might, a letter carrier, say,
or that doctor—if they dared afford to take the risk, if they
          reminded themselves
that you should not be played with, that you deserve . . .
          they'd tell you
the condition of the under-water, the cut-water of anyone,
          including those
who take on themselves
to give you advice,
to tell you, for example,
what not to read

          They'd tell you, because they know (know as the house
                    knows,
wearing its white face, its clapboard mask) who there is will
          not outrage you
in the next edition, who'll not seek, even knowingly, to make
          you
slave

as he is slave
whom you read
as the bus starts off

                    whose slaver
                    would keep you off the sea, would keep
                              you local,
                    my Nova Scotians,
                    Newfoundlanders,
                    Sicilianos,
                    Isolatos

4

Isolated person in Gloucester, Massachusetts, I, Maximus,
     address you
you islands
of men and girls

Maximus, to himself

I have had to learn the simplest things
last. Which made for difficulties.
Even at sea I was slow, to get the hand out, or to cross
a wet deck.
          The sea was not, finally, my trade.
But even my trade, at it, I stood estranged
from that which was most familiar. Was delayed,
and not content with the man's argument
that such postponement
is now the nature of
obedience,

               that we are all late
               in a slow time,
               that we grow up many
               And the single
               is not easily
               known

It could be, though the sharpness (the *achiote*)
I note in others,
makes more sense
than my own distances. The agilities

               they show daily
               who do the world's
               businesses
               And who do nature's
               as I have no sense
               I have done either

I have made dialogues,
have discussed ancient texts,
have thrown what light I could, offered
what pleasures
doceat allows

       But the known?
This, I have had to be given,
a life, love, and from one man
the world.

         Tokens.
         But sitting here
         I look out as a wind
         and water man, testing
         And missing
         some proof

I know the quarters
of the weather, where it comes from,
where it goes. But the stem of me,
this I took from their welcome,
or their rejection, of me

         And my arrogance
         was neither diminished
         nor increased,
         by the communication

   2

It is undone business
I speak of, this morning,
with the sea
stretching out
from my feet

The Ocean

        clay

    Ganesha
                pushed

      into the

      sea (after a single year as worshipped

      God floated out and sunk

      in the Indian Ocean, from

    Bombay

            target area as

    St Sebastian—body as

      shot full of holes for a

      purpose the God punished each year done away with
          knocked off

          the Solar King the Excess—Energy

          transformed. Used. Excessive

      energy

    anyway—in a society like America energy if it is not moral is
        only

    material. Which cannot be destroyed is never destroyed is
        only

    left all over the place. Junk.

                    Gloucester is
        sea-shore where

        Ganesh

        may be

dropped rubbish

into the Harbor cleared away

yearly, to revive the Abstract to make it possible for form

to be sought again. Each year form has expressed itself. Each
    year it too

must be re-sought. There are 70 odd "forms", there are 70
    chances at revealing

the Real. The Real

renews itself each year, the Real

is solar, life is not, life is 13 months long each year. Minus

one day (the day the sun turns) The Sun

is in pursuit of itself. A year

is the possibility, the Real

goes on forever

                                        September 30th 1965

———————

flower of the underworld

to build out of sound the walls of the city
                              & display
in one flower   the underworld   so that,

by such means   the unique
                stand forth   clear itself
shall be made known

———————

I live underneath
the light of day

       I am a stone,
or the ground beneath

My life is buried,
with all sorts of passages
both on the sides and on the face turned down
to the earth
or built out as long gifted generous northeastern Connecticut
       stone walls are
through which 18th century roads still pass
as though they themselves were realms,

the stones they're made up of
are from the bottom such Ice-age megaliths

and the uplands the walls are the boundaries of
are defined with such non-niggardly definition

of the amount of distance between a road in & out
of the wood-lots or further passage-ways, further farms
are given

    that one suddenly is walking

in Tartarian-Erojan, Gaean-Ouranian
time and life love space
    time & exact
analogy   time & intellect   time & mind   time & time
spirit

     the initiation

    of another kind of nation

WINFIELD TOWNLEY SCOTT

(1910–1968)

Crocus Air

Let the crocus air invoke spring.
Gardens are not impossible.
Sun steams on the roofs where
Snow has hung.

The new-straw color of sun,
The sky's thawed blue.
Simple is grass and simple
The dandelion.

I believe in the circling wall,
I believe in the orchard lawn
For you and me and the child,
Though nothing is here at all.

Flowering Quince

If right in front of me,
Slow motion—fast motion really—
The cold branch of the quince
Should all at once
Start with a rash of buds
Then the thin green nudge
The brown back, then the color
Of the waxen flower, the flame,
Open everywhere the same
Golden-centered swirl
Of odor, sweet burning odor—
Performed in one day, one hour
Or even one minute
Which would then hold in it,

For more than sense or praise
Could say, all April's days—
That would set my heart awhirl.
This stratagem
Of instant gold from green
I have never seen
On tree or branch or stem:
Never never never—only once;
Once, and it was a girl.

The U.S. Sailor with the Japanese Skull

Bald-bare, bone-bare, and ivory yellow: skull
Carried by a thus two-headed U.S. sailor
Who got it from a Japanese soldier killed
At Guadalcanal in the ever-present war: our

Bluejacket, I mean, aged 20, in August strolled
Among the little bodies on the sand and hunted
Souvenirs: teeth, tags, diaries, boots; but bolder still
Hacked off this head and under a leopard tree skinned it:

Peeled with a lifting knife the jaw and cheeks, bared
The nose, ripped off the black-haired scalp and gutted
The dead eyes to these thoughtful hollows: a scarred
But bloodless job, unless it be said brains bleed.

Then, his ship underway, dragged this aft in a net
Many days and nights—the cold bone tumbling
Beneath the foaming wake, weed-worn and salt-cut
Rolling safe among fish and washed with Pacific;

Till on a warm and level-keeled day hauled in
Held to the sun and the sailor, back to a gun-rest,
Scrubbed the cured skull with lye, perfecting this:
Not foreign as he saw it first: death's familiar cast.

Bodiless, fleshless, nameless, it and the sun
Offend each other in strange fascination
As though one of the two were mocked; but nothing is, in
This head, or it fills with what another imagines

As: here were love and hate and the will to deal
Death or to kneel before it, death emperor,
Recorded orders without reasons, bomb-blast, still
A child's morning, remembered moonlight on Fujiyama:

All scoured out now by the keeper of this skull
Made elemental, historic, parentless by our
Sailor boy who thinks of home, voyages laden, will
Not say, 'Alas! I did not know him at all.'

Winslow Homer

Fog. He can see only this deep still fog.
Roweled by the falling sun it smoulders westward awhile
But it closes impenetrable curtains: night is fleshed.
No shore, save for the long jut of staggered rock
Shelving a black sharp stair to the burdened, hidden sea.
This he paints in his old age, recording his utter love.
For him there is one canvas, thick with seventy years—
Picture over picture buried, each worked from the last.
Where are the children's faces in the morning schoolroom?
Far under battlefields of the Civil War,
Eaten out by tenser light, man-riddled noon.
Even summer landscape empty kept a memory of people—
Visitors passing and strange. Then one seaman storm-struck.
All vanished now, washed over in a high tide of paint
As though the colors of the world, faster and faster whirling,
Spun this still center of gray; this inevitable mist:
Sun lost, sea filled and covered,
The great stair of black rock deserted, used no more.

BEN BELITT

(b. 1911)

The Orange Tree

To be
intact and unseen,
like the orange's scent
in the orange tree:

a pod of aroma
on the orange's ogive of green
or a phosphorus voice
in the storm of the forge and the hammer:

to climb up a ladder of leaven
and salt, and work in the lump
of the mass, upward and down
in the volatile oils of a wilderness heaven:

to sleep, like the karat,
in the void of the jeweler's glass,
yet strike with the weight of the diamond—
perhaps that is to live in the spirit!

So the orange tree
waits on its stump as the wood of its armature
multiplies: first, the branch, then the twig in the thicket
of leafage, then the sunburst of white in the leaves, the odor's
    epiphany.

All burns with a mineral
heat, all hones an invisible edge of the noonday, while the
    orange's scent
speaks from the tree in the tree to declare what the holocaust
    meant:
to be minimal,

minimal: to diminish excess; to pare it
as a child pares an orange, moving the knife through the peel
in a spiral's unbroken descent, till only the orange's sweat,
a bead of acidulous essence, divides the rind from the steel:

perhaps that is to live in the spirit.

Kites: Ars Poetica

The innocents have come to make their cast
in the sky, fishing upside-down
and flying heraldic signs, Chinese
or Euclidean, with parallel squares
and dotted balsa lines
in vanishing tissue paper—
heart-shapes, shields,
or whatever their breath
can bend to a crossbow of twine
or cut in armorial fields
and make fly—

like that other caster of lightning
paying out bamboo, watching the reel and the spinner
break electrical water,
touch a key in the creel
and blaze for the Philadelphian
with the shock of the trout's phosphorescence—

till, somewhere between the helicopter's star
and a vanishing point in the sea,
I feel myself go up,
unreeling aerial rigging out of my side
and shedding a helix of thread,

an invisible top in the air

a spider climbing the light—

till the whole web bells, and goes tight—

and I am flown by the kite.

ELIZABETH BISHOP

(1911–1979)

The Map

Land lies in water; it is shadowed green.
Shadows, or are they shallows, at its edges
showing the line of long sea-weeded ledges
where weeds hang to the simple blue from green.
Or does the land lean down to lift the sea from under,
drawing it unperturbed around itself?
Along the fine tan sandy shelf
is the land tugging at the sea from under?

The shadow of Newfoundland lies flat and still.
Labrador's yellow, where the moony Eskimo
has oiled it. We can stroke these lovely bays,
under a glass as if they were expected to blossom,
or as if to provide a clean cage for invisible fish.
The names of seashore towns run out to sea,
the names of cities cross the neighboring mountains
—the printer here experiencing the same excitement
as when emotion too far exceeds its cause.
These peninsulas take the water between thumb and finger
like women feeling for the smoothness of yard-goods.

Mapped waters are more quiet than the land is,
lending the land their waves' own conformation:
and Norway's hare runs south in agitation,
profiles investigate the sea, where land is.
Are they assigned, or can the countries pick their colors?
—What suits the character or the native waters best.
Topography displays no favorites; North's as near as West.
More delicate than the historians' are the map-makers' colors.

The Man-Moth*

Here, above,
cracks in the buildings are filled with battered moonlight.
The whole shadow of Man is only as big as his hat.
It lies at his feet like a circle for a doll to stand on,
and he makes an inverted pin, the point magnetized to the
    moon.
He does not see the moon; he observes only her vast properties,
feeling the queer light on his hands, neither warm nor cold,
of a temperature impossible to record in thermometers.

But when the Man-Moth
pays his rare, although occasional, visits to the surface,
the moon looks rather different to him. He emerges
from an opening under the edge of one of the sidewalks
and nervously begins to scale the faces of buildings.
He thinks the moon is a small hole at the top of the sky,
proving the sky quite useless for protection.
He trembles, but must investigate as high as he can climb.

Up the façades,
his shadow dragging like a photographer's cloth behind him,
he climbs fearfully, thinking that this time he will manage
to push his small head through that round clean opening
and be forced through, as from a tube, in black scrolls on the
    light.
(Man, standing below him, has no such illusions.)
But what the Man-Moth fears most he must do, although
he fails, of course, and falls back scared but quite unhurt.

Then he returns
to the pale subways of cement he calls his home. He flits,
he flutters, and cannot get aboard the silent trains
fast enough to suit him. The doors close swiftly.
The Man-Moth always seats himself facing the wrong way
and the train starts at once at its full, terrible speed,
without a shift in gears or a gradation of any sort.
He cannot tell the rate at which he travels backwards.

*Newspaper misprint for 'mammoth.'

Each night he must
be carried through artificial tunnels and dream recurrent
    dreams.
Just as the ties recur beneath his train, these underlie
his rushing brain. He does not dare look out the window,
for the third rail, the unbroken draught of poison,
runs there beside him. He regards it as disease
he has inherited susceptibility to. He has to keep
his hands in pockets, as others must wear mufflers.

If you catch him,
hold up a flashlight to his eye. It's all dark pupil,
an entire night itself, whose haired horizon tightens
as he stares back, and closes up the eye. Then from the lids
one tear, his only possession, like the bee's sting, slips.
Slyly he palms it, and if you're not paying attention
he'll swallow it. However, if you watch, he'll hand it over,
cool as from underground springs and pure enough to drink.

Sleeping on the Ceiling

It is so peaceful on the ceiling!
It is the Place de la Concorde.
The little crystal chandelier
is off, the fountain is in the dark.
Not a soul is in the park.

Below, where the wall-paper is peeling,
the Jardin des Plantes has locked its gates.
Those photographs are animals.
The mighty flowers and foliage rustle;
under the leaves the insects tunnel.

We must go under the wall-paper
to meet the insect-gladiator,
to battle with a net and trident,
and leave the fountain and the square.
But oh, that we could sleep up there. . . .

Roosters

At four o'clock
in the gun-metal blue dark
we hear the first crow of the first cock

just below
the gun-metal blue window
and immediately there is an echo

off in the distance,
then one from the back-yard fence,
then one, with horrible insistence,

grates like a wet match
from the broccoli patch,
flares, and all over town begins to catch.

Cries galore
come from the water-closet door,
from the dropping-plastered henhouse floor,

where in the blue blur
their rustling wives admire,
the roosters brace their cruel feet and glare

with stupid eyes
while from their beaks there rise
the uncontrolled, traditional cries.

Deep from protruding chests
in green-gold medals dressed,
planned to command and terrorize the rest,

the many wives
who lead hens' lives
of being courted and despised;

deep from raw throats
a senseless order floats
all over town. A rooster gloats

over our beds
from rusty iron sheds
and fences made from old bedsteads,

over our churches
where the tin rooster perches,
over our little wooden northern houses,

making sallies
from all the muddy alleys,
marking out maps like Rand McNally's:

glass headed pins,
oil-golds and copper greens,
anthracite blues, alizarins,

each one an active
displacement in perspective;
each screaming, 'This is where I live!'

Each screaming
'Get up! Stop dreaming!'
Roosters, what are you projecting?

You, whom the Greeks elected
to shoot at on a post, who struggled
when sacrificed, you whom they labeled

'Very combative . . .'
what right have you to give
commands and tell us how to live,

cry 'Here!' and 'Here!'
and wake us here where are
unwanted love, conceit and war?

The crown of red
set on your little head
is charged with all your fighting blood.

Yes, that excrescence
makes a most virile presence,
plus all that vulgar beauty of iridescence.

Now in mid-air
by twos they fight each other.
Down comes a first flame-feather,

and one is flying,
with raging heroism defying
even the sensation of dying.

And one has fallen,
but still above the town
his torn-out, bloodied feathers drift down;

and what he sung
no matter. He is flung
on the gray ash-heap, lies in dung

with his dead wives
with open, bloody eyes,
while those metallic feathers oxidize.

St. Peter's sin
was worse than that of Magdalen
whose sin was of the flesh alone;

of spirit, Peter's,
falling, beneath the flares,
among the 'servants and officers.'

Old holy sculpture
could set it all together
in one small scene, past and future:

Christ stands amazed,
Peter, two fingers raised
to surprised lips, both as if dazed.

But in between
a little cock is seen
carved on a dim column in the travertine,

explained by *gallus canit*,
flet Petrus underneath it.
There is inescapable hope, the pivot;

yes, and there Peter's tears
run down our chanticleer's
sides and gem his spurs.

Tear-encrusted thick
as a medieval relic
he waits. Poor Peter, heart-sick,

still cannot guess
those cock-a-doodles yet might bless,
his dreadful rooster come to mean forgiveness,

a new weathervane
on basilica and barn,
and that outside the Lateran

there would always be
a bronze cock on a porphyry
pillar so the people and the Pope might see

that even the Prince
of the Apostles long since
had been forgiven, and to convince

all the assembly
that 'Deny deny deny,'
is not all the roosters cry.

In the morning
a low light is floating
in the backyard, and gilding

from underneath
the broccoli, leaf by leaf;
how could the night have come to grief?

gilding the tiny
floating swallow's belly
and lines of pink cloud in the sky,

the day's preamble
like wandering lines in marble.
The cocks are now almost inaudible.

The sun climbs in,
following 'to see the end,'
faithful as enemy, or friend.

The Fish

I caught a tremendous fish
and held him beside the boat
half out of water, with my hook
fast in a corner of his mouth.
He didn't fight.
He hadn't fought at all.
He hung a grunting weight,
battered and venerable
and homely. Here and there
his brown skin hung in strips
like ancient wall-paper,
and its pattern of darker brown
was like wall-paper:
shapes like full-blown roses
stained and lost through age.
He was speckled with barnacles,

fine rosettes of lime,
and infested
with tiny white sea-lice,
and underneath two or three
rags of green weed hung down.
While his gills were breathing in
the terrible oxygen
—the frightening gills,
fresh and crisp with blood,
that can cut so badly—
I thought of the coarse white flesh
packed in like feathers,
the big bones and the little bones,
the dramatic reds and blacks
of his shiny entrails,
and the pink swim-bladder
like a big peony.
I looked into his eyes
which were far larger than mine
but shallower, and yellowed,
the irises backed and packed
with tarnished tinfoil
seen through the lenses
of old scratched isinglass.
They shifted a little, but not
to return my stare.
—It was more like the tipping
of an object toward the light.
I admired his sullen face,
the mechanism of his jaw,
and then I saw
that from his lower lip
—if you could call it a lip—
grim, wet, and weapon-like,
hung five old pieces of fish-line,
or four and a wire leader
with the swivel still attached,
with all their five big hooks
grown firmly in his mouth.
A green line, frayed at the end

where he broke it, two heavier lines,
and a fine black thread
still crimped from the strain and snap
when it broke and he got away.
Like medals with their ribbons
frayed and wavering,
a five-haired beard of wisdom
trailing from his aching jaw.
I stared and stared
and victory filled up
the little rented boat,
from the pool of bilge
where oil had spread a rainbow
around the rusted engine
to the bailer rusted orange,
the sun-cracked thwarts,
the oarlocks on their strings,
the gunnels—until everything
was rainbow, rainbow, rainbow!
And I let the fish go.

Over 2000 *Illustrations* and a *Complete Concordance*

Thus should have been our travels:
serious, engravable.
The Seven Wonders of the World are tired
and a touch familiar, but the other scenes,
innumerable, though equally sad and still,
are foreign. Often the squatting Arab,
or group of Arabs, plotting, probably,
against our Christian Empire,
while one apart, with outstretched arm and hand
points to the Tomb, the Pit, the Sepulcher.
The branches of the date-palms look like files.
The cobbled courtyard, where the Well is dry,
is like a diagram, the brickwork conduits
are vast and obvious, the human figure

far gone in history or theology,
gone with its camel or its faithful horse.
Always the silence, the gesture, the specks of birds
suspended on invisible threads above the Site,
or the smoke rising solemnly, pulled by threads.
Granted a page alone or a page made up
of several scenes arranged in cattycornered rectangles
or circles set on stippled gray,
granted a grim lunette,
caught in the toils of an initial letter,
when dwelt upon, they all resolve themselves.
The eye drops, weighted, through the lines
the burin made, the lines that move apart
like ripples above sand,
dispersing storms, God's spreading fingerprint,
and painfully, finally, that ignite
in watery prismatic white-and-blue.

Entering the Narrows at St. Johns
the touching bleat of goats reached to the ship.
We glimpsed them, reddish, leaping up the cliffs
among the fog-soaked weeds and butter-and-eggs.
And at St. Peter's the wind blew and the sun shone madly.
Rapidly, purposefully, the Collegians marched in lines,
crisscrossing the great square with black, like ants.
In Mexico the dead man lay
in a blue arcade; the dead volcanoes
glistened like Easter lilies.
The juke-box went on playing "Ay, Jalisco!"
And at Volubilis there were beautiful poppies
splitting the mosaics; the fat old guide made eyes.
In Dingle harbor a golden length of evening
the rotting hulks held up their dripping plush.
The Englishwoman poured tea, informing us
that the Duchess was going to have a baby.
And in the brothels of Marrakesh
the little pockmarked prostitutes
balanced their tea-trays on their heads
and did their belly-dances; flung themselves
naked and giggling against our knees,

asking for cigarettes. It was somewhere near there
I saw what frightened me most of all:
A holy grave, not looking particularly holy,
one of a group under a keyhole-arched stone baldaquin
open to every wind from the pink desert.
An open, gritty, marble trough, carved solid
with exhortation, yellowed
as scattered cattle-teeth;
half-filled with dust, not even the dust
of the poor prophet paynim who once lay there.
In a smart burnoose Khadour looked on amused.

Everything only connected by "and," and "and."
Open the book. (The gilt rubs off the edges
of the pages and pollinates the fingertips.)
Open the heavy book. Why couldn't we have seen
this old Nativity while we were at it?
—the dark ajar, the rocks breaking with light,
an undisturbed, unbreathing flame,
colorless, sparkless, freely fed on straw,
and, lulled within, a family with pets,
—and looked and looked our infant sight away.

The Bight

On my birthday

At low tide like this how sheer the water is.
White, crumbling ribs of marl protrude and glare
and the boats are dry, the pilings dry as matches.
Absorbing, rather than being absorbed,
the water in the bight doesn't wet anything,
the color of the gas flame turned as low as possible.
One can smell it turning to gas; if one were Baudelaire
one could probably hear it turning to marimba music.
The little ocher dredge at work off the end of the dock
already plays the dry perfectly off-beat claves.
The birds are outsize. Pelicans crash

into this peculiar gas unnecessarily hard,
it seems to me, like pickaxes,
rarely coming up with anything to show for it,
and going off with humorous elbowings.
Black-and-white man-of-war birds soar
on impalpable drafts
and open their tails like scissors on the curves
or tense them like wishbones, till they tremble.
The frowsy sponge boats keep coming in
with the obliging air of retrievers,
bristling with jackstraw gaffs and hooks
and decorated with bobbles of sponges.
There is a fence of chicken wire along the dock
where, glinting like little plowshares,
the blue-gray shark tails are hung up to dry
for the Chinese-restaurant trade.
Some of the little white boats are still piled up
against each other, or lie on their sides, stove in,
and not yet salvaged, if they ever will be, from the last bad
     storm,
like torn-open, unanswered letters.
The bight is littered with old correspondences.
Click. Click. Goes the dredge,
and brings up a dripping jawful of marl.
All the untidy activity continues,
awful but cheerful.

At the Fishhouses

Although it is a cold evening,
down by one of the fishhouses
an old man sits netting,
his net, in the gloaming almost invisible
a dark purple-brown,
and his shuttle worn and polished.
The air smells so strong of codfish
it makes one's nose run and one's eyes water.
The five fishhouses have steeply peaked roofs
and narrow, cleated gangplanks slant up

to storerooms in the gables
for the wheelbarrows to be pushed up and down on.
All is silver: the heavy surface of the sea,
swelling slowly as if considering spilling over,
is opaque, but the silver of the benches,
the lobster pots, and masts, scattered
among the wild jagged rocks,
is of an apparent translucence
like the small old buildings with an emerald moss
growing on their shoreward walls.
The big fish tubs are completely lined
with layers of beautiful herring scales
and the wheelbarrows are similarly plastered
with creamy iridescent coats of mail,
with small iridescent flies crawling on them.
Up on the little slope behind the houses,
set in the sparse bright sprinkle of grass,
is an ancient wooden capstan,
cracked, with two long bleached handles
and some melancholy stains, like dried blood,
where the ironwork has rusted.
The old man accepts a Lucky Strike.
He was a friend of my grandfather.
We talk of the decline in the population
and of codfish and herring
while he waits for a herring boat to come in.
There are sequins on his vest and on his thumb.
He has scraped the scales, the principal beauty,
from unnumbered fish with that black old knife,
the blade of which is almost worn away.

Down at the water's edge, at the place
where they haul up the boats, up the long ramp
descending into the water, thin silver
tree trunks are laid horizontally
across the gray stones, down and down
at intervals of four or five feet.

Cold dark deep and absolutely clear,
element bearable to no mortal,

to fish and to seals . . . One seal particularly
I have seen here evening after evening.
He was curious about me. He was interested in music;
like me a believer in total immersion,
so I used to sing him Baptist hymns.
I also sang "A Mighty Fortress Is Our God."
He stood up in the water and regarded me
steadily, moving his head a little.
Then he would disappear, then suddenly emerge
almost in the same spot, with a sort of shrug
as if it were against his better judgment.
Cold dark deep and absolutely clear,
the clear gray icy water . . . Back, behind us,
the dignified tall firs begin.
Bluish, associating with their shadows,
a million Christmas trees stand
waiting for Christmas. The water seems suspended
above the rounded gray and blue-gray stones.
I have seen it over and over, the same sea, the same,
slightly, indifferently swinging above the stones,
icily free above the stones,
above the stones and then the world.
If you should dip your hand in,
your wrist would ache immediately,
your bones would begin to ache and your hand would burn
as if the water were a transmutation of fire
that feeds on stones and burns with a dark gray flame.
If you tasted it, it would first taste bitter,
then briny, then surely burn your tongue.
It is like what we imagine knowledge to be:
dark, salt, clear, moving, utterly free,
drawn from the cold hard mouth
of the world, derived from the rocky breasts
forever, flowing and drawn, and since
our knowledge is historical, flowing, and flown.

The Prodigal

The brown enormous odor he lived by
was too close, with its breathing and thick hair,
for him to judge. The floor was rotten; the sty
was plastered halfway up with glass-smooth dung.
Light-lashed, self-righteous, above moving snouts,
the pigs' eyes followed him, a cheerful stare—
even to the sow that always ate her young—
till, sickening, he leaned to scratch her head.
But sometimes mornings after drinking bouts
(he hid the pints behind a two-by-four),
the sunrise glazed the barnyard mud with red;
the burning puddles seemed to reassure.
And then he thought he almost might endure
his exile yet another year or more.

But evenings the first star came to warn.
The farmer whom he worked for came at dark
to shut the cows and horses in the barn
beneath their overhanging clouds of hay,
with pitchforks, faint forked lightnings, catching light,
safe and companionable as in the Ark.
The pigs stuck out their little feet and snored.
The lantern—like the sun, going away—
laid on the mud a pacing aureole.
Carrying a bucket along a slimy board,
he felt the bats' uncertain staggering flight,
his shuddering insights, beyond his control,
touching him. But it took him a long time
finally to make his mind up to go home.

The Shampoo

The still explosions on the rocks,
the lichens, grow
by spreading, gray, concentric shocks.
They have arranged

to meet the rings around the moon, although
within our memories they have not changed.

And since the heavens will attend
as long on us,
you've been, dear friend,
precipitate and pragmatical;
and look what happens. For Time is
nothing if not amenable.

The shooting stars in your black hair
in bright formation
are flocking where,
so straight, so soon?
—Come, let me wash it in this big tin basin,
battered and shiny like the moon.

Song for the Rainy Season

Hidden, oh hidden
in the high fog
the house we live in,
beneath the magnetic rock,
rain-, rainbow-ridden,
where blood-black
bromelias, lichens,
owls, and the lint
of the waterfalls cling,
familiar, unbidden.

In a dim age
of water
the brook sings loud
from a rib cage
of giant fern; the vapor
climbs up the thick growth
effortlessly, turns back,

holding them both,
house and rock,
in a private cloud.

At night, on the roof,
blind drops crawl
and the ordinary brown
owl gives us proof
he can count:
five times—always five—
he stamps and takes off
after the fat frogs that,
shrilling for love
clamber and mount.

House, open house
to the white dew
and the milk-white sunrise
kind to the eyes,
to membership
of silver fish, mouse,
bookworms,
big moths; with a wall
for the mildew's
ignorant map;

darkened and tarnished
by the warm touch
of the warm breath,
maculate, cherished,
rejoice! For a later
era will differ.
(O difference that kills,
or intimidates, much
of all our small shadowy
life!) Without water

the great rock will stare
unmagnetized, bare,
no longer wearing

rainbows or rain,
the forgiving air
and the high fog gone;
the owls will move on
and the several
waterfalls shrivel
in the steady sun.

The Armadillo

(For Robert Lowell)

This is the time of year
when almost every night
the frail, illegal fire balloons appear.
Climbing the mountain height,

rising toward a saint
still honored in these parts,
the paper chambers flush and fill with light
that comes and goes, like hearts.

Once up against the sky it's hard
to tell them from the stars—
planets, that is—the tinted ones:
Venus going down, or Mars,

or the pale green one. With a wind,
they flare and falter, wobble and toss;
but if it's still they steer between
the kite sticks of the Southern Cross,

receding, dwindling, solemnly
and steadily forsaking us,
or, in the downdraft from a peak,
suddenly turning dangerous.

Last night another big one fell.
It splattered like an egg of fire
against the cliff behind the house.
The flame ran down. We saw the pair

of owls who nest there flying up
and up, their whirling black-and-white
stained bright pink underneath, until
they shrieked up out of sight.

The ancient owls' nest must have burned.
Hastily, all alone,
a glistening armadillo left the scene,
rose-flecked, head down, tail down,

and then a baby rabbit jumped out,
short-eared, to our surprise.
So soft!—a handful of intangible ash
with fixed, ignited eyes.

Too pretty, dreamlike mimicry!
O falling fire and piercing cry
and panic, and a weak mailed fist
clenched ignorant against the sky!

Sestina

September rain falls on the house.
In the failing light, the old grandmother
sits in the kitchen with the child
beside the Little Marvel Stove,
reading the jokes from the almanac,
laughing and talking to hide her tears.

She thinks that her equinoctial tears
and the rain that beats on the roof of the house
were both foretold by the almanac,
but only known to a grandmother.

The iron kettle sings on the stove.
She cuts some bread and says to the child,

It's time for tea now; but the child
is watching the teakettle's small hard tears
dance like mad on the hot black stove,
the way the rain must dance on the house.
Tidying up, the old grandmother
hangs up the clever almanac

on its string. Bird-like, the almanac
hovers half open above the child,
hovers above the old grandmother
and her teacup full of dark brown tears.
She shivers and says she thinks the house
feels chilly, and puts more wood in the stove.

It was to be, says the Marvel Stove.
I know what I know, says the almanac.
With crayons the child draws a rigid house
and a winding pathway. Then the child
puts in a man with buttons like tears
and shows it proudly to the grandmother.

But secretly, while the grandmother
busies herself about the stove,
the little moons fall down like tears
from between the pages of the almanac
into the flower bed the child
has carefully placed in the front of the house.

Time to plant tears, says the almanac.
The grandmother sings to the marvellous stove
and the child draws another inscrutable house.

Sandpiper

The roaring alongside he takes for granted,
and that every so often the world is bound to shake.
He runs, he runs to the south, finical, awkward,
in a state of controlled panic, a student of Blake.

The beach hisses like fat. On his left, a sheet
of interrupting water comes and goes
and glazes over his dark and brittle feet.
He runs, he runs straight through it, watching his toes.

—Watching, rather, the spaces of sand between them,
where (no detail too small) the Atlantic drains
rapidly backwards and downwards. As he runs,
he stares at the dragging grains.

The world is a mist. The world is uniquely
minute and vast and clear. The tide
is higher or lower. He couldn't tell you which.
His beak is focussed; he is preoccupied,

looking for something, something, something.
Poor bird, he is obsessed!
The millions of grains are black, white, tan, and gray,
mixed with quartz grains, rose and amethyst.

Twelfth Morning; or What You Will

Like a first coat of whitewash when it's wet,
the thin gray mist lets everything show through:
the black boy Balthazár, a fence, a horse,
    a foundered house,

—cement and rafters sticking from a dune.
(The Company passes off these white but shopworn
dunes as lawns.) "Shipwreck," we say; perhaps
    this is a housewreck.

The sea's off somewhere, doing nothing. Listen.
An expelled breath. And faint, faint, faint
(or are you hearing things), the sandpipers'
   heart-broken cries.

The fence, three-strand, barbed-wire, all pure rust,
three dotted lines, comes forward hopefully
across the lots; thinks better of it; turns
   a sort of corner . . .

Don't ask the big white horse, *Are you supposed
to be inside the fence or out?* He's still
asleep. Even awake, he probably
   remains in doubt.

He's bigger than the house. The force of
personality, or is perspective dozing?
A pewter-colored horse, an ancient mixture,
   tin, lead, and silver,

he gleams a bit. But the four-gallon can
approaching on the head of Balthazár
keeps flashing that the world's a pearl, *and I,
   I am*

its highlight! You can hear the water now,
inside, slap-slapping. Balthazár is singing.
"Today's my Anniversary," he sings,
   "the Day of Kings."

In the Waiting Room

In Worcester, Massachusetts,
I went with Aunt Consuelo
to keep her dentist's appointment
and sat and waited for her
in the dentist's waiting room.
It was winter. It got dark

early. The waiting room
was full of grown-up people,
arctics and overcoats,
lamps and magazines.
My aunt was inside
what seemed like a long time
and while I waited I read
the *National Geographic*
(I could read) and carefully
studied the photographs:
the inside of a volcano,
black, and full of ashes;
then it was spilling over
in rivulets of fire.
Osa and Martin Johnson
dressed in riding breeches,
laced boots, and pith helmets.
A dead man slung on a pole
—"Long Pig," the caption said.
Babies with pointed heads
wound round and round with string;
black, naked women with necks
wound round and round with wire
like the necks of light bulbs.
Their breasts were horrifying.
I read it right straight through.
I was too shy to stop.
And then I looked at the cover:
the yellow margins, the date.

Suddenly, from inside,
came an *oh!* of pain
—Aunt Consuelo's voice—
not very loud or long.
I wasn't at all surprised;
even then I knew she was
a foolish, timid woman.
I might have been embarrassed,
but wasn't. What took me
completely by surprise

was that it was *me*:
my voice, in my mouth.
Without thinking at all
I was my foolish aunt,
I—we—were falling, falling,
our eyes glued to the cover
of the *National Geographic*,
February, 1918.

I said to myself: three days
and you'll be seven years old.
I was saying it to stop
the sensation of falling off
the round, turning world
into cold, blue-black space.
But I felt: you are an *I*,
you are an *Elizabeth*,
you are one of *them*.
Why should you be one, too?
I scarcely dared to look
to see what it was I was.
I gave a sidelong glance
—I couldn't look any higher—
at shadowy gray knees,
trousers and skirts and boots
and different pairs of hands
lying under the lamps.
I knew that nothing stranger
had ever happened, that nothing
stranger could ever happen.
Why should I be my aunt,
or me, or anyone?
What similarities—
boots, hands, the family voice
I felt in my throat, or even
the *National Geographic*
and those awful hanging breasts—
held us all together
or made us all just one?

How—I didn't know any
word for it—how "unlikely" . . .
How had I come to be here,
like them, and overhear
a cry of pain that could have
got loud and worse but hadn't?

The waiting room was bright
and too hot. It was sliding
beneath a big black wave,
another, and another.

Then I was back in it.
The War was on. Outside,
in Worcester, Massachusetts,
were night and slush and cold,
and it was still the fifth
of February, 1918.

Crusoe in England

A new volcano has erupted,
the papers say, and last week I was reading
where some ship saw an island being born:
at first a breath of steam, ten miles away;
and then a black fleck—basalt, probably—
rose in the mate's binoculars
and caught on the horizon like a fly.
They named it. But my poor old island's still
un-rediscovered, un-renamable.
None of the books has ever got it right.

Well, I had fifty-two
miserable, small volcanoes I could climb
with a few slithery strides—
volcanoes dead as ash heaps.
I used to sit on the edge of the highest one
and count the others standing up,

naked and leaden, with their heads blown off.
I'd think that if they were the size
I thought volcanoes should be, then I had
become a giant;
and if I had become a giant,
I couldn't bear to think what size
the goats and turtles were,
or the gulls, or the over-lapping rollers
—a glittering hexagon of rollers
closing and closing in, but never quite,
glittering and glittering, though the sky
was mostly overcast.

My island seemed to be
a sort of cloud-dump. All the hemisphere's
left-over clouds arrived and hung
above the craters—their parched throats
were hot to touch.
Was that why it rained so much?
And why sometimes the whole place hissed?
The turtles lumbered by, high-domed,
hissing like teakettles.
(And I'd have given years, or taken a few,
for any sort of kettle, of course.)
The folds of lava, running out to sea,
would hiss. I'd turn. And then they'd prove
to be more turtles.
The beaches were all lava, variegated,
black, red, and white, and gray;
the marbled colors made a fine display.
And I had waterspouts. Oh,
half a dozen at a time, far out,
they'd come and go, advancing and retreating,
their heads in cloud, their feet in moving patches
of scuffed-up white.
Glass chimneys, flexible, attenuated,
sacerdotal beings of glass . . . I watched
the water spiral up in them like smoke.
Beautiful, yes, but not much company.

I often gave way to self-pity.
"Do I deserve this? I suppose I must.
I wouldn't be here otherwise. Was there
a moment when I actually chose this?
I don't remember, but there could have been."
What's wrong about self-pity, anyway?
With my legs dangling down familiarly
over a crater's edge, I told myself
"Pity should begin at home." So the more
pity I felt, the more I felt at home.

The sun set in the sea; the same odd sun
rose from the sea,
and there was one of it and one of me.
The island had one kind of everything:
one tree snail, a bright violet-blue
with a thin shell, crept over everything,
over the one variety of tree,
a sooty, scrub affair.
Snail shells lay under these in drifts
and, at a distance,
you'd swear that they were beds of irises.
There was one kind of berry, a dark red.
I tried it, one by one, and hours apart.
Sub-acid, and not bad, no ill effects;
and so I made home-brew. I'd drink
the awful, fizzy, stinging stuff
that went straight to my head
and play my home-made flute
(I think it had the weirdest scale on earth)
and, dizzy, whoop and dance among the goats.
Home-made, home-made! But aren't we all?
I felt a deep affection for
the smallest of my island industries.
No, not exactly, since the smallest was
a miserable philosophy.

Because I didn't know enough.
Why didn't I know enough of something?
Greek drama or astronomy? The books

I'd read were full of blanks;
the poems—well, I tried
reciting to my iris-beds,
"They flash upon that inward eye,
which is the bliss . . ." The bliss of what?
One of the first things that I did
when I got back was look it up.

The island smelled of goat and guano.
The goats were white, so were the gulls,
and both too tame, or else they thought
I was a goat, too, or a gull.
Baa, baa, baa and *shriek, shriek, shriek,*
baa . . . shriek . . . baa . . . I still can't shake
them from my ears; they're hurting now.
The questioning shrieks, the equivocal replies
over a ground of hissing rain
and hissing, ambulating turtles
got on my nerves.

When all the gulls flew up at once, they sounded
like a big tree in a strong wind, its leaves.
I'd shut my eyes and think about a tree,
an oak, say, with real shade, somewhere.
I'd heard of cattle getting island-sick.
I thought the goats were.
One billy-goat would stand on the volcano
I'd christened *Mont d'Espoir* or *Mount Despair*
(I'd time enough to play with names),
and bleat and bleat, and sniff the air.
I'd grab his beard and look at him.
His pupils, horizontal, narrowed up
and expressed nothing, or a little malice.
I got so tired of the very colors!
One day I dyed a baby goat bright red
with my red berries, just to see
something a little different.
And then his mother wouldn't recognize him.

Dreams were the worst. Of course I dreamed of food
and love, but they were pleasant rather
than otherwise. But then I'd dream of things
like slitting a baby's throat, mistaking it
for a baby goat. I'd have
nightmares of other islands
stretching away from mine, infinities
of islands, islands spawning islands,
like frogs' eggs turning into polliwogs
of islands, knowing that I had to live
on each and every one, eventually,
for ages, registering their flora,
their fauna, their geography.

Just when I thought I couldn't stand it
another minute longer, Friday came.
(Accounts of that have everything all wrong.)
Friday was nice.
Friday was nice, and we were friends.
If only he had been a woman!
I wanted to propagate my kind,
and so did he, I think, poor boy.
He'd pet the baby goats sometimes,
and race with them, or carry one around.
—Pretty to watch; he had a pretty body.

And then one day they came and took us off.

Now I live here, another island,
that doesn't seem like one, but who decides?
My blood was full of them; my brain
bred islands. But that archipelago
has petered out. I'm old.
I'm bored, too, drinking my real tea,
surrounded by uninteresting lumber.
The knife there on the shelf—
it reeked of meaning, like a crucifix.
It lived. How many years did I
beg it, implore it, not to break?
I knew each nick and scratch by heart,

the bluish blade, the broken tip,
the lines of wood-grain on the handle . . .
Now it won't look at me at all.
The living soul has dribbled away.
My eyes rest on it and pass on.

The local museum's asked me to
leave everything to them:
the flute, the knife, the shrivelled shoes,
my shedding goatskin trousers
(moths have got in the fur),
the parasol that took me such a time
remembering the way the ribs should go.
It still will work but, folded up,
looks like a plucked and skinny fowl.
How can anyone want such things?
—And Friday, my dear Friday, died of measles
seventeen years ago come March.

One Art

The art of losing isn't hard to master;
so many things seem filled with the intent
to be lost that their loss is no disaster.

Lose something every day. Accept the fluster
of lost door keys, the hour badly spent.
The art of losing isn't hard to master.

Then practice losing farther, losing faster:
places, and names, and where it was you meant
to travel. None of these will bring disaster.

I lost my mother's watch. And look! my last, or
next-to-last, of three loved houses went.
The art of losing isn't hard to master.

I lost two cities, lovely ones. And, vaster,
some realms I owned, two rivers, a continent.
I miss them, but it wasn't a disaster.

—Even losing you (the joking voice, a gesture
I love) I shan't have lied. It's evident
the art of losing's not too hard to master
though it may look like (*Write* it!) like disaster.

Sonnet

Caught—the bubble
in the spirit-level,
a creature divided;
and the compass needle
wobbling and wavering,
undecided.
Freed—the broken
thermometer's mercury
running away;
and the rainbow-bird
from the narrow bevel
of the empty mirror,
flying wherever
it feels like, gay!

J. V. CUNNINGHAM

(1911–1985)

Dream Vision

This dry and lusty wind has stirred all night
The tossing forest of one sleepless tree,
And I in waking vision walked with her
Whose hair hums to the motion of the forest
And in the orbit of whose eyelids' fall
The clouds drift slowly from the starry wharves.
I knew her body well but could not speak,
For comprehension is a kind of silence,
The last harmonic of all sound. Europa,
Iö, and Danäe: their names are love
Incarnate in the chronicles of love.
I trace their sad initials which thy bark,
Gaunt tree, may line with age but not efface,
And carve her name with mine there. The tree is gnarled
And puckered as a child that looks away
And fumbles at the breast—prodigious infant
Still sucking at the haggard teats of time!
Radical change, the root of human woe!

All choice is error, the tragical mistake,
And you are mine because I name you mine.
Kiss, then, in pledge of the imponderables
That tilt the balance of eternity
A leaf's weight up and down. Though we must part
While each dawn darkens on the fortunate wheel,
The moon will not soften our names cut here
Till every sheltering bird has fled the nest.
They know the wind brings rain, and rain and wind
Will smooth the outlines of our lettering
To the simplicity of epitaph.

A Moral Poem

Then leave old regret,
Ancestral remorse,
Which, though you forget,
Unseen keep their course;

Shaping what each says,
Weathered in his style,
They in his fond ways
Live on for a while.

But leave them at last
To find their own home.
Inured to the past,
Be what you become:

Nor ungrudgingly
Youth's hot hours dispense,
Nor live curiously,
Cheating providence.

For My Contemporaries

How time reverses
The proud in heart!
I now make verses
Who aimed at art.

But I sleep well.
Ambitious boys
Whose big lines swell
With spiritual noise,

Despise me not!
And be not queasy
To praise somewhat:
Verse is not easy.

But rage who will.
Time that procured me
Good sense and skill
Of madness cured me.

Montana Pastoral

I am no shepherd of a child's surmises.
I have seen fear where the coiled serpent rises,

Thirst where the grasses burn in early May
And thistle, mustard, and the wild oat stay.

There is dust in this air. I saw in the heat
Grasshoppers busy in the threshing wheat.

So to this hour. Through the warm dusk I drove
To blizzards sifting on the hissing stove,

And found no images of pastoral will,
But fear, thirst, hunger, and this huddled chill.

Selected Epigrams

An Epitaph for Anyone

An old dissembler who lived out his lie
Lies here as if he did not fear to die.

Motto for a Sun Dial

I who by day am function of the light
Am constant and invariant by night.

———

Soft found a way to damn me undefended:
I was forgiven who had not offended.

———

This Humanist whom no beliefs constrained
Grew so broad-minded he was scatter-brained.

Epitaph for Someone or Other

Naked I came, naked I leave the scene,
And naked was my pastime in between.

———

Life flows to death as rivers to the sea,
And life is fresh and death is salt to me.

———

Here lies New Critic who would fox us
With his poetic paradoxes.
Though he lies here rigid and quiet,
If he could speak he would deny it.

———

You wonder why Drab sells her love for gold?
To have the means to buy it when she's old.

———

Good Fortune, when I hailed her recently,
Passed by me with the intimacy of shame
As one that in the dark had handled me
And could no longer recollect my name.

Fear

Love, at what distance mine!
On whose disdain I dine
Unfed, unfamished, I
In your hid counsels lie.
I know your lover, fear.
His presence is austere
As winter air. He trembles
Though the taut face dissembles.
I know him: I am he.

For a Woman with Child

We are ourselves but carriers. Life
Incipient grows to separateness
And is its own meaning. Life is,
And not; there is no nothingness.

Love's Progress

Pal was her friend, her lover, and, dismissed,
Became at last her lay psychiatrist.

To What Strangers, What Welcome

When we parted,
I told her I should see the King again,
And, having seen him, might go back again
To see her face once more. But I shall see
No more the lady Vivian. Let her love
What man she may, no other love than mine
Shall be an index of her memories.
I fear no man who may come after me,
And I see none. I see her, still in green,
Beside the fountain. I shall not go back. . . .
*   If I come not,*
The lady Vivian will remember me,
And say: "I knew him when his heart was young,
Though I have lost him now. Time called him home,
And that was as it was; for much is lost
Between Broceliande and Camelot."

Edwin Arlington Robinson, *Merlin,* 7.425–42

I

I drive Westward. Tumble and loco weed
Persist. And in the vacancies of need,
The leisure of desire, whirlwinds a face
As luminous as love, lost as this place.

2

On either side of the white line
The emblems of a life appear
In turn: purpose like lodgepole pine.
Competitive and thin, and fear

Agile as aspen in a storm.
And then the twilit harboring
In a small park. The room is warm.
And by the ache of travelling

Removed from all immediacy,
From all time, I as time grows late
Sense in disordered fantasy
The sound and smell of love and hate.

3

In a few days now when two memories meet
In that place of disease, waste, and desire
Where forms receptive, featureless, and vast
Find occupation, in that narrow dark,
That warm sweat of a carnal tenderness,
What figure in the pantheon of lust,
What demon is our god? What name subsumes
That act external to our sleeping selves?
Not pleasure—it is much too broad and narrow—,
Not sex, not for the moment love, but pride,
And not in prowess, but pride undefined,
Autonomous in its unthought demands,
A bit of vanity, but mostly pride.

4

You have here no otherness,
Unaddressed correspondent,
No gaunt clavicles, no hair
Of bushy intimacy.
You are not, and I write here
The name of no signature
To the unsaid—a letter
At midnight, a memorial
And occupation of time.

I'll not summon you, or feel
In the alert dream the give
And stay of flesh, the tactile
Conspiracy.
                The snow falls
With its inveterate meaning,
And I follow the barbed wire
To trough, to barn, to the house,

To what strangers, what welcome
In the late blizzard of time.

On the highway cars flashing,
Occasional and random
As pain gone without symptom,
And fear drifts with the North wind.
We neither give nor receive:
The unfinishable drink
Left on the table, the sleep
Alcoholic and final
In the mute exile of time.

5

The Pick-Up

The soft lights, the companionship, the beers,
And night promises everything you lacked.
The short drive, the unmade bed, and night in tears
Hysteric in the elemental act.

6

It was in Vegas. Celibate and able
I left the silver dollars on the table
And tried the show. The black-out, baggy pants,
Of course, and then this answer to romance:
Her ass twitching as if it had the fits,
Her gold crotch grinding, her athletic tits,
One clock, the other counter clockwise twirling.
It was enough to stop a man from girling.

7

A traveller, the highway my guide,
And a little bastard of a dog
My friend. I have pin-ups for passion
As I go moseying about these scenes,
Myself improbable as yucca,
Illusory as the bright desert,
And finally here: the surf breaking,

Repetitive and varied as love
Enacted, and inevitably
The last rim of sunset on the sea.

8

The night is still. The unfailing surf
In passion and subsidence moves
As at a distance. The glass walls,
And redwood, are my utmost being.
And is there there in the last shadow,
There in the final privacies
Of unaccosted grace,—is there,
Gracing the tedium to death,
An intimation? Something much
Like love, like loneliness adrowse
In states more primitive than peace,
In the warm wonder of winter sun.

9

Innocent to innocent,
One asked, What is perfect love?
Not knowing it is not love,
Which is imperfect—some kind
Of love or other, some kind
Of interchange with wanting,
There when all else is wanting,
Something by which we make do.

So, impaired, uninnocent,
If I love you—as I do—
To the very perfection
Of perfect imperfection,
It's that I care more for you
Than for my feeling for you.

10

A half hour for coffee, and at night
An hour or so of unspoken speech,

Hemming a summer dress as the tide
Turns at the right time.
                              Must it be sin,
This consummation of who knows what?
This sharp cry at entrance, once, and twice?
This unfulfilled fulfilment?
                              Something
That happens because it must happen.
We live in the given. Consequence,
And lack of consequence, both fail us.
Good is what we can do with evil.

11

I drive Eastward. The ethics of return,
Like the night sound of coyotes on a hill
Heard in eroded canyons of concern,
Disposes what has happened, and what will.

12

Absence, my angel, presence at my side,
I know you as an article of faith
By desert, prairie, and this stonewalled road—
As much my own as is the thought of death.

13

Nescit vox missa reverti . . .

The once hooked ever after lives in lack,
And the once said never finds its way back.

14

I write only to say this,
In a syllabic dryness
As inglorious as I feel:
Sometime before drinking time
For the first time in some weeks
I heard of you, the casual
News of a new life, silence

Of unconfronted feeling
And maples in the slant sun
The gay color of decay.
Was it unforgivable,
My darling, that you loved me?

ROSE DRACHLER

(1911–1982)

The Evening of the Sixth Day

A Fugue for Tina Meltzer

I search for not knowing in the middle of what I know best.
This is a bottomless well of the inconceivable.
Here is the song of an unseen bird, music turned into flesh.
I reflect on my own powers. Am amazed at the familiar.

By what instrument have I reduced myself to perfection?
Here is the song of a tiny bird, music made flesh
What profound geometry. What exquisite principle.
A walnut is fashioned so like a brain. I laugh. I am afraid.

The song I hear is from an unseen bird. It is flesh made from
    music.
There is a remarkable sort of statistical dissymmetry.
I examine the spatial developments, how they relate
Nothing resembles any other thing exactly.

To say that it is accidental is to say that it exists.
I reflect on my own powers. Am amazed at the familiar.
I can describe what I see in terms of what I saw before
But changes have occurred. By reducing the scale I learn love.

This can go on indefinitely. Of this who would grow weary?
I know nothing of seashells or tiny mushrooms.
I look for the first time and am perplexed. Did I do this?
I reflect on my own powers. Am amazed at the familiar.

The idea of making or remaking is hard to take in.
My own metaphysics and science give me vertigo.
I pretend to know what I know. I go back to the
Beginning of knowing. One can discern a certain construction.

I look for the first time and am perplexed.
There is the work of someone not working at random.
I recognize his work. An unseen bird. Music made flesh.
It is the fruit of humor. A Mozart is playing jokes.

Someone made these for someone else as a partial gift.
To say that it is accidental is to say it exists.
Here is cohesion. Here is reality of matter.
I must disregard their origin and purpose and get to work.

What profound geometry. What guiding principle.
Compare these to small stones. They have something more.
Fragments suggest fragments that were joined to them.
I reflect on my own powers. Am amazed at the familiar

Would it be possible to construct all this consciously
To get the right ingredients, make a plan, proceed step by
        step,
A pre-existing idea guiding the execution
An idea of the work that governs its progress?

Compare these to small stones. They have something more.
They engage my wonder and make me look for a WHOLE.
I divided myself in order to create. Of what else could I make
        them?
And the final result requires unflagging attention.

I am unable to imagine such material, such attention
I cannot even make bread twice the same way.
It is as though the idea of the similar called forth
Endless similarities. I reflect on my own powers.

A thrush is singing an acrobatic song made flesh.
I did this as I lay sleeping. Or not I, someone did this in me
A pre-existing idea directed the execution.
This is surely the work of someone not working at random.
This may go on forever. Of this who would grow weary?

PAUL GOODMAN

(1911–1972)

The Lordly Hudson

"Driver, what stream is it?" I asked, well knowing
it was our lordly Hudson hardly flowing,
"It is our lordly Hudson hardly flowing,"
he said, "under the green-grown cliffs."

Be still, heart! no one needs your passionate
suffrage to select this glory,
this is our lordly Hudson hardly flowing
under the green-grown cliffs.

"Driver! has this a peer in Europe or the East?"
"No no!" he said. Home! home!
be quiet, heart! this is our lordly Hudson
and has no peer in Europe or the East,

this is our lordly Hudson hardly flowing
under the green-grown cliffs
and has no peer in Europe or the East.
Be quiet, heart! home! home!

ROBERT JOHNSON

(1911–1938)

Stones in My Passway

I got stones in my passway
        and my road seem dark as night
I got stones in my passway
        and my road seem dark as night
I have pains in my heart
        they have taken my appetite

I have a bird to whistle
        and I have a bird to sing
Have a bird to whistle
        and I have a bird to sing
I got a woman that I'm loving
        boy but she don't mean a thing

My enemies betrayed me
        have overtaken poor Bob at last
My enemies betrayed me
        have overtaken poor Bob at last
And that's one thing certain
        they have stones all in my pass

    Now you trying to take my life
    And all my loving too
    You laid a passway for me
    Now what are you trying to do
I'm crying please
        please let us be friends
And when you hear me howling in my passway, rider
        please open your door and let me in

I got three legs to truck on
                          boys please don't block my road
I got three legs to truck on
                          boys please don't block my road
I been feeling ashame' 'bout my rider
                          babe I'm booked and I got to go

Hellhound on My Trail

I've got to keep moving
            I've got to keep moving
                        blues falling down like hail
                                    blues falling down like hail
Ummmmmmmmmmmmmmmmmmmmmmm
                        blues falling down like hail
                                    blues falling down like hail
And the days keeps on 'minding me
            there's a hellhound on my trail
                        hellhound on my trail
                                    hellhound on my trail

If today was Christmas Eve
                  If today was Christmas Eve
                              and tomorrow was Christmas Day
If today was Christmas Eve
                  and tomorrow was Christmas Day
                              (aw wouldn't we have a time baby)
All I would need my little sweet rider just
                        to pass the time away
                                    uh huh
                                    to pass the time away

You sprinkled hot foot powder
                        umm around my door
                                all around my door
You sprinkled hot foot powder
                    all around your daddy's door
                                hmmm hmmm hmmm
It keeps me with a rambling mind, rider,
                        every old place I go
                                every old place I go

I can tell the wind is rising
                    the leaves trembling on the trees
                                trembling on the trees
I can tell the wind is rising
                    leaves trembling on the trees
                                umm hmm hmm hmm
All I need my little sweet woman
                    and to keep my company
                        hmmm hmmm hmmm hmmm
                                my company

Me and the Devil Blues

Early this morning
                    when you knocked upon my door
Early this morning oooooo
                        when you knocked upon my door
And I said, Hello Satan
                    I believe it's time to go

Me and the Devil
                    was walking side by side
Me and the Devil oooooo
                        was walking side by side
I'm going to beat my woman
                        until I get satisfied

She said you knows the way
          that I always dog her 'round
            (now baby you know
            you ain't doing me right now)
She said you knows the way oooooo
            that I be dog her 'round
It must be that old evil spirit
          so deep down in the ground

You may bury my body
          down by the highway side
            (now baby I don't care where
            you bury my body
            when I'm dead and gone)
You may bury my body oooooo
          down by the highway side
So my old evil spirit
          can get a Greyhound Bus and ride

JOSEPHINE MILES

(1911–1985)

Housewife

Occasional mornings when an early fog
Not yet dispersed stands in every yard
And drips and undiscloses, she is severely
Put to the task of herself.

Usually here we have view window dawns,
The whole East Bay at least some spaces into the room,
Puffing the curtains, and then she is out
In the submetropolitan stir.

But when the fog at the glass pauses and closes
She is put to ponder
A life-line, how it chooses to run obscurely
In her hand, before her.

All Hallow

The lady in the unbecoming bonnet
Let down her weeping hair.
She saw the broomstick and the witch upon it
Riding there.

The wind was full of bottles and the air
Aggressive as a shell.
The lady watched about her everywhere
The sallyings of hell.

The little boys stopped ringing at the bell
As she came homeward sadly. They had her cat
Spitting and mewing, a black one: lady,
Whose cat is that?

Sale

Went into a shoestore to buy a pair of shoes,
There was a shoe salesman humming the blues
Under his breath; over his breath
Floated a peppermint lifesaver, a little wreath.

I said please I need a triple-A,
And without stopping humming or swallowing his lifesaver
    away
He gave one glance from toe to toe
And plucked from the mezzanine the very shoe.

Skill of the blessed, that at their command
Blue and breathless comes to hand
To send, from whatever preoccupation, feet
Implacably shod into the perfect street.

After noon I lie down
As if my spine were bent from burdens,
My mind from abundance,
Straitening into easy quiet.

After fifty years this is the profit,
That the weight of goods
Dozes me off. But what wakes me
Is the fright that ones thirty, twenty, are sleeping also.

They are yawning against the clatter of the day,
Its rash signs as they read them, and draw
Into a restful silence,
Asleep in the sun.

On the world's other side, the shadow
Darkest before dawn is darkening
Before dawn, and sleepers in their night
Waken with desperation for daylight.

We have it. It crackles down our freeways
As if to consume us. Is in our daylight
Someone awake enough to take, use,
Share its garish inequities?

Album

This is a hard life you are living
While you are young,
My father said,
As I scratched my casted knees with a paper knife.
By laws of compensation
Your old age should be grand.

Not grand, but of a terrible
Compensation, to perceive
Past the energy of survival
In its sadness
The hard life of the young.

KENNETH PATCHEN
(1911–1972)

Street Corner College

Next year the grave grass will cover us.
We stand now, and laugh;
Watching the girls go by;
Betting on slow horses; drinking cheap gin.
We have nothing to do; nowhere to go; nobody.

Last year was a year ago; nothing more.
We weren't younger then; nor older now.

We manage to have the look that young men have;
We feel nothing behind our faces, one way or other.

We shall probably not be quite dead when we die.
We were never anything all the way; not even soldiers.

We are the insulted, brother, the desolate boys.
Sleepwalkers in a dark and terrible land,
Where solitude is a dirty knife at our throats.
Cold stars watch us, chum
Cold stars and the whores

Religion Is That I Love You

As time will turn our bodies straight
In single sleep, the hunger fed, heart broken
Like a bottle used by thieves

Beloved, as so late our mouths meet, leaning
Our faces close, eyes closed
Out there

   outside this window where branches toss
    in soft wind, where birds move sudden wings
Within that lame air, love, we are dying

Let us watch that sleep come, put our fingers
Through the breath falling from us

Living, we can love though dying comes near
It is its desperate singing that we must not hear

It is that we cling together, not dying near each other now

23rd Street Runs into Heaven

  You stand near the window as lights wink
  On along the street. Somewhere a trolley, taking
  Shop-girls and clerks home, clatters through
  This before-supper Sabbath. An alley cat cries
  To find the garbage cans sealed; newsboys
  Begin their murder-into-pennies round.

  We are shut in, secure for a little, safe until
  Tomorrow. You slip your dress off, roll down
  Your stockings, careful against runs. Naked now,
  With soft light on soft flesh, you pause
  For a moment; turn and face me—
  Smile in a way that only women know
  Who have lain long with their lover
  And are made more virginal.

  Our supper is plain but we are very wonderful.

The Figure Motioned with Its Mangled Hand
Towards the Wall Behind It,
and uttered a melancholy cry

It was rumored on the block
Ethel is going to let go tonight.
I made big about it, strutting
Down 5th eyeing the babies over,
Thinking they look like mudhens
Next to my little piece of tail.
She was hard to get. Her old lady
Was saving her for dough, but hell
I had class, want the moon, kid?
And I'd give it to her. Funny thing
Though, this is all a lie, I never
So much as touched her hand, she
Thinks I'm dirt, nobody else ever
Always got the wrong end of the stick.
I'd carry the mail for you, Ethel,
Stop running around with that pup,
He's got a car, sure, and jack to throw
Like water but what does he want?
What do they all want? something easy,
Something that somebody else worked for.
Ethel, lay off rich kids, you'll end dirty.

Join the world and see the army
The slime is quiet tonight, along the Jersey coast
The chippies discuss Democracy in awed tones
Breathes there a heel with man so dead . . .
Shoot the liquidfire to Johnnie, boy
With every rendezvous-with-death we are giving away
An autographed photo of J. P. Morgan taken in the frontline
    trenches

They took him down stone steps
To a cellar thick with rats.
The guard gave him a cigarette
And slapped it out of his mouth.

Moral. Don't ever knock off a cop.
Ethel, looking like a movie queen,
Descended on his cell in a mink coat.
When they fitted the black cap over his head
He knew that he'd never have another chance to be
    president.

The Horses of Yilderin

The great horses of Yilderin!
O the horses of that wild forest!

Flame . . .
Marble . . .
O the blood (the flowing of their proud necks)
    and the tiny hoofs of steel . . .
Flowers of sweat
    on their mating flanks. Awake!
To the running!
To the end of the world!

O hear the terrible horses of Yilderin!
Nobody will sleep in the wood
None shall escape their heat

Call them!
They will kill.

The Origin of Baseball

Someone had been walking in and out
Of the world without coming
To much decision about anything.
The sun seemed too hot most of the time.
There weren't enough birds around
And the hills had a silly look

When he got on top of one.
The girls in heaven, however, thought
Nothing of asking to see his watch
Like you would want someone to tell
A joke—"Time," they'd say, "what's
That mean—time?", laughing with the edges
Of their white mouths, like a flutter of paper
In a madhouse. And he'd stumble over
General Sherman or Elizabeth B.
Browning, muttering, "Can't you keep
Your big wings out of the aisle?" But down
Again, there'd be millions of people without
Enough to eat and men with guns just
Standing there shooting each other.

So he wanted to throw something
And he picked up a baseball.

The Lions of Fire Shall Have Their Hunting

The lions of fire
Shall have their hunting in this black land

Their teeth shall tear at your soft throats
Their claws kill

O the lions of fire shall awake
And the valleys steam with their fury

Because you are sick with the dirt of your money
Because you are pigs rooting in the swill of your war
Because you are mean and sly and full of the pus of your
          pious murder
Because you have turned your faces from God
Because you have spread your filth everywhere

O the lions of fire
Wait in the crawling shadows of your world
And their terrible eyes are watching you

Lonesome Boy Blues

Oh nobody's a long time
Nowhere's a big pocket
To put little
Pieces of nice things that

Have never really happened

To anyone except
Those people who were lucky enough
Not to get born
Oh lonesome's a bad place

To get crowded into

With only
Yourself riding back and forth
On
A blind white horse
Along an empty road meeting
All your
Pals face to face

Nobody's a long time

HYAM PLUTZIK

(1911–1962)

The Airman Who Flew Over Shakespeare's England

A nation of hayricks spotting the green solace
    Of grass,
And thrones of thatch ruling a yellow kingdom
    Of barley.

In the green lands, the white nation of sheep.
    And the woodlands,
Red, the delicate tribes of roebuck, doe
    And fawn.

A senate of steeples guarding the slaty and gabled
    Shires,
While aloof the elder houses hold a secret
    Sceptre.

To the north, a wall touching two stone-grey reaches
    Of water;
A circle of stones; then to the south a chalk-white
    Stallion.

To the north, the wireless towers upon the cliff.
    Southward
The powerhouse, and monstrous constellations
    Of cities.

To the north, the pilgrims along the holy roads
    To Walsingham,
And southward, the road to Shottery, shining
    With daisies.

Over the castle of Warwick frightened birds
    Are fleeing,
And on the bridge, faces upturned to a roaring
    Falcon.

Winter, Never Mind Where

The illusion is one of flatness: the sky
Has no depth, is a sheet of tin
Upon which the blackened branches and twigs
Are corroded, burnt in
By a strong acid:

Hang there, outside the squares of pane—
Work of a gruff but extraordinary artist,
Who has done good things in pastels too,
In summer scenes, leaf-stuff
And the placid

Nuances of snow.
Since, as we know,
Genius is superior to praise or blame,
He will not mind if I suggest:
"Fewer cold subjects please (they do not please!).
Really, your leafy stuff, Sir, is best."

For T.S.E. Only

You called me a name on such and such a day—
Do you remember?—you were speaking of Bleistein our
    brother,
The barbarian with the black cigar, and the pockets
Ringing with cash, and the eyes seeking Jerusalem,
Knowing they have been tricked. Come, brother Thomas,
We three must weep together for our exile.

I see the hunted look, the protestation,
The desperate seeking, the reticence and the brashness
Of the giver of laws to the worshippers of calves.
At times you speak as if the words were walls,
But your walls fell with mine to the torch of a Titus.
Come, let us weep together for our exile.

We two, no doubt, could accommodate ourselves:
We've both read Dante and we both dislike Chicago,
And both, you see, can be brutal—but you must bow down
To our brother Bleistein here, with the unaesthetic
Cigar and the somber look. Come, do so quickly,
For we must weep together for our exile.

O you may enwomb yourself in words or the Word
(The Word is a good refuge for people too proud
To swallow the milk of the mild Jesus' teaching),
Or a garden in Hampshire with a magic bird, or an old
Quotation from the Reverend Andrewes, yet someone or
          something
(Let us pause to weep together for our exile)

Will stick a needle in your balloon, Thomas.
Is it the shape that you saw upon the stair?
The four knights clanking toward the altar? the hidden
Card in the deck? the sinister man from Nippon?
The hordes on the eastern horizon? Come, brother Burbank,
And let us weep together for our exile.

In the time of sweet sighing you wept bitterly,
And now in the time of weeping you cannot weep.
Will you wait for the peace of the sailor with pearly bones?
Where is the refuge you thought you would find on the island
Where each man lives in his castle? O brother Thomas,
Come let us weep together for our exile.

You drew us first by your scorn, first by your wit;
Later for your own eloquent suffering.
We loved you first for the wicked things you wrote
Of those you acknowledged infinitely gentle.
Wit is the sin that you must expiate.
Bow down to them, and let us weep for our exile.

I see your words wrung out in pain, but never
The true compassion for creatures with you, that Dante
Knew in his nine hells. O eagle! master!
The eagle's ways of pride and scorn will not save

Though the voice cries loud in humility. Thomas, Thomas,
Come, let us pray together for our exile.

You, hypocrite lecteur! mon semblable! mon frère!

As the Great Horse Rots on the Hill

As the great horse rots on the hill
    till the stars wink through his ribs;
As the genera of horses become silent,
    the thunder of the hooves receding in the silence;
As the tree shrivels in the wind of time,
    as the wind Time dries the locust tree—
Thus you prepare the future for me and my loved ones.

I have been in many towns and seen innumerable houses,
    also rocks, trees, people, stars and insects.
Thieves, like ants, are making off with them,
    taking them to your old ant-hill.
Thus you prepare the future for me and my loved ones.

What spider made the machine of many threads?

The threads run
    from time's instants to all the atoms of the universe.
In each instant a wheel turns in your head, threads go taut,
    and one of a quintillion atoms is transmuted.
Thus you prepare the future for me and my loved ones.

I observe the ordained explosions on the paper as I write,
The pinpoints of flame in the wood on the table, and on the
    wall
(Like a battlefield at night, or a field where fireflies flicker).
My hand, too, scintillates like a strange fish;
Fires punctuate the faces on the road;
A pox, a fever, burns in the tissues of the hills.
Thus you prepare the future for me and my loved ones.

As the great horse is transmuted on the hill
Till the stars wink through his skull;
As the stars become husk and radiance;
As the locust tree is changed by the wind Time;
As the wind Time too will lapse, will blow from another
　　quarter—
Thus you prepare the future for me and my loved ones.

ANNE PORTER

(b. 1911)

Consider the Lilies of the Sea

Their salt wet life erased, eroded, only
The shells of snails lie on the sand,
Their color darkens toward the whorl's conclusion,
The center is nearly black. Even the fragments
Faithfully observe their tribal custom
Of involution; the motionless whirlpool
Is clearly written on the broken shield.

The two joined petals of a small
Tooth-white clamshell stand ajar, and mimic
The opening of wings or of a song-book;
Leaves that a minute and obscure
Death sprung open in a depth of sea;
Held in one's hand, they still present
The light obedient gesture that let go of time.

And close to these frail, scattered, and abandoned
Carvings which were the armor and the art
Of dark blind jellies that the fish have eaten,
The big Atlantic cumulates and pours,
Flashes, is felled, and streaks among the pebbles
With wildfire foam.

Winter Twilight

On a clear winter's evening
The crescent moon

And the round squirrels' nest
In the bare oak

Are equal planets.

TENNESSEE WILLIAMS

(1911–1983)

The Beanstalk Country

You know how the mad come into a room,
too boldly,
their eyes exploding on the air like roses,
their entrances from space we never entered.
They're always attended by someone small and friendly
who goes between their awful world and ours
as though explaining but really only smiling,
a snowy gull that dips above a wreck.

They see not us, nor any Sunday caller
among the geraniums and wicker chairs,
for they are Jacks who climb the beanstalk country,
a place of hammers and tremendous beams,
compared to which the glassed solarium
in which we rise to greet them has no light.

The news we bring them, common, reassuring,
drenched with the cheerful idiocy of noon,
cannot compete with what they have to tell
of what they saw through cracks in the ogre's oven.

And we draw back. The snowy someone says,
Don't mind their talk, they are disturbed today!

JOHN CAGE

(1912–1992)

2 Pages, 122 Words on Music and Dance

To obtain the value
of a sound, a movement,
measure from zero. (Pay
attention to what it is,   A bird flies.
just as it is.)

Slavery is abolished.

the woods

A sound has no legs to stand on.

The world is teeming: anything can
happen.

sound   movement

Points in   Activities which are different
time, in   love   happen in a time which is a space
space   mirth   are each central, original.
               the heroic
               wonder
The emotions   tranquillity are in the audience.
               fear
               anger   The telephone rings.
               sorrow   Each person is in the best seat.
               disgust

Is there a glass of water?   War begins at any moment.

                              Each now is the time, the space.
          lights

                inaction?
                                        Are eyes open?

                Where the bird flies, fly.   ears?

from
Composition in Retrospect

you can't be serIous she said
we were driNking
a recorD
was bEing played
noT
in thE place
wheRe we were
but in another rooM
I had
fouNd it interesting
And had asked
what musiC it was
not to supplY

a partIcular photograph
but to thiNk
of materials that woulD
makE
iT
possiblE
foR
soMeone else
to make hIs
owN
A
Camera
it was necessarY

for davId tudor
somethiNg
a puzzle that he woulD
solvE
Taking
as a bEginning
what was impossible to measuRe
and then returning what he could to Mystery
It was
while teachiNg
A
Class
at wesleYan

that I thought
of Number 11
i haD
bEen explaining
variaTions
onE
suddenly Realized
that two notations on the saMe
pIece of paper
automatically briNg
About relationship
my Composing
is actuallY unnecessary

musIc
Never stops it is we who turn away
again the worlD around
silEnce
sounds are only bubbles on iTs
surfacE
they buRst to disappear (thoreau)
when we Make
musIc
we merely make somethiNg
thAt
Can
more naturallY be heard than seen or touched

that makes It possible
to pay atteNtion
        to Daily work or play
as bEing
noT
what wE think it is
but ouR goal
all that's needed is a fraMe
a change of mental attItude
amplificatioN
                wAiting for a bus
we're present at a Concert
            suddenlY we stand on a work of art the
                                        pavement

musIc
    Never stops it is we who turn away
i haD
as bEing
noT
surfacE
foR
all that's needed is a fraMe
            It was
amplificatioN
        wAiting for a bus
    my Composing
not to supplY

WILLIAM EVERSON

(1912–1994)

Muscat Pruning

All these dormant fields are held beneath the fog.
The scraggy vines, the broken weeds, the cold moist ground
Have known it now for days.
My fingers are half-numbed around the handles of the shears,
But I have other thoughts.
There is a flicker swooping from the grove on scalloped
    wings,
His harsh cry widening through the fog.
After his call the silence holds the drip-sound of the trees,
Muffling the hushed beat under the mist.
Over the field the noise of other pruners
Moves me to my work.
I have a hundred vines to cut before the dark.

Tor House

Now that I have seen Tor House,
And crouched among the sea-gnawed granite under the
    wind's throat,
Gazing against the roll of the western rim,
I know that I can turn back to my inland town
And find the flame of this blunt headland
Burning beneath the dark beat of my blood.

For I have stood where he has stood,
And seen the same gaunt gulls,
And all the tide come pitching in from Lobos Point
To shatter on this coast.
In going I shall bear the feel of his harsh stone,
The sight of sea-wet wings,

And need no souvenir to rub my memory clean.
There is no keener touchstone I can take
Than my one glimpse of Falcon Tower toothing the Carmel
    sky.

Rainy Easter

Rain: and over the thorned, cliff-eaten,
Ridge-broken hem of the east
Dawn slits its murky eye.
Two thousand years. And the Tomb-breaker
Rose from his nightlong ruin,
Up from the raveling darkness,
Rose out of dissolution,
Heaved off that sealing stone, looked out,
Looks out. The faithful follow.
This day the neighboring churches
Clang up the summons. The faithful rise,
Slosh through the drench to the steep ascent.
Eight days back spring foundered,
Shook off the wintry hand, came on,
Comes on, under the downpour,
Splitting its blind-eyed buds.

A Canticle to the Waterbirds

Written for the Feast of Saint Francis of Asissi, 1950

Clack your beaks you cormorants and kittiwakes,
North on those rock-croppings finger-jutted into the rough
    Pacific surge;
You migratory terns and pipers who leave but the temporal
    clawtrack written on sandbars there of your presence;
Grebes and pelicans; you comber-picking scoters and you
    shorelong gulls;
All you keepers of the coastline north of here to the
    Mendocino beaches;

All you beyond upon the cliff-face thwarting the surf at
    Hecate Head;
Hovering the under-surge where the cold Columbia grapples
    at the bar;
North yet to the Sound, whose islands float like a sown flurry
    of chips upon the sea:
Break wide your harsh and salt-encrusted beaks unmade for
    song
And say a praise up to the Lord.

And you freshwater egrets east in the flooded marshlands
    skirting the sea-level rivers, white one-legged watchers of
    shallows;
Broad-headed kingfishers minnow-hunting from willow stems
    on meandering valley sloughs;
You too, you herons, blue and supple-throated, stately, taking
    the air majestical in the sunflooded San Joaquin,
Grading down on your belted wings from the upper lights of
    sunset,
Mating over the willow clumps or where the flatwater rice
    fields shimmer;
You killdeer, high night-criers, far in the moon-suffusion sky;
Bitterns, sand-waders, all shore-walkers, all roost-keepers,
Populates of the 'dobe cliffs of the Sacramento:
Open your water-dartling beaks,
And make a praise up to the Lord.

For you hold the heart of His mighty fastnesses,
And shape the life of His indeterminate realms.
You are everywhere on the lonesome shores of His wide
    creation.
You keep seclusion where no man may go, giving Him praise;
Nor may a woman come to lift like your cleaving flight her
    clear contralto song
To honor the spindrift gifts of His soft abundance.
You sanctify His hermitage rocks where no holy priest may
    kneel to adore, nor holy nun assist;
And where his true communion-keepers are not enabled to
    enter.

And well may you say His praises, birds, for your ways
Are verved with the secret skills of His inclinations,
And your habits plaited and rare with the subdued
    elaboration of his intricate craft;
Your days intent with the direct astuteness needful for His
    outworking,
And your nights alive with the dense repose of His infinite
    sleep.
You are His secretive charges and you serve His secretive
    ends,
In His clouded mist-conditioned stations, in His murk,
Obscure in your matted nestings, immured in His limitless
    ranges.
He makes you penetrate through dark interstitial joinings of
    His thicketed kingdoms,
And keep your concourse in the deeps of His shadowed
    world.

Your ways are wild but earnest, your manners grave,
Your customs carefully schooled to the note of His serious
    mien.
You hold the prime condition of His clean creating,
And the swift compliance with which you serve His minor
    means
Speaks of the constancy with which you hold Him.
For what is your high flight forever going home to your first
    beginnings,
But such a testament to your devotion?
You hold His outstretched world beneath your wings, and
    mount upon His storms,
And keep your sheer wind-lidded sight upon the vast
    perspectives of His mazy latitudes.

But mostly it is your way you bear existence wholly within the
    context of His utter will and are untroubled.
Day upon day you do not reckon, nor scrutinize tomorrow,
    nor multiply the nightfalls with a rash concern,
But rather assume each instant as warrant sufficient of His
    final seal.

Wholly in Providence you spring, and when you die you look
    on death in clarity unflinched,
Go down, a clutch of feather ragged upon the brush;
Or drop on water where you briefly lived, found food,
And now yourselves made food for His deep current-keeping
    fish, and then are gone:
Is left but the pinion-feather spinning a bit on the uproil
Where lately the dorsal cut clear air.

You leave a silence. And this for you suffices, who are not of
    the ceremonials of man,
And hence are not made sad to now forgo them.
Yours is of another order of being, and wholly it compels.
But may you, birds, utterly seized in God's supremacy,
Austerely living under his austere eye—
Yet may you teach a man a necessary thing to know,
Which has to do of the strict conformity that creaturehood
    entails,
And constitutes the prime commitment all things share.
For God has given you the imponderable grace to *be* His
    verification,
Outside the mulled incertitude of our forensic choices;
That you, our lessers in the rich hegemony of Being,
May serve as testament to what a creature is,
And what creation owes.

Curlews, stilts and scissortails, beachcomber gulls,
Wave-haunters, shore-keepers, rockhead-holders, all cape-top
    vigilantes,
Now give God praise.
Send up the strict articulation of your throats,
And say His name.

Gale at Dawn

Landwind: a gale at dawn scooping down from the hills.
It pours west to the water, hits the foam
Like a counterattack repulsing a beach landing.

But the brute surf stalks in, stupendous breakers
Born out at sea, inexorably arriving.

The landwind, honing them, combs back their furls,
And the low winter light, shining flatly through,
Wreathes the powerful, doomed shoulders,
Gives each lion wave its rainbow mane,
Hackled with gold.

But the wind,
Like a holy terror, rips back those brows.
Plunged in the hollow of each ponderous breast
It explodes into fire.

O wind and water! Like a gale at dawn
Man hits the wave of woman. She arches her throat
For the stab of his lips. Over the wallowing blood
His sudden face divides her life; his terrible gift
Wreathes her with flame.

At dusk
All falls still. The air, curiously spent,
Hangs inert.

We savor salt.

In the immense quietude,
Under the nimbus of sunset, we find by the water
The surf-quenched scoter, the depth-disheveled grebe.

Stone Face Falls

Sheer naked rock. From the high cliff-cut
Straight falling water. Caught halfway down in a stone socket
It checks, boils over, then widens as it drops,
Snaking dreamily into the rockpool below.
Many months back it roared in flood;
Now, in the grip of drought, Big Creek the brawler,
Tamed and gentled, takes this pitch like a gliding dancer,
A shimmering sleeve against dark waterstains,
Storm-trek of the past.

We have come,
The two of us, in the white heat of noon,
To bathe at the fall-foot, a lambent pool
Under the salmon-stopping cliff.
We are struck by silence, the reduction of force,
Recalling those thunderous torrents of the past,
When the wild cataract drove everything before it,
Generating in its plunge a saturating gale,
Sopping a man a hundred feet below,
Drenched to the eyes in stinging spume.
But now, in the drought, the diaphanous film
Ripples down the rock, maidenly, a silken
Scarf, the veil of a bride, as virginal
And as lovely.

Over our heads the great stone face
Juts from the gorge, a chief's visage hewn in raw granite,
Staring north, gazing down the long south-trek of his people,
Ten thousand years from the Bering Strait.
And the mystery keeps, the indomitable spirit

Guarding the secret where the water pulses,
The source, the slowed rhythm at the timeless center,
The heartbeat of earth.

I lower my gaze.
You are standing under the waterfall, nude, your body
An ivory wand against the seamed granite.

It is gleaming there, wreathed in water,
Breasts erect. The woman belly
And the female thighs
Shine in a shimmering ripple of lace,
The circling stream.

I move to meet you.

Suddenly a kingfisher swoops between.
In midflight he sees us, veers sharply,
Utters a sudden electrifying screech,
The ineluctable tension cruxed at the heart of things
Splitting his beak, the mystery
Out of which life springs and from which it passes.
Three times he circles, skirling his fierce
Importunate cry, then climbs the thermal,
The lazy updraft transcending the falls,
And disappears up the canyon.

You hold out your arms.

Dropping my clothes
I enter the pool,
Wade the ripple to where you stand.

It is the longest walk—
Out of the glacial
Past, through the pulsing present,
Into the clenched
Future—man to woman
Through time-dark waters.

Far ahead,
Beyond the stone face of the falls,
The cry of the kingfisher
Pierces the noon.

JEAN GARRIGUE

(1912–1972)

Song in Sligo

I had a bear that danced,
A monkey on a stick,
A dog that begged,
A cat that moused,
And, slouching by a ditch,
A rook in black of silk.
I had those birds that rode
Upon the levels of the cove
At late long twilight in the north
When the brand of sun still burned
Above the shoddy bridges of the Garavogue.
I had a boat that beat
Up levels of the reed-flagged shore
And rock-grained, rack-ruined battlements.
I had a boat and traveled with the birds
That flew against me in the breath of winds,
To each bend of the river its own mews
Of samite-backed and sable-legged young swans
Who winter from the Bay of Rosses here.
I had an island for my own one want,
A ring of prophecy and scent,
Where trees were sloped upon a moss of turf,
One ruined wall that I could sit against
And dip a ragged net to catch a fish
Of rainbowed armor in the scales of night.
I had a love who spoke to me of wars.
It was the summer of the fires.
Blackout by desolating energy.
You silken tatters of the sliding flow,
I had your voices and your leafy pools,
I have these poisons we must choose.

The Grand Canyon

Where is the restaurant cat?
I am lonely under the fluorescent light
as a cook waddles in her smoky region visible through an
    open arch
and someone is pounding, pounding
whatever it is that is being pounded
and a waitress cracks with the cowboys lined up at the
    counter
lumberjacked, weathered and bony
intimates, I would guess, of the Canyon,
like the raven that flies, scouting above it,
of the hooked face and the almost flat sleek wings.

Where is my cat? I am lonely,
knocked out, stunned-sleepy,
knocked out by the terraced massed faces
of the brute Sublime,
color inflamed,
when I came to the edge and looked over:
violaceous, vermillion
great frontal reefs, buttes,
cliffs of rufous and ocher angles,
promontories, projections, jutments, outjuttings
and gnarled mirlitons, so it seemed,
twisting up out of depth beyond depth
gnarled like the juniper tree
rachitic with wind I hung on to
as the raven's wing, glassy in the light of its black,
slid over me

there at the edge of this maw, gash
deepest in the world that a river has made
through an upwarp in the earth's crust,
thickets of tens of thousands of gorges eaten out
by freezing and thawing, tempests, waterspouts,
squalls and falls of the river
with its boulders, pebbles, silt and sand sawing down
through the great cake of geologic time,

eight layers laid bare,
the total effect creating what geometrical effect
in a rocky silence so clear
a bird's voice, even a boy's
is spunged out, sucked up by this stillness
stinging, overpowering the ear,
pure condition of the original echoing soundlessness
this voluminous wrung resonance
welling up out of the handiwork
of the demiurge wrestling down there
in an infinity of imperceptible events
some ten million years,

ages blanching to think of,
taking the switchback trail,
slipping and sliding,
forever slantwise descending
into new confrontations of parapets,
chimneys, mantels, segments of angles,
modelings of rock of slacknesses and accidental tensions
combined with the effects of its weight—
the total effect never total for never can you see it all, not
        even guess
at mazes of the proliferation,
and the river will not be visible
except from a driven angle,
the snaken twists of its rapids looking petrified, frozen
from the distance of a deep mile:

somebody saying a mountain could be plucked up by its
        roots
and dropped head-first down there and it wouldn't dam up
        the river
so that the waters would run over

and that the Washington Monument could be kept out of the
        rain
under one overhanging of an otherwise vertical red wall
where the gold of the light on that chaos of creases nervously
        darts

like the violet-green swallow stitching its leaps and arcs
over the gliding raven,

over the camber of columns, tawny rotundas of ruins
writhed, mottled, crested with shells,
escarpments
downbeaten by frost and rain,
parallel rangings of
rostrums, pulpits and lecterns,
and the mad Tiberius arches groining
cave holes on cave holes in the same wall of limestone, red
from the ironstone drippings,

Aztec pyramidal temples rising in hundreds of steps
to the summit of the seemed shrine
curtained, girdled with snakes and necklaces of hearts,
wet with sacrificial blood,

rusticated building blocks jutting out in warlike ramifications
        of forts,
stockades of black frosted rock,
towers of the baldness mounting like obelisks,
pyramidal forms from the sands of Egypt,
crags vertiginous, cupolas, alcoves,
amphitheatres, arenas, organ pipes, flutings,
porches of rock, wedges of shadow in perforated rock,

and the gold of the light nervously darting
on the Bright Angel shale, pink with long stripes,
on the lavender blue of the Shinumo Quartzite,
on the deeper rose of the Hakatai shale,
on the blond Coconino sandstone
riddled, it's said, with the trails of sea worms,
on the grey Kaibab limestone
with casts of shark teeth and horn coral imbedded
like the Hermit shale of the topmost formation
with footprints of salamanders, insect wings four inches in
        length
and even a dimple left by a raindrop during some era of
        burning

and hailstorm, torrent and drought,
era on era stacked here,
untold era on era,
as the eye like a long-legged insect on a windowpane
slithers and shudders up and down
the banded and ribboned, ribbed systems of rock,
into and out of shadows,
chromatic world of what glitters like phantoms,
corrugations of scaffoldings appointing to chill
over the continuous surface,
assemblies of aggregations
sand-pocked and pitted,
ridged, wind-serrated,
tawny threshholds in the lying out there of the steeps,
in the drinking up of the stillness
pressed in by the gorged rock
deepening in the light of the motes of beams
under those clouds that like water lilies
enclose within them this silence received
that they graze upon and are gone.

Grenoble Café

At breakfast they are sober, subdued.
It is early. They have not much to say
Or with declamations fit only for whisper
Keep under pressure the steam of their joy.
She listens, usually. It is he who talks,
Surrounding her with the furious smoke
Of his looking that simply feeds,
Perhaps, her slightly traveling-away dreams
That, if you judge from her cheek,
Young and incomparably unbroken,
Are rich with the unknowing knowing
Of what he has said the time before
And with the smiles coming down the corridor
Of how it will be for year on year,
Nights as they'll be in his rough arms.

WOODY GUTHRIE

(1912–1967)

Dust Storm Disaster

On the fourteenth day of April
Of nineteen thirty-five
There struck the worst of dust storms
That ever filled the sky.

You could see that dust storm coming
The cloud looked death-like black
And through our mighty nation
It left a dreadful track.

From Oklahoma City
To the Arizona line
Dakota and Nebraska
To the lazy Rio Grande.

It fell across our city
Like a curtain of black rolled down
We thought it was our judgment
We thought it was our doom.

The radio reported
We listened with alarm
The wild and windy actions
Of this great mysterious storm.

From Albuquerque and Clovis
And all New Mexico
They said it was the blackest
That ever they had saw.

In old Dodge City, Kansas,
The dust had rung their knell,
And a few more comrades sleeping
On top of old Boot Hill.

From Denver, Colorado,
They said it blew so strong,
They thought that they could hold out,
They did not know how long.

Our relatives were huddled
Into their oil-boom shacks,
And the children they were crying
As it whistled through the cracks.

And the family, it was crowded
Into their little room,
They thought the world had ended,
And they thought it was their doom.

The storm took place at sundown,
It lasted through the night,
When we looked out next morning
We saw a terrible sight.

We saw outside our window
Where wheatfields they had grown,
Was now a rippling ocean
Of dust the wind had blown.

It covered up our fences,
It covered up our barns,
It covered up our tractors
In this wild and dusty storm.

We loaded our jalopies
And piled our families in,
We rattled down that highway
To never come back again.

Talking Dust Bowl

Back in nineteen twenty-seven
I had a little farm and I called that heaven.
Well, the price was up and the rain come down
And I hauled my crops all into town.
I got the money, bought clothes and groceries, fed the kids
     and raised a family.

Rain quit and the wind got high,
And a black old dust storm filled the sky,
And I swapped my farm for a Ford machine,
And I poured it full of this gasoline.
And I started, rocking and a-rolling over the mountains out
     towards the old peach bowl.

Way up yonder on a mountain road,
I had a hot motor and a heavy load.
I was going pretty fast, I wasn't even stopping,
A-bouncing up and down like a popcorn popping.
Had a breakdown, a sort of nervous bustdown of some kind.
     There was a fellow there, a mechanic fellow, said it was
     engine trouble.

Way up yonder on a mountain curve,
It was way up yonder in the piney woods,
And I give that rolling Ford a shove,
And I was going to coast as far as I could.
Commenced coasting; picking up speed; was a hairpin turn;
     I . . . didn't make it.

Man alive, I'm a-telling you
The fiddles and the guitars really flew.
That Ford took off like a flying squirrel
And it flew halfway around the world.
Scattered wives and childrens all over the side of that
     mountain.

We got out to the West Coast broke,
So dad gum hungry I thought I'd croak,
And I bummed up a spud or two,
And my wife fixed up a 'tater stew.
We poured the kids full of it.
Mighty thin stew, though; you could read a magazine right
 through it.

Always have figured that if it had been just a little bit thinner
 some of these here politicians could have seen through it.

Vigilante Man

Have you seen that Vigilante Man?
Have you seen that Vigilante Man?
Have you seen that Vigilante Man?
I've been hearing his name all over the land.

Well, what is a Vigilante Man?
Tell me what is a Vigilante Man?
Has he got a club in his hand?
Is that a Vigilante Man?

Rainy night down in the engine house,
Sleeping just as still as a mouse,
Man come along and chased us out in the rain,
Was that a Vigilante Man?

Stormy days we'd pass the time away
Sleeping in some good warm place
A cop come along and we give him a little race,
Say, was that a vigilante man?

Preacher Casey was just a working man,
And he said, unite all us working men,
They killed him in the river, some strange man,
Was that your vigilante man?

Oh, why does a vigilante man
Oh, why does a vigilante man
Carry that sawed off shotgun in his hand?
Would he shoot his brother and sister down?

I rambled around from town to town
I rambled around from town to town
And they herded us around like a wild herd of cattle
Was that your vigilante man?

LIGHTNIN' HOPKINS
(1912–1982)

Death Bells

Sound like I can hear this morning
      them bells ringing all in my ear
Sound like I can hear this morning, baby
      them bells ringing all in my ear
 Yes I know I'm gonna leave on a chariot
 Wonder what kind gonna carry me from here

You know every living creeper
      man, was born to die
Yeah you know every living creeper
       was, lord, was born to die
 Yeah, but when that chariot come for you
 They gonna break, run, and try to hide

Yeah, you know my mama told me
      my papa told me too
She: someday, son, you know that chariot's
       coming after you
 I been wondering
    what kinda chariot
 Oh
  gonna take me away from here
 Yes, you know this life I'm living I been living
 Oh lord, for a great many years

MAY SARTON

(1912–1995)

Moving In

I moved into my house one day
In a downpour of leaves and rain,
"I took possession," as they say,
With solitude for my domain.

At first it was an empty place
Where every room I came to meet
Watched me in silence like a face:
I heard the whisper of my feet.

So huge the absence walking there
Beside me on the yellow floor,
That one fly buzzing on the air
But made the stillness more and more.

What I possessed was all my own,
Yet not to be possessed at all,
And not a house or even hearthstone,
And never any sheltering wall.

There solitude became my task,
No shelter but a grave demand,
And I must answer, never ask,
Taking this bridegroom by the hand.

I moved into my life one day
In a downpour of leaves in flood,
I took possession as they say,
And knew I was alone for good.

The Snow Light

In the snow light,
In the swan light,
In the white-on-white light
Of a winter storm,
My delight and your delight
Kept each other warm.

The next afternoon—
And love gone so soon!—
I met myself alone
In a windless calm,
Silenced at the bone
After the white storm.

What more was to come?
Out from the cocoon,
In the silent room,
Pouring out white light,
Amaryllis bloom
Opened in the night.

The cool petals shone
Like some winter moon
Or shadow of a swan,
Echoing the light
After you were gone
Of our white-on-white.

February Days

Who could tire of the long shadows,
The long shadows of the trees on snow?
Sometimes I stand at the kitchen window
For a timeless time in a long daze
Before these reflected perpendiculars,
Noting how the light has changed,
How tender it is now in February
When the shadows are blue not black.

The crimson cyclamen has opened wide,
A bower of petals drunk on the light,
And in the snow-bright ordered house
I am drowsy as a turtle in winter,
Living on light and shadow
And their changes.

VIRGINIA HAMILTON ADAIR

(b. 1913)

Buckroe, After the Season, 1942

Past the fourth cloverleaf, by dwindling roads
At last we came into the unleashed wind;
The Chesapeake rose to meet us at a dead end
Beyond the carnival wheels and gingerbread.

Forsaken by summer, the wharf. The oil-green waves
Flung yellow foam and sucked at disheveled sand.
Small fish stank in the sun, and nervous droves
Of cloud hastened their shadows over bay and land.

Beyond the NO DUMPING sign in its surf of cans
And the rotting boat with nettles to the rails,
The horse dung garlanded with jeweling flies
And papers blown like a fleet of shipless sails,

We pushed into an overworld of wind and light
Where sky unfettered ran wild from earth to noon,
And the tethered heart broke loose and rose like a kite
From sands that borrowed diamonds from the sun.

We were empty and pure as shells that air-drenched hour,
Heedless as waves that swell at the shore and fall,
Pliant as sea-grass, the rapt inheritors
Of a land without memory, where tide erases all.

Exit Amor

You went out with the turning tide
Throwing a few things overboard:
The bound volumes of our years,
O my dear editor, 1933 to '68,
Promises long kept in sickness and health
A date with Ireland
Barrels of ripe plans
Golden garbage for the gulls
To pick from your wake.

What dark eye smiled from the bore?
What siren sang in the short breeze
Of the ball?
You will never answer me more. Nothing at all.

But forever across the bed you sprawl,
And onto my living heart again, again,
You force the dead weight of that panic and pain
Senseless, impure,
Which you could not contain,
Which no one can explain,
Which I must now endure.

CHARLES HENRI FORD

(b. 1913)

The Fox with the Blue Velvet Band

Going from side to side and from place to place
the radio-policemen in a duplex can
harry the fox with the blue velvet band,
darling of No Street, with the finger-printed face.
The hole of whose heart in which she delves
depends on the number of needles the creature
in a dive known as Dreamland, or Second Nature,
jams in the arm of his other self.
Little red fox with the hooves of spring,
little red rose with the teeth of time,
when winter goes pop and the worm goes bing
your blue velvet band will denote the crime
of the dreamer who left the bud to bloom
in the house on Any Street without a room.

The Overturned Lake

Blue unsolid tongue, if you could talk,
the mountain would supply the brain;
but mountains are mummies: the autobus and train,
manmade worms, disturb their centuries.
Tongue of a deafmute, the lake
shudders, inarticulate.

You are like the mind of a man, too:
surface reflecting the blue day.
the life about you seemingly organized, revolving about you,
you as a center,
but I am concerned in your overthrow:
I should like to pick you up, as if you were a woman of water,

hold you against the light and see your veins flow
with fishes; reveal the animal-flowers that rise
nightlike beneath your eyes.

Noiseless as memory, blind as fear,
lake, I shall make you into a poem,
for I would have you unpredictable as the human body:
I shall equip you with the strength of a dream,
rout you from your blue unconscious bed,
overturn your unconcern,
as the mind is overturned by memory, the heart by dread.

I Wouldn't Put It Past You

And you may not have hair as curly as the alphabet
but if your googoo eyes were a bundle of germs
there'd be an epidemic.
With your greenhorn complexion
and your grasswidow ways
you'd make a butcher kill a granite cow
and weigh the gravel out for hamburger.
I mean you'd start the eskimos stripteasing,
give dummies the shakes,
get flyingcircuses to crawl on their hands and knees.
No I wouldn't put it past you.
Just let somebody set you on the fence,
by gosh foulballs would be annulled
and home-runs the rule.
The weather forecast that overlooked you, baby,
sure better watch out for the next cyclone,
seeing how my uptown's flattened,
and my downtown a-waving in the wind.

ROBERT HAYDEN

(1913–1980)

Those Winter Sundays

Sundays too my father got up early
and put his clothes on in the blueblack cold,
then with cracked hands that ached
from labor in the weekday weather made
banked fires blaze. No one ever thanked him.

I'd wake and hear the cold splintering, breaking.
When the rooms were warm, he'd call,
and slowly I would rise and dress,
fearing the chronic angers of that house,

Speaking indifferently to him,
who had driven out the cold
and polished my good shoes as well.
What did I know, what did I know
of love's austere and lonely offices?

Homage to the Empress of the Blues

Because there was a man somewhere in a candystripe silk
    shirt,
gracile and dangerous as a jaguar and because a woman
    moaned
for him in sixty-watt gloom and mourned him Faithless Love
Twotiming Love Oh Love Oh Careless Aggravating Love,

She came out on the stage in yards of pearls, emerging
    like
a favorite scenic view, flashed her golden smile and sang.

Because grey laths began somewhere to show from
    underneath
torn hurdygurdy lithographs of dollfaced heaven;
and because there were those who feared alarming fists of
    snow
on the door and those who feared the riot-squad of statistics,

    She came out on the stage in ostrich feathers, beaded
        satin,
    and shone that smile on us and sang.

Middle Passage

I

Jesús, Estrella, Esperanza, Mercy:

    Sails flashing to the wind like weapons,
    sharks following the moans the fever and the dying;
    horror the corposant and compass rose.

Middle Passage:
        voyage through death
                to life upon these shores.

    "10 April 1800—
    Blacks rebellious. Crew uneasy. Our linguist says
    their moaning is a prayer for death,
    ours and their own. Some try to starve themselves.
    Lost three this morning leaped with crazy laughter
    to the waiting sharks, sang as they went under."

Desire, Adventure, Tartar, Ann:

    Standing to America, bringing home
    black gold, black ivory, black seed.

Deep in the festering hold thy father lies,
of his bones New England pews are made,
those are altar lights that were his eyes.

Jesus   Saviour   Pilot   Me
Over   Life's   Tempestuous   Sea

We pray that Thou wilt grant, O Lord,
safe passage to our vessels bringing
heathen souls unto Thy chastening.

Jesus   Saviour

    "8 bells. I cannot sleep, for I am sick
with fear, but writing eases fear a little
since still my eyes can see these words take shape
upon the page & so I write, as one
would turn to exorcism. 4 days scudding,
but now the sea is calm again. Misfortune
follows in our wake like sharks (our grinning
tutelary gods). Which one of us
has killed an albatross? A plague among
our blacks—Ophthalmia: blindness—& we
have jettisoned the blind to no avail.
It spreads, the terrifying sickness spreads.
Its claws have scratched sight from the Capt.'s eyes
& there is blindness in the fo'c'sle
& we must sail 3 weeks before we come
to port."

    What port awaits us, Davy Jones'
or home? I've heard of slavers drifting, drifting,
playthings of wind and storm and chance, their crews
gone blind, the jungle hatred
crawling up on deck.

Thou   Who   Walked   On   Galilee

"Deponent further sayeth *The Bella J*
left the Guinea Coast
with cargo of five hundred blacks and odd
for the barracoons of Florida:

"That there was hardly room 'tween-decks for half
the sweltering cattle stowed spoon-fashion there;
that some went mad of thirst and tore their flesh
and sucked the blood:

"That Crew and Captain lusted with the comeliest
of the savage girls kept naked in the cabins;
that there was one they called The Guinea Rose
and they cast lots and fought to lie with her:

"That when the Bo's'n piped all hands, the flames
spreading from starboard already were beyond
control, the negroes howling and their chains
entangled with the flames:

"That the burning blacks could not be reached,
that the Crew abandoned ship,
leaving their shrieking negresses behind,
that the Captain perished drunken with the wenches:

"Further Deponent sayeth not."

Pilot   Oh   Pilot   Me

II

Aye, lad, and I have seen those factories,
Gambia, Rio Pongo, Calabar;
have watched the artful mongos baiting traps
of war wherein the victor and the vanquished

Were caught as prizes for our barracoons.
Have seen the nigger kings whose vanity
and greed turned wild black hides of Fellatah,
Mandingo, Ibo, Kru to gold for us.

And there was one—King Anthracite we named him—
fetish face beneath French parasols
of brass and orange velvet, impudent mouth
whose cups were carven skulls of enemies:

He'd honor us with drum and feast and conjo
and palm-oil-glistening wenches deft in love,
and for tin crowns that shone with paste,
red calico and German-silver trinkets

Would have the drums talk war and send
his warriors to burn the sleeping villages
and kill the sick and old and lead the young
in coffles to our factories.

Twenty years a trader, twenty years,
for there was wealth aplenty to be harvested
from those black fields, and I'd be trading still
but for the fevers melting down my bones.

III

Shuttles in the rocking loom of history,
the dark ships move, the dark ships move,
their bright ironical names
like jests of kindness on a murderer's mouth;
plough through thrashing glister toward
fata morgana's lucent melting shore,
weave toward New World littorals that are
mirage and myth and actual shore.

Voyage through death,
                              voyage whose chartings are unlove.

A charnel stench, effluvium of living death
spreads outward from the hold,
where the living and the dead, the horribly dying,
lie interlocked, lie foul with blood and excrement.

Deep in the festering hold thy father lies,
the corpse of mercy rots with him,
rats eat love's rotten gelid eyes.

But, oh, the living look at you
with human eyes whose suffering accuses you,
whose hatred reaches through the swill of dark
to strike you like a leper's claw.

You cannot stare that hatred down
or chain the fear that stalks the watches
and breathes on you its fetid scorching breath;
cannot kill the deep immortal human wish,
the timeless will.

"But for the storm that flung up barriers
of wind and wave, *The Amistad*, señores,
would have reached the port of Príncipe in two,
three days at most; but for the storm we should
have been prepared for what befell.
Swift as the puma's leap it came. There was
that interval of moonless calm filled only
with the water's and the rigging's usual sounds,
then sudden movement, blows and snarling cries
and they had fallen on us with machete
and marlinspike. It was as though the very
air, the night itself were striking us.
Exhausted by the rigors of the storm,
we were no match for them. Our men went down
before the murderous Africans. Our loyal
Celestino ran from below with gun
and lantern and I saw, before the cane-
knife's wounding flash, Cinquez,
that surly brute who calls himself a prince,
directing, urging on the ghastly work.
He hacked the poor mulatto down, and then
he turned on me. The decks were slippery
when daylight finally came. It sickens me
to think of what I saw, of how these apes
threw overboard the butchered bodies of

our men, true Christians all, like so much jetsam.
Enough, enough. The rest is quickly told:
Cinquez was forced to spare the two of us
you see to steer the ship to Africa,
and we like phantoms doomed to rove the sea
voyaged east by day and west by night,
deceiving them, hoping for rescue,
prisoners on our own vessel, till
at length we drifted to the shores of this
your land, America, where we were freed
from our unspeakable misery. Now we
demand, good sirs, the extradition of
Cinquez and his accomplices to La
Havana. And it distresses us to know
there are so many here who seem inclined
to justify the mutiny of these blacks.
We find it paradoxical indeed
that you whose wealth, whose tree of liberty
are rooted in the labor of your slaves
should suffer the august John Quincy Adams
to speak with so much passion of the right
of chattel slaves to kill their lawful masters
and with his Roman rhetoric weave a hero's
garland for Cinquez. I tell you that
we are determined to return to Cuba
with our slaves and there see justice done.
          Cinquez—
or let us say 'the Prince'—Cinquez shall die."

The deep immortal human wish,
the timeless will:

          Cinquez its deathless primaveral image,
          life that transfigures many lives.

Voyage through death
                    to life upon these shores.

Runagate Runagate

I.

Runs falls rises stumbles on from darkness into darkness
and the darkness thicketed with shapes of terror
and the hunters pursuing and the hounds pursuing
and the night cold and the night long and the river
to cross and the jack-muh-lanterns beckoning beckoning
and blackness ahead and when shall I reach that somewhere
morning and keep on going and never turn back and keep on
    going
           Runagate
                    Runagate
                            Runagate

Many thousands rise and go
many thousands crossing over
                    O mythic North
                    O star-shaped yonder Bible city

Some go weeping and some rejoicing
some in coffins and some in carriages
some in silks and some in shackles

        Rise and go or fare you well

No more auction block for me
no more driver's lash for me

        If you see my Pompey, 30 yrs of age,
        new breeches, plain stockings, negro shoes;
        if you see my Anna, likely young mulatto
        branded E on the right cheek, R on the left,
        catch them if you can and notify subscriber.
        Catch them if you can, but it won't be easy.
        They'll dart underground when you try to catch them,
        plunge into quicksand, whirlpools, mazes,
        turn into scorpions when you try to catch them.

And before I'll be a slave
I'll be buried in my grave

North star and bonanza gold
I'm bound for the freedom, freedom-bound
and oh Susyanna don't you cry for me

Runagate

Runagate

II.

Rises from their anguish and their power,

Harriet Tubman,

woman of earth, whipscarred,
a summoning, a shining

Mean to be free

And this was the way of it, brethren brethren,
way we journeyed from Can't to Can.
Moon so bright and no place to hide,
the cry up and the patterollers riding,
hound dogs belling in bladed air.
And fear starts a-murbling, Never make it,
we'll never make it. *Hush that now,*
and she's turned upon us, levelled pistol
glinting in the moonlight:
Dead folks can't jaybird-talk, she says;
you keep on going now or die, she says.

Wanted   Harriet Tubman   alias The General
alias Moses   Stealer of Slaves

In league with Garrison   Alcott   Emerson
Garrett   Douglass   Thoreau   John Brown

Armed and known to be Dangerous

Wanted   Reward   Dead or Alive

    Tell me, Ezekiel, oh tell me do you see
    mailed Jehovah coming to deliver me?

Hoot-owl calling in the ghosted air,
five times calling to the hants in the air.
Shadow of a face in the scary leaves,
shadow of a voice in the talking leaves:

    Come ride-a my train

    Oh that train, ghost-story train
    through swamp and savanna movering movering,
    over trestles of dew, through caves of the wish,
    Midnight Special on a sabre track movering movering,
    first stop Mercy and the last Hallelujah.

    Come ride-a my train

      Mean mean mean to be free.

Soledad

(And I, I am no longer of that world)

Naked, he lies in the blinded room
chainsmoking, cradled by drugs, by jazz
as never by any lover's cradling flesh.

Miles Davis coolly blows for him:
O pena negra, sensual Flamenco blues;
the red clay foxfire voice of Lady Day

(lady of the pure black magnolias)
sobsings her sorrow and loss and fare you well,
dryweeps the pain his treacherous jailers

have released him from for awhile.
His fears and his unfinished self
await him down in the anywhere streets.

He hides on the dark side of the moon,
takes refuge in a stained-glass cell,
flies to a clockless country of crystal.

Only the ghost of Lady Day knows where
he is. Only the music. And he swings
oh swings: beyond complete immortal now.

The Night-Blooming Cereus

And so for nights
we waited, hoping to see
the heavy bud
        break into flower.

On its neck-like tube
hooking down from the edge
of the leaf-branch
        nearly to the floor,

the bud packed
tight with its miracle swayed
stiffly on breaths
        of air, moved

as though impelled
by stirrings within itself.
It repelled as much
        as it fascinated me

sometimes—snake,
eyeless bird head,
beak that would gape
        with grotesque life-squawk.

But you, my dear,
conceded less to the bizarre
than to the imminence
          of bloom. Yet we agreed

     we ought
to celebrate the blossom,
paint ourselves, dance
          in honor of

     archaic mysteries
when it appeared. Meanwhile
we waited, aware
          of rigorous design.

     Backster's
polygraph, I thought,
would have shown
          (as clearly as it had

     a philodendron's
fear) tribal sentience
in the cactus, focused
          energy of will.

     That belling of
tropic perfume—that
signalling
          not meant for us;

     the darkness
cloyed with summoning
fragrance. We dropped
          trivial tasks

     and marvelling
beheld at last the achieved
flower. Its moonlight
          petals were

    still unfold-
ing, the spike fringe of the outer
perianth recessing
    as we watched.

    Lunar presence,
foredoomed, already dying,
it charged the room
    with plangency

    older than human
cries, ancient as prayers
invoking Osiris, Krishna,
    Tezcátlipóca.

    We spoke
in whispers when
we spoke
    at all . . .

Ice Storm

Unable to sleep, or pray, I stand
by the window looking out
at moonstruck trees a December storm
has bowed with ice.

Maple and mountain ash bend
under its glassy weight,
their cracked branches falling upon
the frozen snow.

The trees themselves, as in winters past,
will survive their burdening,
broken thrive. And am I less to You,
my God, than they?

Bone-Flower Elegy

In the dream I enter the house
    wander vast rooms that are
       catacombs midnight subway
          cavernous ruined movie-palace
       where presences in vulture masks
         play scenes of erotic violence
            on a scaffold stage   I want
      to stay and watch but know somehow
I must not linger and come to the funeral
      chamber   in its icy nonlight see
       a naked corpse
          turning with sensual movements
         on its coffin-bed
      I have wept for you many times
      I whisper but shrink from the arms
        that would embrace me
         and treading water reach
arched portals opening on a desert
groves of enormous nameless flowers
      twist up from firegold sand
    skull flowers flowers of sawtooth bone
      their leaves and petals interlock
         caging me for you beastangel
        raging toward me
       angelbeast shining come
          to rend me and redeem

JOHN FREDERICK NIMS

(1913–1999)

The Evergreen

a.

Under this stone, what lies?
    A little boy's thistledown body.
How, on so light a child
    Gravel hefted and hurled?
Light? As a flower entwined
    In our shining arms. Heavy
Laid in this scale—it set
    Wailing the chains of the world.

b.

What did you say? We said:
    Bedtime, dear, forever.
Time to put out the light.
    Time for the eyes to close.
What did he do? He lay
    In a crazyquilt of fever.
His hands were already like grasses.
    His cheek already a rose.

c.

How was that year? His voice.
    Over sun on the rug, slow-turning,
Hung like a seabird lost the
    Lorn and bodiless cry.
Haunting the house. *And then?*
    I remember then. One morning
Silence like knives in the ear.
    A bird gone over the sea.

d.

What of his eyes? Dark glow
    Furling the world's great surface.
Bubbles among tree lights;
    Bubbles of ferny dew.
And his kiss? On our cheek at evening
    Vintage: a fine bursting.
This, and never dreamed his
    Span was a bubble too?

e.

Little head, little head,
    Frail in the air, gold aster—
Why did the great king stoop
    And smoothe those ringlets down?
For a tinsel party-hat?
    It was Christmas then, remember?
I remember grown men wept
    And couldn't lift that crown.

f.

Mother, these tears and tears?
    The better to see you, darling.
Mother, your golden glasses—
    Have a sorry fault,
Being made for things, dear,
    Mostly: carts and marbles.
Mothers wear, for children,
    Better the stinging salt.

g.

What you remember most—?
    Is a way of death with fingers.
How they are cast in tallow
    —Lover!—webbed as one.
Where was he going, with webs?
    A flying child? or a swimming?
He knew, where he went,
    One way back to the sun.

h.

"Tesoro!" implored the maid.
    "Treasure!" the tall signora.
Under a distant heaven
    What struck the famous tower?
Faults in the earth despairing.
    Worlds away, an orchard
Offered violets early.
    And we returned a flower.

i.

Where does he lie? Hill-high
    In a vision of rolling river.
Where the dogwood curls in April
    And June is a dream of Greece.
Like a Christmas scene on china,
    Snow and the stubborn myrtle.
Those flakes from feathery heaven—?
    Deepen all in peace.

j.

Where does he rest, again?
    In a vision of rolling river.
What does he know of river?
    What do we know of sea?
Comfort?—when tomorrow's
    Cheek by jowl with never?
Never . . . in whose garden
    Bloomed the used-to-be.

k.

Under the snow, what lies?
    Treasure the hemlock covers—
Skysail of frost, and riding in
    Starlight keen and steep.
But the boy below? What's here is
    Gear in a sea-chest only.
Stowed for a season, then
    Pleasure-bound on the deep.

MURIEL RUKEYSER

(1913–1980)

The Book of the Dead

These roads will take you into your own country.
Seasons and maps coming where this road comes
into a landscape mirrored in these men.

Past all your influences, your home river,
constellations of cities, mottoes of childhood,
parents and easy cures, war, all evasion's wishes.

What one word must never be said?
Dead, and these men fight off our dying,
cough in the theatres of the war.

What two things shall never be seen?
They: what we did. Enemy: what we mean.
This is a nation's scene and halfway house.

What three things can never be done?
Forget. Keep silent. Stand alone.
The hills of glass, the fatal brilliant plain.

The facts of war forced into actual grace.
Seasons and modern glory. Told in the histories,
            how first ships came

seeing on the Atlantic thirteen clouds
lining the west horizon with their white
            shining halations;

they conquered, throwing off impossible Europe—
could not be used to transform; created coast—
            breathed-in America.

See how they took the land, made after-life
fresh out of exile, planted the pioneer
      base and blockade,

pushed forests down in an implacable walk
west where new clouds lay at the desirable
      body of sunset;

taking the seaboard. Replaced the isolation,
dropped cities where they stood, drew a tidewater
      frontier of Europe,

a moment, and another frontier held,
this land was planted home-land that we know.
      Ridge of discovery,

until we walk to windows, seeing America
lie in a photograph of power, widened
      before our forehead,

Half-memories absorb us, and our ritual world
carries its history in familiar eyes,
planted in flesh it signifies its music

in minds which turn to sleep and memory,
in music knowing all the shimmering names,
the spear, the castle, and the rose.

But planted in our flesh these valleys stand,
everywhere we begin to know the illness,
are forced up, and our times confirm us all.

In the museum life, centuries of ambition
yielded at last a fertilizing image:
the Carthaginian stone meaning a tall woman

carries in her two hands the book and cradled dove,
on her two thighs, wings folded from the waist
cross to her feet, a pointed human crown.

This valley is given to us like a glory.
To friends in the old world, and their lifting hands
that call for intercession. Blow falling full in face.

All those whose childhood made learn skill to meet,
and art to see after the change of heart;
all the belligerents who know the world.

and still behind us falls another glory,
London unshaken, the long French road to Spain,
        the old Mediterranean

flashing new signals from the hero hills
near Barcelona, monuments and powers,
            parent defenses.

Before our face the broad and concrete west,
green ripened field, frontier pushed back like river
            controlled and dammed;

the flashing wheatfields, cities, lunar plains
grey in Nevada, the sane fantastic country
            sharp in the south,

liveoak, the hanging moss, a world of desert,
the dead, the lava, and the extreme arisen
            fountains of life,

the flourished land, peopled with watercourses
to California and the colored sea;
            sums of frontiers

and unmade boundaries of acts and poems,
the brilliant scene between the seas, and standing,
        this fact and this disease.

                    *

You standing over gorges, surveyors and planners,
you workers and hope of countries, first among powers;
you who give peace and bodily repose,

opening landscapes by grace, giving the marvel lowlands
physical peace, flooding old battlefields
with general brilliance, who best love your lives;

and you young, you who finishing the poem
wish new perfection and begin to make;
you men of fact, measure our times again.

*

These are our strength, who strike against history.
These whose corrupt cells owe their new styles of weakness
        to our diseases;

these carrying light for safety on their foreheads
descended deeper for richer faults of ore,
        drilling their death.

These touching radium and the luminous poison,
carried their death on their lips and with their warning
        glow in their graves.

These weave and their eyes water and rust away,
these stand at wheels until their brains corrode,
        these farm and starve,

all these men cry their doom across the world,
meeting avoidable death, fight against madness,
        find every war.

Are known as strikers, soldiers, pioneers,
fight on all new frontiers, are set in solid
        lines of defense.

Defense is sight; widen the lens and see
standing over the land myths of identity,
        new signals, processes:

Alloys begin: certain dominant metals.
Deliberate combines add new qualities,
        sums of new uses.

Over the country, from islands of Maine fading,
Cape Sable fading south into the orange
       detail of sunset,

new processes, new signals, new possession.
A name for all the conquests, prediction of victory
       deep in these powers.

Carry abroad the urgent need, the scene,
to photograph and to extend the voice,
       to speak this meaning.

Voices to speak to us directly. As we move.
As we enrich, growing in larger motion,
       this word, this power.

Down coasts of taken countries, mastery,
discovery at one hand, and at the other
       frontiers and forests,

fanatic cruel legend at our back and
speeding ahead the red and open west,
       and this our region,

desire, field, beginning. Name and road,
communication to these many men,
as epilogue, seeds of unending love.

Ajanta

I—The Journey

Came in my full youth to the midnight cave
Nerves ringing; and this thing I did alone.
Wanting my fulness and not a field of war,
For the world considered annihilation, a star
Called Wormwood rose and flickered, shattering
Bent light over the dead boiling up in the ground,

The biting yellow of their corrupted lives
Streaming to war, denying all our words.
Nothing was left among the tainted weather
But world-walking and shadowless Ajanta.
Hallucination and the metal laugh
In clouds, and the mountain-spectre riding storm.
Nothing was certain but a moment of peace,
A hollow behind the unbreakable waterfall.
All the way to the cave, the teeming forms of death,
And death, the price of the body, cheap as air.
I blessed my heart on the expiation journey
For it had never been unable to suffer:
When I met the man whose face looked like the future,
When I met the whore with the dying red hair,
The child myself who is my murderer.
So came I between heaven and my grave
Past the serene smile of the *voyeur*, to
This cave where the myth enters the heart again.

II—The Cave

Space to the mind, the painted cave of dream.
This is not a womb, nothing but good emerges:
This is a stage, neither unreal nor real,
Where the walls are the world, the rocks and palaces
Stand on a borderland of blossoming ground.
If you stretch your hand, you touch the slope of the world
Reaching in interlaced gods, animals, and men.
There is no background. The figures hold their peace
In a web of movement. There is no frustration,
Every gesture is taken, everything yields connections.
The heavy sensual shoulders, the thighs, the blood-born flesh
And earth turning into color, rocks into their crystals,
Water to sound, fire to form; life flickers
Uncounted into the supple arms of love.
The space of these walls is the body's living space;
Tear open your ribs and breathe the color of time
Where nothing leads away, the world comes forward
In flaming sequences. Pillars and prisms. Riders

And horses and the figures of consciousness,
Red cow grows long, goes running through the world.
Flung into movement in carnal purity,
These bodies are sealed—warm lip and crystal hand
In a jungle of light. Color-sheeted, seductive
Foreboding eyelid lowered on the long eye,
Fluid and vulnerable. The spaces of the body
Are suddenly limitless, and riding flesh
Shapes constellations over the golden breast,
Confusion of scents and illuminated touch—
Monster touch, the throat printed with brightness,
Wide outlined gesture where the bodies ride.
Bells, and the spirit flashing. The religious bells,
Bronze under the sunlight like breasts ringing,
Bronze in the closed air, the memory of walls,
Great sensual shoulders in the web of time.

III—*Les Tendresses Bestiales*

A procession of caresses alters the ancient sky
Until new constellations are the body shining:
There's the Hand to steer by, there the horizon Breast,
And the Great Stars kindling the fluid hill.
All the rooms open into magical boxes,
Nothing is tilted, everything flickers
Sexual and exquisite.
The panther with its throat along my arm
Turns black and flows away.
Deep in all streets passes a faceless whore
And the checkered men are whispering one word.
The face I know becomes the night-black rose.
The sharp face is now an electric fan
And says one word to me.
The dice and the alcohol and the destruction
Have drunk themselves and cast.
Broken bottle of loss, and the glass
Turned bloody into the face.
Now the scene comes forward, very clear.
Dream-singing, airborne, surrenders the recalled,

The gesture arrives riding over the breast,
Singing, singing, tender atrocity,
The silver derelict wearing fur and claws.
O love, I stood under the apple branch,
I saw the whipped bay and the small dark islands,
And night sailing the river and the foghorn's word.
My life said to you: I want to love you well.
The wheel goes back and I shall live again,
But the wave turns, my birth arrives and spills
Over my breast the world bearing my grave,
And your eyes open in earth. You touched my life.
My life reaches the skin, moves under your smile,
And your throat and your shoulders and your face and your
      thighs
Flash.
                  I am haunted by interrupted acts,
Introspective as a leper, enchanted
By a repulsive clew,
A gross and fugitive movement of the limbs.
Is this the love that shook the lights to flame?
Sheeted avenues thrash in the wind,
Torn streets, the savage parks.
I am plunged deep. Must find the midnight cave.

IV—*Black Blood*

A habit leading to murder, smoky laughter
Hated at first, but necessary later.
Alteration of motives. To stamp in terror
Around the deserted harbor, down the hill
Until the woman laced into a harp
Screams and screams and the great clock strikes,
Swinging its giant figures past the face.
The Floating Man rides on the ragged sunset
Asking and asking. Do not say, Which loved?
Which was beloved? Only, Who most enjoyed?
Armored ghost of rage, screaming and powerless.
Only find me and touch my blood again.
Find me. A girl runs down the street

Singing Take me, yelling Take me Take
Hang me from the clapper of a bell
And you as hangman ring it sweet tonight,
For nothing clean in me is more than cloud
Unless you call it. —As I ran I heard
A black voice beating among all that blood:
"Try to live as if there were a God."

V—The Broken World

Came to Ajanta cave, the painted space of the breast,
The real world where everything is complete,
There are no shadows, the forms of incompleteness.
The great cloak blows in the light, rider and horse arrive,
The shoulders turn and every gift is made.
No shadows fall. There is no source of distortion.
In our world, a tree casts the shadow of a woman,
A man the shadow of a phallus, a hand raised
The shadow of the whip.
Here everything is itself,
Here all may stand
On summer earth.
Brightness has overtaken every light,
And every myth netted itself in flesh.
New origins, and peace given entire
And the spirit alive.
In the shadowless cave
The naked arm is raised.

Animals arrive,
Interlaced, and gods
Interlaced, and men
Flame-woven.
I stand and am complete.
Crawls from the door,
Black at my two feet
The shadow of the world.

World, not yet one,
Enters the heart again.

The naked world, and the old noise of tears,
The fear, the expiation and the love,
A world of the shadowed and alone.

The journey, and the struggles of the moon.

The Outer Banks

I

Horizon of islands shifting
Sea-light flame on my voice
　　　　　　　　　　burn in me
　　　　　　　　　　　　Light
flows from the water from sands　islands of this horizon
The sea comes toward me across the sea.　The sand
moves over the sand in waves
between the guardians of this landscape
the great commemorative statue on one hand
　　—the first flight of man, outside of dream,
　　　　seen as stone wing and stainless steel—
and at the other hand
　　banded black-and-white, climbing
the spiral lighthouse.

II

Flood over ocean,
avalanche on the flat beach. Pouring.
Indians holding branches up, to
placate the tempest,
the one-legged twisting god that is
a standing wind.
Rays are branching from all things:
great serpent, great plume, constellation:
sands from which colors and light pass,
the lives of plants.　Animals.　Men.
A man and a woman reach for each other.

III

Wave of the sea.

IV

Sands have washed, sea has flown over us.
Between the two guardians, spiral, truncated wing,
history and these wild birds
Bird-voiced discoverers : Hariot,   Hart Crane,
the brothers who watched gulls.
"No bird soars in a calm,"   said Wilbur Wright.
Dragon of the winds forms over me.
Your dance, goddesses in your circle
sea-wreath, whirling of the event
behind me on land as deep in our own lives
we begin to know the movement to come.
Sunken, drowned spirals,
hurricane-dance.

V

Shifting of islands on this horizon.
The cycle of changes in the Book of Changes.
Two islands making an open female line
That powerful long straight bar a male island.
The building of the surf
constructing immensities
between the pale flat Sound
and ocean ever
birds as before earthquake
winds fly from all origins
the length of this wave goes from the great wing
down coast, the barrier beach in all its miles
road of the sun and the moon to
a spiral lighthouse
to the depth turbulence
lifts up its wave like cities
the ocean in the air
spills down the world.

VI

A man is walking toward me across the water.
From far out, the flat waters of the Sound,
he walks pulling his small boat

In the shoal water.
A man who is white and has been fishing.
Walks steadily upon the light of day
Coming closer to me where I stand
looking into the sun and the blaze inner water.
Clear factual surface over which he pulls
a boat over a closing quarter-mile.

VII

Speak to it, says the light.
Speak to it music,
voices of the sea and human throats.
Origins of spirals,
the ballad and original sweet grape
dark on the vines near Hatteras,
tendrils of those vines, whose spiral tower
now rears its light, accompanying
all my voices.

VIII

He walks toward me.   A black man in the sun.
He now is a black man speaking to my heart
crisis of darkness in this century
of moments of this speech.

The boat is slowly nearer drawn, this man.

The zigzag power coming straight, in stones,
        in arcs, metal, crystal, the spiral
in sacred wet
                        schematic elements of
cities, music, arrangement

spin these stones of home
>   under the sea
return to the stations of the stars
and the sea, speaking across its lives.

IX

A man who is bones is close to me
drawing a boat of bones
the sun behind him
is another color of fire,
the sea behind me
rears its flame.

A man whose body flames and tapers in flame
twisted tines of remembrance that dissolve
a pitchfork of the land worn thin
flame up and dissolve again
>   draw   small   boat

Nets of the stars at sunset over us.
This draws me home to the home of the wild birds
long-throated birds of this passage.
This is the edge of experience, *grenzen der seele*
where those on the verge of human understanding
the borderline people stand on the shifting islands
among the drowned stars and the tempest.
"Everyman's mind, like the dumbest,
claws at his own furthest limits of knowing the world,"
a man in a locked room said.

Open to the sky
I stand before this boat that looks at me.
The man's flames are arms and legs.
Body, eyes, head, stars, sands look at me.

I walk out into the shoal water
and throw my leg over the wall of the boat.

X

At one shock, speechlessness.
I am in the bow, on the short thwart.
He is standing before me amidships, rowing forward
like my old northern sea-captain in his dory.
All things have spun.
The words gone,
I facing sternwards, looking at the gate
between the barrier islands.   As he rows.
Sand islands shifting and the last of land
a pale and open line   horizon
sea.

With whose face did he look at me?
What did I say?   or did I say?
in speechlessness
move to the change.
These strokes provide the music,
and the accused boy on land today saying
What did I say?   or did I say?
The dream on land last night built this the boat of death
but in the suffering of the light
moving across the sea
do we in our moving
move toward life or death

XI

Hurricane, skullface, the sky's size
winds streaming through his teeth
doing the madman's twist

and not a beach not flooded

nevertheless, here
stability of light
my other silence
and at my left hand and at my right hand
no longer wing and lighthouse
no longer the guardians.

They are in me, in my speechless
life of barrier beach.
As it lies open
to the night, out there.

Now seeing my death before me
starting again, among the drowned men,
desperate men, unprotected discoverers,
and the man before me
here.
Stroke by stroke drawing us.
Out there? Father of rhythms,
deep wave, mother.
There is no *out there*.
All is open.
Open water. Open I.

XII

The wreck of the *Tiger*, the early pirate, the blood-clam's ark,
        the tern's acute eye, all buried mathematical instruments,
        castaways, pelicans, drowned five-strand pearl necklaces,
        hopes of livelihood, hopes of grace,
walls of houses, sepia sea-fences, the writhen octopus and
        those tall masts and sails,
marked hulls of ships and last month's plane, dipping his
        salute to the stone wing of dream,
turbulence, Diamond Shoals, the dark young living people:
"Sing one more song and you are under arrest."
"Sing another song."
Women, ships, lost voices.
Whatever has dissolved into our waves.
I a lost voice
moving, calling you
on the edge of the moment that is now the center.
From the open sea.

The Speed of Darkness

I

Whoever despises the clitoris despises the penis
Whoever despises the penis despises the cunt
Whoever despises the cunt despises the life of the child.

Resurrection music,   silence,   and surf.

II

No longer speaking
Listening with the whole body
And with every drop of blood
Overtaken by silence

But this same silence is become speech
With the speed of darkness.

III

Stillness during war, the lake.
The unmoving spruces.
Glints over the water.
Faces, voices.   You are far away.
A tree that trembles.

I am the tree that trembles and trembles.

IV

After the lifting of the mist
after the lift of the heavy rains
the sky stands clear
and the cries of the city risen in day
I remember the buildings are space
walled, to let space be used for living
I mind this room is space
this drinking glass is space
whose boundary of glass

lets me give you drink and space to drink
your hand, my hand being space
containing skies and constellations
your face
carries the reaches of air
I know I am space
my words are air.

V

Between   between
the man : act   exact
woman : in curve   senses in their maze
frail orbits, green tries,   games of stars
shape of the body speaking its evidence

VI

I look across at the real
vulnerable   involved   naked
devoted to the present of all I care for
the world of its history leading to this moment.

VII

Life the announcer.
I assure you
there are many ways to have a child.
I bastard mother
promise you
there are many ways to be born.
They all come forth
in their own grace.

VIII

Ends of the earth join tonight
with blazing stars upon their meeting.

These sons,   these sons
fall burning into Asia.

IX

Time comes into it.
Say it.   Say it.

The universe is made of stories,
not of atoms.

X

Lying
blazing beside me
you rear beautifully and up—
your thinking face—
erotic body reaching
in all its colors and lights—
your erotic face
colored and lit—
not colored body-and-face
but now entire,
colors   lights   the world thinking and reaching.

XI

The river flows past the city.

Water goes down to tomorrow
making its children   I hear their unborn voices
I am working out the vocabulary of my silence.

XII

Big-boned man young and of my dream
Struggles to get the live bird out of his throat.
I am he am I?   Dreaming?
I am the bird am I?   I am the throat?

A bird with a curved beak.
It could slit anything, the throat-bird.

Drawn up slowly.   The curved blades, not large.
Bird emerges   wet   being born
Begins to sing.

XIII

My night awake
staring at the broad rough jewel
the copper roof across the way
thinking of the poet
yet unborn in this dark
who will be the throat of these hours.
No.   Of those hours.
Who will speak these days,
if not I,
if not you?

The Poem as Mask

Orpheus

When I wrote of the women in their dances and wildness, it
    was a mask,
on their mountain, god-hunting, singing, in orgy,
it was a mask; when I wrote of the god,
fragmented, exiled from himself, his life, the love gone down
    with song,
it was myself, split open, unable to speak, in exile from myself.

There is no mountain, there is no god, there is memory
of my torn life, myself split open in sleep, the rescued child
beside me among the doctors, and a word
of rescue from the great eyes.

No more masks! No more mythologies!

Now, for the first time, the god lifts his hand,
the fragments join in me with their own music.

Myth

Long afterward, Oedipus, old and blinded, walked the
roads.   He smelled a familiar smell.   It was
the Sphinx.   Oedipus said, "I want to ask one question.
Why didn't I recognize my mother?"   "You gave the
wrong answer," said the Sphinx.   "But that was what
made everything possible," said Oedipus.   "No," she said.
"When I asked, What walks on four legs in the morning,
two at noon, and three in the evening, you answered,
Man.   You didn't say anything about woman."
"When you say Man," said Oedipus, "you include women
too. Everyone knows that."   She said, "That's what
you think."

DAVID SCHUBERT

(1913–1946)

Monterey

The hills were lush
With rain and youth. I did
What chores were my portion
In the shack I shared with two friends.
It was to be for us
A landmark in our lives, a moment
In our lives to which we returned,
When we were tired out, when
We didn't have anything else to
Do. What a home and parents should
Be.

She came with a friend,
Calling, on the road. She was
Dissatisfied with her lodging.
One of us met them on the
Road, invited them in for lunch.

I loved her not
For herself, but for myself. She
Was, of girls imagined, one.

I am a rugged individualist;
I did not tarry or pretend.

It Is Sticky in the Subway

How I love this girl who until
This minute, I never knew existed on
The face of this earth.

               I sit opposite
Her, thinking myself as stupid as that
Photograph, maudlin in Mumford, of
Orpheus.

        A kinkled adolescent
Defies the Authorities by
Smoking a butt right next to me. He is
Of Romeos the least attractive who
Has played the role.

               He
Smirks, squints, glues his eyes to her
Tightly entethered teeth, scratches
His moist passion on some scratch paper.

       Her eyes
Accuse Plato of non-en
Tity. Most delightful creature of moment's
          above-ground.

Prospect Park

I would like to ask that dumb ox, Thomas
Aquinas, why it is, that when you have said
Something,—you said it—then they ask you
A month later if it is true? Of course it is!
It is something about them I think. They think
It is something about me. It adds up
To my thinking I must be what I don't
Know . . .

        —The park is certainly
Tranquil tonight: lovers, like ants
Are scurrying into any old darkness,
Covert for kisses. It makes me feel
Old and lonely. I wish that I were
All of them, not with any one,
Would I exchange my lot, but the entire
Scene has a certain Breughel quality
I would participate in.—
            Do I have to repeat
Myself. I really mean it.
I am not saying it again to convince myself
But to convince the repressed conviction
Of yourself. I think. I think. I think it.

Victor Record Catalog

Most unexpectedly it happens, just
As you don't know what you say till you
Say it. Sleighbells in the winter of
My discontent.

                    (Like all people, she spoke
By contradiction, so that I had to hear
The negatives of her remarks to find out
How much I liked her. She lived, way up,
In a Kafkalike passageway of bureaucratic
Offices, anonymously ugly, one inside
The other, just like Kafka's temper tantrums.)
She lived there. I didn't like it.

                She looked at me
Alternately too severe and too
Gentle. Why did I hear
Her say that all men are brothers?
"We journey
            under the four winds, past
The enemy's chariot and

Past the river where drown the
Attached. You and I, however,
Are exceptions to every rule. Being glad,
We will survive."

                              Outside the window it was
A hot saggy day in August. The Coast Guard
Drilling at war, far as the Pacific.
As poverty is my taskmaster, as
I study the Victor Record Catalog instead
Of listening to the paragon's
Prerogative: Eugene Ormandy, my

                              Expectancy
Makes me slightly sick, as when years ago,
Hungry for food, I came to friends and they
Talked; now I wait for her to speak
The meanings which I must negate before
I am admitted to the gayest person.

A Successful Summer

The still small voice unto
My still small voice, I listen.
Hardly awake, I breathe, vulnerably,
As in summer trees, the messages
Of telegraphed errands buzz along
July's contour of green.

No Title

A ghastly ordeal it was. In
Retrospect, I am no longer young.
Wise, sad, as unhappy as seeing
Someone you love, with whom life has
Brought suffering, or someone you
Have nothing in common with, yet love,—
Unable to speak a word.

If when I say this I weep, it is not
Because my heart has turned into a
Lachrymose commentator; the
Discus thrower's still
There,—the shining one, quick. It is because
In my moment of rejoicing, I
Thought that one who has suffered with me shall
Rejoice. There was no
One. Not one answered.

Of suffering, who wants to be reminded?

          Sitting on the bench in the
Botanic Garden, watching the charming scene
Beguiled by poplars giving it a fairy tale
Atmosphere

          I was annoyed by someone!
He wanted money. I resented
Him. He disturbed my mood.

          The euphemisms of our age
Make tolerable a universal selfhood,
Which the sick soul, alas, was always sick of.
What but goodnesses' was the dark night
Of the soul, as yet unimmured to its
Failings, sensitive as the snail's an
Tennae?

I stood there on 42nd Street and
Eighth Avenue. I stood there with two
Nickels.

I went to one on whose
Memory I hardly counted; my
Friends—did they care?—and how could I
Ask them, being if a beggar, proud.

How little space there is
Between success and nothing at all.
Watching the passersby
Who fitted in somewhere in what was a
Society.

Outcast. Exiled. Penniless.
Never. Never. Never. Never. Never.
Shall I stand spellbound by the
Reiteration's disaster?
No! What is
Over is over.

DELMORE SCHWARTZ

(1913–1966)

In the Naked Bed, in Plato's Cave

In the naked bed, in Plato's cave,
Reflected headlights slowly slid the wall,
Carpenters hammered under the shaded window,
Wind troubled the window curtains all night long,
A fleet of trucks strained uphill, grinding,
Their freights covered, as usual.
The ceiling lightened again, the slanting diagram
Slid slowly forth.
     Hearing the milkman's chop,
His striving up the stair, the bottle's chink,
I rose from bed, lit a cigarette,
And walked to the window. The stony street
Displayed the stillness in which buildings stand,
The street-lamp's vigil and the horse's patience.
The winter sky's pure capital
Turned me back to bed with exhausted eyes.

Strangeness grew in the motionless air. The loose
Film grayed. Shaking wagons, hooves' waterfalls,
Sounded far off, increasing, louder and nearer.
A car coughed, starting. Morning, softly
Melting the air, lifted the half-covered chair
From underseas, kindled the looking-glass,
Distinguished the dresser and the white wall.
The bird called tentatively, whistled, called,
Bubbled and whistled, so! Perplexed, still wet
With sleep, affectionate, hungry and cold. So, so,
O son of man, the ignorant night, the travail
Of early morning, the mystery of beginning
Again and again,
     while History is unforgiven.

Sonnet: The Beautiful American Word, Sure

The beautiful American word, Sure,
As I have come into a room, and touch
The lamp's button, and the light blooms with such
Certainty where the darkness loomed before,

As I care for what I do not know, and care
Knowing for little she might not have been,
And for how little she would be unseen,
The intercourse of lives miraculous and dear.

Where the light is, and each thing clear,
Separate from all others, standing in its place,
I drink the time and touch whatever's near,

And hope for day when the whole world has that face:
For what assures her present every year?
In dark accidents the mind's sufficient grace.

Far Rockaway

"the cure of souls."
            —HENRY JAMES

The radiant soda of the seashore fashions
Fun, foam, and freedom. The sea laves
The shaven sand. And the light sways forward
On the self-destroying waves.

The rigor of the weekday is cast aside with shoes,
With business suits and the traffic's motion;
The lolling man lies with the passionate sun,
Or is drunken in the ocean.

A socialist health takes hold of the adult,
He is stripped of his class in the bathing-suit,
He returns to the children digging at summer,
A melon-like fruit.

O glittering and rocking and bursting and blue,
—Eternities of sea and sky shadow no pleasure:
Time unheard moves and the heart of man is eaten
Consummately at leisure.

The novelist tangential on the boardwalk overhead
Seeks his cure of souls in his own anxious gaze.
"Here," he says, "With whom?" he asks, "This?" he
        questions,
"What tedium, what blaze?"

"What satisfaction, fruit? What transit, heaven?
Criminal? justified? arrived at what June?"
That nervous conscience amid the concessions
Is a haunting, haunted moon.

Tired and Unhappy, You Think of Houses

Tired and unhappy, you think of houses
Soft-carpeted and warm in the December evening,
While snow's white pieces fall past the window,
And the orange firelight leaps.
                                A young girl sings
That song of Gluck where Orpheus pleads with Death;
Her elders watch, nodding their happiness
To see time fresh again in her self-conscious eyes:
The servants bring the coffee, the children retire,
Elder and younger yawn and go to bed,
The coals fade and glow, rose and ashen,
It is time to shake yourself! and break this
Banal dream, and turn your head
Where the underground is charged, where the weight
Of the lean buildings is seen,
Where close in the subway rush, anonymous
In the audience, well-dressed or mean,
So many surround you, ringing your fate,
Caught in an anger exact as a machine!

In the Slight Ripple, the Mind Perceives the Heart

In the slight ripple, the fishes dart
Like fingers, centrifugal, like wishes
Wanton. And pleasures rise
                  as the eyes fall
Through the lucid water. The small pebble,
The clear clay bottom, the white shell
Are apparent, though superficial.
Who would ask more of the August afternoon?
Who would dig mines and follow shadows?
"I would," answers bored Heart, "Lounger, rise"
(Underlip trembling, face white with stony anger),
"The old error, the thought of sitting still,
"The senses drinking, by the summer river,
"On the tended lawn, below the traffic,
"As if time would pause,
                and afternoon stay.
"No, night comes soon,
"With its cold mountains, with desolation,
                    unless Love build its city."

The Ballet of the Fifth Year

Where the sea gulls sleep or indeed where they fly
Is a place of different traffic. Although I
Consider the fishing bay (where I see them dip and curve
And purely glide) a place that weakens the nerve
Of will, and closes my eyes, as they should not be
(They should burn like the street-light all night quietly,
So that whatever is present will be known to me),
Nevertheless the gulls and the imagination
Of where they sleep, which comes to creation
In strict shape and color, from their dallying
Their wings slowly, and suddenly rallying
Over, up, down the arabesque of descent,
Is an old act enacted, my fabulous intent
When I skated, afraid of policemen, five years old,

In the winter sunset, sorrowful and cold,
Hardly attained to thought, but old enough to know
Such grace, so self-contained, was the best escape to know.

Do the Others Speak of Me Mockingly, Maliciously?

*"As in water face answereth to face,
so the heart of man to man."*

Do they whisper behind my back? Do they speak
Of my clumsiness? Do they laugh at me,
Mimicking my gestures, retailing my shame?
I'll whirl about, denounce them, saying
That they are shameless, they are treacherous,
No more my friends, nor will I once again
Never, amid a thousand meetings in the street,
Recognize their faces, take their hands,
Not for our common love or old times' sake:
They whispered behind my back, they mimicked me.

I know the reason why, I too have done this,
Cruel for wit's sake, behind my dear friend's back,
And to amuse betrayed his private love,
His nervous shame, her habit, and their weaknesses;
I have mimicked them, I have been treacherous,
For wit's sake, to amuse, because their being weighed
Too grossly for a time, to be superior,
To flatter the listeners by this, the intimate,
Betraying the intimate, but for the intimate,
To free myself of friendship's necessity,
Fearing from time to time that they would hear,
Denounce me and reject me, say once for all
That they would never meet me, take my hands,
Speaking for old times' sake and our common love.

What an unheard-of thing it is, in fine,
To love another and equally be loved!
What sadness and what joy! How cruel it is

That pride and wit distort the heart of man,
How vain, how sad, what cruelty, what need,
For this is true and sad, that I need them
And they need me. What can we do? We need
Each other's clumsiness, each other's wit,
Each other's company and our own pride. I need
My face unshamed, I need my wit, I cannot
Turn away. We know our clumsiness,
Our weakness, our necessities, we cannot
Forget our pride, our faces, our common love.

The Heavy Bear Who Goes With Me

"the withness of the body"

The heavy bear who goes with me,
A manifold honey to smear his face,
Clumsy and lumbering here and there,
The central ton of every place,
The hungry beating brutish one
In love with candy, anger, and sleep,
Crazy factotum, dishevelling all,
Climbs the building, kicks the football,
Boxes his brother in the hate-ridden city.

Breathing at my side, that heavy animal,
That heavy bear who sleeps with me,
Howls in his sleep for a world of sugar,
A sweetness intimate as the water's clasp,
Howls in his sleep because the tight-rope
Trembles and shows the darkness beneath.
—The strutting show-off is terrified,
Dressed in his dress-suit, bulging his pants,
Trembles to think that his quivering meat
Must finally wince to nothing at all.

That inescapable animal walks with me,
Has followed me since the black womb held,

Moves where I move, distorting my gesture,
A caricature, a swollen shadow,
A stupid clown of the spirit's motive,
Perplexes and affronts with his own darkness,
The secret life of belly and bone,
Opaque, too near, my private, yet unknown,
Stretches to embrace the very dear
With whom I would walk without him near,
Touches her grossly, although a word
Would bare my heart and make me clear,
Stumbles, flounders, and strives to be fed
Dragging me with him in his mouthing care,
Amid the hundred million of his kind,
The scrimmage of appetite everywhere.

Darkling Summer, Ominous Dusk, Rumorous Rain

1

A tattering of rain and then the reign
Of pour and pouring-down and down,
Where in the westward gathered the filming gown
Of grey and clouding weakness, and, in the mane
Of the light's glory and the day's splendor, gold and vain,
Vivid, more and more vivid, scarlet, lucid and more luminous,
Then came a splatter, a prattle, a blowing rain!
And soon the hour was musical and rumorous:
A softness of a dripping lipped the isolated houses,
A gaunt grey somber softness licked the glass of hours.

2

Again, after a catbird squeaked in the special silence,
And clouding vagueness fogged the windowpane
And gathered blackness and overcast, the mane
Of light's story and light's glory surrendered and ended
—A pebble—a ring—a ringing on the pane,
A blowing and a blowing in: tides of the blue and cold
Moods of the great blue bay, and slates of grey

Came down upon the land's great sea, the body of this day
—Hardly an atom of silence amid the roar
Allowed the voice to form appeal—to call:
By kindled light we thought we saw the bronze of fall.

The Mind Is an Ancient and Famous Capital

The mind is a city like London,
Smoky and populous: it is a capital
Like Rome, ruined and eternal,
Marked by the monuments which no one
Now remembers. For the mind, like Rome, contains
Catacombs, aqueducts, amphitheatres, palaces,
Churches and equestrian statues, fallen, broken or soiled.
The mind possesses and is possessed by all the ruins
Of every haunted, hunted generation's celebration.

"Call us what you will: we are made such by love."
We are such studs as dreams are made on, and
Our little lives are ruled by the gods, by Pan,
Piping of all, seeking to grasp or grasping
All of the grapes; and by the bow-and-arrow god,
Cupid, piercing the heart through, suddenly and forever.

Dusk we are, to dusk returning, after the burbing,
After the gold fall, the fallen ash, the bronze,
Scattered and rotten, after the white null statues which
Are winter, sleep, and nothingness: when
Will the houselights of the universe
Light up and blaze?
                        For it is not the sea
Which murmurs in a shell,
And it is not only heart, at harp o'clock,
It is the dread terror of the uncontrollable
Horses of the apocalypse, running in wild dread
Toward Arcturus—and returning as suddenly . . .

Lincoln

Manic-depressive Lincoln, national hero!
How just and true that this great nation, being conceived
In liberty by fugitives should find
—Strange ways and plays of monstrous History—
This Hamlet-type to be the President—

This failure, this unwilling bridegroom,
This tricky lawyer full of black despair—

He grew a beard, becoming President,
And took a shawl as if he guessed his role,
Though with the beard he fled cartoonists' blacks,
And many laughed and were contemptuous,
And some for four years spoke of killing him—

He was a politician—of the heart!—
He lived from hand to mouth in moral things!
He understood quite well Grant's drunkenness!
It was for him, before Election Day,
That at Cold Harbor Grant threw lives away
In hopeless frontal attack against Lee's breastworks!

O how he was the Hamlet-man, and this,
After a life of failure made him right,
After he ran away on his wedding day,
Writing a coward's letter to his bride—
How with his very failure, he out-tricked
The florid Douglas and the abstract Davis,
And all the vain men who, surrounding him,
Smiled in their vanity and sought his place—

Later, they made him out a prairie Christ
To sate the need coarse in the national heart—

His wife went insane, Mary Todd too often
Bought herself dresses. And his child died.
And he would not condemn young men to death
For having slept, in weakness. And he spoke

More than he knew and all that he had felt
Between outrageous joy and black despair
Before and after Gettysburg's pure peak—

He studied law, but knew in his own soul
Despair's anarchy, terror and error,
—Instruments had to be taken from his office
And from his bedroom in such days of horror,
Because some saw that he might kill himself:
When he was young, when he was middle-aged,
How just and true was he, our national hero!

Sometimes he could not go home to face his wife,
Sometimes he wished to hurry or end his life!
But do not be deceived. He did not win,
And, it is plain, the South could never win
(Despite the gifted Northern generals!)
—Capitalismus is not mocked, O no!
This stupid deity decided the War—

In fact, the North and South were losers both:
—Capitalismus won the Civil War—

—Capitalismus won the Civil War,
Yet, in the War's cruel Colosseum,
Some characters fulfilled their natures' surds,
Grant the drunkard, Lee the noble soldier,
John Brown in whom the Bible soared and cried,
Booth the unsuccessful Shakespearean,
—Each in some freedom walked and knew himself,
Then most of all when all the deities
Mixed with their barbarous stupidity
To make the rock, root, and rot of the war—

"This is the way each only life becomes,
Tossed on History's ceaseless insane sums!"

But on the neighboring range, misty and high,
The past is absolute: some luckless race
Dull with inbreeding and conformity
Wears out its heart, and comes barefoot and bad
    For charity or jail. The scholar
    Sanctions their obsolete disease;
    The gentleman revolts with shame
      At his ancestor.

And the true nobleman, once a democrat,
Sleeps on his private mountain. He was one
Whose thought was shapely and whose dream was broad;
This school he held his art and epitaph.
    But now it takes from him his name,
    Falls open like a dishonest look,
    And shows us, rotted and endowed,
      Its senile pleasure.

Troop Train

It stops the town we come through. Workers raise
Their oily arms in good salute and grin.
Kids scream as at a circus. Business men
Glance hopefully and go their measured way.
And women standing at their dumbstruck door
More slowly wave and seem to warn us back,
As if a tear blinding the course of war
Might once dissolve our iron in their sweet wish.

Fruit of the world, O clustered on ourselves
We hang as from a cornucopia
In total friendliness, with faces bunched
To spray the streets with catcalls and with leers.
A bottle smashes on the moving ties
And eyes fixed on a lady smiling pink
Stretch like a rubber-band and snap and sting
The mouth that wants the drink-of-water kiss.

MAY SWENSON

(1913–1989)

Question

Body my house
my horse my hound
what will I do
when you are fallen

Where will I sleep
How will I ride
What will I hunt

Where can I go
without my mount
all eager and quick
How will I know
in thicket ahead
is danger or treasure
when Body my good
bright dog is dead

How will it be
to lie in the sky
without roof or door
and wind for an eye

With cloud for shift
how will I hide?

Distance and a Certain Light

Distance
and a certain light
makes anything artistic—
it doesn't matter what.

From an airplane, all
that rigid splatter of the Bronx
becomes organic, logical
as web or beehive. Chunks

of decayed cars in junkyards,
garbage scows (nimble roaches
on the Harlem), herds of stalled
manure-yellow boxes on twisting reaches

of rails, are punched clean and sharp
as ingots in the ignition of the sun.
Rubbish becomes engaging shape—
you only have to get a bead on it,

the right light filling the corridor
of your view—a gob of spit
under a microscope, fastidious
in structure as a crystal. No contortion

without intention, and nothing ugly.
In any random, sprawling, decomposing thing
is the charming string
of its history—and what it will be next.

Colors Without Objects

Colors without objects—colors alone—
wriggle in the tray of my eye,

incubated under the great flat lamp
of the sun:

bodiless blue, little razor-streak,
yellow melting like a firework petal,

double purple yo-yo
in a broth of murky gold.

Sharp green squints I have never seen
minnow-dive the instant they're alive;

bulb-reds with flickering cilia
dilate, but then implode

to disks of impish scotomata,
that flee into the void;

weird orange slats of hot thought
about to make a basket—but

there is no material here—they slim
to a snow of needles, are erased.

Now a mottling takes place.
All colors fix chromosomic links

that dexterously mix,
flip, exchange their aerial ladders.

Such stunts of speed and metamorphosis
breed impermanent, objectless acts,

a thick, a brilliant bacteria—
but most do not survive.

I wait for a few iridium specks of idea
to thrive in the culture of my eye.

Unconscious
came a beauty to my
wrist
and stopped my pencil,
merged its shadow profile with
my hand's ghost
on the page:
Red Spotted Purple or else Mourning
Cloak,
paired thin as paper wings, near black,
were edged on the seam side poppy orange,
as were its spots.

UNCONSCIOUS

CAME A BEAUTY

I sat arrested, for its soot haired
body's worm
shone in the sun.
It bent its tongue long as
a leg
black on my skin
and clung without my
feeling,
while its tomb stained
duplicate parts of
a window opened.
And then I
moved.

The Shape of Death

What does love look like?
Death is a cloud, immense
lid is lifted from the
clap of sound. A white
jaw of fright. A
white to gray, like a
and burns— then turns
away, filling the whole
Thickly it wraps, between
moon, the earth's green
 cocoon, its choking
of death. Death is a

We know the shape of death.
and awesome. At first a
eye of light. There is a
blossom belches from the
pillared cloud churns from
monstrous brain that bursts
sickly black, spilling
sky with ashes of dread.
the clean seas and the
head. Trapped in its
breath, we know the shape
cloud. What does love look

like? Is it a particle,
beyond the microscope and
the length of hope? Is
that we shall never dare
color, and its alchemy?
can it be dug? Or
it be bought? Can it be
a shy beast to be caught?
a clap of sound. Love is
nests within each cell,
is a ray, a seed, a note,
our air and blood. It is
our very skin, a sheath

a star, invisible entirely,
Palomar? A dimension past
it a climate far and fair,
discover? What is its
Is it a jewel in the earth,
dredged from the sea? Can
sown and harvested? Is it
Death is a cloud— immense,
little and not loud. It
and it cannot be split. It
a word, a secret motion of
not alien— it is near—
to keep us pure of fear.

Electronic Sound

A pebble swells to a boulder at low speed
                        At 7½ ips a hiss is a hurricane.
                                The basin drain
is Charybdis sucking
                        a clipper down, the ship
                        a paperclip
whirling. Or gargle, brush your teeth, HEAR
                        a winded horse's esophagus lurch
                        on playback at 15/16. Perch
a quarter on edge on a plate, spin:
                a locomotive's wheel is wrenched loose,
                wobbles down the line to slam the caboose,
keeps on snicking over the ties
                        till it teeters on the embankment,
                                bowls down a cement
ramp, meanders onto the turnpike
                                and into a junkhole
                        of scrapped cars. Ceasing to roll,
it shimmies, falters . . .
                                sudden inertia causes
                                pause.
Then a round of echoes
                        descending, a minor yammer
as when a triangle's nicked by the slimmest hammer.

How Everything Happens

(Based on a study of the Wave)

                                       happen.
                                   to
                              up
                       stacking
                    is
               something
When nothing is happening

When it happens
          something
               pulls
                   back
                       not
                         to
                             happen.

When   has happened.
       pulling back   stacking up
            happens

       has happened   stacks up.
When it   something   nothing
                   pulls back while

Then nothing is happening.

                          happens.
                     and
                forward
           pushes
       up
     stacks
   something
Then

Bronco Busting, Event #1

The stall so tight he can't raise heels or knees
when the cowboy, coccyx to bareback, touches down

tender as a deerfly, forks him, gripping the rope-
handle over the withers, testing the cinch,

as if hired to lift a cumbersome piece of brown
luggage, while assistants perched on the rails arrange

the kicker, a foam-rubber band around the narrowest,
most ticklish part of the loins, leaning full weight

on neck and rump to keep him throttled, this horse,
"Firecracker," jacked out of the box through the sprung

gate, in the same second raked both sides of the belly
by ratchets on booted heels, bursts into five-way

motion: bucks, pitches, swivels, humps, and twists,
an all-over-body-sneeze that must repeat

until the flapping bony lump attached to his spine is gone.
A horn squawks. From the dust gets up a buster named
    Tucson.

One of the Strangest

Stuffed pink stocking, the neck,
toe of pointed black, the angled beak,
thick heel with round eye in it upside down, the pate,

swivels, dabbles, skims the soup of pond all day
for small meat. That split polished toe is mouth
of the wading flamingo

whose stilts, the rosy knee joints, bend
the wrong way. When planted
on one straight stem, a big fluffy flower

is body a pink leg, wrung, lifts up over,
lays an awkward shoe to sleep on top of,
between flocculent elbows, the soft peony wings.

Shu Swamp, Spring

Young skunk
cabbages all over
the swamp.

Brownish purple,
yellow-specked
short tusks,

they thicken,
twirl and point
like thumbs.

Thumbs of old
gloves, the nails
poked through

and curled.
By Easter, fingers
will have flipped out

fat and green.
Old gloves, brown
underground,

the seams split.
The nails
have been growing.

Staring at the Sea on the Day
of the Death of Another

The long body of the water fills its hollow,
slowly rolls upon its side,
and in the swaddlings of the waves,
their shadowed hollows falling forward with the tide,

like folds of Grecian garments molded to cling
around some classic immemorial marble thing,
I see the vanished bodies of friends who have died.

Each form is furled into its hollow,
white in the dark curl,
the sea a mausoleum, with countless shelves,
cradling the prone effigies of our unearthly selves,

some of the hollows empty, long niches in the tide.
One of them is mine
and gliding forward, gaping wide.

BIOGRAPHICAL NOTES

NOTE ON THE TEXTS

NOTES

INDEXES

Biographical Notes

Virginia Hamilton Adair (b. February 28, 1913) b. New York City. Studied at Mt. Holyoke (A.B., 1933), Radcliffe (M.A., 1935), University of Wisconsin (1935–37), University of Washington (1953–54), and Claremont Graduate School (1957–58). Published early poems in the *Atlantic* and *The New Republic*. Began teaching at California State Polytechnic University in 1957; became professor of English in 1970. Poetry collection *Ants on the Melon* appeared in 1996, followed by *Beliefs and Blasphemies* (1998).

Helen Adam (December 2, 1909–September 19, 1993) b. Helen Douglas Adam in Glasgow, Scotland; grew up in northeastern coastal region on Moray Firth. Published poetry collections *The Elfin Pedlar and Tales Told by Pixy Pool* (1924), *Charms and Dreams from the Elfin Pedlar's Pack* (1924), and *Shadow of the Moon* (1929). Attended University of Edinburgh for two years; worked as journalist. Came to U.S. in 1939, living in New York before moving to California in 1949. Participated in Robert Duncan's poetry workshops in San Francisco. Was featured in several films of German filmmaker Rosa von Praunheim, including a biographical documentary. Poetry collected in *The Queen o' Crow Castle* (1958), *Ballads* (1964), *Counting-Out Rhyme* (1972), *Selected Poems and Ballads* (1974), *Ghosts and Grinning Shadows* (1977), *Turn Again to Me* (1977), *Gone Sailing* (1980), *The Bells of Dis* (1985), and *Stone Cold Gothic* (1984). The play *San Francisco's Burning*, written with her sister Pat, was produced in 1966.

Léonie Adams (December 9, 1899–June 27, 1988) b. Léonie Fuller Adams in Brooklyn, New York. Attended Barnard, graduating in 1922. Worked as editor at Wilson Publishing Company, 1922–26. Poetry collection *Those Not Elect* published in 1925. Worked as editorial assistant at the Metropolitan Museum of Art, 1926–28. Received Guggenheim Fellowship in 1928; lived in Paris with Allen Tate and his family, and became acquainted with Gertrude Stein and Ford Madox Ford. Published *High Falcon* (1929). Taught at New York University, 1930–32. Married William Troy in 1933. Taught successively at Sarah Lawrence, Bennington, and New Jersey College for Women; lectured at Columbia, 1947–68. Served as Consultant in Poetry at the Library of Congress, 1948–49. *Poems: A Selection* (1954) won Bollingen Prize in 1955. After her husband's death in 1961, collected his work in *William Troy: Selected Essays*, which received National Book Award in 1968.

James Agee (November 27, 1909–May 15, 1955) b. James Rufus Agee in Knoxville, Tennessee. Father died in automobile accident in 1916. Attended St. Andrew's, Episcopal boarding school, where he formed friendship with Father James Herold Flye. After a year at Knoxville High School, transferred to Phillips Exeter Academy. Attended Harvard (1928–32); served as editor-in-chief of *Harvard Advocate*, and contributed to *Harvard Lampoon* and

Crimson. Began writing for *Fortune* in 1932, and continued to work intermittently as reporter and book and film reviewer for *Fortune* and *Time* until 1948. *Permit Me Voyage* published in 1934 in the Yale Series of Younger Poets. An assignment for *Fortune* with photographer Walker Evans on tenant sharecroppers in Alabama evolved into experimental prose work *Let Us Now Praise Famous Men* (1941). Began weekly film column for *The Nation* in 1941. Wrote film scripts including *The Quiet One* (1949), *The African Queen* (1951), and *The Night of the Hunter* (1955). Autobiographical novella *The Morning Watch* published in 1951. *A Death in the Family*, a novel about his father's death, was published posthumously and won the Pulitzer Prize. His film reviews and screenplays were collected in the two-volume *Agee on Film* (1958–60), and his correspondence was published in *The Letters of James Agee to Father Flye* (1962). *The Collected Poems of James Agee*, edited by his friend Robert Fitzgerald, appeared in 1968.

Howard Baker (April 5, 1905–July 25, 1990) b. Philadelphia, Pennsylvania. Graduated from Whittier College in 1927. Attended Stanford (M.A. 1929), where he studied with Yvor Winters, the Sorbonne (1929–31), and University of California, Berkeley (Ph.D. 1937). Taught at Harvard, 1937–43. Grew oranges and olives in California; was director of Lindsay Ripe Olive Company, as well as member of Citrus Advisory Board of California. Poetry collections included *A Letter from the Country* (1941), *Ode to the Sea* (1966), and *Sky Coloured Glasses* (1978).

Mary Barnard (b. December 6, 1909) b. Vancouver, Washington. Educated at local schools and at Reed College. During Depression worked as caseworker for Emergency Relief Administration. Began corresponding with Ezra Pound in 1933; he placed some of her poems in English magazines. *Poetry* published several of her poems in 1935, and awarded her its Levinson Prize. Visited New York City in 1936; met William Carlos Williams, Marianne Moore, Muriel Rukeyser, James Laughlin, and others. Found employment at libraries of University of Buffalo, and started one of the first collections of modern poetry in the country. Returned to New York in 1936 as Carl Van Doren's research assistant. Poetry collection "Cool Country" included in New Directions' *Five Young American Poets 1940;* chapbook *A Few Poems* appeared in 1952. *Sappho: A New Translation* was published in 1958. Published prose study *The Mythmakers* (1966). First book-length poetry collection, *Collected Poems* (1979), won Elliston Award. Later books include a memoir, *Assault on Mount Helicon* (1986), and two book-length poems, *Time and the White Tigress* (1986), a poetic sequel to *The Mythmakers* which won the Western Book Award, and the autobiographical *Nantucket Genesis* (1988).

Ben Belitt (b. May 2, 1911) b. New York City. Raised in Manhattan orphanage and in Lynchburg, Virginia. Educated at University of Virginia. Was assistant literary editor of *The Nation*, 1937–38. Served in U.S. Army (1942–44) and in the Combat Film Section of the Signal Corps Photographic Center; published prose journal "School of the Soldier" (1949) in *Quarterly Review of Literature*. Was professor of literature and languages at Bennington College beginning in 1938. Translated the work of Federico García Lorca, Pablo Neruda, Antonio Machado, Rafael Alberti, Arthur Rimbaud, and others; *Adam's Dream*, a study of translation, appeared in 1978. Poetry collections included *The Five-Fold Mesh* (1938), *Wilderness Stair* (1955), *The Enemy Joy* (1964), *Nowhere But Light* (1970), *The Double Witness* (1978), *Possessions: New and Selected Poems* (1986), *Graffiti* (1989), and *This Scribe, My Hand* (1998).

Stephen Vincent Benét (July 22, 1898–March 13, 1943) b. Bethlehem, Pennsylvania. Siblings were the poets William Rose Benét and Laura Benét. Grew up in a series of army-base homes, in New York, Illinois, California, and Georgia. While attending Yale, published poetry collections *Five Men and Pompey* (1915), *The Drug Shop, Or Endymion in Edmondstown* (1917), and *Young Adventure* (1918); graduated 1919. Novel *The Beginning of Wisdom* appeared in 1921. Won the *Nation* poetry prize in 1923. Received Guggenheim Fellowship in 1925 to write long poem on the Civil War, published as *John Brown's Body* (1928); it became an enduring bestseller and won Pulitzer Prize. Spent three months in Hollywood writing screenplay for D. W. Griffith's *Abraham Lincoln* (1930). Collaborated with his wife on *A Book of Americans* (1933), a series of poems for children. Accepted editorship of the Yale Series of Younger Poets; selected manuscripts by poets including James Agee, Muriel Rukeyser, Reuel Denney, and Margaret Walker. Published *Burning City* (1936). Wrote libretto for Douglas Moore's opera *The Devil and Daniel Webster* (1939), based on Benét's short story. After outbreak of World War II, wrote speeches, radio scripts, and *America*, a brief historical survey for worldwide distribution. *Western Star* (1943), the posthumously published first volume of a projected nine-book narrative poem about the settlement of America, received the Pulitzer Prize.

Elizabeth Bishop (February 8, 1911–October 6, 1979) b. Worcester, Massachusetts. Father died in 1911; mother was often hospitalized thereafter and was permanently institutionalized in 1916. Raised successively by maternal grandparents in Nova Scotia, paternal grandparents in Worcester, and maternal aunt near Boston. Suffered chronic asthma from childhood. Educated at Walnut Hill boarding school and Vassar; graduated in 1934; traveled in Europe and North Africa (1935–37). Formed friendship with Marianne Moore. After 1937, her poems appeared regularly in *Poetry* and *Partisan Review*. In 1938 bought house in Key West, where she spent parts of the next seven years. *North and South*, completed in 1939, appeared in 1946. Lived in New York City during late 1940's; was a close friend of Robert Lowell. Served term as Consultant in Poetry at the Library of Congress. Sailed in 1951 to Rio de Janeiro; moved into her estate in Petrópolis with Lota de Macedo Soares, whom she had met in New York. *Poems: North & South—A Cold Spring* (1955) won Pulitzer Prize. Published *The Diary of Helena Morley* (1957), translation from the Portuguese. Moved with Soares to Rio in 1961. Published poetry collection *Questions of Travel* (1965). Taught at the University of Washington in 1966. Hospitalized for mental exhaustion (1966–67). Soares committed suicide in 1967; Bishop remained in Brazil until 1970. *The Complete Poems* (1969) won National Book Award. Taught at Harvard; became friends with Seamus Heaney, Octavio Paz, and Robert Fitzgerald. Spent summers traveling with Alice Methfessel. Published *Geography III* (1976). Died of cerebral aneurysm.

R. P. Blackmur (January 21, 1904–February 2, 1965) b. Richard Palmer Blackmur in Springfield, Massachusetts. Raised in Cambridge, Massachusetts, where mother ran a boardinghouse. Expelled from Cambridge High and Latin School in 1918, after arguing with headmaster. Worked as soda jerk, bookstore clerk, and clerk at Harvard's Widener Library. Opened a bookstore in Cambridge in 1925 that closed after a year. Became editor of *Hound and Horn* in 1928. Married painter Helen Dickson in 1930. Published critical writings in *The Double Agent* (1935) and poetry collection *From Jordan's Delight* (1937). Awarded Guggenheim Fellowship in 1938 for biography of Henry Adams; lengthy manuscript was never completed. Took position assisting Allen Tate in new creative arts program at Princeton University in 1940. Published book of criticism, *The Expense of Greatness* (1940), and poetry collection *The Second World* (1942). In 1944, named fellow in economics at the Institute for Advanced Study. Published *The Good European* (1947). Promoted to professor in 1951. Published collection of essays on poetry, *Language as Gesture* (1952). Taught at Cambridge University (1961–62).

Louise Bogan (August 11, 1897–February 4, 1970) b. Louise Marie Bogan in Livermore Falls, Maine. Grew up in Milton, New Hampshire, Ballardvale, Massachusetts, and Boston. Attended Girls Latin School in Boston, 1909–15. While in high school, published four poems in *Boston Evening Transcript*. Entered Boston University in 1915. Married Curt Alexander, an army officer, in 1916; joined him in Panama, where he was on duty. Returned to Boston with her seven-month-old daughter in 1918. Moved to Greenwich Village; separated from Alexander, who died of pneumonia soon after. Involved with Alfred Kreymborg's *Others* group; published poems in *The New Republic*, *Vanity Fair*, and *The Measure*. Began a lifelong series of psychoanalytic treatments in the early 1920's. Spent summer of 1922 in Vienna. Published poetry collection *Body of This Death* in 1923. Met Edmund Wilson; became close friend of Rolfe Humphries. Named managing editor of *The Measure*. With her daughter and Raymond Holden, her second husband, moved among Boston, New Mexico, and New York for a period of years; established a home in Hillsdale, New York, in 1929. Published poetry collection *Dark Summer* in 1929. Most of her manuscripts were destroyed when Hillsdale house burned down. Published first book review in *The New Yorker* in 1931; named poetry editor, a position that she held intermittently for 38 years. Underwent treatment at New York Neurological Institute in 1931. Awarded Guggenheim Fellowship in 1932; traveled to Italy. Served as Consultant in Poetry at the

Library of Congress, 1945–46. Published critical collections *Achievement in American Poetry* (1951) and *A Poet's Alphabet* (1970). Maintained friendships with Theodore Roethke, May Sarton, and Morton Dauwen Zabel. Won Bollingen Prize in 1955. Poems collected in *The Blue Estuaries: Poems 1923–1968* (1968).

Arna Bontemps (October 13, 1902–June 4, 1973) b. Arna Wendell Bontemps in Alexandria, Louisiana. Family moved to Los Angeles in 1905. Attended San Fernando Academy, a Seventh Day Adventist school, and afterward Pacific Union College, also affiliated with the church; graduated in 1923. Worked at Los Angeles post office before moving in 1924 to Harlem, where he taught at Harlem Academy, an Adventist high school. Published first poem, "Hope," in *The Crisis* in 1924. Married Alberta Johnson in 1926. In 1926 and 1927 won three poetry prizes given by *Opportunity* and *The Crisis*. Moved in 1931 to Huntsville, Alabama, to teach at Oakwood Junior College. Published novel *God Sends Sunday* (1931). Won prize from *Opportunity* for 1932 short story "A Summer Tragedy." Collaborated with Langston Hughes on *Popo and Fifina: Children of Haiti* (1932), a children's book. Moved to Chicago, where he became principal of an Adventist school. Published novels *Black Thunder* (1936) and *Drums at Dusk* (1939). Edited anthology of African-American poetry for children, *Golden Slippers* (1941), and with Langston Hughes co-edited *The Poetry of the Negro: 1746–1949* (1949). While working for Federal Writers' Project, met Jack Conroy, with whom he collaborated on three children's books. Won scholarships from the Rosenwald Fund; earned master's degree in library science from University of Chicago in 1943. Named head librarian at Fisk University in Nashville, where he remained for the rest of his life. In collaboration with Countee Cullen and composer Harold Arlen, adapted *God Sends Sunday* into the musical *St. Louis Woman* (1946). *The Story of the Negro* (1948) won the Jane Addams Children's Book Award, and was followed by several works of history and biography for children. Poetry collection *Personals* appeared in 1963.

Alter Brody (November 1, 1895–1979) b. Kartushkiya-Beroza, Russia. Came with family to New York City in 1903. Published poetry in *The Seven Arts*, *Atlantic Monthly*, *The Dial*, and other magazines; poetry collected in *A Family Album* (1918), with a foreword by Louis Untermeyer. *Lamentations: Four Folk-Plays of the American Jew* appeared in 1928. As an editor of *Soviet Russia Today*, worked on a number of special publications including *The U.S.S.R. and Finland* (1939), *War and Peace in Finland* (1940), and *Behind the Polish-Soviet Break* (1940). Died at Jewish Home and Hospital for the Aged in New York.

Sterling A. Brown (May 1, 1901–January 13, 1989) b. Sterling Allen Brown in Washington, D.C. Son of the Reverend Sterling N. Brown, religion professor at Howard University. Edited school magazine at Dunbar High School, where teachers included Angelina Grimké and Jessie Redmon Fauset. Studied at Williams College (1918–22); elected to Phi Beta Kappa; earned

M.A. at Harvard in 1923. Taught at Virginia Seminary and College, Fisk University, and Lincoln University; appointed professor of American literature in 1929 at Howard, where he remained for 50 years. Published first book, *Outline for the Study of Poetry of American Negroes* (1931). Published poetry collection *Southern Road* (1932). Was editor on Negro Affairs in the Federal Writers' Project (1936–39); awarded Guggenheim Fellowship (1937–38). Published two critical studies, *The Negro in American Fiction* and *Negro Poetry and Drama*, in 1937. Edited *The Negro Caravan* (1941), an anthology covering nearly 200 years of African-American poetry. His later poetry collections were *The Last Ride of Wild Bill and Eleven Narrative Poems* (1975) and *Collected Poems* (1980).

Stanley Burnshaw (b. June 20, 1906) b. New York City. Son of Eastern European Jews who fled czarist pogroms of the 1880's; raised in Pleasantville, New York. Graduated from University of Pittsburgh in 1925; wrote copy for advertising agency. Started magazine *Poetry Folio* in 1926, and published *Poems* (1927). Attended classes at the Sorbonne; met French poet André Spire. Poetry collection *The Great Dark Love* (1932), privately published, followed by *André Spire and his Poetry* (1933). Worked as advertising manager in New York (1928–32). Earned M.A. from Cornell in 1933. Contributed prolifically to *New Masses*; published *The Iron Land* (1936). Founded Dryden Press in 1939. Published verse drama *The Bridge* (1945), *The Revolt of the Cats in Paradise* (1945), novel *The Sunless Sea* (1948), and poetry collection *Early and Late Testament* (1952). Lectured at New York University (1958–62); co-edited *The Poem Itself* (1960), an anthology of non-English poems with literal translations and analytical gloss; edited *Varieties of Literary Experience* (1962), collection of essays on world literature. Published *The Seamless Web* (1970), study of poetry. Later books include *In the Terrified Radiance* (1972) and *Mirages: Travel Notes in the Promised Land: A Public Poem* (1977).

John Cage (September 5, 1912–August 12, 1992) b. John Milton Cage Jr. in Los Angeles. Valedictorian at Los Angeles High School; attended Pomona College for two years; moved to Europe and began composing music in Majorca. Studied in Los Angeles with Arnold Schoenberg. Lived in Seattle; moved to New York City in 1942; friends included Robert Rauschenberg, Marcel Duchamp, D. T. Suzuki, Jackson Mac Low, and Morton Feldman; collaborated with dancer Merce Cunningham. Early compositions included *Sonata and Interludes for Prepared Piano, String Quartet in Four Parts* (1950), and *Sixteen Dances* (1951). Began using chance operations in composition. Composed *34′ 46.776″: For a Pianist* (1954), *Winter Music* (1957), and *Music Walk* (1958). Co-founded New York Mycological Society. Composed *HPSCHD* (1967–69), an early example of computer-generated music. Writings collected in *Silence* (1961), *A Year from Monday* (1967), and *M* (1973), in which he experimented with mesostics, acrostic poems in which the middle letters of each line spell a word when read vertically. Later writings included

Empty Words (1979), *Themes and Variations* (1982), and *X* (1983); Harvard lectures published as *I–VI* (1990). Extended mesostic text published posthumously as *Composition in Retrospect* (1993).

Emanuel Carnevali (1897–1942?) b. Florence, Italy. Immigrated to United States to avoid conscription in World War I. Worked in Italian restaurants, grocery stores, and hotels in New York City. Met William Carlos Williams at one of Lola Ridge's parties in 1919; Williams dedicated the last issue of *Others* to Carnevali. Served as associate editor of *Poetry*. Published poems in *Poetry*, *Others*, *The Little Review*, *The Modern Review*, and others. Diagnosed with encephalitis; placed in mental ward of St. Luke's Hospital. In 1922 he returned to Italy and was placed in a charity ward in Bazzano. Collection of poetry and prose, *A Hurried Man* (1925), was published by Robert McAlmon's Contact Editions; McAlmon supported him financially for several years. Lived in charity wards for the remainder of his life; died by choking on a piece of bread. *The Autobiography of Emanuel Carnevali*, compiled and edited by Kay Boyle, appeared in 1967.

Constance Carrier (July 29, 1908–December 7, 1991) b. New Britain, Connecticut. Descended from Martha Carrier, who was convicted of witchcraft and hanged during Salem witch trials in 1692. Educated at Smith (B.A., 1929) and Trinity (M.A., 1940). Taught Latin, French, and English in New Britain and West Hartford schools (1931–69). First published poems appeared in *Atlantic Monthly*, *The New Yorker*, and *Poetry*. Published poetry collection *The Middle Voice* (1955). Translated Sextus Propertius' *Elegiae* (1963), *The Poems of Tibullus* (1968), and two plays in Terence's *Works* (1974). Later poetry collections were *The Angled Road* (1973) and *Witchcraft Poems: Salem, 1692* (1988).

Malcolm Cowley (August 24, 1898–March 28, 1989) b. Belsana, Pennsylvania. Entered Harvard in 1915. Contributed poems to *Harvard Advocate*. Drove munitions trucks for French army during World War I. Married Peggy Baird in 1919. Graduated from Harvard in 1920; lived in Greenwich Village for a year, reviewing books and writing advertising copy. Became friend of Allen Tate, Hart Crane, John Wheelwright, and others. With American Field Service scholarship, studied French literature at Université de Montpellier. Traveled with wife to Germany and Paris, where they met André Breton and Louis Aragon. Won *Poetry* magazine's Levinson Prize in 1927; bought farmhouse in western Connecticut. Published poetry collection *Blue Juniata* (1929). Served as editor of *The New Republic*, 1929–44. His literary memoir *Exile's Return* appeared in 1934. Was a co-founder of the League of American Writers in 1935. Moved to Sherman, Connecticut, with second wife and son in 1936. Published poetry collection *The Dry Season* (1941). Worked at Office of Facts and Figures in Washington, D.C. Edited *The Portable Faulkner* (1946), which helped revive William Faulkner's reputation; served as literary adviser to Viking Press from 1948. Held series of visiting professorships between 1950 and 1972, at University of Washington, Stanford, University of

Michigan, University of California, Cornell, Hollins, and University of Minnesota. Served as president of National Institute of Arts and Letters and Chancellor of American Academy of Arts and Letters. Published many prose books including *The Literary Situation* (1954), *A Second Flowering* (1973), *And I Worked at the Writer's Trade* (1978), and *The Dream of the Golden Mountains* (1980). *Blue Juniata: Collected Poems* appeared in 1968.

Hart Crane (July 21, 1899–April 27, 1932) b. Harold Hart Crane in Garrettsville, Ohio. Only child of Clarence Arthur Crane, candy manufacturer who invented the "Life Saver," and Grace Hart Crane. In 1908, after his mother was placed in a sanatorium, Crane was sent to Cleveland to live with his maternal grandmother; his parents divorced in 1917. High school attendance was patchy due to family difficulties. At age 17 began correspondence with Harriet Moody, poet William Vaughn Moody's widow. With promise that his father would support him until he turned 21, left high school during senior year and moved to New York City to concentrate on writing poetry. His mother, then living in Florida, demanded that he write her daily letters; she and Crane's grandmother briefly lived in his one-bedroom apartment. Returned to Cleveland in 1918; worked at munitions factory and as reporter for *Cleveland Plain Dealer*. In New York, served as assistant editor at small literary magazine *The Pagan*; published poems in *The Little Review*, where he worked as advertising manager. Spent summer of 1919 as shipping clerk for one of his father's suppliers, then returned to Cleveland to work for his father; after they quarreled violently in 1921, moved back to New York, where he worked for several advertising firms. Received occasional support from financier Otto Kahn. Visited Cleveland for the last time in 1923. Spent that winter in Woodstock, New York, at the home of friends Edward Nagle and William Slater Brown. In spring of 1924 moved into building in Columbia Heights, Brooklyn, with close view of Brooklyn Bridge; John Dos Passos was a neighbor. The following year lived at Patterson, New York, home of Allen Tate and Caroline Gordon. Published poetry collection *White Buildings* in 1926. That April, with a grant from Kahn, Crane retired to the Isle of Pines in Cuba, where he wrote most of long poem *The Bridge*. Broke permanently with his mother and grandmother in 1928. Lived in Paris for part of 1929. Harry Crosby's Black Sun Press published *The Bridge* (1930); Liveright published the poem a few months later in New York. Awarded Guggenheim Fellowship in 1931; sailed to Mexico with the intention of writing a long poem, but wrote little. Sailed for New York on the *Orizaba* with Peggy Cowley, ex-wife of his friend Malcolm Cowley; committed suicide by jumping overboard.

Harry Crosby (June 4, 1898–December 10, 1929) b. Henry Sturgis Crosby in Boston, Massachusetts. Nephew and godson of J. P. Morgan. Educated at St. Mark's School in Southboro, Massachusetts. Joined American Field Service Ambulance Corps in 1917. Served at Verdun; received Croix de Guerre in 1919. Entered Harvard at his father's insistence; awarded B.A. in 1921. Met Polly Peabody in 1920; she divorced her husband the following year and married Crosby in 1922. Worked briefly at National Shawmut Bank. Moved with Polly and her two children to Paris in 1922 to work at Morgan's Paris bank, Morgan, Harjes et Cie. Encouraged in his literary aspirations by his cousin, Walter Van Rensselaer Berry; quit bank job to devote himself to poetry. Privately published *Anthology* (1924), a collection of his favorite poems. After publishing her book *Crosses of Gold* (1925), Polly changed her name to Caresse; later the same year, Crosby published poetry collection *Sonnets for Caresse*. Traveled through Europe and North Africa over the next two years. Maintained opulent and hedonistic lifestyle. Developed a private religion based on sun-worship. Met other writers and poets, such as Ezra Pound, Ernest Hemingway, Archibald MacLeish, and Eugene Jolas, to whose *transition* Crosby contributed. With Caresse, founded small press Edition Narcisse (later Black Sun Press) in 1927; first two books published were the fourth edition of *Sonnets for Caresse* and Crosby's *Red Skeletons*; in addition to their own work, the Crosbys published volumes by D. H. Lawrence, Jolas, MacLeish, Kay Boyle, Bob Brown, and others. After Walter Berry died in 1927, Crosby inherited most of his 8,000-volume library. Met Josephine Rotch in 1928 (later referred to her in his poetry as "The Mad Queen" and "The Fire Princess"). Refurbished country home in Ermenonville, France, called Le Moulin de Soleil (The Mill of the Sun). Met Hart Crane, who stayed at Le Moulin de Soleil; agreed to publish first version of Crane's *The Bridge*, which appeared in 1930. Met James Joyce and printed sections of *Finnegans Wake* as *Tales Told by Shem and Shaun* (1929). Published four poetry collections in 1929: *Mad Queen, Shadows of the Sun, The Sun*, and *Sleeping Together*. In December, on a visit to the United States, spent several days with Rotch in Detroit; three days after attending a party in his honor given by Crane, shot and killed Rotch and himself in a friend's apartment.

Countee Cullen (May 30, 1903–January 9, 1946) b. Countee Porter in Louisville, Kentucky. Raised by Elizabeth Porter, who may have been his paternal grandmother; after her death in 1918, raised in New York City by the Reverend and Mrs. Frederick Cullen. Educated at De Witt Clinton High School and New York University, where he won 1925 Witter Bynner Prize; published poetry collection *Color* the same year. Won prizes in contests sponsored by *Poetry, Opportunity, The Crisis*, and *Palms*. Earned M.A. from Harvard in 1926. Edited *Caroling Dusk: An Anthology of Verse by Negro Poets* (1927). Wrote column "From the Dark Tower" for *Opportunity*. Published *Copper Sun* and *The Ballad of the Brown Girl: An Old Ballad Retold* (both 1927). Awarded Guggenheim Fellowship in 1928 to study in France. Married Nina Yolande Du Bois, daughter of W.E.B. Du Bois, in 1928; they divorced two years later. Published *The Black Christ* (1929) and novel *One Way to Heaven* (1932). From 1934 taught English and French at Frederick Douglass Junior High School in New York City, where his students included James Baldwin. Published translation of Euripides, *The Medea and Some Poems* (1935), as well as two collections of children's stories. Collected his poems in *On These I Stand* (1945). Collaborated with Arna Bontemps on *St. Louis Woman*, musical adaptation of Bontemps' novel *God Sends Sunday*; died two months before New York premiere.

E. E. Cummings (October 14, 1894–September 3, 1962) b. Edward Estlin Cummings in Cambridge, Massachusetts. Father was a Unitarian minister. Began writing poetry at an early age. Entered Harvard in 1911; joined editorial board of *Harvard Monthly*. Delivered 1915 commencement address, "The New Art," on modernism in painting, music, and literature. Moved to New York City in 1917; worked briefly for a mail order book business. Volunteered for Norton-Harjes Ambulance Service in 1917; with William Slater Brown, a fellow volunteer, abandoned unit in Paris. Detained for three months in Normandy on suspicion of espionage. Shared New York studio apartment with Brown and devoted time to painting. Drafted for army service in 1918; trained for six months at Camp Devens, Massachusetts. Fathered child of Elaine Orr in 1919; they were married in 1924. Toured Europe in 1921 with Harvard friend John Dos Passos; met Ezra Pound in Paris. *The Enormous Room*, a prose account of his incarceration in France, appeared in 1922, followed by the poetry collections *Tulips and Chimneys* (1923), *XLI Poems* (1925), the privately printed *&* (1925), and *Is 5* (1926). Won *Dial* award. Play *Him* produced by Provincetown Playhouse in 1928. Collected stories, epigrams, sayings, and puns in an untitled book (1930). Active throughout his life as visual artist and gave many exhibitions of his paintings. Published book of artwork, *CIOPW* (1931), and poetry collection, *ViVa* (1931). Traveled to Soviet Union in 1931; travel diary published as *Eimi* (1933). Met Marion Morehouse, with whom he entered a common-law marriage. Awarded Guggenheim Fellowship in 1933. Diagnosed with osteoarthritis of the spine. Later poetry collections included *No Thanks* (1935), *Collected Poems* (1938), *50 Poems* (1940), *1 X 1* (1945), *XAIPE* (1950), and *95 Poems* (1958). Lectures at Harvard published as *i: six nonlectures* (1953). Won Bollingen Prize in 1958.

Waring Cuney (May 6, 1906–June 30, 1976) b. William Waring Cuney in Washington, D.C. Educated at Howard University, Lincoln University (where he was a classmate of Langston Hughes), and New England Conservatory of Music; later studied music in Rome and at Columbia University. Published poems in *Fire!!* and in Countee Cullen's anthology *Caroling Dusk* (1927); "No Images" won first prize in *Opportunity*'s 1926 poetry contest. Wrote art and music criticism for *The Crisis*. Collaborated with Josh White on some of the songs on White's 1941 album *Southern Exposure*, including the title song, "Hard Time Blues," and "Jim Crow Train." Served as technical sergeant in South Pacific during World War II. Published several broadsides during the 1950's; co-edited *Lincoln University Poets: Centennial Anthology, 1854–1954* (1954) with Hughes and Bruce Wright. Poetry collected in *Puzzles* (1960) and *Storefront Church* (1973).

J. V. Cunningham (August 23, 1911–March 30, 1985) b. James Vincent Cunningham in Cumberland, Maryland. Attended Jesuit high school in

Colorado; later attended St. Mary's College, Kansas, and Stanford, where he studied with Yvor Winters. Taught English at Stanford, 1937–45. Poetry collected in *The Helmsman* (1942), *The Judge Is Fury* (1947), *Doctor Drink* (1950), *Trivial, Vulgar, and Exalted* (1957), *The Exclusions of a Rhyme* (1960), *To What Strangers, What Welcome* (1964), *Some Salt* (1967), *The Collected Poems and Epigrams* (1971), and *Selected Poems* (1971). Taught at University of Hawaii (1945–46), University of Chicago (1946–52), University of Virginia (1953–76), and Brandeis (1976–80). Published criticism including *The Quest of the Opal* (1950), *Woe or Wonder: The Emotional Effect of Shakespearean Tragedy* (1951), *Tradition and Poetic Structure* (1960), *The Journal of John Cardan* (1964), and *The Collected Essays of J.V. Cunningham* (1976).

Edward Dahlberg (July 22, 1900–July 27, 1977) b. Boston, Massachusetts. Traveled as a child with parents, who were unmarried; father eventually deserted family. Sent in 1912 to Jewish Orphan Asylum in Cleveland. Worked for two years as a Western Union messenger; tramped through the West, supporting himself as a dishwasher, cook, and laborer. Wrote movie scenarios; moved into a Los Angeles YMCA. Enrolled at University of California at Berkeley in 1921; studied philosophy and anthropology. Completed degree at Columbia University. Married Fanya Fass, first of four wives, and moved to Paris, Monte Carlo, and Brussels; wrote novels *Bottom Dogs* (1929) and *From Flushing to Calvary* (1932). Beaten by uniformed Nazis in a Berlin bar; wrote *Those Who Perish* (1934). Helped organize first American Writers' Congress (1935). Formed close friendship with Charles Olson. *Do These Bones Live*, collection of essays on American literature, appeared in 1941. Moved with third wife from New York City to Berkeley, Santa Monica, and Topanga; studied pre-Columbian mythology. Traveled through Europe in 1956, settling in Majorca, where he finished *The Sorrows of Priapus* (1957); also spent time in New York City and Dublin. Wrote *Truth Is More Sacred* (1961) with Herbert Read; published autobiography *Because I Was Flesh* (1964). Moved to Kansas City in 1965 to teach at University of Missouri. Published *Reasons of the Heart* (1965), book of aphorisms, followed by poetry collection *Cipango's Hinder Door* (1966); later books included *The Carnal Myth* (1970), *The Confessions of Edward Dahlberg* (1971), and *The Olive of Minerva* (1976).

Frank Marshall Davis (December 31, 1905–July 26, 1987) b. Arkansas City, Kansas. Studied in Kansas State University's journalism program in 1924. Began writing poetry in freshman year; joined the American College Quill Club. Moved to Chicago in 1927; wrote for various black newspapers, including the *Chicago Evening Bulletin*, the *Whip*, and the *Gary American*. Co-founded and edited *Atlanta Daily World* (1931–34). Published poetry collection *Black Man's Verse* (1935), followed by *I Am the American Negro* (1937), and *Through Sepia Eyes* (1938). Worked as jazz disc jockey in the early 1940's. Was executive editor (1935–47) of Associated Negro Press in Chicago; participated

in League of American Writers, Allied Arts Guild, and South Side Writers'
Group, which included Richard Wright, Arna Bontemps, Fenton Johnson,
and others. Published poetry collection *47th Street* (1948); moved to Hon-
olulu with wife and children; ran wholesale paper business and wrote weekly
column for *Honolulu Record*. Wrote "Waikiki Jungle," unpublished manu-
script on Hawaii. Returned to mainland for reading tour in 1973. Poetry col-
lection *Awakening* appeared in 1978. Memoir *Livin' the Blues* (1992) appeared
posthumously.

H. L. Davis (October 18, 1894–October 31, 1960) b. Harold Lenoir Davis in
Rone's Mill, Oregon. Raised in Dalles, on the Columbia River. Worked as
local tax assessor and as surveyor for U.S. General Land Office, 1912–17.
"Primapara," in April 1919 issue of *Poetry*, won the magazine's Levinson
Prize. Married Marion Lay in 1928 and moved to Bainbridge Island, Wash-
ington. Wrote sketches and stories for *Collier's*, *The Saturday Evening Post*,
and other magazines. Moved to Arizona in 1930. Awarded Guggenheim Fel-
lowship in 1932; moved to Mexico City and later Oaxaca. First novel, *Honey
in the Horn* (1935), won Pulitzer Prize. Bought a ranch near Napa, California,
in 1937; lived there and in Oaxaca. Published poetry collection *Proud Riders*
(1942) and novels *Harp of a Thousand Strings* (1947), *Beulah Land* (1949),
Winds of Morning (1952), and *The Distant Music* (1957). Worked as writer and
researcher for movie studios; essays on the Pacific Northwest collected in
Kettle of Fire (1959).

Alton Delmore (December 25, 1908–June 9, 1964) b. Elkmont, Alabama.
Grew up in sharecropping family. Attended high school in Decatur, Alabama.
Sang and played guitar in local groups. Worked in printer's office. Began
playing at social functions and fiddlers' conventions with younger brother
Rabon, who played four-string "tenor guitar." They successfully auditioned
with Columbia Records in 1931, and made their first record. As the Delmore
Brothers, they made many records for RCA Victor's Bluebird label, 1933–40,
including "Gonna Lay Down My Old Guitar," "Brown's Ferry Blues," and
"Blue Railroad Train." Flourished as cast members of the *Grand Ole Opry*
(1933–38) in Nashville, Tennessee. Toured with Uncle Dave Macon. Per-
formed for WPTF in Raleigh, North Carolina (1938–39), WAPI in Birming-
ham, Alabama (1939–42), and WLW in Cincinnati (1942–45). With Grandpa
Jones and others, Alton performed with gospel group the Brown's Ferry
Four, 1946–52. For Syd Nathan's King label, 1944–50, the Delmore Brothers
recorded songs including "Freight Train Boogie," "Mobile Boogie," "Sand
Mountain Blues," "Trouble Ain't Nothin' But the Blues," and "The Girl by
the River." Worked for WMC in Memphis (1945–47), XERF in Del Rio,
Texas (1950–51), and KPRC in Houston (1951–52). Rabon died of cancer in
1952. Alton continued to write songs, worked as a salesman and postman, and
wrote fiction. He had a radio program in Hattiesburg, Mississippi, in the
early 1960's. His autobiography, *Truth Is Stranger Than Publicity*, was pub-
lished posthumously in 1977.

Edwin Denby (February 4, 1903–July 12, 1983) b. Tientsin, China, where father was American consul. Family moved to Vienna and then Detroit at outbreak of World War I. Educated at Hotchkiss preparatory school and Harvard. Left Harvard twice with classmate Frank Safford, going first to England in 1920, and then to New York City; worked briefly for telephone company; parents financed move to Vienna in 1923. Began psychoanalysis there with Dr. Paul Federn, a colleague of Freud. Took dance classes at the Hellerau-Laxenburg School (1925–28); with dance partner Claire Eckstein, formed small dance company that toured Germany, 1928–33. Spent 1929 at State Theatre of Darmstadt as choreographer and dancer. Met Aaron Copland, Bertolt Brecht, Kurt Weill, and Lotte Lenya. Returned to New York in 1935; lived with photographer Rudy Burckhardt; neighbors included Willem and Elaine de Kooning. Produced adaptations and librettos; worked with Orson Welles, Paul Bowles, Virgil Thomson, Copland, and others; choreographed Weill's *Knickerbocker Holiday* (1938), and appeared in many of Burckhardt's films. Began writing dance reviews; contributed regular dance column to *Modern Music*, and was guest dance critic for New York *Herald Tribune* (1942–45). Published poetry collection *In Public, In Private* in 1948. Awarded Guggenheim Fellowship in 1948; returned to Europe. Published collection of critical writing, *Looking at the Dance* (1949). Became close friend of poet Frank O'Hara. Poetry collection *Mediterranean Cities*, illustrated with Burckhardt's photos, published in 1956. Published critical collection *Dancers, Buildings and People in the Streets* (1965) and novel *Mrs. W's Last Sandwich* (1972); later poetry collections included *Miltie is a Hackie* (1973), *Snoring in New York* (1974), and *Collected Poems* (1975). *Four Plays*, originally written for an Andy Warhol film, produced in 1981 by Eye and Ear Theatre. Committed suicide in Maine summer home by overdose of sleeping pills.

Babette Deutsch (September 22, 1895–November 13, 1982) b. New York City. Educated at Ethical Culture School and Barnard, from which she graduated with honors in 1917. Published article about economist Thorstein Veblen in *Reedy's Mirror*, which led to her being hired by Veblen as his secretary at the New School for Social Research. Poetry collection *Banners* published in 1919. Robert Frost recommended Deutsch for inclusion in Henry Holt's series of volumes by young poets. Married Avrahm Yarmolinsky, head of the Slavonic Division at New York Public Library, in 1921; they collaborated on many translations of German and Russian verse. Published *Honey Out of the Rock* (1925). Won the *Nation* poetry prize for 1926. Published book of criticism, *Potable Gold* (1929); long poem *Epistle to Prometheus* (1931); *Mask of Silenus* (1931), a novel about Socrates; *This Modern Poetry* (1935), a survey of American poetry; poetry collection *One Part Love* (1939); and *Rogue's Legacy* (1942), a novel about François Villon. Also published books for children, including retellings of Russian, Lithuanian, and Finnish folktales. The critical study *Poetry in Our Time* (1952) was followed by *Poetry Handbook: A Dictionary of Terms* (1957). With her husband, she edited the anthology *Two Centuries of Russian Verse* (1966). Taught at Columbia University until 1971.

Thomas A. Dorsey (July 1, 1899–January 23, 1993) b. Thomas Andrew Dorsey in Villa Rica, Georgia. Father was a Baptist minister, mother a church organist. Moved to Atlanta in 1910; briefly attended Morehouse College. Studied at Chicago College of Composition and Arranging during World War I. King Oliver's Creole Jazz Band recorded Dorsey's "Riverside Blues" in 1923. Formed jazz band the Wildcats. As "Georgia Tom," toured and made several recordings with Ma Rainey; collaborated with slide guitarist Tampa Red on many records including the hit "It's Tight Like That" (1928). Worked as arranger and record producer. Co-founded National Convention of Gospel Choirs and Choruses in 1931; thereafter devoted himself exclusively to gospel music. Composed hundreds of songs, including "Take My Hand, Precious Lord," "If I Could Hear My Mother Pray," "There Will Be Peace in the Valley," "When the Last Mile Is Finished," and "Wings over Jordan." Toured with Mahalia Jackson and Roberta Martin.

John Dos Passos (January 14, 1896–September 28, 1970) b. John Roderigo Mason in Chicago, Illinois. Parents married in 1910. Grew up throughout Western Europe and in Washington, D.C. Educated at English boarding school, Choate, and Harvard, where his friends included E. E. Cummings, Gilbert Seldes, and Robert Hillyer. Graduated in 1916; contributed poems to *Eight Harvard Poets* (1917); served with Norton-Harjes Ambulance Service in France and Italy; met Ernest Hemingway. Traveled through Spain and Portugal; settled in New York City. Published novels *One Man's Initiation—1917* (1920) and *Three Soldiers* (1921). Toured Eastern Europe and Middle East. Settled in New York; published *Rosinante to the Road Again* (1922), a travel book about Spain, poetry collection *A Pushcart at the Curb* (1922), and novel *Manhattan Transfer* (1925). Named director of New Playwrights Theatre in 1926, and a number of his plays were produced, including *The Garbage Man* (1926) and *Airways, Inc.* (1929). Reported on case of Sacco and Vanzetti for *New Masses.* Traveled extensively through Mexico, Europe, and Russia; travel accounts published as *Orient Express* (1927). Married Katharine Smith in 1929. Published *U.S.A.* trilogy, comprised of *The 42nd Parallel* (1930), *1919* (1932), and *The Big Money* (1936). Returned to Spain in 1937 to help write script for film about the Civil War; shocked at execution of friend Jose Robles by Communists. Disenchantment with left-wing political movements was expressed in the trilogy of novels consisting of *Adventures of a Young Man* (1939), *Number One* (1943), and *The Grand Design* (1949). In car crash in 1947, his wife died and Dos Passos lost an eye; he remarried in 1949. His later novels included *The Prospect Before Us* (1950), *Chosen Country* (1951), *Most Likely To Succeed* (1954), and *Midcentury* (1961); he also wrote travel books and historical studies.

Rose Drachler (February 11, 1911–July 10, 1982) b. Rose Kaplowitz in Brooklyn, New York. Father was a rabbi. Graduated from Hunter College in 1932; married Jacob Drachler. Taught in New York City public schools, 1933–67. Published poetry collections *Burrowing In, Digging Out* (1974),

Eight Eights (1977), *Amulet Against Drought* (1978), *The Choice* (1978), and *For Witches* (1982).

Richard Eberhart (b. April 5, 1904) b. Austin, Minnesota. Father was vice-president of Hormel Meat Packing. Attended University of Minnesota for a year, then transferred to Dartmouth College in 1923; graduated in 1926. In 1927 embarked on tramp steamer from San Francisco to England. Attended Cambridge; tutors there included F. R. Leavis, Gilbert Murray, and F. L. Lucas; graduated in 1929. Book-length poem *A Bravery of Earth* appeared in 1930. Worked as tutor for Florida family, then for adopted son of the King of Siam. Pursued graduate study at Harvard in 1932. Took teaching position at St. Mark's School in Southboro, Massachusetts. Published poetry collection *Reading the Spirit* (1936). Married Helen Butcher, a teacher, in 1941. Served in the navy, 1942–46. Accepted job with wife's family business, Butcher Polish Company in Boston. Was a co-founder of Poets' Theatre in Cambridge in 1950. Taught at universities including University of Washington, University of Connecticut at Storrs, and Princeton; taught at Dartmouth from 1956 to 1980. Served as Consultant in Poetry at the Library of Congress, 1959–61. Published poetry collections *Undercliff* (1953), *The Quarry* (1964), *Selected Poems 1930–1965* (1965), *Thirty-One Sonnets* (1967), *Fields of Grace* (1972), *Collected Poems 1930–1976* (1976), *Hours, Gnats* (1977), *Ways of Light* (1980), *Florida Poems* (1980), *The Long Reach* (1984), and *New and Selected Poems 1930–1990* (1990). In 1986 he received the Poetry Society of America's Robert Frost Medal.

William Everson (September 10, 1912–June 3, 1994) b. William Oliver Everson in Sacramento, California. Raised in Selma, California. Attended Fresno State intermittently in the early 1930's; worked in canneries and in Civilian Conservation Corps. Left college and planted vineyard; published poetry collection *These Are the Ravens* (1935). Drafted in 1943; as conscientious objector, did forestry work for three years in Waldport, Oregon. Moved to Berkeley in 1946; became involved with group of poets that included Kenneth Rexroth. Founded Equinox Press in 1947. Collected his poetry in *The Residual Years* (1948); that June he married Mary Fabilli. Separated from Mary in 1949; began receiving instruction in Catholicism at St. Augustine's Church in Oakland. Entered Dominican Order at St. Albert's College in Oakland as a lay monk in 1951, adopting the name Brother Antoninus. Moved Equinox Press to Oakland and renamed it Seraphim Press; closed the press in 1954. Published ten volumes of poetry as Brother Antoninus, including *An Age Insurgent* (1959), *The Crooked Lines of God* (1959), *The Hazards of Holiness* (1962), *A Canticle to the Waterbirds* (1968), and *The City Does Not Die* (1969). Took vows in 1964 and 1967. Late in 1969, departed from the order, married Susanna Rickson, and settled in Stinson Beach, California. Published *Man-Fate: The Swan Song of Brother Antoninus* (1974). In 1971, became poet-in-residence at University of Santa Cruz, as well as master printer of the school's Lime Kiln Press. Published critical writings *Archetype West* (1976) and

Earth Poetry (1980). Later poetry collections included *The High Embrace* (1985), *In Medias Res* (1985), and *Mexican Standoff* (1989). Published prose work *The Excesses of God* (1988), as well as *The Engendering Flood* (1990), first volume of autobiographical verse novel.

Kenneth Fearing (July 28, 1902–June 26, 1961) b. Oak Park, Illinois. After his parents divorced, spent most of his childhood with his father's family; raised by an aunt. Attended Oak Park–River Forest High School and University of Illinois in Urbana. Transferred to University of Wisconsin for his junior year; became friend of poet Carl Rakosi and novelist Margery Latimer. Went to New York in 1924 to join Latimer. Worked briefly for the WPA, *Time* magazine, the United Jewish Appeal, and other organizations; wrote pulp fiction under various pseudonyms. Began publishing poetry regularly in periodicals, many of them in *New Masses*. Poetry collection *Angel Arms* appeared in 1929. Married Rachel Meltzer in 1933. Published *Poems* (1935). Awarded Guggenheim Fellowship in 1937; traveled to London. In 1938 spent first of many summers at Yaddo, writers' colony in Saratoga Springs, New York. Published poetry collections *Dead Reckoning* (1938), *Collected Poems* (1940), *Afternoon of a Pawnbroker* (1943), and *Stranger at Coney Island* (1949), and novels including *The Hospital* (1939), *Dagger of the Mind* (1941), *Clark Gifford's Body* (1942), and the successful thriller *The Big Clock* (1946), which was filmed in 1948. Divorced in 1942; married Nan Lurie in 1945 (marriage ended in divorce in 1952). Subpoenaed by the U.S. attorney in Washington in 1950 for questioning on Communist Party affiliations; when asked if he was a party member, replied, "Not yet." Worked on staff of *Newsweek* (1952–54), and as publicist for the Muscular Dystrophy Association (1955–58). Later novels included *Loneliest Girl in the World* (1951), *The Generous Heart* (1954), and *The Crozart Story* (1960); published *New and Selected Poems* (1956).

Thomas Hornsby Ferril (February 25, 1896–October 27, 1988) b. Denver, Colorado. Graduated from Colorado College in 1918. Served in U.S. Army Signal Corps. Was drama critic for Denver *Times,* 1919–21. Worked in movie advertising and as press agent for Great Western Sugar Company, for whom he edited *The Sugar Press.* With his wife, Helen, published and edited *The Rocky Mountain Herald* (1939–72), weekly newspaper which his father had purchased in 1912; journalism collected in *I Hate Thursday* (1946) and *The Rocky Mountain Herald Reader* (1966). In 1979 he was named Poet Laureate of Colorado. Poetry collections included *High Passage* (1926), *Westering* (1934), *Trial by Time* (1944), *New and Selected Poems* (1952), *Words for Denver* (1966), and *Anvil of Roses* (1983).

Dorothy Fields (July 15, 1905–March 28, 1974) b. Allenhurst, New Jersey. Daughter of vaudevillian and Broadway producer Lew Fields. Attended Benjamin School for Girls in New York City. Commissioned to write songs about current events for producer Jack Mills. Met composer Jimmy McHugh in

1927; they collaborated on songs including "I Can't Give You Anything But Love," "On the Sunny Side of the Street," "Exactly Like You," "I Feel a Song Coming on," "Don't Blame Me," and many others. Wrote lyrics for Jerome Kern songs "Lovely to Look At," "I Won't Dance," and "The Way You Look Tonight." Played herself in film *Stage Door Canteen* (1943). Wrote eight librettos for Broadway musicals with brother Herbert, including *Let's Face It* (1941), *Mexican Hayride* (1944), and *Annie Get Your Gun* (1946). Went on to write book and lyrics for *A Tree Grows in Brooklyn* (1951) and *By the Beautiful Sea* (1954); collaborated with Cy Coleman on *Sweet Charity* (1966).

Dudley Fitts (April 28, 1903–July 10, 1968) b. Boston, Massachusetts. Graduated Harvard in 1925. Taught English at Choate (1925–41), and at Phillips Exeter Academy in Massachusetts (1941–68). Collaborated with Robert Fitzgerald on translations of *Alcestis* (1936), *Antigone* (1939), and *The Oedipus Cycle* (1958). Poetry collection *Poems, 1929–1936* appeared in 1937. Other translations included Aristophanes' *Lysistrata* (1954), *The Frogs* (1955), *The Birds* (1957), and *Ladies Day* (1959).

Robert Fitzgerald (October 12, 1910–January 16, 1985) b. Robert Stuart Fitzgerald in Geneva, New York. Educated at Harvard and Cambridge. Wrote for New York *Herald Tribune* (1933–35) and *Time* (1936–49); formed close friendship with James Agee. Served in U.S. Naval Reserve, 1943–46. Taught at Sarah Lawrence (1946–53) and Princeton (1950–52); became regular poetry reviewer for *The New Republic*. Lived in Italy (1953–64). Was Boylston Professor of Rhetoric at Harvard from 1965. Collaborated with Dudley Fitts on translations of *Alcestis* (1936), *Antigone* (1939), and *The Oedipus Cycle* (1958). Published many translations including *The Odyssey* (1961), *The Iliad* (1974), *The Aeneid* (1980), and works by St. John Perse, Paul Valéry, and Jorge Luis Borges. Poetry collected in *Poems* (1935), *A Wreath for the Sea* (1943), *In the Rose of Time* (1956), and *Spring Shade* (1971).

Hildegarde Flanner (June 3, 1899–May 27, 1987) b. June Hildegarde Flanner in Indianapolis, Indiana. Graduated from Short Ridge High School in Indianapolis; after one year at Sweet Briar College, transferred to University of California at Berkeley, where she studied poetry with Witter Bynner. Published poems in the *University of California Chronicle*, *The Occident*, and the *New-York Tribune*. While she was living in New York City, her first poetry collection, *Young Girl* (1920), was published without her knowledge. Settled with her mother in Berkeley in 1922; home was destroyed in Berkeley fire of 1923. Poetry collection *A Tree in Bloom* appeared in 1924. Married in 1926; settled in Altadena. Published collections *Time's Profile* (1929) and *If There Is Time* (1942); won *Poetry*'s Guarantors Prize in 1934. Visited sister Janet Flanner in Paris in 1950 and 1955. Moved to Napa Valley in 1962. Later poems were privately printed in *In Native Light* (1970); *Brief Cherishing*, a collection of essays, appeared in 1985.

Charles Henri Ford (b. February 10, 1913) b. Brookhaven, Mississippi. Published a poem in *The New Yorker* at age 14. Left high school in 1929; started literary magazine *Blues: A Magazine of New Rhythms* with Parker Tyler and Kathleen Tankersley Young. In 1930, moved to New York City with Tyler; they collaborated on a novel, *The Young and Evil* (1933). Sailed to Paris in 1931. Traveled to Italy and later Tangier in 1932; met Paul Bowles, Djuna Barnes, and Russian painter Pavel Tchelitchew. Published poems in *New Review*, *Front*, and Eugene Jolas' *transition*. Published *A Pamphlet of Sonnets* (1936). Poetry collection *The Garden of Disorder* (1938) was followed by *ABC's* (1940). Spent part of each year with Tchelitchew in Paris; joined FIARI, a group of artists. During World War II, divided time between New York City, Vermont, and Connecticut. Edited *View* (1940–47), an art and literary magazine which published work by Wallace Stevens, E. E. Cummings, Henry Miller, Georgia O'Keeffe, and Jorge Luis Borges. Published poetry collections *The Overturned Lake* (1941), *Poems for Painters* (1945), and *Sleep in a Nest of Flames* (1949). Moved to Italy in 1952 with Tchelitchew, who died five years later. Active as photographer and designer. Returned to New York in 1962. Combined word and image for "Poem Posters" exhibit. Published *Spare Parts* (1966) and *Silver Flower Coo* (1968). Wrote and directed film *Johnny Minotaur* (1969). Visit to Nepal in 1972 led to exhibit "The Kathmandu Experience." Later books included *Haiku and Imprints* (1984) and *Handshakes from Heaven* (1985).

Robert Francis (August 12, 1901–July 14, 1987) b. Robert Churchill Francis in Upland, Pennsylvania. Father was a Baptist minister. Raised in New Jersey, Long Island, and Massachusetts. Graduated from Harvard in 1923; taught in preparatory school of the American University in Beirut, Lebanon. Earned Ed.M. from Harvard in 1926. Moved to Amherst, Massachusetts; taught high school and gave violin lessons. First met Robert Frost in 1933. Taught at Mount Holyoke, 1944–45. Taught poetry at Chautauqua Writers' Workshop, 1954–58. Spent a year in Italy, 1957–58. Poetry collected in *Stand with Me Here* (1936), *Valhalla* (1938), *The Sound I Listened For* (1944), *The Face Against the Glass* (1950), *The Orb Weaver* (1960), *Come Out into the Sun* (1965), *Like Ghosts of Eagles* (1974), *A Certain Distance* (1976), *Collected Poems 1936–1976* (1976), and *Late Fire, Late Snow* (1992). Published novel *We Fly Away* (1948) and autobiography *The Trouble with Francis* (1971).

Jean Garrigue (December 8, 1912–December 27, 1972) b. Gertrude Louise Garrigus in Evansville, Indiana. Graduated from University of Chicago; received MFA from University of Iowa in 1943. Changed name upon moving to New York City. Met Delmore Schwartz, who showed her poems to James Laughlin; anthologized in Laughlin's *Five Young American Poets* (1944). Published poetry collection *The Ego and the Centaur* (1947). From the 1950's, taught poetry at Bard, Queens College, the New School for Social Research, University of Connecticut, and Smith. Later poetry collections included *The Monument Rose* (1953), *A Water Walk by Villa d'Este* (1959), *Country Without*

Maps (1964), *New and Selected Poems* (1967), and the posthumously published *Studies for an Actress* (1973). Also published novel *The Animal Hotel* (1966) and critical study *Marianne Moore* (1965).

Ira Gershwin (December 6, 1896–August 17, 1983) b. New York City. Worked in a carnival and in the family-owned bathhouse. First collaborated with brother George in 1918 on "The Real American Folk Song (Is a Rag)." Under pseudonym "Arthur Francis," wrote songs with Vincent Youmans, Raymond Hubbell, and others. Wrote lyrics to George's songs in *Lady, Be Good!* (1924), including "Fascinating Rhythm." They subsequently wrote the musical comedies *Oh, Kay!* (1926), *Funny Face* (1927), *Strike Up the Band* (1927), *Girl Crazy* (1930), *Of Thee I Sing* (1931), and *Let 'Em Eat Cake* (1933). Contributed lyrics to George's opera *Porgy and Bess* (1935). With Vernon Duke, wrote songs for the *Ziegfeld Follies of 1936*, including "I Can't Get Started." With George, wrote songs for two 1937 films starring Fred Astaire and Ginger Rogers, *Shall We Dance?* and *A Damsel in Distress*. Other songs written in collaboration with his brother included "Oh, Lady, Be Good," "The Man I Love," "Someone to Watch over Me," " 'S Wonderful," "Embraceable You," "But Not For Me," "They All Laughed," "Let's Call the Whole Thing Off," "They Can't Take That Away from Me," "A Foggy Day," "Nice Work If You Can Get It," "Love Is Here to Stay," and "Love Walked In." After George's death in 1937, worked with Kurt Weill on *Lady in the Dark* (1941), Jerome Kern on *Cover Girl* (1944), and Harold Arlen on *A Star Is Born* (1954).

Brewster Ghiselin (b. June 13, 1903) b. Webster Groves, Missouri. Graduated from University of California, Los Angeles, in 1927. Attended graduate school at Oxford (1928–29) and University of California at Berkeley (M.A., 1928). Taught briefly at University of Utah before returning to Berkeley, where he became full professor in 1950. Served as poetry editor and associate editor of *Rocky Mountain Review* (later *Western Review*), 1937–49. Edited anthology *The Creative Process* (1952). Poetry collections include *Against the Circle* (1946), *The Nets* (1955), *Country of the Minotaur* (1970), *Light* (1978), *Windrose: Poems 1929–1979* (1979), and *Flame* (1991).

Abraham Lincoln Gillespie (June 11, 1895–September 10, 1950) b. Philadelphia, Pennsylvania. Graduated Germantown Academy in 1912; studied at Pennsylvania State University, Haverford College, and University of Pennsylvania, from which he graduated in 1918. Taught French and Spanish at West Philadelphia High School for Boys. Suffered permanent injury to left leg in automobile accident in 1920. Married Ruth Breslow in New York City in 1923. Went to Paris by himself the following year; lived with composer George Antheil. Became part of group of American and European expatriates at Cagnes-sur-Mer in the late 1920's. Published his linguistic experiments regularly in Eugene Jolas' *transition*. Contributed to the anthology *Readies for Bob Brown's Machine* (1931), a collection of writings prepared for a "reading machine" invented by Brown. Returned to Philadelphia in 1932; received financial support from his family. Lived for a time in Greenwich Village apartment of Maxwell Bodenheim. After suffering a diabetic collapse in New York, was placed under a nurse's care in Philadelphia.

Paul Goodman (September 9, 1911–August 2, 1972) b. New York City. Graduated from City College of New York in 1931; earned Ph.D. from University of Chicago in 1940. Worked as lay psychotherapist; published *Gestalt Therapy* (1951). Short stories appeared in *Partisan Review* and *Kenyon Review*. Published novels *The Grand Piano* (1942), *Parents' Day* (1951), *The Empire City* (1959), and *Making Do* (1963); story collections included *The Facts of Life* (1946), *The Break-Up of Our Camp* (1949), and *Our Visit to Niagara* (1960). Published poems in *Day* (1955) and *The Lordly Hudson* (1962); *Collected Poems* appeared posthumously in 1974. Nonfiction included *Art and Social Nature* (1946), *Communitas* (1947, co-written with brother Percival Goodman), *Growing Up Absurd* (1960), *Compulsory Mis-Education* (1964), the memoir *Five Years* (1966), and *Like a Conquered Province* (1967).

Horace Gregory (April 10, 1898–March 11, 1982) b. Milwaukee, Wisconsin. Tuberculosis of the spine in infancy left him partially paralyzed. Attended University of Wisconsin at Madison, earning B.A. in 1923. Published poems in *Poetry*. Moved to New York City in 1923. Read manuscripts for Horace Liveright; wrote movie reviews for *Amalgamated Garment Maker's Union Weekly*. Married poet Marya Zaturenska in 1925. Published poetry collection *Chelsea Rooming House* (1930); translation *The Poems of Catullus* (1931); and poetry collection *No Retreat* (1933). At invitation of novelist Bryher spent summer of 1934 in England; met H.D., T. S. Eliot, and W. B. Yeats. Taught at Sarah Lawrence. Published *Chorus for Survival* (1935), *Poems, 1930–1940* (1941), and *Medusa in Gramercy Park* (1961); with Zaturenska, wrote *A History of American Poetry, 1900–1940* (1946); translated Ovid's *The Metamorphoses* (1958). *Collected Poems* (1964) received Bollingen Prize. Later books included poetry collection *Another Look* (1976) and autobiography *The House on Jefferson Street* (1971). Died in a nursing home, two months after Zaturenska's death.

Ramon Guthrie (January 14, 1896–November 22, 1973) b. Raymon Hollister Guthrie in New York City. Attended school erratically; worked for Winchester Repeating Arms Factory in 1915. Sailed for France in 1916 as volunteer ambulance driver with American Field Service. Joined 11th Bombing Squadron; participated in raid over La Chausée. Poems first appeared in French magazine *S4N*. Married and returned to United States in 1923; published poetry collection *Trobar Clus* (1923). Taught French at University of Arizona, 1924–26. Returned to France; published novels *Marcabrun* (1926) and *Parachute* (1928), poetry collection *A World Too Old* (1927), and long poem *The Legend of Ermengarde* (1929). Began teaching at Dartmouth in 1930. Published *Scherzo from a Poem To Be Entitled The Proud City* (1933) and *Graffiti*

(1959). Retired from teaching in 1963. Became ill with cancer; published *Asbestos Phoenix* (1968) and *Maximum Security Ward* (1970).

Woody Guthrie (July 14, 1912–October 3, 1967) b. Woodrow Wilson Guthrie in Okemah, Oklahoma. Father's real estate business and political career failed; family moved to Pampa, Texas. Formed musical group the Corncob Trio with friends Matt Jennings and Cluster Baker. Married Jennings' sister Mary in 1933; they had three children. After Oklahoma was devastated by dust storms, moved to California in 1935. Had radio show on KFVD in Los Angeles and performed at Communist Party gatherings. Wrote column for *The Daily Worker*. Moved to New York; met Leadbelly, Pete Seeger, Lee Hays, Cisco Houston, Sonny Terry, and other musicians. Hired to sing on *Back Where I Come From*, CBS radio show. Joined the Almanac Singers, folk group that included Seeger. Separated from Mary; married Marjorie Mazia, a dancer in Martha Graham's troupe, in 1940. Released album *Dust Bowl Ballads*. Published autobiography *Bound For Glory* (1943). Recorded numerous sessions for Moe Asch in 1944. His songs included "Vigilante Man," "Hard Travelin'," "So Long, It's Been Good to Know You," "Talking Dust Bowl," "Dust Storm Disaster," "Pastures of Plenty," and "This Land Is Your Land." Served in merchant marine during WWII. Diagnosed with Huntington's chorea in 1952; spent final 15 years in hospital. During this time his songs were widely recorded by younger musicians including Jack Elliott, The Weavers, Bob Dylan, Richie Havens, and Joan Baez.

Oscar Hammerstein II (July 12, 1895–August 23, 1960) b. Oscar Greeley Glendenning Hammerstein in New York City. Father and grandfather both prominent in New York theatrical world as producers and impresarios. Studied briefly at Columbia Law School. Began working as stage manager in 1917. First play, *The Light* (1919), failed. Collaborated with Herbert Stothart and Otto Harbach on operettas *Tickle Me* (1920), *Wildflower* (1923), *Rose Marie* (1924), and *The Desert Song* (1926). Wrote libretto and lyrics for Jerome Kern's *Show Boat* (1927), including songs "Ol' Man River," "Can't Help Lovin' Dat Man," and "Bill." With Kern, wrote *Sweet Adeline* (1929) and *Music in the Air* (1932). Worked on Hollywood musicals during the 1930's, including *Viennese Night* (1930), *The Night Is Young* (1935), and *High, Wide and Handsome* (1937); collaborated with Kern on song "The Last Time I Saw Paris" (1941). After Lorenz Hart declined to write the lyrics, composer Richard Rodgers invited Hammerstein to collaborate on musical adaptation of the Lynn Riggs play *Green Grow the Lilacs* (1931); *Oklahoma!* (1943) was the first success of an 18-year partnership. Other Broadway shows with Rodgers included *Carousel* (1945), *Allegro* (1947), *South Pacific* (1949), *The King and I* (1951), *Flower Drum Song* (1958), and *The Sound of Music* (1959).

E. Y. Harburg (April 8, 1896–March 5, 1981) b. Isidore Hochberg in New York City. Ira Gershwin was high school classmate. Ran successful appliance business; contributed lyrics to musicals and light verse to Franklin P. Adams's column "The Conning Tower." Went bankrupt in 1929. With Vernon Duke and Gershwin, wrote first successful song, "I'm Only Human After All," for the *Garrick Gaieties* of 1930. Collaborated with Jay Gorney on *Americana* (1932), which featured successful song "Brother, Can You Spare a Dime?" Wrote "Only a Paper Moon" (1932) with Harold Arlen; other hits written with Duke included "April in Paris" (1932) and "I Like the Likes of You" (1934). Traveled regularly to Hollywood with Arlen; collaborated with him on songs for *The Wizard of Oz* (1939); with Kern and Earl Robinson, worked on movie musical *Song of Russia* (1944). Later Broadway shows included *Bloomer Girl* (1946, with Arlen), *Finian's Rainbow* (1947, with Burton Lane), *Jamaica* (1957, with Arlen), and *Darling of the Sun* (1968, with Jule Styne). In 1968, wrote "Silent Spring" with Arlen in memory of Martin Luther King Jr.

Lorenz Hart (May 2, 1895–November 22, 1943) b. Lorenz Milton Hart in New York City. Son of German Jewish immigrants. Met composer Richard Rodgers in 1919, and began writing songs with him; their first successful collaboration was "Manhattan," written for 1925 *Garrick Gaieties* revue. Co-wrote operetta *Dearest Enemy* (1925), followed by Broadway shows *The Girl Friend* (1926), *A Connecticut Yankee* (1927), *Present Arms* (1928), *Spring Is Here* (1929), *Simple Simon* (1930), and *Ever Green* (1930). Worked in Hollywood (1930–35), writing musicals *Love Me Tonight* (1932), *Hallelujah I'm a Bum* (1933), and *Hollywood Party* (1934). Returned to Broadway musicals with *Jumbo* (1935), *Babes in Arms* (1937), *Pal Joey* (1940), and *By Jupiter* (1942). Successful songs included "Mountain Greenery," "Blue Room," "Little Girl Blue," "Where or When," "Thou Swell," "You Took Advantage of Me," "With a Song in My Heart," "Ten Cents a Dance," "The Most Beautiful Girl in the World," "My Funny Valentine," "The Lady Is a Tramp," and "Bewitched, Bothered and Bewildered."

Robert Hayden (August 4, 1913–February 25, 1980) b. Asa Bundy Sheffey in Detroit, Michigan. Raised by William and Sue Ellen Hayden after parents separated. Attended Wayne State University, 1932–36; met Langston Hughes, who attended a production of one of Hayden's plays. Researched black history and folklore for Federal Writers' Project. Published poetry collection *Heart-Shape in the Dust* (1940). Married Erma Inez Morris, concert pianist, in 1940. Pursued graduate work at University of Michigan (1941–46); studied with W. H. Auden. Converted to Baha'i faith. Published *Black Spear* (1942). Began teaching literature and creative writing at Fisk University in 1946. Poetry collection *The Lion and the Archer* (1948), in collaboration with Fisk art curator Myron O' Higgins, followed by *Figures of Time* (1955) and *A Ballad of Remembrance* (1962); *Selected Poems* appeared in 1966. Won Grand Prize in Poetry at First World Festival of Negro Arts in Dakar, Senegal. Edited anthology *Kaleidoscope: Poems by American Negro Poets* (1967). Appointed professor at University of Michigan in 1969. Later collections included *Words in* *the Mourning Time* (1970), *The Night-Blooming Cereus* (1972), *Angle of Ascent* (1975), *American Journal* (1978), and *The Legend of John Brown* (1978). Served two terms as Consultant in Poetry at the Library of Congress (1976–78). Diagnosed with cancer in 1979.

Robert Hillyer (June 3, 1895–December 24, 1961) b. Robert Silliman Hillyer in East Orange, New Jersey. Educated at Harvard, where he was an editor of *Harvard Advocate* and *Harvard Monthly*. Published poetry collection *Sonnets and Other Lyrics* (1917). Joined Norton-Harjes Ambulance Service in France, where he served in same unit as Harvard friend John Dos Passos; awarded Verdun Medal by French government. Returned to Harvard in 1919 as English instructor. Published *The Five Books of Youth* (1920) and *Alchemy: A Symphonic Poem* (1921). Spent 1920–21 in Copenhagen on a fellowship; collaborated with classmate S. Foster Damon on translations in *A Book of Danish Verse* (1922). Taught at Trinity College in Connecticut (1926–28); returned to Harvard as associate professor. Published *The Hills Give Promise, A Volume of Lyrics, Together with Carmus: A Symphonic Poem* (1923), *The Halt in the Garden* (1925), *The Seventh Hill* (1928), and *The Collected Verse of Robert Hillyer* (1933). Named Boylston Professor of Rhetoric and Oratory in 1937. Published novel *My Heart for Hostage* (1942). Left Harvard in 1945; taught at Kenyon College (1948–51) and University of Delaware. Later books included *Poems for Music, 1917–1947* (1947), long poem *The Death of Captain Nemo* (1949), critical collection *In Pursuit of Poetry* (1960), and *Collected Poems* (1961).

John Holmes (January 6, 1904–June 22, 1962) b. John Albert Holmes in Somerville, Massachusetts. Graduated from Tufts College in 1929; returned to Tufts as an instructor in 1934. Early poetry collections were *Address to the Living* (1937), *Fair Warning* (1939), and *Map of My Country* (1943). Taught at New Hampshire Writers' Conference (1940–47, 1954–62); directed Chautauqua Writers' Workshop, 1947–52. Contributed five essays to *Writing Poetry* (1960). Became full professor at Tufts in 1961; students included Anne Sexton and John Ciardi. Later books of poetry included *The Double Root* (1950) and *The Fortune Teller* (1961).

Lightnin' Hopkins (March 15, 1912–January 30, 1982) b. Sam Hopkins in Centerville, Texas; raised in nearby Leona after father was killed in a fight in 1915. One of five children, all of them musicians; learned to play guitar at a young age. Met Blind Lemon Jefferson at a church picnic in Buffalo, Texas, around 1920; later traveled with him. Accompanied his cousin, blues singer Texas Alexander. Married Antoinette Charles in the 1940's. Made first recordings in 1946 with Aladdin label in Los Angeles, and with Gold Star label in Houston. Met blues historian Samuel Charters in 1959; recorded *The Roots of Lightnin' Hopkins*. Collaborated with Brownie McGee, Sonny Terry, and Big Joe Williams on *Down South Summit Meetin'* (1960). Played at numerous folk festivals; performed at Carnegie Hall in 1960 and at American

Folk Blues Festival in Hamburg, Germany, in 1963; traveled frequently in Europe thereafter. Subject of Les Blank documentary, *The Blues Accordin' to Lightnin' Hopkins* (1968). Spent final years in Houston. At the time of his death, over 100 albums of his work had been issued.

Lindley Williams Hubbell (June 3, 1901–October 2, 1994) b. Hartford, Connecticut. Worked at New York Public Library, 1925–46. His first poetry collection, *Dark Pavilion* (1927), was published in the Yale Series of Younger Poets; it was followed by *The Tracing of a Portal* (1931), *Winter-Burning* (1938), *The Ninth Continent* (1947), and *Long Island Triptych* (1947). Corresponded extensively with Gertrude Stein, whom he met on her American tour in 1934. Taught at the Randall School in Hartford from 1946 to 1953. Moved to Japan in 1953; taught Shakespeare and English literature at Doshisha University in Kyoto. Settled there permanently, adopting the name Hayashi Shuseki, and becoming a Japanese citizen in 1960. *Seventy Poems* appeared in 1965; it was followed by many other collections published in Japan, including *Autobiography* (1971), *Climbing to Monfuno* (1977), *Walking Through Namba* (1978), and *The First Architect* (1982). Also published critical essays and translations including *Lectures on Shakespeare* (1958), *The English Lyric in the 17th Century* (1981), and *Translations* (1983). Later taught at Mukogawa University in Kobe, 1970–85.

Langston Hughes (February 1, 1902–May 22, 1967) b. James Mercer Langston Hughes in Joplin, Missouri. Father left family in Hughes' infancy; grew up in Lawrence, Kansas, with his grandmother, and with his mother in Lincoln, Illinois, and Cleveland, Ohio, where he attended Central High School. Visited father in Mexico in 1919 and 1920. Attended Columbia University briefly, 1921–22. Worked on a truck farm on Staten Island. Became a friend of poet Countee Cullen and corresponded with Howard University professor Alain Locke. Worked as a sailor on a freighter to West Africa in 1923; subsequently went to Europe. In Paris, worked as doorman and bouncer at a nightclub, where he heard many black musicians; met Locke in Venice. Published poems in *The Crisis*, *Opportunity*, and *The Buccaneer*. Worked as busboy at New York's Wardman Park Hotel in 1925; received publicity when Vachel Lindsay, to whom he had given some poems while Lindsay was staying at the hotel, read them publicly. Published poetry collection *The Weary Blues* (1926). Studied at Lincoln University in Pennsylvania, 1926–29. With Zora Neale Hurston, Wallace Thurman, and Gwendolyn Bennett, started short-lived literary magazine *Fire!!* Published poetry collection *Fine Clothes to the Jew* (1927) and novel *Not Without Laughter* (1930). Toured the South in 1931; sailed for Cuba and Haiti. Visited Scottsboro Boys in Montgomery, Alabama, jail. Visited Soviet Union in 1932 to participate in abortive film project; toured Soviet Central Asia. Published *The Dream Keeper* (1932) and *Scottsboro Limited: Four Poems and a Play in Verse* (1932). Visited radical Tsukiji Theater in Tokyo; local police accused him of being a Communist spy and pressured him to leave Japan. Lived in Reno, Nevada;

spent winter in Mexico, sharing living quarters in Mexico City with photographer Henri Cartier-Bresson. Won Guggenheim Fellowship. Collected stories in *The Ways of White Folks* (1934). Play *Mulatto* (1935) produced on Broadway. Attended Second International Writers' Congress in 1937 in Paris. Covered Spanish Civil War for the *Baltimore Afro-American*. Rented studio apartment in Harlem in 1938. Founded Harlem Suitcase Theater and New Negro Theater in Los Angeles. Published autobiography *The Big Sea* (1940) and *Shakespeare in Harlem* (1942). From 1942, wrote regular column for the *Chicago Defender*, featuring character Jesse B. Simple (columns later collected in five volumes beginning with *Simple Speaks His Mind*, 1950). Taught creative writing at Atlanta University in 1947; was poet-in-residence at Laboratory School of University of Chicago, 1949–50. Bought a home in Harlem. With Arna Bontemps, co-edited *The Poetry of the Negro: 1746–1949* (1949); published poetry collections *Fields of Wonder* (1947), *One-Way Ticket* (1949), and book-length poem, *Montage of a Dream Deferred* (1951). Questioned by House Un-American Activities Committee. Visited Africa and Europe several times in the 1950's and 1960's. Collaborated with photographer Roy DeCarava on *The Sweet Flypaper of Life* (1955); published second volume of autobiography, *I Wonder As I Wander* (1956). Gospel musical *Tambourines to Glory* opened in New York in 1963. Final poems collected in *Ask Your Mama* (1961) and *The Panther and the Lash* (1967).

Rolfe Humphries (November 20, 1894–April 22, 1969) b. George Rolfe Humphries in Philadelphia, Pennsylvania. Graduated from Amherst in 1915. Served in army during World War I, 1917–18. Worked as high school Latin teacher in San Francisco (1914–23) and Long Island (1925–57). Published poetry collection *Europa* (1929). Awarded Guggenheim Fellowship in 1938; traveled to Mexico and Europe. Published poetry collections *Out of the Jewel* (1942), *The Summer Landscape* (1944), *Forbid Thy Ravens* (1947), *The Wind of Time* (1950), *Green Armor on Green Ground* (1956), and *Coat on a Stick* (1969). Taught at Amherst, 1957–65. Was a prolific translator whose publications included Lorca's *The Poet in New York* (1940), Virgil's *Aeneid* (1951), Ovid's *Metamorphoses* (1955), and Lucretius' *The Way Things Are* (1968). His *Collected Poems* appeared in 1965.

Josephine Jacobsen (b. August 19, 1908) b. Coburg, Ontario. After high school graduation, acted with Vagabond Players in Baltimore; theatrical career ended after marriage to Eric Jacobsen in 1932. Poetry collections include *Let Each Man Remember* (1940), *For the Unlost* (1946), *The Human Climate* (1953), *The Animal Inside* (1966), *The Shade-Seller* (1974), *The Chinese Insomniacs* (1981), *The Sisters* (1987), *Distances* (1991), and *In the Crevice of Time* (1995). Collaborated with William Mueller on critical studies *The Testament of Samuel Beckett* (1964) and *Ionesco and Genet: Playwrights of Silence* (1968). Served as Consultant in Poetry at the Library of Congress, 1971–73; was vice-president of Poetry Society of America, 1979. A short story collection, *A Walk with Raschid*, appeared in 1978.

Blind Lemon Jefferson (July 11, 1897–December 1929) b. Couchman, Texas. Blind from birth. Competed briefly in professional wrestling. Moved to Dallas in 1917. Played guitar and sang at country suppers; playing partners included Leadbelly, Charlie Patton, and Lightnin' Hopkins. Recorded first session at Paramount Records in Chicago in late 1925 or early 1926. Briefly recorded for Okeh Records in 1927. Recorded last session in Richmond, Indiana, on September 24, 1929. Believed by some to have frozen to death on street in Chicago. His recordings included "See That My Grave Is Kept Clean," "Black Snake Moan," "Prison Cell Blues," and "Lonesome House Blues."

Helene Johnson (July 7, 1907–July 7, 1995) b. Boston, Massachusetts. Educated at local schools. Briefly attended Boston University. Moved to New York City in 1926; lived in same building as Zora Neale Hurston, who became a close friend. Studied journalism at Columbia under John Erskine. Returned to Boston around 1929. Between 1925 and 1935, published two dozen poems in magazines including *Opportunity*, *The Messenger*, *The Saturday Evening Quill*, and *Vanity Fair*. Married in 1933; daughter born 1940. Worked for Consumers Union in Mount Vernon, New York. Returned to Manhattan late in life.

Robert Johnson (May 8, 1911–August 16, 1938) b. Hazlehurst, Mississippi. Moved in 1914 to home of stepfather, his mistress, and 12 other children. Spent several years in Memphis, where he learned to play the guitar from his brother, Charles Leroy. Moved back to mother's home in Robinsonville, Mississippi, around 1919. Learned from local musicians Son House and Willie Brown; played jew's harp and harmonica in addition to guitar. His wife died in childbirth in 1930, and Johnson began traveling and performing. Using Memphis, Robinsonville, and other southern towns as bases, he toured the Delta, St. Louis, Chicago, Detroit, and New York, where he played at dances, rent parties, clubs, and met dozens of professional musicians. Met talent scout H. C. Speir in Jackson, Mississippi, in 1936; Speir introduced Johnson to Ernie Oertle, salesman for ARC Records, who took Johnson in 1936 to San Antonio, where he recorded 16 sides; recorded again in Dallas in 1937. Recordings included "Hell Hound on My Trail," "Cross Road Blues," "Me and the Devil," "Stones in My Passway," "Love in Vain," and "Terraplane Blues." Cause of death unknown; believed by some to have been poisoned, possibly by the husband of a woman with whom he was involved.

Eugene Jolas (October 26, 1894–May 26, 1952) b. Union Hill, New Jersey. Raised in Lorraine, France, where parents originated, and in the U.S. Served in U.S. Army, 1916–20. Worked as journalist in Pittsburgh, New York, and Waterbury, Connecticut. Moved to Paris in 1924; worked for Paris branch of *Chicago Tribune*; wrote column "Rambles Through Literary Paris." Married Maria McDonald in 1926. Published poetry collection *Cinema* (1926). In the fall of 1926, started *transition* magazine with former *Tribune* colleague Elliot

Paul; first issue featured work by James Joyce and Gertrude Stein. The magazine serialized sections of Joyce's *Work in Progress* (published as *Finnegans Wake*), and published writings and artwork by Hart Crane, Samuel Beckett, Dylan Thomas, Juan Gris, Man Ray, Pablo Picasso, Hans Arp, and Georges Braque, as well as manifestos and editorials by Jolas, including "Revolution of the Word" in 1929. The final issue of *transition* appeared in 1938. Jolas returned to the U.S. in 1940; began working for the Office of War Information in 1942. His other books included *Secession in Astropolis* (1929), *I Have Seen Monsters and Angels* (1938), *Vertical: A Yearbook for Romantic-Mystic Ascensions* (1941), and *Wanderpoem, or Angelic Mythamorphosis of the City of London* (1946). Returned to Paris after the war; died while working on his autobiography (published as *Man from Babel* in 1998) and translations of Novalis.

Joseph Kalar (1906–1972) Worked in lumber and papermill industries in northern Minnesota. Joined Farmer Labor Party of Minnesota. Reported for *New Masses* during cross-country trip, 1928–30. Published poetry and satire in international journals such as *Red Flag* (published by the German Communist Party), Moscow's *Literature of the World Revolution*, and *International Literature*, as well as in American periodicals such as *New Masses, Left, The Daily Worker, Morada*, and *The Rebel Poet*. Featured in the anthology *We Gather Strength* (1933), along with Sol Funaroff, Edwin Rolfe, and Herman Spector. A selection of his work, *Joseph Kalar, Poet of Protest*, was published by his family in 1985.

Lincoln Kirstein (May 4, 1907–January 5, 1996) b. Rochester, New York. Co-founded literary magazine *Hound and Horn* while a student at Harvard in 1927, serving as editor until 1934. Received M.A. from Harvard in 1930. Published novel *Flesh Is Heir* (1932). Met George Balanchine in Europe in 1933 and persuaded him to come to the U.S. Published poetry collection *Low Ceiling* (1935). Co-founded and directed several ballet schools and companies, including School of American Ballet (1934), American Ballet (1935), and Ballet Caravan (1936–41). Published *Dance* (1935), *Blast at Ballet: A Corrective for the American Audience* (1938), and *Ballet Alphabet* (1939); founded *Dance Index* in 1942. Served in U.S. Third Army, 1943–45. Founded New York City Ballet, of which he was general director from 1948 to 1989. Published *Rhymes of a PFC* (1964) and *More Rhymes of a PFC* (1966). Wrote numerous books and articles on dance, painting, sculpture, and photography; later works included *Movement and Metaphor* (1970), *The New York City Ballet* (1972), *Elie Nadelman* (1973), *Lay This Laurel* (1974), *Nijinsky Dancing* (1975), and *Thirty Years with the New York City Ballet* (1978). *The Poems of Lincoln Kirstein* appeared in 1987.

Stanley Kunitz (b. July 29, 1905) b. Stanley Jasspon Kunitz in Worcester, Massachusetts. Won scholarship to Harvard; graduated 1926. Employed by Wilson Publishing Company in New York City, editing various biographical dictionaries (some under pseudonym Dilly Tante) and *Wilson Bulletin for Librarians*. Published poems in *Poetry, The Nation, The Dial*, and other periodicals; poetry collection *Intellectual Things* appeared in 1930. Served in U.S. Army, Air Transport Command, during World War II (1943–45). Published poetry collection *Passport to the War* (1944). Taught at Bennington College, Potsdam State Teachers College, and New School for Social Research in New York. Was poet-in-residence at University of Washington and Queens College, and taught at Brandeis University. *Selected Poems, 1928–1958* (1958) won Pulitzer Prize. Taught at Columbia University (1963–85). Visited Russia in 1967; translated poetry of Anna Akhmatova and Andrei Voznesensky. In 1968, helped found Fine Arts Work Center in Provincetown, Massachusetts. Published *The Testing-Tree* (1971). Appointed Consultant in Poetry at the Library of Congress (1974–75). Published *A Kind of Order, A Kind of Folly: Essays and Conversations* (1975). Collected poems in *The Poems of Stanley Kunitz, 1928–1978* (1979). Awarded Senior Fellowship by the National Endowment for the Arts in 1984. Later collections include *The Wellfleet Whale and Companion Poems* (1983), *Next-to-Last Things: New Poems and Essays* (1985), and *Passing Through* (1995).

Richmond Lattimore (May 6, 1906–February 26, 1984) b. Paotingfu, China. Graduated from Dartmouth in 1926; published *Hanover Poems* (1927, with A. K. Laing). Won Rhodes scholarship and studied at Oxford University (B.A. 1932). Took Ph.D. in 1934 from University of Illinois, Urbana. Taught classics, English, and philosophy at University of Illinois and Wabash College. Was professor of Greek at Bryn Mawr College (1948–71). Published many translations from the Greek including *The Odes of Pindar* (1947), *The Iliad of Homer* (1951), Aeschylus' *Oresteia* (1953), *Greek Lyrics* (1955), Hesiod's *Works and Days, Theogony, The Shield of Herakles* (1959), *The Frogs of Aristophanes* (1962), *The Odyssey of Homer* (1967), Euripides' *Iphigenia at Tauris* (1973), and *The Four Gospels and the Revelation* (1979). With David Grene edited *The Complete Greek Tragedies*, published by the University of Chicago in 1959. Poetry collected in *Poems* (1957), *Sestina for a Far-Off Summer* (1962), *Selected Poems* (1965), *The Stride of Time* (1966), *Poems from Three Decades* (1972), and *Continuing Conclusions* (1983).

Janet Lewis (August 17, 1899–December 4, 1998) b. Chicago, Illinois. Raised in Oak Park, Illinois. High school classmate of Ernest Hemingway. Educated at University of Chicago; member of Poetry Club, along with Elizabeth Madox Roberts and Yvor Winters. Lived in Paris in 1921; worked for passport bureau of American consulate. Published poetry collection *The Indians in the Woods* in 1922. Contracted tuberculosis in 1922; entered Sunmount Sanatorium in Santa Fe, New Mexico. Corresponded extensively with Winters, who had earlier gone to Sunmount to recover from tuberculosis; they were married in 1926. Moved to Los Altos, California; published collection *The Wheel in Midsummer* (1927). Bred prize-winning Airedale terriers. Published novel *The Invasion* (1932). Read *Famous Cases of Circumstantial Evidence* (1873), anthology of French trials; wrote three novels based on these cases: *The Wife of Martin Guerre* (1941), *The Trial of Søren Qvist* (1947), and *The Ghost of Monsieur Scarron* (1959). Wrote libretto for opera *The Wife of Martin Guerre* (1958), with music by William Laurence Bergsma. After Winters' death in 1968, revisited Southwest. Later poetry collections included *The Earth-Bound* (1946), *Poems, 1924–1944* (1950), *The Ancient Ones* (1979), *Poems Old and New, 1918–1978* (1981), and *The Dear Past* (1994).

Frank Loesser (June 29, 1910–March 28, 1969) b. Frank Henry Loesser in New York City. Worked briefly as newspaper reporter. Published first song in 1931. Moved to Hollywood in 1937; wrote film songs with Burton Lane. With collaborators including Hoagy Carmichael, Frederick Hollander, Joseph Lilley, and Jule Styne, wrote many popular songs including "Two Sleepy People," "On a Slow Boat to China," "Baby, It's Cold Outside," and "I Hear Music." During World War II wrote series of morale-raising songs including "Praise the Lord and Pass the Ammunition," "What Do You Do in the Infantry?," "Roger Young," and "First Class Mary Brown." Scored Broadway musical *Where's Charley* (1948), and wrote music and lyrics to *Guys and Dolls* (1950), highly successful adaptation of Damon Runyon stories. Later shows included *The Most Happy Fella* (1956), *Greenwillow* (1960), and *How to Succeed in Business Without Really Trying* (1961).

Walter Lowenfels (May 10, 1897–July 7, 1976) b. New York City. Worked for family's butter business (later known as Hotel Bar Butter Company). First published poem appeared in Franklin P. Adams's column "The Conning Tower." Published poetry collection *Episodes and Epistles* in 1925. Sailed for Paris in 1926; married Lillian Apotheker. Supported himself as a real estate agent; his clients included Tristan Tzara, Marc Chagall, and Archibald MacLeish; formed friendship with Henry Miller. Co-founded Carrefour Press, dedicated to printing anonymous works. Published poetry collection *Finale of Seem* (1929) and the long poems *Apollinaire an Elegy* (1930), *Elegy in the Manner of a Requiem in Memory of D. H. Lawrence* (1932), and *The Suicide* (1934). Began attending Communist Party rallies in 1932. Moved to Philadelphia in 1938; served as an editor of *The Daily Worker*. FBI raided his home in 1953, and he spent several weeks in jail under the Smith Act. Published poetry collections *The Prisoners* (1954) and *Sonnets of Love and Liberty* (1955) and prose works *To an Imaginary Daughter* (1964) and *The Revolution Is To Be Human* (1973); long poems of the 1930's collected in revised form as *Some Deaths* (1964). Later books included *Translations from Scorpius* (1966), *We Are All Poets, Really* (1967), *Thou Shalt Not Overkill* (1968), *Found Poems* (1972), and *Reality Prime; Pages from a Journal* (1974). Edited several anthologies of antiwar and protest poetry, including *Where Is Vietnam?* (1967), *In a Time of Revolution* (1969), and *The Writing on the Wall* (1969).

David McCord (November 15, 1897–April 13, 1997) b. David Thompson Watson McCord in New York City. Raised in New York, Princeton, and Portland,

Oregon. Graduated Harvard in 1921; took M.A. in romance languages in 1922. Wrote theater reviews for *Boston Evening Transcript*, 1923–28. Served as executive director of Harvard Fund Council, 1925–63. Published *Oddly Enough* (1926), a book of humorous essays, followed by poetry collection *Floodgate* (1927). *The Camp at Lockjaw* (1952) was the first of over a dozen volumes of children's poetry, including *Far and Few, Rhymes of the Never Was and Always Is* (1952), *Every Time I Climb a Tree* (1967), and *Mr. Bidery's Spidery Garden* (1972); *The Star in the Pail* (1975) and *One at a Time* (1977) were nominated for the National Book Award. Frequently gave readings and lectures on poetry for young students.

Phyllis McGinley (March 21, 1905–February 22, 1978) b. Ontario, Oregon. Grew up in Iliff, Colorado, and Ogden, Utah. Attended University of Southern California and University of Utah. After graduation in 1927, taught school in Ogden; moved to New York City in 1929. Taught junior high school; published work in *The New Yorker*. Poetry collections *On the Contrary* and *One More Manhattan* appeared in 1937. Settled with husband and daughter in Larchmont, New York. Published *A Pocketful of Wry* (1940) and *Husbands Are Difficult* (1941). Wrote 17 children's books from 1944 to 1966, including *The Plain Princess* (1945), *Blunderbus* (1951), *The Horse Who Had His Picture in the Paper* (1951), and *Boys Are Awful* (1962). Published further poetry collections including *Stones from a Glass House* (1946), *A Short Walk from the Station* (1951), *The Love Letters of Phyllis McGinley* (1954), and *Times Three: Selected Verse from Three Decades* (1960), which won a Pulitzer Prize. Her essays were collected in *Province of the Heart* (1959), *Sixpence in Her Shoe* (1964), and *Saint-Watching* (1969). Husband died in 1972; moved back to New York City late in life.

Joseph Moncure March (July 1899–February 14, 1977) b. New York City. Graduated from Amherst College, where he studied with Robert Frost. Served in France in World War I. Was first managing editor of *The New Yorker*. Wrote *The Wild Party* (1928), a book-length poem that encountered censorship difficulties in some locations for its depictions of sex and violence. Another narrative poem, *The Set-Up*, was published later the same year. Moved to Hollywood, where he worked on over 20 screenplays, including *Hell's Angels* (1930), *Journey's End* (1930), *Madame Butterfly* (1932), *Jennie Gerhardt* (1933), and *Three Faces West* (1940); *The Set-Up* was filmed in 1949, and *The Wild Party* in 1974.

Johnny Mercer (November 18, 1909–June 25, 1976) b. John Herndon Mercer in Savannah, Georgia. Moved to New York City in 1928 to pursue an acting career. By 1932 he was writing novelty songs with Paul Whiteman for the *Kraft Radio Show*. Acted in *Old Man Rhythm* and *To Beat the Band* (1945). Wrote lyrics and music to "Something's Gotta Give," which was sung by Bing Crosby in *Rhythm on the Range* (1938). With Harry Warren, wrote "Jeepers Creepers" and "You Must Have Been a Beautiful Baby" (1938).

While in Hollywood, hosted a radio show and co-founded Capitol Records. Began collaborating with Harold Arlen in the early 1940's; their songs included "Blues in the Night" (1941), "One for My Baby" (1943), and "Let's Take the Long Way Home" (1944); they also wrote the Broadway musicals *St. Louis Woman* (1946) and *Saratoga* (1959). Had several hit records as a singer, including "Mister Meadowlark" (1940), "Ac-cent-tchu-ate the Positive" (1945), and "Candy" (1945). Wrote Oscar-winning "On the Atcheson, Topeka, and the Santa Fe" (1946); with Hoagy Carmichael, wrote "Skylark" (1942), "How Little We Know" (1944), and the Oscar-winning "In the Cool Cool Cool of the Evening" (1951). With Gene Paul, wrote movie musical *Seven Brides for Seven Brothers* (1954) and Broadway show *Li'l Abner* (1956). Won third and fourth Oscars for "Moon River" (1961) and "Days of Wine and Roses" (1962), written with Henry Mancini.

Josephine Miles (June 11, 1911–May 12, 1985) b. Chicago, Illinois. Raised in California. Suffered from arthritis at a young age. Graduated from Los Angeles High School; earned B.A. from University of California at Los Angeles in 1932 and Ph.D. from University of California at Berkeley in 1938. Published poems in *Trial Balances* (1935), an anthology of new poets. Poetry collection *Lines at Intersection* appeared in 1939. Taught at Berkeley from 1940 until 1978. Published *Poems on Several Occasions* (1941), followed by *Local Measures* (1946) and *Prefabrications* (1955). Wrote critical studies including *The Vocabulary of Poetry* (1946), *The Continuity of Poetic Language* (1951), and *Eras and Modes in English Poetry* (1957). Received Oscar Blumenthal Prize in 1959; published *Poems, 1930–1960* (1960). Her play *House and Home* was performed in Berkeley in 1960. Later poetry collections included *Kinds of Affection* (1962), *Civil Poems* (1966), *Fields of Learning* (1968), and *To All Appearances* (1974). Retired in 1978. *Collected Poems 1930–83* appeared in 1983.

Rosalie Moore (b. October 8, 1910) b. Rosalie Gertrude Moore in Oakland, California. Educated at University of California, Berkeley; graduated in 1932. Was copywriter and announcer on KLX in Oakland, 1935–37. Associated with the Activists, poetic circle whose members included Lawrence Hart and Robert Horan. Married William Brown, a science-fiction writer. Poetry collection *The Grasshopper's Man* (1949) published in the Yale Series of Younger Poets. Awarded Guggenheim Fellowships in 1950 and 1951; lectured at Mexico City College; taught communications at College of Marin in California. Wrote children's books with husband, including *Forest Fireman* (1954), *Whistle Punk* (1956), *Boy Who Got Mailed* (1957), *Big Rig* (1959), *Department Store Ghost* (1961), *Tickley and the Fox* (1962), and *The Hippopotamus That Wanted to Be a Baby* (1963). Later poetry collected in *Year of the Children* (1977), *Of Singles and Doubles* (1979), and *Gutenberg in Strasbourg* (1995).

Vladimir Nabokov (April 23, 1899–July 2, 1977) b. St. Petersburg, Russia. Spent substantial part of childhood on family estates and in Europe; spoke English, French, and Russian at a young age. In childhood began lifelong study of butterflies. Father was active contributor to liberal newspapers and a leader of the Constitutional Democratic party. Privately published a collection of love poems in 1916. After revolution of March 1917, father appointed head of chancellery in Provisional Government. After Bolsheviks seized power in November, father sent family to estate at Yalta. With schoolmate Andrey Balashov, Nabokov published poetry collection *Two Paths* (1918). Family fled Russia in 1919; Nabokov began studying at Cambridge later the same year. Family moved to Berlin in 1920, while Nabokov continued at Cambridge. Father killed by monarchist gunmen in Berlin in 1922. After graduation, settled in Berlin; became part of emigré literary community and published poems and stories in magazines under pseudonym "Vladimir Sirin"; worked as tutor. Married Véra Slonim in 1925; son Dmitri born 1934. Published series of novels in Russian including *Mary* (1926), *The Defense* (1930), *The Eye* (1930), *Glory* (1932), *Laughter in the Dark* (1933), *Despair* (1936), and *Invitation to a Beheading* (1938). Left Germany in 1937, settling in France. Accepted offer of summer teaching job from Stanford; sailed to America in 1940. First novel written in English, *The Real Life of Sebastian Knight*, published in 1941. Lectured on Russian literature at Wellesley, Stanford, Yale, Smith, and other institutions; spent a year studying Lepidoptera as research fellow at Harvard's Museum of Comparative Zoology, 1942–43; began teaching at Cornell in 1947. Published autobiography, *Conclusive Evidence* (later retitled *Speak, Memory*), in 1951. *Lolita* (completed in 1953 and rejected by numerous American publishers) was published in 1955 by Paris-based Olympia Press in their Traveller's Companion series devoted largely to erotica. Published in America in 1958, *Lolita* sold rapidly and became an enduring bestseller. Poetry collected in *Poems* (1959). Resigned from Cornell; traveled through Italy and Sicily; settled with Véra in Montreux, Switzerland. Published novel *Pale Fire* (1962) and annotated translation of Pushkin's *Eugene Onegin* (1963). Later novels included *Ada* (1969), *Transparent Things* (1972), and *Look at the Harlequins!* (1974).

Ogden Nash (August 19, 1902–May 19, 1971) b. Frederic Ogden Nash in Rye, New York. Raised in various East Coast cities. Attended Harvard, 1920–21, then worked as teacher, bond salesman, and advertising copywriter. Co-wrote children's book *The Cricket of Carador* (1925). Between 1925 and 1931 worked as publicist and editor for the publishing companies Doubleday and Rinehart; joined staff of *The New Yorker* in 1929. Collection of light verse *Hard Lines* (1931) followed by *Free Wheeling* (1931), *Happy Days* (1933), and *The Primrose Path* (1935). Married in 1931; had two daughters. Published *The Bad Parents' Garden of Verse* (1936), *I'm a Stranger Here Myself* (1938), *The Face Is Familiar* (1940), *Good Intentions* (1942), and *Many Long Years Ago* (1945). Lived in Hollywood, 1936–42, and wrote screenplays for MGM. Collaborated with S. J. Perelman and Kurt Weill on 1943 musical *One Touch of Venus*. Appeared frequently on television and radio programs, including "Information, Please!" and "Masquerade Party." Published children's poems in *Parents Keep Out: Elderly Poems for Youngerly Readers* (1951), *The Christmas*

That Almost Wasn't (1957), *Custard the Dragon* (1959), and *Girls Are Silly* (1962). Later works included *The Mysterious Ouphe* (1965), *The Cruise of the Aardvark* (1967), and *Bed Riddance: A Posy for the Indisposed* (1970).

Lorine Niedecker (May 12, 1903–December 31, 1970) b. Fort Atkinson, Wisconsin. Spent much of childhood on nearby Black Hawk Island. Studied at Beloit College for two years starting in 1922. Returned to the island to care for her mother. Worked at public library. In 1931, after reading "Objectivists" issue of *Poetry* magazine, guest-edited by Louis Zukofsky, Niedecker started a correspondence with Zukofsky that lasted the rest of her life, and became closely involved with him in the mid-1930's. Published poems and short plays in James Laughlin's *New Directions* anthology (1936). Was a senior writer and research editor for the WPA in Madison, Wisconsin (1938–42), working on the *Wisconsin Guide*; during brief stint as scriptwriter for Madison radio station, adapted William Faulkner's *As I Lay Dying*. Returned to Black Hawk Island in 1942. Began in 1944 as stenographer and proofreader for local journal *Hoard's Dairyman*. Published poetry collection *New Goose* in 1946. Built a one-and-a-half room cabin near her parents' home in 1947. Resigned from *Hoard's* in 1950 after her eyesight deteriorated. Sold family cottages after parents' deaths; supported herself by scrubbing floors at Atkinson Memorial Hospital, 1957–63. Began corresponding in 1960 with Cid Corman, editor of *Origin*. Published collection *My Friend Tree* (1961). Married housepainter Al Millen in 1963; they moved to Milwaukee until her health forced them to return to Black Hawk Island. Later books included *North Central* (1968) and *T&G: The Collected Poems* (1969), expanded and republished as *My Life by Water: Collected Poems, 1936–1968* (1970). *Blue Chicory* (1976), containing poems Niedecker had completed around the time of her death, was published posthumously.

John Frederick Nims (November 20, 1913–January 19, 1999) b. Muskegon, Michigan. Graduated from Notre Dame in 1937. Received Ph.D. from University of Chicago in 1945. Contributed to *Five Young American Poets* (1944). Published poetry collection *The Iron Pastoral* (1947), followed by *A Fountain in Kentucky* (1950) and *Knowledge of the Evening* (1960); translation of *Poems of St. John of the Cross* appeared in 1959. Taught English at universities in Canada, Italy, and Spain, and at Notre Dame (1955–62). Taught poetry at Bread Loaf Writers' Conference (1965–69); edited *Poetry* (1978–84); published textbook *Western Wind: An Introduction to Poetry* (1974). Later collections included *Of Flesh and Bone* (1967), *The Kiss: A Jambalaya* (1982), and *The Six-Cornered Snowflake* (1990); translations collected in *Sappho to Valéry* (1971); *The Complete Poems of Michelangelo* published in 1998.

Charles Olson (December 27, 1910–January 10, 1970) b. Charles John Olson in Worcester, Massachusetts. Vacationed regularly at Gloucester, Massachusetts, during childhood. Educated at Wesleyan University, where he studied with Wilbert Snow, and at Harvard. Became a friend of Edward

Dahlberg. Worked in Foreign Language Division of the Office of War Information, 1942–44, and, during the 1944 presidential campaign, as director of the Foreign Nationalities Division of the Democratic National Committee. Visited Ezra Pound in St. Elizabeth's Hospital. Published *Call Me Ishmael*, a study of Melville, in 1947. Lectured on poetry in California; met Robert Duncan and geographer Carl O. Sauer. Supported presidential bid of Florida senator Claude Pepper at Democratic National Convention in 1948; subsequently withdrew from political activity. Began teaching at Black Mountain College in North Carolina in 1948, where he was part of creative circle that included Robert Creeley, Robert Duncan, Stefan Wolpe, and Josef Albers; served as rector of the college from 1951 until its closing in 1956. Poetry collection *Y & X* published in 1949. The essay "Projective Verse," published as a pamphlet in 1950, was praised by William Carlos Williams, who included part of it in his autobiography. Poetry collected as *In Cold Hell, In Thicket* (1953); *The Distances* (1960), and *Archaeologist of Morning* (1970). Spent first of half of 1951 on the Yucatán Peninsula, studying Mayan glyphs. *Mayan Letters*, written to Robert Creeley, appeared in 1953; the extensive correspondence of Olson and Creeley was collected in nine volumes, 1980–89. The first volume of his life work, *The Maximus Poems*, begun in 1950 and dealing in part with the history and geography of Gloucester, was published in 1953; a complete edition, edited by George Butterick, was published posthumously in 1983. Wrote many theoretical statements on poetry and other matters, some of them collected in *Human Universe and Other Essays* (1960) and *Selected Writings* (1966). Read extensively at universities across the country during the 1960's. Taught at State University of New York at Buffalo, 1963–65.

Elder Olson (March 9, 1909–July 25, 1992) b. Chicago, Illinois. Received Witter Bynner Award in 1927. Published first poem in *Poetry* in 1928, and won the magazine's Guarantor's Award in 1931. Attended the University of Chicago (M.A., 1935). Published poetry collection *Thing of Sorrow* (1934). Taught English at Armour Institute of Technology in Chicago. Published long poem *The Cock of Heaven* in 1940. Began teaching at University of Chicago in 1942; named full professor in 1953. Published critical work *The Poetry of Dylan Thomas* (1954), poetry collection *The Scarecrow Christ* (1954), and *Plays & Poems 1948–58* (1958). Was visiting professor at Indiana University (1955) and the University of the Philippines (1966–67). Published *Collected Poems* (1963). Other books included *The Theory of Comedy* (1968), *Olson's Penny Arcade* (1975), *On Value Judgments in the Arts* (1976), and *Last Poems* (1984). Retired from Chicago in 1977; was visiting professor at University of Houston and University of New Mexico.

George Oppen (April 24, 1908–July 7, 1984) b. George Oppenheimer in New Rochelle, New York. Mother committed suicide when he was four. Family moved to San Francisco in 1918. Expelled from military academy in 1925; entered Oregon State University in 1926. Suspended after violating curfew with fellow student Mary Colby; they left school and were married in 1927. The Oppens hitchhiked across the country, sailed a catboat through the Great Lakes and Hudson River, and lived briefly in New York City, where they met Louis Zukofsky and Charles Reznikoff. Moved to France; started TO Publishers. Visited Ezra Pound in Rapallo, Italy. Published poems in the 1931 "Objectivists" issue of *Poetry*, guest-edited by Zukofsky, and in Pound's *Active Anthology* (1933). TO closed in 1933; the Oppens returned to New York and were involved in the Objectivist Press, which published his *Discrete Series* in 1934. Joined Communist Party in 1935; worked as organizer for Workers' Alliance and aided a Farmers' Union milk strike in Utica, New York. During World War II, trained in anti-tank company; fought in Battle of the Bulge, and was wounded in Alsace in 1945; awarded the Purple Heart. Moved to Redondo Beach, California; worked as housing contractor and carpenter. Visited twice by the FBI; moved in 1950 to Mexico, where he supervised the operation of a furniture factory. Returned to Brooklyn in 1960; resumed writing poetry after long hiatus and published *The Materials* (1962) and *This In Which* (1965). Spent summers in Maine; moved to San Francisco in 1966. *Of Being Numerous* (1968) won Pulitzer Prize. Later collections included *Seascape: Needle's Eye* (1972), *Collected Poems* (1972), and *Primitive* (1978). Diagnosed with Alzheimer's in 1982; died in a nursing home.

Kenneth Patchen (December 13, 1911–January 8, 1972) b. Niles, Ohio. Raised in Warren, Ohio. Graduated from local high school in 1929. Attended University of Wisconsin, where he participated in Alexander Meiklejohn's Experimental College. Traveled throughout the U.S. and Canada, working odd jobs. Met poets Conrad Aiken, John Wheelwright, and Malcolm Cowley in Boston. Married Miriam Oikemus in 1934; moved to Greenwich Village; reviewed books for *The New Republic* and worked for the Federal Writers' Project. Published poetry collection *Before the Brave* (1936). Awarded Guggenheim Fellowship in 1936; spent the year in the southwestern U.S. Moved to Los Angeles in 1937; worked on film scripts and wrote part of a California guide for the WPA. Suffered back injury which had lifelong effects. Joined wife working for James Laughlin's fledgling New Directions; they lived in Laughlin's home in Norfolk, Connecticut. Published poetry collections including *First Will and Testament* (1939), *The Dark Kingdom* (1942), *The Teeth of the Lion* (1942), *Cloth of the Tempest* (1943), *An Astonished Eye Looks Out of the Air* (1945), *Outlaw of the Lowest Planet* (1946), *Selected Poems* (1946), and *Red Wine and Yellow Hair* (1949), as well as prose works including *The Journal of Albion Moonlight* (1941), *Memoirs of a Shy Pornographer* (1945), and *Sleepers Awake* (1946). Underwent spinal fusion in 1950. Moved to San Francisco in the early 1950's. Received second spinal fusion in 1956. Worked with jazz composer and musician Charles Mingus; released several LPs of readings with musical accompaniment. Fell from operating cart during 1959 surgery, causing extreme and almost continuous pain. Awarded grant in 1967 from the National Endowment for the Arts. His experiments in combining words with paintings were featured in 1969 show at the Corcoran

Gallery in Washington, D.C., and in books including *Hallelujah Anyway* (1966) and *Wonderings* (1971). His other poetry collections included *Poems of Humor and Protest* (1954), *Hurrah for Anything* (1957), *Because It Is* (1960), *The Love Poems of Kenneth Patchen* (1960), and *But Even So* (1968); *Collected Poems* published in 1968.

Hyam Plutzik (July 13, 1911–January 8, 1962) b. Brooklyn, New York. Son of Russian immigrants; did not speak English before age seven. Raised in Bristol, Connecticut. Studied at Trinity College; graduated 1932, and won scholarship for graduate study at Yale; awarded Yale Poetry Prize. Worked as newspaper reporter. Collection *Death at the Purple Rim* published privately in 1941. Enlisted in army in 1942; transferred to air force and was commissioned as 2d lieutenant in 1943; married Tanya Roth. Served in England as ordnance officer with the Eighth Air Force and as education and information officer of the Shipdam air base. Appointed to faculty of University of Rochester; became Deane Professor of Poetry and Rhetoric in 1961. Published *Aspects of Proteus* (1949), *Apples from Shinar* (1959), and book-length poem *Horatio* (1961). Published science-fiction novel *Outcasts of Venus* (1952) under pseudonym Anaximander Powell. At the time of his death from cancer he was working on a collection titled *The Unblest Mythmaker*. His *Collected Poems* appeared posthumously in 1987.

Anne Porter (b. 1911) b. Anne Channing in Sherborn, Massachusetts. Married painter Fairfield Porter in 1932; they had five children. After living in New York City for many years, they settled in Southampton, Long Island, in 1949; also spent time on Maine coast. Co-wrote and starred in Rudy Burckhardt film *A Day in the Life of a Cleaning Woman* (1953). For much of the 1960's, the Porters shared their homes with the poet James Schuyler. Fairfield Porter died in 1975. Published poems in *Commonweal, Locus Solus,* and other magazines; her collection *An Altogether Different Language* appeared in 1994.

H. Phelps Putnam (July 9, 1894–July 3, 1948) b. Howard Phelps Putnam in Allston, Massachusetts. Educated at Phillips Exeter Academy and Yale. Suffered severe asthma from childhood, and would later suffer from further lung disorders. His poems were included in the anthology *Parabalou* (1919). Visited New York City frequently; met writers such as Allen Tate and Paul Rosenfeld. Married Ruth Peters. Worked briefly as assistant editor at *Atlantic Monthly,* then as an advertising copywriter for the insurance company where his father was employed; lived in parents' home in Jamaica Plain, a suburb of Boston. Published poetry collections *Trinc* (1927) and *The Five Seasons* (1931); planned a long work, *The Earthly Comedy,* which was never completed. Traveled to the Southwest for his health; became close friend of Senator Bronson Cutting. In the 1930's, lived in farmhouse in Pomfret, Connecticut. Shortly before his death, Putnam was visited by Robert Lowell, who persuaded him to record some of his poems for the Library of Congress.

Carl Rakosi (b. November 6, 1903) b. Berlin, Germany. After parents separated in 1904, father immigrated to U.S. and remarried; Rakosi and his brother joined him in 1910. Raised in Kenosha, Wisconsin. Entered University of Chicago in 1920; transferred in 1921 to University of Wisconsin, where he became friend of writers Kenneth Fearing and Margery Latimer. Worked at family counseling agency in Cleveland and at center for disturbed children in New York City. Published poems in *The Little Review* and *The Nation*. In 1925, returned to University of Wisconsin to study psychology. Legally changed name to "Callman Rawley." Worked as psychologist in personnel department of Milwaukee Electric; returned to New York in 1927 as psychologist for Bloomingdale's. Also worked as family counselor with Massachusetts Society for the Prevention of Cruelty to Children. Beginning in 1928, was successively a graduate student in University of Texas's English department, law school, and medical school. Divided time as high school English teacher in Houston and group worker with Mexican immigrants at Rusk Settlement House. Took courses in social work at University of Chicago. Over the next few years, worked as Director of Social Services in Federal Transient Bureau in New Orleans, and continued studying at Tulane University and University of Pennsylvania, where he received Master of Social Work degree in 1940. Married Leah Jaffe in 1939; a year later, the couple moved to St. Louis, where Rakosi worked at Jewish Family Service. Published *Selected Poems* (1941) and *Two Poems* (1942). Subsequent jobs were in Cleveland and Minneapolis, where he was Executive Director of Jewish Family and Children's Service until 1968. Moved to San Francisco. Began publishing poetry again with *Amulet* (1967). It was followed by *Ere-VOICE* (1971), *Ex Cranium, Night* (1975), *My Experiences in Parnassus* (1977), *History: A Sequence of Poems* (1981), *Droles de Journal* (1981), and *The Collected Poems* (1986). His essays and aphoristic writings were published as *The Collected Prose* (1983). Later poetry collections include *The Beasts* (1994), *Eight Songs and Meditations* (1995), and *The Earth Suite* (1997).

Kenneth Rexroth (December 22, 1905–June 6, 1982) b. Kenneth Charles Marion Rexroth in South Bend, Indiana. Toured Europe in 1912. Grew up in Battle Creek, Michigan, Chicago, and Toledo, Ohio. Mother died in 1916; father died in 1919. Lived with aunt in Chicago; met Sherwood Anderson, Frank Lloyd Wright, and others. Expelled from high school in 1922 for erratic attendance. Frequented burlesque houses; became part owner of the Green Mask, a tea room and performance space. Arrested during police raid on the Green Mask in the early 1920's; followed his court-appointed social worker, Lesley Smith, to Smith College; they later moved to Greenwich Village. In 1924, toured Pacific Northwest and New Mexico, where he met D. H. Lawrence and Witter Bynner. Lived in Holy Cross Monastery in West Park, New York. Served as mess steward on freighter to England and Buenos Aires in 1926. Married painter Andrée Schafer in Chicago in 1927 and moved to San Francisco; helped to set up San Francisco branch of John Reed Club. Louis Zukofsky included Rexroth's work in *An "Objectivists" Anthology* (1932).

Separated from Andrée in 1935. Married Marie Kass, a public health nurse, in 1940. Published poetry collection *In What Hour* (1940). Worked as orderly in San Francisco mental hospital during World War II. Published long poem *The Phoenix and the Tortoise* (1944). Hosted literary salon that included William Everson, Jack Spicer, Muriel Rukeyser, Robert Duncan, and others. Toured Europe on a Guggenheim Fellowship in 1949. Separated from Marie; moved in with Marthe Larsen (they were married in 1958). Published poetry collections *The Art of Worldly Wisdom* (1949), *The Signature of All Things* (1950), *The Dragon and the Unicorn* (1952), and *In Defense of the Earth* (1956), verse play collection *Beyond the Mountains* (1951), translations including *One Hundred Poems from the Japanese* (1955), *One Hundred Poems from the Chinese* (1956), and *Thirty Spanish Poems of Love and Exile* (1956). Became friend of Lawrence Ferlinghetti, poet and publisher. Met Allen Ginsberg, Jack Kerouac, Philip Lamantia, and Michael McClure; emceed their Six Gallery reading in 1955. Was involved in poetry-and-jazz movement. Published essay collections *Bird in the Bush* (1959) and *Assays* (1961), poetry collection *Natural Numbers* (1963), memoir *An Autobiographical Novel* (1966), *The Collected Shorter Poems* (1967), *The Collected Longer Poems* (1968), and the literary studies *Classics Revisited* (1968) and *American Poetry in the Twentieth Century* (1971). Taught at San Francisco State College and University of California, Santa Barbara. Lived in Kyoto, 1974–75. His later poetry appeared in *New Poems* (1974) and *The Morning Star* (1979).

Charles Reznikoff (August 30, 1894–January 22, 1976) b. Brooklyn, New York. Son of Russian Jews who fled pogroms. Graduated high school at age 15; briefly attended University of Missouri School of Journalism. Worked as salesman in parents' hat-manufacturing business. Attended New York University Law School, graduating second in his class in 1916. Published poetry collection *Rhythms* (1918) privately and at his own expense, a practice he continued through most of his career; it was followed by *Rhythms II* (1919), *Uriel Accosta* (1921), the first of a series of short verse plays, and *Five Groups of Verse* (1927). Began working in 1928 for *Corpus Juris*, a law encyclopedia. Published *By the Waters of Manhattan* (1929), a volume of miscellany. The same title was used for a novel he published the following year. Married writer Marie Syrkin in 1930. Became acquainted with poets Louis Zukofsky and George Oppen; Zukofsky published an essay in *Poetry* on Reznikoff's work. Oppen's Objectivist Press published three volumes of Reznikoff's work in 1934: the poetry collections *In Memoriam: 1933* and *Jerusalem the Golden*, and *Testimony*, a prose work based on legal documents and other historical material. Subsequently published *Separate Way* (1937), *Early History of a Sewing-Machine Operator* (1937), written in collaboration with his father, *Kaddish* (1937), and *Going To and Fro and Walking Up and Down* (1941); the historical novel *The Lionhearted* was published in 1944 by the Jewish Publication Society of America. At invitation of close friend Albert Lewin, a film producer, went to Hollywood in 1938 to assist Lewin as researcher and script-reader; returned to New York the following year. After 1941, Reznikoff devoted the majority of his time to editing and research; worked as managing editor of *Jewish Frontier*. The self-published poetry collection *Inscriptions: 1944–1956* appeared in 1959. *By the Waters of Manhattan* (1962), a volume of selected poems, and *Testimony: The United States, 1885–1890: Recitative* (1965) were published by New Directions. Reznikoff reverted to self-publication with *By the Well of Living and Seeing* and *The Fifth Book of the Maccabees* (both 1969). Awarded the Morton Dauwen Zabel prize by the National Institute of Arts and Letters in 1971. Black Sparrow Press published *Testimony: The United States (1891–1900)* (1965), *By the Well of Living and Seeing: New and Selected Poems, 1918–1973* (1974), and *Holocaust* (1975). Gained wider recognition in his later years, and formed friendships with other writers including Milton Hindus, Harvey Shapiro, and Allen Ginsberg. *The Manner Music* (1977), a novel, was published posthumously.

Laura Riding (January 16, 1901–September 2, 1991) b. Laura Reichenthal in New York City. Father was a tailor who had emigrated from Poland; mother was daughter of a peddler. Attended Cornell University, 1918–21. Married history instructor Louis Gottschalk in 1920; left school before completing degree. Moved with husband to Urbana, Illinois, and Louisville, Kentucky (marriage ended in divorce in 1925). Published poems in *The Fugitive*, and met circle of poets associated with the magazine. Accepted invitation in 1926 from Robert Graves and his wife Nancy Nicholson to live with them in England. With Graves wrote *A Survey of Modernist Poetry* (1927). Published poetry collection *The Close Chaplet* (1926) as Laura Riding Gottschalk; changed name to Laura Riding and published *Love as Love, Death as Death* (1928) and *Poems: A Joking Word* (1930); outlined theories of poetry in critical essays collected in *Contemporaries and Snobs* (1928) and *Anarchism Is Not Enough* (1928). Injured when she jumped out a second-floor window in 1929. Left London with Graves and settled in Majorcan village of Deyá; they published small-press editions there under imprint of Seizin Press, including Riding's poetry collections *Though Gently* (1930) and *Laura and Francisca* (1931); other collections included *Twenty Poems Less* (1930), *The Life of the Dead* (1933), and *Poet: A Lying Word* (1933). Also published fiction including *Progress of Stories* (1935), *A Trojan Ending* (1937), and *Lives of Wives* (1939). Established friendships with younger poets including Norman Cameron and Thomas Matthews. Moved with Graves to New Hope, Pennsylvania, in 1936; they lived with Schuyler Jackson, a friend of Thomas Matthews. After Jackson divorced his wife, Riding married him in 1941; they moved to Wabasso, Florida, where Riding studied linguistics. *Selected Poems: In Five Sets* (1970), published under the name Laura (Riding) Jackson, included a manifesto announcing her renunciation of poetry.

Lynn Riggs (August 31, 1899–June 30, 1954) b. Rolla Lynn Riggs, an enrolled Cherokee citizen in Claremore, in northeast Indian Territory of Oklahoma. After high school graduation in 1917, worked as cowpuncher on a cattle train, proofreader for *Wall Street Journal*, and film extra in Hollywood.

Entered University of Oklahoma in 1920. Published first stories and poems in H. L. Mencken's *The Smart Set* in 1922. Became friend of Witter Bynner; lived briefly in Santa Fe before returning to New York City, where he began writing plays. Encouraged by Ida Rauh Eastman, co-founder of Province-town Players. Play *Big Lake* was produced on Broadway in 1927; subsequent plays, mostly set in Oklahoma, were *The Domino Parlor* (1928), *Rancor* (1928), *Roadside* (1930), *A Lantern to See By* (1930), *Green Grow the Lilacs* (1931), and *Sump'n Like Wings* (1931). Poetry collection *The Iron Dish* appeared in 1930. Wrote several screenplays, including *The Garden of Allah* and *The Plainsman* (both 1936). Continued to write plays, including *Russet Mantle* (1936), *A World Elsewhere* (1940), and *The Cream in the Well* (1941). Rodgers and Hammerstein based the musical *Oklahoma!* (1943) on *Green Grow the Lilacs*. Later poems published posthumously in *This Book, This Hill, These People* (1982).

Theodore Roethke (May 25, 1908–August 1, 1963) b. Saginaw, Michigan. Father owned and operated one of largest greenhouses in the state. Graduated from University of Michigan in 1929. After briefly attending Michigan Law School, enrolled at Harvard to pursue a master's degree in literature, studying with Robert Hillyer and I. A. Richards; withdrew in 1931. Taught at Lafayette College, in Pennsylvania, until 1935, also serving as varsity tennis coach. During first semester teaching at Michigan State, suffered first of several mental breakdowns and was hospitalized. Taught at Pennsylvania State University (1936–43). Published poetry collection *Open House* (1941). Began teaching at Bennington College. Suffered another breakdown in 1945, and again returned to Saginaw. Awarded Guggenheim Fellowship in 1945. Spent summer of 1947 at Yaddo writers' colony, where he became a friend of Robert Lowell. Began teaching at University of Washington that fall; students included James Wright and Carolyn Kizer. Published *The Lost Son* (1948) and *Praise to the End!* (1951). Married Beatrice O'Connor, former Bennington student, in 1953. Awarded Pulitzer Prize for *The Waking* (1953). Lived in Italy on Fulbright grant. After hospitalization in 1957, returned to University of Washington. Awarded Bollingen Prize and National Book Award for *Words for the Wind* (1958). Published *I Am! Says the Lamb*, a collection of poems for children, in 1961. *The Far Field* (1964) published posthumously.

Edwin Rolfe (September 7, 1909–1954) b. Solomon Fishman in Philadephia, Pennsylvania. Spent most of childhood in New York City; joined Young Communist League in 1925. Enrolled in 1929 in the Experimental College at the University of Wisconsin at Madison. Returned to New York, joining staff of *The Daily Worker*. Along with Sol Funaroff, Joseph Kalar, and Herman Spector, published poems in anthology *We Gather Strength* (1933). Published poetry collection *To My Contemporaries* (1936). Traveled to Spain to join the Abraham Lincoln Battalion, American unit of the International Brigades in Spanish Civil War; trained at Tarazona in July 1937, then appointed editor of

Volunteer for Liberty, the English-language magazine of the Brigades. Joined field battalion in 1938, and participated in Ebro campaign. Served as Spanish correspondent for *Daily Worker* and *New Masses*. While in Spain met Ernest Hemingway, Langston Hughes, and Rafael Alberti. Wrote poems about the war, many of which were collected in *First Love* (1951). Returned from Spain in 1939. *The Lincoln Battalion*, based on his war experience, was published in 1939. Worked as editor for the New York Office of Soviet News Agency, Tass, from 1940 until 1943, when drafted into U.S. Army; became ill while training at Camp Wolters in Texas and was discharged. Moved to California. Suffered two heart attacks in 1944. With Lester Fuller, wrote mystery novel *The Glass Room*; film rights were purchased by Warner Brothers but film was not made. Suffered third heart attack in 1950. Final book, *Permit Me Refuge*, published posthumously in 1955.

Muriel Rukeyser (December 15, 1913–February 12, 1980) b. New York City. Educated at Fieldston, Vassar, and Columbia. Went to Alabama in 1933 to protest trial of the Scottsboro Boys; reported on mistreatment of tunnel workers in West Virginia mines. Poetry collection *Theory of Flight* (1935) published in Yale Series of Younger Poets. Published *U.S. 1* (1938) and *A Turning Wind* (1939). Published biography *Willard Gibbs* (1942) and critical study *The Life of Poetry* (1949). Taught at Sarah Lawrence; served as vice-president of House of Photography in New York City, 1946–60. Poetry collected in *Wake Island* (1942), *Beast in View* (1944), *The Children's Orchard* (1947), *The Green Wave* (1948), *Orpheus* (1949), *Elegies* (1949), *Body of Waking* (1958), and *Waterlily Fire* (1962). Her translations appeared in *Selected Poems of Octavio Paz* (1963) and *Sun Stone* (1963); published *One Life* (1957), a biography of Wendell Wilkie, and novel *The Orgy* (1965); co-translated *Selected Poems of Gunnar Ekelöf* (1967). Recipient of many awards including the Levinson Prize (1947), the Eunice Tietjens Memorial Prize (1967), and the Shelley Memorial Award (1977). Organized protests against the Vietnam War; later visited Hanoi. Led campaign on behalf of imprisoned South Korean poet Kim Chi-Ha. Later poetry collected in *The Outer Banks* (1967), *The Speed of Darkness* (1968), *29 Poems* (1973), *Breaking Open* (1973), *The Gates* (1976); *The Collected Poems* appeared in 1979.

May Sarton (May 3, 1912–July 16, 1995) b. Eléanore Marie Sarton in Wondelgem, Belgium. Daughter of Belgian father and English mother. At outbreak of World War I, family fled to England and then to Cambridge, Massachusetts. Educated at Cambridge High and Latin School. Became American citizen in 1924. First published poems appeared in *Poetry* when she was 17. Joined Civic Repertory Theater in New York; founded and directed Associated Actors' Theater of Hartford, Connecticut, 1933–36. Published poetry collection *Encounter in April* (1937). Taught creative writing at Stuart School in Boston, 1937–40. Published novel *The Single Hound* (1938) and poetry collection *Inner Landscape* (1939). Wrote scripts for U.S. Office of War Information in 1944; was poet-in-residence at Southern Illinois University in

1945; taught English at Harvard, 1949–52, and lectured at Bread Loaf Writers' Conference, 1951–53. Published poetry collections *The Lion and the Rose* (1948), *The Leaves of the Tree* (1950), *The Land of Silence* (1953), and *In Time Like Air* (1958). Moved to New Hampshire in 1958. Selected poems published as *Cloud, Stone, Sun, Vine* (1961). Taught creative writing at Wellesley, 1960–64. Described travels in Japan, India, and Greece in poetry collection *A Private Mythology* (1966); published *As Does New Hampshire* (1967) and *Plant Dreaming Deep* (1968). Moved to York, Maine, in 1973; later volumes of prose and poetry included *Journal of a Solitude* (1973), *Punch's Secret* (1974), *Crucial Conversations* (1975), *A Walk Through the Woods* (1976), *A World of Light* (1976), *The House by the Sea* (1977), *A Reckoning* (1978), *Halfway to Silence* (1980), *Recovering* (1980), *Writings on Writing* (1981), *Anger* (1982), *A Winter Garland* (1982), *A Seventy* (1984), *Letters from Maine* (1984), and *The Magnificent Spinster* (1985).

Isidor Schneider (August 25, 1896–1977) b. the Ukraine. Immigrated to the U.S. in 1901. Educated at City College of New York. Worked in advertising (1919–28) and as editor at Macauley Co. (1929–33). Published novel *Dr. Transit* (1926), followed by poetry collections *The Temptation of Anthony* (1928) and *Comrade: Mister* (1934). Awarded Guggenheim Fellowships in 1935 and 1937. Other novels included *From the Kingdom of Necessity* (1935) and *The Judas Time* (1947). His essay "Proletarian Poetry" was collected in *American Writers' Congress* (1935), and he was a regular contributor to *New Masses*. Translated *The Autobiography of Maxim Gorky* (1952). Edited anthology *The World of Love* (1964) and *The Enlightenment: The Culture of the Eighteenth Century* (1965).

David Schubert (October 18, 1913–April 1, 1946) b. New York City. Son of Russian immigrants. Mother committed suicide when he was 12. Raised by his aunt. Entered Amherst in 1929; dismissed in his sophomore year for low classroom and chapel attendance. Married Judith Kranes in 1933; they moved to the Chelsea area of Manhattan. Studied at City College of New York. Settled in Brooklyn Heights. Worked on *Bulletin* of the Brooklyn Institute of Arts and Sciences. Assembled manuscript of poems, dedicated to Robert Frost, whom he had met at Amherst, in 1935; failed to find publisher. Formed friendship with Ben Belitt. Began psychoanalytic treatment in 1939. James Laughlin included Schubert's manuscript, titled "Simple Scale," in *Five Young American Poets* (1942). Fired from *Bulletin* in 1942; enrolled in Columbia Library School; became friend of Theodore Weiss. Disappeared after quarrel with Judith in 1943; went to Washington, D.C., where he was admitted to Gallinger Hospital for psychiatric observation. Admitted to Bloomingdale Hospital in White Plains, New York; underwent electric shock treatment. Transferred after a year to Central Islip, where he died of tuberculosis. *Initial A*, a collection of his poetry, appeared in 1961; other poems were published in *David Schubert: Works and Days* (1983), a special publication of *Quarterly Review of Literature*.

Delmore Schwartz (December 8, 1913–July 11, 1966) b. Brooklyn, New York. Studied at University of Wisconsin and New York University, where he earned B.A. in philosophy in 1935. Pursued graduate study at Harvard without earning a degree. Published poems in *Poetry* and *Partisan Review* in 1937. *In Dreams Begin Responsibilities*, a collection including fiction, drama, and poetry, appeared in 1937. Translated Rimbaud's *A Season In Hell*. Awarded Guggenheim Fellowship in 1940; was poetry editor of *Partisan Review*, 1943–47, and *The New Republic*, 1955–57. Published verse play *Shenandoah* (1941), long poem *Genesis: Book One* (1943), *Vaudeville for a Princess* (1950), and *Summer Knowledge: New and Selected Poems, 1938–1958* (1959). At various times from 1946 to 1966, was a visiting lecturer at Harvard, Princeton, Kenyon, Indiana, Chicago, UCLA, and Syracuse. Left Syracuse in 1966; stayed in a mental hospital intermittently, and spent his last days in a succession of hotels. Later work collected posthumously in *The Last and Lost Poems of Delmore Schwartz* (1979).

Winfield Townley Scott (April 30, 1910–April 28, 1968) b. Haverhill, Massachusetts; raised in Newport, Rhode Island. Educated at Brown University. Was assistant literary editor (1931–41) and literary editor (1941–51) of Providence *Journal*. Met Edwin Arlington Robinson, to whom he dedicated *Elegy for Robinson* (1936). Early collections of poems included *Biography for Traman* (1937), *Wind the Clock* (1941), *The Sword on the Table* (1942), *To Marry Strangers* (1945), and *Mr. Whittier* (1948). Long poem *The Dark Sister* appeared in 1958. Settled in Santa Fe and became literary editor of Santa Fe *New Mexican*, 1961–64. Published essays in *Exiles and Fabrications* (1961) and *Alpha Omega* (1972). Later books of poetry included *Scrimshaw* (1959), *Collected Poems 1937–62* (1962), *Change of Weather* (1964), and *Letter to the World* (1966).

Karl Shapiro (b. November 10, 1913) b. Carl Shapiro in Baltimore, Maryland. Attended schools in Baltimore, Chicago, and Virginia. Dropped out of University of Virginia after a year; traveled to Tahiti. Published *Poems* (1935); studied briefly at Johns Hopkins. Attended Enoch Pratt Library School in Baltimore; drafted into army in 1941 before finishing school. Wrote prolifically during military service, 1941–45; published *The Place of Love* (1942); *Person, Place and Thing* (1942), which won *Poetry* magazine's Levinson Prize; the Pulitzer Prize–winning *V-Letter* (1944); and *Essay on Rime* (1945). In 1945, married Evelyn Katz, his literary agent. Served as Consultant in Poetry at the Library of Congress, 1947–48; named associate professor of writing at Johns Hopkins (1948). Edited *Poetry* (1950–56) and *Newberry Library Bulletin* (1953–56). In 1956 became professor at the University of Nebraska and editor of *Prairie Schooner*. Poetry collected in *Trial of a Poet* (1947), *Poems of a Jew* (1958), and *The Bourgeois Poet* (1964), a volume of prose poems. Taught at University of Chicago (1966–68) and University of California at Davis. Published *Selected Poems* and *White-Haired Lover* in 1968; shared Bollingen Prize with John Berryman. Later collections include *Adult Bookstore* (1976),

Collected Poems 1940–1978 (1978), and *The Wild Card* (1998). His essays have been collected in *In Defense of Ignorance* (1960), *To Abolish Children* (1968), and *The Poetry Wreck* (1975).

Bessie Smith (April 15, 1894–September 26, 1937) b. Chattanooga, Tennessee. As singer and dancer, performed with traveling shows in the early 1910's; worked with Ma Rainey. Moved to Philadelphia in 1921. Recorded first sides for Columbia Records in 1923; inaugurated Columbia's "race" catalogue in 1924 with "Chicago Bound Blues," and ultimately recorded more than 150 songs. Collaborated with Louis Armstrong on "St. Louis Blues." Accompanists included Clarence Williams, Fletcher Henderson, Don Redman, and James P. Johnson. Became nationally famous and toured throughout the 1920's; her shows included *Harlem Frolics*, *Yellow Girl Revue*, *Steamboat Days*, and *Happy Times*. Made short film "St. Louis Blues" in 1929. Recorded final session for Okeh Records in 1933. Died in road accident while on tour.

May Swenson (May 28, 1913–December 4, 1989) b. Logan, Utah. Daughter of Swedish immigrants who had converted to Mormonism. Graduated from Utah State University in 1934; worked for local newspapers. Moved to New York City in 1936; worked as oral historian for Federal Writers' Project. After publishing poems in *The Saturday Review* and *New Directions in Poetry and Prose*, spent two-month residence in 1950 at Yaddo, where she became a friend of Elizabeth Bishop. Collection of poems titled "Another Animal" included in *Poets of Today* (1954). Published *A Cage of Spines* (1958). Read manuscripts for New Directions Press, 1959–66. Traveled through France, Spain, and Italy on a fellowship in 1963; published *To Mix with Time* (1963). Collected "riddle poems" for children in *Poems to Solve* (1966). *Half Sun Half Sleep* (1967) included new poems and translations of Swedish poets. Moved to Sea Cliff, New York, where she lived with her companion R. Rozanne Knudson, an author of children's fiction. *Iconographs* (1970), a collection of shaped poems, was followed by children's books *More Poems to Solve* (1971) and *The Guess and Spell Coloring Book* (1976). Was writer-in-residence at Purdue, University of North Carolina, and University of California at Riverside. Later books included *New and Selected Things Taking Place* (1978) and *In Other Words* (1987). Won 1981 Bollingen Prize; awarded MacArthur Fellowship in 1987. *Nature* (1994) published posthumously.

Genevieve Taggard (November 28, 1894–November 8, 1948) b. Waitsburg, Washington. Daughter of missionary schoolteachers. Family moved in 1897 to Hawaii, where her parents founded a public school attended by Hawaiian, Chinese, Japanese, and Portuguese students. Moved to California with family in 1914. Entered University of California at Berkeley; studied poetry with Witter Bynner and edited *The Occident*, college literary magazine. Moved to New York City after graduation; published poems in *The Nation*, *Poetry*, and other magazines. Married Robert Wolf in 1921; daughter Marcia born the following year. With her husband, served as editor of *New Masses* in the 1920's.

Was a co-founder, with Maxwell Anderson and Padraic Colum, of *Measure: A Magazine of Verse*. Poetry collected in *For Eager Lovers* (1922), *Words for the Chisel* (1926), *Traveling Standing Still* (1928); edited anthologies *May Days* (1925), a collection of political poetry, and *Circumference: Varieties of Metaphysical Verse, 1456–1928* (1929). Published biography *The Life and Mind of Emily Dickinson* (1930). After a year in southern France, moved to New England in 1929 to teach at Mount Holyoke. Traveled to Capri, Majorca, and France the following year on a Guggenheim Fellowship. Later taught at Bennington and Sarah Lawrence, where she remained until 1946. Divorced Wolf in 1934; married Kenneth Durant in 1935 and moved to a farm in East Jamaica, Vermont. Later poetry collected in *Not Mine to Finish* (1934), *Calling Western Union* (1936), *Collected Poems* (1938), *Slow Music* (1946), and *Origin: Hawaii* (1947).

Allen Tate (November 19, 1899–February 9, 1979) b. Winchester, Kentucky. Attended Vanderbilt University, where he took courses taught by John Crowe Ransom. Became part of Fugitives group, which included Ransom, Donald Davidson, Robert Penn Warren, and others. Graduated in 1922; left Nashville in 1924 to teach high school in West Virginia. Married novelist Caroline Gordon in 1924. Moved to New York City; worked at *Telling Tales*, a pulp romance magazine. By 1925, Tate had contributed more than 20 poems to *The Fugitive*. Rented farmhouse in Patterson, New York, after birth of daughter Nancy; Hart Crane stayed there with the Tates in 1925. Wrote biographies *Stonewall Jackson* (1928) and *Jefferson Davis* (1929), and published poetry collection *Mr. Pope* (1928). Awarded Guggenheim Fellowship; lived in Paris for over a year; acquaintances there included F. Scott Fitzgerald, Ernest Hemingway, Gertrude Stein, and John Peale Bishop. Contributed to and co-edited Southern Agrarian manifesto *I'll Take My Stand* (1930). Returned to France for a year in 1932, living at Cap Brun outside of Paris. Published *Poems: 1928–1931* (1932), *The Mediterranean* (1936), *Reactionary Essays on Poetry and Ideas* (1936), and *Selected Poems* (1937). Published novel *The Fathers* (1938). Along with Gordon, taught English at the Woman's College in Greensboro, North Carolina, 1938–39. Served as poet-in-residence at Princeton (1939–42), followed by one-year term as the first Consultant in Poetry at the Library of Congress, 1943–44. Published translation *The Vigil of Venus: Pervigilium Veneris* (1943) and poetry collection *The Winter Sea* (1944). Edited *Sewanee Review*, 1944–46. Worked as literary editor at Henry Holt; left in 1948 to teach at New York University. Became tenured professor at University of Minnesota in 1951; won Bollingen Prize. Served as Fulbright Lecturer at Oxford (1953) and Fulbright Professor at University of Rome (1953–54). Edited several anthologies of poetry, fiction and criticism. Published *Collected Poems, 1919–1976* (1977).

Melvin B. Tolson (February 6, 1898–September 3, 1966) b. Melvin Beaunorus Tolson in Moberly, Missouri. Father was a Methodist preacher. Published first poem, on sinking of the *Titanic*, in an Iowa newspaper in

1914. Entered Fisk University in 1918; transferred to Lincoln University, graduating with honors in 1923. Married Ruth Southall in 1922; they had four children. Began teaching at Wiley College in Texas in 1923. Established the Wiley Forensic Society, whose debate teams broke color lines in the Midwest and defeated the University of Southern California in 1935. Took leave from Wiley to study at Columbia University, 1931–32. Completed *A Gallery of Harlem Portraits*, unpublished during his lifetime, in 1932. Wrote weekly column, "Caviar and Cabbage," for *Washington Tribune*, 1937–44. Poem "Dark Symphony" won national contest of American Negro Exposition in Chicago. Received M.A. from Columbia in 1940. Poetry collection *Rendezvous with America* appeared in 1944. Named Poet Laureate of Liberia in 1947. Left Wiley in 1947 for Langston College in Oklahoma. Beginning in 1952, served four terms as mayor of Langston. Published *Libretto for the Republic of Liberia* (1953). Adapted and directed stage version of Walter S. White's *Fire in the Flint* (1924), performed at 1952 NAACP convention. Received permanent fellowship in poetry and drama at Bread Loaf Writers' Conference in Vermont; became friend of Robert Frost. First appointee to the Avalon Chair in humanities at Tuskegee Institute, 1965–66. *Harlem Gallery: Book 1, The Curator*, intended as the first of a five-book series, was published in 1965. Died of abdominal cancer the following year.

Jean Toomer (December 26, 1894–March 30, 1967) b. Eugene Nathan Toomer in Washington, D.C. Father deserted family; raised primarily by grandfather, P.B.S. Pinchback, a former Louisiana politician. Graduated Dunbar High School in 1914. Attended colleges in Wisconsin, Massachusetts, Chicago, and New York. Worked as physical education teacher, car salesman, and shipyard worker. Visited New York in 1919; met Waldo Frank, Kenneth Burke, Hart Crane, and other writers. Took a two-month position in 1921 as acting principal of Sparta Agricultural and Industrial Institute in Sparta, Georgia. Toured the South with Waldo Frank. Published poetry and sketches in *Double Dealer, Broom, The Dial, Opportunity, The Crisis, Nomad*, and *The Little Review*. Published *Cane* (1923), an experimental book combining poetry and prose, based on his experiences in the South. Became a follower of Russian occultist George Gurdjieff; spent time at the Gurdjieff Institute in Fontainebleau, France, in 1924, returning in 1926, 1927, and 1929; led Gurdjieff groups in Harlem (1925) and Chicago (1926–33). Married novelist Margery Latimer in 1931; she died in childbirth a year later. Remarried in 1934; moved to a Quaker community in Bucks County, Pennsylvania, where he spent the rest of his life. Long poem "The Blue Meridian" appeared in the anthology *New Caravan* in 1936. Continued to write prolifically, mostly on spiritual themes, but published only a book of aphorisms, *Essentials* (1931). *The Collected Poems of Jean Toomer* appeared in 1988.

Eve Triem (November 2, 1902–December 26, 1992) b. New York City. Raised in San Francisco. Attended University of California at Berkeley, 1921–24. Married writer Paul Triem in 1924; they had two children. Settled in

Seattle in the 1960's. Published poems in *Parade of Doves* (1946), *Poems* (1965), *The Process* (1976), *Dark to Glow* (1979), *Midsummer Rites* (1981), *New as a Wave* (1984), and *Nobody Dies in Summer* (1992); *Heliodora: Translations from the Greek Anthology* appeared in 1968.

Mark Van Doren (June 13, 1894–December 10, 1972) b. Hope, Illinois. Raised in Urbana, Illinois. Studied at University of Illinois, where he took a B.A. in 1914 and an M.A. in 1915. Published first poem in 1915 in H. L. Mencken's *The Smart Set*. Studied at Columbia University, where his brother Carl taught. Served in infantry during World War I, September 1917–December 1918. Completed Ph.D. thesis on John Dryden's poetry in 1920. Became literary editor of *The Nation* in 1920; began teaching at Columbia. Married Dorothy Graffe, also on *Nation* staff, in 1922. First poetry collection *Spring Thunder* (1924) followed by *7 P.M.* (1926), *Now the Sky* (1928), the long poem *Jonathan Gentry* (1931), *A Winter Diary* (1935), *The Last Look* (1937), and *Collected Poems 1922–1938* (1939), which won Pulitzer Prize. Became full professor at Columbia in 1942. Lectured on the philosophy of education through the 1940's; published *Liberal Education* (1943). Later poetry collections included *The Seven Sleepers* (1944), *The Careless Clock* (1947), *Spring Birth* (1953), *Morning Worship* (1960), *Narrative Poems* (1964), *That Shining Place* (1969), and *Good Morning* (1973). Published a number of critical studies, including *Henry David Thoreau* (1916), *Edwin Arlington Robinson* (1927), *Shakespeare* (1939), and *Nathaniel Hawthorne* (1949). Retired from Columbia in 1959.

Byron Vazakas (September 24, 1905–September 30, 1987) b. New York City. Father died in 1913. Family moved briefly to Chicago, then settled in Lancaster, Pennsylvania. Formal education ended after eighth grade. Family moved to Reading, Pennsylvania, in 1922. In the late 1930's, began publishing poems in magazines such as *Poetry*. Friendship with painter William Baziotes led him to write a number of articles on art. Became a friend of William Carlos Williams, who wrote the preface to Vazakas' first poetry collection, *Transfigured Night* (1946). Moved to Cambridge, Massachusetts, in 1947; met Archibald MacLeish. Lectured occasionally at Harvard. Published *The Equal Tribunals* (1961). Lived in England (1962–64) on Amy Lowell traveling scholarship; completed *The Marble Manifesto* (1966). Returned to Reading, where he remained for the rest of his life. Final poetry collection was *Nostalgias for a House of Cards* (1970).

Robert Penn Warren (April 24, 1905–September 15, 1989) b. Guthrie, Kentucky. Suffered severe eye injury in 1921; entered Vanderbilt University that fall. Professors included John Crowe Ransom and Donald Davidson; roomed with Allen Tate. Became part of Fugitives group; contributed poems to *The Fugitive*. Graduated in 1925; took M.A. from University of California at Berkeley in 1927. Studied briefly at Yale and Oxford. Married Cinina Brescia in 1929; published *John Brown: The Making of a Martyr* (1929). Began teaching at Southwestern College in 1930. Contributed to *I'll Take My Stand*

(1930), anthology of agrarian essays edited by Davidson. Taught at Vanderbilt (1931–34); left eye removed in 1934. Taught at Louisiana State University; with Cleanth Brooks, co-edited *The Southern Review*. Published *Thirty-Six Poems* (1936); textbooks *An Approach to Literature* (1936) and *Understanding Poetry* (1938), both with Brooks; and novel *Night Rider* (1939). Awarded Guggenheim Fellowship in 1939; lived in Italy. Taught at University of Minnesota; served as Consultant in Poetry at the Library of Congress (1944–45). Published *Eleven Poems on the Same Theme* (1942), *Selected Poems: 1923–1943* (1944), and novels *At Heaven's Gate* (1943), *All the King's Men* (1946), which won Pulitzer Prize, and *World Enough and Time* (1949). Named professor of playwriting at Yale. After marriage ended in divorce, married Eleanor Clark. Published long poem *Brother to Dragons* (1953), novels *Band of Angels* (1955) and *The Cave* (1959), essay *Segregation: The Inner Conflict in the South* (1956); and poetry collections *Promises* (1957), which received National Book Award, and *You, Emperors* (1960). Was professor of English at Yale, 1962–73. After novel *Flood* (1964) and essay *Who Speaks for the Negro?* (1965), focused on poetry; late collections included *Selected Poems: New and Old* (1966), *Incarnations* (1968), *Audubon: A Vision* (1969), *Homage to Theodore Dreiser* (1970), *Meet Me in the Glen* (1970), *Or Else* (1974), *Now and Then* (1978), which won Pulitzer Prize, *Being Here* (1980), *Rumor Verified* (1981), and *March* (1985).

John Wheelwright (September 9, 1897–September 15, 1940) b. John Tyler Wheelwright in Milton, Massachusetts. Attended St. George's preparatory school in Newport, Rhode Island. Father was sent to a mental hospital in 1910 and committed suicide two years later. Changed middle name to Brooks, after mother's maiden name. Entered Harvard in 1916; formed friendships with E. E. Cummings, Robert Hillyer, John Dos Passos, and Malcolm Cowley; expelled from Harvard for irregular attendance in 1920. Studied architecture intermittently throughout the 1920's at M.I.T.; established an unsuccessful practice with Zareh Sourian. Edited several issues of Gorham Munson's *Secession*, 1922–23. Poetry collection *North Atlantic Passage* published privately in Florence in 1925. Contributed a number of reviews, poems, and articles to *Hound and Horn* in the early 1930's. Joined Socialist Party of Massachussetts in 1932; was poetry editor of party's journal *Arise*. Poetry collection *Rock and Shell* published in small edition in 1933. Initiated Vanguard Verse Project with Kenneth Porter and Sherry Mangan, sponsoring pamphlet series *Poems for a Dime* and *Poems for Two Bits*, and correspondence course in politically committed poetry. Worked on behalf of American Committee for the Defense of Trotsky. Expelled with other Trotskyites from the Socialist Party in 1937; became a founding member of Socialist Workers Party in 1938. Published poetry collections *Mirrors of Venus* (1937) and *Political Self-Portrait* (1940). Active in League for Cultural Freedom and Socialism. Killed by a drunk driver in Boston. *Collected Poems* published in 1972.

Bukka White (November 12, 1909–February 26, 1977) b. Booker T. Washington White in Houston, Mississippi. Learned to play guitar from father.

Worked on uncle's farm in Grenada, Mississippi. Admired playing of Charlie Patton. Recorded 14 sides at Victor field studio in Memphis, Tennessee, in 1930. Married in 1933 and returned to farming in West Point, Mississippi. Shot a man in 1937; fled to Chicago recording studio while free on bond; Mississippi sheriff arrested him in mid-session. Served two years in Parchman Farm prison; recorded by Alan Lomax for the Library of Congress Folk Song Archive during his incarceration. Recorded 12 sides, most of them composed in jail, in Chicago after release. Lived in Chicago and Memphis; helped cousin B. B. King start music career in Chicago. Recorded in 1963 in Memphis by Berkeley graduate students John Fahey and Ed Denson; moved to California and attempted to earn living as a singer.

Tennessee Williams (March 26, 1911–February 24, 1983) b. Thomas Lanier Williams in Columbus, Mississippi. Raised in St. Louis. Studied briefly at University of Missouri School of Journalism; worked in shoe factory for three years. Had two plays produced at St. Louis theater in 1936. Enrolled at University of Iowa. Moved to New Orleans after 1938 graduation, then to New York City in 1939. *The Long Good-bye* staged at The New School in 1940. Traveled in 1941 to Key West; met Elizabeth Bishop, John Dewey, and Max Eastman; divided time among New York, Key West, and New Orleans. *You Touched Me!*, co-written with Donald Windham, produced at Pasadena Playbox in 1943. Supported by grant from American Academy of Arts and Letters during composition of *The Glass Menagerie*, which opened in 1944. Published *Twenty-seven Wagons Full of Cotton* (1946), a collection of short plays. Became close friend of Carson McCullers. Met longtime companion Frank Merlo in Provincetown in 1947. *A Streetcar Named Desire* (1947), which won the Pulitzer Prize, was followed by *Summer and Smoke* (1948). Published novel *The Roman Spring of Mrs. Stone* (1950). Subsequent plays included *The Rose Tattoo* (1950), *Camino Real* (1953), the Pulitzer Prize–winning *Cat on a Hot Tin Roof* (1955), *Orpheus Descending* (1957), *Suddenly Last Summer* (1958), *Period of Adjustment* (1958), *Sweet Bird of Youth* (1959), *The Night of the Iguana* (1961), and *The Milk Train Doesn't Stop Here Anymore* (1964). His early poems were collected in *In the Winter of Cities* (1956). Suffered health problems exacerbated by chronic use of prescription drugs. Later plays included *Small Craft Warnings* (1972), *The Red Devil Battery Sign* (1974), *Vieux Carré* (1977), *A Lovely Sunday for Creve Coeur* (1979), *Clothes for a Summer Hotel* (1980), and *Something Cloudy Something Clear* (1982). Later poems collected in *Androgyne, Mon Amour* (1977).

Edmund Wilson (May 8, 1895–June 12, 1972) b. Red Bank, New Jersey. Attended Princeton, where he edited *Nassau Lit*; became friend of F. Scott Fitzgerald and John Peale Bishop. Worked as reporter for *New York Evening Sun*. Enlisted with a hospital unit when the U.S. entered World War I; transferred to an intelligence unit in 1918. Joined staff of *Vanity Fair*; later worked for *The New Republic* and *The Dial*. Had wide circle of acquaintants in New York, including Edna St. Vincent Millay, Elinor Wylie, Malcolm Cowley,

Louise Bogan, John Dos Passos, and many others. Early poetry appeared in
The Undertaker's Garland (1922), written in collaboration with John Peale
Bishop. Wife Mary Blair starred in 1924 Provincetown Players' production of
his play *The Crime in the Whistler Room*. Published novel *I Thought of Daisy*
(1929). Established second home at Cape Cod. Published study of literary
modernism, *Axel's Castle* (1931). Reported on the execution of Sacco and
Vanzetti, the trial of the Scottsboro Boys, and coal miners' strikes in Ken-
tucky and West Virginia; collected journalism in *The American Jitters* (1932).
Traveled in 1935 to the Soviet Union to research historical study *To the Fin-
land Station* (1940). Married third wife, novelist Mary McCarthy, in 1938.
Published *The Triple Thinkers* (1938) and *The Wound and the Bow* (1941).
Novel *Memoirs of Hecate County* (1946) encountered censorship problems
and was published in bowdlerized form. Became friend of Vladimir Nabokov.
After World War II, reported for *The New Yorker*; visited Greece, Crete, Italy,
and England. Travel accounts collected in *Europe Without Baedeker* (1947);
literary criticism collected in *Classics and Commercials* (1950), *The Shores of
Light* (1952), and *The Bit Between My Teeth* (1965). Other books included *The
Scrolls from the Dead Sea* (1955), *Red, Black, Blond and Olive* (1956), *A Piece
of My Mind* (1956), *Apologies to the Iroquois* (1960), *Patriotic Gore* (1962), *The
Cold War and the Income Tax* (1963), *O Canada* (1965), *A Window on Russia*
(1972), and *Upstate* (1971). The poems collected in *Poets, Farewell!* (1929) and
Note-Books of Night (1942) were eventually gathered in *Wilson's Night
Thoughts* (1961). Selections from his voluminous diaries were published
posthumously in a series of books beginning with *The Twenties* (1975).

Yvor Winters (October 17, 1900–January 25, 1968) b. Arthur Yvor Winters in
Chicago, Illinois. Raised near Pasadena, California. Attended University of
Chicago (1917–18); in Chicago met writers Marianne Moore and Harriet
Monroe. Contracted tuberculosis and moved to a sanatorium in Santa Fe,
New Mexico. Published poetry collections *The Immobile Wind* (1921) and *The
Magpie's Shadow* (1922). Taught at New Mexico schools (1921–23); attended
University of Colorado; earned B.A. and M.A. in 1925. Taught foreign lan-
guages at University of Idaho (1925–27). In 1926 married Janet Lewis, who
had also gone to Santa Fe for her health. Published *The Bare Hills* (1927); be-
gan graduate study at Stanford University. Corresponded with Hart Crane.
Published poetry collections *The Proof* (1930) and *The Journey* (1931). Earned
Ph.D. from Stanford in 1932; named assistant professor in 1937. Joined de-
fense committee for David Lamson, Stanford employee convicted on circum-
stantial evidence of murdering his wife; Lamson was released after spending
three years in jail. Published poetry collections *Poems* (1940), *The Giant
Weapon* (1943), and *The Brink of Darkness* (1947), and critical studies *Primi-
tivism and Decadence* (1937), *Maule's Curse* (1938), and *The Anatomy of Non-
sense* (1943), later collected in *In Defense of Reason* (1947). Named full
professor in 1949; students included J. V. Cunningham, Edgar Bowers, Thom
Gunn, and Robert Pinsky. Published critical studies *Edwin Arlington Robin-
son* (1946), *The Poetry of W. B. Yeats* (1960), and *The Poetry of J.V. Cunning-*

ham (1961). Won 1961 Bollingen Prize for *Collected Poems* (1952, revised edition 1960). Published critical studies *The Function of Criticism* (1957) and *Forms of Discovery* (1967).

Richard Wright (September 4, 1908–November 28, 1960) b. Richard Nathaniel Wright on plantation in Roxie, Mississippi. Family moved frequently during his early childhood; grew up with various relatives in Natchez, Mississippi, Memphis, Tennessee, Jackson, Mississippi, and other towns in Arkansas and Mississippi. Graduated valedictorian of his junior high school class in 1925, his last year of formal education. Moved in 1927 to Chicago; employed as delivery boy, postal worker, insurance salesman, and ditch digger. Joined local John Reed Club in 1933 and became Communist Party member in 1934. Published poems in *Midland Left*, *International Literature*, *Left Front*, *Anvil*, and *New Masses*. Met James T. Farrell and became member of national council of League of American Writers. Worked on Illinois volume of American Guide Series for Federal Writers' Project; served as literary adviser for Negro Federal Theatre of Chicago; active in South Side Writers' Group along with Frank Marshall Davis, Fenton Johnson, and others. Moved to Harlem in 1937; became Harlem editor of *The Daily Worker* and worked for New York Federal Writers' Project. Published story collection *Uncle Tom's Children* (1938). Awarded Guggenheim Fellowship in 1939; married Ehima Rose Meadman. Published novel *Native Son* (1940), which became a bestseller. Collaborated on stage adaptation of the novel with Paul Green and John Houseman; directed by Orson Welles, it opened in 1941. The same year, published *12 Million Black Voices*, text illustrated with photographs. After breakup of first marriage, married Ellen Poplar. Broke with Communist Party. Published autobiography *Black Boy* (1945), also a bestseller; active in promoting the careers of writers including Gwendolyn Brooks, James Baldwin, and Chester Himes. Visited Paris in 1946, settling there permanently with wife and daughter the following year; met Gertrude Stein, Simone de Beauvoir, Jean-Paul Sartre, André Gide, Léopold Senghor, Aimé Césaire, and Albert Camus. Starred in film version of *Native Son*, shot in Argentina, 1949–50. Traveled extensively within Europe, lecturing and meeting with writers. Published novel *The Outsider* (1953). Visited Gold Coast to research book on Africa, published as *Black Power* (1954); met Kwame Nkrumah. Published novels *Savage Holiday* (1954) and *The Long Dream* (1958); *The Color Curtain* (1956), account of conference of non-aligned nations in Bandung, Indonesia; travel book *Pagan Spain* (1957); and essay collection *White Man Listen!* (1957). Settled in 1959 in London. In his final years, composed nearly four thousand haiku.

Louis Zukofsky (January 23, 1904–May 12, 1978) b. New York City. Youngest child of Lithuanian Jews. Studied engineering at Stuyvesant High School; entered Columbia University in 1919 and shifted focus to humanities. Tutored English as a second language after 1923 graduation. Sent poems in 1926 to Ezra Pound in Italy; Pound printed one in *Exile*, sent others to Harriet Monroe at *Poetry*, and introduced Zukofsky to William Carlos Williams. In 1928, began writing the long poem "*A*," which he outlined in 24 movements. Secured teaching position at University of Wisconsin at Madison. Invited by Monroe to edit the February 1931 issue of *Poetry*, devoted to "Objectivist" poets; he included, along with his own poems and essays, the work of Williams, Charles Reznikoff, George Oppen, Carl Rakosi, Basil Bunting, Kenneth Rexroth, and others (contents later published in expanded form as *An "Objectivists" Anthology*, 1932). Worked as editor for TO Publishers, owned by Oppen. Study of Guillaume Apollinaire published in France as *Le Style Apollinaire* (1934). Went to Europe in 1933 with financial assistance from Pound and violist Tibor Serly; visited Paris, Budapest, and Rapallo. Founded the Objectivist Press, which published the works of Williams, Reznikoff, and others. In 1934, developed poetry textbook for the WPA, later published as *A Test of Poetry* (1948). Corresponded extensively and was closely involved with Lorine Niedecker. Married Celia Thaew, a composer and musician, in 1939. Worked as a high school English teacher, physics lab assistant, technical writer, and editor. Published *55 Poems* (1942). Bought a house in Brooklyn; son Paul born in 1943. Began teaching English at Polytechnic Institute of Brooklyn in 1947. Visited Europe in 1957, met T. S. Eliot and Cid Corman. Taught poetry at San Francisco State College in 1959. Corman financed publication of "*A*" *1–12* in 1959. Later publications included *Bottom: On Shakespeare* (1963), *After I's* (1964), *All: The Collected Short Poems* (1965–66), essay collection *Prepositions* (1967), fictional works *Little: A Fragment for Careenagers* (1967) and *Ferdinand, Including It Was* (1968), translation *Catullus* (1969), "*A*" *13-21* (1969), "*A*" *24* (1972), play *Arise, Arise* (1973), "*A*" *22 and 23* (1975). Retired from teaching in 1965 and moved to Port Jefferson, New York. Final poetic work *80 Flowers* published in 1978.

Note on the Texts

The choice of text for each of the poems selected for inclusion in this volume has been made on the basis of a study of its textual history and a comparison of editions printed during the author's lifetime. In general, each text is from the earliest book edition prepared with the author's participation; revised editions are sometimes followed, in light of the degree of authorial supervision and the stage of the writer's career at which the revisions were made, but the preference has been for the authorially approved book version closest to the date of composition. Texts from periodicals, anthologies, and posthumous sources have been used only when a poem was not printed in one of the author's books during his or her lifetime, or when such a book version is not authoritative. For song lyrics, collected editions (when available) have been preferred over sheet-music texts or new transcriptions.

The following is a list of the sources of all of the texts included in this volume, listed alphabetically by the authors of the poems.

Virginia Hamilton Adair. Buckroe, After the Season, 1942; Exit Amor: *Ants on the Melon* (New York: Random House, 1996).

Helen Adam. Mune Rune; The Huntsman; Shallow-Water Warning: *Selected Poems and Ballads* (New York: Helikon Press, 1974).

Léonie Adams. April Mortality: *Those Not Elect* (New York: Robert McBride and Co., 1925). The Rounds and Garlands Done; The Moon and Spectator; Ghostly Tree; Fragmentary Stars; The Horn; The Figurehead: *High Falcon and Other Poems* (New York: John Day and Co., 1929). Grapes Making: *Poems: A Selection* (New York: Funk & Wagnalls, 1954).

James Agee. "Not met and marred with the year's whole turn of grief"; "So it begins. Adam is in his earth"; "Now stands our love on that still verge of day"; "This little time the breath and bulk of being": *Permit Me Voyage* (New Haven: Yale University Press, 1934). To Walker Evans: James Agee and Walker Evans, *Let Us Now Praise Famous Men* (Boston: Houghton Mifflin, 1941). "Wake Up Threeish": the second of "Three Cabaret Songs" in Robert Fitzgerald (ed.), *The Collected Poems of James Agee* (Boston: Houghton Mifflin, 1968).

Howard Baker. Advice to a Man Who Lost His Dog; Sappho's Leap: *Ode to the Sea and Other Poems* (Denver: Alan Swallow, 1966).

Mary Barnard. Shoreline; Logging Trestle; The Field; Static; The Solitary; Probably Nobody; The Pleiades; Lethe: *Collected Poems* (Portland, OR: Breitenbush, 1979).

Ben Belitt. The Orange Tree: *Nowhere But Light* (Chicago: University of Chicago Press, 1970). Kites: Ars Poetica: *The Double Witness* (Princeton: Princeton University Press, 1978).

Stephen Vincent Benét. *from* John Brown's Body: *John Brown's Body* (Garden City, NY: Doubleday, Doran, 1928). American Names: *Poems and Ballads 1915–1930* (Garden City, NY: Doubleday, Doran, 1931). Cotton Mather; Daniel Boone: *A Book of Americans* (New York: Farrar & Rinehart, 1933), with Rosemary Benét; Metropolitan Nightmare: *The Selected Works of Stephen Vincent Benét. Volume One: Poetry* (New York: Farrar & Rinehart, 1942).

Elizabeth Bishop. The Map; The Man-Moth; Roosters; The Fish: *North & South* (Boston: Houghton Mifflin, 1946). Over 2000 Illustrations and a Complete Concordance; The Bight; At the Fishhouses; The Prodigal; The Shampoo: *Poems: North & South—A Cold Spring* (Boston: Houghton Mifflin, 1955). Song for the Rainy Season; The Armadillo; Sestina; Sandpiper; Twelfth Morning; or What You Will: *Questions of Travel* (New York: Farrar, Straus and Giroux, 1965). In the Waiting Room; Crusoe in England; One Art: *Geography III* (New York: Farrar, Straus and Giroux, 1976). Sonnet: *The Complete Poems 1927–1979* (New York: Farrar, Straus and Giroux, 1983).

R. P. Blackmur. Redwing; "One grey and foaming day"; Mirage; Seas Incarnadine; Since There's No Help . . . : *From Jordan's Delight* (New York: Arrow Editions, 1937). Sunt Lacrimae Rerum et Mentum Mortalia Tangunt; The Communiqués from Yalta: *The Good European* (Cummington, MA: Cummington Press, 1947).

Louise Bogan. Medusa; Sub Contra; Knowledge; Men Loved Wholly Beyond Wisdom; My Voice Not Being Proud; The Alchemist; Women: *Body of This Death* (New York: Robert McBride and Co., 1923). Winter Swan; Cassandra; Song; Late; Dark Summer: *Dark Summer* (New York: Charles Scribner's Sons, 1929). Short Summary; Baroque Comment; Roman Fountain; Evening-Star; Heard By a Girl: *The Sleeping Fury* (New York: Charles Scribner's Sons, 1937). Kept; Several Voices Out of a Cloud; Musician; Zone: *Poems and New Poems* (New York: Charles Scribner's Sons, 1941). The Dragonfly; Night; Morning: *The Blue Estuaries* (New York: Farrar, Straus and Giroux, 1968).

Arna Bontemps. Reconnaissance; Southern Mansion; Dark Girl; A Black Man Talks of Reaping: *Personals* (London: Paul Bremen, 1964).

Alter Brody. Lamentations; Winter Nocturne: The Hospital: *A Family Album and Other Poems* (New York: B.W. Huebsch, 1918).

Sterling A. Brown. Long Gone; Scotty Has His Say; Sister Lou; Southern Road; Memphis Blues; Ma Rainey; Slim in Atlanta; Children's Children; Chillen Get Shoes; Sporting Beasley; Cabaret: *Southern Road* (New York: Harcourt, Brace, 1932). Old Lem: Michael S. Harper (ed.), *The Collected Poems of Sterling Brown* (Evanston, IL: TriQuarterly Books, 1989).

Stanley Burnshaw. End of the Flower-World; Bread: *Early and Late Testament* (New York: Dial Press, 1952).

John Cage. 2 Pages, 122 Words on Music and Dance: *Silence* (Middletown, CT: Wesleyan University Press, 1961). *from* Composition in Retrospect: *Composition in Retrospect* (Cambridge: Exact Change Press, 1993).

Emanuel Carnevali. Sermon; Serenade; Kiss: *A Hurried Man* (Paris: Contact Editions, 1925). Almost a God: *Pagany*, July–September 1931.

Constance Carrier. A Point of View; Clause for a Covenant: *The Middle Voice* (Denver: Alan Swallow, 1955). Elegy; Helianthus; Laudare: *The Angled Road* (Chicago: Swallow Press, 1973).

Malcolm Cowley. Ernest: *The Dry Season* (Norfolk, CT: New Directions, 1941). Winter Tenement: *Blue Juniata: Collected Poems* (New York: Viking, 1968).

Hart Crane. Chaplinesque; For the Marriage of Faustus and Helen; Voyages; Repose of Rivers; The Wine Menagerie; At Melville's Tomb: *White Buildings* (New York: Boni & Liveright, 1925). The Bridge, O Carib Isle!, The Broken Tower: Marc Simon (ed.), *The Poems of Hart Crane* (New York: Liveright, 1986).

Harry Crosby. Vision: *Mad Queen* (Paris: The Black Sun Press, 1929). Photoheliograph: *Chariots of the Sun* (Paris: The Black Sun Press, 1929).

Countee Cullen. Yet Do I Marvel; Atlantic City Waiter; Incident; Heritage; For My Grandmother; For a Lady I Know; For One Who Gayly Sowed His Oats; For Hazel Hall, American Poet: *Color* (New York: Harper & Bros., 1925). From the Dark Tower: *Copper Sun* (New York: Harper & Bros., 1927).

E. E. Cummings. "All in green went my love riding"; "in Just-"; "Tumbling-hair"; "Humanity i love you"; "o sweet spontaneous"; "stinging"; "between green"; "Babylon slim"; "ta"; "Buffalo Bill 's"; "the Cambridge ladies who live in furnished souls"; "god pity me whom(god distinctly has)"; "Dick Mid's large bluish face without eyebrows"; "Spring is like a perhaps hand"; POEM,OR BEAUTY HURTS MR. VINAL; "she being Brand"; "on the Madam's best april the"; MEMORABILIA; "'next to of course god america i"; "lis"; "my sweet old etcetera"; "Among"; "in spite of everything"; "since feeling is first"; "i sing of Olaf glad and big"; "twi-"; "a clown's smirk in the skull of a baboon"; "somewhere i have never travelled,gladly beyond"; "the boys i mean are not refined"; "r-p-o-p-h-e-s-s-a-g-r"; "as freedom is a breakfastfood"; "anyone lived in a pretty how town"; "my father moved through dooms of love"; "plato told"; "pity this busy monster,manunkind,"; "a grin without a": George J. Firmage (ed.), *Complete Poems 1904–1962* (New York: Liveright, 1991).

Waring Cuney. No Images: *Storefront Church* (London: Paul Breman, 1973). The Death Bed; Conception: Langston Hughes and Arna Bontemps (eds.), *The Poetry of the Negro* (Garden City, NY: Doubleday, Doran, 1949).

J. V. Cunningham. Dream Vision; A Moral Poem; For My Contemporaries; Montana Pastoral: *The Helmsman* (San Francisco: The Colt Press, 1942). To What Strangers, What Welcome: *To What Strangers, What Welcome* (Denver: Swallow Press, 1964). Selected Epigrams: *Collected Poems and Epigrams* (Chicago: Alan Swallow, 1971).

Edward Dahlberg. February Ground; Walt Whitman: *Cipango's Hinder Door* (Austin: University of Texas Press, 1965).

Frank Marshall Davis. Christ Is a Dixie Nigger; Sam Jackson: *I Am the American Negro* (Chicago: Black Cat Press, 1937).

H. L. Davis. Proud Riders: *Proud Riders and Other Poems* (New York: Harper & Bros., 1942).

Alton Delmore. The Girl by the River: Transcribed from King Records recording K-3172, March 12, 1951.

Edwin Denby. The Subway; A New York Face; "I had heard it's a fight. At the first clammy touch"; "Smelling or feeling of the several holes": Ron Padgett (ed.), *The Complete Poems* (New York: Random House, 1986).

Babette Deutsch. "To an Amiable Child"; Creatures in the Zoo: *Coming of Age: New and Selected Poems* (Bloomington: Indiana University Press, 1959).

Thomas A. Dorsey. Take My Hand, Precious Lord: Henry Louis Gates Jr. and Nellie Y. McKay (eds.), *The Norton Anthology of African American Literature* (New York: W. W. Norton & Co., 1997).

John Dos Passos. Newsreel LIII: *The Big Money* (New York: Harcourt, Brace, 1936).

Rose Drachler. The Evening of the Sixth Day: *The Collected Poems of Rose Drachler* (New York: Assembling Press, 1983).

Richard Eberhart. This Fevers Me: *A Bravery of Earth* (London: Jonathan Cape, 1930). The Groundhog: *Reading the Spirit* (New York: Oxford University Press, 1937). 'I Walked Over the Grave of Henry James'; The Fury of Aerial Bombardment: *Burr Oaks* (New York: Oxford University Press, 1947). On a Squirrel Crossing the Road in Autumn, in New England: *Great Praises* (New York: Oxford University Press, 1957). La Crosse at Ninety Miles an Hour: *The Quarry* (New York: Oxford University Press, 1964). Gnat on My Paper: *Fields of Grace* (New York: Oxford University Press, 1972).

William Everson. Muscat Pruning; Tor House; Rainy Easter: *The Residual Years* (New York: New Directions, 1948). A Canticle for the Waterbirds: *The Crooked Lines of God: Poems 1949–1954* (Detroit: University of Detroit Press, 1959). Gale at Dawn: *Man–Fate* (New York: New Directions, 1974). Stone Face Falls: *The Masks of Drought* (Santa Barbara, CA: Black Sparrow Press, 1980).

Kenneth Fearing. Green Light; Evening Song: *Angel Arms* (New York: Coward McCann, 1929). 1933; Escape; Dirge: *Poems* (New York: Dynamo, 1935). Portrait; Literary; How Do I Feel?: *Dead Reckoning* (New York: Random House, 1938). American Rhapsody (4): *Collected Poems* (New York: Random House, 1940). Art Review; Reception Good; Beware: *Afternoon of a Pawnbroker* (New York: Harcourt, Brace and Co., 1943). Bryce & Tomlins: *Stranger at Coney Island* (New York: Harcourt, Brace and Co., 1948).

Thomas Hornsby Ferril. Waltz Against the Mountains; Something Starting Over: *Westering* (New Haven: Yale University Press, 1934). Noon: *Trial By Time* (New York: Harper & Row, 1944).

Dorothy Fields. I Can't Give You Anything But Love: Deborah Grace Winer (ed.), *On the Sunny Side of the Street* (New York: Schirmer Books, 1997).

Dudley Fitts. "Ya se van los pastores": *Poems 1929–1936* (Norfolk, CT: New Directions, 1937).

Robert Fitzgerald. Manuscript with Illumination: *Poems* (New York: Arrow Editions, 1935). Horae; Et Quidquid Aspiciebam Mors Erat; Farewell; Souls Lake; Mutations: *A Wreath for the Sea* (New York: Arrow Editions, 1943). South Side; History: *In the Rose of Time* (New York: New Directions, 1956). Spring Shade: *Spring Shade* (New York: New Directions, 1970).

Hildegarde Flanner. Dumb; Moment: *Time's Profile* (New York: Macmillan, 1929). Fern Song; Frog Song; True Western Summer: *The Hearkening Eye* (Boise, ID: Ahsahta Press, 1979).

Charles Henri Ford. The Fox with the Blue Velvet Band: *The Garden of Disorder and Other Poems* (Norfolk, CT: New Directions, 1937). The Overturned Lake: *The Overturned Lake* (Cincinnati: Little Man Press, 1941). I Wouldn't Put It Past You: *Out of the Labyrinth* (San Francisco: City Lights Books, 1991).

Robert Francis. A Broken View; Onion Fields; Earthworm; Slow; By Night; The Curse; While I Slept: *Stand With Me Here* (New York: Macmillan, 1936). The Sound I Listened For; As Easily As Trees: *The Sound I Listened For* (New York: Macmillan, 1944). Waxwings; Pitcher; Cypresses; Swimmer; Farm Boy After Summer: *The Orb Weaver* (Middletown, CT: Wesleyan University Press, 1960). Museum Vase: *Come Out Into the Sun* (Amherst: University of Massachusetts Press, 1965).

Jean Garrigue. Song in Sligo; The Grand Canyon; Grenoble Café: *Studies for an Actress and Other Poems* (New York: Macmillan, 1973).

Ira Gershwin. I Can't Get Started; They All Laughed: Robert Kimball (ed.), *The Complete Lyrics of Ira Gershwin* (New York: Alfred A. Knopf, 1994).

Brewster Ghiselin. Shore Bird; Bath of Aphrodite: *Against the Circle* (New York: E.P. Dutton, 1946). The Food of Birds: *The Nets* (New York: E.P. Dutton, 1955). The Net Breaker; Learning the Language: *Country of the Minotaur* (Salt Lake City: University of Utah Press, 1970).

Abraham Lincoln Gillespie. A Purplexicon of Dissynthegrations: Richard Milazzo (ed.), *The Syntactic Revolution* (New York: Out of London Press, 1980).

Paul Goodman. The Lordly Hudson: *The Lordly Hudson* (New York: Macmillan, 1962).

Horace Gregory. The Cage of Voices: *Selected Poems* (New York: Viking, 1951). *from* Chorus for Survival: *Collected Poems* (New York: Holt, Rinehart and Winston, 1964).

Ramon Guthrie. Elegy for Mélusine from the Intensive Care Ward; Red-Headed Intern, Taking Notes; Scene: A Bedside in the Witches' Kitchen: *Maximum Security Ward* (New York: Farrar, Straus and Giroux, 1970).

Woody Guthrie. Talking Dust Bowl; Dust Storm Disaster; Vigilante Man: Harold Leventhal and Marjorie Guthrie (eds.), *The Woody Guthrie Songbook* (New York: Grosset & Dunlap, 1976). At the request of the rights' holder for these songs, the following emendations to these transcriptions have been made: at 805.4,"of April" is emended to "day of April"; at 805.22–23, "Dakota and Nebraska / To the great mysterious storm." is emended to "The wild and windy actions / Of this great mysterious storm."; at 805.28, "From" is emended to "In"; at 806.4, "They didn't" is emended to "They did not"; at 807.5, "crops into town" is emended to "crops all into town"; at 807.12, "mountains and out" is emended to "mountains out".

Oscar Hammerstein II. Ol' Man River: *Lyrics* (New York: Simon and Schuster, 1949).

E. Y. Harburg. Brother, Can You Spare A Dime?: Harold Meyerson and Ernie Harburg (eds.), *Who Put the Rainbow in the Wizard of Oz?: Yip Harburg, Lyricist* (Ann Arbor: University of Michigan Press, 1993).

Lorenz Hart. Little Girl Blue; Bewitched, Bothered and Bewildered: Dorothy Hart and Robert Kimball (eds.), *The Complete Lyrics of Lorenz Hart* (New York: Alfred A. Knopf, 1986).

Robert Hayden. Those Winter Sundays; Homage to the Empress of the Blues; Middle Passage; Runagate Runagate: *Selected Poems* (New York: October House, 1966). Soledad: *Words in the Mourning Time* (New York: October House, 1970). The Night-Blooming Cereus: *The Night-Blooming Cereus* (London: Paul Breman, 1972) The Ice-Storm: *American Journal*, second edition (Taunton, MA: Effendi Press, 1982). Bone-Flower Elegy: Frederick Glaysher (ed.), *Robert Hayden: Collected Poems* (New York: Liveright, 1996).

Robert Hillyer. Dead Man's Corner: *Collected Verse* (New York: Alfred A. Knopf, 1933).

John Holmes. The Old Professor; Four and a Half: *Map of My Country* (New York: Duell, Sloan and Pearce, 1943).

Lightnin' Hopkins. Death Bells: Eric Sackheim (ed.), *The Blues Line* (New York: Grossman, 1969).

Lindley Williams Hubbell. Ordovician Fossil Algae; Sounds; A student who sat facing me on the Osaka express: *Seventy Poems* (Denver: Swallow Press, 1965). Beer Bottles: *Climbing to Monfumo* (Kobe, Japan: Ikuta Press, 1977). Waka: *The First Architect* (Kobe, Japan: Ikuta Press, 1982).

Langston Hughes. Subway Face: *Crisis*, December 1924. The Negro Speaks of Rivers; Aunt Sue's Stories; When Sue Wears Red; Young Prostitute; Suicide's Note; Summer Night; Sea Calm: *The Weary Blues* (New York: Alfred A. Knopf, 1926). Railroad Avenue: *Fine Clothes to the Jew* (New York: Alfred A. Knopf, 1927). Drum: *Dear Lovely Death* (Aneimia, NY: Troutbeck Press, 1931). My People; I, Too: *The Dream Keeper* (New York: Alfred A. Knopf, 1932). Cubes: *New Masses*, March 13, 1934. Evil: *Shakespeare in Harlem* (New York: Alfred A. Knopf, 1942). Strange Hurt; A House in Taos; Songs: *Fields of Wonder* (New York: Alfred A. Knopf, 1947). Curious:

One Way Ticket (New York: Alfred A. Knopf, 1949). Dream Variations; Little Lyric (Of Great Importance); Luck; American Heartbreak; *from* Montage of a Dream Deferred: *Selected Poems of Langston Hughes* (New York: Alfred A. Knopf, 1959).

Rolfe Humphries. Europa: *Europa, and Other Poems, and Sonnets* (New York: Crosby Gaige, 1928). Test Paper: *The Wind of Time* (New York: Charles Scribner's Sons, 1949). From the Green Book of Yfan: *Green Armor on Green Ground* (New York: Charles Scribner's Sons, 1956).

Josephine Jacobsen. Poems for My Cousin; Yellow: *The Animal Inside* (Athens: Ohio University Press, 1966).

Blind Lemon Jefferson. Long Distance Moan: Eric Sackheim (ed.), *The Blues Line* (New York: Grossman, 1969).

Helene Johnson. Bottled; Sonnet to a Negro in Harlem: Robert T. Kerlin (ed.), *Negro Poets and Their Poems* (Washington, D.C.: Associated Publishers, 1933). Magalu: Countee Cullen (ed.), *Caroling Dusk* (New York: Harper & Bros., 1927).

Robert Johnson. Stones in My Passway; Hellhound on My Trail; Me and the Devil Blues: Eric Sackheim (ed.), *The Blues Line* (New York: Grossman, 1969). "Enemies" at 766.16 and 766.18 are emendations of Sackheim's "innocence," based on Johnson's extant recordings of the song.

Eugene Jolas. Mater Dolorosa: *I Have Seen Monsters and Angels* (Paris: Transition Press, 1938).

Joseph Kalar. Papermill: Sol Funaroff, Joseph Kalar, et. al, *We Gather Strength* (New York: The Liberal Press, 1933).

Lincoln Kirstein. Gloria; P.O.E.: *Rhymes of a P.F.C.* (New York: New Directions, 1964).

Stanley Kunitz. The Science of the Night; The Dragonfly: *Selected Poems 1928–1958* (Boston: Little, Brown, 1958). The Testing-Tree: *The Testing-Tree* (Boston: Little, Brown, 1971). The Catch; The Quarrel; Route Six: *The Poems of Stanley Kunitz 1928–1978* (Boston: Little, Brown, 1978). Touch Me: *Passing Through: New and Selected Poems* (New York: W.W. Norton & Co., 1995).

Richmond Lattimore. North Philadelphia Trenton and New York: *Poems* (Ann Arbor: University of Michigan Press, 1957). Vergil Georgics 1.489–514: *The Stride of Time: New Poems and Translations* (Ann Arbor: University of Michigan Press, 1966).

Janet Lewis. *from* The Indians in the Woods: *The Indians in the Woods* (Evanston, IL: Monroe Wheeler, 1922). Girl Help; The Reader: *The Wheel in Midsummer* (Lynn, MA: The Lone Gull, 1927). Winter Garden: *The Earth Bound* (Aurora, NY: Wells College Press, 1946). Helen Grown Old: *Poems 1922–1944* (Denver: Swallow Press, 1950). The Ancient Ones: Betátakin: *The Ancient Ones* (Portola Valley, CA.: No Dead Lines, 1979). For the Father of Sandro Gulotta; Garden Note I: Los Altos; Garden Note II; March: *Poems Old and New 1918–1978* (Chicago: Swallow Press, 1981).

Frank Loesser: Luck, Be a Lady: *Guys and Dolls* (New York: Frank Music Co., 1953).

Walter Lowenfels. *from* Elegy in the Manner of a Requiem in Memory of
D.H. Lawrence: *Elegy in the Manner of a Requiem in Memory of D.H.
Lawrence* (Paris: Carrefour Press, 1932).

David McCord. Waiter: *Bay Window Ballads* (New York: Charles Scribner's
Sons, 1935). History of Education: *What Cheer* (New York: Modern Li-
brary, 1945).

Phyllis McGinley. Twelfth Night: *A Pocketful of Wry* (New York: Duell, Sloan
and Pearce, 1940). Spring Comes to the Suburbs; The 5:32: *A Short Walk
to the Station* (New York: Viking, 1951). Portrait of Girl with Comic Book:
The Love Letters of Phyllis McGinley (New York: Viking, 1954).

Joseph Moncure March. *from* The Wild Party: *The Wild Party* (Privately
printed, 1929).

Johnny Mercer. Blues in the Night; Midnight Sun: Bob Bach and Ginger
Mercer (eds.), *Our Huckleberry Friend: The Life, Times, and Lyrics of
Johnny Mercer* (Secaucus, NJ: Lyle Stuart, Inc, 1982).

Josephine Miles. Housewife; All Hallow: *Local Measures* (New York: Reynal
and Hitchcock, 1946). Sale: *Prefabrications* (Bloomington: University of
Indiana Press, 1955). "After noon I lie down": *Kinds of Affection* (Middle-
town, CT: Wesleyan University Press, 1967). Album: *Coming to Terms* (Ur-
bana: University of Illinois Press, 1979)

Rosalie Moore. The Mind's Disguise; Memory of Quiet; Height: *The
Grasshopper's Man and Other Poems* (New Haven: Yale University Press,
1949).

Vladimir Nabokov. *from* Lolita: *Novels 1955–1962* (New York: The Library of
America, 1996). On Translating "Eugene Onegin": *Poems* (New York:
Doubleday, 1959).

Ogden Nash. Spring Comes to Murray Hill; Reflection on Ice-Breaking:
Hard Lines (New York: Simon and Schuster, 1931). The Terrible People;
Song of the Open Road: *Happy Days* (New York: Simon and Schuster,
1933). Very Like a Whale; A Necessary Dirge; Portrait of the Artist as a Pre-
maturely Old Man; The Germ: *The Primrose Path* (New York: Simon and
Schuster, 1935). Glossina Morsitans, or the Tsetse; Samson Agonistes: *Se-
lected Verse of Ogden Nash* (New York: Modern Library, 1946). Inter-Office
Memorandum: *Verses from 1929 On* (Boston: Little, Brown, 1959). Which
the Chicken, Which the Egg?: *The Old Dog Barks Backwards* (Boston: Lit-
tle, Brown, 1972).

Lorine Niedecker. "Remember my little granite pail?"; "The clothesline post
is set"; "There's a better shine"; "What horror to awake at night"; "Paul";
"The death of my poor father"; "Woman in middle life"; "He lived—child-
hood summers"; "I rose from marsh mud"; The Graves; "My friend tree";
"The men leave the car"; "My life is hung up"; "Get a load"; Poet's Work;
"I married"; My Life By Water; "Far reach"; "Stone"; Sewing a Dress;
Paean to Place; "Not all harsh sounds displease—"; Darwin: Jenny Lynn
Penberthy (ed.), *The Collected Poetry of Lorine Niedecker* (Berkeley: Uni-
versity of California Press, forthcoming).

John Frederick Nims. The Evergreen: *Knowledge of the Evening* (New Bruns-
wick, NJ: Rutgers University Press, 1960).

Charles Olson. La Préface; These Days; The Moon Is the Number 18; In
Cold Hell, in Thicket; Merce of Egypt; As the Dead Prey Upon Us; Vari-
ations Done for Gerald Van De Wiele: George F. Butterick (ed.), *The Col-
lected Poems of Charles Olson* (Berkeley: University of California Press,
1987). *from* The Maximus Poems: George F. Butterick (ed.), *The Maximus
Poems* (Berkeley: University of California Press, 1983).

Elder Olson. The Four Black Bogmen: *The Scarecrow Christ and Other Poems*
(New York: The Noonday Press, 1954).

George Oppen. Discrete Series: *Discrete Series* (New York: Objectivist Press,
1934). Eclogue; Image of the Engine; From Disaster: *The Materials* (New
York: New Directions, 1962). Psalm; The Occurrences: *This In Which* (New
York: New Directions, 1965). Route: *Of Being Numerous* (New York:
New Directions, 1975). But So As By Fire: *Seascape: Needle's Eye* (Free-
mont, MI: The Sumac Press, 1975). In Memoriam Charles Reznikoff: Sea-
mus Cooney (ed.), *Poems 1918–1975: The Complete Poems of Charles
Reznikoff* (Santa Rosa, CA: Black Sparrow Press, 1989).

Kenneth Patchen. Street Corner College; Religion Is That I Love You; 23rd
Street Runs into Heaven; The Figure Motioned with Its Mangled Hand
Towards the Wall Behind It: *First Will and Testament* (Norfolk, CT: New
Directions, 1939). The Horses of Yilderlin; The Origin of Baseball; The
Lions of Fire Shall Have Their Hunting: *The Teeth of the Lion* (Norfolk,
CT: New Directions, 1942). Lonesome Boy Blues: *Orchards, Thrones &
Caravans* (New York: New Directions, 1952).

Hyam Plutzik. The Airman Who Flew Over Shakespeare's England; Winter,
Never Mind Where; For T.S.E. Only: *Apples from Shinar* (Middletown,
CT: Wesleyan University Press, 1959). As the Great Horse Rots on the Hill:
Hyam Plutzik: The Collected Poems (Brockport, NY: BOA Editions, 1987).

Anne Porter. Consider the Lilies of the Sea; Winter Twilight: *An Altogether
Different Language: Poems 1934–1994* (Cambridge, MA: Zoland Books,
1994).

H. Phelps Putnam. Words of an Old Woman; Bill Gets Burned; Hasbrouck
and the Rose: *The Five Seasons* (New York: Charles Scribner's Sons, 1931).

Carl Rakosi. The January of a Gnat; Amulet; Figures in an Ancient Ink; The
Lobster; Lying in Bed on a Summer Morning; Young Girl; Americana 3;
To an Anti-Semite: *Amulet* (New York: New Directions, 1967). Discover-
ies, Trade Names, Genitals, and Ancient Instruments: *Ere-VOICE* (New
York: New Directions, 1971). Instructions to the Player: *Ex Cranium,
Night* (Los Angeles: Black Sparrow Press, 1975). The Avocado Pit: *The Col-
lected Poems of Carl Rakosi* (Orono, ME: National Poetry Foundation,
1986).

Kenneth Rexroth. Spring, Coast Range: *In What Hour* (New York: Macmil-
lam, 1940). Andrée Rexroth: *The Phoenix and the Tortoise* (New York: New
Directions, 1944). The Signature of All Things; Lyell's Hypothesis Again:

The Signature of All Things (New York: New Directions, 1950). It Is a German Honeymoon: *New Poems* (New York: New Directions, 1974). On Flower Wreath Hill; *from* The Love Poems of Marichiko: *The Morning Star* (New York: New Directions, 1979).

Charles Reznikoff. "On Brooklyn Bridge I saw a man drop dead"; "I met in a merchant's place"; "The shopgirls leave their work"; "How shall we mourn you who are killed and wasted"; "My work done, I lean on the window-sill"; "In the shop, she, her mother, and grandmother"; The Idiot; "She who worked patiently"; Epidemic; "Her work was to count linings"; "The house-wreckers have left the door and a staircase"; Aphrodite Vrania; April; "Out of the hills the trees bulge"; "How difficult for me is Hebrew"; "I have learnt the Hebrew blessing before eating bread"; "After I had worked all day at what I earn my living"; "The Hebrew of your poets, Zion"; "Though our thoughts often, we ourselves"; "Among the heaps of brick and plaster lies"; Epitaphs; Millinery District ["The clouds, piled in rows, like merchandise"]; "A dead gull in the road"; "I like this secret walking"; Rainy Season; "Of course, we must die" "My grandfather, dead long before I was born"; "A grove of small trees, branches thick with berries"; Millinery District ["Many fair hours have been buried here"]; Similes; Epitaph; Free Verse; *from* Early History of a Writer: Seamus Cooney (ed.), *Poems 1918–1975: The Complete Poems of Charles Reznikoff* (Santa Rosa, CA: Black Sparrow Press, 1989).

Laura Riding. As Well As Any Other; Prisms; Lucrece and Nara; O Vocables of Love; Sea, False Philosophy; The Map of Places; Chloe Or...; Take Hands; The World and I; Faith Upon the Waters; The Wind, the Clock, the We; Nothing So Far; Divestment of Beauty; Because of Clothes; With the Face: *Collected Poems* (New York: Random House, 1938). An Ancient Revisits: *First Awakenings: The Early Poems of Laura Riding* (New York: Persea Books, 1992).

Lynn Riggs. Santo Domingo Corn Dance: *The Iron Dish* (Garden City, NY: Doubleday and Co., 1930).

Theodore Roethke. The Heron; The Bat: *Open House* (New York: Alfred A. Knopf, 1941). Cuttings; Cuttings (later); Root Cellar; Old Florist; My Papa's Waltz; The Lost Son: *The Lost Son and Other Poems* (Garden City, NY: Doubleday & Co., 1948). Frau Bauman, Frau Schmidt, and Frau Schwartz; Elegy for Jane; Four for Sir John Davies; The Waking: *The Waking* (Garden City, NY: Doubleday and Co., 1954). I Knew a Woman; A Walk in Late Summer: *Words for the Wind* (Garden City, NY: Doubleday and Co., 1958). The Rose; The Thing; In a Dark Time: *The Far Field* (Garden City, NY: Doubleday and Co., 1958).

Edwin Rolfe. Casualty; First Love: *First Love and Other Poems* (Los Angeles: The Larry Edmunds Book Shop, 1951). Paris—Christmas 1938: Cary Nelson and Jefferson Hendricks (eds.), *Collected Poems* (Urbana: University of Illinois Press, 1993).

Muriel Rukeyser. The Book of the Dead: *U.S. 1* (New York: Covici Friede, 1938). Ajanta: *Beast in View* (New York: Doubleday, 1944). The Outer Banks:

The Outer Banks (Santa Barbara: The Unicorn Press, 1967). The Poem as Mask; The Speed of Darkness: *The Speed of Darkness* (New York: Random House, 1968). Myth: *Breaking Open* (New York: Random House, 1973).

May Sarton. Moving In: *Cloud, Stone, Sun, Vine* (New York: W.W. Norton & Co., 1961). The Snow Light; February Days: *A Durable Fire* (New York: W.W. Norton & Co., 1972).

Isidor Schneider. Insects; A History of the Cæsars: *The Temptation of Anthony* (New York: Boni & Liveright, 1928).

David Schubert. Monterey; It Is Sticky in the Subway; Prospect Park; Victor Record Catalog; A Successful Summer; No Title: *Initial A* (New York: Macmillan, 1961).

Delmore Schwartz. In the Naked Bed, in Plato's Cave; Far Rockaway; Tired and Unhappy, You Think of Houses; The Ballet of the Fifth Year; Sonnet: The Beautiful American Word, Sure: *In Dreams Begin Responsibilities* (Norfolk, CT: New Directions, 1938). In the Slight Ripple, The Mind Perceives the Heart; Do the Others Speak of Me Mockingly, Maliciously?; The Heavy Bear Who Goes With Me; Darkling Summer, Ominous Dusk, Rumorous Rain; The Mind Is an Ancient and Famous Capital; Lincoln: *Summer Knowledge: New and Selected Poems 1938–1958* (Garden City, NY: Doubleday & Co., 1959).

Winfield Townley Scott. Crocus Air: *Collected Poems 1937–1962* (New York: Macmillan, 1962). Flowering Quince; The U.S. Sailor with the Japanese Skull: *To Marry Strangers* (New York: Thomas Y. Crowell, 1945). Winslow Homer: *Mr. Whittier and Other Poems* (New York: Macmillan, 1948).

Karl Shapiro. Homecoming: *Trial of a Poet* (New York: Reynal & Hitchcock, 1947). Auto Wreck; University; Troop Train; Full Moon: New Guinea: *Poems 1940–1953* (New York: Random House, 1953). The Alphabet; The Confirmation; The First Time: *Poems of a Jew* (New York: Random House, 1958). I Am an Atheist Who Says His Prayers; The Funeral of Poetry: *Collected Poems 1940–1977* (New York: Random House, 1978).

Bessie Smith. Empty Bed Blues: Eric Sackheim (ed.), *The Blues Line* (New York: Grossman, 1969).

May Swenson. Question: "Another Animal," in John Hall Wheelock (ed.), *Poets of Today* (New York: Charles Scribner's Sons, 1954). Almanac; The Centaur: *A Cage of Spines* (New York: Rinehart, 1958). Riding the "A"; Distance and A Certain Light: *To Mix With Time* (New York: Charles Scribner's Sons, 1963). Colors Without Objects: *Half Sun Half Sleep* (New York: Charles Scribner's Sons, 1967). Unconscious Came a Beauty; The Shape of Death; Electric Sound; How Everything Happens (Based on a Study of the Wave): *Iconographs* (New York: Charles Scribner's Sons, 1970). Bronco Busting, Event #1; One of the Strangest; Shu Swamp, Spring: *New And Selected Things Taking Place* (Boston: Little, Brown, 1978). Staring at the Sea on the Day of a Death of Another: *Nature: Poems Old and New* (Boston: Houghton Mifflin, 1994).

Genevieve Taggard. Everyday Alchemy; Thirst: *For Eager Lovers* (New York: Thomas Seltzer, 1922). To One Loved Wholly Within Wisdom: *Words for the Chisel* (New York: Alfred A. Knopf, 1926). To Mr. Maunder Maunder, Professional Poet; To the Powers of Desolation; To the Natural World: At 37: *Not Mine to Finish* (New York: Harper & Bros., 1934). Try Tropic; All Around the Town: *Calling Western Union* (New York: Harper & Bros., 1936); Bounding Line: *Collected Poems 1918–1938* (New York: Harper & Bros., 1938). Hymn to Yellow; The Weed: *Slow Music* (New York: Harper & Bros., 1946); Fructus: *To the Natural World* (Boise, ID: Ahsahta Press, 1980).

Allen Tate. Mr. Pope; Ode to the Confederate Dead; The Twelve; Last Days of Alice; The Wolves; Aeneas at Washington; The Mediterranean; Sonnets at Christmas: *Selected Poems* (New York: Charles Scribner's Sons, 1937). The Ivory Tower: *The Mediterranean and Other Poems* (New York: Alcestis Press, 1936). The Swimmers: *Poems* (New York: Charles Scribner's Sons, 1960).

Melvin B. Tolson. *from* Libretto for the Republic of Liberia: *Libretto for the Republic of Liberia* (New York: Twayne Publishers, 1953). *from* Harlem Gallery: *Harlem Gallery* (New York: Twayne Publishers, 1965).

Jean Toomer. Reapers; Cotton Song; Georgia Dusk; Nullo; Evening Song; Portrait in Georgia; Storm Ending; Her Lips Are Copper Wire; Seventh Street: *Cane* (New York: Boni & Liveright, 1923). Gum: *Chapbook,* April 1923. The Gods Are Here: Robert B. Jones and Margery Toomer Latimer (eds.), *The Collected Poems of Jean Toomer* (Chapel Hill: University of North Carolina Press, 1988).

Eve Triem. For Paul: *Dark to Glow* (Seattle: Querencia Books, 1979).

Mark Van Doren. This Amber Sunstream: *A Winter Diary and Other Poems* (New York: Macmillan, 1935). Axle Song: *The Last Look and Other Poems* (New York: Henry Holt and Co., 1937). The Near House; Midland: *The Seven Sleepers and Other Poems* (New York: Henry Holt and Co., 1944). So Simple: *Collected and New Poems 1924–1963* (New York: Hill and Wang, 1963). Where I Saw the Snake; The First Poem: *Good Morning: Last Poems* (New York: Hill and Wang, 1973).

Byron Vazakas. The Pavilion on the Pier; Epitaph for the Old Howard: *Nostalgias for a House of Cards* (New York: October House, 1970).

Robert Penn Warren. The Return: An Elegy; Bearded Oaks; Where the Slow Fig's Purple Sloth; Audubon: A Vision; Birth of Love; Evening Hawk; Heart of Autumn; Vision; Muted Music: John Burt (ed.), *The Collected Poems of Robert Penn Warren* (Baton Rouge: Louisiana State University Press, 1998).

John Wheelwright. Slow Curtain; Why Must You Know?; Would You Think?; Fish Food: An Obituary to Hart Crane; Come Over and Help Us: *Rock and Shell: Poems 1923–1933* (Boston: Bruce Humphries, 1933). Anathema. Maranatha!: *Political Self-Portrait* (Boston: Bruce Humphries, 1940). In the Bathtub, To Mnemosyne; Cross Questions: Alvin A. Rosenfeld (ed.), *The Collected Poems of John Wheelwright* (New York: New Directions, 1971).

Bukka White. Fixin' to Die: A.X. Nicholas (ed.), *Woke Up This Morning* (New York: Bantam Books, 1973).

Tennessee Williams. The Beanstalk Country: *In the Winter of Cities* (New York: New Directions, 1956).

Edmund Wilson. A House of the Eighties; The Omelet of A. MacLeish: *Note-Books of Night* (San Francisco: The Colt Press, 1942). Epitaphs: *Wilson's Night Thoughts* (New York: Farrar Straus & Cudahy, 1953).

Yvor Winters. Two Songs of Advent: *The Immobile Wind* (Evanston, IL: Monroe Wheeler, 1921); The Magpie's Shadow: *The Magpie's Shadow* (Chicago: Musterbrookhouse, 1922). October; The Cold; Nocturne; The Barnyard: *The Bare Hills* (Boston: The Four Seas, 1927). Wild Sunflower; The Fall of Leaves: *The Proof* (New York: Coward McCann, 1930). The Slow Pacific Swell: *The Journey* (Ithaca, NY: The Dragon Press, 1931). To a Young Writer; By the Road to the Sunnyvale Air-Base; Elegy on a Young Airedale Bitch Lost Two Years Since in the Salt Marsh; On Teaching the Young: *Before Disaster* (Tryon, NC: The Tryon Pamphlets, 1934). Time and the Garden: *The Giant Weapon* (New York: New Directions, 1943); The Realization; Apollo and Daphne; The Fable; In Praise of California Wines; To the Moon: *Collected Poems* (Denver: Alan Swallow, 1952). The Solitude of Glass; Vacant Lot: *The Early Poems of Yvor Winters* (Denver: Alan Swallow, 1966).

Richard Wright. I Have Seen Black Hands: *New Masses*, June 26, 1934. The FB Eye Blues: Ellen Wright and Michael Fabre (eds.), *The Richard Wright Reader* (New York: Harper & Row, 1978). Selected Haiku: Yoshinobu Hakutani and Robert L. Tener (eds.), *Haiku: This Other World* (New York: Arcade Books, 1998).

Louis Zukofsky. Poem beginning "The"; "Not much more than being"; "Cocktails"; Ferry; Tibor Serly; "in that this happening"; "To my washstand": *55 Poems* (Prairie City, IL: James A. Decker, 1941). "When the crickets"; "It's hard to see but think of a sea"; "The lines of this new song are nothing"; "Can a mote of sunlight defeat its purpose": *Anew* (Prairie City, IL: James A. Decker, 1946). Xenophanes; "As To How Much"; Shang Cup: *Some Time* (Stuttgart: Jonathan Williams, 1956). (Ryokan's scroll): *I's (pronounced* eyes) (New York: Trober, 1956). "A" 11; *from* "A" 12: *"A" 1–12* (London: Jonathan Cape, 1966). I Sent Thee Late: *I Sent Thee Late* (Cambridge, MA: LHS, 1965).

The following is a list of pages where a stanza break coincides with the foot of the page (except where such breaks are apparent from the regular stanzaic structure of the poem): 2, 10, 12, 14, 16, 27, 28, 72, 95, 102, 103, 107, 108, 109, 111, 112, 115, 117, 129, 132, 147, 162, 168, 176, 190, 193, 195, 199, 200, 207, 210, 211, 221, 223, 227, 229, 236, 242, 246, 261, 269, 292, 295, 296, 306, 312, 314, 316, 319, 321, 333, 337, 339, 354, 356, 357, 358, 363, 365, 372, 375, 407, 413, 417, 442, 443, 446, 449, 461, 468, 470, 471, 475, 477, 478, 487, 491, 512, 535, 536, 537, 539, 542, 543, 544, 547, 549, 551, 553, 557, 558, 562, 566, 582, 589, 592, 601, 602, 604, 606, 607, 613, 614, 615, 621, 622, 623, 655, 667, 671, 673, 680, 682, 686, 689, 694, 695, 696, 699, 700, 702, 707, 708, 710, 712, 714, 747, 749, 767, 768, 769, 774, 783, 794, 818, 819, 820, 822, 825, 826, 856, 859, 874.

This volume presents the texts listed here without change except for the correction of typographical errors; it does not, however, attempt to reproduce nontextual features of their typographic design. Spelling, punctuation, and capitalization are often expressive, and they are not altered, even when inconsistent or irregular. The following is a list of typographical errors in the source texts that have been corrected, cited by page and line number: 125.32, alive; 272.30, sheet-lightening's; 276.23, tytannous; 322.12, whem; 351.10, cute; 470.16, life; 470.25, Mills,"; 470.25, Quetzalcoatl,"; 534.7, exists; 540.20–23, *shadow and . . . shadow / . . . itself with . . . anger. But /;* 603.20, happy!; 609.13, *une*; 715.5, Geaan; 772.26, A sleep.

ACKNOWLEDGMENTS

Great care has been taken to trace all owners of copyright material included in this book. If any have been inadvertently omitted or overlooked, acknowledgment will gladly be made in future printings.

Virginia Hamilton Adair. Exit Amor; Buckroe, After the Season, 1942: From *Ants on the Melon*, copyright © 1996 by Virginia Hamilton Adair. Reprinted by permission of Random House, Inc.

Helen Adam. Mune Rune; The Huntsman; Shallow-Water Warning: Copyright © 1974 by Helen Adam. Reprinted with the permission of the Literary Estate of Helen Adam.

Léonie Adams. April Mortality; Ghostly Tree; The Rounds and Garlands Done; The Moon and Spectator; Fragmentary Stars; The Horn; The Figurehead; Grapes Making: Copyright © 1925, 1954 by Léonie Adams. Reprinted by permission of Judith Farr, literary executrix.

James Agee. "Not met and marred with the year's whole turn of grief"; "So it begins. Adam is in his earth"; "Now stands our love on that still verge of day"; "This little time the breath and bulk of being"; "Wake Up Threeish": Copyright © The James Agee Literary Trust. Reprinted with permission. To Walker Evans: Copyright © 1941 by Houghton Mifflin, Inc. Reprinted with permission.

Howard Baker. Advice to a Man Who Lost His Dog; Sappho's Leap: Copyright © 1966 by Howard Baker.

Mary Barnard. Shoreline; Logging Trestle; The Field; Static; The Solitary; Probably Nobody; The Pleiades; Lethe: Copyright © 1979 by Mary Barnard. Reprinted by permission of the author.

Ben Belitt. Kites: Ars Poetica: Copyright © Virginia Quarterly Review. Reprinted with permission. The Orange Tree: From *This Scribe, My Hand: The Complete Poems of Ben Belitt*, copyright © 1998 by Ben Belitt. Reprinted with permission of Louisiana State University Press.

Stephen Vincent Benét. "American muse, whose strong and diverse heart"; "John Brown's body lies a-mouldering in the grave"; American Names; Cotton Mather; Daniel Boone; Metropolitan Nightmare: Copyright 1927, 1928, 1933 by Stephen Vincent Benét, renewed © 1955, 1956, © 1961 by Rosemary Carr Benét. Reprinted by permission of Brandt & Brandt Literary Agents, Inc.

Elizabeth Bishop. The Map; The Man-Moth; Sleeping on the Ceiling; Rooster; The Fish; Over 2,000 Illustrations and a Complete Concordance; The Bight; At the Fishhouses; The Prodigal; Song for the Rainy Season; The Armadillo; Sestina; Sandpiper; Twelfth Morning; or What You Will; In the Waiting Room; Crusoe in England; One Art; Sonnet: From *The Complete Poems 1927–1979* by Elizabeth Bishop. Copyright © 1979, 1983 by Alice Helen Methfessel. Reprinted by permission of Farrar, Straus & Giroux, LLC.

Louise Bogan. Cassandra; Winter Swan; Dark Summer; Late; Song; Short Summary; Roman Fountain; Evening-Star; Baroque Comment; Kept; Heard by a Girl; Several Voices Out of a Cloud; Musician; Zone; Night; Morning; The Dragonfly: From *The Blue Estuaries: Poems 1923–1968* by Louise Bogan. Copyright © 1968 by Louise Bogan. Reprinted by permission of Farrar, Straus & Giroux, LLC.

Arna Bontemps. Reconnaissance; Southern Mansion; Dark Girl; A Black Man Talks of Reaping: From *Personals* by Arna Bontemps. Copyright © 1963 by Arna Bontemps. Reprinted by permission of Harold Ober Associates Incorporated.

Sterling Brown. Long Gone; Scotty Has His Say; Sister Lou; Southern Road; Memphis Blues; Ma Rainey; Slim in Atlanta; Children's Children; Chillen Get Shoes; Sporting Beasley; Cabaret: From *Southern Road*, copyright 1932, renewed © 1960 by Sterling Brown. Old Lem: From *The Collected Poems of Sterling Brown*, edited by Michael S. Harper, copyright © 1980 by Sterling Brown. Reprinted by permission of HarperCollins Publishers, Inc.

Stanley Burnshaw. Bread: copyright © 1932, 1936 by Stanley Burnshaw. End of the Flower-World: Copyright © 1927, 1936 by Stanley Burnshaw. Reprinted by permission of the author.

John Cage. 2 Pages, 122 Words on Music and Dance: from *Silence*, copyright © 1973 by John Cage, Wesleyan University Press. Reprinted by permission of University Press of New England. *from* Composition in Retrospect: From *Composition in Retrospect*, copyright © 1993 by John Cage. Courtesy of the John Cage Trust. Reprinted with permission.

Constance Carrier. A Point of View; Clause for a Covenant; Elegy; Helianthus; Laudare: Copyright 1955, © 1973 by Constance Carrier.

Malcolm Cowley. Winter Tenement; Ernest: Copyright © Malcolm Cowley. Reprinted with permission.

Hart Crane. Chaplinesque; For the Marriage of Faustus and Helen; Voyages I–VI; Repose of Rivers; The Wine Menagerie; At Melville's Tomb; The Bridge; O Carib Isle!; The Broken Tower: From *Complete Poems of Hart Crane*, edited by Marc Simon. Copyright 1933, © 1958, 1966 by Liveright Publishing Corporation. Copyright © 1986 by Marc Simon. Reprinted by permission of Liveright Publishing Corporation.

Countee Cullen. Yet Do I Marvel; Atlantic City Waiter; Incident; Heritage; For My Grandmother; For a Lady I Know; For One Who Gayly Sowed His Oats; For Hazel Hall, American Poet: From *Color* by Countee Cullen, copyright 1925 by Countee Cullen, renewed © 1953 by Ida M. Cullen. From the Dark Tower: From *Copper Sun*, copyright 1927 by Harper & Brothers, renewed © 1955 by Ida M. Cullen. Reprinted by permission.

E. E. Cummings. "All in green went my love riding"; "in Just-"; "Tumbling-hair"; "Humanity i love you"; "O sweet spontaneous"; "stinging"; "between green"; "Babylon slim"; "ta"; "Buffalo Bill 's"; "the Cambridge ladies who live in furnished souls"; "god pity me whom(god distinctly has)"; "Dick Mid's large bluish face without eyebrows"; "Spring is like a perhaps hand"; POEM,OR BEAUTY HURTS MR. VINAL; "she being Brand"; "on the Madam's best april the"; MEMORABILIA; " 'next to of course god america i"; "lis"; "my sweet old etcetera"; "Among / these"; "in spite of everything"; "since feeling is first"; "i sing of Olaf glad and big"; "twi- / is -Light bird"; "a clown's smirk in the skull of a baboon"; "somewhere i have never travelled,gladly beyond"; "the boys i mean are not refined"; "r-p-o-p-h-e-s-s-a-g-r"; "as freedom is a breakfastfood"; "anyone lived in a pretty how town"; "my father moved through dooms of love"; "plato told"; "pity this busy monster, manunkind"; "a grin without a": From *Complete Poems: 1904–1962* by E. E. Cummings, edited by George J. Firmage. Copyright © 1923, 1925, 1926, 1931, 1935, 1938, 1939, 1940, 1944, 1945, 1946, 1947, 1948, 1949, 1950, 1951, 1952, 1953, 1954, © 1955, 1956, 1957, 1958, 1959, 1960, 1961, 1962, 1963, 1966, 1967, 1968, 1972, 1973, 1974, 1975, 1976, 1977, 1978, 1979, 1980, 1981, 1982, 1983, 1984, 1985, 1986, 1987, 1988, 1989, 1990, 1991 by the Trustees for the E. E. Cummings Trust. Copyright © 1973, 1976, 1978, 1979, 1981, 1983, 1985, 1991 by George James Firmage. Reprinted by permission of Liveright Publishing Corp.

Waring Cuney. No Images; The Death Bed; Conception: Copyright © 1949, 1973 by Waring Cuney.

J. V. Cunningham. Dream Vision; A Moral Poem; For My Contemporaries; Montana Pastoral; Epigrams [selected]; To What Strangers, What Welcome: From *The Poems of J. V. Cunningham*, edited by Timothy Steele. Copyright © J.V. Cunningham. Reprinted with permission of Ohio University Press/ Swallow Press, Athens, Ohio.

Edward Dahlberg. February Ground; Walt Whitman: From *Cipango's Hinder Door* by Edward Dahlberg, copyright © 1965 by Edward Dahlberg. Reprinted by permission of the Harry Ransom Humanities Research Center at The University of Texas at Austin.

Frank Marshall Davis. Christ Is a Dixie Nigger; Sam Jackson: From *I Am the American Negro* by Frank Marshall Davis, copyright © 1937 by Frank Marshall Davis. Reprinted by permission of the Estate of Frank Marshall Davis.

H. L. Davis. Proud Riders: Copyright © 1942 by H. L. Davis. Reprinted with permission of Ahsahta Press.

Alton Delmore. The Girl by the River: Copyright © Country Music Foundation. Reprinted with permission.

Edwin Denby. The Subway; A New York Face; "I had heard it's a fight. At the first clammy touch"; "Smelling or feeling of the several holes": Copyright © Edwin Denby. Reprinted by permission of The Estate of Edwin Denby.

Babette Deutsch. "To an Amiable Child"; Creatures in the Zoo: Copyright © Babette Deutsch. Reprinted with permission of the Estate of Babette Deutsch.

Thomas A. Dorsey. Take My Hand, Precious Lord: Words and music by Thomas A. Dorsey. Copyright © 1938 by Unichappell Music Inc. Copyright renewed. International Copyright Secured. All Rights Reserved. Reprinted by permission.

John Dos Passos. Newsreel LIII: From *U.S.A.* by John Dos Passos, copyright renewed © 1964. Reprinted by permission of the Estate of Elizabeth H. Dos Passos.

Rose Drachler. The Evening of the Sixth Day: Copyright © Rose Drachler. Reprinted by permission of Miriam Eisenstein Drachler.

Richard Eberhart. This Fevers Me; The Groundhog; 'I Walked Over the Grave of Henry James'; The Fury of Aerial Bombardment; On a Squirrel Crossing the Road in Autumn, in New England; La Crosse at Ninety Miles an Hour; Gnat on My Paper: From *Collected Poems 1930–1986* by Richard Eberhart. Copyright © 1960, 1976, 1987 by Richard Eberhart. Used by permission of Oxford University Press, Inc.

William Everson. Muscat Pruning; Tor House; Rainy Easter; A Canticle to the Waterbirds; Gale at Dawn; Stone Face Falls: Copyright © 1997, 1998 & 1999 by Jude Everson and the William Everson Literary Estate and reprinted from *The Residual Years, The Veritable Years,* and *The Integral Years* (Volumes 1–3 of the collected poems) with the permission of Black Sparrow Press.

Kenneth Fearing. Green Light; Evening Song; 1933; Escape; Dirge; Portrait; American Rhapsody (4); Literary; How Do I Feel?; Art Review; Reception Good; Beware; 4 A.M.; Bryce & Tomlins: Copyright © 1994 by Jubal Fearing and Phoebe Fearing. Reprinted by permission of the National Poetry Foundation.

Thomas Hornsby Ferril. Waltz Against the Mountains; Something Starting Over; Noon: Copyright © Thomas Hornsby Ferril, reprinted by permission of the Thomas Hornsby Ferril Literary Trust.

Dorothy Fields. I Can't Give You Anything But Love: Copyright © Dorothy Fields, reprinted with permission of her son, David Lahm.

Dudley Fitts. "Ya se van los pastores": From *Anthology of Contemporary Latin-American Poetry*, edited by Dudley Fitts. Copyright © 1948 by New Directions Publishing Corp. Reprinted by permission of New Directions Publishing Corp.

Robert Fitzgerald. Manuscript with Illumination; Horae; Et Quidquid Aspiciebam Mors Erat; Farewell; Mutations; History; Souls Lake; South Side; Spring Shade: Copyright © 1970 by Robert Fitzgerald. Reprinted by permission of Penelope Laurans Fitzgerald.

Hildegarde Flanner. Dumb; Moment; Fern Song; Frog Song; True Western Summer: Copyright © Hildegarde Flanner. Reprinted with permission of Ahsahta Press.

Charles Henri Ford. The Overturned Lake; I Wouldn't Put It Past You: Copyright © 1991 by Charles Henri Ford. Reprinted by permission of City Lights Books. The Fox with the Blue Velvet Band: Copyright © 1937 by Charles Henri Ford.

Drum; Cubes; Little Lyric (Of Great Importance); Curious; Evil; Songs; Luck; American Heartbreak; *from* Montage of a Dream Deferred: From *Collected Poems* by Langston Hughes. Copyright © 1994 by the Estate of Langston Hughes. Reprinted by permission of Alfred A. Knopf Inc.

Rolfe Humphries. Europa; Test Paper; From the Green Book of Yfan: From *Collected Poems of Rolfe Humphries*, copyright © Rolfe Humphries. Reprinted with permission of Indiana University Press.

Josephine Jacobsen. Poems For My Cousin; Yellow: From *In the Crevice of Time* by Josephine Jacobsen, pgs. 65–68, 87. Copyright © 1995 by Josephine Jacobsen. Reprinted with permission of The Johns Hopkins University Press.

Eugene Jolas. Mater Dolorosa: Copyright © 1935 by Eugene Jolas. Reprinted with permission of the Estate of Eugene Jolas.

Lincoln Kirstein. Gloria; P.O.E: From *Poems of Lincoln Kirstein*, copyright © 1987. Reprinted with permission of Scribner, a Division of Simon & Schuster Inc.

Stanley Kunitz. The Science of the Night; The Dragonfly: copyright © 1953, 1958 by Stanley Kunitz. From *The Poems of Stanley Kunitz 1928–1978*. Reprinted by permission of W.W. Norton & Co., Inc. Touch Me; Route Six; The Quarrel; The Catch: copyright © 1978, 1979, 1995 by Stanley Kunitz. From *Passing Through: The Later Poems New and Selected* by Stanley Kunitz. Reprinted by permission of W.W. Norton & Co.

Richmond Lattimore. North Philadelphia Trenton and New York; Vergil Georgics I.489–514: Copyright © Richmond Lattimore. Reprinted by permission of The Bryn Mawr Trust Company and Alice B. Lattimore.

Janet Lewis. *from* The Indian in the Woods; Girl Help; The Reader; Winter Garden; Helen Grown Old; For the Father of Sandro Gulotta; The Ancient Ones: Betátakin; Garden Note I, Los Altos; Garden Note II, March: From *Poems Old & New: 1918–1978* by Janet Lewis, copyright © Janet Lewis. Reprinted by permission of Ohio University Press/ Swallow Press, Athens, Ohio.

Frank Loesser. Luck, Be a Lady: Copyright © 1950 (renewed) Frank Music Corp., all rights reserved. Reprinted with permission.

Walter Lowenfels. *from* Elegy in the Manner of a Requiem in Memory of D. H. Lawrence: From *Reality Prime: Selected Poems*, edited by Joel Lewis, copyright © 1998 by the Estate of Walter Lowenfels. Reprinted by permission of Manna Lowenfels, literary executrix for the estate of Walter Lowenfels.

Joseph Moncure March. *from* The Wild Party: From *The Wild Party* by Joseph Moncure March, copyright © 1928 by Pascal Covici, Publisher, Inc. Reprinted by permission of Pantheon Books, a division of Random House, Inc.

Phyllis McGinley. Twelfth Night; Spring Comes to the Suburbs; The 5:32; Portrait of Girl with Comic Book: Copyright © 1940, 1951, 1954 by Phyllis McGinley.

Johnny Mercer. Blues in the Night: Copyright 1941 Harms Inc. and Renewed © 1968 Warner Bros./7 Arts. Reprinted by permission of the Johnny Mercer Foundation. Midnight Sun: Copyright 1954 Crystal Music Publishers Inc.; renewed © 1980, 1982 Elizabeth Mercer. Reprinted by permission of the Johnny Mercer Foundation.

Josephine Miles. Housewife; All Hallow; Sale; Album: From *Collected Poems, 1930–1983*. Copyright © 1983 by Josephine Miles. Used with the permission of the University of Illinois Press. "After noon I lie down": Copyright © Wesleyan University Press.

Rosalie Moore. The Mind's Disguise; Memory of Quiet; Height: From *The Grasshopper's Man and Other Poems*, copyright © 1949. Reprinted with permission of Yale University Press.

Vladimir Nabokov. *from* Lolita: From *Lolita* by Vladimir Nabokov, copyright © 1955 by Vladimir Nabokov. Reprinted by permission of Vintage Books, a division of Random House, Inc. On Translating "Eugene Onegin": copyright © the Estate of Vladimir Nabokov. Printed by arrangement with the Estate of Vladimir Nabokov. All rights reserved.

Ogden Nash. Spring Comes to Murray Hill; Reflections on Ice-Breaking; The Terrible People; Song of the Open Road; Very Like a Whale; A Necessary Dirge; Portrait of the Artist as a Prematurely Old Man; The Germ; Glossina Morsitans, Or the Tsetse; Samson Agonistes; Inter-Office Memorandum: From *Verses From 1929 On* by Ogden Nash. Copyright © 1930, 1932, 1933, 1934, 1935, 1942 by Ogden Nash. Reprinted by permission of Little, Brown and Company. Which the Chicken, Which the Egg?: From *The Old Dog Barks Backwards* by Ogden Nash. Copyright © Ogden Nash. Reprinted by permission of Little, Brown and Company (Inc.).

Lorine Niedecker. "Remember my little granite pail?"; "The clothesline post is set"; "There's a better shine"; "What horror to awake at night"; "Paul / when the leaves"; "The death of my poor father"; "Woman in middle life"; "He lived—childhood summers"; "I rose from marsh mud"; The Graves; "My friend tree"; "The men leave the car"; "My life is hung up"; "Get a load / of April's"; Poet's Work; "I married"; My Life by Water; "Far reach / of sand"; "Stone / and that hard / contact-"; Sewing a Dress; Paean to Place; "Not all harsh sounds displease-"; Darwin: From *The Collected Poetry of Lorine Niedecker*, edited by Jenny Lynn Penberthy, copyright © 2000 by The Regents of the University of California. Reprinted with permission of the University of California Press.

John Frederick Nims. The Evergreen: From *Knowledge of the Evening* by John Frederick Nims, copyright © The University of Chicago Press. Reprinted with permission.

Charles Olson. La Préface; These Days; In Cold Hell, in Thicket; The Moon Is the Number 18; Merce of Egypt; As the Dead Prey Upon Us; Variations Done for Gerald Van De Wiele: From *Collected Poems of Charles Olson*, edited by George F. Butterick, copyright © 1987 Estate of Charles Olson. Reprinted with permission of University of California Press. *From* The Maximus Poems: From *The Maximus Poems* by Charles Olson, edited by George F. Butterick, copyright © 1983 by the Regents of the University of California. Reprinted with permission.

Elder Olson. The Four Black Bogmen: From *The Scarecrow Christ* by Elder Olson. Copyright 1954, renewed © 1982 by Elder Olson. Reprinted by permission of Farrar, Straus & Giroux, LLC.

George Oppen. Discrete Series; Eclogue; Image of the Engine; From Disaster; Psalm; The Occurrences; Route; But So As By Fire: From *Collected Poems*, by George Oppen. Copyright © 1975 by George Oppen. Reprinted by permission of New Directions Publishing Corp. In Memoriam Charles Reznikoff: copyright © 1977 by George Oppen. Reprinted from *Poems 1918–1975: The Complete Poems of Charles Reznikoff* with the permission of Black Sparrow Press.

Kenneth Patchen. Street Corner College; Religion Is That I Love You; 23rd Street Runs into Heaven; The Figure Motioned with its Mangled Hand Towards the Wall Behind It; The Horses of Yilderlin; The Origin of Baseball; The Lions of Fire Shall Have Their Hunting; Lonesome Boy Blues: From *The Collected Poems of Kenneth Patchen*. Copyright © 1942, 1957 by New Directions Publishing Corp. Reprinted by permission of New Directions Publishing Corp.

Hyam Plutzik. The Airman Who Flew Over Shakespeare's England; Winter, Never Mind Where; For T.S.E. Only; As the Great Horse Rots on the Hill: Copyright © Hyam Plutzik, reprinted by permission of Tanya Plutzik.

Anne Porter. Consider the Lilies of the Sea; Winter Twilight: Copyright © 1994 by Anne Porter, from *An Altogether Different Language*, Zoland Books, Cambridge, Massachussetts. Reprinted by permission.

H. Phelps Putnam. Words of an Old Woman; Bill Gets Burned; Hasbrouck and the Rose: Copyright © 1931 by H. Phelps Putnam.

Carl Rakosi. The January of a Gnat; Amulet; Figures in Ancient Ink; The Lobster; Lying in Bed on a Summer Morning; Young Girl; Americana 3; To an Anti-Semite; Discoveries, Trade Names, Genitals, and Ancient Instruments; Two Variations on a

Theme; Instructions to the Player; The Avocado Pit: All poems copyright © Carl Rakosi. Reprinted by permission of the National Poetry Foundation.

Kenneth Rexroth. Spring, Coast Range: From *Selected Poems* by Kenneth Rexroth. Copyright © 1940, 1956 by Kenneth Rexroth. Reprinted by permission of New Directions Publishing Corp. The Signature of All Things; Lyell's Hypothesis Again: From *Collected Shorter Poems* by Kenneth Rexroth. Copyright © 1944, 1963 by Kenneth Rexroth. Reprinted by permission of New Directions Publishing Corp. It Is a German Honeymoon: From *New Poems* by Kenneth Rexroth. Copyright © 1974 by New Directions Publishing Corp. Reprinted by permission of New Directions Publishing Corp. Andrée Rexroth: From *Collected Shorter Poems* by Kenneth Rexroth. Copyright © 1944 by New Directions Publishing Corp. Reprinted by permission of New Directions Publishing Corp. On Flower Wreath Hill; The Love Poems of Marichiko: From *The Morning Star* by Kenneth Rexroth. Copyright © 1979 by Kenneth Rexroth. Reprinted by permission of New Directions Publishing Corp.

Charles Reznikoff. "On Brooklyn Bridge I saw a man drop dead"; "I met in a merchant's place"; "The shopgirls leave their work"; "How shall we mourn you who are killed and wasted"; "My work done, I lean on the window-sill"; "In the shop, she, her mother, and grandmother"; The Idiot; "She who worked patiently"; Epidemic; "Her work was to count linings"; "the house-wreckers have left the door and a staircase"; Aphrodite Vrania; April; "Out of the hills the trees bulge"; "How difficult for me is Hebrew"; "I have learnt the Hebrew blessing before eating bread"; "After I had worked all day at what I earn my living"; "The Hebrew of your poets, Zion"; "Though our thoughts often, we ourselves"; "Among the heaps of brick and plaster lies"; Epitaphs; Millinery District ["The clouds..."]; "A dead gull in the road"; "I like this secret walking"; Rainy Season; "Of course, we must die"; "My grandfather, dead long before I was born"; "A grove of small trees, branches thick with berries"; Millinery District ["Many fair hours..."]; Similes; Epitaph; Free Verse; *from* Early History of a Writer: Copyright © 1977 by Marie Syrkin Reznikoff and reprinted from *Poems 1918–1975: The Complete Poems of Charles Reznikoff* with the permission of Black Sparrow Press.

Laura Riding. An Ancient Revisits; As Well As Any Other; Prisms; Lucrece and Nara; O Vocables of Love; Faith Upon the Waters; Sea, False Philosophy; The Map of Places; Chloe or...; Take Hands; The World and I; The Wind, the Clock, the We; Nothing So Far; Divestment of Beauty; Because of Clothes; With the Face: All poems copyright © the Board of Literary Management for Laura (Riding) Jackson and reprinted with permission. In conformity with the late author's wish, her Board of Literary Management asks us to record that, in 1941, Laura (Riding) Jackson renounced, on grounds of linguistic principle, the writing of poetry: she had come to hold that "poetry obstructs general attainment to something better in our linguistic way-of-life than we have."

Lynn Riggs. Santa Domingo Corn Dance: From *The Iron Dish* by Lynn Riggs. Copyright © 1930 by Lynn Riggs. Used by permission of Doubleday, a division of Random House, Inc.

Theodore Roethke. The Heron; The Bat; Cuttings; Cuttings (later); Frau Bauman, Frau Schmidt, and Frau Schwartz; The Lost Son; Elegy for Jane; The Waking; I Knew a Woman; A Walk in Late Summer: Copyright © 1937, 1938, 1947, 1948, 1950, 1952, 1953, 1954, 1957 by Theodore Roethke. Root Cellar: Copyright © 1943 by Modern Poetry Association, Inc. Old Florist: Copyright © 1946 by Harper Brothers. Four for Sir John Davies; My Papa's Waltz: Copyright © 1942 by Hearst Magazines, Inc. The Rose; The Thing; In a Dark Time: Copyright © 1960, 1963 by Beatrice Roethke, Administratrix of the Estate of Theodore Roethke. From *The Collected Poems of Theodore Roethke* by Theodore Roethke. Used by permission of Doubleday, a division of Random House, Inc.

Eve Triem. For Paul: Copyright © 1979 by Eve Triem.

Mark Van Doren. This Amber Sunstream; Axle Song; The Near House; Midland; So Simple; Where I Saw the Snake; The First Poem: Copyright © Mark Van Doren. Reprinted with permission of Hill & Wang, and of Charles and John Van Doren, executors of the Estate of Mark Van Doren. All Rights Reserved.

Byron Vazakas. The Pavilion on the Pier; Epitaph on the Old Howard: Copyright © Byron Vazakas. Reprinted with permission of Donald J. Vazakas and Thomas Vazakas.

Robert Penn Warren. The Return: An Elegy; Bearded Oaks; Where the Slow Fig's Purple Sloth; Audubon: A Vision; Birth of Love; Evening Hawk; Heart of Autumn; Vision; Muted Music: From *New and Selected Poems: 1923–1985* by Robert Penn Warren. Copyright © 1985 by Robert Penn Warren. Reprinted by permission of William Morris Agency, Inc. on behalf of the author.

John Wheelwright. Slow Curtain; Why Must You Know?; Would You Think?; Fish Food; Come Over and Help Us; Anathema. Maranatha!; In the Bathtub, to Mnemosyne; Esprit d'Escalier; Cross Questions: From *Collected Poems of John Wheelwright*. Copyright © 1971 by Louise Wheelwright Damon. Reprinted by permission of New Directions Publishing Corp.

Bukka White. Fixin' to Die: Copyright © 1965 MCA Music Publishing, a division of Universal Studios, Inc. All rights controlled and administered by MCA Music Publishing, a division of Universal Studios, Inc.

Tennessee Williams. The Beanstalk Country: From *In the Winter of Cities* by Tennessee Williams. Copyright © 1956, 1964 by Tennessee Williams. Reprinted by permission of New Directions Publishing Corp.

Edmund Wilson. Epitaphs; A House of the Eighties; The Omelet of A. MacLeish. Copyright 1961 by Edmund Wilson, renewed © 1989 by Helen Miranda Wilson. Reprinted by permission of Farrar, Straus & Giroux, LLC.

Yvor Winters. The Magpie's Shadow; The Solitude of Glass; October; Wild Sunflower: From *Early Poems of Yvor Winters.* Copyright © Yvor Winters. Reprinted with the permission of Ohio University Press/ Swallow Press, Athens, Ohio. The Fable; The Fall of Leaves; To the Moon: From *Collected Poems* by Yvor Winters. Copyright © Yvor Winters. Reprinted with the permission of Ohio University Press/ Swallow Press, Athens, Ohio. Two Songs of Advent; Vacant Lot; The Cold; Nocturne; The Barnyard; The Realization; Apollo and Daphne; The Fall of Leaves; To a Young Writer; By the Road to the Sunnyvale Air-Base; Elegy on a Young Airedale Bitch Lost Some Years Since in the Salt-Marsh; On Teaching the Young; Time and the Garden; In Praise of California Wines: From *Selected Poems of Yvor Winters,* edited by R. L. Barth. Copyright © Yvor Winters. Reprinted with the permission of Ohio University Press/ Swallow Press, Athens, Ohio.

Richard Wright. I Have Seen Black Hands: Copyright © 1934 by Richard Wright. Reprinted by permission of John Hawkins & Associates, Inc. The FB Eye Blues: Copyright © 1978 by Ellen Wright and Michel Fabre. Reprinted by permission of John Hawkins & Associates, Inc. Selected Haiku: Copyright © 1959 by Richard Wright. Published by Arcade Publishing, Inc., New York, NY. Reprinted with permission.

Louis Zukofsky. I Sent Thee Late; Poem beginning "The"; "Not much more than being,"; "Cocktails"; Ferry; Tibor Serly; "in that this happening"; "To my wash-stand"; "When the crickets"; "It's hard to see but think of a sea"; "The lines of this new song are nothing"; "Can a mote of sunlight defeat its purpose"; (Ryokan's scroll); Xenophanes; "As To How Much"; Shang Cup: From *Complete Short Poetry,* copyright © Paul Zukofsky. Reprinted with permission of Johns Hopkins University Press. "A" 11; *from* "A" 12: from *"A,"* copyright © Paul Zukofsky. Reprinted with permission of Johns Hopkins University Press.

Notes

In the notes below, the reference numbers denote page and line of this volume (the line count includes titles). No note is made for material included in standard desk-reference books, such as *Webster's Collegiate Dictionary* or *Webster's Biographical Dictionary*. Quotations from Shakespeare are keyed to *The Riverside Shakespeare* (Boston: Houghton Mifflin, 1974), edited by G. Blakemore Evans. References to the Bible have been keyed to the King James Version.

3.26   the old howard] The Howard Athenaeum, Boston theater built as a church in 1843 by the Millerite sect but abandoned by them the following year; it later became a vaudeville theater and ultimately a burlesque house.

10.7   MR. VINAL] Poet Harold Vinal (1891–1965) founded the poetry quarterly *Voices* in 1921, and continued to edit it until his death. Cummings' poem is a response to Vinal's "Earth Lover."

11.5–6   The Snail's . . . In His andsoforth] Cf. Robert Browning, *Pippa Passes* (1841), 223–28: "Morning's at seven; / The hillside's dew-pearled; / The lark's on the wing; / The snail's on the thorn; / God's in his heaven– / All's right with the world!"

11.24   Nujolneeding] Nujol, a brand of laxative.

14.5   Murano] Town near Venice known for its glass-blowing industry.

14.7–8   nel / mezzo del cammin'] Midway in the road,: cf. Dante, *Inferno*, Canto I, 1.

14.10   cocodrillo] A large stone crocodile, part of the statue of St. Theodore overlooking the Piazza San Marco.

15.10–11   (O to be a . . . triglyph's here)] Cf. Browning, "Home Thoughts from Abroad" (1843): "Oh to be in England / Now that April's here."

28.11–14   a nipponized bit . . . el] The Sixth Avenue elevated railway was demolished in 1939; the United States continued to sell scrap metal to Japan until an embargo was imposed in September 1940.

32.28   *Test Paper*] Originally published as "Laud for Moderns."

33.2   Fadiman] Clifton Fadiman (1904–99), prolific essayist, editor, and anthologist.

974

33.18   *(Cywydd deuair fyrion)*] A rhymed four-syllable couplet. [Humphries' note.] This poem is one of a series employing the 24 traditional meters of Welsh poetry.

42.17   How shall we mourn you] Written for French sculptor Henri Gaudier-Brzeska (1891–1915), killed in World War I.

50.34   one my own age] Albert Lewin, later a film director and producer for Metro-Goldwyn-Mayer and Paramount.

52.10   "we poets . . . gladness."] Cf. Wordsworth, *Resolution and Independence*, VII, 6–7: "We Poets in our youth begin in gladness; / But thereof come in the end despondency and madness."

59.24   *To One . . . Wisdom*] Cf. Louise Bogan, *Men Loved Wholly Beyond Wisdom.*

60.14   Gigadibs] Literary hack in Robert Browning's "Bishop Blougram's Apology" (1855).

63.28   Auslander and Wurdeman] American poets Joseph Auslander (1897–1965), author of *Cyclops' Eye* (1926) and *More Than Bread* (1936), and Audrey Wurdemann (1911–60), the youngest poet ever to be awarded a Pulitzer Prize, for her collection *Bright Ambush* (1934).

66.3   lehua . . . maile] Trees native to Hawaii.

92.11   Mort Homme] Literally "Dead Man," a ridge near Verdun, captured by the Germans in one of the bloodiest battles of World War I, on May 29, 1916. It was retaken by the French on August 20, 1917.

95.1   *The Omelet of A. MacLeish*] Cf. Archibald MacLeish, *The Hamlet of A. MacLeish.*

95.7   Tap Day] At Yale, the day when students are selected for secret societies such as Skull and Bones, of which MacLeish was a member.

95.19   *Anabase*] Long poem by St.-John Perse (1889–1975).

97.16–17   "Social / Credit"] Theory developed by English social economist Clifford Hugh Douglas (1879–1952) and later embraced by Ezra Pound, proposing a social system in which citizens are issued dividends based on the real wealth of the country.

99.3   *Newsreel LIII*] From *The Big Money* (1936), the third novel in Dos Passos' *U.S.A.* trilogy.

107.17   Theatre Guilders] The Theatre Guild (1918–44) was known for its New York productions of challenging and ambitious works such as *Saint Joan* (1923), *Mourning Becomes Electra* (1931), and *Porgy and Bess* (1935).

108.6   Jim Farley] James A. Farley (1888–1976), politician who chaired the Democratic National Committee, 1932–40.

108.17   *Green Pastures*] Play (1930) by Marc Connelly, dramatizing Bible stories in terms of African-American folklore.

108.18   The Siamese Twins] Chang and Eng (1811–74), twins joined at the waist who were exhibited as curiosities in America and later became naturalized American citizens.

108.25   Mr. Lehman] Herbert H. Lehman (1878–1963), partner in Lehman Brothers Bank and governor of New York (1932–42).

111.3   *Elegy . . . Ward*] This, and the following two poems, are from the sequence *Maximum Security Ward* (1970).

111.5   Broceliande] In this vast forest of Brittany the young Vivian laid a spell on her elderly lover Merlin that was to keep him forever captive and visible only to herself. [Guthrie's note.]

111.9   *Viollet-le-Duc's*] *Viollet-le-duc* (1814–1879): Architect who restored many medieval monuments of France. One of the chimeras, often miscalled "gargoyles," with which he decorated the towers of Notre-Dame is a favorite subject of postcards of Paris. [Guthrie's note.]

114.2   Marsyas] Phrygian satyr and flutist who lost a musical contest to Apollo and was flayed alive.

114.18   Epona . . . Venus of Lespugue] Epona, Celtic goddess of horses; Venus of Lespugue, name given to stone statues believed to represent mid-Paleolithic fertility goddesses.

138.25   Build thee less stately mansions] Cf. Oliver Wendell Holmes, "The Chambered Nautilus": "Build thee more stately mansions, O my soul."

143.9   As you drank deep as Thor] During a visit to the land of the giants, Thor failed in a challenge to drain a drinking-horn. He later learned that the horn was perpetually replenished from the sea.

147.23   *Anathema. Maranatha!*] Cf. 1 Corinthians 16:22.

149.1   *Esprit d'Escalier*] A retort conceived after the occasion has passed, literally "staircase wit."

166.15   'Loaf and invite the soul,'] Cf. Walt Whitman, *Song of Myself*, 4: "I loafe and invite my soul."

167.13   Herman Melville of the Customs House] Melville was deputy inspector of customs at the port of New York, 1867–85.

170.4   *Libretto for the Republic of Liberia*] Tolson's notes are printed exactly as they appeared in the first edition (1953) except for the line citations, which are keyed to this volume.

   170.9 *Miserere*. C. Newman, *The Definition of a Gentleman*: ". . . we attended the Tenebrae, at the Sestine, for the sake of the Miserere . . ."

170.13   *Cowled in azure*: the cloak of deceit and false humility. Cf. Hafiz, *The Divan (Odes)*, V, translated by Bicknell.

170.15   *Whale and Elephant*: the symbols Jefferson used to designate Great Britain with her navy under Nelson and France with her army under Napoleon. V. Anderson, *Liberia*, X.

170.20   *Massebôth*: "sacred pillars." Cf. Genesis, XXVIII, xviii. Also the J author.

170.21   *Thou boy of tears*. Cf. Shakespeare, *Coriolanus*, V, v.

170.25   *Lachen mit vastchekes*: "laughing with needles being stuck in you"; ghetto laughter.

170.26   Cf. Blake, *The Tiger*.

170.27   Cf. Hardy. *The Convergence of the Twain*.

171.3   V. Pycraft, *Animals of the World*, 1941–1942. *A fortiori*, the American trotter is "a combination of barb and Arab on English stock."

171.4   V. Christy, *The Asian Legacy and American Life*. This book contains vital facts on Oriental influences in the New Poetry. What I owe the late Professor Arthur A. Christy, a favorite teacher, is not limited to the concept of "the shuttle ceaselessly weaving the warp and weft of the world's cultural fabric."

171.10   *Clochan-na-n'all*: "the blind men's stepping-stones." Cf. Ferguson, *The Welshmen of Tirawley*.

171.14   Cf. Aeschylus, *Agamemnon*.

171.18   Cf. Shakespeare, *Coriolanus*, I, i, 67–76. See also Mr. Traversi's essay on this phrase of the play.

171.20   I came across these words somewhere: "The Ch'in emperor built the Great Wall to keep out Mongolian enemies from the north and burned the books of China to destroy intellectual enemies from within."

171.27   Cf. Akiba: "*Masôreth* is a fence for the sayings of the fathers."

171.29   *Adola mentis*. V. Bacon, *Novum Organum*.

171.30   *Divorcee Art*. Cf. Gourmont: "*Car je crois que l'art est par essence, absolument inintelligible au peuple.*"

172.4   *Pegasus' bomb*. Cf. Dobson, *On the Future of Poetry*.

172.5   V. Joshua VI, i.

172.6   Cf. Treitschke: "The State is Power. Of so unusual a type is its power, that it has no power to limit its power. Hence no treaty, when it becomes inconvenient, can be binding; hence the very notion of arbitration is absurd; hence war is a part of the Divine order." Contrast this idea with Lincoln's premise that the people can establish either a republic of wolves or a democracy of lambs, as instanced in the poem *The Dictionary of the Wolf*. Cf. Bismarck: "The clause *rebus sic stantis* is understood in all treaties."

172.9   *Curtain*. Cf. Crile, *A Mechanistic View of War and Peace, 1915*: France [is] a nation of forty million with a deep-rooted grievance and an iron curtain at its frontier."

172.10   *Sancho's fears.* V. Cervantes, *Don Quixote de la Mancha*, Part
II, translated by Peter Motteux, the episode of the letter: "To Don
Sancho Pança, Governor of the Island of Barataria, to be delivered
into his own hands, or those of his secretary."

172.11   *The Great Fear.* V. Madelin, *French Revolution*, 69.

172.12   Alberti, *Sobre los Angeles.*

172.13   Cf. the aphorism: *"La politique n'a pas d'entrailles."*

172.14   Cf. Meredith, *Lucifer in Starlight.*

172.19   Cf. Hawthorne, *The Scarlet Letter:* "The black flower of civi-
lized society, a prison."

172.23   V. Boccaccio, *The Three Rings.* Cf. Lessing, *Nathan the Wise.*

172.27   *Paseq:* "divider." This is a vertical line that occurs about 480
times in our Hebrew Bible. Although first mentioned in the *Midrash
Rabba* in the eleventh century, it is still the most mysterious sign in
the literature.

172.32   Cf. Cavafy, *Waiting for the Barbarians.*

172.33   *Famed enterprises.* V. Erasmus, *The Praise of Folly,* "Soldiers
and Philosophers," *in toto,* the revised translation by John Wilson.

172.34   *Hearts of rags . . . souls of chalk*: Whitman's epithets for the
"floating mass" that vote early and often for bread and circuses.
Hanorish tharah sharinas: "Man is a being of varied, manifold, and in-
constant nature." V. Della Mirandola, *Oration on the Dignity of Man.*
Cf. Cunha: "The fantasy of universal suffrage [is] the Hercules' club
of our dignity."

172.35   *Zinc buckets of verse.* V. Pasternak, *Definition of Poetry. Sugary
grace.* Cf. Martial, *To a Rival Poet.*

172.38   Cf. Tennyson, *Idylls of the King:*
               "Red Ruin, and the breaking up of laws."
V. Revelation VI. Cf. Jouve, *La Resurrection des Morts.* See the
White Horse, the Red Horse, the Black Horse, and the fourth horse,
the worst:
               "Tu es jaune et ta forme coule à ta charpente
               Sur le tonneau ajouré de tes côtes
               Les lambeaux verts tombent plus transparents
               La queue est chauve et le bassin a des béquilles
               Pour le stérile va-et-vient de la violence . . ."

173.3   *The Leveler.* V. The Acts V, xxxii–xxxvi.

173.7   *Pesiq:* "divided." V. Fuchs, *Pesiq ein Glossenzeichen.* It seems
to me that this linguistic symbol gives us a concrete example of the
teleological—perhaps the only one. By an accident of *a priori* proba-
blility, the sign in itself indicates both cause and effect, and the index
of the relationship is served synchronously by either *paseq* or *pasiq.* Of
course the protagonist of the poem uses them for his own purpose on
another level.

173.9   *Bitter black estates.* Cf. Petrarca, *The Spring Returns, but Not to
Him Returns,* translated by Auslander. *Buzzard.* V. Dryden, *The Hind*

and the Panther. Og. V. Tate, *Second Part of Absalom and Achitophel*, the passage inserted by Dryden.

173.10   V. Rochester, *Satyr against Mankind*. Cf. Cocteau, *Le Cap de Bonne Espérance: "J'ai mal d'être homme."*

173.18   The watchword of Hidalgo, "Captain General of America."

173.20   Cf. Muselli, *Ballade de Contradiction*:
> *"Fiers instants promis à la faux,*
> *Eclairs sombre au noir domaine!"*

173.24   Cf. Camus, *The Artist as Witness of Freedom*: M. Desfourneau's ". . . demands were clear. He naturally wanted a bonus for each execution, which is customary in any enterprise. But, more important, he vigorously demanded that he be given . . . an administrative status. Thus came to an end, beneath the weight of history, one of the last of our liberal professions. . . . Almost everywhere else in the world, executioners have already been installed in ministerial chairs. They have merely substituted the rubber stamp for the axe."

173.26   Cf. Nietzsche, *Thus Spake Zarathustra*, 232.

173.28   *Il Santo and Pero*: respectively, the nicknames of Nietzsche and Trotsky—the first innocently ironical, the second ironically innocent.

173.33   Cf. the remark of Nicholas I to a harassed minister of war: "We have plenty of little gray cattle." The Czar had in mind the Russian peasant.

173.37   *Brain-sick lands.* V. Meredith, *On the Danger of War.*

173.38   In the fable of Antisthenes, when the hares demanded equality for all, the lions said: "Where are your claws?" Cf. Martial, *Epigram XII*, 93: *"Dic mihi, si fias tu leo, qualis eris?"*

174.5   *Höhere.* Cf. Petronius: *"Proecipitandus est liber spiritus."*

174.7   In the Gilded Era, cynics said of Babcock: "He fished for gold in every stinking cesspool." *Galerie des rois.* Cf. Verlaine, *Nocturne Parisien*, the reference to the twenty-eight statues of French kings.

174.8   *The seeking of cows*: this is the literal meaning of the word "battle" among the ancient Aryans who ravaged the Indo-Gangetic plains. The backwardness of their culture is attested by their failure to fumigate and euphemize their war aims. *Apartheid*: the South African system of multi-layered segregation.

174.12   *Deeds hostile all*: these words are from the *Chorus to Ajax*, by Sophocles, which Mr. Forrestal apparently read just before his death. *O Caton*: Cato the Younger commmited suicide in 46 B.C. He had spent the previous night reading Plato's *Phaedo*. Cf. Lamartine, *Le Désespoir.*

174.13   *The walls*: "economic doctrines." The figure is Blok's.

174.16   *Sabotaged world.* Cf. Salmon, *Age de l'Humanité.*

174.17   V. Mitscherlich and Mielke, *Doctors of Infamy*, translated by Norden. Cf. Grotius, *De Jure Belli et Pacis*, "Prolegomena," XVIII:

". . . a people which violates the Laws of Nature and Nations, beats down the bulwark of its own tranquillity for future time."

174.19 Cf. Ronsard, *Le Bocage*. Also Musset, *La Nuit de mai*.

174.20 V. Gautier, *Vieux de la vieille*, the reference to Raffet's *nocturne* showing Napoleon's spirit reviewing spectral troops.

174.21 Plekhanov had Alexander II in mind when he used the trepan figure.

174.23 V. Cendrars, *Eloge de la vie dangereuse*.

174.24 Rimbaud, in a town near the Red Sea, looked toward Khartoum and wrote: *"Leur Gordon est un idiot, leur Wolseley un âne, et toutés leurs entreprises une suite insensée d'absurdités et de déprédations."* But fifty years later, when the Black Shirts entered Harrar, the ex-poet who plotted with Menelik against Italy was not there to hear Vittorio Mussolini's poetic account: "I still remember the effect produced on a small group of Galla tribesmen massed around a man in black clothes. I dropped an aerial bomb right in the center, and the group opened up like a flowering rose. It was most entertaining."

174.27 *Filets d'Arachné*. Cf. Chénier, *Qui? moi? de Phébus te dicter les leçons?*

174.28 *Mal éternel*. Cf. Lisle, *Dies irae*.

174.31 Cf. Baudelaire, *Le Voyage*.

174.32 V. Robinson, the Preface to *The Story of Medicine*.

174.33 *Yofan's studio*: Napoleon's old residence by the Kremlin wall. *Shkola Nenavisti*: a Berlin film on a Dublin subject in a Moscow theater.

174.34 *Otototoi*. See Gilbert Murray's Notes to *Aeschylus*.

174.35 Cf. Ovid, *Tristia*, quoted by Montaigne in *Of Three Commerces*. "Whoever of the Grecian fleet has escaped the Capharean rocks ever takes care to steer clear from those of the Euboean sea."

175.6 Cf. Lamartine: *"Il faut . . . Avec l'humanité t'unir par chaque pore."* Cf. Hugo, the Preface to *Les Contemplations*: "When I speak to you of myself, I am speaking to you of you." And again, Romains: *"Il faut bien qu'un jour on soit l'humanité!"*

175.21 *Black Aethiop*. Cf. Shakespeare, *Pericles*, II, ii:
> "A knight of Sparta, my renowned father,
> And the device he bears upon his shield
> Is a black Aethiop, reaching at the sun;
> The word, 'Lux tua vita mihi'."

175.22 *Nullius in verba*. V. Lyons, *The Royal Society*.

175.31 *Grief-in-grain*. The "grain" I have in mind in this figure consists of the dried female bodies of a scale insect found on cacti in Mexico and Central America. The dye is red and unfading. Cf. Henley, *To James McNeill Whistler, in toto*.

176.8 Cf. Cavafy, *The Footsteps*.

176.9 *Gorii*. The voyage of the Carthaginian general Hanno carried him as far as what is now Liberia. The aborigines he saw were called

Gorii, which later Greek and Latin scholars turned into "gorilla." However, to Hanno's interpreter and in the Wolof language today, the expression means "These too are men."

176.11   *Raya.* In the Turkish conquest of the Southern Slavs, the maltreated people became *raya* or cattle. Conquest salves its conscience with contempt. Among the *raya* for five hundred years, the ballads of the wandering *guslars* kept freedom alive. *Oeil de Boeuf:* a waiting room at Versailles. Cf. Dobson, *On a Fan That Belonged to the Marquise de Pompadour.*

176.12   *Vsechelovek:* "universal man." In spite of its global image, this concept has a taint of *blut und boden.* Ever since Dostoevski, in a eulogy on Pushkin, identified the latter's genius with *vsechelovek*, the term has created pros and cons. Cf. the Latin: "Paul is a Roman and not a Roman." *Descamisados:* "the shirtless ones."

176.13   *The line was suggested by the history of the Crudes and Asados of Uruguay.*

176.14   *Il Duce's Whore.* V. *Ciano Diaries 1939–43*, edited by Gibson. This is one of the "many instances of the vast contempt in which Il Duce held his people."

176.15   Cf. Milton, the outline of *Adam Unparadised.*

170.22   *du-haut-en-bas*]   From top to bottom.

170.33   *elboga*]   West African hallucinogen used ritually by the Bwiti tribe of Gabon; also known as "ibogaine."

170.34   *tribulum*]   A threshing sledge.

172.15   *de las canteras sin auroras.*]   Of songs without dawn.

173.32   *divide et impera*]   Divide and rule.

174.6   *dérèglement de tous les sens*]   Derangement of all the senses. Cf. Arthur Rimbaud, in a letter to Paul Demeny, 1871: "The poet makes himself a seer by a long, immense, and systematic *derangement* of *all the senses.*"

174.18   *la muerte sobre el esqueleto de la nada*]   Death on the skeleton of the void.

177.3   Sir Henry's flap]   The havelock, a cap with a long flap at the back to protect the neck from the sun, invented by British soldier Sir Henry Havelock (1795–1857).

177.5   Hambletonian]   American standardbred horse.

180.35   High Priestess at 27 rue de Fleurus]   Gertrude Stein.

181.27   Comus]   Roman god of merriment, intoxication, and revelry.

190.1   *Faustus and Helen*]   Cf. Christopher Marlowe, *The Tragical History of Doctor Faustus.*

190.10   THE ALCHEMIST]   Comedy (1610) by Ben Jonson.

194.1   Anchises]   Husband of Aphrodite; he was carried to safety by his son Aeneas as Troy burned.

204.3–7   *Venient annis . . . ultima Thule.*]   From Seneca's *Medea*: "A time will come in distant years when Ocean will loosen the bonds of things and the whole earth's surface will be open to view, and Tethys will discover new worlds; Thule will no longer be the outermost limit of the world."

204.9   Luis de San Angel]   Advocate of Columbus's voyage at Queen Isabella's court.

204.15   Juan Perez]   Friar instrumental in arranging Columbus's second meeting with Ferdinand and Isabella.

206.8   Teneriffe's garnet]   The volcano Pico de Teide.

207.3–7   *"—Pocahuntus . . . over."*]   From William Strachey, *History of Travaile into Virginia Britannica* (1615).

210.4   Tintex—Japalac]   Tintex, a brand of dye; Japalac, a varnish.

213.4   Dan Midland]   Legendary hobo who died by falling from a train.

218.14   fifty-nine]   The Colorado gold rush of 1859.

220.3–4   *O . . . no more!*]   Last lines of Herman Melville's *The Temeraire.*

222.27–28   *Taeping? / Ariel?*]   Clipper ships in the tea trade.

224.16   "—Recorders ages hence"]   Title of a poem by Walt Whitman.

224.19   Paumanok]   American Indian name for Long Island.

226.22   Skygak]   Stunt pilot.

228.17   *Panis Angelicus*]   Bread of angels.

229.20   *The one . . . hight.*]   From Christopher Marlowe's *Hero and Leander* (1598).

230.24   *National Winter Garden*]   New York City burlesque theater.

232.16   *Quaker Hill*]   Resort near Pawling, New York, where Crane lived at times, 1925–30.

235.3–4   *To Find . . . Wrath*]   First lines of William Blake's "Morning."

237.12   gigantically down]   Cf. Edgar Allan Poe, "The City in the Sea."

239.3–4   *Music . . . system.*]   From Plato's *Republic* (3.403).

250.8   *Manibush*]   Trickster figure in Ojibwa and other Great Lakes cultures; variants of the name include Manabozho and Nanabush.

254.6   *For the Father of Sandro Gulotta*]   "Written for Vincenzo Gulotta of Milano whose son was dying of leukemia." [Lewis's note.]

255.1   *Betátakin*]   Navajo ruins, discovered in 1909, of a 13th-century village in the Southwest.

263.12   I cannot . . . starling]   From Sterne's *A Sentimental Journey Through France and Italy* (1768), II: "The Passport: Hotel de Paris."

264.1   *vair*]   Gray.

264.3   *Soleil Vert*]   Green Sun.

264.5–8   *L'autre . . . de ta vie?*]   "The other night a cold opera air landed me in bed: / Broken note—whoever trusts that is quite mad! / It is snowing, the decor is crumbling, Lolita! / Lolita, what have I made of your life?" Parody of a passage from IV.ii of Victor Hugo's 1832 play *Le Roi s'amuse*.

265.1   "*Eugene Onegin*"]   Nabokov's annotated translation of Pushkin's poem was published in 1964.

267.12   *Koshari*]   Clowns or "Delight Makers" in Pueblo Indian ceremonies, distinguished by black and white body paint and clay-stiffened hair fashioned into two horns.

275.3   Neoptolemus]   Son of Achilles; sent to Troy by the Greeks after the death of his father, he was among those manning the Trojan horse.

275.3   Atridae]   Sons of Atreus, i.e., Agamemnon and Menelaus.

277.17   *Axel's Castle*]   Edmund Wilson's 1931 critical study of the influence of French Symbolism on modernist poetry and fiction.

277.30   *Quem . . . dolorum?*]   "What end to their troubles, great king, will you give?" Venus' speech to Jupiter in Vergil, *Aeneid I*. 241.

285.29   Pul]   Assyrian king Tiglath-pileser III; cf. II Kings, 15:19.

285.30   Laban]   Cf. Gen. 29–31.

285.32   Erech and Calneh]   Cf. Gen. 10:10.

285.34   Togmarah]   Cf. Gen. 10:3.

286.13   Mamre]   Cf. Gen. 14:13, 24.

288.13   *O saisons, ô châteaux!*]   O seasons, o castles!: cf. Arthur Rimbaud, "Bonheur."

318.27   *O, le bal des belles quarteronnes!*]   Oh, the ball of the beautiful quadroons!

333.1   Edgar Fawcett]   American novelist and poet (1847–1904); his collections of poetry included *Fantasy and Passion* (1878), *Romance and Revery* (1886), and *Songs of Doubt and Dream* (1891).

333.21   Charlotte Perkins Stetson]   Married name of American writer and feminist Charlotte Perkins Gilman (1860–1935).

333.28   Helen Frazee-Bower]   American poet whose religious verse was collected in *Garment of Praise* (1956) and *He Came with Music* (1963).

333.32   George Brandon Saul]   American scholar (b. 1901) who specialized in Irish literature and Yeats.

334.7   *The Light . . . Democracy*]   *The Light of Asia*: Long blank verse poem (1879) on the life of Buddha by Sir Edwin Arnold (1832–1904). *Towards Democracy*: Long poem (1883–1902) by Edward Carpenter (1844–1929), Anglican minister and Socialist.

334.18   *Waka*]   Japanese verse form (also known as tanka) consisting of units of 5, 7, 5, 7, and 7 syllables.

353.12   RFC]   The Reconstruction Finance Corporation, established by Congress in 1932, made loans to businesses, industries, and banks.

356.5   Bowie]   Maryland racetrack.

384.13   Ethical Culture]   School sponsored by the Ethical Culture Society of New York, founded in 1878.

384.15   St. Phillip's]   Episcopal church established in Harlem in 1818.

384.18   409]   Apartment building at 409 Edgecombe Avenue, home to many prominent Harlem residents.

388.22–23   Father . . . Divine]   Father Sheldon Hale Bishop, rector of St. Phillip's church; Duse Efffendi Mohammed, leader of the Pan-African Movement in England at the turn of the century; Rosa Artemisius Horne and Father Divine, Harlem religious leaders.

398.15   the Assyrian . . . on the fold?]   Cf. Byron, "The Destruction of Sennacherib" (1815): "The Assyrian came down like the wolf on the fold, / And his cohorts were gleaming in purple and gold."

399.15   Her little feet . . . petticoat?]   Cf. Sir John Suckling, "A Ballad upon a Wedding" (1641): "Her feet beneath her petticoat / Like little mice, stole in and out, / As if they feared the light."

411.16   *Hazel Hall*]   American poet (1886–1924) who was paralyzed from scarlet fever at an early age and worked most of her life as a seamstress.

438.2   FitzRoy]   Robert FitzRoy (1805–65), commander of *H.M.S. Beagle*, whom Darwin accompanied on his 1831–36 voyage.

438.24–25   Melville . . . a hiss]   Cf. Herman Melville, "The Encantadas" (1854): "No voice, no low, no howl is heard; the chief sound of life here is a hiss."

444.20   *Le mot juste? la branche juste!*]   The precise word? The precise branch!

449.1 *Two Variations on a Theme*] Later published as "What's His Offense?" in *Collected Poems* (1986).

454.26 Luke xxiii, 31] "For if they do these things in a green tree, what shall be done in the dry?"

455.1-2 *Sunt Lacrimae . . . Tangunt*] Cf. Vergil, *Aeneid*, I, 462: "They weep here for how the world goes, and our life that passes touches their hearts."

466.10 *"And out of olde bokes, in good feith"*] Cf. Chaucer, *The Parliament of Fowls*, 24.

474.26 Shagetz] Gentile man.

479.6 *Tibor Serly*] Hungarian-American violist and composer (1901–78), a friend of Zukofsky.

485.8 *Ryokan*] Japanese poet and Buddhist monk, 1758–1831.

493.8 Nicomachus] Son of Aristotle.

498.23 Rosenwald money] The Julius Rosenwald Fund, founded in 1913 by the president of Sears Roebuck, was a major source of private support for black education.

506.13 King Philip's War] War (1675–76) between Wampanoag Indians, led by King Philip (Metacomet), and the New England colonies.

509.21 Ruth Etting] American singer (1896–1978); her most popular number was "Love Me or Leave Me."

513.14 *Sara Crewe*] A novel (1887) by Frances Hodgson Burnett (1849–1924), children's author whose works included *Little Lord Fauntleroy* (1886), *A Little Princess* (1905), and *The Secret Garden* (1911).

516.22 Christian's bundle] In John Bunyan's *Pilgrim's Progress* (1678).

518.20 Nessus' shirt] Shirt made poisonous by being soaked in the blood of the dying centaur Nessus; he tricked Deianira into giving it to her husband, Heracles, causing his death.

519.13 *sempervirens*] *Sequoia sempervirens*, the redwood tree.

520.11–12 Morris / Graves] American painter, born in 1910.

521.1 *Flower Wreath Hill*] Chinese and Japanese euphemism for a cemetery. [Rexroth's note.]

522.6 Mount Hiei] Mount Hiei is the site of the founding temples of Tendai and once, before they were all slaughtered by Nobunaga, contained sixty thousand monks at least. Today there are still many monasteries—but also an amusement park. Kamo River flows close to the edge of the mountains. [Rexroth's note.]

523.28　　Tanabata] Tanabata is Seven-Seven, the seventh day of the seventh month, when the Cowboy, Altair, crosses the Milky Way to lie for one night only with the Weaving Girl, Vega. Magpies link wings and form a bridge for him to cross, but there are many Chinese and Japanese dawn poems which would indicate that he rowed himself back. [Rexroth's note.]

523.35　　Kegonkyoyama] Kegonkyo (Flower Wreath Sutra) is the Avatamsaka Sutra, by far the most profound and the most mystical of the sutras of Mahavana. [Rexroth's note.]

524.33　　sotoba] Important Japanese graves or family burial lots (only the ashes are buried) are often marked by a stupa (Japanese: *sotoba*) consisting of four and sometimes five stones, a cube, a sphere, a lune, a triangle, and sometimes a little shape on top of the triangle. [Rexroth's note.]

527.4　　Matsukaze and Murasame] Matsukaze and Murasame were two lovers of a prince exiled to the shore of Suma. They were salt girls who evaporated sea water over burning dried seaweed and driftwood, and who saw the moon one night after the prince had left, each in her own water pail or pails. [Rexroth's note.]

527.8　　Net of Indra] The Flower Wreath Sutra is known in Hinduism as the Net of Indra. [Rexroth's note.]

527.19　　gopis] The gopis are the nineteen thousand milkmaids who dance to Krishna's flute. [Rexroth's note.]

527.21　　*The Love Poems of Marichiko*] Rexroth later acknowledged that the female poet Marichiko was his own creation.

528.4　　shoji] Sliding doors or windows with "panes" of paper.　　[Rexroth's note.]

528.27　　Uguisu] The uguisu, often translated "nightingale," is not a nightingale and does not sing at night. It is the Japanese bush warbler, *Horeites cantans cantans*, or *Cettia diphone*. [Rexroth's note.]

529.7　　Kannon] Both forms of Kannon (Avalokitesvara) are common statues. Sanjusangendo, across from the Kyoto Art Museum, is a hall of over a thousand such, each very slightly different. [Rexroth's note.]

531.4　　pachinko] Pachinko is a form of vertical pinball—and immense pachinko parlors, crowded with hypnotized players, litter Japan. It is a symbol of total immersion in the world of illusion, ignorance, suffering, and grasping. [Rexroth's note.]

533.21–22　　*Madame X*] Play by Alexandre Bisson, filmed a number of times in the 1920s and '30s.

533.26　　*Old Howard*] See note 3.26.

542.17   *II. The Dream He Never Knew the End Of*]   For the source of this narrative, cf. John James Audubon, "The Prairie," in *Ornithological Biography* (1831–39).

580.1   *P.O.E.*]   Port of Embarkation.

583.10   *Laudare*]   To praise.

591.8   Maude Blessingbourne]   Cf. Henry James, "The Story in It" (1902).

605.7   *Veritas sequitur*]   Truth follows.

606.21   *Wen Fu* of Lu Chi]   Poetic teatise on the art of letters, by Chinese poet Lu Chi (261–303).

666.14   Tibidábo]   Mountain on the northwest border of Barcelona where, during the Spanish Civil War, Republican anti-aircraft guns were placed.

671.23   *Horae*]   In Greek mythology, goddesses of the seasons.

673.17   *Et . . . Erat*]   "Whatever I beheld was death." Cf. Augustine, *Confessions*, Book IV, chapter 4.

675.1   *Farewell*]   Translation of Catullus, *Carmina* 11.

684.20   DPs]   Displaced Persons.

688.18   selva oscura]   Dark forest.

692.17   *Merce*]   Dancer and choreographer Merce Cunningham (b. 1919), a friend of Olson.

702.1   *Gerald Van De Wiele*]   One of Olson's students at Black Mountain College.

702.2   *Le Bonheur*]   Happiness.

702.24   O saisons, o chateaux!]   See note 288.13.

706.27   Cressy's]   Cressy's Beach on Freshwater Cove, near Stage Fort Park, Gloucester.

707.6   Fresh Water Cove]   On the southwest side of Gloucester Harbor; named by Champlain when he landed there in 1606.

707.22   the Races]   The International Fishermen's Races held annually off Gloucester and Halifax, Nova Scotia, from 1920 to 1938.

707.23   San Pietro]   Fiesta of Saint Peter, held annually by the Italian community of Gloucester.

710.24   *achiote*]   The seed of the annatto tree, which yields a reddish dye.

711.5   doceat]   Teaching.

712.3   Ganesha] Elephant-headed god of the Hindu pantheon, son of Siva and Parvati.

726.22–23   St. Peter's sin . . . Magdalen] For Peter's denials of Christ, see Luke 22:54-62; for Christ's healing of Mary Magdalen, see Luke 8:2.

727.7–8   *gallus canit; / flet Petrus*] The cock crows; Peter weeps.

731.29   Volubilis] Ancient Roman city in Morocco.

744.15   Osa and Martin Johnson] Osa Johnson (1894–1953) and Martin Johnson (1884–1937), explorers who specialized in filming and photographing their travels in the South Seas, Africa, and elsewhere.

753.3   *Dream Vision*] Published as "All Choice Is Error" in *Collected Poems and Epigrams of J. V. Cunningham* (1971).

762.23   *Nescit vox missa reverti*] The word sent forth can never return: Horace, *Ars Poetica*, 390.

782.4   Bleistein] Cf. T. S. Eliot, "Burbank with a Baedeker: Bleistein with a Cigar."

783.3   You, hypocrite . . . frère!] Cf. Eliot, *The Waste Land*, 76, itself a quotation of Baudelaire's *Les Fleurs du Mal*.

789.14   davId tudor] David Tudor (b. 1926), pianist and experimental composer who frequently collaborated with Cage.

792.17   *Tor House*] Stone cottage built by Robinson Jeffers in Carmel, California.

808.27   Preacher Casey] Labor organizer in John Steinbeck's *The Grapes of Wrath*.

818.18   *Empress of the Blues*] Bessie Smith (1894–1937).

819.12   *Jesús, Estrella, Esperanza, Mercy*] Slave ships.

821.4   barracoons] Slave quarters.

821.30–31   Fellatah, / Mandingo, Ibo, Kru] West African tribes.

827.23   *O pena negra*] Oh dark pain.

827.24   Lady Day] Jazz singer Billie Holiday (1915–59).

830.12   Tezcátlipóca] Aztec creator god.

839.22   *Ajanta*] Caves discovered in 1819 in the state of Maharashtra, containing Buddhist chapels, monasteries, frescoes, and sculptures dating from c. 200 B.C.–A.D. 650.

841.17   *Les Tendresses Bestiales*] Bestial endearments.

844.5   *The Outer Banks*] This country, the Outer Banks of North Carolina, is a strong country of imagination: Raleigh's first settlements, in which

Thomas Hariot the scientist served a year in the New World, were here; the Wright Brothers flew from here; Hart Crane's "Hatteras" is set among these sand-bars, these waters. Several journeys here, the last one for the sake of the traces of Thomas Hariot (toward a biography I am writing) led me to this poem. The *Tiger*, in the last part of the poem, is one of the ships sent out by Raleigh. The quotations are from Selma, Alabama, in 1965. The truncated wing is a monument to the Wright Brothers. The spiral lighthouse is Hatteras light. [Rukeyser's note.]

845.19   the Book of Changes] The *I Ching*, one of the Chinese Five Classics, a book used to predict the future.

847.20   *grenzen der seele*] Limits of the soul.

865.5–6   *"As in water . . . to man."*] Proverbs 27:19.

866.12   *"the withness of the body"*] In a later version of the poem, Schwartz attributes this phrase to Alfred North Whitehead.

868.15   "Call us . . . love."] Cf. John Donne, "The Canonization."

869.18   at Cold Harbor . . . away] Grant's defeat at Cold Harbor, Virginia, on June 3, 1864, cost 7,000 men killed and wounded, compared to less than 1,500 for the Confederate army.

880.4   Mu] Lost continent said to have sunk into the Pacific Ocean.

891.5   Charybdis] Maelstrom that sucks in and casts out water three times per day. Cf. *Odyssey*, XII.

Index of Titles and First Lines

Index of Poets

Library of Congress Cataloging-in-Publication Data

American poetry. The twentieth century.
    p.   cm. — (The Library of America ; 115–116)
   Includes bibliographical references (p.) and index.
   ISBN 1–883011–77–9 (v. 1 : alk. paper) —
   ISBN 1–883011–78–7 (v. 2 : alk. paper)
   1. American poetry—20th century.   I. Series.
PS613.A4 2000
811'.50821—dc21   99–043721

THE LIBRARY OF AMERICA SERIES

The Library of America fosters appreciation and pride in America's literary heritage by publishing, and keeping permanently in print, authoritative editions of its best and most significant writing. An independent nonprofit organization, it was founded in 1979 with seed money from the National Endowment for the Humanities and the Ford Foundation.

This book is set in 10 point Linotron Galliard,
a face designed for photocomposition by Matthew Carter
and based on the sixteenth-century face Granjon. The paper is
acid-free Ecusta Nyalite and meets the requirements for permanence
of the American National Standards Institute. The binding
material is Brillianta, a woven rayon cloth made by
Van Heek-Scholco Textielfabrieken, Holland.
The composition is by The Clarinda
Company. Printing and binding by
R.R.Donnelley & Sons Company.
Designed by Bruce Campbell.